Building English Skills

Yellow Level

Building English Skills

Purple Level

YELLOW LEVEL

Blue Level

Orange Level

Green Level

Red Level

Gold Level

Silver Level

Aqua Level

Brown Level

Plum Level

Pink Level

Cherry Level (K)

THE McDOUGAL, LITTELL ENGLISH PROGRAM

Building English Skills

Yellow Level

Joy Littell, EDITORIAL DIRECTOR

McDougal, Littell & Company
Evanston, Illinois
New York Dallas Sacramento

Prepared by the Staff of
THE WRITING IMPROVEMENT PROJECT

Joy Littell, Editorial Director, McDougal, Littell & Company

Sylvia Z. Brodkin, formerly, West Hempstead High School, West Hempstead, New York

Eric Kraft, Writer and Editor, Stow, Massachusetts

Robert J. Lumsden, Evanston Township High School, Evanston, Illinois

Elizabeth J. Pearson, formerly, West Hempstead High School, West Hempstead, New York

Agnes Stein, English Department, Bloomfield College, Bloomfield, New Jersey

Marcia Baldwin Whipps, East High School, Salt Lake City, Utah

The Staff wishes to thank the more than 1500 students who contributed samples of their writing for analysis.

Consultants

Dr. Patsy M. Davis, Assistant Professor, College of Education, Department of Curriculum and Instruction, University of Tennessee, Knoxville, Tennessee

Beth Johnson, English Department Chair, Polk County School District, Lakeland, Florida

Karen Kutiper, Language Arts Coordinator, Alief Independent School District, Houston, Texas

Adrian W. McClaren, English Consultant, Memphis City Schools, Memphis, Tennessee

Julia S. Nichols, English Department Chair, North Area II, Memphis, Tennessee

Harry H. Raney, Teacher, Memphis School District, Memphis, Tennessee

Carolyn C. Walter, Educational Consultant and Writer, Chicago, Illinois

ISBN: 0-86609-316-8 TE ISBN: 0-86609-317-6

Acknowledgments: Simon & Schuster, Inc.: For the entry *heavy* from *Webster's New World Dictionary,* Students Edition; copyright © 1981 by Simon & Schuster, Inc. Macmillan Publishing Company: Chapters 1, 3, 4, 6, and the Handbook contain, in revised form, some materials that appeared originally in *English Arts and Skills, Grade 11,* by Ronald J. Wilkins et al, copyright © 1965, 1961 by The Macmillan Company. Used by arrangement. (Acknowledgments are continued on page 820.)

Box 1667, Evanston, Illinois 60204

85 86 87 / 9 8 7 6 5 4 3

Contents

Handbook

1.0 The Classification of Words 425

2.0 The Parts of a Sentence 469

3.0 Sentence and Clause 518

4.0 Complete Sentences 550

5.0 Verb Usage 571

6.0 Agreement of Subject and Verb 602

7.0 Pronoun Usage 623

8.0 Adjectives and Adverb Usage 651

9.0 The Right Word 670

10.0 Capitalization 688

11.0 End Marks and Commas 703

12.0 The Semicolon, the Colon, the Dash, and Parentheses 725

13.0 The Apostrophe 738

14.0 Quotations 750

15.0 Spelling 763

16.0 The Plurals of Nouns 782

17.0 Good Manuscript Form 792

18.0 Outlining 809

Chapter 1

Developing Your Vocabulary

What do you do when you encounter a word that you do not know in your reading? Do you stop dead in your tracks? Do you skip the section where the word appears and try to pick up at some later point? If so, you probably realize that you have missed something and that your comprehension has suffered because of what you have missed. You know that you *should* check the meaning of the word that stopped you, but it is not always possible or practical to run to a dictionary. How else can you understand the meaning of an unfamiliar word?

The purpose of this chapter and the next is to give you tools to pry loose the meanings of words that you do not know. Learning to use these tools will help you to interpret what you read and hear. It will also increase the number of words available to you for use in your own speaking and writing.

Part 1 How Context Reveals Meaning

Getting the meaning of a word from its **context,** or the passage in which it occurs, is not new to you. When you were learning to talk, you learned new words and their meanings by hearing them in context. When you were learning to read, many words that you did not know became clear because of surrounding words that you did know. Because context clarifies the meanings of unfamiliar words, learning to use context clues can be a powerful tool for developing your vocabulary.

Sometimes context clarifies the meaning of a word in a very deliberate manner. You can almost sense as you read that the writer knew that a word would be unfamiliar to you and took the trouble to help you understand it. A writer can do this in any of several ways.

Restatement

If a writer suspects that readers will not understand a word, he or she may restate the concept; that is, the writer may put the concept in other words. Certain phrases and words signal a restatement of a thought. These words and phrases may be used in other ways as well, but when they follow an unfamiliar word, you can consider them signals of a restatement.

in other words	this means	that is
to put it another way	which is to say	or

> Gandhi used Thoreau's technique of *civil disobedience;* **that is,** he passively refused to comply with government regulations that affected his personal life.

Notice how the words *that is* signal that a restatement follows.

Another kind of restatement is the appositive, in which the signal is usually a pair of commas.

> Thomas Jefferson, our third President, is responsible for the decimal money system we have today.

The appositive tells you that "Thomas Jefferson" and "our third President" are one and the same.

The simplest kind of restatement uses a form of the verb *be* to connect the unfamiliar word to a restatement of it.

> A rapier **is** a straight, two-edged sword with a narrow, pointed blade.

This type of restatement you know as a definition.

Example

Sometimes it is hard to define a word simply, but giving an example makes the meaning clear. The words listed below, though they may be used in other ways, are often a writer's way of saying "let me give you an example."

such as	for example
such	for instance
like	other
as	this *or* these
especially	(followed by a synonym)

Notice in the following examples how the signal words and the restatements they introduce work to clarify the meanings of the words in italics.

> **Like other** mental illnesses, *paranoia* can prevent a person from living a normal life.

Both *like* and *other* signal that paranoia is a mental illness.

> As an apprentice baker, Andy practiced making elaborate *confections*. Unfortunately, **these** tarts, eclairs, and cream pies were often judged inedible by the pastry chef.
>
> *Ginseng* and **other** herbs are valued for the vitality they are supposed to impart.
>
> The speaker's remarks were largely *derogatory*. **For instance,** he charged the candidate with being insensitive to the problems of unemployment, sky-rocketing property taxes, and the high cost of energy.

Comparison

Like an example, a comparison gives you information about an unfamiliar word, but does not provide a definition. Comparisons show associations between two words or concepts. These associations can suggest meanings to you. Some of the words that signal an example also signal a comparison.

like	in the same way
as	the way
similar to	

The following example shows how comparison works to provide clues to meaning.

> This change in policy could have **as** *cataclysmic* an effect on the downtown area **as** an earthquake.

The word *cataclysmic* is not defined, but you are told that an earthquake is cataclysmic. This provides a clue to the meaning of the word.

Contrast

In a contrast, the *dissimilarity* of two things gives you a clue to the meaning of a word. In effect, you work backwards to find the meaning of the word. A contrast tells you not what a word means, but something that it does *not* mean. Again, certain words often signal a contrast.

but	on the other hand
although	as opposed to
on the contrary	unlike

Notice how the signal words and the contrasts they introduce give clues to the italicized words in the following examples.

> Mr. McCabe introduced the judge with words of praise, **although** in private his words had been quite *disparaging*.

The word *although* signals that words of praise are different from disparaging words.

Exercises How Context Reveals Meaning

A. For each numbered sentence, choose the letter of the answer that best explains the italicized word. Following the letter, write the context clue or clues that led you to the answer you chose.

1. He had lived a life of *rectitude* in the service of the public, but his biographer uncovered some private wrongdoings.

   a. luxury c. virtue
   b. triumph d. difficulty

2. By studying her *genealogy*, or family tree, Caroline discovered that she was a descendant of John Adams.

   a. family history c. political documents
   b. genetics d. biography of a famous person

3. To operate in the black, a private college must have a sizeable *endowment;* that is, it must supplement tuition income with gifts from private donors.

   a. administration building c. private donations
   b. alumni organization d. government grant

4. The *porgy* was much more colorful than the other fish.

   a. pig c. aquatic mammal
   b. fish d. seaweed

5. The mime troupe, dramatic club, and other local *thespians* will convene Saturday for a day-long workshop.

   a. organizations c. singers
   b. Greeks d. actors

6. The optometrist, unlike the *ophthalmologist,* cannot prescribe drugs or perform surgery.

   a. dental technician c. one who fits glasses
   b. M.D. eye specialist d. pharmacist

7. Within the atom are particles like the *positron* that exist for only a very short time.

   a. brief moment c. subatomic particle
   b. atom d. experiment

8. A cow is an *herbivore;* that is, it feeds on plants.

a. botanist c. cannibal
b. mystic d. vegetarian

9. The pears she had picked looked *succulent,* although there were many still on the tree that were hard and unripe.

a. green c. hard
b. juicy d. large

10. Pewter is a combination of copper, tin, and antimony. This *alloy* is quite soft and presents some problems to the metalsmith.

a. mixture of metals c. hardware
b. bowl d. chemical

B. The sentences that follow are from an article on cell biology. Write each italicized word and a definition for it based on what you can learn from context clues. Then list the clues that led you to your definition. Finally, compare your definition with a dictionary definition for the word.

1. Cells use hormones—*insulin,* for example—to order other cells to respond to such conditions as too much sugar in the blood.
2. Eventually it should be technically possible to make limitless copies, or *clones,* of desirable microorganisms.
3. *Lysosomes* also serve as cell janitors, aiding in the removal of old or defective cells from the system.
4. When your antibodies win the battle with invading cold germs they make you *immune.* On the other hand, when they lose the battle, you come down with a cold.
5. Some scientists say that cancer is caused by *mutations,* alterations in a cell's DNA, that prevent key genes from working properly.

C. Begin keeping a vocabulary notebook. Include all of the words studied in this chapter, and their meanings. Add words from other subject areas. Review this notebook periodically. It will serve as excellent preparation for many of the standardized tests you will be taking. Also, when writing a composition, use words from your notebook.

Part 2 Inferring Meaning from Context

You will not always be able to pluck the meaning of a word from its context as you did in the examples you just worked. More often, you will have to probe and hunt and put many small clues together to get the meaning of a word from its context. You will have to work your way bit by bit from the known to the unknown; that is, you will have to **infer** meaning.

Inference from Form

The form or structure of the context sometimes gives clues to the meaning of a word. A repeated sentence pattern may suggest associations between words, as in this example.

> High inflation foreshadows an economic slowdown. High unemployment *portends* less spending for consumer goods.

The word *portends* is linked to the word *foreshadows* by the structure of the sentences. Both sentences follow the same pattern, with *portends* and *foreshadows* fitting into the same places in the pattern.

If an unfamiliar word appears in a list, you may sometimes be able to determine its meaning from what you know about the meanings of other words in the list.

> On one game farm you can see a herd of elephants, a *pride* of lions, and a pack of wolves in their natural habitats.

The word *pride* is structurally linked to the words *herd* and *pack*, and their meanings are linked as well.

The repetition of key words may clarify the meaning of an unfamiliar word.

> The development of motor coordination in a child is *antecedent* to the development of judgment. This gap in development is a time of great trial for the child's parents, who will find the child ready to scale the heights of stairways and furniture but not yet ready to judge the dangers involved.

Here the repetition of the word *development* makes a connection between motor coordination and judgment. The repetition of key words related to time—*development, gap, time, ready, not yet ready*—should show you that the connection is one of time. From the sense of the second sentence, which uses the same time sequence as the first, you should be able to tell that *is antecedent to* means "comes before."

Look also for connecting words that give some clue to an unfamiliar word. Words like *besides, however, but, yet, nevertheless,* and *despite* establish positive or negative connections between two words and the thoughts they represent. These connectives tell you whether to expect similarity or dissimilarity between the thoughts and words they connect.

> Besides *migraines,* Millie also suffered from arthritis.

You can see that the word *besides* makes a positive connection between migraines and arthritis. You cannot conclude from the context that a migraine is a headache, but you can see that it is some sort of illness.

> When Maria began to sing, she was very aware of the audience, and her voice was *tremulous*. However, as she continued she began to get involved in the music, and her voice became strong and clear.

The word *however* should suggest to you a negative connection between a tremulous voice and a strong and clear one.

Inference from Content

In trying to understand an unfamiliar word, ask yourself questions about the content or message of the context.

1. Does the main idea of the passage shed some light on the meaning of the word?
2. Are there descriptive words, phrases, or clauses that apply to the word?
3. Is there a hidden restatement, example, comparison, or contrast—one not highlighted by a signal word?

Ask yourself each of the questions as you read these examples and try to determine the meanings of the italicized words.

> There is much to be said for a *rototiller*, even for the backyard gardener. It turns out and aerates the soil, rips up roots that would steal soil nutrients from the vegetables to be planted, and mixes lime and fertilizer throughout the top layer of soil.

The entire passage reveals what a rototiller is and what it does; the function of the rototiller is the main idea of the passage.

> Behind the auction barn was a corral for *feral* horses. One could hear them halfway across the town, kicking and snorting whenever someone approached, opposing their unnatural captivity with natural savageness and fury.

The meaning of the word *feral* is implied by the phrases *unnatural captivity* and *savageness and fury*. In addition, the second sentence gives examples of the actions of *feral* horses, showing that they snort and kick and are unused to people.

Exercises **Inferring Meaning from Context**

A. The following passages contain italicized words for you to define. Try to discover a meaning for each word from its context. Be ready to explain what clues led you to your definition.

1 There are long periods of silence where one hears only the *winnowing* of snipe, the hoot of a distant owl, or the nasal clucking of some amorous coot.—ALDO LEOPOLD

2 Now, returning from my *foray* into the grasshopper meadow, I was back where I started, on the bank that separates the cottage from the top of the dam.

—ANNIE DILLARD

3 The French Revolution has given pleasure to all *subsequent* generations, because it was an outstanding event which afterwards proved never to have happened.

—REBECCA WEST

4 A bramble caught hold of her skirt, and checked her progress. When she began to *extricate* herself it was by turning round and round, and so unwinding the prickly switch.—THOMAS HARDY

5 And his laugh was frankly vulgar; he seemed in his *hilarity* to be recklessly trying to rip down all the illusions that one supposed him to have been at such pains to build up. —LOUIS AUCHINCLOSS

6 Hunting is sometimes thought to represent a basic "instinct" in human nature, and certainly there is something *elemental* and primitive in the thrill of the chase. —MARSTON BATES

7 The adventures of the evening so *disconcerted* me, that I could not sleep all night.—FANNY BURNEY

8 From the weighing tanks the raw milk is pumped through a *clarifier* that whirls out fine dust particles as well as blood cells from the cow that are often present in the milk.—CAROLYN MEYER

B. Look up each of the words in the list below. Write a sentence or two using each word in a way that will make its meaning clear.

pellucid fulminate judicious
penchant eulogize mandate

Part 3 Gaining Precision in the Use of Words

The launching of a rocket, the assembly of an automobile engine, and the service of a tennis ball must all be done with *precision* to be done well. Precision is also a mark of skill in writing and speaking.

If you say more or less what you mean, you will be more or less understood. If you say precisely what you mean you will be precisely understood, and your words will have force and impact. To develop precision in your use of language, you must select your words carefully. To be able to select your words carefully, you must be aware of multiple meanings given in dictionary entries and of synonyms and antonyms. They hold the key to accuracy of word choice.

Using Words with Multiple Meanings

One way to increase your vocabulary and gain precision in your language is to take advantage of multiple meanings of words that you already know. Look at the entry for the word *heavy* in *Webster's New World Dictionary, Students Edition*.

Dictionary Entry for *heavy*

heav·y (hev′ē) ***adj.*** **heav′i·er, heav′i·est** [OE. *hefig* < base of *hebban*, to HEAVE + *-ig*, -Y²] **1.** hard to lift or move because of great weight; weighty **2.** of great weight for the size [lead is a *heavy* metal] **3.** above the usual or a defined weight **4.** larger, greater, rougher, more intense, etc. than usual [a *heavy* blow, a *heavy* vote, a *heavy* sea, *heavy* thunder, *heavy* features] **5.** going beyond the average; to a greater than usual extent [a *heavy* drinker] **6.** serious; grave [a *heavy* responsibility] **7.** oppressive; burdensome [*heavy* demands] **8.** hard to do or manage; difficult [*heavy* work] **9.** hard to bear [*heavy* sorrow] **10.** burdened with grief; sorrowful [a *heavy* heart] **11.** burdened with sleep or fatigue [*heavy* eyelids] **12.** hard to digest [a *heavy* meal] **13.** not leavened properly [a *heavy* cake] **14.** clinging; penetrating [a *heavy* odor] **15.** cloudy; gloomy [a *heavy* sky] **16.** tedious; dull [*heavy* humor] **17.** clumsy; awkward [a *heavy* gait] ☆**18.** steeply inclined [a *heavy* grade] **19.** designating any large, basic industry that uses massive machinery **20.** designating, of, or equipped with heavy weapons, armor, etc. ☆**21.** [Slang] very good or pleasing: a general term of approval ☆**22.** [Slang] important, significant, profound, etc. **23.** *Chem.* designating an isotope of greater atomic weight than the normal or most abundant isotope **24.** *Theater* serious, tragic, or villainous —***adv.*** heavily [*heavy*-laden] —***n.**, pl.* **heav′ies** **1.** something heavy **2.** *Theater* *a*) a serious, tragic, or villainous role *b*) an actor who plays such roles —**hang heavy** to pass in a slow, boring way; drag: said of time —**heavy with child** pregnant

SYN.—**heavy** implies greater weight than is usual for its size [a tiny box which was surprisingly *heavy*] and is used to suggest a pressing down on the mind or spirits [*heavy* sorrow]; **weighty** implies absolute rather than relative heaviness and is used to suggest great importance [*weighty* matters of state]; **ponderous** applies to something that is very heavy because of its bulk and is used to suggest dullness and a lack of grace [a *ponderous* lecture, full of complicated sentences]; **massive** stresses great size and solidness but not necessarily great weight and suggests an impressiveness due to great scope [a *massive* study of pollution control]; **cumbersome** applies to something that is difficult to handle because it is heavy and bulky, and suggests clumsiness [*cumbersome* rules that hinder change] —***ANT.*** **light**

For this one common word, twenty-six separate meanings are given. Some of these meanings are familiar. Others are not. By learning the less familiar meanings of the word *heavy* as applied to *industry, chemistry,* or *theater*, you can, in effect, increase your vocabulary without learning a new word. Because less familiar meanings tend to be precise applications of a word to a particular area of endeavor, learning these meanings will also help to increase the precision of your vocabulary.

Using Synonyms

Synonyms are words that have similar meanings. Most synonyms do not mean exactly the same thing. Knowing the small differences in meaning between two synonyms enables you to use each word precisely.

Learning sets of synonyms through attentive listening and reading is a slow and gradual process. A more direct method is to study synonymies in a dictionary or thesaurus. A **synonymy** lists synonyms and points out slight differences in meaning among them.

To get an idea of how a synonymy works, look at the preceding entry for the word *heavy*. Following the definitions listed for the word is a synonymy comparing the meanings of *heavy, weighty, ponderous, massive,* and *cumbersome*.

If you had looked up the word *massive* instead of the word *heavy,* you would have found the note "see **SYN.** at HEAVY." This cross-reference will be found at the entry for each word appearing in a synonymy. The synonymy itself is given at the entry for the word with the broadest meaning.

After studying the differences among the meanings of the words listed as synonyms for *heavy,* you will see that synonyms cannot be used interchangeably. You might speak of a massive building, but not a heavy one. You might talk about a cumbersome package rather than a weighty one. Each of these words has its own uses, though they share the same general meaning. Try writing a sentence for each word in which you employ the special meaning of the word. Then try substituting the others in the sentence to see how the meaning is distorted.

If you were not aware of these synonyms, you might use the word *heavy* when you meant to express the meaning specific to one of its synonyms. You would have settled for a general word when a specific one would have made your point forcefully. Learning synonyms will help you broaden your vocabulary, expanding the range of words available to you, and enabling you to express your ideas with precision.

Exercises **Using Words Precisely**

A. Answer the following questions by checking all of the meanings of each italicized word in a dictionary.

1. What does it mean to *wash* a photograph?
2. What does the term *relief* mean in painting?
3. For what purpose would a florist use a *frog*?
4. What does the verb *to stem* mean to a person who can paddle a canoe?
5. What is *principal* to a banker?
6. What is a *shell* in the fashion industry?
7. What is the difference between an *exhibit* in an art gallery and an *exhibit* in a court of law?
8. What does the word *down* mean to a football player?
9. What does it mean to *call* a loan?
10. What is a *movement* of a symphony? What is a political or artistic *movement*?

B. In the following sentences words have been used that do not convey a precise and appropriate meaning. Find more accurate and forceful synonyms for the italicized words in each sentence.

1. Her generosity would *get* her the reputation of having a deep concern for all in the community.
2. When the bowl dropped, it *crashed* into numberless pieces.
3. When her dog died, she became *hopeless* and brooded over its death for months.
4. The warden *asked* the prisoners about the events leading to the disruption.
5. After failing to win the judges' approval for the third time, Michael felt *sad* and resolved never to play the piano again.

C. Write a sentence using each word in a way that conveys a precise meaning that could not be conveyed by its synonyms.

1. sincere, unaffected, heartfelt
2. show, display, exhibit, expose, flaunt
3. expect, anticipate, hope, await
4. contain, hold, accommodate
5. rational, reasonable, sensible

Using Antonyms

Antonyms are words that are opposite in meaning. An antonym of *shy* is *bold*. An antonym of *cold* is *hot*. The word *warm* contrasts with *cold,* but is not an antonym for it.

You will find antonyms listed at the ends of some synonymies in dictionaries. These antonyms are roughly opposite in meaning to all the words in the synonymy. Remember, however, that a rough meaning is not what you want to convey; you want to convey a precise one. You will have to note the differences in meaning among the antonyms and choose carefully.

Exercises Using Antonyms

A. Answer the questions. Use a dictionary as necessary.

1. While making your first salad dressing, you discover that oil and vinegar are immiscible. You are surprised. What had you expected the ingredients to do?

2. If your blood is deficient in iron, what does that mean? What would describe the opposite condition?

3. Describe a person with base motives. Describe a person with the opposite characteristics. What word would you use to describe the second person's motives?

4. A pessimist expects the worst. Who takes the view that everything will work out for the best?

5. If you still cannot add and subtract, you are inept with numbers. If you spend your spare time doing differential calculus, what word would describe your way with mathematics?

B. Decide which of the pairs of words are true antonyms.

1. belief—distrust
2. dark—white
3. rural—suburban
4. young—senile
5. tall—shallow
6. inimical—friendly
7. convivial—unsociable
8. dexterity—maladroitness
9. intermittent—continuous
10. antithetical—identical

C. Think of an antonym for each of the following words and use it in a sentence.

1. antagonistic
2. tentative
3. volatile
4. verbose
5. extinct
6. predilection
7. jocose
8. mitigate
9. phlegmatic
10. trepidation

Part 4 Using Prefixes

You have learned how to use context clues, synonyms, antonyms, and the multiple meanings of words to develop your vocabulary and to determine the meanings of unfamiliar words. Another technique that you can use is the analysis of the parts from which words are made. Every English word is made up of one or more of the following parts:

Prefix a word part that is added to the beginning of another word or word part

Suffix a word part that is added to the end of another word or word part

Base Word a complete word to which a prefix and/or a suffix can be added

Root a word part to which a prefix and/or a suffix may be added. Roots cannot stand alone.

The word *unfruitful*, for example, is made up of the prefix *un-*, the base word *fruit*, and the suffix *-ful*. The word *inoperative* is made of the prefix *in-*, the root *operis*, and the suffix *-ative*.

Most of the prefixes used to form English words have more than one possible meaning. However, each of the prefixes in the list below has just one meaning. These prefixes, therefore, are reliable clues to the meanings of the words in which they appear.

Prefixes with a Single Meaning

Prefix	Prefix Meaning	Example
bene-	good	beneficial
circum-	around	circumnavigate
equi-	equal	equivalent
extra-	outside	extracurricular
inter-	between	interstate
intra-	within	intramural
intro-	into	introduction
mal-	bad	malformation
mis-	wrong	misinformed
non-	not	nonconformist
pre-	before	premature

The prefixes below are so common that you should learn them even though they have more than one possible meaning.

Common Prefixes with Multiple Meanings

Prefix	Prefix Meaning	Example
in- ir- il- im-	not, in	inept, inject
un-	not, the opposite of	unnoticed, untie
dis-	the opposite of, away	disqualify, dislodge
sub-	under, less than	submerge, substandard
super-	above, more	superstructure, superfine
re-	back, again	recall, restart

Exercises **Prefixes**

A. Give the meaning of the prefix in each word below.

1. irreligious
2. noncommittal
3. reupholster
4. unseat
5. discover
6. extraordinary
7. imperfect
8. subhuman

B. You have seen that the prefixes *non-*, *un-*, and *in-* (and its forms *il-*, *ir-*, and *im-*) can mean "not." In most cases, only one of these can be used in a particular word. Decide which prefix can be used with each of the base words below and write the new word.

1. delicate
2. opportune
3. existent
4. complete
5. lucky
6. direct
7. able
8. payment
9. dependent
10. mature
11. resident
12. secure
13. reasonable
14. combatant
15. interested
16. adequate
17. broken
18. visible

C. The prefixes *mal-* and *mis-* both mean "bad" or "wrong." Usually only one can be attached to a particular word. Decide which to add to each of the following base words. Write the new words.

1. spell
2. guided
3. practice
4. deed
5. content
6. took
7. adventure
8. function
9. managed
10. conduct
11. adjusted
12. demeanor

D. Determine the meanings of the prefix and the whole word.

1. The lawyer assured her client that there would be a speedy *disposition* of his case, now that the trial date was set.

2. The *subtotal* of her bill did not include the tax.

3. At the climax of the piece, the hall *reverberated* with the clash of cymbals, and the music paused until the last echo had died away.

4. There were no local taxes to pay or officials to elect. The settlement had so few residents that it was still *unincorporated*.

5. We did not practice because of the *inclement* weather.

Part 5 Using Suffixes

Suffixes provide better clues to word meaning than prefixes do. Most of the suffixes that are useful for determining word meaning appear in nouns and adjectives.

Noun Suffixes

Some suffixes are used only to make nouns from other parts of speech; they add little or nothing to the meaning of a word. A great many noun suffixes, however, have a single meaning that they give to every word in which they appear. Some of the most common of these are listed below. If you see one of these suffixes in a word you do not know, think of what it means in a word you do know. You will then have made a start toward learning the meaning of the new word.

Noun Suffixes with Single Meanings

Suffix	Suffix Meaning	Example
-ana	a collection of material on a certain subject	Americana
-archy	form of government	monarchy
-ard -art	one who does something to excess	braggart
-cide	killer, killing	germicide
-ee	receiver of an action or benefit	employee
-fication	state or action of creating or causing	ratification
-ics	science or skill	athletics
-itis	inflammation	appendicitis

The noun suffixes in the following list also have single, specific meanings. They all indicate an agent. That is, they all mean "one who is something" or "one who does something."

Noun Suffixes Indicating an Agent

Suffix	Example
-eer	auctioneer
-ess	waitress
-ician	technician
-ist	pianist
-ster	gangster

The suffix *-ess* indicates that the agent is female.

The suffixes *-er*, *-or*, and *-an* or *-ian* also frequently indicate an agent, but they are also used in other ways.

Exercises Noun Suffixes

A. Give the meaning of the suffix in each of the following words. Then give the meaning of the whole word.

1. genocide
2. patriarchy
3. divorcee
4. justification
5. appointee
6. arthritis
7. anarchy
8. politics
9. laryngitis
10. Victoriana
11. drunkard
12. unification

B. What is a person called who is involved in each of the following fields? Use a suffix indicating an agent to make the new word.

1. politics
2. psychiatry
3. biology
4. geology
5. statistics
6. conducting
7. editing
8. photography
9. pamphlet writing
10. magic

C. From the context and the suffix, determine the meaning of each word in italics.

1. A half-dozen mean-looking *buccaneers* boarded the ship and proceeded to rob the crew of their possessions.

2. This new *herbicide* will kill all the weeds in the field without hurting the fish in the pond.

3. General Washington showed himself a superb *tactician* in the battle of Valley Forge.

4. As a student of *aesthetics*, Frank was concerned less with whether a piece of art was genuine than with why it was considered beautiful.

5. The fact that the remains of Egyptian pharaohs are still well preserved attests to the advanced state of the art of *mummification* at that time.

Adjective Suffixes

A number of adjective suffixes have specific meanings. Because they almost always have the meanings given below, the suffixes listed are good clues to the meanings of unfamiliar words.

Adjective Suffixes with Specific Meanings

Suffix	Suffix Meaning	Example
-fic	causing or producing	honorific
-fold	specified number of times as much	twofold
-ward	in the direction of	homeward
-less	without	worthless
-able -ible -ble	capable of being, or having qualities of	comfortable

Four adjective suffixes mean "full of" or "having."

Adjective Suffixes Meaning "Full of" or "Having"

Suffix	Example
-acious	audacious
-ful	wonderful
-ose	verbose
-ous	dangerous

A number of adjective suffixes have the general meaning "pertaining to." They can be translated "connected with," "tending to," or "like."

Adjective Suffixes Meaning "Pertaining to"

Suffix	Example
-ive	protective
-ative	talkative
-ish	impish
-aceous	herbaceous
-ic	caloric
-al	original

The last two suffixes in this group, *-ic* and *-al,* are also found in nouns, where they have different meanings.

Exercises Adjective Suffixes

A. Give the meaning of the suffix in each of the following words. Then give the meaning of the whole word. Use a dictionary for help as needed.

1. legible
2. guileless
3. fallacious
4. prolific
5. manifold
6. treacherous
7. authoritative
8. tenacious
9. boorish
10. cherubic
11. envious
12. leeward
13. comatose
14. arboreal
15. formative

B. From the context and the suffix, determine the meaning of each italicized word.

1. As the debate on censorship proceeded, it appeared that the main argument between the opponents was *semantic;* they could not agree on the meaning of the words "free speech."

2. On the day students were to elect a new student body president, Sarah, who was favored to win, felt *magnanimous* toward her hardrunning opponent and treated him to a hamburger.

3. When the guards filled the moat and pulled up the drawbridge, the castle was all but *impenetrable*.

4. As the finishing touch to her model of the Santa Maria, Amy added a *diminutive* Christopher Columbus.

5. Senator McNally had a *soporific* way with words that put half his audience to sleep before he had finished his remarks.

Part 6 Using Roots and Word Families

If you cut off the prefix and suffix from a long word, you are sometimes left with a word part that cannot stand alone. Such a word part is a root. Sometimes, identifying the root or roots combined in an unfamiliar word will help you to understand what the word means. Consider the word *cryptic*. This word may appear unfamiliar, but if you remove the suffix *-ic*, you reveal the root *crypt*. If you know that *cryptos* is the Greek word for *secret* or *hidden* and that *-ic* is an adjective suffix, you will be able to figure out the meaning of *cryptic*.

Sometimes a single root will be used in many different words. These related words make up a **word family.** By learning the meaning of one root, you can determine the meanings of the many words in which the root occurs.

Latin and Greek Roots

Many of the roots used in English words originally came from Latin or Greek. Some of these are presented in the lists below. Use these lists for reference. The point is not to memorize the Latin and Greek roots, but to see how their meanings are contained in the English words that are derived from them. If you can accomplish this, you will be able to understand other English words built from the same roots. Because the lists are long, they have been divided into groups. The exercises that follow the groups will give you practice in recognizing the roots in English words.

Latin Roots and English Derivatives (I)

Root	Meaning	English Words
alius	other	alienate
amicus	friend	amicable
animus	mind, spirit	animate
bellum	war	rebellious
bonus	good	bonny
credere, creditus	believe	incredible
cor, cordis	heart	concord
corpus, corporis	body	corporation
crux, crucis	cross	crucifixion
dicere, dictus	say, tell	diction
dormire	sleep	dormitory
errare, erratus	wander	erratic
facere, feci, factus	make, do	factory

Latin Roots and English Derivatives (II)

Root	Meaning	English Words
fluere	flow	fluid
gratia	kindness, favor	gratitude
grex, gregis	flock	gregarious
jungere, junctus	join	junction
jus, juris	law, right	justice
juvenis	youth	juvenile
lumen, luminis	light	illuminate
mandare	command	commandment
manus	hand	manual
multus	much, many	multiple
opus, operis	work	operate
pendere, pensus	hang	pendant

Exercises Latin Roots

A. Find the root in each of the following words. Give the meaning of the root and the meaning of the word.

1. corpulent
2. cordial
3. corpuscle
4. crux
5. coronary
6. belligerent
7. erroneous
8. unanimous
9. amity
10. credence
11. dormant
12. inalienable
13. dictation
14. incorporate
15. bellicose
16. amiable
17. malefaction
18. corporeal

B. Find the root in each of the following words. Give the meaning of the root and the meaning of the word.

1. ingratiate
2. fluent
3. jury
4. congregation
5. mandatory
6. manipulate
7. luminary
8. operant
9. pendulous
10. rejuvenate
11. conjugal
12. multimedia
13. congratulate
14. adjunct
15. cooperate
16. pendulum
17. affluent
18. manufacture

Latin Roots and English Derivatives (III)

Root	Meaning	English Words
rapere, raptus	seize	rapacity
rumpere, ruptus	break	rupture
sequor, secutus	follow	sequence
solus	alone	solitary
somnus	sleep	somnolent
stringere, strictus	bind	stringent
tempus	time	temporal
tenere, tentus	hold	tenure
terminus	end, boundary	terminal
unus	one	unity
videre, visus	see	visible
vincere, victus	conquer	invincible

Exercise Latin Roots

Identify the root in each of the following words. Give the meaning of the root and the meaning of the word.

1. restrict
2. insomnia
3. rapture
4. victorious
5. consecutive
6. retention
7. temporary
8. video
9. solitude
10. terminate
11. disrupt
12. unifying

Greek Roots and English Derivatives (I)

Root	Meaning	English Words
anthropos	human	anthropology
autos	self	automatic
biblos	book	Bible
bios	life	biology
chronos	time	chronological
cosmos	world, order	cosmic
cryptos	secret, hidden	cryptic
demos	people	democracy
dynamis	power	dynamic
ethnos	race, nation	ethnic
ge, geos	earth	geology
graphein	write	graphic
gramma	something written	grammatical

Exercise Greek Roots

Identify the meaning of the Greek root or roots in each of the following words. (Some words have more than one root.) Give the meaning of the root or roots and the meaning of the word.

1. autobiography
2. autonomous
3. cosmopolitan
4. demagogue
5. chronic
6. ethnology
7. dynamite
8. philanthropy
9. bibliography
10. biosphere
11. cryptogram
12. geography

Greek Roots and English Derivatives (II)

Root	Meaning	English Words
homos	same	homogenized
iatr	heal	psychiatry
logos	word, thought	logical
metron	measure	metric
micro	small	microscope
monos	alone, single	monotonous
neos	new	neoclassical
neuron	nerve	neurotic
onyma	name	anonymous
orthos	right	orthopedic
osteon	bone	osteopath
pathos	suffering	pathetic

Greek Roots and English Derivatives (III)

Root	Meaning	English Words
phobos	fear	phobia
phone	sound	phonics
pneuma	air, breath	pneumatic
polis	city	police
polys	many	polygamy
psyche	breath, soul, mind	psychology
scope	seeing, watch	telescopic
syn, sym	with	synchronize
tele	far, distant	television
therme	heat	thermal
techne	art	technology

Exercises **Greek Roots**

A. Identify the Greek roots in the following words. Give their meanings and the meanings of the words. Use a dictionary for help as needed.

1. neurology
2. monogram
3. pathological
4. pseudonym
5. orthodox
6. homonym
7. neologism
8. podiatrist
9. microcosm
10. logistics
11. monometer
12. neuroscience

B. Give a definition for each of the following words.

1. phobic
2. pneumonia
3. polyphony
4. cosmopolitan
5. phonetic
6. psychopath
7. macroscopic
8. sympathy
9. thermometer
10. telegraph
11. technical
12. symbiosis

Additional Words for Vocabulary Study

1. abeyance
2. acquiesce
3. adamant
4. advent
5. affluent
6. aggregation
7. alienation
8. altercation
9. amicable
10. aristocratic
11. articulate
12. ascribe
13. aspiration
14. assimilate
15. augment
16. austere
17. beneficent
18. burgeoning
19. coerce
20. coherent
21. complement
22. conjecture
23. consensus
24. correspondent
25. deduction
26. degradation
27. delegation
28. demoralize
29. deplete
30. deportment
31. diabolical
32. duplicity
33. economic
34. emancipation
35. empathy
36. enigmatic
37. entity
38. equitable
39. escalate
40. exemplify
41. explicit
42. extrapolate
43. fiscal
44. gaunt
45. grandiose
46. immerse
47. imply
48. import
49. incipient
50. induce
51. inhibition
52. initiate
53. integrity
54. irreversible
55. latitude
56. lethargy
57. litigation
58. magnitude
59. manifest
60. marginal
61. melancholy
62. millennium
63. morale
64. mundane
65. negotiate
66. nutrient
67. obliterate
68. peremptory
69. perturbation
70. pious
71. poignant
72. polyglot
73. postulate
74. precedent
75. prerequisite
76. profound
77. provincial
78. purport
79. reactionary
80. recompense
81. reconcile
82. recur
83. replete
84. repress
85. revenue
86. seclusion
87. serenity
88. sinister
89. solicit
90. soliloquize
91. solvent
92. tantamount
93. tenant
94. transaction
95. tumult
96. universal
97. validate
98. vicarious
99. vocation
100. volatile

SUMMARY AND APPLICATIONS

1. By developing your vocabulary, you will increase your understanding of what you read and hear and become better equipped to express your own ideas clearly and precisely.
2. Careful attention to context clues such as restatement, example, comparison, and contrast will help you to determine the meanings of unfamiliar words.
3. A second method for determining meaning and improving your vocabulary is inference from form or content.
4. Learning synonyms, antonyms, and the multiple meanings of words can also aid in vocabulary development.
5. Analyzing word parts—prefixes, suffixes, base words, and roots—can help you to unlock the meanings of words.
6. Use these methods of vocabulary analysis on the vocabulary sections of standardized tests.

Applications in Other Subject Areas

All Subjects. Whenever you are studying for an examination in one of your classes, make a separate list of vocabulary items that you will need to know. Look these words up in a dictionary, and make a chart showing prefixes, suffixes, base words, and roots.

Vocabulary for Science Exam

① geo + therm + al = geothermal

"earth" + "heat" + adjective suffix = having to do with the heat of the earth's interior

② geo + morph + ology = geomorphology

"earth" + "form" + word study = study of the forms (features) of the earth's surface

Chapter 2

Dialects and the Levels of Language

No two people speak or write in exactly the same way. Language is an amazingly varied and flexible instrument, offering many ways of expressing any given idea. Nowhere is the variety in language more evident than with its dialects. Americans, for example, speak many distinct forms of their common tongue, depending upon the areas of the country in which they live and the social groups to which they belong. These dialects have enriched American English tremendously, reflecting the diversity of the American people and making possible rich and colorful regional literatures.

In this chapter you will learn about the nature and origins of American dialects. You will also learn about the ways in which language varies from person to person, group to group, and situation to situation. This will increase your appreciation of the range of expression possible in English and help you to choose language that is precise, colorful, and appropriate for particular audiences and occasions.

Part 1 The Nature of Dialects

A **dialect** is any of the distinct forms of a language spoken in a particular region or by a particular social group. The people who speak a given dialect make up a speech community, which may vary in size from a few hundred people to many millions. Because people in a speech community speak more frequently to one another than to people outside the community, they develop habits of speech that are unfamiliar to outsiders. A dialect appears when enough of these habits of speech develop to set one speech community off from others in which a different form of the same language is spoken.

How Dialects Differ

A dialect differs from other dialects of the same language in predictable ways. Typically, two dialects will contain variations in each of the following areas:

pronunciation or accent
vocabulary
grammar or sentence structure

American English, for example, differs from the standard dialect spoken in Great Britain in all three ways. An American pronounces the word *schedule* with a hard *c*, as in *ski*. A British speaker, on the other hand, pronounces the initial cluster of consonants without the hard *c*, as in the word *shoe*. An American transports goods by *truck*. An English man or woman sends them by *lorry*. In the areas of grammar and usage, Americans tend to use articles and prepositions differently than English speakers. For example, an American would "go on *a* vacation" while an English individual would drop the article and simply "go on holiday."

How Dialects Originate

The chief cause of dialectical variation is the isolation of speech communities. If two speech communities are separated from one another by distance, by geography, or by customs or beliefs, they tend to change in different ways. If the separation continues, these changes are preserved. Americans, for example, are isolated from the British by a great body of water, the Atlantic Ocean. The descendants of the men and women who first brought English to this continent therefore developed the dialect known as American English. This dialect was the result of three basic processes:

1. alteration of existing words and methods of expression
2. invention of new words and grammatical forms
3. borrowing from other languages, chiefly Spanish, French, Dutch, and the languages of the American Indians.

Similar processes of change have resulted in several variations within American English. These regional and social dialects will be discussed in the following parts.

Part 2 Regional Dialects

There are two main kinds of dialects in America: **regional** and **social.** The first reflects the part of the country a person lives in or lived in when he or she learned to speak. The second reflects the speaker's membership in particular social groups. These groups are determined by the origins of the speaker's ancestors, the occupations that are common in the speech community, and the level of education the speaker has attained. In actual speech, regional and social dialects are not separate.

This is because most people belong to both the speech community of the region in which they are living, and various social communities made up of family, friends, co-workers, neighbors, and other associates.

Origins of Regional Dialects

The regional dialects of America result from migrations of speech communities, first across the Atlantic Ocean, and then across the continent. During early colonial times, the various settlements in America had little contact with one another. They were separated by distance, geographical barriers, unfriendly natives, and opposing religious and political views. In fact, there was often more communication across the ocean with England than among the colonies themselves.

Because of their isolation and various origins, colonists in different areas of the country developed different ways of speaking. This resulted in three distinct regional dialects, which have been identified by experts in language as **Northern, Southern,** and **Midland.** The boundaries for these regional dialects are indicated by the heavy black lines on the map on page 35. In addition, some experts speak of a **Western** region, made up of a combination of other dialects and covering most of the continent west of the Mississippi.

Northern and Southern Dialects. During the seventeenth century, many settlers immigrated to America from England. The English they spoke was the type common in London and in the southern and eastern counties of England. These settlers established colonies in what are now the states of Massachusetts, Rhode Island, Connecticut, New York, New Jersey, Pennsylvania, Delaware, Maryland, Virginia, and South Carolina.

These same regions also received immigrants from other areas of England. For example, Western New England had settlers from Northern England and the area just north of London. Eventually, these seventeenth-century colonists split into two main groups, and each group began to develop unique speech characteristics. This resulted in the Eastern and Southern dialects of today. Major cities in the areas in which these dialects developed included Boston and New York in the North and Richmond and Charleston in the South.

Midland Dialect. In the early eighteenth century, many Scotch-Irish people came to western New York and to the Midland region, the area that lay between the established regions of the North and South. These pioneers pushed the frontier west and southwest, over the Appalachian mountains and into the Shenandoah Valley and the western portions of what are now the Carolinas and Georgia. Migrating westward, they carried their speech patterns with them, eventually creating the Midland dialect. During the same period, Germans arrived and settled in Pennsylvania (See "Pennsylvania Dutch," pages 38-39).

After these initial migrations, many settlers followed the Scotch-Irish to the frontier. Settlers from the Midland region continued to expand the frontier, west into what is now Kentucky, and north into Indiana, southern Ohio, and southern Illinois. Pioneers from western New England and western New York migrated into the Great Lakes area. There was also a slow and irregular migration of Southerners west into the Gulf States. The spread of the three major east coast dialects was, therefore, roughly horizontal across the continent, though there was considerable movement north and south as well, particularly of the Midland dialect.

Western Dialects. Eventually, settlers from the East moved into the extreme western parts of the United States. Because these settlers came from various dialect regions, there was a great deal of mixing of dialects in the American West. This is why it is virtually impossible to define distinct dialect boundaries in most western states. The situation is further complicated by the fact that Western speech also shows the influence of the languages of many immigrant groups. The Scandinavians in the Dakotas, for example, have contributed considerably to local speech patterns, as have the Spanish in Texas. Other groups that have influenced Western speech include the Orientals and Spanish in California, the Czechs in Nebraska, and the Poles and Hungarians in Minnesota.

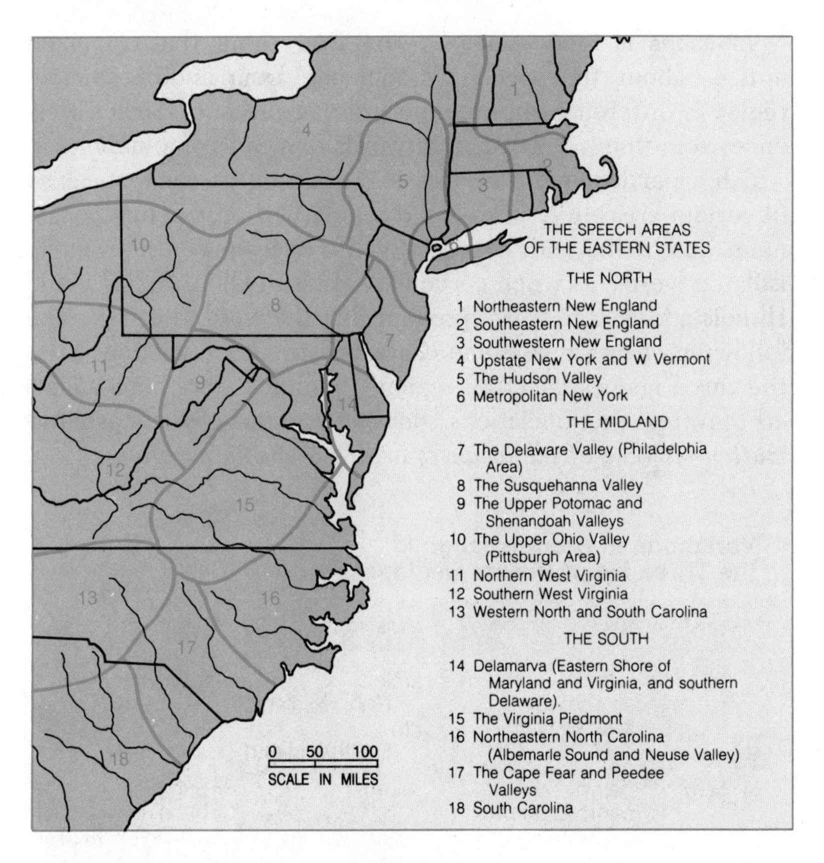

—KURATH, HANS. A World Geography of the Eastern United States. Studies in American English 1. University of Michigan Press, 1949, Fig. 3.

Variations in Regional Dialects

The regional dialects of America display differences in pronunciation, vocabulary, and grammar, as well as variations in rhythm, in pace, and in gestures and facial expressions.

When generalizing about the speech of any speech community, it is important to remember that there is also great diversity within communities. Thus, a statement about the characteristic speech of a particular region may not be true of specific places, people, or social groups within the region.

The following pages present a few characteristics found in the speech of the three major dialect regions in America.

Variations in Pronunciation. The first thing that a person notices about the speech of someone from another dialect region is differences in pronunciation, or "accent." Such differences sometimes appear in all words or word combinations in which a particular sound occurs. For example, some speakers in certain areas of New England regularly drop *r* before consonants and at the ends of words. Differences may also occur in isolated words, as when certain speakers in Ohio, Indiana, and Illinois add an *r* in *wash*, pronouncing the word as *warsh*. The following chart shows some characteristic pronunciations from the three major dialectical regions. Spellings have been adapted to reflect pronunciations. *Remember, none of these generalizations is true of all speakers or areas within a region.*

Variations in Pronunciation in the Three Major Dialect Regions

Word	North	Midland	South
creek	krĭk krēk	krēk (North Midland) krĭk (South Midland)	krĭk
barn	bahrn bahn (Eastern North)	bahrn	bahrn bahn (East Coast)
on	ahn	awn	awn
hoarse	hawrs	hawrs, hōrs	hawrs, haws
beard	bĭrd bĭuhd (Eastern North)	bĭrd	bĭuhd
put	pŭt	pŭt	pŭt, puht
new	noo	noo, nyoo	nyoo
poor	pŭr pŭuh (Eastern North)	pŭr	pŭuh pōuh pō
this	thĭs dĭs (urban)	thĭs	thĭs
greasy	grēsĭ	grēzĭ	grēzĭ
Mrs.	mĭsĭz	mĭsĭz	mĭzĭz, mĭz

Variations in Vocabulary. Also common in the three major dialects are variations in the vocabulary. Such regional differences are readily recognizable in the names given to foods. A sandwich that is made on a very large, elongated roll and filled with a variety of cold meats and cheeses may be called a *hero,* a *grinder,* a *poor boy,* a *hoagie* or a *submarine,* depending on the dialect of the speaker. Similarly, if you want to order a glass of carbonated water, you will have to decide whether to ask for *soda water, tonic, fizzy water,* or *seltzer,* depending on where you are when thirst strikes. The following chart shows a few of the objects and actions that are given different names by some speakers in different parts of the country:

Variations in Vocabulary in the Three Major Dialect Regions

Item	North	Midland	South
paper container	bag	sack	sack
faucet	faucet	spigot spicket	faucet spigot
insect	firefly (urban) lightning bug (rural)	lightning bug	lightning bug
insect	darning needle sewing bug dragonfly	snake feeder snake doctor dragonfly	snake feeder snake doctor mosquito hawk
container	pail	bucket	bucket
shelf above fireplace	mantel mantel piece	fireboard mantel board	shelf mantel
type of vegetable	string beans	green beans string beans	snap beans snaps
siding on house	clapboards	weatherboards weather-boarding	weatherboards weather-boarding
creek	brook	run	branch
bone from fowl	lucky-bone (New England) wish-bone	pully-bone	pully-bone

Variations in Grammar. In addition to variations in pronunciation and vocabulary, the three major dialect regions also show some variations in grammar and usage. For example, many speakers of Southern dialect use the phrase *you all* in place of the second person plural personal pronoun. Speakers of Northern dialect, on the other hand, sometimes use *hadn't ought* in place of such forms as *shouldn't have*. Other common variations are shown in the following chart:

Variations in Grammar in the Three Major Dialect Regions

	North	Midland	South
Trouble comes all ______ once.	to at	at	at
He's sick ______ his stomach.	to	at on in	at
I have two ______ of shoes.	pair	pairs	pair pairs
She ______ into the pool.	dove	dived	dived
I will ______ to the door.	take you escort you	take you see you	carry you see you
He lives ______ Pennsylvania Avenue.	in	on	on
They'll stand ______ line for hours.	on	in	in

Local Dialects Within Regions

The map on page 35 indicates that there are smaller speech communities within each of the three major dialect areas. One local dialect that has developed along the East coast, Pennsylvania Dutch, is a particularly interesting example of this type of smaller speech community. Because its members live in a fairly isolated manner, their speech has not been strongly influenced by contact with other dialects. Pennsylvania Dutch therefore shows more variation than other dialects and is harder for people outside the speech community to understand.

The name of the dialect derives from the word *Deutsch*, which is the German word for *German*. This dialect is characterized by special words that are not used by outsiders, such as *smearcase* for *cottage cheese* and *doodle* for *haystack*. The sentence structure that is used often reflects the German language, as in *I down the stairs fell*.

Exercises **Regional Dialects**

A. The regional dialects of America have made possible the creation of a lively and colorful regional literature that employs dialectical speech on the part of its characters. The following is a sample passage taken from a work of regional fiction. Study the passage. Then, write a composition analyzing the passage for unusual dialectical variations in pronunciation, vocabulary, and grammar.

> "No, Joanna was Joanna and there she lays on her island where she lived and did her poor penance. She told mother the day she was dyin' that she always used to want to be fetched inshore when it come to the last; but she'd thought it over, and desired to be buried on the island, if't was thought right. So the funeral was out there, a Saturday afternoon in September. 'T was a pretty day, and there wa'n't hardly a boat on the coast within twenty miles that didn't head for Shell-heap cram-full o' folks, an' all real respectful, same's if she'd always stayed ashore and held her friends. Some went out 'o mere curiosity, I don't doubt,—there's always such to every funeral; but most had real feelin' and went purpose to show it."—SARAH ORNE JEWETT,

B. With the other members of your class, put together a "dialect notebook" that compares the vocabularies of different regions. Interview each other, as well as relatives, friends, and neighbors, for interesting variations such as the ones shown on page 38. Discuss possible reasons for these differences.

Part 3 Social Dialects

Much of the research on dialects that has been done in the past few decades has concentrated on the dialects of city-dwellers. Studies conducted in the 1960's showed that, within the confines of a single metropolis, New York City, a variety of dialects are spoken. Such dialects reflect the social groups to which individual speakers belong. These groups consist of people of the same ethnic background, the same level of employment, or the same level of education.

One of the most important social dialects in America is Black English. Black English may vary a little from one region of the country to another, but the most significant element contributing to an individual's use of this dialect is not *where* he or she lives, but rather his or her membership in the black community. Sometimes this dialect is used unconsciously, and at other times it is consciously adopted as a means of identification with the community. Many blacks, of course, do not speak Black English at all.

Like other dialects, Black English has regular patterns of pronunciation and grammar that are observed by its speakers. These variations give Black English a distinctive sound and character. However, speakers of this or any other dialect often find themselves faced with a problem: how to reconcile their speech patterns with the patterns accepted in other speech communities. This concern will be discussed in Part 4.

Exercise Social Dialects

Each of the stories below makes use of dialects. Read one of the stories, noting examples of dialectical variations in pronunciation, vocabulary, or grammar. Then, write a composition describing how social dialect adds to the color and vividness of the tale.

William Faulkner, "Barn Burning"
Richard Wright, "The Man Who Saw the Flood"
Toni Cade Bambara, "Blues Ain't No Mockin' Bird"
John Updike, "A & P"

Part 4 Attitudes Toward Dialectical English

Many linguists, or experts in language, believe that all dialects are equally correct and worthy of study. This is because all dialects can be equally useful for communicating ideas. However, in order for different groups to communicate effectively, there must be some agreement as to what constitutes "correct" language. Thus, there are certain pronunciations, vocabulary items, and grammatical forms that educators and linguists have labeled as "standard," just as there are certain widely agreed-upon or "standard" spellings for words.

During the past century, American English has become increasingly standardized due to the influence of travel, public education, and the mass media. For this reason, standard English is today expected of most people in formal, institutional, or public settings. In fact, employers and teachers often make important judgments based upon the ability of their employees or students to communicate in accurate, standard English.

This situation presents a problem for all speakers: How does one meet the public demand for standard English and still retain the dialect that is used at home or among friends? For many speakers, the solution to this problem is **style-shifting**—using more than one type of speech and switching from one to another as the situation demands.

Part 5 Levels of Language

As you learned in Part 4, speakers often adapt their language to suit particular audiences and situations. Even speakers of the most widely used dialects choose different **levels of language** for different occasions. To choose appropriate language, you must first identify both your situation and audience. Once you have this information, you can then select the appropriate level of English.

Standard English

Standard English is language that is acceptable at all times and in all places. There are two levels of standard English: formal and informal.

Formal English is language that is suited to serious, dignified, or ceremonial occasions. It is the language most often used for sermons, lectures, and speeches. In addition, scholarly journals, legal documents, business reports, and textbooks are generally written in formal English, as is the following example.

> In such an expression as "We must listen to *both* sides of every question," there is an assumption, frequently unexamined, that every question has, fundamentally, only two sides. We tend to think in opposites, to feel that what is not "good" must be "bad" and that what is not "bad" must be "good." This tendency to see things in terms of two values only, affirmative and negative, good and bad, hot and cold, love and hate, may be termed the *two-valued orientation*.
>
> —S.I. HAYAKAWA
> *Language in Action*

Informal English is appropriate for use in everyday situations. Also known as **colloquial English,** it is the language of conversation and of informal talks. It is also widely used in newspaper and magazine articles. The following is an example.

> "Where's my pet monkey Mimi?" squeaked an elderly woman wrapped in a bright pink kimono. "Someone's stolen my wallet, and I can't buy myself a train ticket home," moaned a lanky teen-ager. For the two officers stationed at the Ochanomisu police box in the heart of Tokyo, the complaints were typical. Within fifteen minutes they had soothed the woman with a promise to be on the lookout for her pet (it was found) and lent the penniless youth 560 yen ($2.33) from a special emergency fund in exchange for a signed IOU. . . . Said Sergeant Shigeo Takahashi, grinning with satisfaction: "You stand here for a quarter of an hour, and you can do as deep a study of life as is possible."—*Time*

The following chart describes the differences between formal and informal English and suggests the appropriate uses and audiences for each.

Characteristics of Formal and Informal English

	Formal	Informal
Tone	Serious, reserved, academic, ceremonial	Personal, friendly, casual
Vocabulary and Mechanics	Sometimes uses longer or more complicated words Avoids contractions, clipped words, and slang Uses correct grammar, spelling, and punctuation	Uses simpler words Often uses contractions and clipped words Avoids slang Uses correct grammar, spelling, and punctuation
Organization	Uses longer, carefully constructed sentences	Uses sentences of a great variety of length Is similar to conversational English
Appropriate Uses	Reports or serious essays Legal, academic, religious, or other professional documents Formal speeches, debates, or interviews	Writing intended for a general audience Conversations, letters Informal talks
Audience	Readers of scholarly material Readers of professional documents Persons in positions of authority	Friends, co-workers Most general audiences

Nonstandard English

Nonstandard English is language that does not conform to accepted standards of grammar, usage, and mechanics. It is chiefly a form of spoken English. If it appears in print, it is usually in the dialogue of a character in a story or a play.

Slang is one kind of very informal language that is not accepted as standard English. It contains many newly coined words, or altered forms of old words used in new ways. One of two things happens to most slang: It becomes widely used, people tire of it, and then it is discarded; or it becomes a permanent part of our vocabulary. For example, few people today use the words *groovy* or *far-out,* slang terms associated with the 1960's. However, many people do use the words *hot dog, varsity,* and *jazz,* all of which originated as slang, but are now accepted as standard English. Because most slang usually disappears after a short period of time, it is best to avoid using it.

Gobbledygook is another kind of language that is not accepted as standard. It is characterized by overloaded sentences and vague, abstract, uncommon, or technical words. Writing of this sort is often found in business or government publications. The following is an example:

> The dealer and/or his/her authorized representative, from the effective date shown, for the period of time of the contractual agreement described herein or for the accumulated actual miles indicated above, whichever shall first occur, agrees to repair, replace (or reimburse if unable to repair or replace) the listed covered component parts of the vehicle described herein, which shall fail to perform its intended purpose, subject to all other terms of this contract.

What this means, quite simply, is this: If any of the following parts of your car break down while this contract is in effect, the dealer agrees to fix the parts, replace them, or reimburse you.

Avoid gobbledygook by using language that is simple and direct. Do not use words and constructions that are unnecessary, overly elaborate, too formal, or too unfamiliar; and avoid packing too much information into a single sentence.

Exercises Levels of Language

A. The following composition contains a mixture of levels of language, including elements of formal English, informal English, and slang. Identify those elements and then rewrite the composition, making the language suitable for a school report.

Surrealism is a movement in art and literature that began in Paris in 1924. The aim of the movement was to kind of get people to respond to plain old everyday things by presenting these everyday things in odd, dreamlike combinations.

Two really weird surrealist painters are René Magritte and Salvador Dali. Magritte painted some really neat stuff, including pictures of birds and people made of stone, apples that fill entire rooms, and men in bowler hats kind of hanging in the sky. In this respect, the works of Magritte and Dali are similar, for Dali also presents images in wild combinations. Several of his canvases, for example, depict melting clocks, burning giraffes, and objects propped up by leafless sticks or branches.

Perhaps because of these peculiarities, the works of Magritte and Dali are still immensely popular, especially among young people. Though artists generally don't work in the surrealist mode any more, copies of the works of surrealists like Magritte and Dali are still being sold.

B. Translate the following passages of gobbledygook into simple, direct English. Use a dictionary as necessary.

1. To preserve and maintain the viability of flora within the confines of a private residence or domicile, position said flora in areas such that there is properly contingent illumination and irrigate sufficiently to prevent dehydration.

2. As writing utensils are requisite to the completion of innumerable tasks assigned at all levels of secondary education, and as provision of these utensils lies not within the scope of the stated obligations of most academic institutions, it is necessary that you personally procure the aforesaid utensils and place them among your personal effects.

SUMMARY AND APPLICATIONS

1. Learning about dialects and the levels of language will help you appreciate the flexibility of English. It will also help you to adapt your writing and speech to suit particular occasions.
2. Dialects, which are regular patterns of variation found within particular speech communities, differ from one another in pronunciation, vocabulary, and, less frequently, in grammar or sentence structure.
3. There are three major regional dialects in America: Northern, Midland, and Southern. The speech of the Western part of the United States contains elements of these and other dialects.
4. Use of a social dialect is determined by a speaker's membership in a particular social group. Social dialects reflect the ancestral language, occupation, and level of education of the speaker.
5. A speaker or writer may choose between informal or formal standard English, depending on his or her audience and purpose. Gobbledygook is rarely appropriate to any occasion and should therefore be avoided.

Applications in Other Subject Areas

Mass Media. Choose two or three television programs that feature speakers from various social groups and areas of the country. Listen carefully to an episode of each of these programs, noting examples of dialectical speech. Write down several of these examples, spelling the words as they are pronounced. Then, choose one program, and write a brief composition explaining how the use of dialect adds to the color and realism of the show.

Fine Arts / Music. Choose a favorite work of art or piece of music and write a brief composition, in formal English, explaining why you think this work has artistic merit. Then, rewrite your comments in informal English, as though you were including them in a letter to a friend.

Chapter 3

Writing Effective Sentences

Using the right word at the right time is the secret of a fresh and vigorous style. As your vocabulary develops, the expression of your judgments and feelings will become more precise. The *effectiveness* of your expression, however, depends upon how you put words together. In English, meaning is not conveyed by words alone; it is conveyed by words working together in groups—in phrases, clauses, and sentences.

Successful writing is therefore largely a matter of effective sentences. When you have learned to write clear, straightforward sentences, your writing will do what you intend it to do.

The authors of this text have studied over three thousand samples of student writing. They have analyzed these samples to determine the kinds of sentence problems that occur most frequently. Chapters 3–6 set forth those sentence problems and show ways of avoiding or correcting them. These chapters will also introduce you to revision, an important step in the process of writing that you will study in detail in Chapter 7.

Part 1 Avoiding Empty Sentences

The function of a sentence is to convey facts, ideas, and feelings.

Writing cannot be done well in haste. It cannot be done well without thought. Sentences like the following result from haste and from failure to think before beginning to write.

> Schools are too crowded because there are too many students and classes are overcrowded and the schools are too small as well as the incredible population growth.

This sentence begins well: "Schools are too crowded because . . ." The writer promises to explain why schools are too crowded. What is the reason given? ". . . there are too many students . . ." That is no reason. The writer is simply saying, "Schools are too crowded because they are too crowded."As an afterthought, she adds something about the school size and population growth. The sentence says nothing; it is an empty sentence.

Lack of classroom space and population growth are important points. They are directly related to the problem. The writer's task is to think through the relationship and to express it clearly. If she had thought first, she might have written this:

> Inadequate classroom space and incredible population growth are responsible for our overcrowded schools.

Here is another example of an empty sentence:

> Young people find rock music appealing because they really enjoy it.

This sentence says only that young people like rock music because they like rock music. Why do they like it? If the writer had reasons, these reasons should have been given. If the writer did not have reasons, the sentence should have merely expressed the opinion without pretending to offer an explanation. By using "because" the writer has led the reader to expect reasons and details. The following sentence corrects this.

> Young people find rock music appealing because they like its beat, and the lyrics express their feelings.

Exercise Avoiding Empty Sentences

Rewrite the following empty sentences. In some cases you will need to shorten the sentences. In other cases, you will need to add facts or ideas.

1. In this play you have to have imagination, for there is no scenery and you have to supply the scenery from your own mind by using your imagination.
2. I'd like to be a commercial airline pilot because that is what I've always wanted to be.
3. Bob is planning to go to agricultural school so he will have a good background in scientific farming before he goes into it.
4. It may cost more money to go to college than we can afford, and that is one drawback that might hinder me.
5. A football player must have a quick mind as well as quick feet, and his mind must be clear as a bell as well.
6. I like the book because it is the kind of book I read.
7. Most of the inhabitants of India are Hindus, but not all the inhabitants are.
8. Reggae is a popular form of music because it has a quality of rhythm and melody that makes it a popular form of music.
9. I was glad to have a chance to see the TV program.
10. Scientists say that foods eaten as soon as possible after picking contain more vitamins, and that prolonged cooking or canning causes foods to have fewer vitamins than if they are freshly picked and eaten.
11. Experience with many kinds of people is an important part of education, and I think that everybody should have this kind of experience.
12. I think that America should build a permanent space station soon because I believe that building one would be a good thing for our country.
13. I'd like to be a basketball coach because I'd love to do that and get paid for it too.
14. Put stereo speakers at least ten feet apart from each other since ten feet apart is the best distance for them to be.
15. I know I did well on the test because the test was easy for me to do well on and I did so without any trouble.

Part 2 Avoiding Overloaded Sentences

The guides to writing effective sentences are few and simple to learn.

1. Say one thing at a time.
2. Say it clearly and directly.

Everyone has the experience of writing sentences that try to say too much. They become so crowded that the writer cannot remember what he started to say, and the reader becomes fatigued from trying to follow the thought. Even professional writers make this mistake. You do not see many of their overloaded sentences because professional writers revise their work before publication. Here is one from the editorial pages of *The New York Times*.

> To execute the mandate of the New York constitution that the state budget must be balanced and at the same time to expand the state aid to political subdivisions and individuals that he feels the growing needs and rights of the people require, the Governor proposed a record rise of $575 million in state taxes.

This passage might better have been written as follows:

> (1) The New York state constitution requires that the state budget be balanced. (2) At the same time, the Governor feels that the growing needs and the rights of the people require an expansion of state aid. (3) To meet these conflicting requirements, he has proposed an increase of $575 million in state taxes.

When you find an overloaded sentence in your own writing, examine it carefully. Look for the main idea; look for the subject and verb that make the framework of this idea. Start over again with this subject-verb combination. Drop irrelevant details entirely. If the left-over details are important, start with a new subject-verb combination and pull the details together around it.

OVERLOADED: As it would cost too much for all the renovations needed for my concept of a perfect school the only alternative is that we be allowed to go to our lockers any time and thus the time between classes would have to be lengthened.

IMPROVED: The cost of renovations needed for my concept of a perfect school would be impossible to meet. The only alternative is to lengthen the time between class periods and allow us to go to our lockers whenever necessary.

Exercise Avoiding Overloaded Sentences

Rewrite the following overloaded sentences. There may be more than one right way to improve them. You may need to add words and details.

1. While I am covering these various news stories, I will be able to learn many new things as well as understand things I know even better, and also help the paper's readers to be able to learn and understand different things that happen in the world better.

2. A salesperson must have a number of different approaches in order to interest the customer in more than one product, in that way giving the customer a choice and giving the salesperson an opportunity to show the customer the need for one product or the other.

3. When Charles Goodyear dropped a piece of rubber mixed with sulphur on a hot stove, he accidentally discovered a new process, which was how rubber could be vulcanized.

4. When the nasturtiums did not grow, the gardener used nitrogen, and when that didn't work he used peat moss, which he worked into the soil.

5. Kutztown is in the Pennsylvania Dutch country, and it is the scene of a folk festival every year, which is a unique event.

6. Some of the ancestors of the Pennsylvania Dutch came from Holland, but most of them came from Germany and Switzerland, which you may already know.

7. Basketball was invented in 1891 by James A. Naismith, who was a Y.M.C.A. instructor and who needed an indoor game for winter play, so he nailed peach baskets at either end of a gymnasium and used a soccer ball for play.

8. If we had had trained actors, they would have remembered their lines, and if we had had a prompter handy, she could have prompted the actors, but we didn't.

9. Through the city of Chicago run two branches of the Chicago River, which is known as "the river that flows backward" because the flow was reversed by an amazing scientific feat.

10. I read that the world's highest mountain is not Mount Everest but a mountain in the Hawaiian Islands called Mauna Kea, which is partly submerged in the Pacific and is 33,476 feet high.

Part 3 Avoiding Wordiness

A sentence that uses more words than necessary is boring. The extra words smother the meaning. The writer with a sharp eye can spot excess words and delete them during revision of the work.

One kind of wordiness arises from needless repetition of a word or from needless use of words with similar meanings.

> Many people like the *modern* artists of *today*.
> Life is *not easy* but involves many *hardships*.
> The *magnificence* of the scene awed me with its *grandeur*.

Another kind of wordiness arises from the repetition of *that*.

> You knew *that* if you failed *that* you could not be on the team.
> I promised *that* when I returned *that* I would call her.

In the last two sentences, the second *that* may be dropped.

In general, wordiness results simply from the use of too many words. The writer may use a phrase or a clause when a single word would suffice. Methods of avoiding or repairing wordiness are considered in Chapter 4 under the heading *Reducing Sentences To Eliminate Wordiness*.

Awkward Repetition

Sentences lose their effectiveness if a word or phrase is repeated carelessly. Sometimes there is no substitute for a word, and it must be repeated. Awkward repetition is the use of a word or phrase a second or third time when it need not be repeated. Such awkward repetition can be corrected by using a synonym, by using pronouns in place of nouns, or by rewriting the entire sentence.

AWKWARD: During prime time there are more *silly situation comedies* than there are serious dramas and news programs. Many of these *silly situation comedies* are simply boring.

IMPROVED: During prime time, silly situation comedies, many of which are simply boring, outnumber serious dramas and news programs.

AWKWARD: Try studying for one month without the *television and radio on* and you will see how your grades improve because you have not been distracted by having the *television and radio on*.

IMPROVED: Try studying for one month without the distractions of television and radio, and you will notice an improvement in your grades.

Exercise Avoiding Wordiness

Revise the following sentences, correcting wordiness.

1. During an ice storm, the car slipped on the ice and slid into a ditch.
2. As a general rule I'm usually at home by 4:00 P.M. in the afternoon whenever possible.
3. The Senator answered all of the questions unhesitatingly and without any reservations.
4. The essential requirements necessary for employment are carefully outlined in this thorough pamphlet which tells you everything you will need to know.

5. To my way of thinking, I think it is time to discuss salaries and working conditions.

6. I saw a person who was a suspicious-looking character crossing the street.

7. The statement is almost self-explanatory itself, so I will not try to explain it.

8. The start of English literature had its beginning in the Anglo-Saxon period, which was from the year 449 to 1066.

9. Banks recommend that you save a part of your paycheck regularly and that you make a habit of doing this.

10. Would you mind repeating the question again?

Part 4 Avoiding Awkward Beginnings

The normal, easily readable pattern of English sentences is subject—verb—complement. A great many awkward sentences occur when this pattern is abandoned. Certain expressions, if used at the beginning of a sentence, create awkwardness. They delay the thought, and they add nothing to it. Usually, they are not needed at all. The most common of these offending expressions are *The fact that, What I believe is, What I want is, Being that, The reason is*.

AWKWARD: *What I believe is* that the honor system has worked.

BETTER: I believe that the honor system has worked.

EVEN BETTER: The honor system has worked.

AWKWARD: *Being that* Bill never sets his alarm clock, he is often late for class.

BETTER: Since Bill never sets his alarm clock, he is often late for class.

AWKWARD: *The fact that* you want to learn should make you study.

BETTER: Wanting to learn should make you study.

AWKWARD: *What the* officers object to is the lack of cooperation.

BETTER: The officers object to the lack of cooperation.

AWKWARD: *The reason* the jet crashed *was because* of a storm.

BETTER: The jet crashed because of a storm.

Exercise Revising Sentences with Awkward Beginnings

Revise these sentences to remove their awkward beginnings.

1. The fact that I am late is because I had a flat tire.
2. Nothing looks better to me than to see a beautiful sunrise in the morning.
3. The reason he failed to run with the ball was due to the fact that he had sprained his ankle.
4. The thing I am looking forward to being is a geologist.
5. The reason our team lost the opening game is because the field was wet.
6. What *stalemate* is is when a player cannot move without moving into check.
7. What everyone with children should have is a playroom.
8. The fact that I had to get a check cashed at the supermarket is why I am late.
9. The reason some students never get an education is because they work for marks only.
10. Being that I had seen the picture, I went to another.
11. What I am looking forward to becoming is an interior designer.
12. It is an actual fact that India has well over two hundred languages.
13. When the pilot began to worry was when she was becoming low on fuel.
14. What you call a squeeze play is when the batter bunts to score a runner from third.
15. The reason the mayor lost the election was because his record of administration had been very poor.

SUMMARY AND APPLICATIONS

1. Learning to write effective sentences will help you to achieve clarity of expression in your writing.
2. To correct an empty sentence, think through the relationship that you are attempting to express. Then, shorten the sentence or add additional facts and ideas.
3. To correct an overloaded sentence, look for the main idea, express this idea in a separate sentence, drop any irrelevant details, and place any important details that remain in a new sentence.
4. To correct a wordy sentence, look for repeated or unnecessary ideas and delete them.
5. Avoid awkward sentence openings that add no essential information.

Applications in Other Subject Areas

Vocational or Industrial Arts / Home Economics. In applied sciences such as Home Economics or Vocational or Industrial Arts, precise descriptions and explanations are extremely important, especially with regard to the use of tools and machinery. Choose a tool that is used in cooking, sewing, woodworking, or any other applied science. In a brief composition, describe the tool and its uses. Be precise, clear, and economical in your use of words.

Science / Health. Because of their complexity, scientific concepts present special problems to writers who attempt to explain them. Among the most common pitfalls in scientific writing are wordiness and overloaded sentences. Choose one of the following scientific concepts and research it. Then, write an explanation of the concept. Make your explanation clear and straightforward enough that it might be included in an encyclopedia for children.

Photosynthesis	Nuclear fission	Cell division
Metabolism	Entropy	Carbon dating

Chapter 4

Revising Your Sentences

Everyone is called upon at times to speak without preparation. In conversation and discussion, in class meetings, faculty meetings, or business conferences, a question will arise on which you must say something. In these situations there is little time to arrange your thoughts. You do your best, and the quality of your "best" depends upon previous experience and training.

In writing, the situation is different. There is always a point at which you can go back over what you have written and put it in order. You can reorganize; you can rearrange your paragraphs; you can revise your sentences. This chapter deals with the kinds of revisions you will find it profitable to make in your sentences.

Part 1 Omitting Unrelated Details

The function of a sentence is to state an idea, to present facts, or to describe feelings. When unrelated details appear in a sentence, they interrupt the flow of thought. They are as distracting as an orange flower on a pink dress or as tennis shoes worn with a tuxedo.

In sentence revision, keep your mind on the main idea. Delete any detail that is not closely related to this idea.

> I would like to be a pilot like my uncle, who owns a motorboat and flies from coast to coast each week.

Clearly, the motorboat has nothing to do with being a pilot. It might have something to do with "my uncle's" success as a pilot, but his success is another matter. It belongs in another sentence.

> The colorful spectacle of the opening of the Olympics, which we follow closely, still includes the Greek custom of lighting the torch.

Following the Olympics closely has nothing to do with its colorful ceremonies. If it seems important to include this idea, do so in another sentence.

Exercise Omitting Unrelated Details

Rewrite these sentences, omitting details that are not related to the main idea.

1. We often go to Maine, which is known as the Pine Tree State, because we enjoy sailing and fishing.
2. Because of the parking problem, it is easier to shop at the shopping center outside our town, which has a population of 10,000.
3. The service station attendant told us that Mac's Garage would repair our odometer, which registered 26,000 miles.
4. *Sherlock Holmes*, the Broadway play, received unfavorable comments from the critics, who got free tickets to opening night.

5. The book club, which has a thousand members, has chosen this novel for summer reading.

6. Our sub-compact, which is metallic blue, has two advantages over large cars: it is easy to park and economical to run.

7. We had a sneak preview of the Manet exhibit at The Art Institute of Chicago, which is a beautiful building.

8. The alumni reunion at my parents' college, which is one of the oldest institutions in the country, takes place each June.

9. The trip to Washington, which we took last year and which we are planning to take again this year, will be well worthwhile if you see nothing but cherry blossoms in bloom.

10. From lookout towers, where two of my friends have jobs, rangers maintain a constant check on forest fires.

11. "Road rash," "nose wheelies," and "360's" are key words for skateboard enthusiasts, who seem to dominate our block, which is near Ohio Stadium.

12. Do you realize what you could have bought for a nickel in 1915 when all nickels were the Indian-head type?

13. Carlton Fisk struck out, and Greg Luzinski, who has made a number of television commercials, hit a grounder to second base.

14. Theodore Roosevelt loved boxing, Lincoln enjoyed wrestling, and Jackson, whose nickname was "Old Hickory," owned a racing stable.

15. Birds range in size from the tiny hummingbird, which weighs less than a penny, to the ostrich, which weighs up to 300 pounds and lays eggs that some people think are quite tasty.

Part 2 Keeping Related Sentence Parts Together

Certain sentence parts derive much of their meaning from their relation to each other: subject and verb; verb and complement; the parts of a verb phrase. When these related sentence parts are widely separated by intervening words, the sentence is difficult to read. In general, keep closely related sentence parts together.

AWKWARD: *Sarah,* after she watched a new TV show, *wrote* a letter of complaint to the local station. (subject and verb separated)

REVISED: After she watched a new TV show, Sarah wrote a letter of complaint to the local station.

AWKWARD: The visitor to Rome *was,* as she surveyed the city, *struck* by its mixture of ancient and modern. (parts of a verb phrase separated)

REVISED: As she surveyed the city, the visitor to Rome was struck by its mixture of ancient and modern.

AWKWARD: TV *exerts,* for good or bad, an *influence* on the public. (verb and object separated)

REVISED: For good or bad, TV exerts an influence on the public.

Exercise **Keeping Related Sentence Parts Together**

Revise these sentences to bring related parts closer together.

1. He is the last person, for all we know, who saw her alive.
2. He enjoys, unfortunately, every motion picture and television program he watches.
3. The climbers were, having spent the whole day crossing the mountain pass, tired enough to go straight to sleep.
4. The coach, in all her years at camp, had never seen such fine sportsmanship.
5. The car finally, after twenty years of faithful service, had to be towed to the junkyard.
6. The date, the place, and the weather, as I remember, were the reasons that the outdoor show was so poorly attended.
7. Hannah's action, to put it mildly, was inconsiderate.
8. The ceiling beams had, after many years' wear, begun to show signs of dry rot.
9. The air conditioner, for some reason or other, went completely out of commission.
10. Life expectancy, according to modern surveys, has increased from 40 to 70 years since 1850.

11. The speaker presented after dinner a history of computation from finger-counting to microcomputer.

12. Weasels kill more animals than they can eat often.

Part 3 Avoiding Stringy Sentences

Some sentences become overloaded because the writer strings a number of ideas together, placing *and's* between ideas. The result is that no one idea stands out; there seems to be no organization. You can revise stringy sentences in two ways.

1. Choose the conjunction that will show the real relationship between the ideas you are presenting.
2. Divide the sentence into two or more sentences.

STRINGY: The class discussed the question of morality in a literary work and mentioned the problem of censorship that is so controversial today and offered their own opinions about the wisdom of imposing it by law.

REVISED: The class discussed the question of morality in a literary work. They mentioned the problem of censorship, so controversial today, and offered opinions about the wisdom of imposing it by law.

STRINGY: Innsbruck is a city and lies in the valley of the Inn River in the Austrian Tyrol and is an ideal location for winter sports and it has numerous and fast downhill courses which are a great challenge for the skiers who go there to compete in international championships.

REVISED: Innsbruck, a city in the Austrian Tyrol, lies in the valley of the Inn River. It is an ideal location for winter sports competition because of its numerous and fast downhill courses. These courses are a great challenge for the skiers who go there to compete in international championships.

Exercise Revising Stringy Sentences

The following sentences have too many *and*'s. Revise each sentence. In each instance, you will need to make two or more sentences.

1. Many people fear old age, and they think it means becoming debilitated, and they don't try to take steps to keep themselves useful members of society.
2. Most children like to draw, and they draw freely with imagination unless some adult interferes with their work, and then they become self-conscious and their work becomes more inhibited and less creative.
3. It is better to spend less than you earn, and then you can start a bank account and save some money.
4. The northern lights, which are huge rays of bluish-green, pink, yellow, or white light in the northern sky, are a real sight to see, and they are also called the aurora borealis.
5. The northern lights are caused by electrified particles from the sun, and these particles strike rare gases in the earth's upper air and make them glow.
6. The earth's most abundant form of animal life finally has a zoo of its own, and it is located at the Smithsonian Institution in Washington and is called the Insect Zoo.
7. A new magazine about the film industry is now being published in the United States, and it is called *The Movies*.
8. There is a magazine for Italian-Americans, and it is called *I-AM*, and it was the first magazine ever published for Italian-Americans.
9. I was calmly waiting to make a deposit into my savings account, and the bank was suddenly transformed into a confusing scene of alarms, sirens, police, and frightened employees, and it turned out that one of the employees had pushed the alarm button by mistake.
10. The early settlers in what is now the state of Colorado first wanted to call it Jefferson, and then tried to have it named Idaho, and finally settled for the original Spanish name that the conquistadors had used, which was Colorado, and that means "reddish" or "colored."

Part 4 Subordinating Ideas in Sentences

All sentences contain one or more clauses. A **clause** is a group of words that contains a subject and a verb. The **main clause** provides the basic structure in the sentence. It states the main idea. Modifying clauses and phrases are used to add details or to explain the conditions that define or limit the meaning of the main clause. (See Section 3.3 in the Handbook.)

You alone know what the main idea is in each sentence you write. If all of your sentences contain only main clauses, you give your reader no guidance; hence, the effectiveness of what you are saying is lost.

Main Idea	Limiting, Explaining, or Defining Details
He has a right to protest (at any time?)	if the rules are violated. (under this condition)
June will be sent for (why?)	to serve as a witness. (explanation)
The actor achieved his ambition (how?)	playing the role of Hamlet. (defining details)

To provide guidance to the reader, materials of less importance can be subordinated (given less importance) by use of **subordinate clauses.** These are clauses that cannot stand alone. They must be connected to a main clause with a subordinating conjunction, such as *because, since, after,* or *when*. (See Sections 3.3, 3.4, and 3.5 in your Handbook.)

When a sentence contains two main clauses that are connected by *and,* the sentence can often be improved by changing one of the clauses to a subordinate clause. This involves deciding which of the two ideas is less important and then introducing it with a subordinating conjunction that expresses the relationship between the two ideas.

FAULTY: The visibility was poor, and all flights had to be canceled.

REVISED: *Because* the visibility was poor, all flights had to be canceled. (The *and* was eliminated, and the word *Because* was added to one of the clauses.)

FAULTY: I handed in my composition, and my teacher suggested revision.

REVISED: *After* I had handed in my composition, my teacher suggested revisions. (The *and* was eliminated, and the word *After* was added to a clause.)

FAULTY: The restaurant serves some of the finest French food found in America, and it is near Chicago.

REVISED: The restaurant, which is near Chicago, serves some of the finest French food found in America. (The word *it* was replaced by *which*.)

In each of the preceding examples, the writer has joined two clauses that are obviously not of equal importance. The *and* placed between the clauses does not mean "in addition to." It has been replaced by a subordinating conjunction that clearly expresses the relationship between the two clauses.

The same kind of improvement can sometimes be made by converting a clause into a participial phrase. Such a phrase modifies one of the words in the main clause.

WEAK: Amy knew the facts, *and* she answered all the questions clearly and completely.

REVISED: *Knowing* the facts, Amy answered all the questions clearly and completely. (The *and* was eliminated, and the first clause was turned into a phrase beginning with the word *Knowing*.)

WEAK: Big Jake was pinned under the fallen tree, *and* he shouted for help.

REVISED: *Pinned* under the fallen tree, Big Jake shouted for help. (The *and* was eliminated, and the first clause was turned into a phrase beginning with *Pinned*.)

Materials of less importance can also be subordinated by the use of **appositives,** which are words or phrases that repeat an idea in different words.

FAIR: The video recorder is a useful teaching aid. It makes our science lessons exciting and profitable.

BETTER: The video recorder, *a useful teaching aid,* makes our science lessons exciting and profitable. (The *and* was eliminated, and the first clause was made into an appositive phrase.)

Upside-Down Subordination

Upside-down subordination is the fault of placing an important idea in a subordinate clause or phrase.

FAULTY: Lightning struck the car, *killing the driver*. (The killing of the driver is more important.)

REVISED: When lightning struck the car, the driver was killed.

FAULTY: The game, *which gave us the championship,* was our last of the season.

REVISED: The game, which was our last of the season, gave us the championship.

REVISED: We clinched the championship when we won the last game of the season.

Exercises Subordinating Ideas

A. Combine each pair of sentences, converting one into either a phrase or a subordinate clause. Avoid upside-down subordination.

1. The brakes froze. The car crashed into the lane divider.
2. Last night we were watching TV. Our cat rushed into the room and sprang onto the set.
3. We were parked on the wrong side of the street. A police officer gave us a ticket.

4. The judge was busy taking notes. She did not see the demonstration the witness was putting on.

5. The teacher looked into his desk. A small white mouse jumped out onto his lap.

6. The author is only twenty-three. Her book has won widespread recognition.

7. Be sure to save the weekend of June 17 and 18 for the convention. The convention will be held in Cincinnati.

8. My birthday party for Mother was a great success. I served her favorite dishes.

9. Beth is studying chemistry. She wants to become a research chemist.

10. Luis canceled his violin lessons. He broke his wrist.

B. Change the following compound sentences by subordinating one of the clauses. You may change it to either a subordinate clause or a phrase.

1. In the Virgin Islands, the climate is temperate, and the temperature varies only ten degrees throughout the seasons.

2. The Boers were defeated by the British, but they still retain their authority in South Africa.

3. The course in creative writing is given on Wednesdays, and it is well attended.

4. The jeweler cleaned the watch thoroughly, and the watch kept better time.

5. Ms. Howard has held important positions in Turkey and Iran, and she is now working in Beirut.

6. Veterans Day used to be called Armistice Day, and it is a legal holiday.

7. Dad lost his car key, and ever since he has kept a duplicate key under the hood.

8. The newest ocean liners are equipped with stabilizers, and these stabilizers reduce the roll to two degrees.

9. An old-fashioned delicacy is rose-petal jam, and you can still buy it in fancy food stores.

10. President McKinley was attending the Pan-American Exposition in Buffalo, and he was assassinated.

C. Correct the upside-down subordination in these sentences.

1. Debra was taking a walk in the woods when she saw a rattlesnake.
2. The next morning I called the gardener, telling him that he had planted my shrubs in the wrong place.
3. Although he was a minibike racing champ, he was only eleven years old.
4. The plane, which made a crash landing, came from Detroit.
5. The Coast Guard plane, searching for survivors of a ditched oil tanker, flew low over Atlantic waters.
6. The train, which was three hours late because of a power failure, was en route to Boston from New York.
7. The tenement, which was gutted by fire, had corridors filled with rubbish.
8. The children, who were saved, were carried down fire escapes and ladders by the neighbors.
9. Whenever Dad plays golf, he has a free weekend.
10. Walking onto the stage, he whistled under his breath.

Part 5 Reducing Sentences To Eliminate Wordiness

Reduction is the means by which bulky sentences are made compact and effective. Reduction can be achieved by changing a clause to a phrase or a phrase to a single modifier.

CLAUSE: I go to a school *that has closed-circuit television.*

PHRASE: I go to a school *with closed-circuit television.*

PHRASE: One of the old programs *on radio* was revived.

WORD: One of the old *radio* programs was revived.

CLAUSE: Swift wrote *Gulliver's Travels, which is a satire.*

APPOSITIVE: Swift wrote *Gulliver's Travels, a satire.*

If two clauses have the same subject or verb, they can be reduced by combining these similar sentence parts with *and*.

SAME SUBJECT: The freshmen followed her advice, *and they decided to take industrial arts*.

REDUCED: The freshmen *followed* her advice and *decided* to take industrial arts.

SAME SUBJECT: The box weighs too much, *and it is awkward to carry*.

REDUCED: The box *weighs* too much and *is* awkward to carry.

SAME VERB: The fragile ornaments were packed carefully. The *figurines* were carefully packed, too.

REDUCED: The *fragile ornaments and figurines* were packed carefully.

Exercise **Reducing Sentences**

Rewrite these sentences, reducing the italicized words to a shorter construction.

1. The university, *which has a research department*, will publish its findings in a scientific report.
2. The anthropologist, *who is a specialist in Indian life*, read a paper before the historical society.
3. The O'Keeffe Center for the Performing Arts, *which is a non-profit theater located in Toronto*, cost $12,000,000.
4. Dr. Baker, *who is a psychoanalyst and is well known*, will handle this case.
5. The blunder was mine, *but the blunder was yours, too*.
6. Wordsworth is often called a poet of nature, *and he was one of the Lake poets of England*.
7. A conference on new sources of energy was held in August, and *the conference was at Sugar Loaf Mountain*.
8. Nobody knows precisely what makes rain, *and it is one of the commonest of weather phenomena*.
9. The report, *which was long and tedious*, was delivered to an audience *that was altogether bored*.

10. Fund raising, *which is a business in itself,* is handled by experts in the field.

11. The Constitution states that the census must be taken every ten years, *and the first census was taken in 1790.*

12. Golf, *which was a favorite game of James I and Charles I, who were Stuart kings,* became known as "the royal and ancient game."

13. The cliché, *which is a trite or hackneyed expression,* should be avoided whenever possible.

14. Puerto Rico, *which is a self-governing Commonwealth associated with the United States,* is a beautiful tropical island.

15. Reading, *which is a delightful pastime,* is also an important source of knowledge.

Part 6 Making Sentence Parts Parallel

The word *and* joins sentence parts of the same kind. It may join two nouns, two prepositional phrases, and so on. Similar sentence parts so joined are **parallel**. If the sentence parts joined by *and* are not the same kind, **faulty parallelism** has occurred.

FAULTY: Will enjoys *reading* and *to go to the theater.* (noun joined to phrase)

REVISED: Will enjoys *reading* and *going* to the theater.

FAULTY: No one told Meg *to bring a note* and *that she had to go to the office.* (phrase joined to clause)

REVISED: No one warned Meg *to bring* a note and *to go* to the office.

FAULTY: Tim wondered about the *car* and *if he could repair it.* (phrase joined to clause)

REVISED: Tim wondered *if he could repair the car.* (If a parallel is impossible, change the sentence.)

FAULTY: Beth is *tall, fast,* and *good coordination.*

REVISED: Beth *is tall, is fast,* and *has good coordination.*

And Which, and Who

A special kind of faulty parallelism occurs with *which* and *who*. The *and* should never appear before these words unless *which* or *who* appears earlier in the sentence.

NONSTANDARD: In the park is a lovely bridle path *and which* winds through scenic woods.

STANDARD: In the park is a lovely bridle path, *which* winds through scenic woods.

NONSTANDARD: We went to interview the actor *and who* answered our questions willingly.

STANDARD: We went to interview the actor, *who* answered our questions willingly.

Exercise Making Sentence Parts Parallel

Correct the faulty parallelism in these sentences.

1. Linda is enthusiastic, ambitious, and has seemingly unlimited energy.
2. Meg thought about her clothes and if her denim skirt and jacket would be suitable.
3. On the boat were young people dancing, older people playing shuffleboard, and others who were seated and talked.
4. Every child needs good food, plenty of sleep and exercise, and to feel he or she is loved.
5. The auctioneer, a persuasive man and who knows how to arouse interest, sold many articles quickly.
6. All pedestrians crossing at the intersection and who don't obey the traffic lights, will receive tickets.
7. The storm cut off the lights, stopped the pump, and the furnace stopped going.
8. I have brown hair, brown eyes, and wear reading glasses.
9. He was an actor with a funny face but who hated comedy.
10. Moby Dick was a big white whale with a mouth as long as thirty feet and would hold twenty men in it.
11. Her duties were hiring personnel and sometimes to evaluate programs.

12. David tried playing football in the afternoon and his homework at night.

13. The new baby is plump, fair, and light hair.

14. Cottonseed oil is used in steel-making, palm oil in tin-plating, and linseed oil to make paint.

15. Henderson has speed, height, size, and a great all-round basketball player.

Part 7 Avoiding Omissions of Necessary Words

Omission of *That*

In some sentences the *that* introducing a clause must be stated to avoid confusion.

CONFUSING: The director realized the scene with Jimmy would have to be reworked.

REVISED: The director realized *that* the scene with Jimmy would have to be reworked.

CONFUSING: Lou heard the parade, scheduled for the next day, had to be postponed.

REVISED: Lou heard *that* the parade, scheduled for the next day, had to be postponed.

CONFUSING: The principal understood all the students were excited about the holiday.

REVISED: The principal understood *that* all the students were excited about the holiday.

Omission of Part of a Compound Verb

Sometimes two or more verb phrases are combined using *and*, *or*, or *but*. If the verbs combined in this way differ in number or tense, the sentence must be revised so that the verbs are parallel.

CONFUSING: The chairs were stacked and the room swept. (chairs *were;* room *was*)

REVISED: The chairs *were* stacked, and the room *was* swept.

CONFUSING: The meeting was called, and the officers elected. (meeting *was;* officers *were*)

REVISED: The meeting *was* called, and the officers *were* elected.

Omission of Words in Idioms

An idiom is a group of words with a meaning different from the literal meanings of the words taken one by one.

The diver *put on* his helmet.
The club *put on* a big celebration.

In the first sentence above, the words *put on* have their usual meaning. In the second sentence, the same words are an idiom meaning "to stage."

Many idioms like *put on* are composed of a verb followed by an adverb. Here are some idioms:

Idioms with *on*	**Idioms with *for***	**Idioms with *in***
put on	desire for	interest in
turn on	admiration for	confidence in
pile on	respect for	pride in

Idioms with *off*	**Idioms with *out***	**Idioms with *up***
turn off	find out	pick up
hold off	carry out	hold up
take off	pull out	give up

When two idioms are used together in a compound construction, there is a temptation to drop the preposition from one of them. This omission is awkward and confusing.

FAULTY: There was no preparation or hint of a party.

IMPROVED: There was no preparation *for* or hint of a party.

FAULTY: We were listening and worrying about the news.

IMPROVED: We were listening *to* and worrying about the news.

FAULTY: I am interested and proud of your career.

IMPROVED: I am interested *in* and proud of your career.

Exercises Avoiding Omissions of Necessary Words

A. Revise these sentences to correct the omissions.

1. We heard the committee was going to buy the prizes.
2. The bus was loaded, and the children driven to school.
3. I noticed a dozen wasps had paid me a visit.
4. The coach saw the player had injured his ankle.
5. She had no love or pride in her work.
6. On the way home from school I remembered the birthday of a friend of mine was the next day.
7. I have a fear and antagonism toward most insects.
8. The grounds were cleared and a picnic table set up.
9. I discovered our old house had been painted pink.
10. The door was locked and the windows barred.

B. Revise these sentences to correct omissions.

1. He told me before I left the job was mine.
2. The coach was given a banquet and the players taken to New York.
3. Lee discovered all his change had slipped through a hole in his pocket.
4. We knew over a hundred students would be in the cheering section.
5. A charter has been drawn up and bylaws prepared.
6. I have no respect or confidence in such a man.
7. We read a good stereo would cost two hundred dollars.
8. The tubes were tested and the antenna installed.
9. He has both admiration and trust in his doctor.
10. We heard the cargo ships would be reaching the harbor within a few hours.

Part 8 Placing Modifiers Properly

A single adjective is usually placed just before the word it modifies. An adjective phrase or clause follows immediately after the word it modifies. The only exception is the sentence in which both a phrase and a clause modify the same word. In this situation, the phrase precedes the clause.

We cheered the boy in the class who saved the child's life.
phrase clause

Many adverb modifiers can be moved from one place in a sentence to another without a change of meaning. Occasionally, however, moving an adverb produces unexpected effects. In general, be careful to place adverb modifiers so that they will express your meaning exactly.

CONFUSING: Jean was *attentively* trying to listen.
REVISED: Jean was trying to listen *attentively*.

CONFUSING: I *only* ate the spaghetti.
REVISED: I ate *only* the spaghetti.

CONFUSING: The boys were warned about reckless driving *by the coach*.
REVISED: The boys were warned *by the coach* about reckless driving.

CONFUSING: Rina practiced for the audition *in the gym*.
REVISED: Rina practiced *in the gym* for the audition.

Exercises The Placement of Modifiers

A. Revise these sentences to correct the misplaced modifiers.

1. Marcia nearly ran the 100-meter dash in twelve seconds.
2. We saw the full moon, coming home last night.
3. My parents thought that I would die of pneumonia several times when I was a child.

4. We can hear the waves lapping on the beach in our cottage.
5. Vitamin C prevents scurvy, which is in citrus fruits.
6. Everyone couldn't get into the Volvo.
7. It is a myth that Lincoln wrote the Gettysburg Address while traveling to Gettsyburg on the back of an envelope.
8. I could only find one ripe banana in the grocery store.
9. I bought a hat for my mother with a flower on top.
10. Take the suit to the cleaner with the narrow lapels.

B. Revise these sentences to correct the misplaced modifiers.

1. The tackle was stored in the rowboat under the seat.
2. My uncle was arrested for jaywalking by the sheriff.
3. She only wanted to do it to prove that she could.
4. The shore was littered with debris along the bay.
5. For three days I almost ate nothing.
6. The player was praised by the coach who kicked the winning goal.
7. My uncle bought a house last week in the country.
8. The boat has a heavy cargo that is gliding downstream.
9. Joe almost agreed with everything the teacher said.
10. I found a purse on the sidewalk stuffed with money.

Part 9 Avoiding Dangling Modifiers

When a phrase or clause is placed next to a word that it cannot modify sensibly, it is called a **dangling modifier.** Dangling modifiers often appear at the beginnings of sentences.

PARTICIPLE: Changing the tire, the car rolled down the road. (This says the *car* changed the tire.)

INFINITIVE: To be healthy, vacations are needed. (This says that *vacations* are trying to be healthy.)

ELLIPTICAL CLAUSE: While sketching the scene, rain poured down. (This says that the *rain* sketched the scene.)

To correct a dangling participle (See Section 2.15 in your Handbook.), supply a word for it to modify sensibly, or change the participle to a main verb and give it a subject. The phrase is thus turned into a clause.

FAULTY: Riding past the castle, Arthur's gaze fell upon Guinevere.

REVISED: As he was riding past the castle, Arthur's gaze fell upon Guinevere.

FAULTY: Reading the paper, many facts can be learned.

REVISED: Reading the paper, I can learn many facts.

FAULTY: Running fifty yards, a touchdown was scored.

REVISED: Jack ran fifty yards, scoring a touchdown.

To correct a dangling infinitive, supply a word that can modify the phrase sensibly.

FAULTY: To get a license, a test must be passed.

REVISED: To get a license, you must pass a test.

FAULTY: To fix this pipe, a wrench is needed.

REVISED: To fix this pipe, the plumber needs a wrench.

Exercises **Avoiding Dangling Modifiers**

A. Revise these sentences to correct the dangling modifiers.

1. While eating lunch, the telephone rang.
2. Coming down with flu, Mom gave Larry some medicine.
3. Climbing up, the trees get smaller.
4. While setting the table, the soup can be heated.
5. When browned on one side, turn the fish over.
6. Looking out of the plane, the clouds resemble the sea.
7. To have a good time, the hotel runs weekly dances.
8. Picking her up in his arms, the child was rushed to the doctor.
9. To really fit well, you should take in the bodice seams of this dress.
10. After analyzing the problem, the solution was simple.

B. Revise these sentences to correct the dangling modifiers.

1. While baby-sitting, the dog ate my sandwich.
2. Sitting in the pilot's seat, my mind wandered.
3. After biting the postman, I sold my dog.
4. To assemble the toy rocket, the directions must be followed carefully.
5. Playing chess for three hours, my brain stopped working.
6. To rest properly, the bed must be clean, comfortable, and not too soft.
7. After agreeing to cut the grass, the lawn mower broke down.
8. To become a guitar player, practice is necessary.
9. Taking me out into the garage, there was a twinkle in Dad's eye.
10. After canceling the program, I sent a strong protest to the network.

Exercise Misplaced and Dangling Modifiers

Revise these sentences to correct the misplaced and dangling modifiers.

1. I knocked over a plant, waltzing on the porch.
2. I spotted some wild ducks, eating my lunch in the park.
3. Swarming over the grass and climbing up the plants, I saw some strange-looking insects.
4. Letting out the clutch, the car shot forward.
5. Leaning back in a comfortable chair, the magazine on the table attracted my attention.
6. To get a television contract, considerable talent is required.
7. Being deaf when he wrote them, Beethoven's later works are all the more remarkable.
8. To get to Times Square or Lincoln Center, two subway trains must be taken.
9. A doctor should be seen twice a year in order to stay healthy.
10. Rising vertically from the earth, the rocket's upward speed was breathtaking.

SUMMARY AND APPLICATIONS

1. The revision techniques that you have learned in this chapter will help you to write sentences that state ideas clearly and sensibly.
2. When revising your sentences, watch for and correct the following errors:

unrelated details	improper parallelism
related but separated sentence parts	omissions of necessary words
stringy sentences	misplaced modifiers
improper subordination	dangling modifiers
wordiness	

Applications in Other Subject Areas

All Subjects. The revision techniques that you have learned in this chapter can be used whenever you write for any of your classes. Analyze a piece of writing that you have done for a class in science, social studies, business, fine arts, journalism, or speech. Identify and correct any problems in sentence construction that appear in this piece of writing.

Drama. The personality of a character in a book or play can often be defined by the way he or she speaks. A child, for example, might speak using long stringy sentences. A gossipy character might punctuate his or her speech with unrelated details and a great deal of wordiness. Write a short scene using three or four characters that speak in ways such as those described above. Then rewrite the dialogue, revising the sentences. Perform both skits with the help of some classmates. How do the characters change?

Chapter 5

Combining Ideas in Sentences

Just as two sculptures may represent the same subject yet differ vastly in both form and execution, so two pieces of writing may express the same ideas yet differ greatly in style. For example, one writer might produce a paragraph like this:

> We reached the summit. We stood for a while. We admired the mountains below us. They were smaller. We admired the lakes too. They seemed numberless. They shimmered in the noon sunlight.

The paragraph is grammatically correct, but its short, simple sentences create a choppy and monotonous effect. The passage can be improved by combining some sentences.

> When we reached the summit, we stood silently for a while, admiring the smaller mountains below us and the numberless lakes shimmering in the noon sunlight.

The combined sentence flows more smoothly and shows more clearly how the ideas of the original paragraph are related to each other.

In this chapter you will learn how to use sentence combining techniques to produce interesting, sophisticated sentences. These techniques will provide you with many alternate ways to express your ideas in speech and in writing.

Part 1 Joining Sentences and Sentence Parts

One way to avoid a choppy, monotonous style is to join together sentences or sentence parts that express ideas of equal importance. This can be done by using the coordinating conjunctions *and*, *or*, *nor*, and *but*. When complete sentences are joined using these conjunctions, a comma is placed before the conjunction unless the sentence is very short, such as, "Mary sang and Tom danced."

Sentences or sentence parts that express similar ideas of equal importance can usually be joined by using the word *and*. Ideas that are repeated, such as those represented by italicized words in the following sentences, can be deleted.

> The actors froze in their positions. The narrator walked downstage center to deliver the epilogue.
>
> The actors froze in their positions, and the narrator walked downstage center to deliver the epilogue.
>
> Albert Schweitzer was a medical missionary in French Equatorial Africa. *He was also* a renowned authority on the music of J. S. Bach.
>
> Albert Schweitzer was a medical missionary in French Equatorial Africa and a renowned authority on the music of J. S. Bach.

Sentences or sentence parts that express contrasting ideas of equal importance can usually be joined using the word *but*.

Ben Franklin was a leader of the American Revolution. He could not convince William, his son, to support the cause.

Ben Franklin was a leader of the American Revolution, but he could not convince William, his son, to join the cause.

Our new lineman is talented. *However, he is* inexperienced.

Our new lineman is talented but inexperienced.

Sentences or sentence parts that express choices of equal importance can usually be joined using the word *or*.

Did the space shuttle launch occur on schedule? Did the weather delay it?

Did the space shuttle launch occur on schedule, or did the weather delay it?

Erosion of topsoil may be caused by wind. *It may also be caused by* rain.

Erosion of topsoil may be caused by wind or by rain.

Exercises **Joining Sentences**

A. Join sentences or sentence parts by following the directions in parentheses. Eliminate any italicized words.

1. Can we finish painting the billboard before dark? Should we plan on working tomorrow? (Join with **, or**.)
2. Dr. Mendoza has traveled in India. *He has traveled* in China, *too*. (Join related parts with **and**.)
3. The candidate pictured on the campaign poster seemed vaguely familiar. I still can't figure out why. (Join with **, but**.)
4. The United States will have to develop new energy sources. *Otherwise, it will have to* import more oil from Mexico and the Middle East. (Join related parts with **, or**.)
5. The unexpected plot twists will keep you on the edge of your seat. The ending is sure to surprise you. (Join with **, and**.)
6. Lisa has found the bug in her program. *She* hasn't corrected it yet. (Join related parts with **, but**.)
7. The temperature on Mercury can reach 800°F. On Pluto temperatures remain below -300°F. (Join with **, but**.)

8. Bob Fosse choreographed the dance routines. *He* rehearsed the dancers, *too*. (Join related parts with **and**.)

9. Don went into the game in the fourth quarter. *He* scored the winning touchdown. (Join related parts with **and**.)

10. Shrimp are found everywhere along the coast. Most of the catch comes from the Gulf of Mexico. (Join with **, but**.)

B. Join each of the following pairs of sentences in one of two ways. You may join complete sentences using **, or**, **, and**, or **, but**, or you may join related sentence parts by eliminating unnecessary words and using conjunctions.

1. Christina set up the lights. She attached the cables to the video camera.

2. Lyndon Baines Johnson enjoyed being President. He did not seek a second term.

3. Should we open the curtains before the audience arrives? Should we open them after the audience is seated?

4. The variety show produced by the junior class will raise money for the scholarship fund. It will also raise money for the spring dance.

5. In movies such as *King Kong*, gorillas are made to appear aggressive. Research in the wild has shown that they are actually rather gentle.

Part 2 Adding Words

Sometimes the second sentence in a pair repeats material from the first sentence, adding only one new word that is important to the meaning. In such cases, the repeated material can usually be eliminated, and the one important word can be added to the first sentence.

Ms. Rivers nervously handed the master of ceremonies an envelope. *It was* sealed.

Ms. Rivers nervously handed the master of ceremonies a sealed envelope.

Sometimes the main sentence is followed by several other sentences, each of which adds one important word. In such cases, the sentences can be combined by adding each of these important words to the sentence that expresses the main idea.

Many perfumes are made from the petals of flowers.

The perfumes are expensive. *The flowers are* common.

Many expensive perfumes are made from the petals of common flowers.

Sometimes you will have to use a comma when you add more than one word to a sentence.

Ahead of us was a path. *It was* narrow. *It was* steep. *It was* rocky.

Ahead of us was a narrow, steep, rocky path.

In each of the preceding examples, words were added without any changes in their form. Sometimes, however, you cannot add a word without making a change. You may have to end the word with *-ing*.

Those brakes may need new linings. *They* squeal.

Those squealing brakes may need new linings.

At other times you may have to end the word with *-ly*.

When Maria made the free throw, the fans cheered. Their cheers were wild.

When Maria made the free throw, the fans cheered wildly.

There may be more than one place in the sentence where the word ending in *-ly* can be placed.

The park warden and the veterinarian approached the sedated grizzly. They were cautious.

The park warden and the veterinarian approached the sedated grizzly cautiously.

Cautiously, the park warden and the veterinarian approached the sedated grizzly.

Exercises Adding Words

A. Combine the following groups of sentences by adding important words to the sentence that expresses the main idea. Eliminate the italicized words and follow any directions in parentheses.

1. During World War II, some Londoners actually became accustomed to the sirens that preceded the air raids. *The sirens were* wailing.
2. Ed suggested that reggae would not be appropriate music for a slide-tape presentation on Eskimo culture. *He was* tactful *about it*. (Add **-ly**.)
3. Though they had only a month to rehearse, the dancers still gave a performance. *The performance was* polished. *It was* professional. (Use a comma.)
4. There are many trails at the wildlife refuge. *They will* fascinate *you*. (Add **-ing**.)
5. Dorothea Dix's work led to the establishment of mental hospitals. *Her work was* valuable.
6. The award presented to the student who placed first in the debate contest was a trophy. *The trophy was* beautiful. *It was made of* gold. (Do not use a comma.)
7. The driver's manual says that you should check the water level in the battery. *It says that you should do this every* week. (Add **-ly**.)
8. The senator referred her colleagues to a report on the levels of lead pollution in the air. *The report could* disturb *readers*. (Add **-ing**.)
9. Andy worked throughout the canned food drive. *He was* tireless. (Add **-ly**.)
10. The explorers avoided the water above the falls. *The explorers were* careful. (Add **-ly**.) *The water* whirled. (Use **-ing**.)

B. Combine each of the following sets of sentences by adding the important word from the second sentence.

1. The company underwent an inspection by agents of the Nuclear Regulatory Commission. It was a surprise.
2. The gem stones gradually grew smoother under the cloth. The stones had been rough. The cloth was used to polish them.

3. Rain forced us to postpone the game. The rain was torrential. The game was for the championship.

4. The stagehands moved the piano and several other set pieces during the blackout. They were quiet.

5. Robots now perform tasks on assembly lines. The robots are efficient. The tasks are simple. They are also repetitive.

Part 3 Adding Groups of Words

You have seen how single words may be added to sentences. Similarly, a group of words from one sentence can often be added to another sentence. Usually, the group of words gives more information about something in the first sentence. It is added near the word that identifies the person or thing.

> The note said that Mr. Perkins would return at 4:00. *It was* taped to the door.
>
> The note taped to the door said that Mr. Perkins would return at 4:00.

Sometimes the added group of words restates an idea presented in the original sentence. Such groups of words are called **appositives** and are set off by commas.

> Buddy Layman finds water by using a "witching rod." *Buddy Layman* is a character in Jim Leonard's *The Diviners*.
>
> Buddy Layman, a character in Jim Leonard's *The Diviners*, finds water by using a "witching rod."

When you add a group of words, you will occasionally have to change the form of one of the words by adding *-ing*.

> A dancer entered the medicine circle. She wore special ceremonial beads.
>
> A dancer wearing special ceremonial beads entered the medicine circle.

Notice that the word *wore* was changed to *wearing* and that the word *She* was eliminated. Notice also that the resulting phrase, *wearing special ceremonial beads*, is used to modify the word *dancer*.

Sometimes one word in a sentence refers to the whole idea expressed in another sentence, as does the word *this* in the following example.

> *You should* exercise daily. *This* will help you to stay in good mental and physical condition.

In such cases, you can often combine the two sentences by substituting a phrase beginning with *-ing* for the word that refers to the whole idea.

> Exercising daily will help you to stay in good mental and physical condition.

The word *exercise* was changed to *Exercising*, and the italicized words were eliminated.

Another way to add a group of words is to begin the group with the word *who*.

> The official asked to remain anonymous. *He* leaked the story to the press.
>
> The official who leaked the story to the press asked to remain anonymous.

The word *who* replaces *He* in the second sentence. The group of words is then inserted into the first sentence to add information about the official.

When a group of words adds information about a thing instead of a person, you may have to add the word *that*.

> The toys will be distributed to the children of needy families. They were collected by the fire department.
>
> The toys that were collected by the fire department will be distributed to the children of needy families.

The word *that* replaces the word *they*. The group of words is used to add information about the toys to the first sentence.

In the examples that you have seen so far, the group of words added to the first sentence in each pair is necessary to make the meaning clear. Without the added words, it would not be clear which official and which toys were meant. In other sentences, however, the added group of words is not necessary. These words add information, but the information is not necessary to make the meaning clear. When the group of words just adds information, combine with a comma and *who* or with the word *which* instead of *that*.

Mr. Williams has many stories to tell about his experiences as a musician. *He* once played with Duke Ellington.

Mr. Williams, who once played with Duke Ellington, has many stories to tell about his experiences as a musician.

Holography produces three-dimensional pictures. *It* is a photography technique that uses laser light.

Holography, which is photography that uses laser light, produces three-dimensional pictures.

Exercises Adding Groups of Words

A. Combine the following sentences by adding groups of words. Eliminate the italicized words and follow any special directions.

1. In the attic, Richard discovered a crate. *It was* full of diaries. *They* had been kept by his grandparents. (Use **that**.)
2. I heard Theresa's story about her fishing trip. I enjoyed *that*. (Begin your sentence with *I enjoyed* and add **-ing** to the verb in the first sentence.)
3. I have been reading about Harry Houdini. *He* was well known for his escapes and illusions. (Combine with **, who**.)
4. The old legend mentioned a griffin. *The griffin* is a mythological beast with the head and wings of an eagle and the body of a lion. (Use **, which**.)
5. I glanced in the rear view mirror. *This* enabled me to see the two cars. (Use **-ing**.) *They* were approaching quickly. (Use **, which**.)
6. The art students lined the walls of the auditorium with paintings. They had done *the paintings* themselves. (Combine with **that**.)
7. William Butler Yeats lived in an old castle. Yeats was one of the greatest poets of our century. (Combine using commas.)

8. Many computer systems use a dot-matrix printer. *It* forms letters made of many tiny dots. (Combine with **, which**.)

9. The director was Alfred Hitchcock. *He* created the modern horror film. (Combine with **, who**.)

10. The polar bears provided quite a spectacle for the children at the zoo. *They* fought playfully among themselves. (Combine with **-ing**.)

B. Combine the following sentences by adding groups of words. Decide on your own what words you should eliminate and what words or endings you must add.

1. The relatives of the returning heroes waited for the arrival of the plane. They waited together in the fog.

2. The Seine is a river. It flows northwest, through Paris, and into the English Channel.

3. The scientist stared through the microscope for hours. This gave him a painful case of eyestrain.

4. Hemlock looks much like parsley. It is a poisonous herb.

5. The Boston Museum and the Chicago Museum of Art contain several Oriental carvings made of lapis lazuli. Lapis lazuli is a semiprecious stone. The stone is prized for its azure-blue color.

Part 4 Combining To Show a Sequence of Events

Often in writing you will want to explain to your readers when or in what order certain events occurred. Clearly demonstrating the sequence of events is especially important in directions, stories, and reports of actual or imaginary events. When two sentences state events that occur in a certain sequence, combining them effectively may make the sequence of events clearer. Notice how different methods of combining the following two sentences affect the meaning.

Tony arrived at home. He telephoned Anita.
As soon as Tony arrived at home, he telephoned Anita.
After Tony arrived at home, he telephoned Anita.

The following are some words and phrases that can be used when combining sentences to show a sequence:

after	as soon as	by the time	while
as	before	when	until

Exercise Combining To Show a Sequence of Events

Combine each of the following pairs of sentences by following the directions in parentheses.

1. The tornado struck. The residents of the community had already fled to safety. (Begin the first sentence with **By the time**.)
2. Alexander the Great reached the age of seventeen. He had already built an empire. (Begin the first sentence with **Before**.)
3. Betsy saw the look on my face. She could tell that I had something important to tell her. (Begin the first sentence with **As soon as**.)
4. Robert Frost returned from England in 1913. He published the American edition of *A Boy's Will,* his first book of poems. (Begin the first sentence with **After**.)
5. The viewer cannot be sure who is guilty. The detective identifies the thief in the final scene. (Begin the second sentence with **Until**.)
6. The news commentator stalled for time. A group of technicians tried to reestablish contact with the Lebanese correspondent. (Combine with **While**.)
7. The piñata burst. Confetti and glitter fell upon the assembled guests. (Combine with **When**.)
8. The President stepped from the plane and waved. A security guard motioned to the crowd to move back. (Begin the second sentence with **as**.)
9. The delegates studied such documents as the Iroquois Constitution. They drafted a constitution of their own. (Begin the second sentence with **Before**.)
10. The Aborigines agreed to limited mining and exploration on their land. The Australian government made assurances that companies would not be allowed to violate sacred territory. (Begin the second sentence with **after**.)

Part 5 Combining To Show Cause and Effect

To show your readers why something happened, you need to make statements of cause and effect. One way to do this is to place the cause in one sentence and the effect in another. However, it is usually better to combine the cause and effect in a single sentence so that your reader can see the relationship between the ideas more clearly.

Chippewa is a difficult language to learn. It has approximately six thousand verb forms.

Chippewa is a difficult language to learn because it has approximately six thousand verb forms.

In the preceding example, *because* was added before the sentence that states the cause. Another way to show a cause-effect relationship is to add a word or group of words before the effect. You may add the words *so*, *as a result*, *consequently*, or *therefore*. If you use *as a result*, *consequently*, or *therefore*, you will also have to place a semicolon (;) before the added word and a comma after it.

Chippewa has approximately six thousand verb forms; therefore, it is a difficult language to learn.

Chippewa has approximately six thousand verb forms, so it is a difficult language to learn.

Exercise Combining To Show Cause and Effect

Combine each of the following pairs of sentences twice. First, use **because** or **since.** Then, use **as a result, consequently,** or **therefore**.

1. When Ms. Mangus was in the Peace Corps, she was stationed in India. She knows a great deal about Hinduism.
2. Ken hasn't seen his cousin Emily in six years. He isn't sure that he will recognize her.
3. The water vapor in warm air condenses as the temperature falls. Dew forms overnight.

4. Videos are extremely popular. They combine elements of music, theater, and dance.

5. The flying fish has long fins that resemble a bird's wings. It can glide above the water for as much as a quarter of a mile.

Part 6 Using Combining Skills in Revision

Whenever you write a paragraph or composition, you should always look for ways to improve your expression of ideas. Remember that while any idea may be expressed in several different ways, one way is often more effective than another.

Your sentence combining skills can provide you with one method of improving your writing. Look for relationships among your ideas. If two or three related ideas appear in separate sentences, you may be able to combine them to make the relationship clearer. Study the following rough draft.

> When people hear the word *autograph*, they usually think of "signatures." Actually, the term comes from the Greek words *autos* and *graphein*. *Autos* means "self." *Graphein* means "to write." Therefore, all handwritten materials may be considered autographs. These materials include unsigned letters, manuscripts, notes, and musical scores.
>
> Collecting such handwritten artifacts is a hobby. The hobby is ancient. The hobby is popular. There are many collectors in the United States. They are wealthy. They pay enormous prices for the autographs of Presidents. They pay enormous prices for the autographs of artists. They also pay enormous prices for the autographs of composers and other famous figures. However, one does not have to be wealthy to collect autographs. Many people keep albums. These people are not wealthy. These albums contain the autographs of their friends. Such an album used to be called an *album amicorum*. This means "album of friends" in Latin.

This composition can be improved by combining many of the ideas that it contains.

When people hear the word *autograph*, they usually think of "signatures." Actually, the term *autograph* comes from the Greek words *autos*, meaning "self," and *graphein*, meaning "to write." Therefore, all handwritten materials, including unsigned letters, manuscripts, and musical scores, may be considered autographs.

Collecting such handwritten artifacts is an ancient and popular hobby. There are many wealthy collectors in the United States who pay enormous prices for the autographs of Presidents, artists, composers, and other famous figures. However, one does not have to be wealthy to collect autographs. Many people who are not wealthy keep albums that contain the autographs of their friends. Such an album used to be called an *album amicorum*, which means "album of friends" in Latin.

Exercises **Applying Combining Skills**

A. Revise the following paragraph using combining skills.

A noise had been keeping me awake. This had happened for several nights. The noise thumped. I was determined to stop it. I stood beside the outside wall of my bedroom. The outside wall of my bedroom was where the noise seemed to come from. I pressed my ear to the wall. That helped me hear the sound better. I still heard the thump. Now I heard a scratching sound too. I opened the window. I looked out. I saw what made the noise. I laughed. A kite was caught on the roof. It swung against the house.

B. Revise the following paragraph using sentence combining techniques.

The cormorant is a bird. It is large. It is related to the pelican. Its feathers contain less oil than a duck's feathers do. Consequently, the cormorant is able to submerge itself. It does this quite easily. It swims well underwater. This enables the cormorant to catch fish. You may see a cormorant dive. It will be sudden. It will go beneath the surface. The cormorant finally returns to the surface. It may be a hundred yards away.

Review Exercises **Combining Ideas in Sentences**

A. Combine each pair of sentences by joining sentences or sentence parts using **or**, **and**, or **but.** Eliminate the italicized words and insert commas as necessary.

1. Many wild mushrooms are edible. Some are deadly.
2. Charlotte Brontë wrote *Jane Eyre*. Her sister, Emily, wrote *Wuthering Heights*.
3. The counter person at the hardware store said that you can nail the panels in place. *You can also* hang them with adhesive.
4. One of the researchers has invented an electronic fire alarm. *She has also invented* a safer type of automobile brake.
5. The weather on the day of the yacht race will be clear. *It will be* windy. *It will* not *be* very warm.

B. Combine each of the following pairs of sentences by adding the important word or words. Eliminate the italicized words, and follow any special directions in parentheses.

1. Richard Adams wrote a novel on the subject of life in a rabbit colony. *This was an* unusual *subject for a novel.*
2. A team of miners discovered a woolly mammoth in the Siberian tundra. *The woolly mammoth was* frozen.
3. Across the moors one could hear the cry of the hound of the Baskervilles. *The hound* howled. (End the important word with **-ing**.)
4. Eileen prompted us from her position behind the curtain. *She was* unobtrusive. (End the important word with **-ly**.)
5. We dipped our hands into the spring and drank the water. *Our hands were* cupped. *The water was* cool. *It was* refreshing. (Use a comma.)

C. Combine the following sentences by adding groups of words. Eliminate the italicized words and follow any special directions.

1. There is a note for you. *It is* on the bulletin board. *The bulletin board is* in the coach's office.
2. *Eve* visited her sister at the University of Texas. *That* gave Eve a first-hand view of college life. (Combine with **-ing**.)

3. Golda Meir once taught school in Wisconsin. *She* was Prime Minister of Israel from 1969 to 1974. (Combine with **, who**.)

4. The mayor unveiled her development plan. *It* is considerably different from the city council's. (Combine with **, which**.)

5. The television pictures were taken by a weather satellite. *They* showed the progress of the hurricane. (Combine with **that**.)

D. Combine the pairs of sentences by following the directions in parentheses.

1. John White returned to the Roanoke colony in 1590. He could find no trace of 117 settlers whom he had left there three years before. (Combine with **When**.)

2. The performers sang one last rousing song. One of their assistants passed a hat through the audience to collect donations. (Begin the first sentence with **As**.)

3. Several flights were delayed. Crews worked to clear ice and snow from the runways. (Begin the second sentence with **While**.)

4. The star arrived on the set. Dense fog had rolled in from the sea, and shooting had to be postponed. (Begin the first sentence with **By the time**.)

5. Rolanda finished serving. It looked as though nothing could keep us from winning the game and the tournament. (Begin the first sentence with **After**.)

E. Combine each of the following pairs of sentences in two ways. First use **because** or **since.** Then use **therefore, as a result,** or **consequently.**

1. The trail is unfamiliar to many of you. Be careful to stay within sight of the other hikers.

2. Tickets for the free concert are going quickly. You should get yours today.

3. Tomato plants will grow in flower pots or in buckets. They are ideal for a city vegetable garden.

4. Fran plans to go to a veterinary school. She was delighted to get a part-time job at an animal hospital.

5. Heat can damage records. It is not a good idea to store records near a radiator.

SUMMARY AND APPLICATIONS

1. Applying sentence combining techniques will help you to achieve variety in your speech and writing. These techniques will also help to clarify relationships between ideas.
2. Sentences and sentence parts of equal importance can often be combined by using *or*, *and*, or *but*.
3. Often single words from one or more sentences can be added to another sentence. When doing this, you may have to add *-ly* or *-ing* to the borrowed word or words.
4. Groups of words may also be added to sentences. The first word in the group may have to be put in its *-ing* form. At other times, you may have to add *who*, *which*, or *that* to the beginning of the group of words.
5. Sentences may sometimes be combined to show cause and effect or a sequence of events.

Applications in Other Subject Areas

Business. A *memorandum* or *memo* is simply a note used in businesses and other organizations to communicate information that does not require a lengthy report.

When writing a memo, it is a good idea to keep your audience in mind. If you are writing a memo to be read by many different kinds of people, then you should keep your sentences short and use simple words. If you are writing a memo to a specific individual whom you know to be a good reader, you can use a more sophisticated vocabulary and longer, more complex sentences.

Imagine that you are the president of a large record company. Write two memos, one addressed to all of your employees, and one addressed to the vice president of one of your departments.

Science. Statements of cause and effect are often used in explanations of scientific procedures or processes. Write a paragraph explaining a simple laboratory experiment or a common occurrence in nature. In your paragraph use what you have learned in this chapter about expressing relationships of cause and effect.

Chapter 6

Achieving Sentence Variety

Good writing and speaking require not only a logical movement from one idea to another, but also the presentation of these ideas in a way that is rhythmically pleasing. If the pattern and length remain the same in every sentence, the rhythm becomes monotonous. When the pattern and length of sentences are varied, the rhythm is more interesting.

You can achieve a variety of sentence rhythm in the following three ways:

1. By varying sentence beginnings
2. By varying sentence structure
3. By varying sentence length

Because a writer's first job is to get ideas down on paper, the above methods of achieving sentence variety are best used in revision. The writer who sets out in a first draft to begin each sentence in a different way is likely to find that concern with sentence structure interferes with natural speech rhythms, producing self-conscious and awkward passages.

Part 1 Variety of Sentence Beginnings

When every sentence in a passage begins in the same way, the effect can be monotonous. A succession of sentences beginning with the same word or with the same kind of phrase or clause can bore the reader. In the first passage below, note the irritating repetition of the word *it*. In the second passage, note how your interest lags from the sameness of each sentence.

Sentences beginning with the same word

> Then the fog came. *It* did not roll in like a wave; *it* came from nowhere. *It* was not there—then *it* was. *It* wove its gray veil with shocking speed. *It* surrounded our island silently. *It* smothered sunlight and sound. *It* isolated us.

Sentences beginning with the same kind of phrase

> *Stepping out of the boat*, we landed on Spirit Island. *Pulling the boat up on the beach*, we began to explore. *Picking our way along the beach*, we could feel the stillness watching us, waiting for us.

Sentence variety can be achieved by beginning a succession of sentences in different ways—with adverb modifiers, phrases, or clauses.

The cat carefully stalked the unsuspecting robin. (subject—verb)
Carefully, the cat stalked the unsuspecting robin. (adverb modifier)
With infinite care, the cat stalked the unsuspecting robin. (prepositional phrase)
To avoid alerting the unsuspecting robin, the cat stalked it carefully. (infinitive phrase)
Moving slowly and carefully, the cat stalked the unsuspecting robin. (participial phrase)
Until it was ready for a final charge, the cat carefully stalked the unsuspecting robin. (adverb clause)

Exercises Varying Your Sentence Beginnings

A. Rewrite the following sentences, beginning each in accordance with the suggestion in parentheses.

1. Marcia's drawing has improved recently. (Begin with **recently**.)
2. Charles Blondin crossed Niagara Falls on a tightrope in 1859. (Begin with **in**.)
3. The Steelers won the championship during the first minute of a sudden-death overtime period. (Begin with **during**.)
4. The street-repair people were following their usual schedule; they began tearing up the pavement outside my hotel room at 2:00 A.M. (Begin with **following**.)
5. The clouds had gone by midmorning. (Begin with **by**.)
6. The chairperson continued to bang her gavel, and the delegates gradually quieted down. (Begin with **as** or **when**.)
7. Gondolas have been used on the canals of Venice for over eight hundred years. (Begin with **for**.)
8. Mr. Smith fell and hurt himself as he ran to catch his bus. (Begin with **running**.)
9. Mary forgot to buy a ticket in her hurry to board the train. (Begin with **in**.)
10. Frontenac became a well known-summer resort after the Civil War. (Begin with **after**.)

B. Follow the directions for Exercise A.

1. A limestone marker, with the initials "MD" carved on it, stands a few paces off the road. (Begin with **a few paces**.)
2. The little town nestles comfortably against the bluff and seems content to dream the years away. (Begin with **nestling**.)
3. The young actor left for Los Angeles the next day. (Begin with **the next day**.)
4. This hatchback model must be considered the "best buy," because it combines high performance and low cost. (Begin with **combining**.)
5. Galileo made the first practical use of the telescope in 1609. (Begin with **in**.)

6. The workers' summer output was very poor until air conditioning was installed. (Begin with **until**.)

7. Andrés Segovia is undoubtedly the greatest classical guitarist the world has ever known. (Begin with **undoubtedly**.)

8. Sonia seemed very pleased when she was offered the scholarship. (Begin with **when**.)

9. Stephen Crane died of tuberculosis at the age of twenty-eight. (Begin with **at**.)

10. The arctic tern is the champion migrant bird; it travels 11,000 miles from the Arctic to winter in the Antarctic. (Begin with **traveling**.)

Part 2 Variety of Sentence Structure

In student writing, a monotonous style occurs chiefly from overuse of compound sentences. Compound sentences occur when independent clauses—groups of words that contain a subject and a verb and can stand alone as sentences—are joined by such conjunctions as *and, or,* or *but*. The compound sentence is a good and useful tool, but overuse dulls its edge. A succession of compound sentences is boring because the rhythm is so monotonous. As you read this passage, note the unvarying stop-and-go effect.

> We reached Trinidad, Colorado, in the evening, and in the morning we headed south through Raton Pass. We ate lunch at Eagle's Nest, New Mexico, and then we took a roundabout route through the mountains. The gravel road was better than we expected, and the mountains were strikingly beautiful.

A succession of compound sentences can be avoided by changing one of the clauses. The clause may be made into a subordinate clause or a participial phrase. (See Sections 2.15 and 3.3.) Some compound sentences can be changed into simple sentences with a compound predicate. (See Section 2.11.)

COMPOUND SENTENCE	We visited Taos Pueblo, and we were deeply impressed by this vigorous survival of an older civilization.
PARTICIPIAL PHRASE	Visiting Taos Pueblo, we were deeply impressed by this vigorous survival of an older civilization.
SUBORDINATE CLAUSE	When we visited Taos Pueblo, we were deeply impressed by this vigorous survival of an older civilization.
COMPOUND PREDICATE	We visited Taos Pueblo and were deeply impressed by this vigorous survival of an older civilization.

Exercises Varying Sentence Structure

A. Rewrite the following sentences, changing one of the clauses in each in accordance with the suggestion in parentheses.

1. Mrs. Lambert enjoys good music, and she is a generous benefactor of the symphony orchestra. (compound predicate)
2. The house lights dimmed, and quiet settled on the audience. (subordinate clause beginning with **as**)
3. The hydrant was turned on, and the firefighters discovered that there was not enough water pressure to fight the fire. (subordinate clause beginning with **when**)
4. Paul worked as a drugstore delivery boy during the school year, and he was a lifeguard at the city pool during the summer. (compound predicate)
5. The compromise offer was acceptable to the union leadership, but it was voted down by the members of the local. (subordinate clause beginning with **although**)
6. The town lies several miles off the main highway, and it is easy to miss. (participial phrase beginning with **lying**)
7. The speaker seemed ill at ease, and he appeared to depend entirely on his written text. (compound predicate)
8. The crew has made no effort to reforest the stripped acres, and the residents have protested that the development is an eyesore. (subordinate clause beginning with **because**)

9. We felt starved and weary, and we gratefully grounded our canoe on a small island. (participial phrase beginning with **starved**)

10. Liz revved the motor, and the rest of us pushed hard on the front bumper and fenders. (subordinate clause beginning with **as** or **while**)

B. Follow the directions for Exercise A.

1. A truck crashed through the fence and onto the practice field, and the coach canceled further outdoor practice. (subordinate clause beginning with **because**)

2. The desert sun had been unbearably hot, but the night brought a biting chill. (subordinate clause beginning with **although**)

3. The city council could not raise enough money, and the construction of the new park had to be delayed. (subordinate clause beginning with **since**)

4. He doesn't understand the importance of compromise, and he will never be a good politician. (subordinate clause beginning with **because**)

5. The octopus has eight tentacles, covered with suckers, a horny beak, and almost human eyes, but it has internal characteristics that make it remarkably like a clam. (subordinate clause beginning with **although**)

6. The President spent the weekend at Camp David, and then he flew to Washington for talks with the new Russian ambassador. (compound predicate)

7. The harbor pilot climbed aboard the sleek cruise ship *Margaret B. Perrin*, and he guided it into San Francisco Bay. (participial phrase beginning with **climbing**)

8. The TV station interrupted the program, and it issued a severe weather warning. (participial phrase beginning with **interrupting**)

9. No one claimed the $100,000, and the boy who had reported it suddenly found himself very wealthy. (subordinate clause beginning with **because**)

10. Raindrops act like prisms; they refract sunlight to produce rainbows. (participial phrase beginning with **acting**)

Part 3 Variety of Sentence Length

A passage in which all the sentences are of about the same length, whether long or short, is monotonous. An occasional sentence of different length varies the rhythm and revives the interest of the reader. In the following passage from Albert Einstein's *Out of My Later Years*, note how the short sentences are relieved by long sentences.

> I do not consider myself the father of the release of atomic energy. My part in it was quite indirect. I did not, in fact, foresee that it would be released in my time. I believed only that it was theoretically possible. It became practical through the accidental discovery of chain reaction, and this was not something I could have predicted.

Avoiding a Series of Short Sentences

Monotony is created especially by a succession of short sentences. There are times when a conscious series of short sentences is very effective, as in narrative, when it has the effect of building up suspense. The unconscious use of a succession of short sentences, however, creates an awkward effect.

Short sentences may be combined in a number of ways.

1. By using a compound sentence

   TWO SENTENCES Residents reported a huge flying saucer. It was only a hole in the clouds.

   COMBINED Residents reported a huge flying saucer, but it was only a hole in the clouds.

2. By using a simple sentence with a compound predicate

   TWO SENTENCES A huge meteor struck Siberia in 1906. It plunged far down into the earth's crust.

   COMBINED A huge meteor struck Siberia in 1906 and plunged far down into the earth's crust.

3. By using a subordinate clause

TWO SENTENCES I entered the store. A camera caught my eye.

COMBINED As I entered the store, a camera caught my eye.

TWO SENTENCES My aunt has just received a research grant. She is a chemist.

COMBINED My aunt, who is a chemist, has just received a research grant.

4. By using a participial phrase

TWO SENTENCES The comedian was shaking with laughter. He could hardly speak.

COMBINED Shaking with laughter, the comedian could hardly speak.

5. By using a prepositional phrase

TWO SENTENCES Howie is relaxing. He has had a hard day in the classroom.

COMBINED Howie is relaxing after a hard day in the classroom.

The following passage is an example of how the monotony of too many short sentences can be avoided by combining sentences.

ORIGINAL I returned to my room in the dormitory. There was a note under my door. It was from Bill. He said that he had just returned from auditions. He didn't know yet whether he had gotten a part. He was sorry to have missed me.

REWRITTEN When I returned to my room in the dormitory, I found a note from Bill under the door. He said that he had just returned from auditions, but didn't know yet whether he had gotten a part. He added that he was sorry to have missed me.

Exercises Varying Sentence Length

A. Combine the sentences following each number. Make one effective sentence.

1. Front Street was flooded this morning. Water from a broken main did it.
2. A police officer reports on rush-hour traffic on the expressway. He is in a helicopter.
3. The central human character in *Moby Dick* is Captain Ahab. He is captain of the *Pequod*.
4. Jacqueline Auriol was the first woman to fly the jet. The jet was a supersonic Concorde.
5. In 1946 *All the King's Men* was written. Robert Penn Warren wrote the book.
6. Mr. Smith is in San Francisco. He is house-hunting. His family is staying in Connecticut.
7. The parade went past the state capitol. It looked like a river. It lasted for hours.
8. Some shippers are storing wheat on the open ground. They dump it in huge piles. There is a shortage of railroad cars.
9. Robin Yount swung at the low pitch. He drove the ball out of the park.
10. We went to a drive-in restaurant. We went there after the movie. We had hamburgers, onion rings, and French fries.

B. Rewrite the following paragraph, making changes in sentence structure to create fluent, readable prose.

> Many of the nation's new housing developments are monotonous and dull. They are advertised as the ultimate in modern living. They consist of badly built houses with fancy facades and rickety carports. The developments have pastoral names like Pine Acres and King's Forest. Trees have been bulldozed to make way for roads and parking lots. The advertisements call these developments "communities." There is no community center—a large park, green, or lake—within walking distance of the homes. Shops, theaters, bowling alleys are all miles away. People cannot "rub elbows" with their neighbors. There is no sense of community.

SUMMARY AND APPLICATIONS

1. Varying the pattern and length of your sentences will make your speaking and writing more natural and pleasing.
2. One way to achieve sentence variety is to vary the types of words with which you begin your sentences.
3. Another way to achieve sentence variety is to vary the structure of your sentences.
4. Yet another way to achieve sentence variety is to vary the length of your sentences.
5. All of these methods may be used when you revise any type of writing.

Applications in Other Subject Areas

Home Economics / Vocational Arts / Science. There are two ways to write directions. If the sole purpose of your writing is to convey information, you may simply state the facts, beginning every sentence with a verb:

> *Preheat* the oven. *Mix* the batter. *Coat* the bottom of the cake pan with butter or shortening.

Directions written in this way have the advantage of being direct and easy to follow. However, they are also monotonous. If you are writing directions in a context in which the writing itself must be interesting, as in a magazine article, you can avoid such monotony by applying the techniques for achieving sentence variety that are discussed in this chapter. Try writing directions for performing some task such as sewing a hem or changing a tire. Write a rough draft in which you begin most of your sentences with verbs. Then, revise your composition by varying the beginnings, structure, and length of your sentences.

Speech. Find a copy of a famous speech such as Lincoln's "Gettysburg Address" or Chief Joseph's "I Will Fight No More Forever." Explain, in writing, what techniques the speaker has used to achieve sentence variety. Give examples of these techniques.

Chapter 7

The Process of Writing

Hidden beneath the surfaces of some of the art world's greatest masterpieces are some fascinating surprises—more paintings. X-rays reveal the same scene or portrait repeated several times on a canvas, each one showing slight changes of position, form, or shadow. Apparently, the artists had to work through several versions of their paintings before achieving products with which they were satisfied.

Experienced writers also rework their material several times in order to realize their goals. They begin with a rough idea and then take it through a thoughtful process of development and revision. This **process of writing** has three stages: pre-writing, writing the first draft, and revising. In this chapter, you will learn how to apply each stage of the process to your own writing. Later chapters will develop the finer aspects of writing paragraphs and compositions.

Part 1 Pre-Writing

An inexperienced writer often makes the mistake of beginning in the middle of the writing process. Rather than take the time to generate and organize ideas, the writer begins composing immediately. He or she develops one idea for a while and then branches off as a new thought or point of view presents itself. The resulting piece of writing is often unstructured and disjointed, frustrating to both writer and reader in that it does not communicate its ideas effectively.

The planning stage of the writing process, pre-writing, keeps this sort of situation from occurring. During pre-writing you select and refine your topic as well as identify your audience and purpose. At this stage you also gather ideas and organize them in a meaningful way. Each of these steps is important to a coherent, well-organized piece of writing.

Complete each of the following steps as part of the pre-writing process. You will find that the effort spent on pre-writing activities will make the writing of your paper much easier.

Select and Refine Your Topic

Choosing a Topic. Often you will be writing in response to an assignment or in order to satisfy some other specific requirement. Sometimes, however, you will be given the opportunity to choose and develop your own topic. If this is the case, you can begin to generate a list of possible topics by taking an informal inventory of your interests, ideas, and experiences. Answering the following questions may provide you with possible paper topics.

–What are my specific areas of expertise?

–What areas would I like to explore or learn more about?

–What knowledge do I have from my reading and past experience?

–What is happening to me or around me that I could observe or record?

The techniques listed in the chart below suggest other possibilities for discovering interesting and enjoyable subjects for writing.

Pre-Writing Techniques

Journal Writing. Keep a spiral notebook in which you record interesting ideas, thoughts, feelings, impressions, and experiences. Write in your journal on a regular basis. Such a book can become a valuable resource for writing ideas.

Reading. Skim magazines, books, and newspapers for intriguing topics or for stories that trigger your imagination. Keep a list of possible subjects or maintain a writing file in which you save the clippings.

Discussions and Interviews. Other people are often a source of fascinating ideas. Remember that every individual has unique experiences and knowledge to share. Listen carefully to what others have to say and ask questions about opinions and stories that emerge.

Brainstorming. This technique may be done alone or with others. It involves starting with one general idea and then building on it or branching out from it. The topic "sports," for example, could eventually lead to topics as varied and interesting as "the founding of the NFL," "teaching soccer fundamentals," or "my first home run."

Clustering. Clustering is actually a type of brainstorming. Begin by writing a word or phrase on a piece of paper. Circle it. Now, outside this circle, write down any word or phrase that you associate with that "nucleus" word. Put each new idea in its own circle and connect it with the nucleus. Branch out from the new circles in a similar manner. When a brand-new train of thought begins, start again at the nucleus.

Limiting and Refining a Topic. Topics may need to be narrowed or expanded so that they are appropriate for the paper you want to write. To check the feasibility of a topic, ask yourself if it can be fully developed within the specified length. If the topic is too broad, your writing may result in lists and generalizations. On the other hand, if your topic is too narrow, you may find yourself "stretching" information or padding sentences. Look at the example below. It illustrates how one writer might complete these first pre-writing steps. Throughout the chapter, you will see how the same writer handles other stages of the process of writing.

EXAMPLE: Topic

One writer identified "exercise" as an area of general interest. He realized, however, that he could not write an effective short composition on such a broad topic. Brainstorming about the idea "exercise" led him to consider several sports in which he had participated. As a member of his school's cross-country team, the writer knew a great deal about running. However, temporary injuries had sidelined him, and it occurred to him that his current exercise alternative, walking, had some unique and underrated benefits.

At this point, "The Benefits of Walking" can still lead the writer to many different types of writing. Determining the purpose and audience for his composition will help him to focus his narrowed subject even further.

Determine Your Purpose

Any topic can be approached in several different ways. In order to focus your ideas more accurately, you need to decide on the purpose of your paper. In other words you must determine what you want your writing to accomplish.

General Purposes	Purposes Relating to Topic	
to entertain	to define	to describe
to inform	to explain	to analyze
to persuade		

Once you have clarified your purpose, you may find it helpful to further refine your topic by writing a one-sentence **statement of purpose.** This is sometimes called a **thesis statement.**

Many decisions in writing are interrelated. As you make some firm decisions about your topic and purpose, for example, you will find that you have already determined to some extent the types of details you will use to develop your topic, as well as the types of organization that are possible. You may also find yourself making decisions about the following pre-writing considerations.

Point of View. Will you use first- or third-person point of view? With first-person narration, your narrator is part of the action. With third-person narration, the narrator is outside the action and can perceive as much as the writer wishes.

Tone. Tone is the attitude a writer takes toward the subject. The tone may be serious, critical, amused, sentimental, or angry.

Mood. Mood is the atmosphere or feeling that the reader experiences as he or she reads. For example, the writer can work to create a mood of joy, tranquility, terror, or confusion.

EXAMPLE: **Purpose**

The writer of "The Benefits of Walking" considered several possible ways of handling his topic. He considered writing an entertaining narrative about the time he discovered Christmas gift ideas for his whole family by looking in display windows as he walked through a shopping district early one morning. He also thought he might write a description in which he related all the sensory delights of a brisk walk on a crisp autumn morning. The writer also realized that, using the explanatory approach, he could give reasons why walking is such a beneficial exercise.

After some consideration, the writer of "The Benefits of Walking" decided that his paper would be an explanatory composition that tells why walking is a beneficial form of exercise. He also decided to adopt a "light" tone toward his subject and to create a humorous mood by contrasting it with a more popular exercise, running.

Identify Your Audience

If your writing is to have the impact you wish it to have, you must clarify in your mind exactly who your readers are. There are several reasons for this. First of all, identifying what your readers know and don't know will help you to determine how much background material you need to provide on your topic. Knowing their attitudes, opinions, and concerns will help you select appropriate supporting details.

Your audience will also determine the type of vocabulary and level of language you should use. (See Chapter 2.)

EXAMPLE: Audience

The writer of the sample composition determined that he was writing for his peers. Since this was the case, he felt he could write more informally. He could also assume that their concerns would be similar to his own.

Gather Supporting Information

As you have seen, your topic, purpose, and audience help to determine the type of additional material you will gather for writing. Supporting information can be classified in four ways:

Sensory details appeal to the readers' senses of sight, hearing, touch, smell, and taste. These details would include vivid descriptions of all the sounds, smells, and visual and tactile experiences one would encounter in a given situation.

Facts and statistics are statements and numbers that are verifiable. They provide data and support ideas and opinions.

Incidents or anecdotes are very short stories that illustrate a point. They are effective in informal, or personal compositions.

Specific examples are also useful to lend support to or illustrate a topic. They can clarify a general concept or term.

The techniques you use for gathering additional material are similar to those you used in identifying a topic. Details come from your own knowledge as well as from outside sources.

EXAMPLE: Pre-Writing Notes

The writer of "The Benefits of Walking" used his own experiences to come up with a list of possible supporting details. He recorded these details, as well as other decisions he made during pre-writing, in the following pre-writing notes.

1. Possible Topics:
   running · walking *(benefits of?)
   weight lifting · exercise workouts
2. Purpose: to explain why walking is beneficial
   — compare walking with running?
   — humorous tone?
3. Audience: classmates (informal writing)
4. Details:
   ran for five years
   took up walking one month ago
   benefits of both—physical fitness?
   walking a safe form of exercise
   aware of surroundings when walking
   everyone can walk
   speed and time a concern when running
   must be in good shape to run
   equipment needed for both? shoes? clothes? (cost?)
   thirty-minute walk all that is necessary
   once bitten by a dog when running!

Evaluate and Organize Information

Your lists and notes have been composed spontaneously as ideas occurred. To you, they may make perfect sense, but you need to consider what will make the most sense to your readers. Take time to assess your material. Look for gaps in your information or for other details that could be added for clarity. Look also for material that may have to be deleted because it does not really fit your topic or purpose.

In deciding how your material can most effectively be organized, again consider your purpose, audience, and supporting information. Then look for relationships among your ideas.

It is often helpful to make organizing a multi-step process. First, simply group together details that seem to relate naturally to one another. In longer papers, such groupings may indicate possible paragraph divisions. Try to identify the main idea that ties each group together and write this idea down.

Once the ideas are grouped, decide on a specific method of organization for your major points. Base your decisions upon what would be easiest for your readers to follow. You may choose from among these possible orders:

Chronological Order. With this order, you arrange your details in the order in which they happened or should happen. This organization is generally used in writing developed by an incident or anecdote, or in writing that explains a process.

Spatial Order. This type of organization presents details in the order in which a viewer might notice them. Spatial order might proceed from side to side, from top to bottom (or the reverse), or from near to far (or the reverse). Spatial organization is useful in presenting visual details.

Least to Most Important Idea. A paper organized using this technique presents ideas so that the strongest is presented last. Thus, the writer can build to a climax or emphasize an important point. This type of organization is useful when you are trying to persuade your audience or make a point.

Most to Least Familiar Idea. With this method of organization, you first present familiar ideas and then move to new concepts.

Comparison or Contrast. This type of organization works well whenever you want to point out similarities or differences.

EXAMPLE: **Evaluation and Organization**

The writer of the sample composition followed through with his original idea and began by grouping his ideas under the headings "running" and "walking." This allowed him to identify similarities and differences, which led him to consider organization by comparison and contrast. However, the writer also realized that his details about walking fit into three categories of benefits: physical, economic, and incidental. These suggested possible paragraph groupings. He reorganized his ideas within these three categories and then organized the categories from least to most important. However, each paragraph within the paper was organized by comparison and contrast.

As the reworked notes indicate, the writer began the process of refining and revising his ideas at the pre-writing stage, even before he wrote his first complete sentence. In addition to organizing the notes, the writer deleted some he felt were inappropriate. As we shall continue to see, this process of adding, deleting, and reorganizing is an ongoing one.

order {
③ physical benefits
② economic benefits
① incidental benefits

Specific Details

Walking	Running
~~walking for one month~~	~~running for five years~~
~~safe form of exercise~~	~~may be bitten by dog~~
① concern for/aware of surroundings (collect leaves for botany project) ⟷	concerned with speed and time
③ physical fitness (by-product?) ⟷	physical fitness (main goal?)
~~everyone can walk~~	~~must be in good shape~~
② no special equipment required ⟷	special equipment—expensive shoes and clothes
③ 30 min. brisk walk	

Order of Details

least to most important—overall
comparison and contrast—within paragraphs

Exercises Pre-Writing: Preparing To Write

A. Consider "A Rainy Day" as a possible topic for developing pre-writing notes. For this general topic, develop a narrowed topic and a purpose. Identify a specific audience, tone, and mood. Consider the types of supporting details you would include and a possible order for those details. Write these notes in the form shown in the example on page 112.

B. Make a pre-writing plan similar to the one illustrated on page 112. You might begin by brainstorming to generate possible topics for a general category such as "My Favorite Pastime." Rework these notes, following the example on page 114. Incorporate all decisions about supporting information and organization.

Part 2 Writing a First Draft

The first draft is a starting point for translating all your ideas and careful planning from the pre-writing stage into an actual piece of writing. At this point in the process, simply write to get the ideas from your pre-writing notes down on paper in sentence and paragraph form. Do not make the mistake of trying to produce a final piece of writing at this point. This step in the process of writing should be relaxed and spontaneous. Focus on your topic, but also allow yourself the freedom to incorporate new ideas as they may occur to you. Do not worry about details such as spelling and punctuation. You can correct these errors later, during revision. To make revision easier, however, leave space between the lines of your rough draft.

Your first draft is an important link between your ideas and your final product. You are trying out your ideas to see if they are workable. Experiment with your material and techniques as you write. Add and delete ideas and details if such changes seem appropriate as your writing progresses. Don't be afraid to reorder ideas or even to start over with an entirely new plan. As long as your changes remain consistent with the topic, purpose, and audience, you will have a unified piece of writing.

EXAMPLE: First Draft

Here is the first draft of a composition written from the pre-writing notes on pages 112 and 114.

The Benefits of Walking

The reason that I discovered the joys of walking was that I was recently sidelined myself from running by heel spurs and shin splints.

Like other runners, I was primarily always interested in improving my speed and time. Since taking up walking, I have, however, learned the virtues of a slower pace. I am much more aware of my surroundings now. Not only have I collected all the leaf specimen for my botany project on my daily walks, but I also have had time to smile at any people waiting for their busses each afternoon along my route, too.

Walking also has its economic benefits. While running, I require a lot of special equipment: not only special shoes but also sweat suits and running shorts. For walking, I need only a comfortable pair of shoes.

By walking rather than running, however, I have not abandoned physical fitness. By walking at a brisk pace for thirty minutes each day, I can still keep fit. My focus has just shifted. I am "stretching myself" rather than "pushing myself" and competing with myself and fittness has become a by-product of walking along with finishing my botany project, people-watching, and having more money in my pocket.

For all these reasons, walking is beneficial!

Compare this rough draft to the pre-writing notes in Part 1. Notice that the writer has expanded his idea of being interested in his surroundings while walking. However, he has also deleted other details that did not seem to fit into his writing plan as it developed. Although this is a good beginning, the composition still needs a great deal more work before it will read smoothly and capture a reader's interest. The writer may need to work through several rough drafts before achieving a good piece of writing.

Exercise Writing the First Draft

Use your pre-writing notes from Exercise B in Part 1 to write a rough draft. Remember that changes and revisions in your plan are not only possible but desirable at this point. Keep your first draft for use later in this chapter.

Part 3 Revising

By definition, a process is "a continuing development involving many changes." In the writing process, these changes, or revisions, occur at every stage. For instance, the writer of the sample composition on walking made changes as he worked on both his pre-writing notes and his rough draft. He added, deleted, and rearranged details as ideas on his topic continued to develop.

At the revising stage of the process, think critically about what you have written. You are no longer writing to free your ideas and to get them down on paper. Now you are working more carefully and thoughtfully in order to improve what you have already composed.

Since there are many aspects to consider in the revision process, read through your paper several times. Ask yourself only a few of the following revision questions during each reading.

1. Do I like what I have written? Will it appeal to a reader? Does my writing "come alive," or is it static?
2. Have I accomplished my **purpose?**
3. Have I included **adequate detail?** Can anything be added to make my ideas clearer or more complete?
4. Is the writing **unified?** Do all the supporting details relate to the topic and purpose of the paper? Do they relate to each other?
5. Is the writing **coherent?** Do my ideas flow smoothly? Are they clearly expressed? Is the writing organized logically? Is there a beginning, middle, and end to the development of the ideas?

6. Are the **tone** and **mood** consistent? Does each word in the writing contribute to the tone and mood of the entire composition?
7. Is the language appropriate to the audience? Have I used terms that are too informal or too technical for my readers to understand?

In addition to these points, use your knowledge of sentence construction to improve your writing. (See Chapters 3 through 6.) Is there variety in your sentence structure? Have you avoided empty, padded, or unclear sentences? Are ideas combined into sentences so that the relationships are clear? Does each sentence move smoothly into the next?

During revision, all good writers check these aspects of writing. They know revision is vital to developing the best in their writing. Be prepared to work through several drafts as you polish each aspect of your work.

Proofreading

One final consideration in revision is proofreading. After you have finished your content revisions, proofread your paper specifically to correct mistakes in grammar, usage, capitalization, punctuation, and spelling. You will find that many of these types of errors will have been corrected as you worked through your drafts. Use reference texts and correct any errors that remain. You may also wish to use the proofreading symbols shown on page 124, as well as the Sections on grammar, usage, and mechanics that appear at the back of this book.

EXAMPLE: Revision

Study the revised, rough draft on the following page. Notice how the writer has added an incident to his introduction that catches his readers' attention. This addition also adds to the humorous tone. By changing his title and referring to the introductory incident in his conclusion, the writer has also improved the unity of his writing.

The other day I almost tripped a friend who was jogging, but the impulse was without malice. I really had her best interests at heart.

Confessions of a Sidelined Runner

~~The Benefits of Walking~~

~~The reason that~~ I discovered the joys of walking ~~was that I was~~ recently sidelined ~~myself~~ from running by heel spurs and shin splints.

have

In the past,

Like other runners, I was primarily always interested in improving my speed and time. Since taking up walking, I have, however, ~~learned~~ the virtues of a slower pace. I am much more aware of my surroundings ~~now~~. Not only have I collected all the leaf specimen for my botany project on my daily walks, but I ~~also have time to smile at any people waiting for their busses each afternoon along my route, too.~~

in competition with myself.

discovered

Now

have had time for a little people-watching, too.

Walking also has its economic benefits. ~~While~~ running, I ~~require~~ a lot of ~~special~~ equipment: ~~not only~~ special shoes ~~but also~~ sweat suits ~~and~~ running shorts. For walking, I need only a comfortable pair of shoes.

When I'm running,

use

arch supports, heel lifts, Shoe Goo, and even a jogger's wrist wallet.

Most importantly,

By walking rather than running, however, I have not abandoned physical fitness. By walking at a brisk pace for thirty minutes each day, ~~I can~~ still keep fit. My focus has ~~just~~ shifted. I am "stretching myself" rather than "pushing myself" ~~and~~ competing with myself and fitness has become a by-product of walking along with finishing my botany project, people-watching, and having more money in my pocket.

having to

me in good condition.

For the time being,

move to ¶ 2

Maybe I should have tripped that friend!

~~For all these reasons, walking is benefitial!~~

Exercises Revising the First Draft

A. Look at the revised composition on page 119. Compare it with the first draft. In addition to the changes discussed in the text, several changes were made in revising sentence structure. Find these changes. Why were they made? In what ways have the sentences been improved?

B. Revise the content of the rough draft of the composition you wrote for the exercise in Part 2. Proofread your paper for errors in grammar, usage, and mechanics.

Part 4 Preparing the Final Copy

When you are satisfied that your writing is clear and correct, write it in its final form. Write carefully. Make your work as neat as possible. Be sure to follow the manuscript form that your teacher requires, including a proper heading and proper margins. For additional information about manuscript form, see Section 17 in your Handbook.

When you have finished your final copy, proofread your work again. Read your writing aloud, to yourself, one final time.

EXAMPLE: Final Copy

Now look at the final version of the sample composition.

Confessions of a Sidelined Runner

The other day I almost tripped a friend who was jogging, but the impulse was without malice. I really had her best interests at heart. Recently sidelined from running by heel spurs and shin splints, I have discovered the "joys of walking."

In the past, like other runners, I was always interested primarily in improving my speed and time and in competing with myself. Since taking up walking, however, I have discovered the virtues of a slower pace. Now I am much more aware of my surroundings. Not only have I collected all the leaf specimens for my botany project on my daily walks, but I have had time for a little people-watching, too!

Walking also has its economic benefits. When I'm running, I use a lot of equipment: special shoes, arch supports, heel lifts, sweat suits, running shorts, Shoe Goo, even a jogger's wrist wallet. For walking, I need only a comfortable pair of shoes.

Most importantly, however, I have not abandoned physical fitness by having to walk rather than run. Walking at a brisk pace for thirty minutes each day still keeps me in good condition. For the time being, my focus has shifted. I am "stretching myself" rather than "pushing myself."

Fitness has become a byproduct of walking—along with finishing my botany project, people-watching, and having more money in my pocket. Maybe I should have tripped that friend!

Exercise Preparing the Final Copy

Prepare a final copy of the writing that you have been developing throughout this chapter.

Guidelines for the Process of Writing

Pre-Writing

1. Select a topic that interests you.
2. Refine the topic until it can be developed in a specific length.
3. Decide on your purpose, audience, point of view, tone, and mood.
4. Gather and list details that you could use to develop your topic. Consider the following types of details:

sensory details	incidents and anecdotes
facts and statistics	specific examples

5. Evaluate and organize your list of details. Delete unrelated ideas. Add new ones that would develop your ideas. Put your details into a logical order, such as one of the following:

chronological order	least to most important idea
spatial order	most to least familiar idea
	comparison or contrast

Writing the First Draft

1. Keeping your audience and purpose in mind, begin to write.
2. Let your thoughts flow freely. Modify your initial plans for content and organization if necessary. Do not be too concerned with grammar and mechanics at this point.

Revising

Read what you have written. Answer the following questions:

1. Did you stick to your topic?
2. Did you include everything you wanted to?
3. Are there any unnecessary or unrelated details?
4. Is each idea clearly expressed and thoroughly developed?
5. Do tone, mood, and level of language remain consistent?
6. Is your writing unified and coherent?
7. Is your writing organized logically, with a beginning, a middle, and an end? Are the ideas presented in an order that makes sense?
8. Is your writing interesting and lively? Is there variety in the type and structure of your sentences?
9. Is your word choice vivid and precise?
10. Do the language and content suit your audience?
11. Have you accomplished your purpose?

Revise as necessary. Then proofread, using the Checklist on page 123.

Proofreading Checklist

Proofread your paper by answering the questions below. Additional instruction on each concept may be found in the indicated Sections.

Grammar and Usage

Are compound and complex sentences written and punctuated correctly? (Sect. 3)
Are there any sentence fragments or run-ons? (Sect. 4)
Have you used verb tenses correctly? (Sect. 5)
Do all verbs agree with their subjects? (Sect. 6)
Have you used the correct form of each pronoun? (Sect. 7)
Have you used adjectives and adverbs correctly? (Sect. 8)

Capitalization

Did you capitalize first words and all proper nouns and adjectives? (Sect. 10)
Are titles capitalized correctly? (Sect. 10)

Punctuation

Does each sentence have the proper end mark? (Sect. 11)
Are marks such as commas, colons, semicolons, apostrophes, hyphens, and quotation marks used correctly? (Sect. 12, 13, 14)

Spelling

Are plurals and possessive forms spelled correctly? (Sect. 13, 16)
Did you check all unfamiliar words in the dictionary? (Sect. 15)

Form

Were corrections made neatly? (Sect. 17)
In your final copy, is the writing legible?
Have you used the proper heading and margins?
Did you follow the manuscript form required by your teacher?

Proofreading Symbols

SYMBOL	MEANING	EXAMPLE
∧	insert	would have gone
≡	capitalize	United states
/	make lower case	our club President
∾	transpose	theif
ℓ	delete	finished the the race
¶	make new paragraph	. . . be complete. ¶ Another reason
⁀‿	close up space	head line
⊙	period	. . . and stop⊙ Before going . . .
∧,	add comma	Once that was settled the next
∨" ∨"	add quotation marks	the poem Autumn
∨'	add apostrophe	the childrens needs
/=/	add a hyphen	the copilot
⊂⊃	connect sentences	To finish your statue, you must complete this final step. Take a brush and dip it in

SUMMARY AND APPLICATIONS

1. The process of writing consists of three stages: pre-writing, writing the first draft, and revising. This process is essential to good composition. It is also a means of training yourself to think through problems thoroughly and logically.
2. Careful attention to pre-writing steps makes actual writing much easier. Pre-writing includes choosing a topic, deciding on the audience and purpose for the writing, and gathering and organizing ideas.
3. The first draft is the writer's opportunity to experiment with the ideas developed during pre-writing. Attention to mechanical details is not important at this time.
4. Revising and proofreading are the final stages of the process of writing. The writer checks for complete coverage; a consistent tone, mood, and level of language; sound organization; and a precise vocabulary. Finally, the writer proofreads for errors in grammar, capitalization, punctuation, and spelling.

Applications in Other Subject Areas

All Subjects. The writing stages of planning, drafting, and revision can be applied to almost any task. Such an approach can help you to organize and simplify your work.

Select a long-term assignment, such as a science experiment or a group project, in one of your other classes. Break it down into the three stages described above. Identify the particular elements you should consider or complete in each stage.

Fine Arts. As noted in the introduction of this chapter, many creations in the fine arts are also the result of a long and careful process. Try to identify the steps of the process involved in any of the following activities. Write a short composition that explains the procedure.

creating a painting
choreographing a dance
composing an unusual photograph
composing a piece of music
creating a character in a play
sculpting an object or figure

Chapter 8

Writing the Paragraph

In Chapter 7, you studied the three stages of the process of writing. This process is essential to all good writing. It is, however, only the beginning. If you want a piece of writing to be well crafted and uniquely your own, you must also learn some of the subtler aspects of composing and ways to apply them to your own work.

You should begin this learning process with the paragraph. Good paragraphs are important to good writing. They develop ideas that are impossible to convey in a single sentence. Good paragraphs working together are the building blocks of compositions—and of books. In this chapter you will learn what the basic characteristics of a good paragraph are. You will also learn about the subtler elements that can make a paragraph special.

Part 1 Defining the Paragraph

A paragraph is a group of related sentences that develop a single idea. In this short definition, the two adjectives "single" and "related" differentiate a paragraph from a random collection of sentences. Each sentence within the paragraph must state or develop a *single* main idea. This results in a **unified** group of sentences. The sentences must also be *related* to each other logically, so that the ideas they present are easy to follow. In other words, the paragraph as a whole must be **coherent.**

Thus, to expand on the original definition, a paragraph is a group of sentences that demonstrate *unity* and *coherence*.

A paragraph usually has a topic sentence that states the main idea. The body of a paragraph presents the subordinate ideas that support or explain the main idea in the topic sentence. While the topic sentence gives you the idea of the paragraph in a neat little package, the body opens the package so you can see what it contains. The body should always be long enough to develop the main idea adequately.

The sample paragraphs in this chapter either fit the above definition of a paragraph or are examples of poorly written paragraphs that do not conform to the prescribed pattern.

EXAMPLE 1

Ballet dancing is designed to give the impression of lightness and ease. Nothing in classic dancing should be convulsive or tormented. Derived from the seventeenth- and eighteenth-century court dances, the style is kingly, a series of harmonious and balanced postures linked by serene movement. The style involves what appears to be a total defiance of gravity. The illusion is achieved first by an enormous strengthening of the legs and feet to produce great resilient jumps and second by a coordination of arms and head in a rhythm slower than the rhythm of the legs which have no choice but to take the weight of the body when the body falls. But the slow, relaxed movement of head and arms gives the illusion of sustained flight.—AGNES DE MILLE

The preceding paragraph begins with a topic sentence that refers to the illusion of ease that ballet creates. The rest of the sentences build on this idea or explain how the illusion is achieved. All of the sentences work to create a unified whole and conclude with a restatement of the main idea.

EXAMPLE 2

Decide if the following paragraph fits the definition of an ideal paragraph.

> Half of Mexico is under eighteen. We are young and full of *inquietudes*. We also have long roots in the soil. Our bronze-faced ancestors were not movie Indians, hunting buffalo and sleeping in teepees, but pioneers in agriculture, mathematics, and city building. They put poems to music and danced to please both the gods and themselves. Not waiting for America to be discovered in 1492, they founded our great capital.

The topic sentence, while interesting, is not really clear in its meaning. What is actually meant, of course, is that half of the people in Mexico are under eighteen years of age. The writer begins to clarify the meaning in his second sentence, but in the third sentence he shifts to a new subject—the roots of the Mexican people. By the fourth sentence he is involved in a description of the achievements of ancestors, which has no relationship to the idea in the topic sentence.

Exercise Analyzing Paragraphs

Study the following paragraphs. Identify those that fit the definition of an ideal paragraph and those that do not. Write a sentence or two explaining each answer.

1. Many Native American peoples cherished a belief in a Golden Age when people and animals had lived and talked together. Northwest Coast families proudly proclaimed their descent from the eagle, the raven, and the wolf. Medicine men in nearly every tribe were initiated into their roles as mystical healers and prophets by animal instructors who

had appeared to them in visions. Through elaborate ceremonies refined over centuries, young Indian men and women learned how to revere the sacred forces of animals and all the rest of the living, natural world. The yearning for a dimly remembered time of wholeness, when human beings lived in peaceful harmony with all of nature, was part of their highest rituals as well as in the activities of their everyday lives.

2 It required more skill to hunt the deer than any other animal. We never tried to approach the deer except against the wind. Frequently we would spend hours in stealing upon grazing deer. If they were in the open we would crawl long distances on the ground, keeping a weed or brush before us, so that our approach would not be noticed. Often we could kill several out of one herd before the others would run away. Their flesh was dried and packed in vessels and would keep for many months. The hide of the deer was soaked in water and ashes and the hair removed, and then the process of tanning continued until the buckskin was soft and pliable. Perhaps no other animal was more valuable to us than the deer.

3 In summer, the countryside blossoms into a stretch of heaven. Magnolia trees fill the breezes with sweet scent for long miles. Days are slumberous, and the skies are high and thronged with clouds that ride fast. At midday the sun blazes and bleaches the soil. Butterflies flit through the heat; wasps sing their sharp, straight lines; birds fluff and flounce, piping in querulous joy. Nights are covered with canopies sometimes blue and sometimes black, canopies that sag low with ripe and nervous stars. The throaty boast of frogs momentarily drowns out the call of crickets.

4 We sat in front of the fire and pretended to see pictures in the dancing flames. The neighbors next door were not home, but their dog, a huge Irish setter, was barking insistently. As we got up to investigate the noise, Mother came in with hot cocoa. Looking back, it seems like all the winters of my childhood were warmed with hot cocoa.

Part 2 Pre-Writing: Choosing and Refining a Topic

In Chapter 7, you learned various techniques for generating topic ideas. You also learned to choose from among these ideas by focusing on those that could be developed around your own areas of expertise, or which appeal to your sense of curiosity. Finally, you learned to refine a subject by limiting its scope and selecting a purpose and audience for your writing.

This initial step of choosing and refining a topic affects the rest of the writing process. Learning to write a strong topic sentence can help you with this step by sharpening the focus of your topic even more.

Using the Topic Sentence To Focus Ideas

A topic sentence functions in many ways within a paragraph. Its most obvious job, as you have learned, is to present the main idea of the paragraph. In this capacity, it should demonstrate the following characteristics.

1. **The topic sentence must present a general statement.** In other words, it must lend itself to being supported by other more specific ideas, examples, and details.
2. **The topic sentence must limit the scope of the paragraph.** The idea it presents must not be too broad or too narrow to be developed within a given length.
3. **The topic sentence must catch the reader's attention.** If the topic sentence is not interesting, the reader will have no incentive to read further.

All three of these characteristics are important, and you probably incorporate them automatically. However, the topic sentence must do more than state the main idea of a paragraph in an interesting manner. To completely prepare the reader for what is to come, the topic sentence should also set the **tone** of the paragraph. This means that it should suggest the writer's attitude toward the subject.

Beginning writers often start writing a paragraph, only to discover that they cannot go beyond a sentence or two. Usually this happens because the topic sentence does not set a tone that can be developed further. For example, consider the following topic sentence.

> The Sears Tower is in Chicago.

While this sentence is about something—the Sears Tower—it expresses no feeling or attitude about it. Once the writer has stated that the building is in Chicago, she has little more to say. She could add a sentence giving the address, but that would be all. The following is a reworking of the same sentence.

> The Sears Tower is one of the most exciting buildings in Chicago.

This sentence presents an attitude about the subject, expressed by the word *exciting*. The writer now has literally dozens of supporting ideas from which to choose. She could, for example, focus on the architecture—the sheer mass of the building, the crispness of its style, the magnificent interior design. She might choose to discuss the excited reactions of first-time visitors to the building or the vital business transacted in its many offices. In other words, the idea of excitement is expandable; it can be explained or supported.

Placement of the Topic Sentence. A writer could choose to start a paragraph with "The Sears Tower is in Chicago" and then follow it with a second sentence that reads "It is one of the most exciting buildings in the world." However, the second sentence, not the first, would be the topic sentence for the paragraph. This order of sentences brings out the fact that a topic sentence does not have to be the first sentence in a paragraph. Although the topic sentence usually *is* the first sentence, it can also be positioned somewhere in the middle of the paragraph, or even at the end.

Just as it is desirable to use sentences of various lengths and structures, so it is desirable to place topic sentences in various positions. By doing so, you introduce variety into your paragraph structures and avoid a certain monotony of style.

Exercises Working with Topic Sentences

A. Here are ten sentences that would make good topic sentences for paragraphs. Copy them. Put one line under the main idea and two lines under the word or words that express the tone, like this: Spring rains brighten nature.

1. The craftsmanship shown on that table is superb.
2. Would you be surprised if you found oil in your yard?
3. Roller skating is becoming remarkably popular once again.
4. A hurricane devastated the coast of Southern Florida.
5. The cuddly appearance of bears can be fatally deceptive.
6. Day in and day out I follow the same tedious pattern of life.
7. Raymond's Kitchen is the worst restaurant in the Midwest.
8. Do you believe in ESP (extrasensory perception)?
9. I learned to treasure books when I was very young.
10. Swimming is the best all-around exercise for your body.

B. Pre-Writing. Generate a list of ten topics and write a topic sentence for each of them. Make certain that you have a specific audience and purpose in mind. Also be sure that each sentence states a main idea, is interesting, and expresses an attitude toward the subject. Keep your sentences for use later in the chapter.

Part 3 Pre-Writing: Gathering Information

The topic sentence identifies your topic and sets a tone for the rest of the paragraph. It is the body of your paragraph, however, that develops the main idea. The information included in the body of your paragraph may come from your own knowledge, experience, and observation; from others whom you interview; or from conventional information sources, such as books, magazines, and newspapers. The types of information you use to develop the idea expressed in the topic sentence might include any of the following, either alone or in combination:

sensory details
facts or statistics
examples
incidents or anecdotes

See Chapter 7, Part 1, for a more in-depth treatment of this part of the writing process.

The body of the following paragraph is developed using specific examples.

> Motion pictures, the phonograph, radio, and television have all radically changed the way we live and the way we encounter the world. The movies deeply affected the theater, effectively killing the "popular" stage and leaving only a "legitimate" theater that is constantly striving for survival. The phonograph, which made it possible to preserve musical performance and speech for an indefinite period, brought sounds and words into the home that previously could be heard only in large auditoriums with large audiences. The radio brought a "radio culture" of its own, constructed entirely on sound, and consisting of home-delivered music, drama, news coverage, political speeches, and much more. Most recently, television added picture to the sound, making it possible as never before to bring the entire world into the home—this in a literal sense after the launching of satellites around the world that pick up signals from any part of the globe.

The topic sentence of the paragraph states the main idea, which is that four inventions—motion pictures, the phonograph, radio, and television—have radically changed the way we live and the way we encounter the world. The rest of the paragraph summarizes the unique impact of each invention. Since each specific example explains how and why one of the inventions changed life so drastically, each detail develops the main idea of the paragraph and contributes to a unified piece of writing.

No matter what type of development you choose for your paragraph, make certain that the details all support the main idea and reflect the purpose for which you are writing.

Exercises Gathering Supporting Information

A. In each of the following paragraphs, identify the main idea that is expressed in the topic sentence. Next, identify the types of supporting information—sensory details, facts and statistics, examples, incidents or anecdotes—that are used in each paragraph. (Remember that more than one type may be used.) Explain how this information develops the main idea of the paragraph.

1 Most mysterious was the Indian reverence for land. For centuries the Indians had lived off the land as hunters, taking and giving in their dances and ceremonies. Earth, they believed, was mother of all. Most important was the land on which their particular tribe dwelt. The Crow are a good example of the Indian religious love for land. The Crow have a long prayer that thanks the Great Spirit for giving them their land. It is not too hot, they say, and not too cold. It is not too high and snowy and not too low and dusty. Animals enjoy the land of the Crow; men and women enjoy it also. The prayer ends by declaring that of all the possible lands in which happiness can be found, only in the land of the Crow is true happiness found.

—VINE DELORIA, JR.

2 Durant Motors, Inc., grew by leaps and bounds. Facilities were built in Flint and Lansing and in Oakland, California. The Sheridan plant in Muncie, Indiana, was bought to produce the "Durant Six." The bankrupt Locomobile Company of Bridgeport, Connecticut, was purchased to add to the Durant line a luxury car with a long-standing, prestigious reputation. Chrysler and Studebaker were outbid at $5.25 million to acquire the new Willys plant at Elizabeth, New Jersey, the most modern automobile factory in the world. Then, on February 15, 1922, Durant announced that he would bring out the "Star," which at a price of $348 would compete with the Ford Model T. Some sixty thousand people flocked to see the Star at its first showing in New York City, and by January 1, 1923, Durant had accepted cash deposits on orders for 231,000 Stars, a full year's production.—JAMES J. FLINK

3 It often comes as a shock to Asians to realize that they are not human beings. At least they are not, as represented by movies and TV. The greatest educational and propaganda devices ever devised by mankind still depict Asians in the stereotype created in the early 1900's. With rare exceptions, Asians are always portrayed as waiters, laundrymen, cooks, villains, warmongers, geishas, house servants, gardeners, and karate experts. Movies and TV have failed to reflect the achievements of Asian-Americans in medicine, finance, music, or any other field.—IRVIN PAIK

4 When I was six or seven years old, growing up in Pittsburgh, I used to take a precious penny of my own and hide it for someone else to find. For some reason I always "hid" the penny along the same stretch of sidewalk up the street. I would cradle it at the roots of a sycamore, say, or in a hole left by a chipped-off piece of sidewalk. Then I would take a piece of chalk and, starting at either end of the block, draw huge arrows leading up to the penny from both directions. After I learned to write I labeled the arrows: SURPRISE AHEAD or MONEY THIS WAY. I was greatly excited, during all this arrow drawing, at the thought of the first lucky passer-by who would receive in this way, regardless of merit, a free gift from the universe. However, I never lurked about. I would go straight home and not give the matter another thought, until some months later, I would be gripped again by the impulse to hide another penny.

—ANNIE DILLARD

5 On the dock everyone was busy. There were women selling things to eat and children waiting for sailors to come ashore. Winches rattled, and the cranes lifted up their loads of palm oil and cocoa beans. Ebony-black men, naked to the waist, the sweat pouring off them, loaded the rope hampers before they swung up and over and down into the dark hole of the big ship. Their sweat fell from shining black bodies onto the bags of cocoa beans and went away to England and came back in gold for the white people to count in banks as though it were the most precious thing in the world.—LANGSTON HUGHES

B. Pre-Writing. Look at the list of ten topic sentences that you created for Exercise B, page 132. Decide what types of details could be used to develop each topic sentence. Select one sentence and develop complete pre-writing notes for it. Be sure to identify your audience and purpose and to develop a full list of specific details. Refer to Chapter 7, "The Process of Writing," for help with each of these steps.

Part 4 Pre-Writing: Organizing Information

Once you have gathered information for your paragraph, the next step is to establish a logical relationship among your details.

The idea of logical order should not imply that there is one, absolutely correct order for the ideas in any given paragraph. For example, a paragraph about the pleasures of skiing could probably describe those pleasures in any order. In a paragraph using sensory details to describe a sunny day in June, it most likely would not matter if the singing of the birds was described first and the greenness of the grass second, or the other way around. A paragraph developed by facts or examples does not have to follow any particular order if the facts or examples are of equal importance.

On the other hand, a paragraph should demonstrate some sort of pattern that is determined by the nature of the subject and by the approach to that subject chosen by the writer. Without such a pattern, the paragraph would not be coherent. The most frequently used ways of ordering or arranging details to form a pattern are the following:

chronological order
spatial order
order of importance
comparison and contrast

You were introduced to each of these orders in Chapter 7. Now you will examine them in greater detail.

Chronological Order

Chronological order is the order of time. For example, in relating an incident, you would arrange the details in the order in which they happened. In explaining the steps in a process, you would arrange the steps in the order in which they should be done. The following paragraph provides an example of a paragraph in which the details are arranged in chronological order.

> At the age of nine or ten, I became a businesswoman, having discovered that the mustard and dandelion greens that my mother was so fond of were also loved by all of her churchgoing friends who did not live on farms. I picked the greens by the basket in the morning and had sold two or three baskets by early afternoon. I soon expanded my marketable produce to include strawberries, blackberries, and raspberries in season. I took on a business rival as a partner: my cousin Marlene, who, barefoot the same as I, would accompany me down the hot highways as we made our daily business rounds. The quarters of profit we immediately sank into the local movie house, where three times a week we sat through the delightful and terrifying horror of old and new Wolfman and Frankenstein films. Always, we remembered too late that afterwards we would have to run more than a half mile out of town down a pitch-black road to get home. Nevertheless our business flourished—as did our fright—until we outgrew both.—VIRGINIA HAMILTON

Spatial Order

Spatial order is the position of things in space and is usually used in descriptive writing. In describing a scene, for example, you would arrange the details so that the reader would know their positions in relation to the narrator or to the central object in the scene. You might also arrange details in the order in which a viewer would notice them. In the paragraph on the next page, the writer uses spatial order to describe a clinic.

> One must descend to the basement and move along a confusing, mazelike hall to reach it. Twice the passage seems to lead against a blank wall; then at last one enters the brightly lighted auditorium. And here, finally, are the social workers at the reception desks; and there, waiting upon the benches rowed beneath the pipes carrying warmth and water to the floors above, are the patients. One sees white-jacketed psychiatrists carrying charts appear and vanish behind screens that form the improvised interviewing cubicles. All is an atmosphere of hurried efficiency, and the concerned faces of the patients are brightened by the friendly smiles and low-pitched voices of the expert workers. One has entered the Lafarque Psychiatric Clinic.—RALPH ELLISON

Order of Importance

The order of importance is often used in a paragraph of explanation or persuasion. Generally, you would begin with the least important fact or reason and end with the most important one, thus providing a strong conclusion to your paragraph. Sometimes, however, you might choose to do just the opposite—start with your strongest or most compelling fact or reason and then support it with ideas arranged in their descending order of importance. In either case, your reader should be able to understand the relative importance of the ideas. Note how the ideas in the following paragraph build to a climax.

> There are three kinds of book owners. The first has all the standard sets and best sellers—unread, untouched. (This deluded individual owns woodpulp and ink, not books.) The second has a great many books—a few of them read through, most of them dipped into, but all of them as clean and shiny as the day they were bought. (This person would probably like to make books his or her own, but is restrained by a false respect for their physical appearance.) The third has a few books or many—every one of them dog-eared and delapidated, shaken and loosened by continual use, marked and scribbled in from front to back. (This person owns books.)
>
> —MORTIMER J. ADLER

Comparison and Contrast

If the main idea of a paragraph is to show how persons, things, or events are alike or different, the most effective method of organization might involve comparison or contrast. A paragraph organized by comparison emphasizes the similarities between subjects by placing them side by side. A paragraph organized by contrast emphasizes the differences between subjects by using this same strategy. Comparison and contrast paragraphs do not always have an alternating presentation of facts or details. These details can be grouped. Also, a paragraph may include both similarities and differences and use a combination of these two methods. The following paragraph is developed by making a comparison of facts.

> The deaths of President Lincoln and President Kennedy are alike in several ways. Both Lincoln and Kennedy were attacked suddenly by an assassin on a Friday, and each in the presence of his wife. Each man was shot in the head; in each instance, crowds of people watched the shooting. Lincoln's secretary, named Kennedy, had advised him not to go to the theater where the attack occurred. Kennedy's secretary, named Lincoln, had advised him not to go to Dallas where the attack occurred.

Exercises Using Logical Order in Paragraphs

A. Determine the type of organization used in each paragraph that follows and be ready to explain your decision.

1 They reached the junction some time before the train was due to arrive and stood about two feet from the first set of tracks. Mr. Head carried a paper sack with some biscuits and a can of sardines in it for their lunch. A coarse-looking, orange-colored sun coming up behind the east range of mountains was making the sky a dull red behind them; but in front of them it was still gray, and they faced a gray, transparent moon, hardly stronger than a thumbprint and completely without light. A small tin switch box and a black fuel tank were all there was to mark the place as a junction; the tracks were double and did not converge again until they were hidden behind the bends at either end of the clearing. Trains passing appeared to emerge from a tunnel of trees and, hit for a second by the cold sky, vanish terrified into the woods again.

—FLANNERY O'CONNOR

2 When we moved to Signal Mountain fourteen years ago, this was still a fairly woodsy area. Vacant lots were grown up to weeds and sassafras. Possums trundled in the ditches, at night little foxes crossed the road in the headlights of cars, and toads trilled from every direction on summer evenings. In this short time the trees have gone, the vacant lots have been cleared and built upon, the wet-weather springs dug up and blasted out and rechanneled. Foxes and possums come no more; the toads no longer sing; I must travel miles to hear a whippoorwill. It had been two years now since yellow jackets nested in my yard—those bright, harmless, sturdy wasps with their tiny-horned goat-heads, which once gave me so much pleasure. My children's children will likely never see their lovely curving flight against the shrubbery.

—MARY Q. STEELE

3 An old tale accounts for the origin of the cat family in a thoroughly unscientific way. Not long after Noah had loaded the Ark with animals and set sail on his memorable voyage, he found that the vessel was overrun with mice. The original pair had multiplied so rapidly that their offspring were adding greatly to the discomforts of an already overcrowded passenger list. Even more serious were the terrific inroads the hungry rodents were making in the food supply. Noah in desperation went to the lion and asked his advice. After a moment's thought, the resourceful king of beasts took a deep breath, humped his back, and brought forth a mighty sneeze. Out from his mouth popped a pair of house cats! Needing no urging, they immediately went to work. Soon all but one pair of mice had disappeared.

—CARL BURGER

4 Every attempt must be made to preserve the Spanish language in the United States. It is the instrument that makes the English language available to the Spanish-speaking child through well trained bilingual teachers. Bilinguals also work effectively in government and industry. They are a human resource that must not be allowed to dry up, for the voice of America must be bilingual if it is to be understood by our Spanish-speaking friends to the south, with whom our destiny is inextricably interwoven.

—SABINE A. ULIBARRI

B. Pre-Writing. Determine the best method of organization for the list of details that you prepared for Exercise B on page 136. First group and then number your specific details in the order you would present them in a paragraph. As a pattern begins to take shape, eliminate details that seem to be unrelated to your topic. Add additional ideas that might aid in the development.

Part 5 Writing the First Draft

Now that you have thought about your topic sufficiently, you are ready to write your first draft. Using your pre-writing notes to guide you, let your ideas and feelings flow on paper. Do not stop to correct mistakes or to try to make anything perfect.

As you write, add new details that occur to you and delete others that do not fit into your ideas as they develop. At this point, you can still reorganize your ideas or even start over with a modified topic or different tone. Remember, this is only your first draft. It is simply the framework for your writing. You will take time to revise later on in the writing process.

Exercise Writing the First Draft

Use the notes that you developed and organized in Exercise B above to write a rough draft of a paragraph. Add, delete, and rearrange details as long as your changes are consistent with your subject, point of view, audience, and purpose.

Part 6 Revision: Incorporating Adequate Detail

Revision may be the most important part of the composing process. At this stage, you might compare yourself to a sculptor who has fashioned the rough shape of a statue and who must now concentrate on adding just the right details of character, line, and form.

Revision should be done in several stages. Concentrate on one aspect of the paragraph at each stage.

One of the first and most important aspects for which to check is adequate detail. Details are important in all types of paragraphs, for they are the means by which a writer elicits a response from a reader. If a paragraph is developed without sufficient detail, a reader has great difficulty maintaining interest in the subject and is unable to visualize, understand, agree, or disagree with the writer's ideas.

The following is an example of a paragraph that lacks adequate detail.

> Harriet Tubman was a slave. She was born in 1821, the same year that Denmark Vesey led a slave uprising. Harriet learned a song made popular by Vesey called "Go Down Moses." In later years, it became Harriet's song.

The paragraph contains few details and is, therefore, flat and uninteresting. In contrast, the revised paragraph on the same subject contains plentiful details.

> Harriet Tubman was a slave, born to slave parents and owned by a Maryland master. She was born in 1821, the year of the great slave uprising in South Carolina led by Denmark Vesey. All through that year, and for many years to come, Vesey's name was whispered in slave cabins throughout the South. His exploit frightened some slaves because masters became harsher, but it excited others to hope. As a very small girl, Harriet was taught to sing a song that Vesey had made popular.

> Go down, Moses
> Way down to Egypt land!
> And tell old Pharaoh
> To let my people go!
>
> It was a dangerous song to sing. It had to be sung under the breath even when no white person was around, but in the years to come, it became Harriet's song.
>
> —HENRIETTA BUCKMASTER

By reading this paragraph, you learn many biographical facts about Harriet Tubman and Denmark Vesey. You learn the origin of a song that is still sung today, and you get at least an impression of what the life of a slave was like. If you compare this paragraph with its rough draft, you can see the importance of including adequate detail in your own writing.

Exercises Supplying Adequate Details

A. Here are some "rough drafts" that lack sufficient detail. Choose three and amplify them. Stick to the subject but supply enough details to develop them into substantial paragraphs.

1. Some exams are "bad news." I have a real fear of examinations in some of my subjects. The worst subjects for me are science and math.
2. I would like to travel more. I have made trips to a few places in my lifetime. I always had a good time.
3. I love a parade. The last parade I saw had a number of floats. It also had bands and other enjoyable things to see and listen to.
4. I used to be easily embarrassed. Several things that happened to me embarassed me at the time. Sometimes I would cringe for weeks when I thought about them.
5. The train usually runs late. It is hard to have to depend upon public transportation.
6. There are some jobs around the house that I detest. I try to avoid them whenever I can. Sometimes, however, circumstances demand that these tasks be completed.

B. The following rough drafts also lack adequate detail. Choose two and, from your own imagination, revise them by supplying details that will develop them into good paragraphs.

1. The squad car, with its siren screaming, pulled up beside the battered truck. A scene of devastation met the eyes of the trooper. For years afterward, he would remember that awful night.
2. The flood waters spewed through the hole in the dam, which widened even as we watched it. Then, with fury, the water hurled itself down the stream bed toward the town below. It destroyed everything in its path.
3. It was hard to tell who had started the fight. Both boys looked terrible and refused to talk. Eventually, we found out the truth.
4. The directions were explicit. Phyllis confidently began to put the bicycle together.
5. The lake was so polluted you could almost walk on it. It was unfit for swimming.

C. Revision. Reread the rough draft you wrote for the exercise on page 141. What details can you add to help your reader visualize, understand, agree with, or disagree with your ideas?

Part 7 Revision: Achieving Unity

Paragraphs differ in many ways—in purpose, style, and length, for example. However, every well written paragraph shares one vital quality. That quality is unity. In a unified paragraph, all the sentences relate to one single idea. There are no "extra" sentences that distract or lead away from the purpose of the paragraph.

In your own writing, you can sometimes find and remove unrelated details when you are still in the pre-writing stage. This can be accomplished as you study your pre-writing notes. At other times, you may not become aware of these "extra" ideas until you are well into the drafting stage. Many writers find it hard to delete any of their ideas once they are written down on paper. However, for the sake of unity, you must train yourself to read your rough draft with a critical eye in order to delete those unrelated sentences.

The following paragraph has some unneeded sentences. Look for them as you read.

> Perhaps the only tiresome thing about being an American is that one is continually being told by foreigners what is wrong with this country. Fortunately, most Americans seem rather to enjoy this type of criticism and wisely so because, after all, criticism is a form of homage. I have a history teacher who always criticizes me, so I know what it is like to be criticized. I get B's, but she thinks I should get A's. One criticizes only that which seems potentially perfect. There is a long history of people criticizing each other.

This paragraph exemplifies a common pitfall in all types of writing. A word or a phrase or the subject matter itself suggests a thought to the writer who then goes off in a new direction.

In the sample paragraph, the word *criticism* diverts the writer from her purpose. She has a complaint against a teacher, and that word reminds her of it. She then presents two sentences on the new topic of her teacher's criticism, a topic that is only indirectly related to the main idea of the paragraph. The writer is not able to stick with the new topic either, for, after returning briefly to her original idea, she concludes with a random thought about people criticizing each other. She will need to delete these extra details and generate new ones that relate more closely to her original purpose.

Exercises **Achieving Paragraph Unity**

A. Read the following paragraphs carefully. For each paragraph, pick out the sentences that do not work with the others to develop the main idea or the tone of the paragraph.

1 The reputation of the lion as a killer has been greatly exaggerated. By and large it is a peaceable, good-natured beast and does not attack human beings unless molested. Wolves have a bad reputation, too. People mistakenly believe that they run in packs and chase humans. However, a lion is dangerous when aroused or when, as sometimes happens, it has acquired a taste for human flesh. Lions once held up the building of the Uganda Railway for nine months, during which time they killed a great many laborers. There are no wolves in Uganda.

2 Our last football game was wild. Up until the very last play in the game we were tied 0-0. On the last play, Jackson, our quarterback, kept the ball and plowed right through the middle for a score. Jackson is an All-Conference choice. During the past two seasons, he has played outstanding ball for our school. Jackson is so tall that he is easily recognized in the corridors.

3 My family rented a houseboat on the Mississippi for a weekend. If prizes were given for rotten weekends, that weekend would win them all. There were a few good things. The scenery was beautiful despite the rain. The mosquitoes didn't bite much in the part of the river to where we drifted after losing our anchor. The weekend was cheap; it cost only thirty dollars. My sister insists that we should take the same kind of trip again next year.

B. Check for unity in the paragraph you wrote for Part 5. Does every element contribute to the development of your main idea? Do these elements reinforce the tone of the paragraph? Make additions and deletions as necessary.

Part 8 Revision: Reinforcing Coherence

By definition, a good paragraph is coherent. The ideas are presented in a logical order and are clearly linked to one another so that the train of thought is easy to follow.

Because coherence is so important to any piece of writing, you have been concerned with it since the pre-writing stage when you determined a method of organization for your pre-writing notes. During revision, check your draft to make sure that your organization is effective. It is not too late to rearrange your ideas if another method of organization would better suit your audience or purpose.

There is also one more step you can take to make sure that your ideas flow well. Even good organization can be enhanced by the addition of linking words and expressions that reinforce coherence by showing relationships among the ideas. These words and expressions, called **transitional devices,** help the reader to follow the writer's line of thought from one idea or concept to another.

Transitional Devices

The use of **pronouns** is one way of contributing to the coherence in a paragraph. Pronouns such as the following refer to persons, places, things, or ideas in preceding sentences, thereby connecting the sentences.

he, him, his	they, them, their
she, her, hers	this, that
it, its	these, those

In the paragraph that follows, notice how the words in italics refer to someone or something mentioned in a previous sentence.

> I saw Lorraine in her hospital bed, as she was dying. *She* tried to speak; *she* couldn't. *She* did not seem frightened or sad, only exasperated that *her* body no longer obeyed *her;* *she* smiled and waved. But I prefer to remember *her* as *she* was the last time I saw *her* on *her* feet. *We* were at, of all places, the PEN Club. *She* was seated, talking, dressed all in black, wearing a very handsome wide, black hat, thin, and radiant. I knew *she* had been ill, but I didn't know, then, how seriously. I said, "Lorraine, *you* look beautiful. How in the world do *you* do *it?*" *She* was leaving, I have the impression *she* was on a staircase, and *she* turned and smiled that smile and said, "It helps to develop a serious illness, Jimmy!" and waved and disappeared.—JAMES BALDWIN

Linking expressions, or connectives, also can help to move the ideas in a paragraph smoothly from one sentence to another. Linking expressions are used in the following ways.

Linking Expressions

TO ADD IDEAS

and	in addition	and then	equally important
also	likewise	further	in the same fashion
too	again	furthermore	moreover
besides	nor	as a result	

TO LIMIT

but	however	at the same time	in contrast
yet	although	on the other hand	as opposed to

TO CONTRADICT

and yet	nevertheless	on the contrary
still	otherwise	nonetheless

TO ARRANGE IN TIME OR PLACE

first	finally	soon	here
second (etc.)	at this point	before	near
next	meanwhile	afterward	below
presently	eventually	at length	above

TO EXEMPLIFY OR SUM UP

for example	in short	for the most part
for instance	in brief	in any event
in fact	on the whole	in any case
in other words	to sum up	as I have said

Finally, repeating words or phrases from a previous sentence is another excellent means of providing coherence. Use this or any of the above methods whenever you write.

Exercises Using Linking Words and Expressions

A. Study this paragraph. Identify pronouns and other transitional devices that reinforce coherence. Copy them, numbering each with the number of the sentence in which it appears.

> 1. For people with offices in the towers, especially on their upper floors, working in the World Trade Center is radically different from working anywhere else. 2. In the first place, many of them admit to being nagged by a constant fear of fire—what the Port Authority casually refers to as "The Towering Inferno" syndrome. 3. For the most part, this fear is irrational, for the WTC is constructed entirely of fireproof materials. 4. On the other hand, the WTC has already had a major fire, on February 13, 1975, when a blaze set by a disgruntled cleaning person on the eleventh floor of the North Tower caused more than a million dollars' worth of damage. 5. What burned, however, wasn't the building itself but drapes, carpets, and furnishings, although the heat of the fire did blow out windows and cause some minor structural damage. 6. Luckily, no one was injured and the fire didn't spread to any other floors, but it nonetheless proved that the towers were somewhat less fireproof than the Port Authority had been claiming.—THOMAS MEEHAN

B. Check the rough draft of your paragraph for coherence. Do all details relate to one another? Does your writing have a beginning, a middle, and an end? Can you improve coherence?

Part 9 Revision: Achieving Emphasis

The entire writing process involves making choices. In the pre-writing stage, you began by choosing a topic and main idea for your paragraph. Now, at the point of revision, you need to determine which ideas and details you wish to highlight in order to emphasize the main idea. You must also decide which specific strategies you will use to achieve that emphasis.

Many devices can be used to make a whole paragraph or certain parts of it emphatic. For instance, you can use a strong style with short, muscular sentences and many active words. You can write at length about what is important and give only a little space to what is less vital to the development of an idea. You can employ striking words that connote brutality or beauty. You can repeat words or phrases. You can choose a central place or object and present details in relation to it.

Read the following paragraph. What are the topic, main idea, and tone? How are they emphasized?

> The whole history of our continent is a history of the imagination. Our ancestors imagined land beyond the sea and found it. No force of terror, no pressure of population, drove them across this continent. They came, as the great explorers crossed the Atlantic, because of the imagination of their minds—because they imagined a better, a more beautiful, a freer, happier world; because they were people not only of courage, not only of strength and hardiness, but of warm and vivid desire; because they desired; because they had the power to desire.—ARCHIBALD MACLEISH

Emphasis is achieved in this paragraph through a long series of reasons. These reasons state and restate the idea of the importance of the imagination of our ancestors. The words used are glowing and positive. Also, the repetition of the word "desire" strengthens the positive tone and mood.

Exercises Analyzing and Adding Emphasis

A. Read each of the following paragraphs. What idea is the writer trying to emphasize? How is this emphasis achieved?

1 Always when he looked in the mirror, his eyes were different. Sometimes they peered from out of the broken glass asking an unanswerable question, sometimes they were angry and damning, sometimes they were silent and brooding. Too often they were the eyes of a dead man, jellied and black. His long, fleshy nose with its countless red pinpricks would expand and contract in time to his breathing, and the gray-striped lips that refused to open over the severe outward slant of the front teeth would strain themselves into the subtlest kind of smile. Thus he could stand, sometimes for over an hour, a silent, ugly man who could no longer tell whether he was inside the mirror or inside himself.—WILLIAM DEMBY

2 He was a man, a border man. What did he look like? Well, that is hard to tell. Some say he was short and some say he was tall; some say he was Indian brown and some say he was blond like a newborn cockroach. But I'd say he was not too dark and not too fair, not too thin and not too fat, not too short and not too tall; and he looked just a little bit like me. But does it matter so much what he looked like? He was a man, very much of a man; and he was a border man. Some say he was born in Matamoros; some say Reynosa; some say Hidalgo County on the other side. And I guess others will say other things. But Matamoros, or Reynosa, or Hidalgo, it's all the same border; and short or tall, dark or fair, it's the man that counts. And that's what he was, a man.—AMÉRICO PAREDES

3 It was the best of times, it was the worst of times, it was the age of wisdom, it was the age of foolishness, it was the epoch of belief, it was the epoch of incredulity, it was the season of Light, it was the season of Darkness, it was the spring of hope, it was the winter of despair, we had everything before us, we had nothing before us, we were all going direct to Heaven, we were all going direct the other way—in short, the period was so far like the present period, that some of its noisiest authorities insisted on its being received, for good or evil, in the superlative degree of comparison only.—CHARLES DICKENS

4 It must have been a day in April. What other month could give me such blue and white, such sun and wind? The clothing on the lines was horizontal and shuddering: the sharp, carved clouds hurried; the sun spattered from the soap suds in the gutter; the worn bricks were bright with a

dashing of rain. It was the sort of wind that gives grown-ups headaches and children frantic exultation. It was a day of shouting and wrestling, a day aflame and unbearable, without drama and adventure. Something must happen.

—WILLIAM GOLDING

B. Determine what ideas you want to emphasize in the paragraph you are writing. Select words and phrases that help to strengthen your emphasis.

Part 10 Revision: Developing Tone

At some time, you may have played the game in which you take a simple sentence and explore its possible shades of meaning by accenting the first word, then the second, and so on throughout the sentence. Take this sentence, "He is my best friend." You can say, "*He* is my best friend," then "He *is* my best friend," then "He is *my* best friend," and so on. You have still other possibilities if you change the statement to a question or vary your tone of voice. You might say one of the sentences angrily, insistently, mockingly, scornfully, or in disbelief. As you speak, you would be communicating your attitude toward your subject by your tone of voice.

In writing also, tone is the writer's attitude toward a subject and the coloration that results from that attitude. A writer, for instance, might take a satirical, angry, humorous, disgusted, insulting, ironic, flippant, or businesslike approach to a subject. He or she would then give that particular coloration to a paragraph on the subject by many means: by a careful choice of words and details, by sentence organization, by the rhythms of words and phrases, and by figurative language, repetition, and omission.

Note how the writer has achieved the tone in the following description.

The hedgerow was beaded with silver. In the English November fog, the leaves dripped with a deadly intensity, as if each falling drop were a drop of acid.

The phrases "deadly intensity" and "drop of acid" create evil images in your mind. The overall tone of these lines is malevolent and somewhat ominous, a tone created by the careful choice of words and by figurative language.

As you revise your writing, check for a consistently developed tone. Add words, phrases, and ideas that reinforce your tone, and delete others which are inconsistent. One careless, mischosen word can greatly confuse your reader.

Exercises Analyzing and Developing Tone

A. Determine the tone of these paragraphs. Then explain how the tone is created by listing some of the specific words, phrases, or ideas that keep the tone consistent.

1 A child was standing on a street corner. He leaned with one shoulder against a high board fence and swayed the other to and fro, all the while kicking carelessly at the gravel. Sunshine beat upon the cobbles, and a lazy summer wind raised yellow dust that trailed in clouds down the avenue. Clustering trucks moved with indistinctness through it. The child stood dreamily gazing.

—STEPHEN CRANE

2 My childhood landscape was not land but the end of the land—the cold, salt, running hills of the Atlantic. I sometimes think my vision of the sea is the clearest thing I own. I pick it up, exile that I am, like the purple "lucky stones" I used to collect with a white ring all the way round, or the shell of a blue mussel with its rainbowy angel's fingernail interior; and in one wash of memory the colors deepen and gleam, the early world draws breath.—SYLVIA PLATH

3 Hunger stole upon me so slowly that at first I was not aware of what hunger really meant. Hunger had always been more or less at my elbow when I played, but now I began to wake up at night to find hunger standing at my bedside, staring at me gauntly. The hunger I had known before this had been no grim, hostile stranger; it had been a normal hunger that had made me beg constantly for bread, and when I ate a crust or two I was satisfied. But this new hunger baffled me, scared me, made me angry and insistent.—RICHARD WRIGHT

4 On the day before Thanksgiving, toward the end of the afternoon, having motored all day, I arrived home and lit a fire in the living room. The birch logs took hold briskly. About three minutes later, not to be outdone, the chimney itself caught fire. I became aware of this development rather slowly. Rocking contentedly in my chair, enjoying the stupor that follows a day on the road, I thought I heard the dull-fluttering roar of a chimney swift, a sound we who live in this house are thoroughly accustomed to. Then I realized that there would be no bird in residence in my chimney at this season of the year, and a glance up the flue made it perfectly plain that, after twenty-two years of my tenure, the place was at last afire.—E. B. WHITE

B. Ask yourself what specific tone you are trying to create in the paragraph you are writing. Now look at your paragraph and make any revisions necessary to strengthen tone. Finally, write two or three sentences describing your paragraph's tone and explaining how you achieved it.

Part 11 Revision: Creating Mood

Students sometimes confuse *tone* with *mood*. Tone, you remember, is the writer's attitude toward a subject. Mood, on the other hand, is the feeling that is evoked in the reader. For example, Franz Kafka's short story "The Metamorphosis" begins with these famous lines.

As Gregor Samsa awoke one morning from uneasy dreams, he found himself transformed in his bed into a gigantic insect. He was lying on his hard, as if it were armor-plated, back, and when he lifted his head a little he could see his dome-like brown belly divided into stiff, arched segments on top of which the bed quilt could hardly keep in position and was about to slide off completely. His numerous legs, which

> were pitifully thin compared with the rest of his bulk, waved helplessly before his eyes.

In this paragraph the tone is one of acceptance, of naturalness, as if turning into an insect were an everyday occurrence. It is a tone of detachment. However, the mood (which is what the reader feels) is one of horror and revulsion.

In the following paragraph, determine both the tone and the mood. Then try to explain how each is achieved.

> "It is not good for man to be alone," Papa used to say, quoting from the Poor Man's Almanac of Rationalizations—so we slept in various sets: four in a bed (the group plan); three in a bed (semiprivate, unless one of the three had a contagious disease, in which case he was allowed to sleep with only one, preferably one who had never had a disease); two in a bed (double-header); and one in a bed (critical list). Hopeless cases slept in Mama's bed. Chairs and floors also served as beds. Floors were preferred because you could not fall off.
>
> —SAM LEVENSON

Here the tone is lighthearted and amusing. The writer describes the poverty of his childhood with cleverness and good humor. The reader, while responding to the sense of fun, also feels the mood of compassion for the poverty and crowded conditions in which the writer's family lived.

As you work on your writing to develop mood, keep your audience in mind. Answer the following questions:

1. Who are your readers?
2. How do you want them to react to your writing?
3. What changes can you make to reinforce the mood you are trying to create for your reader?

Exercise Creating Mood

Revise your paragraph so that it evokes a specific mood in your reader. Have you involved the reader in the writing through your word choice and sentence structure? Remember that the mood can either parallel the tone or provide a contrast to it.

Part 12 Making the Final Copy

Once you are completely satisfied with the content of your paragraph, it is time to make a final copy. Just before doing so, check your most recent rough draft for any errors in grammar, usage, and mechanics. The Proofreading Checklist on page 123 will help guide you in this step. Make any corrections using the appropriate proofreading symbols. Remember, even small errors can seriously detract from an otherwise excellent piece of writing.

After you have isolated and corrected any remaining errors, make your neat, final copy. Follow all requirements for proper manuscript form. When you paper is complete, proofread it one final time.

Exercise Making the Final Copy

Read over the most complete rough draft of the paragraph you have been revising, looking for errors in grammar, usage, and mechanics. Correct these errors and make a neat, final copy.

SUMMARY AND APPLICATIONS

1. A paragraph is the building block from which compositions, reports, and even novels are built. It is essential, therefore, that you learn to create paragraphs with unity and coherence.
2. Paragraphs usually begin with a topic sentence that states the main idea, catches the reader's interest, and sets a tone for the rest of the paragraph.
3. Paragraphs may be developed using sensory details, facts, statistics, incidents, or anecdotes. This information may be organized in order of importance, order of familiarity, or by comparison and contrast.
4. Revision may be the most important stage of paragraph development. Handle revision in several stages, checking only one or two aspects of it at a time. These aspects include adequate detail, unity, coherence, emphasis, tone, and mood.

Applications in Other Subject Areas

History. Historians often speak of the *tone* and *mood* of a certain period in history. In general they are referring to the attitudes people had toward existing policies of government, as well as the ways these people had of expressing themselves socially and culturally. Do some research on any of the following time periods. How would you describe the tone and mood of that time?

The Revolutionary Period	The Roaring '20's
The Neo-Classic Age	The 1960's
Era of Western Expansion	The 1980's

Mass Media. A story for a newspaper may be presented in any of several ways, depending on the purpose of the writer. The story may be a purely objective news story, or it may be a more creatively written feature article, displaying all of the elements of tone, mood, and emphasis.

Find a short, objective news story concerning a dramatic event such as a fire or a competition of some sort. Rewrite the story as a feature article that demonstrates a distinct mood and tone.

Chapter 9

Different Types of Paragraphs

Whenever you write a paragraph or longer composition, you are trying to communicate ideas to your reader. Sometimes you simply want to relate a story or describe something you've seen. At other times, you hope to explain a difficult concept or persuade others to accept a plan or idea in which you believe strongly.

The purpose of a piece of writing affects almost every prewriting and revision choice a writer makes. In particular, the purpose determines the manner in which a paragraph is developed. All of these decisions are, to some extent, made instinctively. However, a conscious understanding of the different types of paragraphs and paragraph development may help you to make some of these decisions a little more confidently. Also, since a paragraph seldom exists independently, an increased awareness of the wide variety of paragraph types will help you to add variety and interest to longer compositions.

Part 1 The Paragraph of Narration

Narration is the telling of a story or anecdote. A narrative can be as long as a novel or as short as a paragraph. It may relate a real incident or spring solely from the imagination of the writer. Following is an example of a paragraph of narration:

> Hopping freight trains on my way west, I had one bad afternoon. A shack (hobo for brakeman) had ordered me off an open coal car where I was crouched. When the train started, I got on again. The train was running full speed when he climbed down from the car ahead and another shack followed him. He put his face close to mine. "I told you to stay off the train. Now you'll come through with two bits or you'll take what you get." It was my first time with a shack of that kind. I had met brakemen who were not small-time grafters, and one who spotted me in a boxcar corner said, "If you're going to ride, keep out of sight." I figured I might owe the railroad money for fare, but the shack wasn't a passenger-fare collector, so I didn't come through with the two bits. He outweighed me by about forty pounds, and when his right fist landed on my left jaw and his left fist slammed into my mouth, I went to the floor. As I slowly sat up, he snarled, "Stay where you are or you'll get more." Then, as he and his partner turned to go, he gave me a last look and laughed, "You can ride; you've earned it."—CARL SANDBURG

Applying the Process of Writing

Pre-Writing. In writing a narrative paragraph, your topic will come from your own experience or from the experience of someone you know. The topic may also come entirely from your imagination. As you reflect upon experiences that you may want to write about, try to choose one that would have a high level of interest to your reader, or one that has some special significance to you. Questions such as the following may help you to choose such a topic:

- What experience stands out from the rest? Why?
- From which experience have I learned something about myself or about life?
- Which experience is most likely to interest or teach something to my reader?
- Is there an idea or concept that is important to me and that I could illustrate with a story?

These questions will help you to choose and limit a topic and to identify your purpose. Once this has been accomplished, you will want to make decisions about the particular tone and mood you want to convey in your story, as well as the point of view you will use.

After you have made these preliminary writing decisions, gather and organize your details. Recall or create all of the actions, sensory details, and details of setting and character that your reader would need to visualize the incident. Also choose those details that would reinforce the tone and mood and create a specific impression. Avoid details that are not relevant to your story or that would interrupt the flow of ideas.

Once you have gathered your details, you will probably arrange them in chronological order. Do not hesitate, however, to adapt your organization to suit your purpose. You might, for example, begin with the end result of some unusual event and then explain the circumstances leading up to it.

First Draft and Revision. As with any rough draft, this is the time to put your ideas in paragraph form. Concentrate primarily on telling your story as clearly as possible. Try to incorporate transitional devices to make the flow of ideas clear. (See Chapter 8, pages 147–148.)

After you have written your first draft, ask yourself the following questions:

- Does every detail contribute to my purpose in telling the story? (Unity)
- Are the details arranged so that events can easily be followed by the reader? Have transitional devices been used effectively? (Coherence)
- Are the tone and point-of-view consistent throughout?

- Does the narrative evoke a strong and consistent mood? Will the reader sense whatever feeling—for example, confusion or terror or acceptance—the narrative is meant to convey?
- Are lively verbs and strong modifiers used to recreate the event as vividly as possible?

Exercises Writing Paragraphs of Narration

A. Not all subjects can be made into narrative paragraphs. Below is a list of subjects. Some of them can be developed as narrative paragraphs and others cannot. Identify those subjects that lend themselves to development by narration. Be ready to describe the kinds of stories or anecdotes that you might relate.

1. I remember the night I learned what terror is.
2. Lake ______ is thoroughly polluted.
3. A laser beam can do a number of things.
4. I think I have ESP.
5. A fisherman can get by with very little equipment.
6. When Arnie saw the car, it was love at first sight.
7. There are positive ways to improve your grades.
8. I don't think I will ride with Carole again.
9. We have done a number of things to improve our house.
10. Vandalism is a costly crime.
11. Mr. Nichols is as unusual as his strange old house.
12. I always seem to be assigned the less attractive chores.
13. The farewell party was over almost before it began.
14. I saw one bad accident and do not wish to see another.
15. Game shows on TV reveal the greed of the contestants.

B. Choose one of the narrative subjects from Exercise A or make up a subject of your own. Write a paragraph of narration by completing the following steps.

Pre-Writing: After you have selected your general topic, narrow it by determining the special significance or peak point of the experience. Identify the tone and the mood you want to create for your readers. Choose an appropriate point of view.

Write a topic sentence that identifies your experience and establishes a tone and mood. Make a list of specific details that relate directly to the experience and reinforce the impression you want to make on the reader. Organize these details in chronological order or in another order that suits your topic.

First Draft: Using your pre-writing notes as a guide, get your ideas down on paper. Add and delete details as your ideas take shape. Use transitions to improve the flow of the narrative.

Revision: Go over your rough draft several times. Add vivid details that emphasize the impression you are trying to create. Delete details that do not contribute directly to the purpose of your story. Check for coherence in your organization of details and add transitional words and expressions where necessary. Refer to the Guidelines on pages 122 and 182.

Part 2 The Paragraph of Description

A paragraph developed by description can have as its subject a person, a place, or a thing. For such a paragraph to be effective, the writer must not only describe the external characteristics of a subject, but must also convey an impression of its internal qualities as well. Suppose, for example, that you are describing your school. You might say that it is built of red brick and has two hundred windows and twenty outside doors. These statistics are fine, but they are not enough. They do not convey an impression of the school. You might go on to describe it as "fortress-like" and as "grim and forbidding," or you might choose to describe it as "smiling in the sunshine" and as having a "welcoming warmth." You would incorporate into your paragraph those details that would create a specific impression in the mind of the reader.

Before you write a description, you must think about the impression the subject creates in your own mind and about the details that will communicate this same impression to your readers. For example, suppose you have chosen the Lincoln Memorial in Washington, D.C., as your subject. For you, the Memorial has an elusively haunting quality. The statue of Lincoln is brooding and troubled. He looks like a man who has suffered. Yet, he exudes quiet dignity and determination. For your paragraph, then, you would select details that would convey your feelings about the Memorial to your readers. You might include physical proportions, such as dimension, weight, and color, in your description, but you would not concentrate on them exclusively.

Describing a Person

Read the following description of a person.

> He was, morning or evening, very correct in his dress. I have no doubt that his whole existence had been correct, well ordered and conventional, undisturbed by startling events. His white hair brushed upwards off a lofty forehead gave him the air of an idealist, of an imaginative man. His white mustache, heavy but carefully trimmed and arranged, was not unpleasantly tinted a golden yellow in the middle. The faint scent of some very good perfume, and of good cigars (that last an odor quite remarkable to come upon in Italy) reached me across the table. It was in his eyes that his age showed most. They were a little weary, with creased eyelids. He must have been sixty or a couple of years more, and he was communicative. I would not go so far as to call it garrulous—but distinctly communicative.—JOSEPH CONRAD

The writer of this paragraph uses external details as the vehicle through which he reveals the essence of a man. The man's neat appearance indicates that he is fastidious. The good perfume and good cigars reveal his expensive tastes and suggest his ability to indulge them. He is obviously sophisticated, a man of the world with a comfortable and well ordered life. That he is communicative but not garrulous is a sign of dignity and intelligence. The weariness of his eyes is perhaps due not only to age but also to a kind of world-weariness.

Describing a Place

The following paragraph describes a room in the Babbitts' home in Floral Heights.

> It was a room that observed the best Floral Heights standards. The gray walls were divided into artificial paneling by strips of white-enameled pine. From the Babbitts' former house had come two much-carved rocking-chairs, but the other chairs were new, very deep and restful, upholstered in blue- and gold-striped velvet. A blue velvet davenport faced the fireplace, and behind it was a cherrywood table and a tall piano-lamp with a shade of golden silk. (Two out of every three houses in Floral Heights had before the fireplace a davenport, a mahogany table or imitation, and a piano lamp or a reading lamp with a shade of yellow or rose silk.)
>
> —SINCLAIR LEWIS

While at first, the room seems quite ordinary, its essence is captured in the last sentence, in which the writer sneers at the owners' lack of originality and taste. The effect is heightened by the understated tone in which it is presented.

Describing a Thing

In describing a thing, as in describing a place, you must select detail skillfully and make use of one or more of the senses. You might also find it helpful to use comparisons. For example, if you wish to describe a perfume (a thing), you will discover that it is difficult, if not impossible, to describe its fragrance. You would find it comparatively easy, though, to say it smells *like* something; for instance, like roses.

The following paragraph is a description of a thing. As you read, be aware of the writer's skill in using details that capture the nature of the fish. Watch also for the several comparisons that are used in the paragraph.

> When we got the lamp lighted, Herman was sitting in triumph with his hand gripping the neck of a long, thin fish that wriggled in his hands like an eel. The fish was over

three feet long, as slender as a snake, with dull black eyes and a long snout with a greedy jaw full of long, sharp teeth. The teeth were as sharp as knives and could be folded back into the roof of the mouth to make way for what was swallowed. Under Herman's grip, a large-eyed white fish, about eight inches long, was suddenly thrown up from the stomach and out of the mouth of the predatory fish, and soon after up came another like it. These were clearly two deepwater fish, much torn by the snakefish's teeth. The snakefish's thin skin was bluish violet on the back and steel blue underneath, and it came loose in flakes when we took hold of it.

—THOR HEYERDAHL

Did you note the comparisons? They are "wriggled like an eel," "slender as a snake," and "sharp as knives."

There are several types of comparisons that you can utilize to heighten sensory awareness in your writing. Refer to Chapter 11, "Using Figurative Language," for further examples and explanations of this special use of language.

Mixing Descriptions

You might choose one person, place, or thing as the subject for a description. You might also choose to write a mixed description, a description in which two, or even all three, types of subjects are treated. For example, you might describe a rock musician, the auditorium in which he is playing, and the jostling and screaming crowd. You might describe both a gardener and the garden she is tending, or you might describe a bird or animal and its surroundings. It is important to remember that the subjects in a mixed description must be closely related to each other and to the single, unifying idea of the paragraph.

The following paragraph is a mixed description of a place, people, and dogs. Note the careful choice of words and the strong sensory appeal that create a vivid impression of the writer's childhood.

I remember the cold, quiet nights and the stifling hot summers, starched summer suits and the smell of talcum, sweet-smelling black people in white dresses—my "nurses," who could be adoring and gentle and then impatient and rough—tugs at my hand and a high, rich voice telling me, "If you don't behave, boy, the police gonna put you *under* the jail." There were three big bird dogs named Tony, Sam, and Jimbo, their warm licks and loud barks, the feel of their bodies against mine in front of a black stove, the way they bounded into my bed to get me out to play, the taste of gingerbread and hot corn on the cob, and my whispered words, "God bless everybody and me."—WILLIE MORRIS

Applying the Process of Writing

Pre-Writing. When you decide to write a descriptive paragraph, the entire world is your potential topic! Selectively narrowing your subject is your first task. As you consider various possibilities, ask

- –What person, place or thing has made a lasting impression upon me? Why?
- –If I were to observe a particular person, place or thing as though for the first time, what about it would have the strongest impact on me?
- –What is my attitude toward these possible subjects? What tone would I want to convey?

Answering questions like these will help you to narrow your topic and to determine the dominant impression and mood you wish to create for your readers. Also keep your audience in mind as you generate your pre-writing list of sensory details. Use questions such as the following:

- –How do I perceive my subject through each of the five senses?
- –Which sensory details are most important to the impression I want to create? Those of sight? of smell? of sound?
- –What comparisons might help to make the subject come alive?
- –What details could reinforce the tone and mood?

Arrange these details in logical order. If a description is primarily visual, spatial order is often the best method of organization. However, you may want to consider other methods, depending upon your subject. For example, chronological order might suit a description of a sunset, while comparison and contrast might work best for a description of twins.

First Draft and Revision. As you write your first draft, keep in mind the dominant impression that you want to create. Add any words and details that would reinforce your tone and mood. Provide transitional devices to strengthen the organization. After you have completed your first draft, consider the following points:

- Does the paragraph include enough sensory details so that the reader can vicariously experience what you directly experienced? (Adequate Detail)
- Does every detail contribute to the primary impression created by the subject? (Unity)
- Do the sentence structure, word choice, and organization work together to highlight the most important features of your description? (Emphasis)

Exercises Writing Paragraphs of Description

A. Write a paragraph describing someone you like, respect, or find interesting for some other reason. You may also want to create a totally imaginary character. Try to capture some of that person's inner qualities. Complete the following steps.

Pre-Writing: After you have selected a subject, narrow your focus by determining exactly *why* you feel as you do about your subject. List those physical characteristics, actions, and traits that contribute to your impression. Identify a logical order for presenting these details to your reader.

First Draft: Use your pre-writing notes to get your ideas down on paper. Write a topic sentence that will prepare your reader for the description that is to come. Use vivid language that paints a striking word picture of your subject. Make the order of your details clear through the use of transitional devices.

Revision: Go over your rough draft several times. Add sensory details and examples that will help your readers visualize the subject. Delete details that do not contribute to the characteristics you want to emphasize. Strengthen your word choice and sentence structure to highlight the important impressions. When you are satisfied with the content, proofread your writing. Refer to the Guidelines on pages 122 and 182.

B. Write two paragraphs, each describing the same place. In one paragraph, describe the place as though you are fond of it, and in the other describe the place as though you dislike it intensely. For each paragraph, complete the steps in Exercise A. In the prewriting stage, be sure to identify your tone and mood. Carefully choose details that will reinforce the impression you want to create.

C. Choose a particular thing that you think would lend itself to an interesting description. For a change of pace, you may want to choose an item or animal from another country or time period. Follow the steps in Exercise A. As you make your list of details, write your first draft, and revise, try to use unusual comparisons and sensory appeal that will make your description vivid.

Part 3 The Expository Paragraph

A paragraph that is written to explain something or convey information is called an **expository,** or **explanatory,** paragraph. Most expository paragraphs can be put into one of four main categories, according to their differing purposes and methods of development.

Paragraphs That Explain a Process

One common type of expository paragraph has as its purpose the step-by-step delineation of a process. Such a paragraph may tell how something is done, or how something works. Each step of the process is presented along with detailed facts and examples. These are organized chronologically to facilitate the reader's ability to duplicate or understand the process. The following paragraph, for example, explains how to repot a plant.

> Certain procedures should be followed in repotting a plant. First, select a pot only slightly larger than the one the plant is in now, with a hole in the bottom for drainage. If it is a clay pot, soak it in water for several hours before using it. Place a piece of broken pot over the drainage hole so the soil does not leak out and add a small layer of new soil. Second, tap the potted plant on the bottom to loosen the soil. Then, holding your hand over the soil on top, turn the pot sideways and tap it gently as you turn it. When the soil is loosened, slowly withdraw the plant, keeping the ball of soil as intact as possible. Carefully set the root ball into the new pot and fill in new soil around it. Tap down the soil to remove any air pockets and water the plant thoroughly.

Paragraphs That Define

A second type of expository paragraph clarifies the meanings of a term, object, or idea that might not be completely understood by the readers. Sometimes a writer may develop a paragraph of definition for a commonplace object or basic concept. In this case, the writer simply wants to explore the object or concept in complete detail. At other times, the writer may want to explore a difficult topic in a more analytical or personal way. Such a subject requires the fuller development of a paragraph due to its complexity, its far-reaching connotations, or its importance within the experience of the writer.

A paragraph of definition first places the term to be defined in a general category and then identifies several distinguishing characteristics of the term. To make the description precise, sensory details, facts, and statistics are often used. Following is an example of a paragraph of definition.

> My first task is to define the concept of revolution as precisely as I can. A revolution, first of all, involves a rapidly escalating struggle for power. This culminates in the forced displacement of the social groups who have held economic

> and political power, by another social group who has previously been ruled by those in power. Second, a revolution involves the destruction of one form of social organization that has been developed to meet the needs of a given society but which has obviously failed to meet the needs of a significant section of that society. This organization is displaced by another system which purports to meet these needs. These two conditions are not all that is involved in a revolution. Without them, though, what we are talking about may be a revolt, a movement, a rebellion, but it is not a revolution.
>
> —GRACE LEE BOGGS

This definition of revolution is broader and more personal than the dictionary definition of the same word. The writer sets forth the two conditions for revolution in such a specific way that the reader clearly understands her use of the term.

Paragraphs That Give Reasons

The purpose of the third type of exposition is to give reasons for something that happened—why your car overheated, why you were late to a party, or why many senior citizens are not getting adequate medical care. The explanation can also give reasons for a decision that was made—why the party is being held the day before Halloween or why the city changed from a mayoral to a city manager form of government. In the following paragraph, Coretta Scott King explains why the Ebenezer Baptist Church was chosen as the site for the funeral of Dr. Martin Luther King, Jr.

> Martin's funeral was held at Ebenezer Baptist Church on Tuesday, April 9, 1968. The church would hold only seven hundred and fifty of the one hundred fifty thousand who had come to pay their respects to him, and we were deeply sorry that they could not all be accommodated. This was his church, his father's, and his grandfather's. There he was baptized, and had grown up, and been imbued with the deep religious faith which had guided his life and informed his

spirit; there he and his family had preached for three generations. Ebenezer was one of Martin's great loves. It was only fitting that it should be the scene of his funeral.

Paragraphs That Support Opinions

In a fourth type of exposition, reasons are given to support a conclusion that is open to question. The topic sentence for this kind of paragraph presents an opinion. The other sentences strive to justify the opinion with valid, logical reasons. Following is an example of such a paragraph.

> I believe that photographs are a true interpretation. One photograph might lie, but a group of pictures can't. I could have taken one picture of sharecroppers, for example, showing them toasting their toes and playing their banjos and being quite happy. In a group of pictures, however, you would have seen the cracks on the wall and the expressions on their faces. In the last analysis, photographs really have to tell the truth; the sum total is a true interpretation. Whatever facts a person writes have to be colored by his prejudice and bias. With a camera, the shutter opens and it closes, and the only rays that come in to be registered come directly from the object in front of you.—MARGARET BOURKE-WHITE

Usually, the reasons that support an opinion are organized from least to most important to build to a point. However, you may encounter an expository paragraph that supports an opinion by leading you through the writer's reasoning process. In this case, reasons and facts are organized chronologically.

Applying the Process of Writing

Pre-Writing. An expository topic arises from a desire or need to inform others. If you explain a process or define a term, you communicate your knowledge and understanding to your readers. If you write to give reasons or to support an opinion, you explain your ideas, concerns, or beliefs to others.

In determining a topic for an expository paragraph, ask the following questions:

–What are my special areas of expertise?
–What definite ideas and opinions do I have? What led to my having them? Why do I hold them?

Deciding which type of expository paragraph you will write defines your purpose and helps to narrow your focus. Identifying your audience further clarifies the level of language and the types of details you will use. In developing your list of pre-writing details, consider these points:

–What types of details best develop my subject? The steps of a process? An incident or anecdote? Facts and statistics?
–What examples might clarify my explanation?

The best method of organization for your details will vary according to the type of paragraph you are writing. Choose one that will present your ideas so that they have the most impact.

First Draft and Revision. Using your pre-writing notes, get your ideas down on paper. As you write, add any additional details that would clarify your explanation for your readers. Use transitional devices to make the order of your ideas clear.

After you have written your first draft, pay particular attention to adequate detail, unity, and coherence in the revision process. Use the following guidelines:

–Are there enough details so that the reader can understand the explanation completely? (Adequate Detail)
–Does every detail add to the reader's knowledge? (Unity)
–Are the details arranged logically to facilitate the reader's understanding? (Coherence)

Exercises Writing Expository Paragraphs

A. Write a paragraph that explains a process. Explain how to baste a turkey, how a fluorescent tube produces light, how a cake rises, or how a band makes patterns on a football field. If you would rather choose a subject of your own, you may do so, but be certain that in developing the subject you will be describing a process. Complete the following steps as you write.

Pre-Writing: Determine a narrowed topic that can be adequately explained in a paragraph. Have your purpose clearly in mind and identify the background and concerns of your audience. Develop a list of details that will fully illustrate your topic. Decide on a method of organizing these details.

First Draft: Use your pre-writing notes to get your ideas down on paper. Try to be precise and specific in developing your details so that they are as informative as possible.

Revision: Go over your rough draft several times. Check to see that your topic and purpose are clearly presented. Make sure that each of your points is fully developed and that your explanation is complete. Each detail should be logically related to the topic in general and specifically linked to the points that come before and after it. Make additions and deletions to improve the unity and coherence of your writing. When your explanation is complete, proofread your paper carefully. Use the Guidelines on pages 122 and 182.

B. Choose an abstract concept such as loyalty, friendship, integrity, or bravery, and write a paragraph of definition. Follow the steps that are outlined in Exercise A. In the pre-writing process, determine all of the characteristics and conditions of your topic. As you revise, make sure that you have included enough specific detail to differentiate your term from other closely related ones.

C. Some of the following subjects describe events or decisions; others present opinions. Choose one of the subjects or one of your own and write a paragraph in which you develop the subject by giving reasons. Complete the steps that are outlined in Exercise A. In your first draft and revision, add adequate details to fully support each reason.

1. The commercialization of holidays is steadily increasing.
2. The development of rock videos has had a major impact on the music business.

3. Good recreational facilities almost guarantee the stability of a neighborhood.

4. Stress can be as dangerous as any disease.

5. The movies released in a given year often reflect the attitude of the people during that time.

6. Inflation is a serious threat to people on fixed incomes.

7. Going steady in high school can be a mistake.

8. Last week she quit her after-school job.

9. At times it is good to be alone.

10. Television has been absent from our house for nearly a month.

Part 4 The Paragraph of Persuasion

In Part 3, you studied the type of expository paragraph in which a writer presents an opinion along with reasons to support that opinion. The writer's purpose in developing such a paragraph is to convince readers of the rationality of his or her way of thinking. He or she attempts to elicit aknowledgment, but not necessarily agreement, from the reader.

The paragraph of persuasion is closely related to this type of explanation in that it, too, presents a writer's point of view on a debatable topic. However, the goal of the persuasive paragraph is to inspire an action or to convert a reader to the writer's point of view. In a persuasive paragraph, for example, you might try to persuade someone to support a program, to buy a product, or to vote for a particular candidate. You might try to persuade that person to accept your point of view on women's rights, TV programming, or professional football. You would draw on facts, statistics, examples, anecdotes, comparisons, contrasts, and any other kind of information that would contribute to the effectiveness of your presentation. Whichever type of detail you use, your organization should leave your reader with a strong and clear impression.

Read the following paragraph. What is its purpose?

Although many parents are justly concerned about letting their nine- to twelve-year-old sons play tackle football, youth tackle football has its good points. First, many of the negative feelings toward youth football are unfounded. Extensive studies have shown that there are more serious injuries in youth soccer, and there are many injuries in Little League as well. Secondly, a major favorable aspect of youth football is that the weights are controlled so that the players are all basically the same size. This is not true in most other youth sports, and there are great differences in size at the ages of nine through twelve. With this in mind, it may be advantageous to have youths learn to block and tackle with players their own age and size before they enter high school. There they will be playing against upper-classmen who are more experienced and much more mature physically.

—PAT MCINALLY

The writer of this paragraph begins by defining his audience, those with reservations about youth tackle football. He builds an effective case by first addressing the other side's major concern, injuries. Next, the writer points out how the regulations of youth tackle football protect against injuries and how early experience may actually prevent injuries later in players' careers. Notice, too, how the writer makes his points by effectively contrasting tackle football and other sports.

Applying the Process of Writing

Pre-Writing. In writing a paragraph of persuasion, your topic will come from your own convictions. In daily living, everyone develops ideas and opinions, but convictions involve *strong* beliefs for which you not only have good reasons but on which you are also ready to take a stand. Ask yourself the following questions:

–What causes or ideas do I strongly believe in?
–Do I have information to support my position?
–Can I answer arguments of the opposition?

The answers to questions like these will help you to identify a topic for a persuasive paragraph. They will also help you to analyze your audience, a crucial consideration in this type of writing. The audience is important because in order to present effective arguments, you must understand what the opposing side believes and why they believe it.

Once you have your audience clearly in mind, you are ready to generate reasons that will move them to action or agreement. Do not resort to empty, emotional appeals. Your reasons will be stronger if you rely upon solid data, concrete examples, and verifiable facts. Consider these points:

–What reasons will be most convincing to my audience?
–What specific details illustrate and support my reasons?

A strong organization is especially important in a persuasive paragraph. Without it, your arguments may not have their greatest impact on the reader. There are five main ways of organizing a persuasive paragraph:

1. Present the weakest argument first, building up to the strongest argument as a forceful conclusion.
2. Use the strongest argument to gain the reader's attention and support at the beginning, then present other supporting arguments.
3. Begin with an argument your readers are most likely to agree with and gradually lead them to those ideas that they may take exception to.
4. Show weaknesses in the argument(s) against your position, then follow with arguments in favor of your position. This is a form of comparison and contrast.
5. Start with arguments in favor of your position and follow with a discussion of the weaknesses in arguments against your position. Again, this is another order of comparison and contrast.

First Draft and Revision. Your first step in composing a persuasive paragraph is to write a topic sentence that is a definite proposition of belief. In other words, you must write a clear statement of your opinion. This statement should then be followed by the reasons you have identified.

As you write, remember that the opinions held by others are also valid. Never attack an opposing view by using slanted or harsh language. Let your reasons argue for you. See Chapter 15, "Critical Thinking," for further discussions of the elements of persuasion.

As you revise your draft, check the following points:

–Does every reason and illustrative detail directly support the stated opinion? (Unity)

–Are the reasons presented in a logical sequence? (Coherence)

–Has the audience been considered? Does the paragraph emphasize those reasons which will be most convincing to them? (Emphasis)

Exercise Writing a Paragraph of Persuasion

Write a paragraph of persuasion in which you develop your point of view on some controversial issue. You might choose something you have read, a social or political issue, or a school-related topic as your subject. Complete these steps.

Pre-Writing. Determine a specific issue on which you have an opinion. Write a topic sentence that clearly states the topic and your opinion. Identify your audience and their opinions. Generate reasons that would be convincing to your audience. Support your reasons with specific details. Organize your reasons effectively.

First Draft: Use your pre-writing notes to get your ideas down on paper. Use reasons and language that appeal to logic rather than emotion.

Revision: Go over your rough draft several times. Add further details that develop your reasons. Delete any details or reasons that do not specifically support your opinion. Check the logical presentation of your ideas. When you are satisfied with the content of your writing, proofread for mechanical corrections. Use the Guidelines on pages 122 and 182.

Part 5 The Paragraph of Comparison or Contrast

As you become more sophisticated in your writing skills, you realize that each decision you make affects many others. For example, the purpose for your writing may lead you to want to create a certain impression, or mood. To create this impression, you may decide to emphasize certain types of details over others. This, in turn, may affect your organization.

Sometimes, your purpose may be to point out the similarities and differences between two things. This decision results in a paragraph of comparison or contrast. Such a paragraph may, in addition, be a descriptive or expository paragraph. It is distinguished by the fact that the points of comparison or contrast are highlighted. If your purpose is comparison, your development focuses on the similarities between two or more people, places, things, ideas, or reasons. Contrast, on the other hand, highlights differences between subjects.

In the paragraph below, the writer's purpose is to point out how people and machines are actually quite similar.

> Machines and tools have always been created in the image of human beings. The hammer grew from the balled fist, the rake from the hand with fingers outstretched for scratching, the shovel from the hand hollowed to scoop. As machines became more than simple tools, outstripping their creators in performance, demanding and obtaining increasing amounts of power, and acquiring superhuman speed and accuracies, their outward resemblance to the natural model disappeared. Only the names of the machines' parts showed vestiges of their human origin. The highly complex machinery of the modern industrial age has arms that swing, fingers that fold, legs that support, and teeth that grind. Machines feed on material, run when things go well, and spit and cough when they don't.—JOHN H. TROLL

In your everyday life, you probably rely on a combination of comparison and contrast more often than on either one or the other exclusively. For example, you would most likely consider both the similarities and differences between two stereos or between two mayoral candidates before making a decision.

In writing also, comparison and contrast often are combined. The following paragraph, for instance, describes similarities and differences between English people and Americans.

> To the American who dwells for a season within these stout and well-fortified coasts, there are probably no such irritating people under the sun as the English. Perhaps this fact lies in another, namely that because many of us are sprung from them, we expect them to be more like us than they are. The initial exasperation comes when we discover immediately that this is at once a complete and baffling misconception. Our common language, the physical characteristics common to us both, many other elements of our common inheritance—all would seem to afford points of similarity between us. However, these things have not resulted in resemblance or even in affinity. Three hundred years of a totally different environment and development have set us apart from them, and this must be coupled by the knowledge that each decade in their island only serves to make them more uncompromisingly what they are.—MARY ELLEN CHASE

Applying the Process of Writing

Pre-Writing. To write a paragraph of comparison or contrast, you need to identify two subjects in which you perceive either similarities or significant differences. Your topic may originate from a unique observation on your part or from a careful analysis of two clearly related subjects.

Once you have determined a topic, you can generate specific details by asking yourself these questions:

- –How are these two subjects alike? Of what significance are these similarities?
- –How are these two subjects different? Why are these differences important?
- –What do I want to accomplish by comparing these subjects?

The points of comparison or contrast within a paragraph may be presented by discussing all the points of one subject and then all the points of the other. On the other hand, you may compare or contrast the subjects directly with respect to each point.

First Draft and Revision. The first draft of a paragraph of comparison or contrast requires careful thought because of its complex content. Begin with a topic sentence that presents not only the subjects to be compared, but also the point you are trying to make with this comparison. Then try to present the supporting ideas so that they flow naturally from one subject to the other. Avoid the disjointed, choppy effect of simply listing similarities and differences one after another. After you have written your first draft, pay particular attention to this consideration as well as the following ones.

–Are the points of comparison or contrast easy to identify and follow? (Coherence)
–Is there enough detail to identify clearly the comparison or contrast being made? (Adequate Detail)
–Do the details help to emphasize the point the paragraph is trying to make? (Emphasis)
–Can linking words or phrases such as "on the other hand," "similarly," or "in contrast," be employed to highlight differences or similarities? (Coherence)

Exercises Writing Paragraphs of Comparison and Contrast

A. Write a paragraph in which you compare or contrast two people you know well. Complete the following steps.

Pre-Writing: Identify your two subjects. Generate a list of specific details for each suject. Compare the two lists. What are the identifiable points of comparison or contrast between the two lists? Of what significance are these similarities or differences? What would be the most effective means of organizing these points?

First Draft: Use your pre-writing notes to get your ideas down on paper. Write a topic sentence that identifies your subjects and the point you are trying to make about them. Develop both subjects adequately, tying in each detail to the purpose of the paragraph.

Revision: Ask yourself if your paragraph achieves its purpose in presenting the comparison. Then check to see that your points of comparison or contrast are easily identifiable and fully developed. Make sure that you have developed both subjects thoroughly. Add linking words and expressions to improve coherence. After you are satisfied with your paragraph's content, proofread for mechanical correctness. Use the Guidelines on pages 122 and 182.

B. Choose one of the following subjects, or one of your own, and develop it into a paragraph. Complete the steps outlined in Exercise A. In the pre-writing stage, determine whether you will emphasize similarities, differences, or a combination of both. Write a topic sentence that reflects your purpose.

1. Badminton and tennis are somewhat alike. (Choose any two sports.)
2. Today's astronaut is like yesterday's Western pioneer.
3. Though gerbils and rats are both rodents, I like gerbils and dislike rats.
4. Road racing is different from track racing.
5. Two books I have read recently have similar (or different) themes/plots.
6. The clothing styles of today are similar to those of the ______.
7. Private and public schools are quite different.
8. Although they are close friends, his lifestyle is totally different from hers.
9. TV police stories are alike, yet different. (Choose two specific shows.)
10. I like ______ movies but dislike ______ movies.

Guidelines for Writing and Revising Paragraphs

These Guidelines will help to remind you of the qualities necessary for good paragraphs. However, your writing procedure should also follow the steps in the Guidelines for the Process of Writing on page 122.

1. Does the paragraph deal with only one main idea?
2. Does the paragraph have a topic sentence that states the main idea?
3. Does the topic sentence have a subject? Does it express some tone or attitude toward the subject?
4. Does the body of the paragraph support or explain the main idea in the topic sentence?
5. Is the paragraph coherent? Are the ideas presented in a logical order and clearly linked to one another? Is the order of ideas appropriate for the subject of the paragraph?
6. Are there transitional words and expressions that reinforce coherence by showing relationships among the ideas in the paragraph?
7. Are there enough details to engage the reader's interest?
8. Does the paragraph work to evoke the desired mood?
9. Are tone, mood, and point of view consistent throughout the paragraph?
10. Does the paragraph have a carefully determined emphasis?
11. If it is a paragraph of narration, does the story or anecdote achieve the purpose of the paragraph?
12. If it is a paragraph of description, does it capture the essence of what is being described?
13. If it is an expository paragraph, do the details adequately explain the main idea? If explaining a process, does the paragraph follow a step-by-step order? If explaining something that happened, are the reasons convincing? If defining a concept, does it clarify a concept or a term for the reader? If supporting an opinion, are the reasons logical and valid?
14. If it is a paragraph of persuasion, is it developed by the kinds of information that would effect your purpose?

SUMMARY AND APPLICATONS

1. There are several different types of paragraphs that a writer may use to present ideas: narrative, descriptive, expository, persuasive, and comparison/contrast.
2. Narrative paragraphs relate stories or anecdotes. They are generally organized in chronological order.
3. Descriptive paragraphs create word pictures through sensory details. These details are usually organized in spatial order.
4. Expository, or explanatory, paragraphs can explain a process, give definitions, or offer reasons to support an idea. The persuasive paragraph is a special type of expository paragraph. The most common methods of organization for expository writing are most familiar to least familiar idea and least important to most important idea.
5. Paragraphs of comparison or contrast point out the similarities or differences of two or more people, places, or things.

Applications in Other Subject Areas

History. Choose any historical event that interests you. Write two paragraphs about some incident connected with that event, such as the signing of a treaty. The first paragraph should be completely expository, recounting the incident as though for a history text. The second paragraph should be written in narrative form, as a story.

Computer Science. Compare two types of "computer language," such as BASIC, PASCAL, or COBOL. Keep your comparison both simple and general, as though you were writing for an audience completely unfamiliar with computers.

Science. Scientific research depends on the researchers' abilities to observe a subject closely and record what they see accurately. Choose a subject for observation, such as a plant, a microscopic animal, or a crystal. Record everything that you notice about it. Look past the obvious details to the minor ones that you don't notice except after long study. Write up your findings in a paragraph.

Chapter 10

Writing a Composition

In the previous chapter, you learned how to compose several different types of paragraphs. The value of being able to shape a variety of paragraphs becomes more apparent when you consider the fact that paragraphs are seldom used in isolation. Instead, they are often combined into a longer piece of writing—the composition.

The composition enables a writer to explore a topic or idea in much greater depth than he or she would be able to in a single paragraph. Many different aspects of a topic can be covered, and different types of paragraphs can be utilized to present these ideas. The writing that results is an interesting and comprehensive treatment of a subject.

The process of writing a composition is no different from the process you have been using all along. The three stages of prewriting, writing the first draft, and revising still apply. In this chapter, you will learn exactly how you can use the process to create a composition of your own.

Part 1 What Is a Composition?

A composition is, in essence, an expanded paragraph. Both types of writing concern a single main idea, and both are characterized by unity and coherence. Even the types of compositions parallel the types of paragraphs—narrative, descriptive, and expository. The main difference between paragraphs and compositions is that a paragraph is a group of sentences that concerns a main idea, while a composition is a group of paragraphs.

The paragraphs that make up a composition are usually of three basic kinds. The **introductory paragraph** presents the main idea of the composition. The **body paragraphs** explain or support the main idea. Body paragraphs may be developed in different ways. For example, an explanatory composition might include descriptive paragraphs that present a picture of the object being explained, and narrative paragraphs that advance the explanation with an anecdote. Lastly, the **concluding paragraph** restates the main idea, summarizes the information that has been presented in preceding paragraphs, or makes a final comment on the information that has been presented.

Read the following example of a composition.

ICEBERGS ON THE MOVE

As the population of the world increases and the standard of living rises, the need for water—for homes and cities, industry and agriculture—grows steadily too. Even though water covers three-quarters of the earth's surface, about ninety-seven percent is salt water, which is of little use to human development on land. Most of the remaining three percent is frozen as glaciers, "rivers of ice" that creep down cold mountain valleys and drain off the frigid land in broad ice sheets. Many glaciers melt while still on land, but some reach the coast, where large pieces break off from the glacial sheet and fall into the ocean to form icebergs. For more than a century, both dreamers and realists have thought about towing icebergs thousands of miles to the coasts of warm, dry areas where they would provide water for thousands, perhaps millions, of people. So far the obstacles to such an undertaking have proven to be nearly overwhelming.

The most obvious obstacle is that icebergs are extremely dangerous to approach. If you look at an ice cube floating in a glass of water, you will see that most of the cube is beneath the surface. As it melts, it changes shape, and its center of gravity shifts. An iceberg does much the same thing. As its weight and shape change, it may roll over suddenly, churning the water violently and bringing large, submerged parts into the air—endangering any vessel nearby.

Even if an iceberg could be approached and prepared for transportation, several obstacles still remain. One problem is the melting that occurs when an iceberg reaches warm water. Only if it could be steered directly to a desired location, with no loss of time, might it still be large enough to yield a substantial volume of water. Glacier ice is colder than regular ice, so it melts more slowly. However, only a very large iceberg could be worth transporting, and that would cost an enormous amount of money. Then, even if this iceberg could be brought to its destination, it could not be towed in close to shore. Because eighty-five to ninety percent of an iceberg is underwater, it would be grounded on the ocean floor far from land. Even from this distant position, an iceberg would probably change the environment somewhat. It might create cool breezes or fog and lower the air and water temperature. The decrease in water temperature, along with the changes in the salt content of the water, could affect the marine plants and animals in the area.

Recently the National Science Foundation developed an elaborate plan for towing icebergs from Antarctica to Los Angeles. The plan seems to surmount many of the major obstacles, particularly those involved in moving the icebergs and in getting water from iceberg to shore. Satellites, photographing earth from space, would be used to spot icebergs of the desired size and shape for towing. Several large, solid, flat, streamlined bergs would be linked together with cables, like a string of barges. They would be insulated with quilted plastic sheeting to slow melting, so that in the year-long trip to Los Angeles, less than one-tenth of the ice would melt. Power would be drawn from escort ships. Tugs, helicopters, and a crew would travel with the iceberg train. At Los Angeles the train would serve as a long breakwater or be taken apart. Melt-water would be collecting in floating dams, or pieces of quarried ice could be brought inland, perhaps on a conveyor belt. Water might also be channeled into hollows or collection points on the berg.

Despite great physical and financial risks, iceberg importing, once a fantastic dream, may become a reality. Someday, glistening white icebergs may float in warm harbors through the world.—GWEN SCHULTZ

This composition deals with one main idea—the problems of transporting icebergs for use as a source of fresh water. The introductory paragraph introduces this idea and presents some background on it. The first two body paragraphs deal with some of the problems involved in transporting icebergs. The third body paragraph describes a possible solution. The conclusion sums up the main ideas and provides a feeling of finality.

Part 2 Pre-Writing: Choosing Your Subject

Your first step in writing a composition is to decide on a subject. What are you interested in? Do you know enough about a subject you are interested in to write about it at some length? If not, are you sufficiently interested in it to find more information about it? Do you know where to find more information?

If you are interested in ecology, you might want to write about the conversion of open fields to industrial sites or shopping plazas, an action which is depriving ground birds of nesting sites. You might want to write about the importance of planned reforestation of timberland or burned-over areas, or the efforts to control water pollution. On a more personal level, you may decide to tell about your own conservation efforts.

If you play tennis, you could write about the spirit of competition, the role of women in tennis, or the origins of the sport. Remember that your interest in the topic will enliven your writing. The reverse is also true: a lack of interest will produce a composition that will fail to interest your readers.

Limiting Your Subject

This chapter will discuss the five-paragraph composition, which is approximately 500 words. When you limit the expansion of an idea to that length, you can easily see that subjects that are too broad cannot be adequately developed. You need to limit your subject. There are several methods you can use to accomplish this. If the subject is personal, or from your imagination, techniques such as brainstorming and clustering might lead you to some possible topics. If the subject is more objective, try reading an encyclopedia article or scanning the index or table of contents of a book on the subject.

As one example of the narrowing process, consider the subject of transportation. That is an almost unlimited field, and many books would have to be written to cover it adequately. To limit the subject, you might proceed as follows:

UNLIMITED:	Transportation
SLIGHTLY LIMITED:	Early Methods of Transportation
2,000-WORD LIMITATION:	Electric Railroads
1,000-WORD LIMITATION:	The Trolley
500-WORD LIMITATION:	The Disappearance of the Trolley

Exercise Choosing and Limiting the Subject

Here is a list of broad subjects. Within each subject, find three narrow subjects suitable for a composition of 500 words. Keep these subjects for a later exercise.

1. Mass Media
2. Politics
3. Unidentified Flying Objects
4. Endangered Species
5. Senior Citizens
6. The Space Age
7. Careers
8. Music
9. Health
10. Historical Sites

Determining the Purpose

As you select and limit your subject, you will find yourself making some other preliminary decisions about how you want to treat that subject, and about what you want to accomplish with your composition. You may decide that you simply want to inform your reader by presenting a clear explanation of your subject. If so, you would be writing an expository composition. On the other hand, you may want to tell a story about your subject or describe it in detail. In this case, you would write a narrative or descriptive composition.

As you consider these options, you would also identify your audience and make some initial decisions about the tone and mood you want to convey. Your **audience,** you remember, will help determine the type and amount of background information and supporting details you will need to provide. It will also guide you as to how formal and technical your language can be. The **tone** is your attitude toward the subject and the attitude you may want to communicate to your reader. The **mood** is the feeling or atmosphere you want your audience to experience as they read.

Once these pre-writing decisions have been made, you should have a fairly clear idea of the controlling purpose of your composition:

> The controlling purpose of this composition is to explain the circumstances that led to the disappearance of the trolley.

Notice that this sentence includes not only a statement of the topic, but also the word *explain,* which shows that the subject will be developed as an expository composition. This sentence will be a constant reminder of what you are going to write about and the direction you are going to take.

You may wish to include a revised version of the controlling statement in the composition itself. Such a sentence is sometimes called a **thesis statement.** A thesis statement is especially useful in a persuasive paper or a report, in which you want your topic and purpose to be extremely clear from the outset.

Other Pre-Writing Choices

In addition to the decisions described above, you will have to make some other pre-writing choices based on the type of composition you are writing. The most important of these are discussed in the following paragraphs.

The Narrative Composition. To tell a story effectively, you need to have every detail of it clear in your own mind. Consider and write down ideas for the following aspects of a narrative:

CHARACTER: the people or animals in the story

SETTING: the place where the events in a narrative occur. This includes the time frame of the story.

CONFLICT: the struggle or problem that is central to the narrative

THEME: the dominant impression or idea the writer wants to convey to the reader

POINT OF VIEW: the eyes and mind through which the story is told. The writer may choose to use **first-person point of view,** where the narrator is a part of the action and refers to himself or herself as *I*, or **third-person point of view,** where the narrator is outside the action of the story.

The Descriptive Composition. To create a vivid picture in the "mind's eye" of your reader, consider the following points:

DOMINANT IMPRESSION: the feature of the subject that affects you the most. This is the detail that would be the center of emphasis in the composition.

PHYSICAL POINT OF VIEW: the position from which you will view the scene, object, or person. Details must be limited to those things that can be seen, heard, touched, tasted, and smelled from that particular vantage point.

The Expository Composition. There are several different types of expository compositions, each with its own particular purpose: the composition that explains a process, the composition that defines, the composition that gives reasons, and the composition that persuades. Make certain that you clearly identify which type of composition you are developing and make appropriate pre-writing choices. (See Part 3 in Chapter 9.)

Exercises Determining the Controlling Purpose

A. In the exercise on page 188 you limited each of ten broad subjects to three possible compositions of 500 words. Choose three of these limited subjects and write (1) an appropriate title for each and (2) a statement of the controlling purpose that you would follow. Keep this work for a later assignment.

B. Choose a subject to write about in a composition. Limit your subject sufficiently for a 500-word paper. Consider your audience, as well as the tone and mood you want to convey. Then write a one-sentence controlling purpose for your subject.

Part 3 Writing Down Your Ideas

Now that you have chosen your subject, limited it, and stated your controlling purpose, the next step is to write down your ideas on your subject. These may include sensory impressions, facts and statistics, examples, incidents, or anecdotes.

If the subject is personal, your ideas can be generated through brainstorming or clustering. If the subject is more objective, you may need to do some research. Perhaps you need to check the accuracy of some points in reference books or other source material. Perhaps you need to do more extensive reading on the subject in general. (See Chapter 14.)

As you gather your details, write them down in note form. Because you do not want to interrupt your flow of ideas, jot down whatever ideas come to mind. Do not worry about order or phrasing or style. Just get your ideas on paper. At the top of your paper, write your tentative title and the statement of your controlling purpose so that when you begin to arrange your ideas and eliminate unnecessary ones, you can do so in terms of your controlling purpose.

Your first list of ideas might look something like this (pay no attention to the asterisks):

TENTATIVE TITLE: Who Killed the Trolley?

CONTROLLING PURPOSE: The controlling purpose of this composition is to explain the circumstances that led to the disappearance of the trolley.

SUPPORTING DETAILS:

trolley was attractive and comfortable
shift to automobiles
trolleys deteriorate
*rise of auto industry
cheap trolley fares
network of trolley lines
trolley was quiet and relaxing
could we use trolleys today?
automobiles compete with trolley
improvements in automobiles
*auto shows
*foreign cars
trolley was dependable
*rising cost of auto maintenance
*cost of gas and oil
auto always available
traffic problems
automobile new and exciting
*family auto trips
*camping sites
rise in use of autos
automobile threatens trolley
trolleys went on excursions
trolley was popular
jobs for motormen
jobs in auto repair shops
trolley car disappears

Now analyze the details that you have listed. Is each one related to your topic? Will every detail fit the type of composition you are writing and match your controlling purpose?

You can see how some of the ideas in the preceding list have no relationship to the topic and controlling purpose of the composition. These unrelated ideas, marked with asterisks, should be eliminated at this point so that your composition does not go off in the wrong direction. "Rise of auto industry," "auto shows," "foreign cars," "family auto trips," and "camping sites" are broad topics that cannot be handled adequately in a five-paragraph composition. "Rising cost of auto maintenance" and "cost of gas and oil," also marked with asterisks, have nothing to do with the purpose of the composition.

The job of deleting inappropriate or unmanageable material is an important step in sorting out and evaluating your material. In some cases, an idea may seem important enough to retain at the moment, but you may find that it is of no value when you begin to organize your ideas.

Exercises Writing Down the Ideas

A. In Exercise A on page 191, you wrote a title and a controlling purpose for three limited subjects. Select two of these titles and controlling purposes and list under them all the ideas that come to your mind for developing that subject. After studying your lists, cross out those ideas that would be unmanageable or irrelevant. Keep these lists for a later assignment.

B. Do the same as above for your own composition.

Part 4 Organizing Your Ideas

You have tested your ideas against your controlling purpose and have eliminated those that are too broad to handle and those that are irrelevant. You are now ready to organize your ideas. First look for related details that could be grouped together into idea "clusters." Then try to identify the major point that each cluster represents. Sometimes a detail within the cluster will state this main point for you. At other times you will need to add a statement of the main point.

In the final list of ideas concerning the trolley car, you will notice that certain ideas begin to emerge as major points: "*shift to automobiles*" is an important point in developing the idea of the controlling purpose. Ideas related to this one are "auto always available," "automobile new and exciting," and "automobile threatens trolley."

Another major point seems to be "*automobiles compete with trolley,*" and related ideas are "trolleys deteriorate," "improvements in automobiles," "traffic problems," "rise in use of autos," and "trolley car disappears."

A third point is "*trolley was popular,*" and related ideas are "trolley was attractive and comfortable," "cheap trolley fares," "network of trolley lines," "trolley was quiet and relaxing," "trolley was dependable," and "trolleys went on excursions."

That leaves three ideas not accounted for. "Jobs for motormen" and "jobs in auto repair shops" are unrelated to any of the main points and should be deleted. The idea "could we use trolleys today?" seems like the germ of an idea for a conclusion. This idea may be set aside and reconsidered later.

You now have three major points to develop—just the right number for the body of a five-paragraph theme:

shift to automobiles
automobiles compete with trolley
trolley was popular

With the identification of these main ideas, you might adjust your statement of the controlling purpose as follows:

> The controlling purpose of this composition is to explain why the decline of the trolley was caused by the advent of the automobile.

Determining the Best Order

The final problem is to determine the order of the three main headings and the details within them. When you plan a composition, you must present your ideas to the reader in some kind of logical order. Here are some guidelines:

Chronological Order. This is the most natural type of organization. It involves presenting ideas in the order in which they occurred. This order is often used in narrative compositions.

Spatial Order. This type of order is usually used in descriptive compositions. Details are presented in the order in which a writer wishes the reader to "notice" them.

Order of Importance. When an expository composition presents ideas or arguments to explain a subject, the writer often chooses to organize these ideas from least to most important. Thus, the strongest idea is presented last. The writer may also choose to begin with the most important idea and then support it.

Most Familiar to Least Familiar, or Simple to Complex. Both of these types of organization use the strategy of beginning with ideas with which the audience is most comfortable and then proceeding to more difficult concepts. This type of organization is extremely useful for persuasive compositions and compositions that explain unfamiliar concepts.

Comparison and Contrast. This is actually two types of organization. The writer may choose to compare two subjects point by point, with each paragraph covering one of these points for both subjects. On the other hand, the writer may decide to discuss several aspects of one subject and then proceed to a discussion of the second subject as it relates to the first.

These guidelines can be helpful, but in reality you must use some logic of your own to select the best method of organization. Ideas that are not closely related can move from least important to most important or from simple to complex. However, ideas that depend on other ideas to be clearly understood must be presented in logical order. If Point B cannot be understood without Point A, then Point A must come first.

Let's see if logical order applies to the three major points of the composition about trolleys. The controlling purpose, you remember, is as follows:

> The controlling purpose of this composition is to explain why the decline of the trolley car was caused by the advent of the automobile.

It seems obvious that before you can talk about automobiles, you have to discuss the trolley car because it came first. The shift from the trolley car to the automobile obviously comes next, followed by the automobile competing with the trolley. Thus, the logical order of ideas for the development of the body of the paragraph is as follows:

trolley was popular
shift to automobiles
automobiles compete with trolley

The next step is to organize the related ideas under each main point in their logical order of development. You organize these ideas as you would the ideas in any paragraph. When you are done, the completed, organized list becomes the writing plan for your composition. Look at the example below.

trolley was popular

- cheap trolley fares
- trolley was dependable
- trolley was attractive and comfortable
- trolley was quiet and relaxing
- trolley went on excursions
- network of trolley lines

shift to automobiles

- automobile new and exciting
- automobile always available
- automobile threatens trolley

automobiles compete with trolley

- trolleys deteriorate
- improvements in automobiles
- rise in use of autos
- traffic problems
- trolley car disappears

leftover good idea: could we use trolleys today?

You may wish to put your writing plan into outline form. See Section 18 in the Handbook for a discussion of outlines.

Exercises Organizing the Ideas

A. Continuing your work with the lists in Exercise A on page 193, organize the ideas under both subjects into the major points and their related ideas in the order you would develop each of them in a composition. Save this work for a later assignment.

B. Do the same as above with your own composition.

Part 5 Writing the First Draft

You now have a working title that you may wish to revise later. You have a statement of your controlling purpose, and you have a writing plan to work from. You have also identified your audience and, if appropriate, decided on a tone and mood. You are now ready to write your first draft.

With all this preliminary work behind you, it would seem that the actual writing should be easy. That is not always true, however. There are still many decisions to be made about the presentation of your ideas. Remember, the rough draft is an opportunity to explore different approaches to your material.

Often one of the most difficult parts of writing the first draft is getting started. In fact, many writers initially find themselves unable to write an introduction. If you find yourself in this situation, begin writing with the second paragraph, which is information that you have at hand. You can always work on the introduction later, after you have become involved in the act of writing and have clarified your thoughts.

The most important thing is to begin somewhere and keep writing. Do not worry at this point about sentence structure, word choice, or punctuation. You can concentrate on those aspects when you revise your composition.

Your composition will have three basic parts—a beginning, a middle, and an end; in other words, an introduction, a body, and a conclusion. That may seem like an obvious statement, but each of the parts plays a crucial role in an effective composition. The writing of each part will be considered in turn.

The Introduction

The introduction ordinarily has two functions: to *introduce* the reader to the subject and to *interest* the reader in it. A five paragraph composition usually devotes one paragraph to an introduction. Sometimes the introductory paragraph begins immediately with a statement of the main idea and then outlines the information that is to follow. Usually, however, an introductory paragraph leads the reader gradually from general information to the specific topic. Effective introductions of the second type can be constructed around quotations, startling statistics, or interesting anecdotes.

The following introductions are three possible ways of beginning the composition on the trolley.

QUOTATION: I want to hire out as the Skipper
(Who dodges life's stresses and strains)
Of the Trolley, the Toonerville Trolley,
The Trolley that Meets all the Trains.

—DON MARQUIS

Don Marquis would be out of luck in the city of Babbington today. The trains are barely running, and the trolley has been a long time gone. Only the automobiles are running.

STATISTIC: In the city of Babbington in 1910 nearly a hundred trolleys were operating on 198 miles of track. Today none of the track remains, and the only trolley has been made into a diner. The automobile has taken over.

ANECDOTE: Last month, the street that I live on was torn apart for resurfacing, and I discovered, buried beneath the pavement, the remains of what was once a genial and reliable public servant—The Babbington and Hargrove Street Railway. The resurfacing was necessary, of course, because the automobiles had worn down the road.

Besides getting attention, each of these introductions tells the reader precisely what the composition is about, namely that the trolleys that once ran in Babbington no longer operate, and that the automobile has taken over. The beginning of a composition should never be a dull, flat statement of intent like the following:

> In this paper I will describe the decline of the trolley and show how the automobile caused this decline.

Such a statement might be an appropriate statement of purpose to use as a guide, but it does little to interest a reader.

Exercises Writing an Effective Introduction for a Composition

A. Rewrite and expand three of the following introductions to heighten the appeal for the reader and inform the reader of the subject of the composition. Use a quotation, a statistic, or an anecdote.

1. We all use a great deal of paper every year, but most of us take it for granted.
2. I'll never forget the time I tried to learn to juggle.
3. Many people think that sightings of unidentified flying objects began in the twentieth century. They're wrong.
4. Compiling a dictionary requires a lot of work.
5. Something must be done about the cat and the dog population explosion.
6. In 1905 President Theodore Roosevelt threatened to ban football. It was too violent.

B. With the preceding possibilities for introductions in mind, write a beginning paragraph for your composition that introduces the subject and captures your reader's interest. Be sure to test it against your controlling purpose to be sure you have included all aspects of your purpose in your introduction. For example, if the introductions for the composition on the trolley had failed to include the automobile, the reader would think you were going to discuss only the trolley car.

The Body

The middle part of the composition, or the body, is the longest section. In a five-paragraph theme it would consist of three paragraphs. It is here that the writer must accomplish his or her purpose. In writing the body of your composition, be sure to observe the following points.

1. Use your writing plan, or outline, as a guide. Remember that the purpose of your writing plan is to establish a clear and appropriate pattern for the development of your ideas. If you ignore the plan, you may lose the organizational clarity you have worked to achieve. However, do not be afraid to adapt the plan as new ideas or a better type of organization occurs to you.

2. Keep your purpose and audience in mind. Work to achieve what your controlling purpose promises. If you set out to explain something, be certain that you explain it clearly. Keep your language and material suitable to your audience.

3. Divide your writing into paragraphs. Using your writing plan as a guide, devote a paragraph to each main topic. Begin each paragraph with a topic sentence. Develop each topic fully, including all subtopics.

4. Provide clear transitions. A transitional device at the beginning of a paragraph indicates how the idea to be dealt with relates to ideas in preceding paragraphs. There are a number of ways to establish smooth transitions. The use of the following transitional devices will help your reader follow your ideas.

Using Transitional Devices

Transitional Words and Phrases. In Chapter 8 you studied linking expressions, or connectives, that are used to achieve coherence with a paragraph and to help the reader move smoothly from one idea to another. Certain words and phrases are also important to help the reader move smoothly from one paragraph to another. The following transitional words and phrases are used to indicate specific relationships.

Time Relationships

before	earlier	once	sooner or later
during	later	then	at this point
after	soon	in time	at the same time
afterward	first	eventually	
at last	next	finally	

Logical Relationships

since	besides	furthermore
therefore	consequently	and then
because	inevitably	as a result

Similarity

as	also	similarly	in the same way
like	again	another	equally important
and	likewise	moreover	
too	equally	in addition	

Contrast

but	still	otherwise	in contrast
yet	nevertheless	however	on the contrary
nor	nonetheless	although	on the other hand

Each of the following sentences is the first sentence of a paragraph. Notice how the transitional devices serve, in each case, to link the new topic to that of the preceding paragraph. You can even guess what the preceding paragraph was about.

> *First* he would have to have the roof fixed, or they would not be able to stay there for long.
>
> The prospect of widespread crop failure is *equally* threatening to countries that escape it, since they will be compelled to share their provisions with less fortunate nations.

Pronouns. You can use a pronoun to refer to an idea in the preceding paragraph. *This, that, these,* and *those* are frequently used as transitional words, either as pronouns or as adjectives.

However, when these words are used as adjectives, they must be followed by a noun that clarifies the reference for the reader. For example, if you say, "This was open to criticism," and the reader has to ask, "This what?" you are not communicating your ideas. Say "This policy," or "This action," or whatever specifically you are referring to.

Other pronouns also operate as transitional devices. Study the sentences that follow, all of which are opening sentences of paragraphs, to see how the device works.

> Brad approached *them* and tried to become one of their group, but they didn't make it easy.
>
> *This* crisis was only the beginning.
>
> Jamie had taken *that* train for weeks without noticing who his companions were.

Repetition. Using a strategic word from one paragraph in the opening sentence of the following paragraph preserves the flow of meaning from one paragraph to the next. Notice how repetition is used as a transition in the following examples.

1 Modern-day homesteaders are wondering what they can live in that will be an efficient structure for conserving energy and yet will suit their aesthetic tastes. They have put up all sorts and shapes of houses from log cabins to foam domes.

For those who choose to live in a log cabin, there is actually a log cabin kit that looks like a giant Lincoln Log set.

2 In 1972 the governor of Vermont proposed a new source of fuel for electricity. The new source was to be found just about everywhere in Vermont, and he proposed that it was more reasonable to use a cheap, plentiful source than to buy costly and vanishing foreign oil. He was talking about trees.

The trees the governor proposed to feed to the furnaces were not the virgin forests that people yearn to see in Vermont every fall, but surplus timber and deformed trees that prove worthless as lumber.

Sometimes a writer will repeat more than a single word; he will make use of a whole idea from one paragraph to start off the next. In this case the repetition refers directly and deliberately to the preceding paragraph. This use of repetition provides a transition and, at the same time, underscores a major idea about the subject of the composition.

3 Most meteorologists will admit to not being taken seriously by their audience. They present their visions of the upcoming weather every day, and if ten percent of the time they are completely wrong, the public casts doubts on every forecast.

The weather forecaster's credibility problem is only one of the characteristic trials of the profession.

4 A fisherman can get so hooked on his pastime that even fantastically adverse conditions cannot keep him home. In mid-February the lakes of northern New England are dotted with figures swathed in goose down, toting their gear to chosen spots where they will drill for water.

Ice fishing is a surprisingly simple undertaking, requiring no fancy equipment and only the most basic of skills.

Exercises Writing the Body of the Composition

A. Choose a magazine article that interests you and write the opening sentences of ten paragraphs that employ transitional devices discussed in this section. Explain how the devices work in each example.

B. Write the body of your composition, which will consist of three paragraphs. Here are points to remember.

1. Keep your controlling purpose in front of you.
2. Use your outline as your guide.
3. Develop your three paragraphs completely.
4. Provide clear paragraph transitions.

The Conclusion

The conclusion of the composition should "wrap things up." It should bring your key points together and leave the reader with a sense of completeness. The single most effective way to achieve a sense of completeness is to return in the conclusion to the ideas you used in your introduction. This procedure gives the reader the feeling of having come full circle. If you like, you may think of the composition as something like a sightseeing tour. The writer promises the readers an interesting tour; the readers climb aboard, and the writer conducts the tour; and then at the end the writer brings the readers back to the point where they started.

The composition on the trolley might have a conclusion like the following, if the writer has chosen the anecdote for her introduction.

> The street I live on has been repaired and repaved, and the tracks are buried once again. Traffic struggles along as it did, but now the automobile is in trouble. Will something new come along to replace it? I don't think so. I think something old will come along to replace it. I look forward to sitting on the curb sometime soon and watching a crew install tracks on top of the pavement—trolley tracks, of course.

Notice how the writer has returned to the anecdote she chose to open her composition. She recalls the image of the tracks being dug up by having them buried again. The reader has learned why the automobile caused the decline of the trolley, and the possibility of new tracks being laid over the old gives the reader something new to think about.

Exercise Writing an Effective Conclusion

You are now ready to complete the final step of your first draft. Write the concluding paragraph of your composition, returning to the method you used for the beginning. Try to achieve a sense of completeness by including all the necessary ideas in your controlling purpose.

Part 6 Revising the Composition

It is in this last step of the process of writing that the careful writers are separated from the careless. In revision, a merely acceptable piece of writing can become something really good. It is a good idea to work through your composition several times, concentrating on only one or two aspects of revision on each reading. The suggestions below will help you to produce a revision that is a definite improvement over your first draft.

1. **Read your composition aloud.** The importance of this step cannot be overemphasized. Nothing else will show you so clearly where your ideas were not fully developed or where your thinking was fuzzy or where your sentences were awkward. Reading aloud will also make you aware of the rhythm and variety of your sentences. If possible, read your work to someone who will be critical of it. Use the criticism in your revision.

2. **Revise for content.** Is your purpose for writing clear from the outset? Have you said enough to accomplish your purpose? Is your information accurate? Are your ideas laid out as clearly as possible?

3. **Revise for unity.** Does each paragraph relate directly to the topic and controlling purpose of the composition? Do the details within each paragraph support the topic sentence?

4. **Revise for coherence.** Have you organized your composition clearly and logically? Have you given each main idea its own paragraph and introduced it with a topic sentence? Is each individual paragraph coherent? Are all your ideas clearly related to each other? Have you made connections between ideas by using transitional devices?

5. **Check for a consistent tone, mood, and point of view.** Once you have chosen the way you want to present your material, make sure that there is no shift in approach from one paragraph to the next.

6. **Revise for wording.** Is your level of language appropriate? Have you used the most precise words to express your ideas? Review the information on synonyms and antonyms in Chapter 1. Use a dictionary or thesaurus to check the meaning of key words in your composition and to locate synonyms. If you find new words with meanings closer to what you intended, revise the wording. Have you used figurative language where appropriate, to make your writing more vivid? See Chapter 11 for a discussion of figurative language.

7. **Proofreading: Check grammar, usage, capitalization, punctuation, and spelling.** Obviously, faults of these kinds will distract your reader from what you are saying. If necessary, consult Sections 10–15 in your Handbook.

Sample Revision

Below is one of the body paragraphs from the composition on trolleys. Try to analyze the writer's revisions.

Then, *along came* the automobile ~~arrived.~~ *This machine* ~~The automobile~~ would take you wherever you wanted to go *whenever you felt like going there,* with no waiting*, no transfers, no crowds.* ~~Even today, this is one of the automobile's most attractive features.~~ Little by little, the trolley began to seem less attractive *and the automobile more so.* The loss of pa*s*sengers on the B & H me*a*nt a loss of income, and this me*a*nt that the equip~~t~~ment *could not be kept in good repair.* ~~fell apart.~~ The trolleys bec~~o~~*a*me less dependable and *less attractive,* ~~not as good looking,~~ and more people *abandoned* ~~left~~ the trolley for private cars. ~~Even though the automobile~~ *It* was nois~~e~~y and uncomfortable*,* and unreliable, *but* it ~~had~~ caught the public's fancy from the first.

Notice the following improvements that were made in this paragraph.

1. In line 5, the statement concerning the trolley was tied in to the purpose of the composition, which was to show how the automobile contributed to the trolley's decline.
2. Unity was strengthened by deleting the unrelated idea in lines 2 and 3.
3. Coherence was also improved. The last sentence was moved to a place in the paragraph where, chronologically, it is more appropriate. The transitional phrase "This machine" in line 1 also improved the flow of ideas.
4. More precise words were substituted for weak ones. For example, "less attractive" replaced "not as good looking," and "abandoned" replaced "left."
5. Errors in grammar, usage, and mechanics were corrected throughout the paragraph.

Final Copy: A Model Composition

Once you are satisfied with your revised composition, make a final, clean copy. Be sure to follow proper manuscript form.

Following is a revised, completed composition based on the writing plan that appears on page 196. This is the last step in the process of writing. Read the composition critically. Notice the ways in which the writer has achieved unity and coherence. Analyze the tone, mood, and point of view. Be aware of the language used and the rhythm of the sentences.

WHO KILLED THE TROLLEY?

Last month, as jackhammers split the blacktop on my street to uncover some pipes, workmen laid open the grave of a bit of local history. Beneath my street, and beneath streets all over town, lie the tracks of the Babbington and Hargrove Street Railway. The once beloved

The introduction offers an anecdote and asserts the purpose of the composition: to recount how the trolley, which was enjoyed in its day, has been supplanted by the automobile.

and reliable trolleys are gone, driven underground by the automobile.

When it was in its prime, the trolley was cheap, dependable, and attractive. A rider could go a long way on a few cents. The schedule was so regular that people sent messages and even groceries with the conductor to be picked up at the other end of the line. People rode in comfort on the upholstered seats. The cars were electric, and so were quiet and smokeless. The ride was slow, and passengers had a chance to get to know each other and to take in the sights as they rode. In the summer, open cars with wicker seats were added, and on holidays special excursion cars took families to amusement parks on the edge of town. The B & H allowed easy transfer to other lines, and it was actually possible, though certainly not efficient, to travel from New York to Boston on the network of trolley lines. People regarded the trolley as an ideal means of transportation.

The first paragraph of the body of the composition corresponds to the first section of the writing plan. The first setence is the topic sentence, and the rest of the paragraph illustrates what the topic sentence states.

Then along came the automobile. It was noisy and uncomfortable and unreliable, but it caught the public's fancy from the first. This machine would take you wherever you wanted to go whenever you felt like going there, with no waiting, no transfers, no crowds. Little by little, the trolley began to seem less attractive and the automobile more so. The loss of passengers on the B & H meant a loss of income, and this meant that the equipment could not be kept in good repair. The trolleys became less dependable and less attractive, and

The first word of this paragraph suggests a time relationship between this paragraph and the last. The writer is advancing chronologically. The first sentence also reminds the reader of the controlling purpose of the composition, that the automobile was the undoing of the trolley system.

more people abandoned the trolley for private cars.

While the trolley companies were struggling with declining revenues and ailing equipment, automobiles were becoming more reliable and more plentiful. Automobile traffic was competing with trolley traffic in the streets. Intersections often became confusing, and cars were becoming numerous enough to create traffic jams. Eventually the cars crowded the trolleys off the streets, and the tracks were paved over to make a wider and smoother surface for traffic.

Again, the first word of this paragraph provides a transition between this paragraph and the one before it. It indicates a time relationship.

The street I live on has been repaired and repaved, and the tracks are buried once again. Traffic struggles along as it did before, but there is talk of getting people out of their cars and into some other kind of transportation. The automobile is not quite so wonderful as people first thought. Will something new replace it? I hope not. I hope something old will replace it. I look forward to looking out to the street one day soon and watching a crew install tracks on top of the blacktop—trolley tracks, of course.

The final paragraph constitutes the conclusion of the composition, and as such brings the reader full circle—back to the street in front of the writer's house. The "tour" is complete. After reviewing the past, the writer projects her imagination into the future, which she envisions as repeating the past, and leaves the reader with something to think about.

Exercise Revising a Composition

Revise your composition, following the suggestions in this section. Prepare a clean, final version.

Guidelines for Writing and Revising Compositions

As you write a composition, follow the steps in the Guidelines for The Process of Writing on page 122. Use the Guidelines below after you have written your first draft.

1. Has the subject been narrowed to a topic that can be covered in a few paragraphs?
2. Does the composition deal with a single topic or idea?
3. Does the composition follow your writing plan? Have you used your major topics as the main idea of each paragraph? Have you used the subtopics to develop the main idea of each paragraph? Does the composition have an introduction, a body, and a conclusion?
4. Does the introduction present the main idea of the composition? Does it catch the reader's interest?
5. Does the body explain or support the main idea?
6. Does the conclusion restate the main idea, summarize the information, or comment upon it? Does it leave the reader with a sense of completeness?
7. Do the paragraphs work together to develop the single topic or idea that is the subject of the composition?
8. Is the composition appropriate for the audience for which it is intended? Is the purpose clear? Is the level of language suitable?
9. Does the composition have unity? Are the supporting ideas in each paragraph related to the topic sentence? Is each paragraph directly related to the main idea in the introductory paragraph? Does the composition relate directly to the idea set forth in your controlling purpose?
10. Is the composition coherent? Are the ideas presented in a clear, logical order?
11. Are there transitional devices that tie the paragraphs together?
12. Are the tone, mood, and point of view consistent?
13. Could any words or phrases be replaced with more vivid or precise language?
14. Is the title meaningful and interesting?
15. Are there any errors in grammar, usage, and mechanics?

SUMMARY AND APPLICATIONS

1. A composition is a group of paragraphs that develops a single idea. There are three main types of compositions: narrative, descriptive, and expository.
2. A composition has three main parts. The introduction tells what the composition will be about. The body paragraphs develop this idea. The final paragraph, or conclusion, summarizes the information or comments on it.
3. Limit the subject of the composition to an idea that can be covered within the specified limits of the paper.
4. To further clarify your topic, write a statement of your controlling purpose. Also identify your audience and select a tone, mood, and point of view.
5. Organize information for a composition by taking notes, identifying main ideas, grouping details under these main ideas, and putting the material in logical order.
6. As you write rough drafts, remember that this is the time to experiment with your material. Change and new ideas are expected, even desirable, at this point.
7. Revise for content, unity, and coherence. Check for a consistent tone, mood, and point of view and proofread your material.

Applications in Other Subject Areas.

Fine Arts. Choose an area of the fine arts in which you are interested. Narrow the area to a limited topic, such as a famous dancer or musician. Look in magazines, newspapers, reference materials, and books for examples of different types of writing on this topic. Analyze the different types of writing for changes in tone, language, and methods of development.

Science / Social Studies. The next time you write for one of your classes, look for an unusual way to develop the topic. For example, you might do a history report as a first-person narrative. You might record some scientific observations in the form of a descriptive essay. Be sure to get permission from your teachers, first.

Chapter 11

Using Figurative Language

Sometimes a speech or a composition uses words correctly, obeys the rules of grammar, follows accepted patterns of organization, and yet remains dull or lifeless. The speaker or writer's message is clearly expressed, but in a way that does not excite curiosity or interest. Such speech or writing can be dramatically improved by the use of **figurative language**—images of sight, sound, touch, taste, and smell that make ideas come alive by appealing to the imagination.

The techniques of figurative language, known as the **figures of speech,** include the following:

onomatopoeia	metaphor	hyperbole
alliteration	simile	personification
assonance	symbol	

Learning to use these techniques will enable you to capture and sustain the interest of those to whom you speak and write, making your language more vivid, precise, and appealing.

Part 1 Onomatopoeia

Onomatopoeia is a Greek word meaning "the making of poetry." As a literary device used today, onomatopoeia means "using words whose sounds mimic, or echo, their meanings." The word is a mouthful, but if you separate it into its syllables, you see how appropriate it is for naming a figurative device: *on/o/mat/o/poe/ia*. With its wavy rhythm, repetition of vowel sounds, and suggestive ending, the sound of the word *onomatopoeia* echoes its own meaning: poetry.

Some words seem to have originated as imitations of sounds.

whirr   squash   rumble   crackle   murmur   pop

Onomatopoetic words are used by advertising copywriters, headline writers, sports reporters, and writers in general to produce sounds in the imaginations of their readers.

In this example, you not only hear but feel the sound.

> Casey Jones was the throttle-puller of the Illinois Central's crack Cannonball.

The words pulse and throb with the sound and rhythm of a fast train moving over steel rails. The image of another sound is added with the repetitive *t*'s of throttle. Each time Casey Jones pulls the throttle to control the flow of engine fuel, a bursting, explosive sound is released that is related to the sound of a cannonball as it is fired. Try to imagine the sounds in your mind.

Exercises Using Sounds That Echo Their Meaning

A. In the following examples taken from the sports pages, find the onomatopoetic words and show how they are appropriate.

1. When he shot the puck into the net for the winning goal, the audience exploded with excitement.
2. With a man on second and third, he cracked a single into center field.
3. On the jump shot just before the buzzer, he swished in the winning two points.

B. In the following, state what sounds echo their meaning, and what the meaning is.

1. The thunder roared overhead, then rolled and rumbled through the cave of the sky.
2. The moan of doves in immemorial elms,
   And murmuring of innumerable bees.
3. The small sticks hissed and sputtered.

C. What feelings do the sounds of the italicized words arouse?

1. The sharp *scratch* of a match on the bricks startled him.
2. The soggy leaves were *squashed* beneath her foot.
3. *Sizzling* hot dogs greeted his ears and nose.
4. The garden was alive with the *buzz* of bees.
5. The bow *twanged* jarringly and the arrow *hissed* toward the target.

D. Write a sentence describing the motion of a car, cycle, or plane, using words that mimic the sound each makes.

E. Write a sentence using onomatopoetic words to describe the following. Make each word sound as vivid as you can.

a fire	a storm	a lawn sprinkler
a fountain	a crowd of people	a window breaking
a whip	a ringing phone	someone crying
a bird	a whistle	inside a cave

Part 2 Alliteration and Assonance

Alliteration and assonance are related types of sound imagery. In **alliteration,** identical or similar consonant sounds are repeated, usually at the beginnings of words that are close to each other, such as the following:

a bend of birch trees	the rolling rumble of rocks
the silver sweep of the sea	a Monday morning meeting

Assonance repeats vowel sounds, usually within words that are close to each other, such as the following:

moaning and groaning	a red felt headdress
snap, crackle, and rattle	about the house

Alliteration and assonance may be used separately, or jointly, as in "One could do worse than be a swinger of birches," in which both vowel sounds (*worse, birches*) and consonant sounds (*be, birches*) are repeated.

A pulsating effect occurs when the same sounds return to strike our ears. When the repetition is joined to the sound mimicry of onomatopoeia, it adds intensity. Listen to the "beat, bang, blow" of the hammer, or the "ding-dong" of bells.

Headline writers recognize the value of repetitive sounds. Alliteration in bold print catches the prospective reader's attention: EARTHQUAKE TREMORS TROUBLE PEKING. The repetition of sounds, whether in headline writing, sports reporting, or writing in general, is pleasing to the eye and ear. It adds flavor and makes the reader more responsive.

Exercises Using Alliteration and Assonance

A. Examine the following for alliteration and assonance. Some sentences may combine both; others contain only one. Explain how the sound effect works, whether as (1) decoration, (2) catchy attention-getter, (3) evocation of atmosphere or action, or a combination.

1. Fall foliage takes a final fling.
2. Join the Jippi Jappa Festival in Jamaica.
3. For her, the newly formed leaves were bursting buds of promise.
4. The dismal dusk of darkening days is with us now.
5. Bigger—Better—Busier was once the ethic of the nation.
6. Dogged Determination Drives Winner
7. WHAT A SEASON OF SPARKLING SPECIALS
8. Baggy Bravado from Big Name Jeans

B. Search the advertising pages of your newspaper or listen to TV commercials for catchy sound effects. Bring them to class and discuss them.

C. Listen to the lyrics of your favorite songs for assonance. Bring in examples. Is there a mood that the assonance strengthens? What is it?

D. Write three sentences using alliteration, assonance, or both. You may choose your own subject or write about the sights, sounds, smells, or tastes of the place in which you are.

Part 3 Metaphor

Metaphor (from the Greek "transfer") is a figure of speech that superimposes one image on another. The characteristics of one object or event are transferred to another object or event, even though literally this cannot be the case. Metaphor occurs only when the assertion is preposterous because the two images involved are dissimilar.

Song lyrics often make use of metaphor. For example, the American songwriter Randy Newman used metaphor in the following lines:

> You're the song that the trees sing
>   When the wind blows.
> You're a flower; you're a river;
>   You're a rainbow.

Of course, Newman did not mean, literally, that the person to whom the song is addressed is a sound, a flower, a river, or a rainbow. Instead, he meant that this person shares the qualities of various objects in nature. The person is fresh and beautiful and, in a word, natural. Likewise, when people described the son of King Henry II of England as *Richard the Lion-Hearted*, they did not mean, literally, that he had a lion's heart in his body. They meant that he shared the lion's qualities of nobility and courage. In other words, one image, Richard, is described as having the qualities of another image, the lion.

Metaphor is useful to writers and speakers because it enables them to show new relationships and new insights. Have you ever seen a crowd of people in the way described by Ezra Pound in the following poem?

> In a Station of the Metro
> The apparition of these faces in the crowd;
> Petals on a wet, black bough.

In these two lines, Pound uses two metaphors. First, he describes the scene in the Paris subway, which is called the *Metro,* as an *apparition*. In other words, it is like a ghostly vision. Second, he describes the faces of the people in the station as being like the petals of flowers, standing out in sharp contrast to the darkness of the rest of the scene. By using these vivid metaphors, the poet enables us to see in a new and interesting way.

After long and repeated usage, metaphor loses its original force, and, used literally, becomes incorporated into the language. When you "thread your way" through the crowd you no longer think of the original image. The "legs" of a table belong to it as certainly as the legs of a dog; and the "head of state" or the head of any organization brings no image of heads to mind. With tongue in cheek, the humorist-poet Ogden Nash makes fun of such overused metaphors:

> Then they always say things like after a winter storm the snow is a white blanket. Oh it is, is it? All right then, you sleep under a six-inch blanket of snow and I'll sleep under a half-inch blanket of unpoetical blanket material and we'll see which one keeps warm.

After repeated use in a specific field, metaphor becomes the *jargon* of that field. When a golfer "shoots" a 68 or when a tennis player "breaks" service, the images are literal in that the original *breaking* and *shooting* figures no longer come to mind. When a metaphor becomes so commonplace that people no longer recognize its metaphorical quality, it is referred to as a **dead metaphor.**

Mixed Metaphor

Mixed metaphors form in those phrases where the original image has slipped away. Coming too quickly to the writer's pen, a phrase mixes with others to produce contradictory or uncongenial images:

> You've buttered your bread; now lie in it.
> The hand that rocked the cradle has kicked the bucket.

In some writing, mixed images may nevertheless create a unified impression. In sports writing, for instance, hard-hitting verbs may be of mixed imagery: Jets Snap Slump.

Sometimes the metaphor may refer to two different images that reinforce each other. In the following, connect the "gunning" metaphor with both "gear" and "Bullets."

> The Washington Bullets played their best game of the season last night as they got their fast break in gear and outgunned their rivals at Capitol Centre.

Cliché

Clichés are overused metaphors. When the original image is lost, repeated phrases, emptied of meaning, strike hollowly at your ears. *Spilled milk, dogged determination, ladders of success, sands of time* are figureless phrases. When they serve as apt expressions to communicate meaning quickly, they may be regarded as a kind of shorthand.

Exercises Analyzing the Use of Metaphor

A. Explain the following metaphors.

1. We must all hang together or assuredly we shall all hang separately.—BENJAMIN FRANKLIN
2. An escalator rides on dinosaur spines.—BARBARA HOWES
3. His eyes were gun barrels.—JON STALLWORTHY
4. O serpent heart, hid in a flow'ring face!
—WILLIAM SHAKESPEARE

B. "He had that spark of talent that made him look so natural weaving down a court with a basketball in his hand." Can you connect "weaving" with "spark"? Are the metaphors well suited?

C. In what way is the term "running mate" an accurate image of the vice-presidential candidate?

D. Explain the metaphors in the following sentences by showing what two things are being compared.

1. Everything in nature is closing up shop for the season.
2. All ignorance toboggans into know/and trudges up to ignorance again.—E. E. CUMMINGS
3. Apartments are tenanted tight as hen-houses, people roosting in every cupboard.—BARBARA HOWES

E. "I hope that as the weather gets colder his heart gets warmer." This was said of a legislator with reference to tax relief on fuel costs. What makes the imagery particularly appropriate?

F. Give examples of five metaphors from sports or songs.

G. In the following mixed metaphors, take the metaphorical images literally to show how they make each other ludicrous.

1. Realizing that he had a finger in every pie, gave me food for thought.
2. He turned tail and fell into the well of despair.

Part 4 Simile

Simile is a figure of speech closely related to metaphor. Again, the characteristics of one object or event are joined to those of another in a way that is literally not true. Simile differs from metaphor in that the comparison made between two things is indicated by connectives such as *like, as,* or *than;* or by verbs such as *resemble*. "My love is a rose" is a metaphor; "My love is like a rose" is a simile. In this case, the metaphor would be a more forceful statement than the simile. Often, however, the simile is preferred to the metaphor because it can state directly what the shared characteristic is.

When someone writes: "Mr. Smith is as crafty as a fox" or "Mr. Smith is as swift as a fox," we know exactly what qualities Mr. Smith shares with the fox. However, when we say, "Mr. Smith acts like a true friend," we are no longer using figurative language because the statement may be literally true.

Attaching animal characteristics to human beings has long been a feature of figurative writing. The American humorist James Thurber cites several such similes of praise: "as brave as a lion, as proud as a peacock, as lively as a cricket, as graceful as a swan, as busy as a bee, as gentle as a lamb," and points out that most of these similes have become dog-tired. Similes, if not overused, do have the potential to make writing and speech much more vivid and interesting. A newspaper article says of a character at a neighborhood meeting that "he drifted through the shaded room like ectoplasm clothed in blue jeans." What does this simile tell you about the character? What sort of picture do you visualize in your imagination?

Exercises Analyzing the Use of Simile

A. In each of the following sentences, pick out the simile and explain the comparison made between the two terms.

1. A line of elms plunging and tossing like horses.
—THEODORE ROETHKE

2. Birds flickered like skipped stones across the vast inverted pond of heaven.—RAY BRADBURY

3. An automatic smile flashed across her face as if it were an electronic scoreboard.

4. My Mama moved among the days like a dreamwalker in a field.—LUCILLE CLIFTON

5. Second-hand sights, like crumpled, mud-smudged post-cards.—CAROLYN M. RODGERS

6. What happens to a dream deferred? Does it dry up like a raisin in the sun?—LANGSTON HUGHES

7. Objects arranged like rows of fine teeth.—ISHMAEL REED

B. In the following examples, both metaphor and simile are used. Find each and explain the comparisons being made.

1. The bus was trapped like a fly in the web of traffic.
2. If I can bear your love like a lamp before me,/When I go down the long steep Road of Darkness,/I shall not fear the everlasting shadows.—SARA TEASDALE
3. His fortunes moved up and down like a horse on the merry-go-round of life.

C. Complete the following similes.

1. Prices are rising like ______.
2. He felt as if he were a ______.
3. The beach was as hot as ______.
4. Our team ran over the opposition like a ______.
5. In the blizzard the landscape resembled a ______.
6. As he read the new directions, his thoughts whirled faster than a ______.

D. For the following similes, substitute comparisons that are both more original and more to the point.

1. busy as a bee
2. gentle as a lamb
3. crazy as a loon
4. fierce as a lion

Part 5 Extended Metaphor

When an image created by a metaphor occurs repeatedly in a passage, the metaphor is said to be extended. The **extended metaphor** emphasizes the point being made. Notice how the poet Karl Shapiro extends the metaphor in the following passage.

The ambulance at top speed floating down
Past beacons and illuminated clocks
Wings in a heavy curve, dips down,
And brakes speed, entering the crowd.

Two entirely different images, an ambulance and a large bird, have been superimposed upon one another. The metaphor has been extended by describing the movement at different stages. Here is another extended metaphor.

> The sea—quick pugilist—
> uses for a pun
>   ching
>   ball
> the restless little boats.
>
> With the towel of the wind,
> even rubs down the boxer's
> sweaty body.
>
> The buildings—
> ringside fans—
> crowd close to watch
> the big training.—
>
> —DEMETRIO HERRERA

What are the two dissimilar images in this metaphor? What characteristics of the sea does the boxer image describe?

In the following passage, Patrick White extends an image of "trumpeting corn" to make more vivid the immensity of field after field of corn stretching beyond the horizon.

> All through the middle of America there was a trumpeting of corn. Its full, yellow, tremendous notes pressed close to the swelling sky. There were whole acres of time in which the yellow corn blared as if for judgment.

The shape of the corn and its color suggest a trumpeting image that is repeated in the "tremendous notes pressed close to the swelling sky" and in the figure of corn that "blared as if for judgment." The blaring "as if for judgment" refers to the horn waking the dead on judgment day and may be read here as emphasizing the strength of the corn's statement.

When you write an extended metaphor, you must be very sure that the characteristics of one image can be superimposed upon the other in a believable way.

Exercises Analyzing Extended Metaphor

A. The following passages are extended metaphors. Determine what the metaphor is and how it has been extended.

1. The progress of science is strewn, like an ancient desert trail, with the bleached skeletons of discarded theories that once seemed to possess eternal life.—ARTHUR KOESTLER

The preceding may be read omitting the adjectives *ancient, bleached, eternal*. What do these adjectives add?

2. The straw poll is the fastest growing political crop in the land. State political parties, hopeful candidates, television networks, and newspapers fertilize and nurture them.

3. These great brown hills move in herds, humped like bison, before the traveling eye. Massive above the farms, they file and hulk daylong across every distance; and bending come as the sun sinks (orange and small) beyond their heavy shoulders, shaggy at evening, to drink among the shadowy lakes.—ROBERT WALLACE

B. In the following passage, what extends the "ice flow" simile? What is metaphor and what is simile?

> His approach to tennis is as cold as winter, as methodical as an ice flow. If indeed, there are passions that churn within him, they are locked away and rumble unnoticed.—Article on Bjorn Borg in *The New York Times*

C. Here is a simple metaphor. Determine exactly what two images are being compared. Then extend the metaphor, selecting those characteristics of each that will superimpose believably on each other to reveal new relationships between them.

> About an excavation
> a flock of bright red lanterns
> has settled.—CHARLES REZNIKOFF

D. Write a paragraph using the extended metaphor. For example, "March raced in like a wild stallion bursting from the corral." Then make every sentence, adjective and vivid verb apply to this comparison.

Part 6 Symbol

In a metaphor or simile, a writer or speaker uses an image for comparison only. The image is meant to be taken figuratively, but not literally. For example, if you say that someone is "sharp as a tack," you do not mean, literally, that this person has a sharp, pointed shape. You mean that the person's mind has a quality that is shared by tacks.

In contrast, **symbols** *are* meant to be taken both literally and figuratively. They are presented in speech or in writing as objects that exist in their own right, but that also represent things beyond themselves. Most symbols also have denotation and connotation. Denotation means a literal or dictionary definition. Connotation refers to the feelings and emotions that a particular word brings forth.

Objects in everyday life often act as symbols: an American flag is a symbol of our country; uniforms are symbols of professions; a golden crown is a symbol of royalty, a rose is a symbol of beauty or of love. By referring to objects that have traditional symbolic meanings, writers and speakers can arouse the emotions of their audiences and suggest complex ideas in a very few words.

In speech or writing, symbols may be used in different ways. Sometimes, a well-known symbol may be used much as a synonym would be, as a more interesting way of expressing a common idea. For example, a writer may speak of "the white dove hovering uncertainly over a country tired of war." Since the white dove has become a symbol of peace, the writer is actually saying that peace is about to come to a struggling nation.

Symbols may also be used in a subtler way that must be interpreted by the reader. A setting that involves smoke or fog, for example, may become symbolic of a confusing situation in the story. A growing tree may come to represent the growth of a person, or even a country. Wandering in a maze may be symbolic of a person's search for some elusive goal. In such cases, the symbolism is not stated directly. Instead, the writer designs it subtly to reinforce a character or situation. Such a device is a powerful way to add meaning and depth.

Exercises Analyzing Symbols

A. Determine what the following images symbolize.

blue skies	a donkey	a white flag
a heart	an elephant	a halo
a red cross	a dollar sign	a wedding ring

B. In the following passage, Charles Dickens describes an occurrence in Paris shortly before the outbreak of the bloody French Revolution. Explain what image is used in this passage as a symbol and why this image is particularly appropriate:

> A large cask of wine had been dropped and broken in the street. . . . It had stained many hands . . . and many faces, and many naked feet, and many wooden shoes; and one tall joker, his head more out of a long squalid bag of a nightcap than in it, scrawled upon a wall with his finger dipped in muddy wine lees—BLOOD.
>
> The time was to come when that wine, too, would be spilled on the street stones and when the stain of it would be red upon many there.

Part 7 Hyperbole

Hyperbole (from the Greek, "overshooting") is a figure of speech that uses bold and obvious exaggeration.

> GM's Sale To End All Sales
> Place Kickers: It's Do or Die in Seconds

These statements are obviously figurative. General Motors is not going to end its sales this year or next. The place kicker may perform, but he will not die if he does not.

Although hyperbole is used to make something bigger than life, smallness too can be exaggerated.

> He was so miserly that he wouldn't even give you the time.
> She was so thin she could have hidden behind a parking meter.

Hyperbole is not intended to deceive anyone, nor is it in any sense a realistic description. The writer or speaker exaggerates a quality to emphasize it or to infect the reader with his or her enthusiasm. The writer of advertising copy does not expect you to believe that the circus coming to town is the greatest event in history. The writer is merely arousing your enthusiasm with the largeness of the claim. As propaganda, of course, hyperbole is an effective tool.

Exercises Analyzing Hyperbole

A. In the following sentences, explain in greater detail what makes these figures hyperbole. How would you describe the effect they may have on the reader?

1. He's so crooked he has to screw his socks on.
2. In that great cavern of his mind a thought is as lost as a gull on the high seas.
3. That's as exciting as watching paint dry.
4. Let us spend one day as deliberately as Nature, and not be thrown off the track by every nutshell and mosquito's wing that falls on the rails.—HENRY DAVID THOREAU

B. What other figure of speech is used in the preceding sentences besides hyperbole?

C. Search for examples of hyperbole in newspaper advertisements and TV commercials. Select the truly effective ones and list those whose claims are so trite, colorless, or absurd that you would ignore the product.

D. Write a sentence about each of the following, using hyperbole in your statement.

1. a good friend
2. the performance by a musician, dancer, or actor
3. the action of a sports event, either live or televised
4. a TV comedy or movie
5. your pet or some other animal

6. the record of some athletic team
7. a car or cycle that you admire
8. your talents in a game or activity in which you excel

Part 8 Personification

Personification gives to a concept, or to an inanimate object, the qualities of a living thing, either animal or human.

> The mountains rose majestically.
> Earth wears a green velvet dress.

Speaking literally, can you say of mountains or earth that they "do" anything of their own volition? Mountains (except in cases of extreme natural agitation) do not move at all, and the earth does not wear clothes. By endowing these inanimate things with lifelike qualities, the writer is again using figurative language. Because these characteristics are often associated with persons, the figure is called *personification*.

As a way of humanizing events, personification proves useful for making abstract ideas more vivid.

> Education, that great liberator of the human spirit, cannot be overvalued.

Personification engages your attention. You are more likely to respond to the personal than to the impersonal. In ascribing personal characteristics to inanimate objects, the writer or speaker involves your feelings and your sensations. The moon "in all her glory" becomes a creature in whose radiance you take pleasure. When you read, "the wind blew and blew until its breath was spent," your own breathing feels the difficulty.

In its long history, language has taken many figures, such as personification, and put them into its standard lexicon. Running was once an animal and human characteristic. Today brooks run, stockings run, time runs, and thoughts run, among others. Overuse, as in other figures, has robbed many images that were once vividly pictured.

With proper care not to use the obvious, personification remains a rich source of figurative meaning. Try using it to make your writing come to life.

Exercises Using Personification

A. "The bottom was deep, soft clay; he sank in, and the water clasped dead cold around his legs."—D. H. LAWRENCE
What is the image you feel?

B. Write sentences that give the quality of life to the following items:

1. rain
2. kitchen
3. classroom
4. school
5. a sports event

C. Name several products personified in TV commercials.

D. In the following, what are the personified qualities?

1. forbidding buildings
2. moaning seas
3. lonely city streets
4. throbbing machines
5. roar of traffic
6. scarred landscapes

Review Exercises Using Figurative Language

A. Each of the following sentences contains one or more of the literary figures discussed in this chapter. Identify the figures and be prepared to explain them. In some cases a word or phrase may be part of more than one figure.

1. I am a miner for a heart of gold.—NEIL YOUNG
2. Its mouth gaped, exposing a fence of teeth like daggers.
3. Rono's Running Is as Good as Gold.

4. Come to a Whale of a Sale at the mall!

5. The leaves scattered as if the wind were the enemy.

6. The ferocious sea growled at the borders of the shore.

7. There was a sweet sadness in the air that sang of the last rose of summer.

8. The buzz saw snarled and rattled in the yard.

—ROBERT FROST

9. Her halo tarnished under the merciless questioning.

10. The audience exploded with applause.

11. By now most of the sumacs at the roadside and in the corner of the back pasture begin to look like Sioux war bonnets and are ready to lead the parade right into Indian summer.—*The New York Times*

12. Farmers heap hay in stacks and bind corn in shocks against the biting breath of frost.—MARGARET WALKER

B. The following literary passages combine several figures to create impressions, atmosphere, or the formation of an idea. Identify the figures and state the emotional effect created.

1 No man is an island, entire of itself; every man is a piece of the continent, a part of the main. If a clod be washed away by the sea, Europe is the less, as well as if a promontory were, as well as if a manor of thy friend's or of thine own were. Any man's death diminishes me because I am involved in mankind, and therefore never send to know for whom the bell tolls; it tolls for thee.—JOHN DONNE

2 Let the sea-gulls wail
For water, for the deep where the high tide
Mutters to its hurt self, mutters and ebbs.

—ROBERT LOWELL

3 if i were a poet
i'd kidnap you
put you in my phrases and meter
you to jones beach
or maybe coney island
or maybe just to my house
lyric you to lilacs—NIKKI GIOVANNI

4 I feel the sun on the stone above me; it's striking, striking, like a hammer on all the stones and it's the music, the vast music of noon, air and stones vibrating.—ALBERT CAMUS

5 Here and there, near the glistening blackness of the water, a root of some tall tree showed amongst the tracery of small ferns, black and dull, writhing and motionless, like an arrested snake. . . . Darkness oozed out from between the trees, through the tangled maze of the creepers, from behind the great fantastic and unstirring leaves; the darkness, mysterious and invincible; the darkness scented and poisonous of impenetrable forests.—JOSEPH CONRAD

C. Write a paragraph, or short account, of a recent emotional experience, using figurative language as much as possible. You may use one of the following topics or select your own.

1. a party
2. a school sport victory or defeat
3. an automobile drive in traffic
4. a movie or TV show
5. an accident in which you or someone close to you was involved
6. an important event in your family, such as a birth, death, wedding, graduation
7. a personal outdoor adventure, such as a hike or camping trip
8. the habits of your pet
9. your successful accomplishment of something done with great difficulty
10. a long-held wish finally obtained

SUMMARY AND APPLICATIONS

1. Figurative language can help make your writing and speaking more vivid and interesting.
2. Onomatopoeia, alliteration, and assonance can be used to create striking effects of sound.
3. Metaphors and similes can be used to transfer the vivid characteristics of one image to another, dissimilar image.
4. Symbols, images that can be taken both literally and figuratively, can be used to suggest complex emotions or ideas in a few words.
5. Hyperbole, or exaggeration, can be used to emphasize a quality or to communicate enthusiasm about a subject.
6. Personification can be used to give inanimate objects interesting, lifelike qualities.

Applications in Other Subject Areas

Business / Speech / Mass Media. Figurative language is often used in commercials and in advertisements to arouse the emotions of potential buyers. Choose a product and write a commercial for it. Use at least three figures of speech, and perform your commercial in class.

Social Studies / Journalism. When reporting political events, journalists generally avoid using figurative language because such language tends to be emotionally-charged. However, when writing editorials, journalists are free to express emotional attitudes and, therefore, often do use figurative language. Write a brief newspaper article describing an event at your school such as a student council election. In your article, simply report the facts without using figurative language. Then, rewrite the article as an editorial expressing your attitudes toward the event. In your revised version, use figurative language. Which version is more interesting? Which is more accurate? Why?

Chapter 12

Writing Paraphrases and Summaries

Sometimes it is necessary to create altered or shortened versions of material written or spoken by others. Two such versions of material originally produced by someone else are the **paraphrase** and the **summary,** or **précis.** The paraphrase and the summary can be used to study important information contained in complex reading assignments. They can also be used during the pre-writing stage of the process of writing to adapt material for presentation in a report or research paper.

Like notetaking, the paraphrase and summary are used to record the essential information in a written or spoken selection. Unlike notetaking, they provide a prose version of the original. You will find a use for paraphrases and summaries both in school and in your future work. This chapter will provide a guide to these useful skills.

Part 1 The Paraphrase

Whenever you put the ideas of another person into your own words, you are using a technique known as paraphrasing. This technique requires careful reading and rephrasing of the *original* material. Paraphrasing difficult reading assignments will help you to understand and remember them. You can also use paraphrase to adapt material for a report or research paper.

Before putting a concept into your own words, you must understand it thoroughly. That is why paraphrasing is an excellent way to master complex ideas. The paraphrase simplifies; it does not necessarily shorten the selection. The procedure below, will show you how to approach this type of writing.

How To Write a Paraphrase

1. Pre-Writing

a. Read the selection once to get the central meaning.
b. Look up any words you do not understand.
c. Reread the selection at least twice more. Think of simple words to substitute for any long or difficult ones.

2. Writing

a. Follow the same order that the writer uses in presenting the ideas.
b. Put the material into your own words. Shorten long sentences. Use simple vocabulary.

3. Revision

a. Check your paraphrase to be sure that it expresses the ideas of the original. Revise as necessary.
b. Proofread your revised paraphrase for errors in spelling, grammar, usage, and punctuation. It is especially important that names and unfamiliar terms have been spelled correctly and that numbers are accurate.

A Sample Paraphrase

Read the paragraph below. Then work through the steps that lead to a finished paraphrase.

> Dominating the mind of primitive human beings is the belief that behind the world they see before their eyes is another hidden universe peopled by beings of great power. It is these beings who bring life-giving rain, germinate the seeds, and protect the crop until the harvest; and since they seem to rule the domain of the spirit world like powerful chiefs, the awe-struck savages accord them the respect they do their own tribal leader. If they are friendly they must be flattered; if unfriendly, outwitted; but where they are malevolent, bringing death and disease in their train, they must be overcome, and for this purpose one who has the power to invoke an even mightier spirit is required, a specialist in magic, the witch doctor.—ERIC MAPLES

Applying the Techniques

Step 1. Reread the paragraph for the central meaning. Note that the first and last sentences really clinch the main idea. The writer is explaining how the primitive fear of the unknown makes the witch doctor an important member of a society.

Put into your own words, the idea of the paragraph might read like this:

> Primitive human beings view with great awe and respect the witch doctor who can control mighty, unseen spirits.

Although this sentence may not appear in your finished paraphrase, it is helpful to keep it in front of you as you work. It will give focus and coherence to your writing.

Step 2. The original paragraph contained some words you may need to look up. The dictionary gives more than one synonym. Checking the context will help you choose the most appropriate one. Whenever possible, choose the word with which you are familiar and comfortable.

For example, *to accord* is defined in the dictionary as (1) to bring into agreement (2) to award (3) to grant as suitable or proper. Clearly it is the last of these that the writer means.

Following is a list of the more difficult words in the selection and their appropriate synonyms.

peopled	populated by
germinate	produce; cause to develop
domain	area; realm
malevolent	evil
invoke	to call forth

Step 3. In rereading the selection, substitute the synonyms given. What else might be simplified or even omitted?

Writing the Paraphrase

Step 1. In your paraphrase, follow the same order of ideas that the writer uses. Begin your paragraph by talking about the hidden universe that primitive human beings believe in. Expand this by identifying the specific areas in which the unseen beings are powerful. Conclude with the statement about the need for and the power of the witch doctor.

Step 2. Make a clean final copy. Following is the completed paraphrase.

> Primitive human beings believe that behind their own world is an unseen one, populated by powerful beings. These beings bring the all-important rain, cause the seeds to develop, and guard the crops from danger until they can be gathered. Since these unseen spirits are mighty and powerful in the area they rule, primitive human beings, in fear and reverence, grant them as much respect as they do the leader of their own tribe. They try to please those that are friendly and to be cleverer than those that are not. However, the forces that bring death and disease must be beaten. This is the job of the witch doctor, the specialist who has the power to call forth a spirit even more powerful than the ones against which he is struggling.

Exercises Practice in Writing Paraphrases

A. Paraphrase this selection on juggling. Follow the pre-writing steps that are outlined after the selection. Then write your paraphrase.

> Juggling, the continuous tossing and catching of objects in the air, is an excellent example of humans' extraordinary capacity for play. Some other animals, such as the seal, have been trained to balance objects, but true juggling seems beyond the abilities of even the higher primates (despite occasional circus posters that falsely picture chimpanzees juggling). That juggling is unique to humans should not be surprising since it involves not only the use of the hands but also complex spatial perception and cognitive skills.
>
> —MARCELLO TRUZZI

Step 1. Find the sentence that states the central idea. Rephrase it in your own words.

Step 2. Are there words that need defining? What synonyms can you substitute for *capacity, primates, unique, complex, spatial, perception,* and *cognitive?*

Step 3. Reread the selection and in your mind substitute the synonyms you have selected. Does it sound right? Now rewrite the paragraph as simply and clearly as you can.

B. Using the same procedure, paraphrase each of the following selections.

1 Just as the heat may pose a hazard to your physical and emotional health, it can also have a stultifying effect on your work. Researchers have repeatedly found that productivity peaks in cool, dry temperatures—with 60 to 65 degrees Fahrenheit considered the ideal stimulus. On hot, sizzling days, stenographers are said to transcribe their notes more slowly, and students score lower on their tests at school. Physical performance, too, may not be quite up to par. While muscles generally become more flexible and limber with the application of heat, strength and stamina may be appreciably undermined, so don't be surprised if your running or jogging time is considerably slower in July than in September.—JILL NEWMAN

2 Remarkable physical adaptations over the long years have enabled dolphins to separate themselves from their terrestrial ancestors and embark on their zoological adventure in the undersea—to become one of the most specialized and efficient marine creatures that has ever existed. This all sounds like work. The dolphin prefers to play. When all else failed to amuse him, ages ago, the dolphin invented body-surfing—and in many parts of the world can be seen rollicking in the breakers in groups of four or more. With the advent of the steamship, the dolphin discovered another game—riding the bow waves. Perfectly calculating the speed of the ship, the contours of waves, winds, and currents, one or more dolphins take up a position in front of a fast-moving boat and, with next to no expenditure of energy on their part, hitch a ride. Let humans do the work!

Unlike us, dolphins have found no need to develop their territory by constructing huge habitation complexes. They are content to play, perpetuate their species, and take from nature only what they need. Such animals have no enemy in the sea except for their cousins the killer whales. And, alas, humans, who cheat—with net, harpoon, and gun!—JACQUES COUSTEAU

3 Dinosaurs were unintelligent machines; their actions were automatic, and lacking in the flexibility needed to cope with unfamiliar situations. Flexibility means intelligence, and the dinosaurs had little. Their small brains held a limited repertoire of behavior, with no room for varied response. The brain of a dinosaur was devoted mainly to the control of its huge bulk; it served simply as a telephone switching center, receiving signals from its body and sending out messages to move its head and limbs in unthinking reaction. If the eye of Tyrannosaurus registered a moving object, it pursued it; but its hunt lacked

cunning. If the eye of Brontosaurus registered movement, it fled; but its flight was mechanical and mindless. Some other dinosaurs were still less intelligent; Stegosaurus, a ten-ton vegetarian, had a brain the size of a walnut. Dinosaurs were stupid animals; incapable of thought, moving slowly and ponderously, they waded through life like walking robots. Their mechanical responses were sufficient for coping with the familiar problems of their serene, friendly environment. There was no need for greater intelligence in their lives, and therefore it never evolved.

—ROBERT JASTROW

4 Whatever else may be said about India, it is one of the few countries in the world that has resisted homogenization. Its peoples, their costumes and customs, remain as varied and fascinating as their myriad languages and the diverse topography of their homelands. Visitors react to India in many different ways, but never with indifference.

Of all India's cities, New Delhi, its capital, is the core, or heart, where millenia of cultures meet and mold. By archeological count, there were seven distinct ancient cities that rose, not layer upon layer in the usual way, but side by side, so that many of the principal monuments (well over a thousand) still stand to capsulate the sweep of history in stone.—GERO TROTTA

Part 2 The Summary, or Précis

Unlike the paraphrase, the summary, also known as the précis, cuts a selection down to about one-third of its original length. Its purpose is to condense without sacrificing the basic meaning of the original.

You read and listen to summaries daily. The lead paragraph of a news article is a summary. Radio and TV broadcasts present important events of the day in brief, summarized form. The last paragraph of a textbook chapter often summarizes the main points. Summaries may be used in the conclusion of a composition, report, or research paper. They can also be used to rework material contained in complex reading assigments.

How To Write a Summary

1. Pre-Writing

a. Read the selection carefully. Can you find a key sentence that states the writer's main point? A topic sentence may summarize a whole paragraph for you.

b. Note the important ideas, the order in which they occur, and the way the writer has connected them. You may want to write these ideas in your own words.

2. Writing

a. Omit unnecessary details, examples, anecdotes (little stories that illustrate a point) and repetitions.

b. Rephrase the material. You may retain some of the key words or technical language of the original, but the bulk of the summary should be in your own words.

3. Revision

a. Read your first draft. Does it include all the important ideas of the original? Have you omitted the unnecessary or repetitious details?

b. You may need to revise. Your final summary should be about one-third the length of the original. It should give the essential information in a way that the reader can use without referring to the original.

c. Proofread your summary for errors.

A Sample Summary

Read the following paragraph. Then work through the steps that lead to a finished summary.

> Lions and tigers are always associated together in the minds of the zoo or circus goer, yet in temperament and

appearance the two could hardly be more different. The lion is a naturally lazy, and a ponderous beast; the tiger, with its broad, powerful shoulders and immensely strong hind limbs, is like a huge and impressively powerful spring and has a seventeen-foot leap. It is a very nervous, highly strung animal, and hates shouting or sharp words of command. Blaring bands disturb it, but quiet music can soothe. Its hearing is sharp, and its sense of smell far more accurate than the lion's—and it can attack from the crouching position or even when lying down, so quick are its reactions. Unlike the lion, which fights with one front paw at a time (the other it uses to keep its balance), the tiger fights, almost boxes, with both paws at a tremendous speed, using its hindquarters to propel it forward. In the wild, the tiger is a natural climber and will often lie along a branch or sit on a rock. This habit means that it learns to climb onto its circus tub far more quickly than the lion. More cunning and more daring than the lion, the tiger is generally quicker to learn. It is also a more cynical creature, cannot be bluffed as easily as the lion, and requires different handling—the metaphor of the heavy, powerful car and the light racer has been used more than once. The conduct of a mixed act of lions, tigers, and leopards is in some ways a performance of opposites, and once one understands this, the true genius of the animal trainer with his or her mixed act becomes apparent, especially as lions do not like tigers and vice versa, and both dislike leopards, which they consider inferior beasts.—PETER VERNEY

Applying the Techniques

Step 1. As you reread the paragraph, you will see that the first sentence expresses the basic idea—a contrast between lions and tigers in the circus. Although the writer describes both animals, his emphasis is on the tiger. The contrasting qualities of the lion are often implied. The writer develops his paragraph by presenting points of difference between the two animals. A brief listing of those points of difference is on the following page.

	TIGER	LION
Physical Qualities	strong and agile keen sense of smell keen sense of hearing	lazy and heavy less acute sense of smell
Temperament	nervous and quick	(implied difference)
Fighting Style	can attack from crouch can fight with both paws	(implied difference) fights with one paw
Behavior in Ring	climbs tub quickly daring, clever, quick to learn, cynical	slower to climb lesser degree of these qualities

The final sentence of the paragraph relates these differences to the task of the animal trainer.

Step 2. By omitting unnecessary details, examples, and repetitions, you can reduce phrases and whole sentences.

Original	Summary
Sentence 2—"The tiger, with its broad, powerful shoulders and immensely strong hind limbs, is like a huge and impressively powerful spring and has a seventeen-foot leap."	strong and agile
Sentences 3 and 4—"It is a very nervous, highly strung animal, and hates shouting or sharp words of command. Blaring bands disturb it, but quiet music can soothe."	nervous

The following is the finished summary.

Although people think of lions and tigers as similar, there are important differences between them. The lion is lazy and slow compared with the strong, agile, and more keen-scented tiger. Nervous and quick to react, the tiger can attack from a crouch and, unlike the lion, fight with both front paws. Being a natural climber, he can mount his tub faster than the lion. More daring than the lion and cleverer, the tiger is quicker at learning tricks. He presents a different problem, however, being cynical and hard to bluff. It takes a skilled trainer to make these very different animals perform in a mixed act.

Exercises **Practice in Writing Summaries**

A. Summarize this selection. Follow the steps below it.

George Washington wore a perfumed, powdered wig at his inauguration. Most of the other men present were similarly bedecked; it was standard fashion for upper-class men of that period. Women of the same class were more elaborately adorned and went to greater extremes to be fashionable. Their ghostly pallor was not always due to delicate health, but to ceruse, a white lead paint, known to be toxic. In spite of the horror stories about the slow death and ruined complexions of its users, some women braved the consequences. They used rouge, too, and their hair—real and false, powdered and pomaded—reached heights of a foot or more above their heads. A Philadelphia newspaper of that time advertised hair dressing with "construction of rolls" to raise heads to the desired "pitch." No attempt was made by either sex to conceal the wearing of cosmetics, since their use was the mark of the aristocrat.—ESTELLE KLEIGER

Step 1. Reread the selection.

a. Look for a sentence that expresses the basic idea. You will find that in this paragraph it is not the first sentence.
b. List the important ideas in the order in which they occur.

Step 2. Summarize the selection in your own words.
a. Omit unnecessary details.
b. Read your summary and check for accuracy. Revise as necessary.

B. Using the same procedure, summarize each of the following:

1 The ballad, or folksong, was the world's first newspaper and informal history book. It came into being as a sort of tabloid record of battles, adventures, and scandals in the days when an illiterate community depended for its news on the minstrels who roamed the countryside. The form of the folk song served a practical purpose. The minstrel, having much news to report, could not rely entirely on his memory. A ballad stanza, by its rhyme scheme and general circumscribed framework, helped him to supply details that might otherwise be forgotten—to give accurate versions of names and times and places, and to recall the sequence of an event as it really happened.

Even today, when the newspaper and the radio flourish in almost every community, the ancient, news-bearing quality of the ballad has not been lost. The recent war, for instance, produced many songs. The much-popularized, too-sentimental ones will die with their occasion. Some will have a longer life: the songs of the underground fighters of France and Norway, the guerrillas of Russia and China, and the marching fighting songs of the world's armies. These have the austerity and imagination-catching qualities of the older ballad. In a future peaceful century they will survive, as much of a record of the world's conflict as is the printed page. They will probably more truly convey the doubts, fears, and hopes of the world's people.

—FIRESIDE BOOK OF FOLK SONGS

2 The most dangerous place to dive is inside the earth—into caves filled with fresh water, cold as winter and darker than night. The darkness contrasts with the sunlit waters outside. In such explorations the greatest challenge is finding the way out before the air supply is depleted. In sea caves, underwater flashlights are easy to use because the organisms in suspension in the water give substance to the beam of light. In a freshwater cave, on the contrary, there is no life. The cold water is numbing and strength-sapping. The interior of the cave is jagged, etched by centuries of water scouring the softer stones, sharpening the harder ones. A flashlight is almost useless, for the crystal-clear water seems to eat light unless it falls by chance on the rocks of the wall; but if mud is stirred up, then one is left with no visibility.—JACQUES COUSTEAU

3 Not often does a literary work inspire a series of films. It is rare indeed that one becomes a continuing screen effort to the point that, in effect, it establishes careers for a large number of actors. But that is exactly what Edgar Rice Burroughs's *Tarzan of the Apes* has achieved.

ERB's fantastic creation has (in all likelihood) directly affected more lives than any other character in fiction. "How much would heredity," ERB mused on a sleepless night in 1911, "influence character if the infant were transplanted to an entirely different environment and raised there?" For his fictional experiment, he put a babe of the English nobility into the jungles to be brought up by apes. ". . . and the boy-child was called Tarzan," which is ape-talk for "white-skin."

Little did ERB realize then the potential of his fictional hero. He could not have guessed that Tarzan would become an international figure, idolized by millions. He could not have known that his brainchild would make him wealthier than in his most satisfying dreams. In fact, he thought the story poor and doubted its salability, until *All-Story Magazine* purchased it in 1912 for seven hundred dollars.—GABE ESSOE

SUMMARY AND APPLICATIONS

1. Paraphrases and summaries can be used when you are studying difficult reading material and when you are recording or adapting material for inclusion in a report or research paper.
2. A paraphrase presents the ideas of another person in different words. It simplifies, but does not necessarily shorten, the selection from which it is drawn.
3. A summary, or précis, presents the basic meaning of a selection in fewer words. It is usually about one-third the length of the original.
4. When writing paraphrases and summaries, try to reflect the content of the original selection as accurately as possible.

Applications in Other Subject Areas

Social Studies / Science. Choose a difficult selection from one of your textbooks, a passage that you need to study for a test. Try writing a summary or précis of the passage, following the procedure described in this chapter. Writing such a summary will help you to understand and remember the content of the passage.

Social Studies / Mass Media. Imagine that you are the editor of a "News-in-Brief" section of a weekly newspaper. Choose two news reports from television and two from a daily newspaper, all from the same week. Write a summary of these four news items, using no more than two hundred words. Make certain that you credit your sources.

Chapter 13

Writing a Research Paper

Introduction

A research paper is longer and more formal than a composition. The subject of the paper is one that requires research into reliable sources of information, mainly books and magazine articles. While research is vital to a paper of this kind, you must organize and shape your gathered information with your own thinking and judgment.

You must search for suitable source materials related to your subject. You must plan and write your paper according to the procedures studied in writing a composition. All this requires an extended period of time. In order to use your time wisely, each step of the planning, research, and writing must be carefully controlled along the way.

A thorough research paper takes weeks to complete. Choosing a subject for which reference books and articles are not readily available can be a costly error in terms of time. Careful attention to planning and organizing your paper is also important because mistakes become increasingly difficult to correct once you are involved in the actual writing. You must allow enough time to read your source materials and to judge the usefulness of that reading for your subject. You must allow enough time to write and revise your paper; and, finally, you must prepare accurate footnotes and a final bibliography.

While a research paper is a more ambitious undertaking than a composition, footnotes and a bibliography are the only aspects that are entirely new. When your teacher makes the research paper assignment, work out a time schedule, with your teacher's guidance, that will help you work through each stage in a thorough and unhurried way.

This chapter will discuss the process of writing as it applies to a research paper. The basic steps are these:

The Process of Writing a Research Paper

1. Choose and limit your subject.
2. Prepare a working bibliography.
3. Prepare a preliminary outline.
4. Read and take notes.
5. Organize your notes and write the final outline.
6. Write the first draft.
7. Revise the first draft.
8. Write the final draft with footnotes.
9. Write the final bibliography.

Part 1 Pre-Writing: Choosing Your Subject

Choosing the right subject is extremely important to the success of your paper. To start your thinking, you may wish to make a list of ten subjects that come to mind as possibilities for a research paper. Check your list against the following guidelines.

1. **Choose a subject that interests you.** Choose a subject that you want to learn more about. If your subject does not really interest you, your paper will probably not be interesting.

2. **Choose a subject for which a wide range of source materials is readily available.** Subjects that are too recent in development, or too technical in nature, will have few, if any, source materials. If you have doubts about source materials for a subject, consult your school librarian to find out how much information the library has. Also check the card file, vertical file, and *Readers' Guide to Periodical Literature*.

3. **Choose a subject of some significance.** A subject of lasting interest will be challenging and gratifying to pursue. After all, you will be spending much time and effort on this assignment, and what you learn should be a significant addition to your store of knowledge as well as that of the reader.

4. **Choose a subject that can be presented objectively.** Your purpose is to sift through and reshape an accumulated body of information. To achieve this, you must write your entire paper in the third person, avoiding the subjective use of *I*, *me*, or *my*. This does not mean that you cannot write a paper of argument or persuasion. You can. However, the challenge of research is to find and use the opinions of authorities.

5. **Avoid straight biography.** Biography requires long, intensive research involving letters, interviews, and unpublished material. If the person is well known, biographies already exist and using them as resource material results merely in a rehashing of already published information. If you do wish to write about some interesting figure, try to choose an unusual angle or unique viewpoint.

Limiting Your Subject

Limiting your subject is of vital importance in writing a good paper. A research paper will be approximately 2,000 words in length. Your subject must be limited so that the coverage of your subject can be thorough, yet handled in the space allotted. To limit your subject, do some general reading in an encyclopedia or other reference book. You may also want to scan the indexes or tables of contents of some books on the subject.

As you limit your subject, try to focus on the purpose of the paper as well. This will actually make the task of narrowing the topic much easier. A clear purpose will tell you what kind of paper you are writing, and may provide you with an interesting angle as well. In general, you will probably decide on one of the following three types of purposes:

1. To *inform* your audience about your topic
2. To *analyze* the topic
3. To *compare or contrast* your topic with another

EXAMPLE 1

Suppose you were interested in electronics. Limiting your paper might proceed in the following steps:

1. Electronics
2. History of electronics
3. The electronics industry

At this point, stop to consider whether your subject can be handled in a 2,000-word paper. Obviously, the electronics industry is far too large to be covered in that length, so you will have to narrow it further.

4. Home computers
5. Vacuum tube
6. Solid state device

If you examine the last two subjects, you will probably realize that your source material may be too limited to cover either of the subjects adequately. Whatever information you could find would tend to be repetitious and therefore frustrating. Subject number 4 might be exactly right. It has enough breadth for you to move around in, yet it is specific enough to concentrate on.

Now you must focus on your purpose, or what you want to say about the subject. If your purpose is to inform, you may simply want to tell your audience how a home computer works. If you want to analyze the topic, you might decide to write about whether home computers will have a positive or negative impact on the users. If you wonder what kinds of computers are most useful in the home, you could compare or contrast several types.

EXAMPLE 2

Here is another example of a subject for a research paper. Suppose you were interested in television. Limiting your subject might proceed like this:

1. Television
2. Television shows
3. Daytime television shows
4. Children's television shows

You have worked your way down to what seems to be a manageable subject: a special kind of show. However, the subject is still too general because there are countless ways in which to discuss children's shows. You need to focus on a particular aspect of children's shows that you feel will lend itself to a wide variety of source materials. You also want to clarify your purpose somewhat. You decide on the following subject:

The effects of television viewing on preschool children

Exercise Limiting Your Subject

Bring to class three possible subjects for a research paper. By doing some preliminary research, limit each one properly and be sure that each one can be adequately researched. You will probably have to work in the library to complete this assignment. It is a vital first step in your research paper.

Part 2 Pre-Writing: Making a Working Bibliography

When you have decided on your subject, in consultation with your teacher, your next step is to search for and collect your source material. While the *Readers' Guide to Periodical Literature* and specialized reference books will be your best sources, you should first read an article in a good encyclopedia for a general overview of your subject.

If you have limited your subject properly, you may not find an article on your specific subject. Look for a general article on the larger subject of which yours is a part. This overview of the whole subject may suggest related ideas that you will want to consider as your subject takes shape. It may also suggest a modification in your original subject. While a shift in idea is not serious at this point, consult your teacher for approval.

Recommended Sources

At this point, you may wish to review Chapter 14 so that you can use your library time wisely. The following sources are the most important for a research paper.

1. **The card catalog.** Suppose you are doing a paper on Wildlife Conservation. You would first look for any subject cards on wildlife. However, many books that may have informative chapters on conservation may not be entered. Look at "Animals," "Animal Conservation," "Animal Protection," "Wild Animals," "Wildlife Societies," "Zoos," and any other subjects that may seem related. The description of the book on the card will tell you if the book is worth investigating.

2. **The *Readers' Guide to Periodical Literature.*** This source will list current magazine articles on your subject. For most subjects, past articles may be as useful as present ones, and the library has cumulative bound volumes of past years.

3. **Specialized reference books.** In the reference section of your library you will find encyclopedias on general and on specific subjects. See whether any relate to your subject. They often suggest additional books that may be useful.

4. **Other sources.** Do not neglect interviews, television and radio shows, and graphic aids as possible sources of material. These often provide valuable information and unique insights on a subject.

In preparing a working bibliography, your objective is to accumulate as many books and articles as you think might be helpful to you in some way. Because you cannot always tell whether the information on a catalog card or in the *Readers' Guide* or in a bibliography will be helpful to you, it is wise to include sources you may be doubtful about at the moment. If some sources turn out to be of little help, you can later drop them from your bibliography.

Guidelines for Selecting Source Materials

The following guidelines will help you in selecting source materials.

1. **Is the author an authority on the subject?** While you may not know this at the beginning, an author who has written several books or whose name is included in various bibliographies may be an authority on the subject. As you read, be on the alert for writers whose opinions are mentioned or quoted.

2. **Is the author unbiased?** Try to decide whether the material in the source will be presented objectively. A book on a famous scientist, written by a friend or relative, may not be as accurate as one written by an authority on scientific thinking.

3. **Is the source up-to-date?** A book on the space age published in 1958 may not be as useful as one published in the last few years. A third edition of a book would be more valuable than the first or second edition. Recent material is especially important for topics on which research is still being done.

4. **If a magazine article looks promising, what kind of magazine did it appear in?** In general, popular interest magazines, such as those on the newsstand, are not suitable sources for a research paper.

5. **If a book looks promising, for what audience is it intended?** Many interesting books are actually intended for younger readers. The simplification of the material in them means they are not suitable for research papers. Books of a highly technical nature are usually not useful either. They are too detailed and too complex to be meaningful for the average reader.

6. **Are additional books or articles included in any of the bibliographies you have consulted?** In addition to the bibliographies in reference books, many of the books from the card catalog will contain their own bibliographies. When you find such a bibliography, examine the entries closely. If the same books or authors appear in various bibliographies, they are probably worth investigating.

Bibliography Cards

For each bibliography source, use a 3″ × 5″ card or slip of paper. Because you will be referring to each card time and again for specific information, be sure you fill out each card carefully and completely. Bibliography cards have three purposes.

1. To record all the information needed to find the reference in the library when you are ready to take notes from it
2. To record the information needed to prepare the footnotes for your paper
3. To record the information needed to prepare the final bibliography for your paper

Here are the correct forms of bibliography cards from three different kinds of sources: a book, a magazine article, and an encyclopedia article.

BOOK

Author — Mayer, Martin. — (1) — Source Number

Title — About Television.

Publishing Information — New York: Harper and Row, 1972.

Call Number — 338.5544 M 452 A

Public Library — Location

MAGAZINE ARTICLE

Author	Singer, J.L. and D.G. Singer. ②	Source Number
Title	"Come Back, Mr. Rogers, Come Back."	
Magazine, Volume, if any, Date, and Pages	Psychology Today, March 1979, pp. 56-60.	
	Public Library	Location

ENCYCLOPEDIA ARTICLE

Title	"Television." ③	Source Number
Reference	The World Book Encyclopedia.	
Date	1979 ed.	
Call Number	Ref. 0 31 En 7	
	School Library	Location

On these cards, note that the titles of books are underlined and the titles of articles are enclosed in quotation marks. Note also the correct abbreviations and punctuation.

Here is some additional information that will be helpful in preparing bibliography cards.

1. When you first locate a source, find the correct bibliography form for this source by checking the sample bibliography entries on pages 280–287. Then, write a bibliography card, making certain that you include all the information that you will need in your final bibliography entry.

2. If a book has an editor rather than an author, use *ed.* (editor) or *eds.* (editors) after the name: *Todd, William, ed.*
3. If no publication date is given, use the copyright date.
4. If neither publication nor copyright date is given, use the abbreviation *n.d.* (no date).
5. Information such as the above is usually found on the title page of a book, encyclopedia, or pamphlet. Sometimes pamphlets have the information on front or back covers or on the last page. Magazines may have the information on the front covers or on one of the first few pages.
6. The source number in the upper right-hand corner of your card is important because it will save you a great deal of time as you are writing the first draft of your paper. Instead of having to write out all the information on the bibliography card every time you credit the use of an idea or a quotation, you can merely jot down the number of the card to identify the source.

As you continue the work on your paper, you will understand the importance of including the complete bibliographical data for each source.

Exercise Preparing a Working Bibliography

Using all available facilities, prepare a working bibliography for your subject. Use 3″×5″ note cards to record your sources.

Determining the Controlling Purpose of Your Paper

You have chosen your subject, prepared your working bibliography, and done some background reading. You are now ready to formulate a controlling purpose for your paper—a formal, exact statement of what your paper is going to be about. You began this process when you limited your topic. Now, based on some of the initial reading you have done, you must refine your controlling purpose to the extent that it presents your purpose clearly. You can then use it to direct your notetaking, and to help you write a good outline and paper.

It is possible that as you continue your research you will want to revise your controlling purpose. Stating it as clearly as possible now, however, will help you select the right material for your note-taking. Material that does not relate directly to your controlling purpose does not belong in your paper or your notes.

You will recall that on page 250, the student interested in television decided to write a paper on the effects of television viewing on preschool children. While this statement may be suitable as a title, it is not sufficiently focused for a statement of controlling purpose. Clarifying the type of effects would help. The statement must also be recast into one that requires proof, such as the following:

> *Controlling Purpose:* to discuss the potentially harmful effects of television viewing on preschool children.

As you begin to write your report, you may want to include a revised version of this statement in your introductory paragraphs. Such a sentence is sometimes called a **thesis statement.**

Exercise Stating the Controlling Purpose

Write out the controlling purpose for your paper, stating it as exactly as you can at this point in your procedure.

Part 3 Pre-Writing: Preparing a Preliminary Outline

The clear statement of your controlling purpose and the nature of the resources in your stack of working bibliography cards will help you prepare a preliminary outline for your paper. (See Section 18 for more information on preparing an outline.) At this stage your outline will be only tentative and rough in form, but the major divisions and some subdivisions will suggest themselves. The first major topic will be devoted to your introduction and the last major topic to your conclusion, so at the present you need be concerned only with the topics in between.

This preliminary outline will function merely as a general guideline to your reading. As your reading progresses and you gain more information, you will revise and extend your outline accordingly. If you find that your source material does not contain enough information to develop a major topic sufficiently, you may have to delete that topic entirely and substitute one that is better covered. Your reading may also suggest an entirely new topic that you may want to develop. Make notes or revisions on your outline as you pursue your reading, so you have all the information in one place when you are ready to prepare your final outline.

Keep the statement of your controlling purpose before you at all times. This will enable you to judge the relevance of your material when preparing your preliminary outline and also when taking notes on your reading. If, as a result of your reading, you find that major topics need revising, you may need to revise your controlling purpose accordingly.

Here is an example of how a rough preliminary outline of the paper on children's television programs might look.

Television: What Is It Doing to Preschool Children?

Controlling Purpose: to discuss the potentially harmful effects of television viewing on preschool children.

I. (Introduction—to come)

II. Time spent
  A. Children
  B. Adults

III. Program quality
  A. Attention span
  B. Hypersensitivity
  C. Violence

IV. Reality and unreality
    A. Television
    B. Real world
    C. Parents' help

V. Commercials
    A. Children's market
    B. Exploitation
    C. Friction

VI. (Conclusion—to come)

Exercise Preparing a Preliminary Outline

Prepare a preliminary outline for your paper in form.

1. Put the title of your paper at the top.
2. Below the title, write your controlling purpose.
3. Follow standard outline form.
4. Keep the details of your outline to a minimum so you can revise and expand more easily as your reading progresses.

Part 4 Pre-Writing: Reading and Taking Notes

As you read and take notes, keep referring to your controlling purpose and your preliminary outline so you can keep a strong control over the direction of your paper. Take notes on 4″ × 6″ cards so they do not get mixed up with your 3″ × 5″ bibliography cards. Be sure to use a separate card for each note or for each set of related facts about one topic from the same source. Remember that the grouping of your cards under separate topics will be necessary when you write your final outline. If you have two different ideas on one card, you may need them in different places in your paper. Sorting out your cards would be almost impossible with both ideas on one card.

A Sample Note Card

Here is a sample note card showing proper position and spacing.

Guideline — TV Violence

(4) — Source Number

Note — Children tend to accept everything they see as real. "Studies indicate that children who have witnessed televised violence view the world as a more violent place."

page 1 — Page Reference

Here is an explanation of the parts of a sample note card.

1. **The guideline** is a heading that identifies the note on the card. It corresponds to a topic or subtopic on your preliminary outline. Include on the card only ideas pertaining to the guideline and use a different card for each source. If your reading does not yield enough information for your guideline, you may need to delete the topic and discard the corresponding note cards. If your reading yields new or different information, revise your outline and your guideline.

   As you work, you will probably keep cards with similar guidelines together. You may even try to put these cards in logical order. You may shift the order several times, but you will also be simplifying the task of organization that comes later.

2. **The source number** corresponds with the number of your working bibliography card and is the source from which the note was taken. By checking the card in the working bibliography, you can obtain all the information on the source whenever you need it.

3. **The page reference** must be exact for two reasons: (1) You may want to refer again to the source to verify the facts, and (2) you may need the page reference for footnotes.

4. **The note,** of course, is the most important part of the card because it is this part that you are going to use in writing your paper. Except for direct quotations, all notes should be paraphrased. (See Chapter 12 "Writing Paraphrases and Summaries.")

The purpose of paraphrasing is twofold. First, it helps you to take notes more quickly and efficiently. Second, it ensures that you avoid plagiarism.

Plagiarism

Because plagiarism is intellectually dishonest and therefore a form of stealing, it is an extremely serious offense and can result in severe penalties, even no credit for the course. The following forms of plagiarism are the most frequent:

1. **Failure to document with quotation marks any material copied directly from other sources**
2. **Failure to acknowledge paraphrased material (someone else's ideas)**
3. **Failure to provide a bibliography**
4. **Use of others' work as one's own, particularly in the creative arts**
5. **Use of others' ideas as one's own for themes, poems, musical compositions, or art work**

Improving Your Skill at Taking Notes

Here are some suggestions to improve your skill in taking notes.

1. Keep your topic, purpose, and audience in mind at all times. Do not bother recording material that is unrelated to your topic, that will not help you accomplish what you

want to in your paper, or that is too basic or too technical for your audience.

2. Be accurate. Double-check statistics and facts to make sure you have them right. When you summarize or paraphrase a writer's words, be sure you do not misinterpret or distort his meaning.
3. Distinguish between fact and opinion. (See Chapter 15, "Critical Thinking," for an in-depth discussion of fact and opinion.) Label opinions: "Dr. Graves thinks that . . ." or "According to Grace Jackson, . . ." Be careful to note differences in opinion and to point out such differences in your notes.
4. Take notes as quickly as possible. Omit all words or phrases not essential to meaning; use abbreviations. Be careful, however, not to take notes so brief that when you need to use them you cannot understand them.
5. Copy a direct quotation exactly, including punctuation, spelling, and grammar. Be sure to use quotation marks both at the beginning and at the end of the quotation so that you can easily separate the quotation from paraphrased material.
6. Any words inserted by the writer in the text of a quotation must be enclosed in brackets. (See Section 12.13 in your Handbook.) Parentheses must not be used. Insert brackets in ink if your typewriter does not have them.
7. Indicate the omissions of nonessential parts of a quotation by ellipses. (See Section 12.14 in your Handbook.)
8. If you cannot get all the information on one side of a card, write *over* in parentheses at the bottom of the card, flip the card over and continue on the back. If you have more than two lines, you probably have too much material for one card.

Exercise **Reading and Taking Notes**

Finish your reading and complete your note cards. Adjust or revise your preliminary outline as you do your research, and make any final revisions of your controlling purpose.

Part 5 Pre-Writing: Organizing Your Material

A research paper is longer and more complex than a short composition and your outline will be the same. Remember, however, that much of your work has already been done. The guidelines on your note cards reflect the divisions and subdivisions of your outline, which you have been modifying as you did research. You will now organize these note cards so that you can write your first draft by referring to them.

Put each note card with the same guideline into a separate pile. You may already have begun this process during your research. Each of these piles of cards should relate to one of the major or minor divisions of your preliminary outline. Study these piles of cards to see what information each contains. Also determine the extent to which the information conforms to the information on your preliminary outline. Refer to your controlling purpose often as you study your cards.

Gradually, some groups of ideas will emerge as major divisions of your subject, some as subdivisions and others as sub-subdivisions. (This part of the organization process is exactly the same as in shorter compositions, except that you are dealing with more material.) If some cards reveal insufficient material on a subdivision but you feel that the subdivision is important, you may have to do more reading. If the subdivision is not important, you can either combine it with another subdivision or delete the information and the card entirely.

This is the point at which you decide exactly what you are going to include in your paper and what you are going to leave out. Keep checking your controlling purpose to see that all your usable material is relevant to your subject. Do not be afraid to delete information that is not relevant. The decisions you make at this point will be reflected in your paper.

Finally, when you have chosen your main topics and subtopics and tested each note card for relevance to your controlling purpose, begin to organize the topics for your final outline. Try to decide in what order your topics would move most logically toward the conclusion you have determined in your controlling purpose. Feel free to move an entire main topic from one place to another or to shift the note cards within a group to different positions. See Chapters 7 and 8 for a review of possible types of organizations.

Write down your main topics in various orders and study them, thinking about how logically you can make transitions between topics. If a transition from one topic to another seems forced, something is probably wrong. Either you need to rearrange your topics or you need to revise the emphasis or the direction of one of them.

When you are finally satisfied with the order of your material, test it once more against your controlling purpose in the following ways:

1. Does it begin at the beginning and move logically to the conclusion?
2. Are the main topics the most important ideas?
3. Do the subtopics relate specifically to the main topics?
4. Is there unnecessary duplication of topics or subtopics?
5. Do all main topics relate clearly to the controlling purpose?
6. Will the transition from one topic to the next be logical?
7. Will the conclusion correspond to the controlling purpose?
8. Is there too much information on any one idea that upsets the balance of the paper?
9. Is enough information included to develop each idea?

When you are satisfied with the answers to these questions, you are ready to write your final outline. Include all of the major groupings and subgroupings in the order you have devised. If you have any doubts about standard outline form, see Section 18 in the Handbook. Remember that a good outline is not necessarily a long, elaborate one. Try to keep it within reasonable bounds.

Exercise Organizing Notes and Writing the Final Outline

Organize your note cards and write your final outline.

Part 6 Writing the First Draft

At this point you have the title of your paper, the statement of your controlling purpose, your final outline, and your note cards sorted to fit your outline. With all these in front of you, you are ready to write your first draft. This is the time to get all your information on paper as fully and freely as you can. Do not worry about style and form or the mechanics of punctuation. Your main purpose is to get all your ideas down in a form that you will be able to follow when you are ready to revise and polish your paper.

Follow your outline and keep your controlling purpose in mind. Begin a new paragraph for every topic and subtopic on your outline. Make some attempt at paragraph transitions, although you can work these out more carefully later.

Write your entire paper in the third person. Never use *I*, *me*, or *my* because you will be in danger of injecting your own opinion. The only opinions you should use to prove your argument are those of authorities. These opinions, as was mentioned earlier, should be attributed to the experts either directly or through a footnote. Use the information on your note cards as you write, and be sure to follow this information with the source number from the upper right-hand corner of your note card. You will need these sources for your footnotes. To save time, you can write only the first few words of a direct quotation in your rough draft. The source number will help you locate the quotations very quickly when you need to copy it carefully and completely on your final draft.

Stay alert to the possibility of using maps, charts, diagrams, and other graphic aids as a concise way to present some of your information. You can reproduce a graphic aid from one of your sources, or you can create one of your own. Just be certain to credit the source of the material.

As you write, keep in mind that the first paragraph of your paper should be your introduction and should set forth your controlling purpose. Your final paragraph should round up all your ideas in a restatement of your controlling purpose.

Exercise Writing the First Draft

With your controlling purpose and your outline before you, write the first draft of your paper. Use the information from your note cards as you write.

Part 7 Revising the First Draft and Adding Footnotes

Before writing your final draft, you may wish to review the section on Revising on pages 117-118 in Chapter 7, "The Process of Writing." Also review the recommendations for manuscript form in Section 17 of your Handbook. Because you have spent so much time and effort thus far, you will want to do your best job on revising and polishing your paper.

Long Quotations

As you write your final draft, you will be including the complete form of the direct quotations you are using. If direct quotations are more than three typed lines long, indent them five spaces from both the left and the right margins. Single space each line and do not use quotation marks. If the quotation is the beginning of a paragraph in the source, indent the first word an additional two spaces.

Footnotes

Uses

1. To indicate the source of material that is directly quoted
2. To give credit for other people's ideas even though you write them in your own words
3. To give the source of graphic aids, figures, or statistics that are referred to

Numbering

Number footnotes consecutively throughout the paper, beginning with number 1. Use Arabic numerals placed slightly above the material to be footnoted, usually after the last word of a sentence or a direct quotation. For example:

Most children will have watched 20,000 hours of television and seen 350,000 commercials while growing up.[1]

Position

Footnotes may appear in a paper in one of two ways: at the bottom of each page or on a separate page at the end. The actual form of each is the same.

If footnotes are to appear on each page, you must be careful to allow enough room at the bottom of each page for all the footnotes on that page. This will also include a one-inch margin of blank space at the bottom of each page.

When you have typed the last line of text on a page, skip a line. Then type a line that extends across the page, from the left margin to the right. Skip another space, and then type your first footnote. The bottom of your page will look like this:

When children get their life experiences through television, they lose the ability to learn from actual experience, which is much more complicated. Besides, in real life, nobody comes in at the end to explain it all.[1]

---

[1]Martin Mayer, About Television (New York: Harper and Row, 1972), p. 128.

Form

1. Number each footnote with an Arabic numeral to correspond to the material in the text (See above).

2. Indent each footnote five spaces, just as you do for paragraphs. Observe the text margin at the right. If the footnote runs to a second or third line, bring those lines back to the left margin.
3. Single space each footnote, but double space between footnotes.
4. Place a period at the end of each footnote.

The following guidelines will provide you with all of the information you need to write footnotes of your own. As you study the models, keep in mind that underscores are used to identify books, magazines, and other longer works. Quotation marks are used for chapters, stories, and similar shorter pieces. (See Section 14 in the Handbook.)

Parenthetical Documentation of Sources

The 1984 edition of the *MLA Handbook for Writers of Research Papers* suggests a simplified method for citing sources. When using this method, known as **parenthetical documentation,** list the author's name and the page number of the source in parentheses after the paraphrased or quoted material.

> Most children will have watched 20,000 hours of television and seen 350,000 commercials while growing up (Mayer 128).

At the end of the paper, include a list of "Works Cited" containing complete bibliography entries for all the sources you have referred to (See Part 8 of this chapter).

Basic Forms for Footnotes

Whole Books

A. One author:

[1]Marion Meade, Eleanor of Aquitaine: A Biography (New York: E.P. Dutton, 1980), p. 54.

B. Two authors:

[2]Alice Marriott and Carol K. Rachlin, American Indian Mythology (New York: New American Library, 1972), p. 27.

C. Three authors:

[3]Bertram L. Linder, Edwin Selzer, and Barry M. Berk, A World History: The Human Panorama (Chicago: Science Research Associates, 1983), pp. 276–77.

D. Four or more authors:

[4]Rodney F. Allen and others, Deciding How to Live on Spaceship Earth, Values Education Series (Evanston, Ill.: McDougal, Littell, 1978), p. 46.

Instead of the words *and others*, you may use the Latin abbreviation *et al.*

E. No author given:

[5]Literary Market Place: The Directory of American Book Publishing, 1984 ed. (New York: R.R. Bowker, 1984), p. 76.

F. An editor, but no single author:

[6]James Woodress, ed., American Literary Scholarship, 1981 (Durham, N.C.: Duke University Press, 1981), p. 10.

Basic Forms for Footnotes

G. Two or three editors:

[7]Jane Sherrod and Kurt Singer, eds., Folk Tales of Mexico (Minneapolis, Minn.: T.S. Dennison, n.d.), p. 142.

[8]Francis Lee Utley, Lynn Z. Bloom, and Arthur F. Kinney, eds., Bear, Man, and God: Eight Approaches to Faulkner's "The Bear" (New York: Random House, 1971), p. 117.

H. Four or more editors:

[9]Norris McWhirter and others, eds., Guinness 1983 Book of World Records, (Toronto: Bantam Books, 1983), p. 37.

Instead of the words *and others,* you may use the Latin abbreviation *et al.*

I. A translator:

[10]Ovid, Metamorphoses, trans. Rolfe Humphries (Bloomington: Indiana University Press, 1973), pp. 279-80.

J. Author, editor, and translator:

[11]Jorge L. Borges, Introduction to American Literature, trans. Robert O. Evans and L. Clark Keating, ed. Robert O. Evans and L. Clark Keating (Lexington: University Press of Kentucky, 1971), p. 102.

K. A particular edition of a book:

[12]Laurence Perrine, Sound and Sense: An Introduction to Poetry, 6th ed. (New York: Harcourt Brace Jovanovich, 1982), p. 40.

Basic Forms for Footnotes

L. A book or monograph that is part of a series:

[13]Marion Kesselring, Hawthorne's Readings, Studies in Hawthorne, Vol. 15 (New York: Haskell House, 1975), p. 22.

M. A particular volume of a multi-volume book:

[14]David Daiches, A Critical History of English Literature, 2nd ed. (New York: Ronald, 1970), II, 776–77.

N. A volume with its own title that is part of a work of several volumes under a different title:

[15]Winston S. Churchill, The New World, Vol. II of A History of the English-Speaking Peoples (New York: Dodd, Mead, 1983), pp. 131–32.

Parts Within Books

A. A poem, short story, essay, or chapter from a collection of works by one author:

[16]Gilbert Highet, ''How to Torture an Author,'' Explorations (New York: Oxford Univ. Press, 1971), pp. 270–71.

When the name of the author of the work appears in the title of the collection, you may omit the first mention of the author's name:

[17]''Song for a Summer's Day,'' Sylvia Plath: The Collected Poems, ed. Ted Hughes (New York: Harper and Row, 1981), pp. 30–31.

B. A poem, short story, essay, or chapter from a collection of works by several authors:

[18]Anne Bradstreet, ''Upon the Burning of Our House, July 10th, 1666,'' in McDougal, Littell Literature: Yellow Level, ed. Donald T. Hollenbeck and Julie West Johnson (Evanston, Ill.: McDougal, Littell, 1984), p. 34.

C. A novel or play from a collection of novels or plays published under one cover:

[19]Ruth Wolff, The Abdication, in The New Women's Theatre: Ten Plays by Contemporary American Women, ed. Honor Moore (New York: Random House, 1977), p. 437.

D. An introduction, preface, foreword, or afterword written by the author of a work:

[20]Ray Bradbury, Introduction, The Wonderful Ice Cream Suit and Other Plays (New York: Bantam Books, 1972), p. vii.

E. An introduction, preface, foreword, or afterword written by someone other than the author of a work:

[21]W. H. Auden, Introduction, The Star Thrower, by Loren Eiseley (New York: Harcourt Brace Jovanovich, 1978), pp. 16–17.

Magazines, Encyclopedias, Reports, Pamphlets, Newspapers

A. An article from a quarterly or monthly magazine:

[22]Donna Haupt, ''Nature Under Siege,'' Life, July 1983, p. 106.

Basic Forms for Footnotes

B. An article from a weekly magazine:

[23]John Underwood, ''Gone with the Wins,'' Sports Illustrated, 24 Oct. 1983, p.42.

C. A magazine article with no author given:

[24]''Bearish on the Grizzlies,'' Time, 6 June 1983, p. 63.

D. An article from a daily newspaper:

[25]Kevin Anderson, ''Home Computers: Who's on Top?'' USA Today, 26 July 1983, Sec. B, p. 1, col. 2.

If no author is given, begin with the title. If the paper is not divided into sections, omit section information.

E. An editorial in a newspaper:

[26]''For a Tough Ethics Law,'' Editorial, Chicago Sun-Times, 29 April 1984, Views, p. 3, cols. 1-2.

F. An article in a journal that has continuous page numbers throughout the annual volume:

[27]Robert Halpern, ''Early Childhood Programs in Latin America,'' Harvard Educational Review, 50 (1980), 484.

The volume number, the date, and the page number follow the title of the journal.

G. An article in a journal that numbers the pages of each issue separately:

[28]Febe Portillo Orozco, ''A Bibliography of Hispanic Literature,'' The English Journal, 71, No. 7 (1982), 58-59.

The volume number, the number of the issue, the date, and the page number follow the title of the journal.

H. An encyclopedia article;

[29]''Industrial Revolution,'' The World Book Encyclopedia, 1983 ed.

I. A signed review:

[30]Paul Gray, ''Telling the Birth of a Nation,'' rev. of France and England in North America, by Francis Parkman, Time, 25 July 1983, p. 70.

J. An unsigned, untitled review:

[31]Rev. of Harry and Son, dir. Paul Newman, American Film, March 1984, p. 78.

K. A report or a pamphlet:

[32]American Medical Association, Medical Relations Under Workmen's Compensation (Chicago: American Medical Association, 1976), p. 3.

Other Sources

A. An interview:

[33]Personal interview with Robert Hughes, Director, New Playwright's Workshop, University of Washington, Bellingham, Washington, 6 Feb. 1984.

B. A letter that has not been published:

[34]Letter from Hon. Jimmy Carter, President of the United States, Washington, D.C., 22 May 1977.

C. Information in private files:

[35]Guidelines For Experimental Theatre, by Maurice Dixon and members of The Theatre Company at Purdue University Calumet, Hammond, Indiana, 26 Oct. 1983 (in the Files of the Department of Communication and Creative Arts).

D. A thesis or dissertation:

[36]H.L. Reynolds, The Number of Commas in Early Renaissance Poetry, (unpublished Ph.D. dissertation, Department of English, University of Chicago), p. 78.

E. A quotation:

[37]Richard Ellmann, as quoted in Harold Bloom, Yeats (London: Oxford University Press, 1970), p. 128.

F. A film:

[38]Richard Attenborough, dir., Gandhi, with Ben Kingsley, Columbia Pictures, 1982.

G. A work of art:

[39]Pablo Picasso, Guernica, Museum of Modern Art, New York.

H. A television or radio program:

[40]''A Desert Blooming,'' writ. Marshall Riggan, Living Wild, dir. Harry L. Gorden, prod. Peter Argentine, PBS, 29 April 1984.

I. A musical composition:

[41]Tchaikovsky, Symphony No. 5 in E minor, op. 64.

Subsequent Reference Footnotes

To refer to sources already cited in previous complete footnotes, use a shortened form.

A. In most cases, the author's last name, followed by the relevant page numbers, is sufficient.

[42]Rosemary Agonito, History of Ideas on Woman: A Source Book (New York: G.P. Putnam's Sons, 1977), p. 23.

[43]Agonito, p. 74.

B. If references by other authors with the same last name are used, you will also have to include the author's first name or initials.

[44]Tennessee Williams, ''This Property Is Condemned,'' Twenty-Seven Wagons Full of Cotton (New York: New Directions, 1966), p. 197.

[45]Selma R. Williams, Demeter's Daughters: The Women Who Founded America (New York: Atheneum, 1976), p. 12.

[46]Tennessee Williams, p. 199.

C. If more than one work by the same author has been referred to, then you should write the author's last name and the title. The title may be in shortened form.

[47]John C. Gardner, Grendel (New York: Alfred A. Knopf, 1971), p. 24.

[48]John C. Gardner, Dragon, Dragon and Other Timeless Tales (New York: Alfred A. Knopf, 1975), p. 6.

[49]Gardner, Dragon, Dragon, p. 91.

Reference Words and Abbreviations Used in Footnotes

Here are some of the more common reference words and abbreviations used in footnotes. Some of these words and abbreviations are no longer used in writing footnotes and bibliography entries, but are provided here for reference.

bk., bks.	book or books
ca. (or *c.*)	circa, "about" or "near." Used with approximate dates: *ca.* 1776; "*ca.*" is preferable to "*c.*," which can also mean "chapter" or "copyright."
cf.	*confer*, "compare." Used, for example, when you wish to have your reader compare footnotes 22 and 23, which follow: *cf.* footnotes 22 and 23 or *cf.* Ernest Hemingway, *The Sun Also Rises*, p. 15.
c., ch., chs., (or chap., chaps.)	chapter(s)
col., cols.	column(s)
comp.	compiles or compiler
ed., eds.	editor(s), edition(s)
e.g.	*exempli gratia*, "for example"
esp.	especially (as in "pp. 208–232, esp. p. 220")
et al.	*et alii*, "and others"
et seq.	*et sequens* and *et sequentes*, "and the one following," "and those that follow." But cf. "f.," "ff."
ex., exs.	example and examples
f., ff.	and the following page(s) or line(s). These abbreviations are replacing *et. seq*.

fig., figs.	figure(s)
fn.	footnote (Cf. "n.")
ibid.	*ibidem,* "in the same place"; i.e., the single title cited in the note immediately preceding.
idem	(no period; sometimes *id.*) "the same." Used in place of *ibid.* when the footnote is to the same source on exactly the same page as that referred to in the note immediately preceding.
i.e.	*id est,* "that is"
illus.	illustrated, illustrator, illustration(s)
l., ll.	line, lines
ms.	manuscript
mss.	manuscripts
n. or nn.	note or notes (as "p. 48, n. 2")
n.b., N.B.	nota bene, "note well"
n.d.	no date
no., nos.	number(s)
op. cit.	*opere citato,* "in the work cited." If several different items have come between the first mention of a book and a subsequent reference to it in a footnote, the last name of the author is repeated, followed by *op. cit.* and the page number.
p. or pp.	page(s)
par., pars.	paragraph(s)
passim	"throughout the work, here and there" (as pp. 79, 144, *et passim*)
pref.	preface
pseud.	pseudonym, a pen name: e.g., Mark Twain, pseud.

rev.	review, reviewed; revised, revision
sec. (or sect.), secs.	section(s)
ser.	series
sic	"thus, so". If the word "*sic*" in brackets [*sic*] is inserted in a quotation, it shows that you are recognizing and pointing out an error or a questionable statement. For example: "There were nine [*sic*] men on the bench at that time." Your own additions to quotations are shown by bracketing those words added: "He [Wouk] was a member of the New York Writers' Club."
st.	stanza
trans. (or tr.)	translator, translation, translated by
vol., vols.	volume(s)
vs.	*versus*, "against"; also verse

Exercise Writing the Final Draft with Footnotes

Write the final draft of your paper with the footnotes. Leave a three-inch margin at the top of your first page and number each page beginning with page two. Check the following:

1. Does your introductory paragraph engage the reader? Is it well developed? Does it state the controlling purpose?
2. Does your paper follow your outline exactly? Is it well paragraphed? Do your ideas flow logically?
3. Are your paragraph transitions natural and logical?
4. Does your conclusion sum up your ideas and restate your purpose? Is it a logical result of what you set out to prove?
5. Have you numbered all the ideas and direct quotations in the text and footnoted them correctly?
6. Have you tested the force and accuracy of specific words? Do you have interesting sentence variety?
7. Have you checked spelling, punctuation, and usage?

Part 8 Writing the Final Bibliography

Most research papers have at the end a bibliography, a list of references actually used in writing the paper. (Sources listed on your bibliography cards that were consulted but not referred to in the paper are not listed.) This bibliography serves two purposes: (1) it shows what research was done; (2) it provides a list of references for those who may be especially interested in your topic and wish to investigate it further.

General Guidelines

1. Arrange all bibliography entries alphabetically by the last name of the author or editor.
2. If you wish to do so, you may divide your bibliography into separate sections for books, magazines, and other sources. If this is done, each section should be alphabetized separately and should begin with a centered subheading reading, in upper and lower case letters, *Books, Magazines,* or *Other Sources*.
3. If no author or editor is given, alphabetize each entry by the first word of the title. If the first word of the title is *A, An,* or *The,* begin with the second word of the title.
4. Begin the first line of each entry at the left margin. If the entry runs to a second or third line, indent those lines five spaces.
5. Single space each bibliography entry, but double space between entries.
6. Place a period at the end of each entry.
7. Bibliography entries contain page numbers only when they refer to parts within whole works. For example, an entry for a chapter in a book or an article in a magazine should contain page numbers for the complete chapter or article.

The following pages show correct bibliography form for various types of entries.

Basic Forms for Bibliography Entries

Whole Books

A. One author:

Meade, Marion. Eleanor of Aquitaine: A Biography. New York: E.P. Dutton, 1980.

B. Two authors:

Marriott, Alice, and Carol K. Rachlin. American Indian Mythology. New York: New American Library, 1972.

C. Three authors:

Linder, Bertram L., Edwin Selzer, and Barry M. Berk. A World History: The Human Panorama. Chicago: Science Research Associates, 1983.

D. Four or more authors:

Allen, Rodney F., and others. Deciding How to Live on Spaceship Earth. Values Education Series. Evanston, Ill.: McDougal, Littell, 1978.

E. No author given:

Literary Market Place: The Directory of American Book Publishing. 1984 ed. New York: R.R. Bowker, 1984.

F. An editor, but no single author:

Woodress, James, ed. American Literary Scholarship, 1981. American Literary Scholarship Series. Durham, N.C.: Duke University Press, 1981.

This form may be used when you have cited several works from a collection.

G. Two or three editors:

Sherrod, Jane, and Kurt Singer, eds. Folk Tales of Mexico. Minneapolis, Minn.: T.S. Dennison, n.d.

Utley, Francis Lee, Lynn Z. Bloom, and Arthur F. Kinney, eds. Bear, Man, and God: Eight Approaches to Faulkner's ''The Bear.'' New York: Random House, 1971.

H. Four or more editors:

McWhirter, Norris, and others, eds. Guinness 1983 Book of World Records. Toronto: Bantam Books, 1983.

Instead of the words *and others*, you may use the Latin abbreviation *et al.*

I. A translator:

Ovid. Metamorphoses. Trans. Rolfe Humphries. Bloomington: Indiana University Press, 1973.

J. Author, editor, and translator:

Borges, Jorge L. Introduction to American Literature. Trans. Robert O. Evans and L. Clark Keating. Ed. Robert O. Evans and L. Clark Keating. Lexington: University Press of Kentucky, 1971.

K. A particular edition of a book:

Perrine, Lawrence. Sound and Sense: An Introduction to Poetry. 6th ed. New York: Harcourt Brace Jovanovich, 1982.

L. A book or monograph that is part of a series:

Kesselring, Marion. Hawthorne's Readings. Studies in Hawthorne, Vol. 15. New York: Haskell House, 1975.

M. A particular volume of a multi-volume book:

Daiches, David. A Critical History of English Literature. 2nd ed. New York: Ronald, 1970.

Note that the bibliography entry is for the entire work.

N. A volume with its own title that is part of a work of several volumes under a different title:

Churchill, Winston S. The New World. Vol. II of A History of the English-Speaking Peoples. New York: Dodd, Mead, 1983.

Parts Within Books

A. A poem, short story, essay, or chapter from a collection of works by one author:

Highet, Gilbert, ''How to Torture an Author.'' Explorations. New York: Oxford University Press, 1971, pp. 267-73.

When the name of the author appears in the title of the collection, you may omit the first mention of the author's name. Alphabetize the entry by the title, ignoring A, An, or The.

''Song for a Summer's Day.'' Sylvia Plath: The Collected Poems. Ed. Ted Hughes. New York: Harper and Row, 1981, pp. 30-31.

B. A poem, short story, essay or chapter from a collection of works by several authors:

Bradstreet, Anne. ''Upon the Burning of Our House, July 10th, 1666.'' In McDougal, Littell Literature: Yellow Level. Ed. Donald T. Hollenbeck and Julie West Johnson. Evanston, Ill.: McDougal, Littell, 1984, p. 34.

C. A novel or play from a collection of novels or plays published under one cover:

Wolff, Ruth. The Abdication. In The New Women's Theatre: Ten Plays by Contemporary American Women. Ed. Honor Moore. New York: Random House, 1977, pp. 339–454.

The Moon is Down. In The Short Novels of John Steinbeck. New York: The Viking Press, 1963, pp. 273–354.

D. An introduction, preface, foreword, or afterword written by the author of a work:

Bradbury, Ray. Introduction. The Wonderful Ice Cream Suit and Other Plays. New York: Bantam Books, 1972, pp. vi–xiv.

E. An introduction, preface, foreword, or afterword written by someone other than the author of a work:

Auden, W.H. Introduction. The Star Thrower. By Loren Eiseley. New York: Harcourt Brace Jovanovich, 1978, pp. 15–24.

Basic Forms of Bibliography Entries

Magazines, Encyclopedias, Reports, Pamphlets, and Newspapers

A. An article from a quarterly or monthly magazine:

Haupt, Donna. "Nature Under Siege." Life, July 1983, pp. 106–11.

B. An article from a weekly magazine:

Underwood, John. "Gone with the Wins." Sports Illustrated, 24 Oct. 1983, pp. 42–49.

C. A magazine article with no author given:

"Bearish on the Grizzlies." Time, 6 June 1983, p. 63.

D. An article from a daily newspaper:

Anderson, Kevin. "Home Computers: Who's on Top?" USA Today, 26 July 1983, Sec. A, p. 1, col. 2.

If no author is given, begin with the title. If the paper is not divided into sections, omit section information.

E. An editorial in a newspaper:

"For a Tough Ethics Law." Editorial. Chicago Sun-Times, 29 April 1984, Views, p. 3, cols. 1–2.

F. An article in a journal that has continuous page numbers throughout the annual volume:

Halpern, Robert. "Early Childhood Programs in Latin America." Harvard Educational Review, 50 (1980), 481–95.

The volume number, the date, and the page numbers follow the title of the journal.

Basic Forms of Bibliography Entries

G. An article in a journal that numbers the pages of each issue separately:

Orozco, Febe Portillo. "A Bibliography of Hispanic Literature." <u>The English Journal</u>, 71, No. 7 (1982), 58–59.

The volume number, the number of the issue, the date, and the page numbers follow the title of the journal.

H. An encyclopedia article:

"Industrial Revolution." <u>The World Book Encyclopedia</u>. 1983 ed.

I. A signed review:

Gray, Paul. "Telling the Birth of a Nation." Rev. of <u>France and England in North America</u>, by Francis Parkman. <u>Time</u>, 25 July 1983, p. 70.

J. An unsigned, untitled review:

Rev. of <u>Harry and Son</u>, dir. Paul Newman. <u>American Film</u>, March 1984, p. 78.

If the review is unsigned but has a title, use the form for a signed review, but delete the author's name.

K. A report or a pamphlet:

American Medical Association. <u>Medical Relations under Workmen's Compensation</u>. Chicago: American Medical Association, 1976.

If the report is by an individual author rather than by an association or committee, begin with the author's name.

Other Sources

A. An interview:

Hughes, Robert. Director, New Playwright's Workshop, University of Washington. Personal interview. Bellingham, Washington. 6 Feb. 1984.

B. A letter that has not been published:

Letter from Hon. Jimmy Carter, President of the United States, Washington, D.C., 22 May 1977.

C. Information in private files:

Guidelines for Experimental Theatre. Maurice Dixon and members of the Theatre Company at Purdue University Calumet. Hammond, Indiana. 26 Oct. 1983. In the files of the Department of Communication and Creative Arts.

D. A thesis or dissertation:

Reynolds, H.L. "The Number of Commas in Early Renaissance Poetry." Unpublished Ph.D. dissertation, Department of English, University of Chicago.

E. A quotation (See page 274, item E):

Bloom, Harold. Yeats. London: Oxford University Press, 1970.

F. A film:

Attenborough, Richard, dir. Gandhi. With Ben Kingsley. Columbia Pictures, 1982.

Basic Forms of Bibliography Entries

G. A work of art:

Picasso, Pablo. Guernica. Museum of Modern Art, New York.

H. A television or radio program:

"A Desert Blooming." Writ. Marshall Riggan. Living Wild. Dir. Harry L. Gorden. Prod. Peter Argentine. PBS, 29 April 1984.

I. A musical composition:

Tchaikovsky. Symphony No. 5 in E minor, op. 64.

Exercise Writing the Final Bibliography

Following the correct form of your entries, prepare your final bibliography. Assemble your research paper in the following order:

1. Title page in form your teacher requires
2. Page containing title at top, statement of controlling purpose beneath it, followed by your final outline
3. The text of your paper
4. The final bibliography

TELEVISION:
WHAT IS IT DOING
TO PRESCHOOL CHILDREN?

by

Loriann Moravec

[The following is a high school student's complete research paper. Use it as a model for preparing your own paper.]

3 English
Ms. Gibson
March 15

Television: What Is It Doing to Preschool Children?

Controlling Purpose: to discuss the potentially harmful effects of television viewing on preschool children.

I. Television Viewing
   A. Experience
   B. Factors
II. Time spent in watching television
   A. Preschool children
   B. Adults
III. Poor Quality of Programs
   A. Shortens attention span
   B. Leads to hyperactivity
   C. Encourages violence
IV. Reality versus fantasy
   A. Television as real world
   B. Real-life experience
   C. Role of parents
V. Advertising
   A. Specialized market
   B. Exploitation of children
   C. Family friction
VI. Concern for improvement
   A. Education
   B. Action for Children's Television (ACT)

> No sane parent would present a child with a fire engine, snatch it away in thirty seconds, replace it with a set of blocks, snatch that away thirty seconds later, replace the blocks with clay, and then replace the clay with a toy car. Yet, in effect, a young child receives that kind of experience when he or she watches television.[1]

Television in America greatly affects the lives of preschoolers today, and these effects are determined by many different factors. The most significant factors are the amount of time spent in watching television, the poor quality of the children's television programs, the inability of preschool children to understand what they see, and the exploitation of the children's market by the advertisers. Because television occupies almost all young children's lives, these factors are of increasing concern.

Statistics vary in the time that preschool children spend in watching television. One survey has shown that the average preschool child in the United States spends four to six hours a day watching television. By the time this child is in college, he or she will have spent more time in front of a television set than in school, in church, or in conversation or play with parents.[2] Other nationwide studies have shown that preschool children average three and one-half hours a day watching television. This three and one-half hours is a major part of their

---

[1]J.L. Singer and D.G. Singer, "Come Back, Mister Rogers, Come Back," Psychology Today, March 1979, p. 56.

[2]K. Mason, "Revamping Saturday Morning Children's Television," Vital Speeches, 15 Jan. 1979, p. 205.

waking hours.[3] Most children will have watched 20,000 hours of television and seen 350,000 commercials while growing up.[4]

In view of the time spent in watching television, the quality of the programs can be a determining factor in their effect on a child. American television puts emphasis on extremely short action sequences, frequent interruptions, and drastic changes in the visual field. "It's actually creating a psychological orientation in children that leads to a shortened attention span, a lack of reflectiveness, and an expectation of rapid change in the broader environment."[5] The rapid-fire tempo of television programs like "Sesame Street" shortens the attention span of young children and inhibits their ability to understand and keep new information.[6] This type of motion can have an even more serious effect on some children. The back-and-forth action, the fast movement without purpose, is a major cause of hyperactivity. After the television set is turned off, the physical energy created by the images comes bursting outward. After quietly watching television, children tend to become overactive, irritable, and frustrated.[7] It would help if producers of children's shows provided children with longer

---

[3]Robert M. Liebert et al., The Early Window: Effects of Television on Children and Youth (New York: Pergamon Press, 1973), p. 9.

[4]Personal interview with Maurice Dixon, Associate Professor of Communication and Creative Arts, Purdue University Calumet, Hammond, Indiana, 6 Oct. 1983.

[5]Singer, p. 56.

[6]Singer, p. 56.

[7]Jerry Mander, Four Arguments for the Elimination of Television (New York: William Morrow and Co., 1978), p. 167.

sequences, slower pacing, and more personal communication.[8]

Another kind of problem with quality is the cartoons, which take up much of preschool children's viewing time. Many cartoons are filled with senseless violence. Children are bombarded with hitting, chasing, blowing up, and other forms of painful torture.[9] This kind of television experience can lead to violent activity on the part of the child, usually containing the content of the program.[10] Research studies have shown that after children have viewed acts of violence on television, they are stimulated to imitate aggressive behavior.[11] Children are too young to understand violence on television. When people are hurt, they appear to recover very quickly. This rapid recovery gives children the impression that people are not easily hurt by a punch, a shove, a thrown brick, or a bullet wound. Children seeing these acts of violence do not realize that they really do hurt. They think that violence is the way to solve problems.[12] The reality of television to preschoolers is transferred to real life.

Before the age of five, a young child's sense of time, distance, space, and language is undeveloped; this is also true of

---

[8]Singer, p. 59.

[9]Marilyn C. Blossom, "Children and Television: Part I," Home Economics Guide, September 1972, p. 2.

[10]Mander, p. 4.

[11]Lynette Kohn Friedrich and Aletha Huston Stein, Aggressive and Prosocial Television Programs and the Natural Behavior of Preschool Children, Monographs of the Society for Research in Child Development (Chicago: University of Chicago Press, 1973), p. 56.

[12]Liebert, p. 1.

he ability to distinguish reality from fantasy.[13] Young children pproach the world literally; they believe what they see. They annot understand that something can be "unreal." They find it ifficult to understand that actors or actresses play the parts f people, and that they are not "real" people. Children see the dults on television as models of behavior. They watch a human eing perform powerful feats, and they expect themselves to be ble to do the same things.[14] What they see on television can asily develop an uncritical and unrealistic view of the world.[15]

Unfortunately, television is becoming more and more a child's irst exposure to real-life experience. The more limited the hild's actual real-life experience, the more likely the child rusts what he or she sees on television. Children who watch elevision constantly are affected in their intellectual development because they have little or no time for participating in ctual life.[16] Talking, going places, doing things, and relating o others are real-life experiences that are critical for young hildren. When children spend thirty-five hours per week in ront of television, it is impossible for them to get the full ange of real-life experience that they must have.[17]

Human beings undergo their greatest emotional development

---

[13] Lillian Ambrosino, "Do Children Believe TV?" Children Today, Nov.-Dec. 1972, p. 19.

[14] Liebert, p. 1.

[15] Grant Noble, Children in Front of the Small Screen London: Constable, 1975), p. 69.

[16] Noble, pp. 65-66.

[17] Mander, p. 265.

during the age of three or four, and the only way to develop emotionally is through actual experience. This development does not occur by watching television.[18] When children get their life experiences through television, they lose the ability to learn from actual experience, which is much more complicated. In real life, nobody comes in at the end to explain it all.[19] "Children need time with parents or other 'live' care-givers who talk with them, listen to what they say, and encourage their imaginative development by telling stories, singing songs, or playing pretend games."[20]

Too often parents rely on television as a babysitter for their children. They do not engage their children in conversation about the programs they watch. Children need someone there to answer their questions, to explain, and to put things into perspective for them.[21] "To the many tasks of parents and teachers, television has added a new job: helping children sort truth from fiction on the television screen."[22]

Although it is a great help for parents to view television with their children, a continuing problem remains--the television commercials. Advertising and programming practices in commercial children's television are a specialized market that makes children natural targets for profitable integration into the television ad-

---

[18]Mander, p. 265.

[19]Martin Mayer, About Television (New York: Harper and Row, 1972), p. 128.

[20]Singer, p. 60.

[21]Blossom, p. 2.

[22]Ambrosino, p. 19.

vertising medium.[23] This is especially true on weekends when many children watch television. The network weekend children's television has become a specialized market for a specialized group of advertisers, with advertising messages uniquely directed to children's audiences.[24] The special treatment of children as television viewers is based not upon the needs or interests of the children, but upon the effective exploitation of profitable markets.[25] The advertiser's only concern is that the commercial will successfully sell the product. "Children are continually sold fads and useless toys because the advertiser knows perfectly well that tiny kids are impractical, open to suggestion, and fickle."[26]

This specialized market is so profitable because the child is actually tricked into believing the commercial. Young children often cannot tell the difference between a commercial and program content.[27] Many advertisements deceive the child into believing that the commercial is actually part of the program. For example, advertisers use animated advertisements with animated programs.[28] Advertisements tend to be loud, bright, and action-oriented, and are blended as closely as possible into the program so that the children do not lose interest. This reduces the chance of losing

---

[23] William Melody, Children's TV (New Haven, Conn.: Yale University Press, 1973), p. 81.

[24] Melody, p. 95.

[25] Melody, p. 83.

[26] Melody, p. 65.

[27] Liebert, p. 129.

[28] Melody, p. 60.

the child's attention at the time of the advertising break.[29]

In addition, advertising can actually cause problems for the child and the child's family. "The frequent repetition of ads reflects consideration of the relatively short memory spans of children."[30] These ads create peculiar needs and anxieties in the preschool child. Advertisers in the children's television market concentrate heavily on products like cereals, candies, snack foods, and toys.[31] Eating habits encouraged by ads for these non-nutritive foods promote unhealthy patterns of nutrition, and these habits are likely to remain throughout life.[32] The concentration on these products also influences the behavior of the child viewer toward the purchasing habits of parents.[33] Consequently, advertising directed at children creates more problems for families in the form of children nagging at parents and causing family friction.[34] Since children are not the ones who must actually purchase the product, it is unethical to encourage children to pressure their parents into it.[35]

While children will always be exposed to advertising, they should be protected from being singled out as the most vulnerable

---

[29] Melody, p. 59.

[30] Melody, p. 60.

[31] Melody, p. 61.

[32] Liebert, p. 122.

[33] Melody, p. 86.

[34] Liebert, p. 125.

[35] Melody, p. 86.

and malleable target for direct attack by television advertisers.[36] It should be possible for advertisers to produce commercials for children that provide the child with helpful information. The advertising industry should get together and agree on a way to introduce a cluster of commercials, so that children can be helped to understand what they are seeing.[37] Until then, advertising will continue to create problems for young children and parents alike.

Because television continues to be a large part of the life of preschool children, many groups have been formed to study the effects it is having on these children. Some educators think that heavy television watching can cause children to be passive, withdrawn, or apathetic. These children are often less imaginative than children who watch little television. They also seem to have trouble following any but the simplest directions.[38] One group, Action for Children's Television (ACT), is an effective force in children's television. Today it has 11,000 members and is campaigning nationwide against violence and commercialism in children's programs. It is striving for quality and diversity.

> ...there is just no way a person interested in the future of this country can sit in front of a television set on a typical Saturday morning from 9:00 A.M. to 12:00 noon and not be visually and mentally disappointed by the lack of intellectual content in most of the scripts, the lack of mechanical animation employed in most of the programs, and the frequency, the blatancy, and often the sheer idiocy of so many of the commercials.[39]

---

[36]Melody, p. 86.

[37]Mason, p. 205.

[38]Dixon, 1983.

[39]Mason, p. 205.

BIBLIOGRAPHY

Ambrosino, Lillian. "Do Children Believe TV?" Children Today, Nov.-Dec. 1972, pp. 18-19.

Blossom, Marilyn C. "Children and Television: Part I," Home Economics Guide, Sept. 1972, pp. 1-2.

Dixon, Maurice. Associate Professor of Communication and Creative Arts. Purdue University Calumet. Hammond, Indiana, 6 Oct. 1983.

Friedrich, Lynette Kohn, and Aletha Huston Stein. Aggressive and Prosocial Television Programs and the Natural Behavior of Preschool Children. Monographs of the Society for Research in Child Development, Vol. 38, Chicago: University of Chicago Press, 1973.

Liebert, Robert M., et al. The Early Window: Effects of Television on Children and Youth. New York: Pergamon Press, 1973.

Mander, Jerry. Four Arguments for the Elimination of Television. New York: William Morrow and Company, 1978.

Mason, K. "Revamping Saturday Morning Children's Television." Vital Speeches, 15 Jan. 1979, pp. 204-07.

Mayer, Martin. About Television. New York: Harper and Row, 1972.

Melody, William. Children's TV. New Haven, Conn.: Yale University Press, 1973.

Noble, Grant. Children in Front of the Small Screen. London: Constable, 1975.

Singer, J.L., and D.G. Singer. "Come Back, Mr. Rogers, Come Back." Psychology Today, March 1979, pp. 56-60.

SUMMARY AND APPLICATIONS

1. When writing a research paper, follow the process of writing.
2. Begin by choosing and limiting your subject. The subject should be significant, objective, and represented by a wide range of source materials. Once your subject is limited, it should clearly reflect the purpose of the paper.
3. Prepare a working bibliography by consulting the card catalog, the *Readers' Guide*, and other reference works.
4. Write a preliminary outline to be used as a guide for the reading to be done during your research.
5. Take notes on information related to your controlling purpose and to the divisions of your preliminary outline.
6. Organize your notes and write a final outline.
7. Using the information on your note cards, write your rough draft. Follow your outline. Be careful to avoid plagiarism.
8. Revise your rough draft and add footnotes in proper form.
9. Write a final bibliography listing all sources actually referred to in your paper.

Applications in Other Subject Areas

All Subjects. Bibliographies are often supplied at the ends of books on scientific, political, historical, artistic, or literary subjects. These bibliographies can be of enormous value to students doing research. Go to the library and locate two bibliographies in books from a field of study that interests you. Based on these bibliographies, compile a list of books that you would like to read.

Journalism / Mass Media. Reporters must be very careful to attribute paraphrased or quoted material to the right sources. They also must take care to quote or paraphrase their sources accurately. Find two or three current newspaper articles containing quoted or paraphrased material. How do reporters go about documenting their sources? How do their methods of documentation differ from the methods used by writers of research papers?

Chapter 14

Using the Library and Reference Materials

Knowing how to use the library resources quickly and efficiently is of great practical value not only for your work in English but for all your studies. You will find the library an indispensable ally as you do research in literature, history, science, and other subjects.

To make effective use of the library, however, you need to know (1) how books are classified and arranged, and (2) how you can find them by using the card catalog.

You also need to know how to find and use the many kinds of reference materials the library contains. These include dictionaries, encyclopedias, almanacs, catalogs, atlases, biographical reference books, literary reference books, and magazines.

This chapter will give you the basic information you need to make the best use of the library.

Part 1 The Classification and Arrangement of Books

To find any book in the library, you know that you must first locate that book in the card catalog. Every book is listed on at least three cards: the **author card,** the **title card,** and the **subject card.** Once you have found the card for the book you are interested in, you must then find that book on the library shelves. A knowledge of how books are classified and how they are arranged will help you locate the material you need.

The Classification of Books

Fiction. Novels and anthologies of short stories are usually arranged in alphabetical order by author. When there are two or more books written by the same author, you would find them shelved alphabetically by title. For example, John Steinbeck's books would be found under *S*. His *East of Eden* and *The Grapes of Wrath* would be followed by *Of Mice and Men*.

Nonfiction. Most libraries—including high school libraries—use the Dewey Decimal System of classifying nonfiction books. This system is named for its originator, the American librarian, Melvil Dewey. There are ten major classifications in the Dewey Decimal System; all books fit into one of these classifications. The ten major classifications are these:

000–099	**General Works**	(encyclopedias, handbooks, almanacs, etc.)
100–199	**Philosophy**	(includes psychology, ethics, etc.)
200–299	**Religion**	(the Bible, theology, mythology)
300–399	**Social Science**	(sociology, economics, government, education, law, folklore)
400–499	**Language**	(languages, grammars, dictionaries)
500–599	**Science**	(mathematics, chemistry, physics, biology, etc.)

600–699	**Useful Arts**	(farming, cooking, sewing, nursing, engineering, radio, television, gardening, industries, inventions)
700–799	**Fine Arts**	(music, painting, drawing, acting, photography, games, sports, amusements)
800–899	**Literature**	(poetry, plays, essays)
900–999	**History**	(biography, travel, geography)

As you can see from the major categories of the Dewey Decimal System, each discipline has a classification number. For example, all books on the fine arts are classified between 700 and 799, and all literature books will be found between 800 and 899. The system becomes more detailed as each of these major groups is subdivided.

900–999 History

910 General geography and travel
920 General biography
930 Ancient history
940 European history
950 Asian history
960 African history
970 North American history
980 South American history
990 General history of other parts of the world

970 North American history

971 Canada
972 Middle America-Mexico
973 United States
974 Northeastern United States
975 Southeastern United States
976 South central United States
977 North central United States
978 Western United States
979 Great Basin and Pacific Slope regions of the United States

The numbers in a particular classification, combined with the letter of the author's last name, make up the **call number.** The call number helps you locate the book on the shelf once you have found it in the card catalog.

Arrangement of Books on the Shelves

You can see that books are arranged on the shelves numerically in order of classification. Most libraries prominently mark their shelves with the numbers indicating the books to be found in each particular section. Like fiction books, nonfiction books are arranged alphabetically by authors' last names.

Biographies are one of the most popular kinds of books in libraries. The Dewey Decimal System division for them is 920. However, large libraries will often place biographies in a separate section because of the large number of these books. In this case, they will have a "B" on the spine of the book and on the catalog card. If you are looking for a particular biography and are unable to locate the 920 division, ask for assistance.

Reference Books are located in the library's reference room or area. They are classified according to the Dewey Decimal System and often with the letter "R" or "Ref" above the classification number. Usually, a reference book may not be checked out of the library.

Exercise The Classification and Arrangement of Books

Using the Dewey Decimal Classification summary on pages 301 and 302, assign the correct classification number to each of the following books.

1. *Fun with Mathematics*, by Jerome Meyer
2. *Dictionary of Classical Mythology*, by J. F. Zimmerman
3. *The Theatre*, by Sheldon Cheney
4. *Garden Flowers in Color*, by Daniel Foley
5. *Words and Ways of American English*, by Thomas Pyles
6. *The Magic of Black Poetry*, comp. Raoul Abdul
7. *Television News*, by Irving Fang
8. *Invitation to Skiing*, by Fred Iselin
9. *Your Legal Rights as a Minor*, by Robert Loeb, Jr.
10. *Outdoor Photography*, by Erwin Bauer
11. *Life in a Medieval Castle*, by Joseph Gies
12. *Alternatives in Education*, by Vernon Smith

Part 2 Finding Information in a Book

You must often skim a book to see whether it will be a useful source. If you are familiar with the parts of a book, you will be able to determine this quickly.

The Parts of a Book

The **title page** generally gives the complete title of the book, the names of authors or editors, the name of the publisher, and the place of publication.

The **copyright page** gives the copyright dates, the names of the copyright holders, the dates of editions or printings, and the Library of Congress catalog card number.

The **foreword, preface, or introduction** is a written commentary that supplies necessary background information.

The **table of contents** is a summary or outline of the contents of the book, arranged in order of appearance.

The **text** is the body of the book. It may be divided into chapters or sections.

The **appendices** contain additional information, such as maps, charts, tables, illustrations, or graphs.

The **notes** section contains footnotes to works cited or explanations of statements made in the text.

The **bibliography** is a list of works that have been used in preparing the book or that may be of interest to readers who want more information on the subject.

The **glossary** is a dictionary of unusual or technical terms used in the text of the book.

The **index** is an alphabetical list of subjects covered in the book. Each entry is followed by page numbers.

Exercise Using the Parts of a Book

Answer the following questions. For questions 1–4, refer to the appropriate parts of this textbook.

1. According to the table of contents, what chapter of this book will give you information on writing a summary or précis?
2. According to the index, what pages of this book deal with proper footnote form?
3. What is the copyright date of this book?
4. In what cities are the offices of the publisher of this book located?
5. Suppose that you are reading a science textbook and encounter a term that you do not understand. Where might you look in the book for a definition of the term?
6. In a book entitled *Everyday Life in Colonial America,* where might you find a list of other sources on the same subject?
7. In a book on the political and economic history of Italy, where might you look for maps of Italy and tables of statistics?
8. Suppose that, while reading a book, you come across a quotation followed by a footnote number. Where are you most likely to find information on the source of this quotation?

Part 3 Using Reference Materials

One of the best ways to obtain information on a particular topic is to consult a reference work. Libraries have either a reference section or a reference room. It is here that you will find just about everything you want, from a *Time* article on the Secretary of State to an encyclopedia article on solar energy.

Reference works include the following: dictionaries; encyclopedias; pamphlets, handbooks, and catalogs; almanacs and yearbooks; atlases; biographical reference books; literary reference books; and magazines.

Most reference works have prefaces that describe how information is arranged, show sample entries, and explain the symbols and abbreviations used in the book. Before using any reference work for the first time, skim the preface.

Dictionaries

The most widely used reference books in the library are the general dictionaries. General dictionaries fall into three major categories.

1. **Unabridged** dictionaries are dictionaries with over 250,000 entries.
2. **"College"** or **"desk"** dictionaries generally carry 130,000 to 150,000 entries.
3. **Concise** or **"pocket"** dictionaries are those with a smaller number of entries.

Unabridged Dictionaries. An unabridged dictionary may contain up to 500,000 words. It gives uncommon, as well as common meanings of many words, and explains in detail how they are used. The best known unabridged dictionaries are these.

Webster's Third New International Dictionary
The Random House Dictionary of the English Language, Unabridged Edition

You will find at least one—if not both—of these in your school or community library.

College or Desk Dictionaries. A college or desk dictionary is a quick and convenient reference. It provides information you would normally need about definitions, spellings, pronunciations, and matters of usage. It usually contains a special section that gives biographical information, and articles on such topics as pronunciation, spelling, and dialects.

Your school or local library probably carries several different college dictionaries. The best known are these.

The American Heritage Dictionary of the English Language
The Macmillan Dictionary
The Random House Dictionary of the English Language, College Edition
Thorndike-Barnhart Dictionary
Webster's New Collegiate Dictionary
Webster's New World Dictionary of the American Language

Dictionaries About Language. Another group of dictionaries is available to you. Each of these deals with a specific aspect of our English language: synonyms and antonyms, rhymes, slang, Americanisms, etymology, and so forth.

As a young writer, you need to be concerned with precision in your writing. A help in finding the precise word you are looking for is a **thesaurus,** or dictionary of synonyms.

A thesaurus should be used only as a "memory-jogger" to help you find words that are already in your vocabulary. You are treading on dangerous ground if you select from a thesaurus a word you do not know in place of word you do know. From your study of Chapter 1, you know that most synonyms are not interchangeable. A list of reliable thesauruses follows.

Roget's International Thesaurus
Roget's Thesaurus in Dictionary Form
Roget's Thesaurus of English Words and Phrases
Webster's Collegiate Thesaurus
Webster's Dictionary of Synonyms

Additional dictionaries dealing with our language are these.

Abbreviations Dictionary: (Abbreviations, Acronyms, Contractions, Signs, and Symbols Defined)
Acronyms, Initialisms, and Abbreviations Dictionary
Brewer's Dictionary of Phrase and Fable
A Dictionary of American Idioms
Dictionary of American Slang
Dictionary of Literary Terms
A Dictionary of Slang and Unconventional English
A Dictionary of Word and Phrase Origins (3 Volumes)
Harper Dictionary of Contemporary Usage
Mathews Dictionary of Americanisms
The Oxford Dictionary of English Etymology
Wood's Unabridged Rhyming Dictionary

Special-Purpose Dictionaries. Also, there are some special-purpose dictionaries that deal exclusively with music, medicine, foreign language, biography, and many other subjects. Check your library as to the availability of the many titles in print.

Encyclopedias

General Encyclopedias. An encyclopedia (from the Greek *enkyklios paideia,* which means "general education") is a collection of articles alphabetically arranged in volumes on nearly every conceivable subject. It is designed for quick reference, and provides you with general information on various fields or branches of learning.

Guide letters on the spine of each volume and guide words at the top of the pages assist you in finding information. It is best, however, to check the general index. It may list several good sources. For up-to-date information on a topic, check the yearbook that many encyclopedias include.

Never use an encyclopedia as your only source. Use it only to obtain a general survey of your subject. The library is a storehouse of information; an encyclopedia should be used only as a door to that storehouse.

Most libraries include the following encyclopedias in their reference section.

GENERAL ENCYCLOPEDIAS

Collier's Encyclopedia (24 volumes)
Publishes *Collier's Yearbook;* Volume 24 includes a Bibliography and Index

Encyclopaedia Britannica (30 volumes)
Publishes *Britannica Book of the Year;* includes separate Index and Atlas for the set (more details follow)

Encyclopedia Americana (30 volumes)
Publishes *Americana Annual*

World Book Encyclopedia (22 volumes)
Publishes annual supplement; Volume 22 includes Research Guide and Index

The *Encyclopaedia Britannica* is unique in its organization. In dealing with the great amounts of knowledge known to humankind, the *Britannica* has broken down its encyclopedia into three parts: the *Propaedia* (*pro* meaning "prior to"), the *Micropaedia* (*micro* meaning "small") and the *Macropaedia* (*macro* meaning "big").

The *Propaedia*, or Outline of Knowledge and Guide to the *Britannica*, presents more than 15,000 different topics, arranged according to fields or areas of knowledge. For each topic in the Outline, there are references to the *Macropaedia* of three kinds: (1) whole articles, (2) sections of articles, (3) other references. These references make possible systematic study or reading on any subject in the encyclopedia.

The *Micropaedia*, consisting of 10 volumes, is a ready reference and index to the entire encyclopedia. As a ready reference, it is a short entry encyclopedia. Its more than 100,000 entries, arranged in alphabetical order, give the most important and interesting facts about their subject. Often this is all you will want to know. But when a subject is also treated in depth in the *Macropaedia*, the *Micropaedia* is an index.

The *Macropaedia*, which contains knowledge in depth, is the main body of the *Britannica*. The *Macropaedia's* 19 volumes contain 4,207 long articles by world-renowned contributors on major subjects.

Encyclopedias on Specific Subjects. Encyclopedias on a wide variety of specific subjects fill library shelves. To give you some idea of the diversity, here is a partial list.

ENCYCLOPEDIAS ON SPECIFIC SUBJECTS

ART

Encyclopedia of Modern Art
LaRousse Encyclopedia of Byzantine and Medieval Art
LaRousse Encyclopedia of Prehistoric and Ancient Art
LaRousse Encyclopedia of Renaissance and Baroque Art

HISTORY

An Encyclopedia of World History
Encyclopedia of American History
Illustrated Encyclopaedia of the Classical World

HOBBIES AND INTERESTS

Encyclopedia of Gardening
Encyclopedia of Sailing
The Illustrated Encyclopedia of World Coins
The International Encyclopedia of Cooking

LITERATURE

The Concise Encyclopedia of English and American Poets and Poetry
The Concise Encyclopedia of Modern Drama
LaRousse Encyclopedia of Mythology
McGraw Hill Encyclopedia of World Biography (12 volumes)
McGraw Hill Encyclopedia of World Drama (4 volumes)

SCIENCE AND MATHEMATICS

Encyclopedia of Animal Care
The Encyclopedia of Chemistry
Grzimek's Animal Life Encyclopedia (13 volumes)
The Illustrated Encyclopedia of Aviation and Space
International Encyclopedia of Social Sciences (17 volumes)
Universal Encyclopedia of Mathematics

Pamphlets, Handbooks, and Catalogs

The Vertical File. Pamphlets, handbooks, booklets, and clippings on a variety of subjects are available in most libraries. These subjects include information about vocations, travel, census data, and program schedules. It is here you may find college catalogs, too. All of this information is kept in a set of file cabinets called the **vertical file.**

A main feature of the vertical file is that the information in it is current. This file can be an invaluable source to you when writing a report on a contemporary topic, seeking current statistics, or looking up information on various careers.

Information About Vocations, Colleges, and Universities. The reference section of the library can be a starting point in seeking information about careers and about colleges. Here is a list of some resources you might use.

Encyclopedia of Careers and Vocations
Barron's Guide to the Two-Year Colleges
Barron's Profiles of American Colleges
Lovejoy's College Guide

The 300 section of your reference area will provide related material. Many libraries also have on reserve a large number of college catalogs.

Almanacs and Yearbooks

Published annually, almanacs and yearbooks are useful sources of facts and statistics on current events, as well as on matters of historical record in government, economics, population, sports, and other fields.

Guinness Book of World Records
Information Please Almanac, Atlas and Yearbook
Statesman's Yearbook
Statistical Abstract of the United States
Women's Rights Almanac
World Almanac and Book of Facts

Atlases

We usually think of an atlas mainly as a book of maps, but it also contains interesting data on a number of subjects. The excellent *National Geographic Atlas of the World*, for example, lists some of the following topics in its table of contents: "Great Moments in Geography," "Global Statistics," and sections on population, temperature, oceans, and place names. Below is a list of other widely used atlases.

Atlas of World History
Atlas of World Wildlife
The Britannica Atlas
Collier's World Atlas and Gazetteer
Goode's World Atlas
Grosset World Atlas
The International Atlas from Rand McNally
Rand McNally Commercial Atlas and Marketing Guide
The Times Atlas of the World
Webster's Atlas with Zip Code Directory

Biographical References

There are brief biographical notations in dictionaries and longer biographical articles in encyclopedias. Often, however, a better source is one of the specialized works listed below.

Current Biography. Biographies of current newsworthy individuals are published here monthly. Each issue is indexed. All copies are bound in an annual volume with a cumulated index of people in that particular volume as well as previous annual volumes. Also found at the end of the annual volumes are the names of the people in *Current Biography* according to their professions. Biographies of internationally known persons are found here, but Americans are well represented throughout this reference.

Dictionary of American Biography. This is the most famous and most reliable of all American biographical dictionaries. Alphabetically arranged, this twenty-two-volume work carries articles on the lives and accomplishments of prominent deceased Americans. The work contains 14,870 biographies of Americans from the colonial days to 1940. The length of the articles varies from half-page to chapter-length essays.

Dictionary of National Biography. This multi-volume dictionary is the most famous and the most reliable of British biographical dictionaries. Its accurate and concise information makes it a most valuable source.

The International Who's Who. Alphabetically listed, this source provides brief biographical sketches of prominent living people of all nations. This publication includes thousands of personalities and provides a valuable source for current biographies.

Webster's Biographical Dictionary. This is a source of biographical facts about noteworthy people, past and present. More than 40,000 individuals are listed alphabetically, and pronunciation keys are given for each name.

Who's Who. Principally concerned with British personalities, this source provides a very brief description of the life and accomplishments of each individual included. You would probably need to refer to another source if you needed detailed information.

Who's Who in America. This source, alphabetically listed, provides biographical sketches of prominent living Americans who are known either for their positions or their accomplishments. Published every two years, this is a reference book that can guide you to other sources in seeking detailed information about a particular person.

Who's Who in America also has regional editions: *Who's Who in the Midwest, Who's Who in the South and Southwest,* and *Who's Who in the West.*

Who's Who in American Women. This book not only lists outstanding American women, but women of international acclaim.

Books About Authors. For biographical information about authors, and critical evaluations of their works, the following sources are especially useful.

American Authors: 1600–1900
British Authors Before 1800
British Authors of the Nineteenth Century
Contemporary Authors
Cyclopedia of World Authors
European Authors: 1000–1900
Twentieth Century Authors
Twentieth Century Authors: First Supplement
World Authors: 1950–1970
Writers at Work

Literary Reference Books

The following are valuable reference books on the history of literature, on quotations and proverbs, for locating poems and stories, and for finding information about writers.

Bartlett's Familiar Quotations
Book Review Digest
Contemporary Poets
Cyclopedia of Literary Characters
A Dictionary of Literature in the English Language
Encyclopedia of World Drama

Granger's Index to Poetry and Recitations
Illustrated Encyclopedia of the Classical World
A Literary History of England
A Literary History of the United States
Mencken's *A New Dictionary of Quotations*
The Oxford Companion to American Literature
The Oxford Companion to Classical Literature
The Oxford Companion to English Literature
The Oxford Companion to the Theatre
Poetry Handbook

From the above list, three widely used reference works are the following:

Bartlett's Familiar Quotations. This is one of the best known of the dictionaries of quotations. Its completeness and accuracy have made it notable for over a century.

Quotations are arranged chronologically by author in the main section of the book. A shorter section of passages from the Bible, the Koran, and the Book of Common Prayer follow. To find the complete source of a quotation, use the main index in the back of the book. Whether you know the entire quotation or simply have a general idea of its topic, you would be able to find it in the index.

For example, study this quotation by Carl Sandburg.

The fog comes
on little cat feet.
It sits looking
over the harbor and city
on silent haunches
and then moves on.

You may find this quotation in three places.

1. under Carl Sandburg entries in the main index of the book
2. in the index under the first line of the quote
3. under the subject of Fog

Whatever your recollection or your need for a quotation on a particular subject may be, *Bartlett's* is an excellent source.

Book Review Digest. Arranged alphabetically by authors of the book reviewed, this digest gives short quotations from selected reviews from many popular American and English periodicals. If a work of fiction has had four or more reviews or a work of nonfiction has had two or more reviews, and if the book is hard-bound and has been published in the United States, it will appear in this digest. It is published monthly and cumulated annually.

You will find this to be a good source in finding both unfavorable and favorable reviews of particular books.

Granger's Index to Poetry and Recitations. This source includes an index of first lines as well as an index of authors to assist you in finding a poem if its title is unknown to you. By using this reference book, you will also be able to locate not only a quotation but an entire short work. For example, let us say you need to find an anthology or book containing the poem "Song of the Open Road" by Walt Whitman. You would look up this title in the *Index* and under the title you will find listed a number of books containing this poem. The titles, however, are coded. The code explained in the front of the book.

Granger's Index to Poetry and Recitations is a standard, worthwhile source for any student of literature.

Magazines

When you are writing about a current topic, magazines are an important resource. The *Readers' Guide to Periodical Literature* lists the titles of articles, stories, and poems published during the preceding month in more than one hundred leading magazines. It is issued twice a month from September through June and once a month in July and August. An entire year's issues are bound in one hard cover volume at the end of the year. Articles are listed alphabetically under *subject* and *author* (and *titles* when necessary). You will find the *Readers' Guide* invaluable when looking for articles on a subject for a composition.

The excerpt from the *Readers' Guide* on the following page illustrates how articles are listed.

Excerpt from the *Readers' Guide*

ALPS

Mount Blanc and Chamouni; Bolsson and Montavert or Sea of Ice glaciers. P. B. Shelley. Earth Sci 32:53-5 Spr '79

ALSCHULER, Alfred, and Flinchum, Betty

Raising minimum competencies. il Phi Delta Kappan 60:678-9 My '79 — title of article

ALSTON, Elizabeth

Between the lines. il Redbook 153:40 Je '79 — name of magazine

ALTER, Norah Lee

I won't apoligize for being a housewife. Ladies Home J 96:24+ Je '79 — volume number

ALTER, Robert — author entry

Literary lives. Commentary 67:56-62 My '79

ALTERNATING Current Synthesizers. See Frequency changers

ALTERNATIVE newspapers. See Newspapers

ALTIMETERS

Remote sensing of surface ocean circulation with satellite altimetry; use of Geodynamics Experimental Ocean Satellite radar altimeter. R. S. Mather and others. bibl il maps Science 205:11-17 Jl 6 '79 — page reference

Seasalt altimeter calibration: initial results; radar altimeter. B. D. Tapley and others. bibl il Science 204-1410:12 Je 29 '79 — date of magazine

ALTMAN, Robert

Robert Altman: a young Turk at 54. W. Grigsby, por Macleans 92:4-5+ Ap 23 '79*

ALTRUISM

Good Samaritans at age two? work of M. R. Yarrow and C. Zahn-Waxler. M. Pines. bibl il Psychol Today 13:66-8+ Je '79 — illustrated article

ALUM, Manuel, Dance Company. See Dance companies

ALUMINA

Fast ionic transport in solids. G. C. Farrington and J. L. Briant. bibl il Science 204:1371-9 Je 29 '79

ALUMINUM canoes. See Canoes—Materials

ALUMINUM industry — subject entry

Export-import trade

Aluminum walkout threatens U.S. supply; Canadian strike. Bus W p47-8 Je 18 '79

Canada

See also

Alcan Aluminum, Ltd — "see also" cross reference

United States

See Also

Kaiser Aluminum & Chemical Corporation

ALUMINUM industry strikes (Canada) See Strikes—Canada — "see" cross reference

Computers, Microfilm, and Microfiche

Recent technology has made several new sources of information available to students doing research. For example, many libraries store books, magazines, pamphlets, newspapers, and other materials on **microfilm** or **microfiche.** These are types of film on which printed documents are reproduced in miniature. To read these documents, you must place the film into a projector to enlarge the miniature print. Check with libraries in your area to see if they store information in either of these ways. Your librarian will help you to learn how to use the microfilm or microfiche projector.

If you have access to a home computer equipped with a **modem**—a device for communicating with other computers via telephone lines—still other sources of information are available to you. Several companies in the United States offer information services that can be purchased by home computer users. A student with a home computer can use these services to gain access to reports on current events and to information from encylopedias. To find out more about these computer services, consult a reference librarian in your community or a local dealer in home computer software.

Exercises Using Reference Materials

A. Dictionaries and Encyclopedias. Using the dictionaries and encyclopedias listed on pages 306–310, indicate the best source for answers to these questions. Include the page reference.

1. Find an article listing important events in France during the Eighteenth Century.
2. Give a definition and examples of a limerick.
3. Who is Merlin?
4. What were the "Jim Crow" laws?
5. Who wrote the ballet "Slaughter on Tenth Avenue"?
6. Give two examples of twentieth century fables.
7. What is meant by the expression "French leave"?
8. What do the following abbreviations mean?

SHAPE EKG USAF SALT

9. Compare the form of the Miltonic sonnet with that of the Shakespearean sonnet.

10. What are the techniques for reproducing color?

11. Find a copy of the Greek alphabet.

12. What was the original meaning of the word *johnnycake?*

13. What is the plot of Eugene O'Neill's play *Mourning Becomes Electra?*

14. When was the guillotine used?

15. Find an explanation of a dangling participle.

B. Almanacs, Yearbooks, and Atlases. Using the almanacs, yearbooks, and atlases listed in this chapter, indicate the best source for answers to these questions. Include the page reference.

1. How many Americans have been awarded the Nobel Prize for Literature?
2. Where are the National Seashores?
3. What is the literacy rate in India?
4. How can you obtain a passport?
5. Where can you find illustrations of the different American Revolution flags?
6. Compare life-expectancy rates of men and women in the United States.
7. Find a copy of the Bill of Rights.
8. Who made the first orbital flight?
9. What are the provisions of the Campaign Finance Act?
10. Find a map showing the density of world population.
11. What are the four time zones in the United States?
12. How many miles long is the Mississippi River?

C. Biographical References. Using the biographical references listed in this chapter, give the best source for answers to these questions. Include the page reference.

1. Find a list of the rulers of the British Empire.
2. When did Sir Edmund Hillary climb Mount Everest?
3. Was James Thurber's *My Life and Hard Times* autobiographical?
4. What was the family background of Charlotte Brontë?

5. How did Alfred Eisenstadt achieve his reputation as a famous photographer?

6. How do you pronounce the name of the French aviator and writer Antoine de Saint Exupéry?

7. Which of James Michener's writing does he think will survive the longest?

8. For what historical works is Carl Sandburg famous?

9. What were Frederick Jackson Turner's views on the significance of the frontier in American history?

10. Why were Ogden Nash's writings so popular?

D. Literary Reference Books. Use the literary reference books listed in this chapter to find answers to the following questions. Write the name of the reference book you used.

1. From what source did Aldous Huxley take the title *Brave New World?*

2. In what American novel is Carol Kennicott a character?

3. How were the reviews of Richard Wright's *Black Boy?*

4. What is the title of the poem that begins "Some say the world will end in fire"?

5. Who coined the phrase "the lost generation"?

6. What plays did the Irish dramatist, Sean O'Casey, write for the Abbey Theatre?

7. What is the setting of Stephen Vincent Benét's poem "John Brown's Body"?

8. Who were the nine muses?

9. Who was the founder of *The New Yorker* magazine?

10. Where did Sir Winston Churchill say, "Never in the field of human conflict was so much owed by so many to so few"?

11. Find a poem on the subject of pride.

12. List the volumes of poetry written by Mark Van Doren.

E. *Readers' Guide to Periodical Literature.* Use the excerpt from the *Readers' Guide* on page 316 to answer these questions.

1. Under what subject will you find articles on aluminum canoes?

2. Which magazine articles will have pictures of oceanic research?

3. Give the volume and pages of the *Macleans* article on "Robert Altman: a Young Turk" by W. Grigsby.

4. To which magazines do the abbreviations Earth Sci, Ladies Home J, Psychol Today, and Bus W refer?

5. How many issues of *Science* have articles on altimeters?

F. Using Reference Materials for a Research Paper. You are doing a research paper on John Steinbeck's place in American literature. Using the reference sources listed in this chapter, find the specific books that give the answers to these questions. Include the page references.

1. Reviews of *The Grapes of Wrath, Cannery Row, Of Mice and Men, The Pearl.*
2. Comprehensive biographical information.
3. A bibliography of his writings.
4. The text of his acceptance speech upon receiving the Nobel Prize for Literature.
5. His experience as a war correspondent.
6. The sources of the titles of these novels: *The Grapes of Wrath, The Winter of Our Discontent.*
7. His novels that were made into movies.
8. The area in California that is the background for many of his stories.
9. The plot of his novel *Tortilla Flat.*
10. A list of the books by Steinbeck that are in your school library.

SUMMARY AND APPLICATIONS

1. In libraries you can find sources on every conceivable subject. Mastering library skills will help you do research efficiently.
2. Libraries arrange works of fiction in alphabetical order, according to the author's last name.
3. Most libraries arrange works of nonfiction according to the Dewey Decimal classification system.
4. Alphabetically-organized cards for materials contained in a library can be found in the card catalog. Books may be listed by author, title, and subject cards.
5. Books are commonly organized into the following parts:

   title page
   copyright page
   forward, preface, or introduction
   table of contents
   text
   appendices
   notes
   bibliography
   glossary
   index

6. Most libraries mark reference works with an "R" and keep them in a separate section.

Applications in Other Subject Areas

Fine Arts. Choose one of the following artists. Find information concerning this artist in as many different kinds of resource materials as possible. Record your sources.

Vincent Van Gogh
Georgia O'Keeffe
Grandma Moses
Pablo Picasso

Business. To find up-to-date information on businesses, you can refer to newspaper articles and to the many business-related magazines currently available. Choose a particular company in one of the following industries and find articles in at least two different magazines concerning the company or industry that you have chosen. Report on any recent developments in this company or industry.

the automobile industry
the record industry
the petroleum industry
the movie industry

Chapter 15

Critical Thinking

Whenever we communicate, we share or exchange ideas with others. As we do so, we learn what other people think. Sometimes we also learn more about what we ourselves believe. This exchange of ideas, therefore, can enable us to learn and grow, to absorb existing concepts and discover new ones. Unless we know how to analyze and evaluate the facts and opinions that are presented to us, however, we cannot take full advantage of the opportunities to learn. We may also be misled into accepting weak or dangerous ideas.

In this chapter you will learn how to apply some basic principles of critical thinking that will help you to use the information you acquire. You will learn how to use critical thinking skills when you are reading or listening to determine whether the ideas being presented are true or false, reasonable or unreasonable. You will also learn how to present ideas in your own speech and writing.

Part 1 Understanding Fact and Opinion

Every statement that you read or hear is either a fact or an opinion. A **fact** is a statement that can be proved true or false. An **opinion** is a statement that cannot be proved. Study the following examples.

FACT: Plankton, the microscopic life found in oceans, can be harvested for food.

OPINION: Plankton should be developed as a primary food source.

The first statement can be proved true if one observes small-scale harvesting of plankton that is being done today. Therefore, it is a fact. The second statement, however, cannot be proved. It is simply someone's belief about how plankton should be used. Therefore, the statement is an opinion.

Both facts and opinions can be further classified for easier identification. First of all, there are two main types of facts: those that can be proved by **definition,** and those that can be proved by **observation.** Study the following examples:

TRUE BY DEFINITION: A fiord is a narrow inlet of the sea.

TRUE BY OBSERVATION: The planets Jupiter and Saturn both have rings.

The first statement is a definition of the word *fiord*. To prove that it is true, you do not have to look beyond the statement itself. The meaning has already been evaluated and agreed upon by experts.

The second statement is not a simple definition. It makes a claim about the world that can be proved only by observation. To prove that this statement is true, you must actually look at the planets Jupiter and Saturn or depend upon the observations of other people who have studied these planets.

If a statement fits into neither of these two categories of fact, then it is an opinion. The most common types of opinions are judgments, statements of obligation, and predictions.

A **judgment** is an opinion that expresses the attitude of a speaker or writer toward a subject. Judgments contain words of approval or disapproval such as *wonderful, terrible, beautiful, ugly, interesting, boring,* or *nice*. The meanings of such words vary from speaker to speaker. Therefore, they cannot be proven, and cannot be considered facts.

JUDGMENT: Colonizing the moon is an excellent idea.

A **statement of obligation** is an opinion in which the speaker states what he or she believes should be done or should happen. Words such as *should, ought to,* or *must* are used.

STATEMENT OF OBLIGATION: We ought to reduce the amount of funds allocated for the space program.

A **prediction** is an opinion about the future. Such opinions make claims that cannot be proved until the events that they predict come to pass.

PREDICTION: Eventually, the people of the world will communicate using one common language.

Evaluating Facts and Opinions

Both facts and opinions may be used effectively to present and support ideas. If these statements are weak or inaccurate, however, they can also destroy the believability of a concept or argument. It is therefore important that you learn how to evaluate the statements you hear, read, and present.

Evaluating Facts. To evaluate a fact, first determine whether it is a definition. If it is, you can determine whether it is true by consulting a dictionary. Look at the following example.

A spider is a type of insect.

If you consult *Webster's New World Dictionary: Students Edition,* you will find that an *insect* is an animal with three pairs of legs, and that a *spider* is an animal with eight legs. Therefore, the statement "A spider is a type of insect" is false.

If a statement of fact is not a definition, you can determine whether it is true by making an observation or by consulting a reliable source. This source may be human authority or a reference work. Look at the following example.

Most women in India dress in a long garment called a *sari*.

To determine the truth of this statement you must rely on actual observation. Since you probably have no means of checking this fact yourself, you would have to ask someone who has been to India, or you could consult a reliable encyclopedia or an authority on Indian culture.

Whenever you attempt to verify a statement of fact by consulting a reference work or other authority, keep the following guidelines in mind.

1. **Make certain that your source is up-to-date.** Always check the copyright date of written sources to ensure that they contain the most recent information available. A statement that was true in the 1940's may no longer be true now.

2. **Make certain that your source is reliable and unbiased.** Depend upon sources that are compiled by experts and that have a reputation for truth. Avoid sources that might have reason to present a slanted or prejudiced view of reality. For example, a soup manfacturer's statements about the nutritional value of soups may be slanted somewhat to increase sales, not to improve people's diets.

3. **Make certain that statements made by your source are consistent with other known facts.** When a statement contradicts what you know to be true, then the statement must be false. For example, the statement that dumping raw sewage into lakes is harmless is contradicted by the fact that several lakes have become contaminated by such practices.

Evaluating Opinions. The techniques used to evaluate an opinion are different from those used to evaluate facts. An opinion, you remember, cannot be proven true or false. It can, however, be shown to be sound or unsound.

An opinion is sound if it can be supported by facts. An opinion is unsound if it cannot be supported by facts. Look at the following statement of opinion.

Cities should monitor their water supplies carefully.

This opinion is sound because it is supported by facts such as the following:

Water is necessary to human life.
Many cities are not experiencing water shortages and problems with water pollution.
By monitoring water supplies, cities can detect overuse or contamination of their water supplies.

The opinion that cities should not spend money to monitor water supplies is unsound because it is contradicted by all of these facts.

When you evaluate an opinion, attempt to identify the facts that are used to support it. If the opinion is well supported by statements of fact, and if these statements can themselves be proved true, then the opinion is sound.

Exercises Using Facts and Opinions

A. Identify each of the following statements as a fact or an opinion. If the statement is a fact, tell whether it is true by definition or by observation. If the statement is an opinion, tell if it is a prediction, a judgment, or a statement of obligation.

1. The California redwoods should be preserved for the benefit of future generations.
2. The redwood is a type of evergreen tree.
3. The English language will probably change considerably over the next fifty years.
4. Zithers, psalteries, and hammer dulcimers are all stringed instruments with shallow sound boxes.
5. Tracks of an elephant were found on Mt. Kilimanjaro at an altitude of fifteen thousand feet.
6. George Henri Schmidt, the former Chief of the United Nations Terminology Section, is fluent in nineteen languages.

7. We should not allow any portion of our national parks to be developed commercially.

8. Meryl Streep is among the most talented actresses of the 1980's.

9. Students in the next century will do most of their homework by computer.

10. The underdeveloped nations of the world must begin placing a higher priority on educating their young.

B. Check each of the following statements of fact by consulting the reference work listed in parentheses. Then, label each statement *True* or *False*.

1. "Bed of roses" is a colloquialism. (dictionary)
2. The Caucasus Mountains are located in France. (atlas)
3. Delaware was the first state to ratify the United States Constitution. (encyclopedia)
4. Gwendolyn Brooks won the Pulitzer Prize for Poetry in 1950. (encyclopedia, almanac)
5. Brazil is the largest country in South America. (atlas)
6. The first liquid-fueled rocket was launched in 1913. (encyclopedia)
7. French and Flemish are the official languages of Belgium. (encyclopedia, almanac)
8. The coffee plant is a tall tropical shrub with bean-like seeds. (dictionary, encyclopedia)
9. Two Presidents of the United States have had the first name *John* and the last name *Adams*. (encyclopedia, textbook)
10. *Sol* was the Greek sun god. (dictionary, encyclopedia)

C. Study the following statements and the information that is provided about their sources. Then, explain why each statement is questionable or false.

1. "No American woman has ever traveled in space." (Source: book about the United States space program, copyright 1980)
2. "Scientists have discovered a cure for cancer, but the cure has been suppressed by officials of the United States government." (Source: independently produced newsletter)

3. "Studies have shown that Panacea-Brand Cold Remedy is 50% more effective than its leading competitor." (Source: magazine advertisement)

4. "There can be no doubt that our party has begun to lead our country toward economic recovery." (Source: candidate running for political office during a severe economic depression)

D. Tell whether each of the following opinions is a prediction, a judgment, or a statement of obligation. Then write two facts that support or contradict each opinion.

1. All students should study mathematics.
2. Books will be obsolete in a few generations.
3. One of the truly fascinating things about America is the diversity of its people.
4. The United States must develop new sources of energy.
5. Most professional athletes are overpaid.

E. A report, or research paper, must consist only of facts. The following is a list of statements that might be found by a student during research for a paper on the American author Shirley Jackson. Which of these statements might be used in the paper?

1. Shirley Jackson's "Charles" is one of the most entertaining stories ever told.
2. Shirley Jackson was born in San Francisco and educated at Syracuse University.
3. Shirley Jackson's stories have been widely anthologized.
4. Jackson's best novel is *The Haunting of Hill House*.
5. *The Haunting of Hill House* will become a classic.
6. Many of Shirley Jackson's stories deal with psychological horror caused by bizarre situations.
7. Shirley Jackson's fiction should be read by everyone who is interested in horror stories.
8. "The Lottery" is a masterpiece worthy of Edgar Allan Poe.
9. Jackson's *Raising Demons* is a collection of short stories based upon her family life.
10. "The Lottery" is a frightening and intriguing tale set in a seemingly ordinary American town.

Part 2 Using Inductive Reasoning

Evaluating statements of fact and opinion is only the first step toward more advanced critical thinking. In order to benefit most from facts and opinions, you must also learn to draw conclusions from them. When you gain the ability to do this, you become more than a receptacle for other people's ideas. You develop instead into an individual capable of presenting fresh ideas, developing unique insights, and finding new applications for old concepts.

One of the most basic types of reasoning is known as **induction.** This is the process of arriving at a general conclusion based upon specific facts. A simple example of induction may be illustrated as follows:

1. First, you observe several specific facts.

   In the past, candidate Smith has always voted in favor of federally-funded jobs programs.
   In a speech before the League of Women Voters, candidate Smith expressed his support for federally-funded day care centers.
   In a news conference, candidate Smith stated that he plans to introduce legislation that will provide federal assistance to pay the utility bills of people who need help.

2. Then, having noticed a similarity between these specific facts, you draw a conclusion.

   Candidate Smith usually supports federally-funded social programs.

The conclusion that is drawn through inductive reasoning is called a **generalization.** The group of specific facts on which the generalization is based is called a **sample.**

You use induction whenever you make an observation based upon specific facts drawn from observation or past experience. For example, if you make the statement that your school's baseball team always plays better at home, you are drawing a general conclusion based upon your observation of past games. If you say that a certain journalist is guilty of biased reporting, you are drawing a general conclusion based upon past observations of the unreliability of that reporter's news stories. Without inductive reasoning, you would be unable to learn from past experience.

Overgeneralization

Any type of reasoning is only as good as the facts that are used. Therefore, when you use the inductive method, you must be careful about your sample. Study the following example.

> *The Time Machine,* by H.G. Wells, is science fiction.
> *The Invisible Man,* by H.G. Wells, is science fiction.
> *The War of the Worlds,* by H.G. Wells, is science fiction.
> Therefore, books by H.G. Wells are science fiction stories.

The above sample includes three books by H.G. Wells. However, Wells wrote many other books, many of which were not science fiction. The generalization based upon this sample is too broad. In other words, it is an overgeneralization because the sample on which it is based is too limited.

Overgeneralizations can also result from samples that are unrepresentative. For example, an airline company once presented a commercial which stated that, in a recent survey, nine out of ten people preferred their company to any other airline with flights to Europe. The conclusion was obviously that this airline was best, for it was chosen by an overwhelming majority of travelers. However, the survey was taken only among the passengers who were already using that airline. It ignored those who traveled with other companies. Thus, the sample was unrepresentative, and the conclusion invalid.

These rules will help you to avoid making overgeneralizations.

1. **Keep your sample as large and as representative as possible.**
2. **Never make a statement about an entire group unless you are certain that the statement applies to each individual or object within the group.** For example, the statement "all adults hate video games" is an overgeneralization because it is not true of all adults.

3. Use qualifying words to limit the scope of your generalizations. Instead of using absolute words such as *all, every, each, none,* or *never,* use less sweeping words such as *most, many, some, a few,* and *occasionally.* In other words, instead of making a statement like "Everyone enjoys a good comedy," make a qualified or less-sweeping statement such as "Most people enjoy a good comedy." Qualified statements are usually more accurate than unqualified ones.

Stereotyping

The most dangerous kind of overgeneralization is the **stereotype.** This is a generalization made about all people of a particular sex, race, social or professional group, ethnic origin, or religious background. Stereotypes ignore the existence of individual choice and variation. They lead to inaccuracies and misunderstandings. Even scientists who study differences in human populations are extremely wary of making generalizations. Any group is likely to be so large and diverse that an accurate generalization about members of the group is impossible.

Exercises Using Inductive Reasoning

A. Using the inductive method, draw general conclusions from the following related facts.

1. The brachiosaurs, the largest animals that ever lived, were plant eaters.
   African brush elephants, the largest living animals, are plant eaters.
   Giraffes, the tallest living animals, are plant eaters.
2. *T. V. Guide* has the largest circulation of any weekly magazine.
   Adults watch an average of 23.3 hours of television each week.
   Ninety-eight percent of the homes in the United States have at least one television set.

3. One cold remedy claims in its television commercials that it is the most effective decongestant available.
   Another cold remedy claims in its magazine advertisements that it is the most effective decongestant.
   Yet another cold remedy claims on its label that it is the most effective decongestant available.
4. Hemingway chose France during World War I as the setting for his novel, *A Farewell to Arms*.
   Hemingway chose a bullfighting festival in Pamplona, Spain, as the setting for his novel, *The Sun Also Rises*.
   Hemingway chose an African safari as the setting for his story, "The Short, Happy Life of Francis Macomber."

B. The following statements are all examples of overgeneralization. List all absolute words and words referring to entire groups of people that you find in these statements. Rewrite each statement, making it a valid generalization by using words from the list of qualifiers given on page 331. Finally, write one statement of fact that can be used to support each revised generalization.

1. Until recently, everyone in America drove big cars.
2. Advertisements are always deceptive.
3. People who eat well-balanced meals live long, healthy lives.
4. The movies coming out of Hollywood these days are made to appeal to young people.
5. All doctors are wealthy.

C. Using the library, research one of the following people. Do not gather opinions about this person. Instead, gather a list of facts describing the person's actions or accomplishments. Then, based upon these facts, make a generalization about this person's life. Use your generalization as the main idea for a paper on the person whom you have chosen. In the body of your composition, support your generalization by providing specific facts from your research.

Thomas Alva Edison
Mother Theresa
Eleanor Roosevelt
John F. Kennedy
Simón Bolívar

Part 3 Using Deductive Reasoning

You know that in inductive reasoning, you start with a group of specific facts from which you form a generalization.

Inductive Reasoning

Specific fact	Copperheads have fangs and are poisonous.
+	
Specific fact	Rattlesnakes have fangs and are poisonous.
+	
Specific fact	Coral snakes have fangs and are poisonous.
+	
Many more specific facts	(observations of other poisonous snakes)
↓	
Generalization	Therefore, snakes that have fangs are poisonous.

In **deduction,** you start with a generalization and then derive a specific fact from it.

Deductive Reasoning

Generalization	Snakes that have fangs are poisonous.
+	
Related Fact	The asp viper has fangs.
↓	
Specific Fact	Therefore, the asp viper is poisonous.

Notice that the generalization with which a deductive argument begins can itself be the product of inductive reasoning. It can also be a general definition:

> A bird is a warm-blooded, egg-laying creature with feathers and wings.
>
> The osprey is a bird.
>
> Therefore, the osprey is a warm-blooded, egg-laying creature with feathers and wings.

The above arguments are presented in the form of syllogisms. A **syllogism** is a specific type of argument used in deductive reasoning. Although you may never have to present a formal argument in this manner, understanding the syllogism will help you to understand a reasoning process with which you can draw conclusions from a given set of facts.

A syllogism is made up of three statements: the **major premise,** the **minor premise,** and the **conclusion.** It is useful to draw a diagram or illustration that shows the relationships between the elements in the argument. Study the following argument.

MAJOR PREMISE: All ballads are poems.
MINOR PREMISE: "Barbara Allen" is a ballad.
CONCLUSION: Therefore, "Barbara Allen" is a poem.

Another way of stating the major premise of this argument is to say that "the forms of literature called ballads are contained within a group called poems." You can illustrate this in a diagram, as follows:

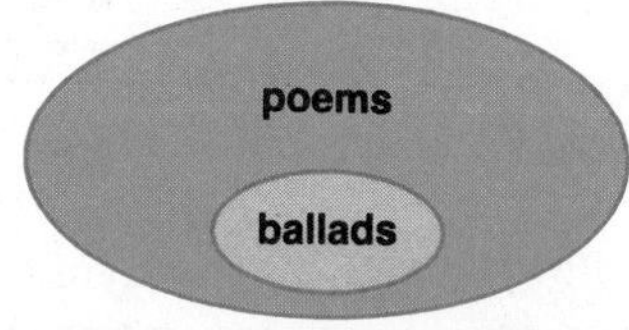

Another way of stating the minor premise is to say that "Barbara Allen" is contained within the group of ballads. This can also be illustrated on the diagram:

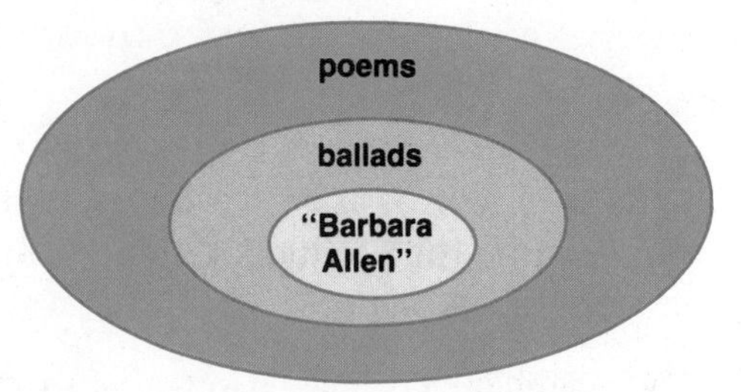

Once you have drawn a diagram illustrating the major and minor premises of the argument, you can see that the conclusion is also illustrated:

"Barbara Allen" is contained within the group of poems.

The way in which such a diagram is drawn depends upon what relationships are expressed in the statements that make up the argument. Study the following example.

MAJOR PREMISE: No Democrats are in favor of the new tax.
MINOR PREMISE: Senator Byrd is a Democrat.
CONCLUSION: Therefore, Senator Byrd is not in favor of the new tax.

The major premise can be illustrated by drawing two circles, one for Democrats and one for people in favor of the new tax. The circles are not connected because the two sets contain no members in common.

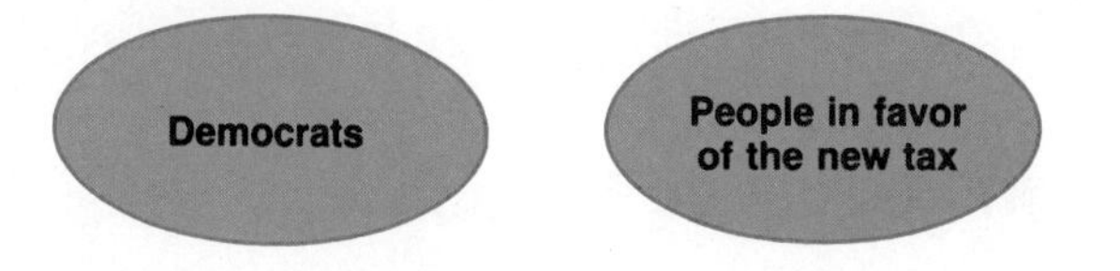

The minor premise is shown by drawing a circle inside the circle for Democrats.

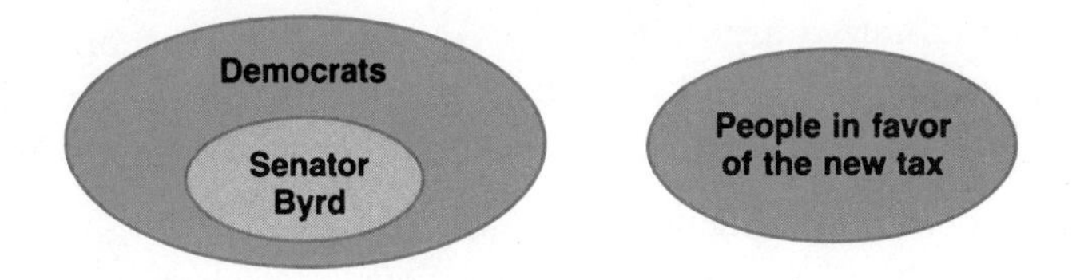

Because the circles for Democrats and people in favor of the new tax are separate, if Senator Byrd is placed within the circle of Democrats, he cannot be in the circle for people who favor the new tax. Therefore, the conclusion is true.

Exercise Deductive Reasoning

Draw diagrams to illustrate the following major and minor premises. Then state your own conclusions.

1. MAJOR PREMISE: All conifers produce cones.
   MINOR PREMISE: Spruces and pines are conifers.

2. MAJOR PREMISE: All primates are mammals.

MINOR PREMISE: The chimpanzee is a primate.

3. MAJOR PREMISE: Everyone on the speech team will be going on the field trip.

MINOR PREMISE: Ali and Steve are on the speech team.

4. MAJOR PREMISE: The jury came to a unanimous decision that the defendant was innocent.

MINOR PREMISE: Ms. Jefferson was a member of the jury.

5. MAJOR PREMISE: Folk tales do not have well-rounded, fully-developed characters.

MINOR PREMISE: "Jack and the Beanstalk" is a folk tale.

Errors in Deductive Reasoning

You saw in Part 2 how weak inductive arguments can lead to faulty conclusions. Errors in deductive reasoning can also result in inaccurate statements.

In a deductive argument, the conclusion is true only when two conditions are met. First, both of the premises must be true. Second, the argument must have a **valid** or logical form.

MAJOR PREMISE: Some mammals lay eggs.

MINOR PREMISE: The horse is a mammal.

CONCLUSION: Therefore, horses lay eggs.

Both the major and minor premises of this argument are true. Some mammals, the platypus and the echidna, for example, do lay eggs. It is also true that the horse is a mammal. However, the conclusion of this argument is false because the argument has an invalid form. You can see this by drawing a diagram of the major premise:

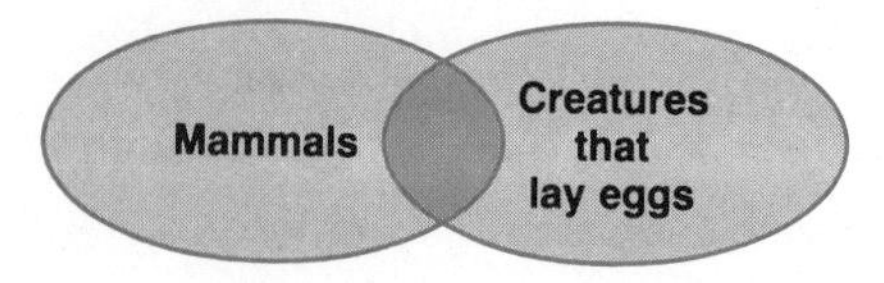

The major premise states that *some* mammals lay eggs. In other words, the two groups, *mammals* and *creatures that lay eggs*, contain elements in common. These elements are represented by the shaded area on the diagram. The minor premise says only that a horse is a mammal, but it does not tell us whether to place the horse inside or outside the shaded area of the circle for mammals. Therefore, the argument does not have a valid or logical form.

A deductive argument also fails if one of its premises is false.

All teenagers love loud music.
Rolanda is a teenager.
Therefore, Rolanda loves loud music.

A diagram can prove that this argument follows proper form.

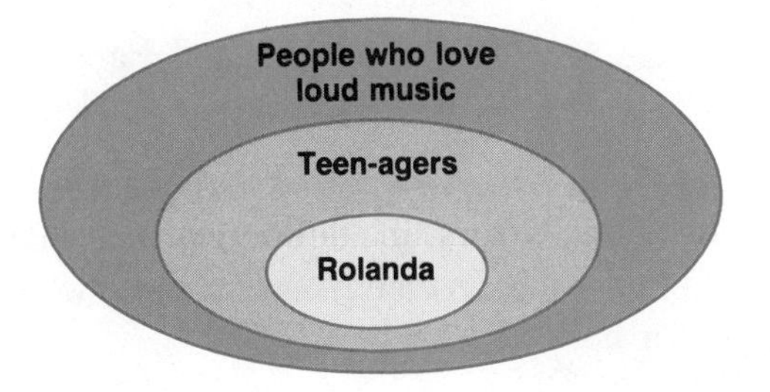

However, the conclusion of this argument has not been proved because the major premise, "All teenagers love loud music," is untrue.

The conclusion of a deductive argument is definitely true only when the argument has a valid form and both of its premises are true.

Exercises Avoiding Errors in Deductive Reasoning

A. For each of the following pairs of statements, draw a set diagram to see whether a valid conclusion is possible. If such a conclusion is possible, write it. If no valid conclusion is possible, write "no conclusion possible."

1. MAJOR PREMISE: Many Eskimo artists depict the myths and activities of the Eskimo people.

   MINOR PREMISE: Kenojuak is an Eskimo artist.

2. MAJOR PREMISE: All lawyers must pass a bar exam.
MINOR PREMISE: Barbara Vicevich is a lawyer.

3. MAJOR PREMISE: Classical guitarists play guitars that have nylon strings.
MINOR PREMISE: Sandy plays a guitar that has nylon strings.

4. MAJOR PREMISE: The people who ate the meat loaf became sick.
MINOR PREMISE: The restaurant manager became sick.

5. MAJOR PREMISE: People who attended grammar school in sixteenth-century England learned to read Latin.
MINOR PREMISE: Shakespeare attended grammar school in sixteenth-century England.

B. Each of the following arguments contains at least one major error. Tell whether each argument has an invalid form, contains false premises, or both.

1. MAJOR PREMISE: Workers must have social security cards.
MINOR PREMISE: Clair has a social security card.
CONCLUSION: Clair is a worker.

2. MAJOR PREMISE: Few Americans speak Thai or Vietnamese.
MINOR PREMISE: Mr. Margolis speaks Vietnamese.
CONCLUSION: Therefore, Mr. Margolis is not an American.

3. MAJOR PREMISE: To learn how to drive, a person must take driver's education.
MINOR PREMISE: All of the teachers in this school know how to drive.
CONCLUSION: All of the teachers in this school took driver's education.

4. MAJOR PREMISE: Eating vegetables is good for you.
MINOR PREMISE: Pears are a kind of vegetable.
CONCLUSION: Eating pears is good for you.

5. MAJOR PREMISE: A professional deep-sea diver can go without breathing for hours.
MINOR PREMISE: Rolfe Washington is a professional deep-sea diver.
CONCLUSION: Rolfe Washington can go without breathing for hours.

Part 4 Other Fallacies in Reasoning

An error in reasoning is called a **fallacy.** Overgeneralization and stereotyping are two fallacies of inductive reasoning. False premises and invalid form are two fallacies of deductive reasoning. Such fallacies can lead to lost arguments, mistaken conclusions, and unsound judgments or beliefs. There are several other types of fallacies that you may encounter. By learning to recognize them, you will be able to identify such errors in the reasoning of others. You will also be able to avoid them in your own speaking and writing.

Study the types of fallacies on the following chart:

Errors of Reasoning

Fallacy	Description	Example
THE SINGLE CAUSE FALLACY	An event that has several causes is incorrectly described as having only one.	Central H.S. won a close football game. A fan told the team's kicker, who had scored a two point field goal, "We owe it all to you."

Fallacy	Description	Example
POST HOC, ERGO, PROPTER HOC (after this, therefore, because of this)	An event is assumed to have caused a second event simply because it preceded the second event in time.	"For two weeks I had a terrible cold. Then, one day, I had some tomato soup. A few hours later, the cold was gone. Tomato soup is the best treatment for colds."
THE EITHER/OR FALLACY	It is assumed that there are only two alternatives when there are more.	Auto racing is a peculiar sport. You either love it or you hate it.
FALSE ANALOGY	A false conclusion is drawn from an observed similarity.	Life is like an elaborate play. People are never really sincere; they just pretend to be.
CIRCULAR REASONING	An attempt is made to prove a statement simply by reasserting it in different words.	Steinbeck is a fine writer because his novels and short stories are so well written.
BANDWAGON	An attempt is made to pressure people to adopt some belief simply in order to conform. If the pressure is to conform to the ideals of an elite group, this fallacy is called **snob appeal.**	"This year, everyone will be wearing our fabulous false furs. Don't be left out. Come on down and see our selection."

Fallacy	Description	Example
TRANSFER	An attempt is made to relate positive feelings that people have about one thing to another idea that is actually unrelated.	At Gimix Products, the spirit of the American pioneer lives on. Gimix Products—making our country strong.
UNRELIABLE TESTIMONIAL	An endorsement is made by someone who is not necessarily qualified to make the endorsement.	"When I crossed the finish line I knew that I was a winner. Today, I'd like to tell you about another winner, Hendrix's Appliances."

Exercise Identifying Fallacies

Identify the fallacies in these passages by choosing its name from among those provided in parentheses.

1. When I wear this T-shirt, I do well on tests. This must be my lucky T-shirt. (post hoc, either/or, false analogy, bandwagon)

2. Coach Watson said that our team should be like a family, so why don't you let me borrow your new sweater? I mean, you borrow your brother's clothes, don't you? (single cause, post hoc, either/or, false analogy, unreliable testimonial)

3. There are two types of politicians: those who support the wealthy, and those who support the poor. (single clause, post hoc, either/or, circular reasoning, snob appeal)

4. Dine at Sarti's—Where the Elite Meet to Eat. (single cause, either/or, false analogy, circular reasoning, snob appeal)

5. If you are tired of winter, bring a May Morning into your home—new May Morning Air Freshener. Feel your house leap into spring. (post hoc, bandwagon, transfer, unreliable testimonial)

6. The colonists came to America because of poor economic opportunities in Europe. (single cause, either/or, circular reasoning, unreliable testimonial)

7. As a professional singer, I can't afford to get a sore throat. That's why I use So-o-o-the Sore Throat Lozenges. Get a pack of So-o-o-the and then you'll know. And tell them your favorite singer sent you. (single cause, either/or, circular reasoning, bandwagon, unreliable testimonial)

Part 5 Avoiding Errors in Meaning

Many errors in reasoning result from the misuse of individual words. To identify such errors, you must understand the different kinds of meanings that a word can have.

Denotation and Connotation

Consider the following statements:

Movie stars are fabulously wealthy.
Movie stars are filthy rich.

In one sense, these statements mean the same thing. They both tell us that movie stars have great financial resources. However, in another sense, these statements do not mean the same thing at all. The first statement implies admiration. The second statement implies disapproval. The phrases *fabulously wealthy* and *filthy rich* have the same **denotative** meaning. In other words, they refer to the same thing. However, they have different **connotative** meanings. That is, they carry different associations and suggest different attitudes.

Vague or Undefined Terms

One common fallacy is the use of **vague or undefined terms.** A term is vague if it has no clear denotation. Using such terms can lead to statements that are unclear or even meaningless.

This fallacy often occurs in judgments. Judgment words such as *good, bad, right, wrong,* or *dangerous* have different connotations for different people and in different contexts. For example, if you say that the ideas in a certain speaker's presentation are *dangerous,* no one can be sure what you mean. Do you mean that the ideas could be physically harmful? Do you mean that they could be detrimental to certain existing ideas? Or do you simply mean that you disagree with the speaker's ideas and are attempting to influence the opinions of others?

Be cautious about using vague terms in your own speech and writing. To avoid vagueness, always define terms that are unclear and, whenever possible, provide specific, concrete examples to illustrate your meaning. Otherwise your arguments may be perceived as weak or even inflammatory.

Equivocation

Equivocation occurs when one takes unfair advantage of the fact that some words have more than one denotative meaning. Suppose, for example, that you read the following headline:

SCIENTIST ADMITS: "I COMMUNICATE WITH ALIENS"

When you read the article, you find out that it is about a linguistic scientist who works for the government immigration service as a translator. The newspaper has taken unfair advantage of the fact that *alien* can mean both "a foreign-born resident who has not become a citizen" and "a creature from outer space."

Loaded Words

Loaded words are words that have powerful positive or negative connotations. The following passage demonstrates how such loaded words can affect the meaning. Read the speech twice. On the initial reading, insert the first word of each pair. On the second reading, insert the remaining word.

My friends, the (*parasite, person*) sitting on my right is, as you know, a (*notorious, famous*) (*politician, statesman*). He is familiar to you, my friends, both as a (*cunning, skillful*) (*bureaucrat, administrator*) and as a (*would-be, distinguished*) (*dictator, public servant*). He is a (*lackey, friend*) of (*big business, free enterprise*) and a (*crony, friend*) of (*union bosses, labor officials*). His (*pigheaded, persevering*) (*fanaticism, dedication*) played a key role in (*brainwashing, persuading*) Congress to pass the (*Slave-Labor, Right-To-Work*) Law that we (*despise, revere*). After hearing him (*rant, speak*) you will return to your homes in (*disgust, pride*) that America could (*spawn, produce*) such a (*creature, man*) . . . .

Loaded words that have powerful positive connotations, like *statesman* or *pride*, are called **purr words**. They are used to sway people to feel positively toward the subject being discussed. Loaded words that have powerful negative connotations, like *lackey* or *fanaticism*, are called **snarl words**. They are used to sway people to feel negatively toward the subject. Whenever you hear or read a passage that contains many such loaded words, you should recognize that the speaker or writer is not supplying any real information. Instead, he or she is simply trying to influence how you feel.

Exercise Avoiding Errors in Meaning

Write two versions of a brief article on one of the topics given below. In the first version, use undefined terms, equivocation, and loaded language. Then rewrite the article, substituting reasonable, unbiased, and accurate language for the slanted words.

1. A controversial issue in the news
2. A school or governmental policy that you would like to change
3. A person, living or dead, whom you greatly admire
4. Your qualifications for a class or club office at your school

SUMMARY AND APPLICATIONS

1. The principles of critical thinking can help you to evaluate the facts, opinions, and arguments that you read and hear. They can also help you to ensure the truth, reasonableness, and validity of facts, opinions, and arguments presented in your own speech and writing.
2. Facts can be proved by observation or by reference to a reliable source. Opinions cannot be proved, but they can be supported by facts.
3. There are two major kinds of reasoning: induction, which derives general conclusions from specific facts; and deduction, which derives specific conclusions from general facts.
4. Learn to recognize and avoid the following logical fallacies:

single clause	*post hoc, ergo propter hoc*
either/or	false analogy
bandwagon	circular reasoning
transfer	unreliable testimonial

5. Learn to recognize and avoid vague or undefined terms, equivocation, and loaded words.

Applications in Other Subject Areas

Mathematics. This subject makes extensive use of deductive reasoning (arguing from general principles to specific conclusions). In a mathematics textbook, find several examples of deductive reasoning. What kind of statements are mathematical statements? Are they facts that are true by definition or by observation?

Science. Scientists use inductive reasoning when they compose a general law to govern specific facts that they have observed. Find a report of a scientific experiment in a textbook or in the science section of your library. Explain what specific facts are observed in the experiment and what general conclusions are drawn as a result of these observations.

Chapter 16

College Entrance Examinations and Other Tests

You have always known how important tests are in school. You are probably also aware of the role that they can play in achieving such personal goals as finding a job, obtaining a driver's license, and getting into most college and vocational programs. This is why it is essential for you to learn how to make the most of the knowledge and abilities that you bring to any particular test.

In this chapter you will learn about some basic types of tests, including college entrance examinations. You will also learn specific strategies for preparing for tests, reducing pre-test anxiety, and answering the most common types of test questions. These strategies will increase your chances of receiving acceptable scores on tests of all kinds. They will also enable you to view tests, not as obstacles or burdens, but as doors to achievement in school and in later life.

Part 1 Tests in Specific Subject Areas

Most of the tests that you take in high school are designed to measure how much you have learned about a specific subject during a particular period of time. To do well on such tests, you must use proper study techniques when preparing for them. In addition, you must apply particular strategies to each of the various kinds of questions that such tests contain.

Preparing for Tests

Because most tests that you take cover specific material studied for your classes, the best way to prepare for them is to make sure that you do not fall behind in studying this material. To accomplish this goal, you must establish good study habits.

1. Keep an assignment notebook and complete all assignments that you are given. Do not procrastinate and then try to complete all the assignments at once.
2. Follow all assignment directions exactly. Pay particular attention to action words used in these directions, such as *explain, list, calculate, estimate,* or *write.*
3. Take thorough notes on all of your schoolwork both in and out of class. These notes should include material from your lectures, discussions, and reading.

4. Set aside regular times for study outside of class. A good rule of thumb is to allot at least twenty minutes per day for every class that you have.
5. Study in an area that is quiet and well-lighted. Keep pens, pencils, paper, and a dictionary by your side.
6. Begin each outside study session with a quick review of the material covered in your classes since your last study session. You may wish to recopy your notes or to make lists of key terms, definitions, names, dates, events, formulae, theories, and concepts.

Another important element of proper preparation for tests is following a logical procedure when reviewing for them.

1. Before you begin, make sure that you know the date of the test, the material to be covered, and what types of questions it will contain.
2. Make a list of study questions on the material to be covered by the test. Combine this list with any study guides supplied by your teachers. Keep a separate list of key terms, definitions, names, dates, events, formulae, theories, and concepts covered by the test.
3. Review all sources of information for the test, including textbooks, notes, returned quizzes, and papers. Reread as many of these sources as time permits. Pay particular attention to chapter headings and summaries, topic and concluding sentences in paragraphs in your texts, and any material that was repeated or emphasized in class.
4. Answer your list of study questions verbally or in writing. You may find it helpful to use flashcards or to have someone else quiz you.
5. Review your notes, study guides, and other materials several times before the day of the test.
6. Prepare yourself mentally and physically for the test by eating well and getting enough sleep. Cope with anxiety by thinking of the test as an opportunity to display your knowledge. If possible, do some light exercise to clear your mind and relieve tension. If you are nervous just prior to taking a test, try relaxing your body, breathing slowly and deeply, and counting your breaths.

Taking Tests

You have already seen a number of strategies for use before tests. The following strategies will be useful to you as you actually take examinations.

1. Survey the test and budget your time. Read all directions before beginning and estimate the amount of time you can devote to the various parts of the test.
2. Answer first those questions that are worth the most points and those that are easiest. Save difficult questions for last.
3. Before answering a question, read it through carefully. Look for words that tell you what to do, such as *describe, find,* or *list*. Know what sort of answer you are expected to give.
4. Save time for review, proofreading, and revision.

In addition to these general guidelines, there are specific strategies you can use on different kinds of test questions. The following hints and techniques can be useful as you answer the kinds of questions found in tests over specific subject areas.

True/false tests

a. If any part of a statement is false, the entire statement is false.
b. Statements containing absolute words, such as *all, never, everyone,* and *always,* are frequently false.
c. Statements containing qualifiers, such as *a few, sometimes, many,* and *occasionally,* are frequently true.

Matching tests

a. Check the directions to see how many times each item can or must be used.
b. Read all items before matching any of them.
c. Match items that you are certain about first.
d. Cross out items as you match them.

Multiple choice tests

a. Read all the choices before answering.
b. Eliminate incorrect answers first.
c. Choose the answer that is *most* complete and accurate.
d. Be skeptical about choices that contain absolute words, such as *totally, always, all,* or *never.*
e. Pay particular attention to negative words, such as *not* or *no,* and to choices, such as *none of the above* or *all of the above.*

Completion, or fill-in-the-blank, tests

a. Make sure your answer fits grammatically.
b. If several words are required to answer the question, give all of them.
c. Write legibly, and proofread your answer for proper spelling, grammar, punctuation, and capitalization.

Short answer tests

a. Answer in complete sentences.
b. Answer all parts of the question.
c. Write legibly and proofread your answer.

Essay tests

a. Read the question carefully, looking for words like *compare* or *interpret* that tell you what information your essay should contain.
b. If the essay question is divided into parts, organize your essay into corresponding parts.
c. Before beginning, write a statement of the main idea and make a quick outline of the major points and supporting details that your essay will contain.
d. Make sure that your essay contains an introduction, body, and conclusion.
e. Use transitions to tie ideas together.
f. Proofread your completed essay for errors in grammar, usage, and mechanics.

Exercises Tests in Specific Subject Areas

A. Find two or three old tests on which you answered some questions incorrectly. Examine these incorrect answers; then, write a paragraph explaining what mistakes you made and how you could have avoided them. Be specific. Refer to the test-taking strategies presented in Part 1 of this chapter.

B. Prepare a list of study questions covering the material presented in Part 1 of this chapter.

C. Explain in one paragraph how you would go about preparing for each of the following:

1. A quiz on a list of spelling and vocabulary words
2. An essay test on the major themes in a novel or play
3. A true/false and multiple choice test on the important people and events of the Civil War

Part 2 College Entrance Examinations

Most colleges require applicants to take entrance examinations. These may be **aptitude tests** that measure basic skills used in many different subject areas or **achievement tests** that measure knowledge of a specific subject such as history or biology. Colleges use scores from such examinations to determine whether applicants meet admission requirements or should receive college credit for work completed in high school. Scholarship committees, including the ones awarding National Merit Scholarships, use these same scores to identify students who should be considered for financial awards. Because of their importance to both college admissions and scholarships, you need to familiarize yourself with the various college entrance examinations now in use. You should also learn how to prepare yourself for taking these exams.

Types of College Entrance Examinations

The two most widely-used college entrance examinations are the Scholastic Aptitude Test (the S.A.T.) and the test of the American College Testing Program (the A.C.T.). Both are three-hour, multiple choice exams.

The S.A.T. is divided into sections on verbal and mathematical abilities and is scored on a scale of 200-800. It is accompanied by the Test of Standard Written English, a multiple choice test used to measure your ability to recognize language that is free of errors in grammar and composition. To prepare for the S.A.T., you can take the Preliminary Scholastic Aptitude Test/ National Merit Scholarship Qualifying Test (P.S.A.T./ N.M.S.Q.T.). This is a practice test containing questions like those on the S.A.T. Taking this test is important not only because it provides practice for the S.A.T., but because its results are used to determine eligibility for National Merit Scholarships.

The A.C.T. consists of two parts, one a series of four separate tests on English, mathematics, the natural sciences, and social studies; and the other a series of questions about your achievements, goals, and special interests. Each part of the A.C.T. is scored on a scale of 0 to 36. Both the S.A.T. and the A.C.T. are commonly used, along with high school scores and letters of recommendation, as a basis for deciding upon applications for admission to college.

In addition to or in place of the S.A.T. and the A.C.T., many schools require applicants to take achievement tests such as the English Composition Test or the College Board Achievement Test in Physics. These tests are often used to place students in courses suited to their level of competence in particular subjects. The College Entrance Examination Board (the C.E.E.B.) offers fifteen such tests on various subjects. Each test is one hour long. Colleges that require achievement tests often ask their applicants to take any three of the fifteen.

In addition, the C.E.E.B. offers Advanced Placement Tests in some subjects. These are college level examinations that enable high school students to receive college credit for work they have already completed.

Preparing for College Entrance Examinations

Aptitude tests such as the S.A.T. and the A.C.T. measure skills that are gained over a period of many years. Consequently, it is impossible to study for them in the usual sense. In other words, you cannot simply sit down a few days before one of these exams and learn everything that you need to know for them. Instead, you must begin now to develop the skills that these tests measure, including, for both the S.A.T. and A.C.T., your vocabulary; your reading and computational skills; your ability to think reasonably and critically; and your understanding of the basic principles of English.

The following guidelines will help you to increase your skills.

Long-Term Preparation for College Entrance Examinations

1. Study the vocabulary sections of this textbook. Keep lists of all unfamiliar words that you encounter in your reading or listening. Try to learn at least ten new words every week.
2. Devote as much time and energy as you can to classwork in the following areas: English grammar, usage, mechanics, and composition; mathematics; natural sciences; and social studies.
3. Read as much as possible on your own. Keep a journal and take notes on your reading. Include in your notes definitions or explanations of any key terms, ideas, themes, theories, or concepts that you encounter.
4. Write often and write a great deal. This writing can be on any subject that interests you. The one essential element is that you spend time doing revisions. During the revision process, force yourself to examine your language carefully. Such a regimen can improve your English skills tremendously.

Long-term preparation guidelines have one thing in common: they require that you make learning a habit. You need to read, write, and learn new vocabulary words, and study for your classes on a regular basis. Schedule your time carefully and establish goals.

During the period immediately preceding the exam you should aim to further sharpen your skills and increase your confidence. The following guidelines will help.

Short-Term Preparation for College Entrance Examinations

1. **Make use of practice materials.**
   a. The test applications for both the S.A.T and A.C.T. contain sample questions and guidelines for answering them. Read these carefully and answer the practice questions.
   b. Various commercially-prepared test-taking manuals are available in libraries or at bookstores. These contain practice questions and explanations of the questions that may increase your understanding of the material.
   c. If you are going to take the S.A.T., you can choose to take the Preliminary Scholastic Aptitude Test beforehand. This is a practice test that contains questions like those on the S.A.T.
2. **Review question types and strategies.** (See Part 3 of this chapter for more information on these.)
3. **Prepare yourself mentally and physically.**
   a. On the night before the test, relax and get plenty of sleep.
   b. Eat well on the night before and the morning of the exam.
   c. Follow the guidelines for reducing nervousness given on page 348.

Taking College Entrance Examinations

The following guidelines will help you to convert your pretest preparation into a successful test experience.

Beginning the Test

1. Equip yourself with the necessary materials. These are detailed in the informational booklet accompanying your registration form. Typically, you will need several sharpened pencils, your properly-completed admission ticket, a recognized form of personal identification, and a watch to aid you in making efficient use of time.
2. Arrive at the test center approximately half an hour before the test is scheduled to begin. Settle into your assigned seat and accustom yourself to the surroundings.
3. Listen carefully to the oral instructions of the test supervisor. Be alert to announcements instructing you on how and where to supply the requested information on the answer form. Further announcements will direct you to the appropriate page in the examination booklet. Before the test begins, you will be given an opportunity to ask questions.
4. Wait for the command to begin. Do not attempt to direct yourself and do not anticipate commands.

Filling Out the Answer Key

1. The answer key will look something like this:

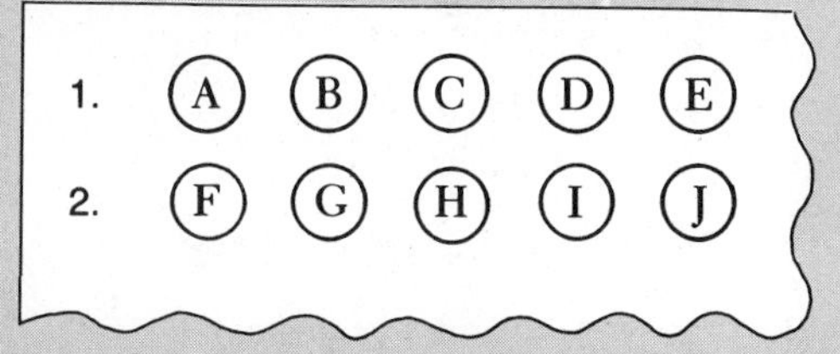

2. Indicate your answer by darkening the circle on the answer key that corresponds to the correct answer in your test booklet. Check regularly to make sure that you are marking the correct spaces on the answer sheet.
3. Make sure that circles are completely darkened. Erase any stray marks that you make on the answer sheet. These marks may be interpreted as answers.
4. If you wish to change an answer, be sure to erase your initial answer completely.

Selecting Your Answers

1. S.A.T. scores reflect the number of questions answered correctly minus a penalty for questions answered incorrectly. It is not in your best interest to guess unless you can eliminate two or three incorrect answers.
2. A.C.T. scores do not reflect a penalty for guessing.
3. As you begin the test, note the number of questions and the time available. Check your watch regularly to make certain that you are not wasting time on difficult questions. Remember that you are not expected to answer every question correctly.
4. Answer easy questions as you come to them.
5. Place a "+" on your answer sheet next to any question that seems answerable but requires a great deal of time.

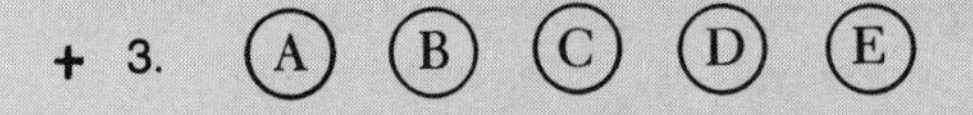

Place a "−" on your answer sheet next to any question that appears to be too difficult to answer.

− 4. (F) (G) (H) (I) (J)

After answering all of the easy questions, go back to the ones marked with a "+" and answer them. Once you have answered these, attempt to answer the ones you marked with a "−."

Make sure that you save time to erase your "+" and "−" marks. Otherwise, these may be read as answers.

Part 3 Types of Standardized Test Questions

To prepare for college entrance examinations, familiarize yourself with the types of questions that they contain. These include *antonyms*, *analogies*, *sentence completion*, *sentence correction*, *reading comprehension*, and *usage questions*.

Antonyms

An **antonym** is a word that is opposite in meaning to another word. Antonym questions provide a single word and ask you to select from a list of words the one that is most opposite in meaning. A typical antonym question looks like this:

EXAMPLE: Antonyms

DEPRESS: (A) force (B) allow (C) clarify (D) elate (E) loosen

To answer an antonym question, use the following strategies.

1. Look for a word that is opposite in meaning. Do not be thrown off by any synonyms—words that are similar in meaning—that are included among the choices.
2. Before looking at the choices, be sure that you know the meaning of the first word. Define it using any of the following methods.

   a. Think of another word or group of words that means the same thing.
   b. Think of a sentence or sentences that use the word, then try to arrive at an exact definition.
   c. Try analyzing the parts of the word. See Chapter 1 for more information.

3. Once you know the meaning of the first word, look at the choices. If none of these is obviously the correct antonym, try either or both of the following strategies.

   a. Eliminate any obviously incorrect answers.
   b. Remember that many words have more than one meaning. If none of the choices seems to be opposite in meaning, think of other meanings of the first word.

The answer to the sample question is D.

Analogies

Analogies are words that are related to each other in some way. In an analogy question, you are given two words that are related, and you must determine what this relationship is. You then choose a second pair of words that are related in the same way. A typical analogy question looks like this:

EXAMPLE: Analogies

SONG: REPERTOIRE:: (A) score: melody (B) solo: chorus (C) instrument: artist (D) suit: wardrobe (E) benediction: church

There are strategies to use in answering analogy questions.

1. First determine the relationship between the first pair of words by creating a sentence containing both of them.

   Several *songs* make up a *repertoire*.

Common relationships found in analogy questions include:

Type of Analogy	Example
action to object	play: clarinet
cause to effect	sun: sunburn
item to category	iguana: reptile
object to its function	pencil: writing
object to its material	curtains: cloth
part to whole	page: book
time sequence	recent: current
type to characteristic	dancer: agile
word to antonym	help: hinder
word to synonym	provisions: supplies
worker and creation	artist: sketch
worker and tool	lumberjack: saw

2. Then, find a second pair of words that you can substitute for the original pair.

   Several *suits* make up a *wardrobe*.

Sentence Completion

Sentence completion questions measure both your vocabulary and your ability to recognize relationships between parts of a sentence. You are given a sentence from which one or two words have been removed. You must choose words that best fit the meaning of the rest of the sentence. A typical sentence completion question looks like this:

> **EXAMPLE: Sentence Completion**
>
> The author was determined to . . . his own conclusion, so he . . . any information that did not support it.
>
> (A) uphold . . . ignored (B) revise . . . destroyed
> (C) advance . . . devised (D) disprove . . . distorted
> (E) reverse . . . confiscated

To answer sentence completion questions, use the following strategies.

1. Read the incomplete sentence carefully, noting any key words. Pay particular attention to words that indicate contrast (*but, however, on the other hand*) or similarity (*and, another, the same as*).
2. Try each of the choices in the sentence, eliminating any that make no sense or that are grammatically incorrect.
3. Do not be misled by answers that contain only one word that fits well into the sentence. Incorrect answers often contain one word that makes sense and another one that doesn't. In the example, the first word in answer C makes sense, but the second word does not. Answer A is correct.
4. Look for grammatical clues in the sentence. Does the sentence call for a verb, an adverb, a noun? If a verb is

required, what should its tense be? By asking such questions, you can sometimes eliminate incorrect answers.

Sentence Correction

Sentence correction questions test the ability to recognize errors in sentences. Some part or all of a sentence is underlined. If the underlined material contains no errors, you mark "A," which repeats the underlined material exactly. If the underlined material contains one or more errors, you choose the word or group of words that produces a correct sentence. A typical sentence correction question looks like this:

EXAMPLE: Sentence Correction

The shorter bearpaw snowshoes are the best choice if you are looking for an easy to lift and maneuver model.

(A) an easy to lift and maneuver model
(B) a model that is easy to lift and maneuver
(C) an easy model as far as lifting and maneuvering goes
(D) a model with ease of lifting and also maneuver
(E) an easily lifted and also maneuvered model

The following strategies will help you to answer sentence correction questions.

1. Identify the error before looking at the answers. Look for the errors of the following kinds.
   a. Errors in grammar
   b. Errors in word choice
   c. Errors in punctuation or capitalization
   d. Awkwardness or vagueness
   e. Ambiguity (double meaning)
2. Check your answer by inserting it and then reading the entire sentence. The underlined phrase in the example is awkward. Choice B best corrects the sentence.

Usage Questions

Usage questions require that you recognize writing that is not standard written English. In usage questions, four words or phrases are underlined and lettered. You must either choose the underlined part that contains an error or mark the answer corresponding to *no error*. Here is a typical usage question.

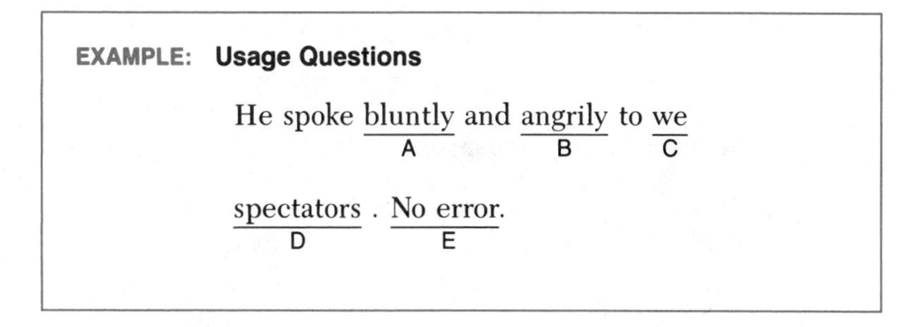
EXAMPLE: Usage Questions

He spoke bluntly (A) and angrily (B) to we (C) spectators (D). No error. (E)

Use the following strategies to answer usage questions.

1. Read the sentence in its entirety.
2. Look for errors of the following kinds:

    a. Incorrect word choice
    b. Errors in punctuation
    c. Errors in capitalization
    d. Errors in grammar
    e. Improper, awkward, or unclear sentence structure

3. Common grammatical errors found in usage questions include the following: incorrect verb tenses, improper agreement of pronoun and antecedent or of subject and verb, improper form of the pronoun, and use of an adjective for an adverb or an adverb for an adjective. Common errors in sentence structure include fragments, dangling modifiers, improper parallelism, and run-ons caused by comma faults. See the Handbook for further information.
4. Remember that the error, if there is one, appears in one of the underlined sections of the sentence. The correct answer to the example question is C. The object pronoun *us* should follow the preposition.

Reading Comprehension

The **reading comprehension** questions on both the S.A.T. and the A.C.T. measure your ability to understand various kinds of reading passages. These passages are taken from such fields as the biological and physical sciences, the humanities, and the social sciences. After reading a passage, you must then answer questions about it. A typical reading comprehension passage looks like this:

EXAMPLE: Reading Comprehension

Aside from the large number of purely imaginary beings which people the regular folk tales of Europe and western Asia, and which the tellers normally recognize as unreal, there exist in every country a considerable number of such beings, human or animal in form, devoutly believed in by both storyteller and listener. It is not easy to draw a sharp line between the creatures of fiction and of actual belief. But psychologically there is a great difference, for the creatures of belief are a part of the unlettered man's view of the natural world.

Each country has such beliefs. Many are doubtless related to those of neighboring lands, but exact equations of similar imaginary creatures are usually inaccurate. Each country has its own favorite groups. The *sidhe,* or kindly fairies, of Ireland; the terrible *baba yagas* of Russia; the malevolent *glaestigs* of the Scottish Highlands; the *jinns* of the Near East; and the *rakshasas* of India—these creatures set the tone for the whole world of supernatural beings which they dominate.

According to the passage, the sidhe, baba yagas, glaestigs, jinns, and rakshasas are all examples of:

(A) folk tales
(B) dangerous creatures
(C) kindly creatures
(D) imaginary creatures

To answer reading comprehension questions, use the following strategies.

1. Expect questions on the following:

   a. The central thought of the passage
   b. Specific details in the passage
   c. Conclusions that can be made based upon information provided in the passage
   d. The meanings of words in the passage
   e. The mood of the passage
   f. Specific techniques used by the writer of the passage
   g. Relationships between things in the passage

2. As you read the passage, identify the main idea and pay particular attention to transitions and other words that show relationships.
3. Read all the choices before you select an answer.
4. Answer the questions based on material in the passage, not on your own knowledge or opinions.
5. Do not choose an answer simply because it is true. Make certain that you answer the question being asked.
6. Do not be misled by answers that are partially correct.
7. Budget your time. Set a time limit for reading each passage and answering questions on it. Do not waste time on impossibly difficult questions. Refer to your watch to make sure that you are not spending too much time. The correct answer to the question is D.

Exercises Taking College Entrance Examinations

The following test questions were taken from preparation materials created by the College Entrance Examination Board for students taking the S.A.T.

A. Antonyms. Each question below consists of a word in capital letters, followed by five lettered words or phrases. Choose the word or phrase that is most nearly *opposite* in meaning to the word in capital letters. Since some of the questions require you to distinguish fine shades of meaning, consider all the choices before deciding which is best.

1. WILT: (A) prevent (B) drain (C) expose (D) revive (E) stick
2. ISSUE: (A) dilute (B) revolve (C) depend (D) substitute (E) retract
3. PREMEDITATED: (A) spontaneous (B) conclusive (C) disruptive (D) vindictive (E) strenuous
4. SUMMARY: (A) bracing (B) accented (C) detailed (D) animated (E) disconcerting
5. WOE: (A) honesty (B) obedience (C) generosity (D) happiness (E) cleverness
6. RABID: (A) poignant (B) circular (C) skillful (D) dense (E) calm
7. AIR: (A) conceal (B) conform (C) detain (D) mislead (E) satisfy
8. CIRCUMSCRIBED: (A) unbounded (B) imperfect (C) injurious (D) readily evaded (E) barely legible
9. RANCOR: (A) carelessness (B) restlessness (C) inexperience (D) kindness (E) self-consciousness
10. PERIPHERAL: (A) colossal (B) central (C) condensed (D) subsequent (E) adjacent

B. Analogies. Each question consists of a related pair of words or phrases, followed by five lettered pairs of words or phrases. Select the lettered pair that *best* expresses a relationship similar to that expressed in the original pair.

1. COW : BARN :: (A) pig:mud (B) chicken:coop (C) camel:water (D) cat:tree (E) horse:racetrack
2. LEAVE : LINGER :: (A) manipulate:manage (B) warrant:employ (C) surprise:astonish (D) cease:prolong (E) flout:violate
3. NOTES : SCALE :: (A) solos:harmony (B) sentences:punctuation (C) attitudes:fact (D) fractions:numerator (E) letters:alphabet

4. APPAREL : PERSON:: (A) plumage:bird (B) prey:animal (C) water:fish (D) insignia:officer (E) scenery:theater

5. SONG : RECITAL:: (A) author:bibliography (B) episode:series (C) coach:team (D) intermission:play (E) poetry:prose

6. ANALGESIC : PAIN:: (A) vaccination:injection (B) anesthetic:sleep (C) antidote:poisoning (D) prescription:medication (E) liniment:ointment

7. FEINT : ILLUSION:: (A) insanity:hallucination (B) decoy:enticement (C) ambush:cache (D) impasse:exit (E) ploy:vengeance

8. BURNISH : LUSTER:: (A) resist:aggression (B) preserve:area (C) accelerate:rapidity (D) pivot:reflex (E) plunge:distance

9. HEIRLOOM : INHERITANCE:: (A) payment:currency (B) belongings:receipt (C) land:construction (D) legacy:bill (E) booty:plunder

10. PHILISTINE : CULTIVATED:: (A) regionalist:authoritarian (B) anarchist:disorderly (C) capitalist:greedy (D) visionary:practical (E) eccentric:artistic

C. Sentence Completion. Each sentence below has one or two blanks, each blank indicating that something has been omitted. Beneath the sentence are five lettered words or sets of words. Choose the word or set of words that *best* fits the meaning of the sentence as a whole.

1. He claimed that the document was ___ because it merely listed endangered species and did not specify penalties for harming them.

   (A) indispensable (B) inadequate (C) punitive (D) aggressive (E) essential

2. The author makes no attempt at ___ order; a scene from 1960 is followed by one from 1968, which, in turn, is

followed by one from 1964.

(A) an impartial (B) an innovative (C) a motley (D) a chronological (E) an extemporaneous

3. Traditionally, countries with __ frontiers requiring __ must maintain a large army and support it by imposing taxes.

(A) historic..markers (B) vulnerable..defense
(C) vague..exploration (D) unwanted..elimination
(E) contested..estimation

4. The ability to estimate distance comes only with __; a baby reaches with equal confidence for its bottle or the moon.

(A) tranquility (B) talent (C) experience
(D) assurance (E) distress

5. She undertook a population census of the island with the __, if not always the enthusiastic support, of the authorities.

(A) objection (B) elation (C) suspicion
(D) acquiescence (E) disdain

D. Sentence Correction. In each of the following sentences, some part or all of the sentence is underlined. Below each sentence you will find five ways of phrasing the underlined part. Select the answer that produces the most effective sentence, one that is clear and exact, without awkwardness or ambiguity. In choosing answers, follow the requirements of standard written English. Choose the answer that best expresses the meaning of the original sentence.

1. Because dodo birds could not fly, so they were killed by the hogs and monkeys brought to the islands by the explorers.

(A) fly, so they were killed
(B) fly, they were killed
(C) fly and they were killed
(D) fly, and this allowed them to be killed
(E) fly, killing them

2. Performing before an audience for the first time, fear suddenly overcame the child and she could not remember her lines.

   (A) fear suddenly overcame the child and she could not remember her lines
   (B) the lines could not be remembered by the child because she was overcome by fear
   (C) the child was suddenly overcome by fear and could not remember her lines
   (D) the child was suddenly overcome by fear, she could not remember her lines
   (E) suddenly the child was overcome by fear, and consequently not remembering her lines

3. Violin makers know that the better the wood is seasoned, the better the results for the tone of the instrument.

   (A) better the results for the tone of the instrument
   (B) better the tone of the instrument
   (C) better the result is for the instrument's tone
   (D) resulting tone will be better
   (E) result will be a better instrument tone

4. Although today many fabrics are made from synthetic fibers, at one time all natural fibers were used in their manufacture.

   (A) all natural fibers were used in their manufacture
   (B) all fabrics were made of natural fibers
   (C) they were making them all of natural fibers
   (D) they made fabrics all of natural fibers
   (E) their manufacture was of all natural fibers

5. Between three and four percent of children born with hearing defects serious enough to require treatment.

   (A) born with hearing defects
   (B) being born with hearing defects that are
   (C) are born with hearing defects
   (D) are born with hearing defects, these are
   (E) born with hearing defects which are

E. Usage Questions. The following sentences contain problems in grammar, usage, diction (choice of words), and idiom. Some sentences are correct. No sentence contains more than one error. You will find that the error, if there is one, is underlined and lettered. Assume that elements of the sentence that are not underlined are correct and cannot be changed. In choosing answers, follow the requirements of standard written English. If there is an error, select the *one underlined part* that must be changed to make the sentence correct. If there is no error, select choice E.

1. Most people listen to the weather forecast every day, but (A) they know hardly nothing (B) about (C) the forces that influence (D) the weather. No error (E)

2. Him (A) and the other (B) delegates immediately (C) accepted the resolution drafted by (D) the neutral states. No error (E)

3. The foundations of (A) psychoanalysis were established by Sigmund Freud, who begun (B) to develop (C) his theories in (D) the 1880's. No error (E)

4. In her novels, Nella Larson focused on (A) the problems of young black women which (B) lived in (C) Europe and America during (D) the 1920's. No error (E)

5. During the early Middle Ages, before the development
A
of the printing press, virtually the only books were those
B C
that are laboriously copied by monks. No error
D E

F. Reading Comprehension. The passage below is followed by questions based on its content. Answer the questions following the passage on the basis of what is stated or implied in the passage.

Mars revolves around the Sun in 687 Earth days, which is equivalent to 23 Earth months. The axis of Mars's rotation is tipped at a 25° angle from the plane of its orbit, nearly the same as the Earth's tilt of about 23°. Because the tilt causes the seasons, we know that Mars goes through a year with four seasons just as the Earth does.

From the Earth, we have long watched the effect of the seasons on Mars. In the Martian winter, in a given hemisphere, there is a polar ice cap. As the Martian spring comes to the Northern Hemisphere, for example, the north polar cap shrinks, and material in the planet's more temperate zones darkens. The surface of Mars is always mainly reddish, with darker gray areas that, from the Earth, appear blue-green. In the spring, the darker regions spread. Half a Martian year later, the same process happens in the Southern Hemisphere.

One possible explanation for these changes is biological: Martian vegetation could be blooming or spreading in the spring. There are other explanations, however. The theory that presently seems most reasonable is that each year during the Northern Hemisphere springtime, a dust storm starts, with winds that reach velocities as high as hundreds of kilometers per hour. Fine, light-colored dust is blown from slopes, exposing dark areas underneath. If the dust were composed of certain kinds of materials, such as limonite, the reddish color would be explained.

1. It can be inferred that one characteristic of limonite is its

(A) reddish color
(B) blue-green color
(C) ability to change colors
(D) ability to support rich vegetation
(E) tendency to concentrate into a hard surface

2. According to the author, seasonal variations on Mars are a direct result of the

(A) proximity of the planet to the Sun
(B) proximity of the planet to the Earth
(C) presence of ice caps at the poles of the planet
(D) tilt of the planet's rotational axis
(E) length of time required by the planet to revolve around the Sun

3. It can be inferred that, as spring arrives in the Southern Hemisphere of Mars, which of the following is also occurring?

(A) The northern polar cap is increasing in size.
(B) The axis of rotation is tipping at a greater angle.
(C) A dust storm is ending in the Southern Hemisphere.
(D) The material in the northern temperate zones is darkening.
(E) Vegetation in the southern temperate zones is decaying.

1. To take tests successfully in specific subject areas, you must develop good study habits and follow a logical procedure for review.
2. The most widely used standardized aptitude tests are the S.A.T. and the A.C.T. In addition, many schools require that students take achievement tests. Other standardized tests that you may choose to take include the P.S.A.T./N.M.S.Q.T. and the Advanced Placement Tests in particular subjects.
3. Long term preparation for college entrance exams involves studying vocabulary, devoting time and energy to classwork, and doing independent reading and writing.
4. Short term preparation for college entrance exams involves making use of practice materials and learning strategies for answering different types of questions.

Applications in Other Subject Areas

All Subjects. Check with your college adviser or guidance counselor to get a list of achievement tests offered by the College Entrance Examinations Board. Discuss the possibility of taking achievement tests in your areas of specialization. Such tests may allow you to receive college credit for your high school work.

Mathematics / Natural Sciences / Social Studies. In addition to containing sections on English skills, the S.A.T. and A.C.T. have sections covering the following areas.

S.A.T.	A.C.T.
Mathematics, including basic arithmetic, algebra, and geometry	Natural Sciences Social Sciences

Discuss these sections with your math and science teachers. Ask for their suggestions on preparing for these sections, and report your findings to your class.

Chapter 17

Language Skills and Your Future

Up to this point, you have used your skills in writing, speaking, and listening primarily to complete school assignments or to communicate casually with friends. Soon, however, you will find different uses for these skills in a new context—the world of your future. Suddenly your language abilities will become the tool with which you conduct important business. It will also be the means through which you begin a career or secure a place in college. Your ability to communicate may very well determine how much success you have in all of these areas.

This chapter will introduce you to some of the ways that the language skills you already have may be applied in these new situations. Use this information as you begin making decisions about what you will do after high school.

Part 1 Writing Business Letters

The business letter is an important and efficient means of communication. Its primary purpose is to convey accurately important information, such as orders, instructions, or requests. The business letter also communicates one other important idea to the reader—an impression of the person who wrote the letter. When the letter is the only link between these two people, as in the case of a letter of application, the impression that is created becomes extremely important.

In order to create a positive impression of yourself when you write a business letter, you must understand the basic features of good form and effective content.

The Parts of a Business Letter

To write a good business letter, you must first understand its form. Every good business letter contains six main parts.

1. **The heading** is made up of three lines: The first line contains your street address; the second gives your city, state, and ZIP code; and the third tells the date of your letter.

1335 N. Jefferson Street
Van Nuys, California 94213
August 15, 1985

2. **The inside address** contains the following information: on the first line, the name and title of the person to whom you are writing (or the name of the department, if you are not writing to a specific person); on the second line, the name of the organization; on the third line, the street or mailing address; and, on the fourth line, the city, state, and ZIP code.

Ms. Stephanie Lach, Service Representative
Consumer Service Department
Pacific Stereo, Inc.
1001 Oceanside Blvd.
Santa Monica, California 96722

Whenever possible, direct your correspondence to a specific person. If this person has a title, use it. If not, use a courtesy title such as Mr., Miss, Ms., or Mrs.

3. **The salutation** follows the inside address. One line is left blank before and after the salutation. The following are salutations commonly used in business letters:

For a Department or Company	For a Specific Person Name Unknown
Gentlemen:	Dear Sir:
Ladies and Gentlemen:	Dear Madam:
Dear Sir or Madam:	Dear Sir or Madam:

4. **The body** is the most crucial part of your letter. In this part of your letter, you state your message as clearly and concisely as possible. In a polite and businesslike tone, say what you have to say without including unnecessary information.

5. **The closing** should be kept as simple as possible. The first word should be capitalized, and the last word should be followed by a comma. Leave one blank line between the body and the closing. Then, skip four lines below the closing and type or print your name.

Some closings are more formal than others. In choosing an appropriate closing, let your audience be your guide.

FORMAL: Yours respectfully,
Respectfully yours,
Yours very respectfully,

BUSINESSLIKE: Yours truly,
Yours very truly,
Very truly yours,

LESS FORMAL: Sincerely,
Yours sincerely,
Sincerely yours,

6. **The signature** should appear in the space between the closing and your name.

Whenever you write a business letter, make a copy for yourself by using carbon paper or a duplicating machine.

Organizing the Parts of a Business Letter

Every business letter must contain all of the parts mentioned on the previous page, and these parts must be organized in an accepted form. The two most common organizations for business letters are block form and modified block form. In letters written in block form, all six parts begin at the left margin. (See the letter on page 392.) In modified block form, the heading and closing are moved to the right, and the paragraphs of the letter are indented. (See the letter on page 397.)

Types of Business Letters

Business letters are used for a number of purposes. They can help you to get an interview, order a product, or settle a claim. To ensure that your letters accomplish the purposes for which they are written, they must be clear and easy to read. This requires not only proper grammar, punctuation, and spelling, but well-organized and significant content as well.

As you learned previously, the primary message of a business letter is contained in the body. This content will vary, but you should always follow a few general rules:

1. **Make certain that your message is well-organized.** Good business letters have a definite beginning, middle, and end.
    a. Begin your letter by stating your purpose simply and directly.
    b. Follow this introduction by supplying the reader with any necessary information or specific details related to your purpose.
    c. End your letter by asking the reader to take some action that accomplishes your purpose.

2. **Be brief and to the point.** Readers of business letters do not have time to read messages that wander.
    a. Before writing, make an outline of your letter by listing the major points that you wish to communicate.
    b. After writing, revise your letter to eliminate any unnecessary information.

3. **Establish a polite and businesslike tone.** Even if you are writing a letter of complaint, make certain that you remain courteous and reasonable. If your letter is written in a pleasant manner, your reader is more likely to take the actions that you have requested.

Letters Requesting Information. One common type of business letter is the request for information. Such letters are used to gain information about colleges, employment opportunities, and specific products or services. They are also used to gather information during research.

When writing a letter requesting information, state as clearly as possible what information you need and why you need it. You may wish to include an itemized list of this information in the body of the letter. Also, make sure that you include all information your reader will need to answer your letter.

Letters Ordering Merchandise. Whenever you write a letter to order merchandise, you should make your letter as complete as possible. Be sure to include the names, sizes, colors, and catalog numbers of the products you are ordering. Also include the prices of these products and the total dollar amount of your order. (For clarity, put these items in list form.) Check to determine whether you or the company will pay for postage. If you are expected to pay, be sure you add this amount to the order. Also check the instructions about sales tax. Any errors on your part will cause delays in the delivery or receipt of unwanted items. Keep a copy of your letter in case mistakes are made in filling your order.

Letters of Complaint. At times you will need to write a letter of complaint to resolve a conflict or settle a claim. In such a situation, you can usually get the manufacturer's address from the label on the box used to ship the product to you. If not, you can obtain the necessary information through your local store. Before you write the letter, remember that the manufacturer did not intend to send you damaged merchandise. Therefore, keep your tone polite and reasonable. Your purpose is to settle a claim; the tone of your letter should reflect your willingness to cooperate in settling this claim.

Letters of Application. When applying to a school or for a job, you will need to write a letter of application. A letter of application to a college is usually accompanied by an application form containing most of the essential application information. Therefore, the letter may be brief. Simply state your intentions and refer the reader to any accompanying materials.

Body of a Letter to a College

```
Dear Sir or Madam:

Please consider me a candidate for admission to
the freshman class at Indiana University this
fall. Enclosed you will find my completed appli-
cation form, letters of recommendation, and high
school transcripts. I have instructed the Col-
lege Board to send my S.A.T. scores to your
office. Thank you for considering my applica-
tion.

Sincerely,
```

A letter of application to an employer should state the position for which you wish to be considered and your related experience and skills. Refer the employer to your résumé for references and for further information on your background. Invite the employer to send you an application form or to contact you by mail or telephone to set up an interview. (See pages 395-397 for further information and a sample letter.)

Exercise Writing Business Letters

Choose one of the following subjects and write a letter using your own return address. Be sure to use the proper form.

1. Write a request for information to the Chamber of Commerce in some city. Be specific as to why you need this informa-

tion (you are planning to move to the city, you are interested in vacationing there, or you are researching the city as part of an assignment).

2. Write to a college or university requesting information regarding any courses that are offered for high school students. Specify your interests and grade level.

3. Write a letter ordering a specific product.

4. Write a letter of complaint to the manufacturer of some defective product that you have recently purchased.

5. Write to a company asking about summer employment. Include all necessary information.

Part 2 Preparing for the Future

During the next year or so, you will be making several important decisions concerning what you will do after high school. In Part 1 you learned about one basic communication tool—the business letter—that will help you gather the information necessary to make those decisions. There are several other sources to which you can refer for this information. The first of these is you.

Assessing Your Interests and Skills

To assess the values and preferences of people who come to them for advice on choosing a career or a field of study, professional counselors often conduct an interest inventory. This involves asking questions to determine the work environments and areas of occupational and academic endeavor for which people are best suited by their interests and values. The chart on the following page illustrates the types of items found on such an interest inventory. An answer of 3 means that you do not have a preference for either of the alternatives presented. Answers of 2 or 4 indicate moderate committment to one of the choices, while responses of 1 or 5 show a strong committment to one of the two alternatives. If you would like to complete an interest inventory, see your school counselor.

Interest Inventory

To determine the types of jobs that are suited to you, rank yourself on a scale of one to five in regard to each of the following questions.

Question		
1. Which do you prefer most, mental labor or physical labor?	mental	physical
	1 2 3 4 5	
2. Which do you prefer most, working with other people or by yourself?	by myself	with others
	1 2 3 4 5	
3. Which do you prefer most, working with words or with numbers?	words	numbers
	1 2 3 4 5	
4. Which do you prefer most, working outdoors or indoors?	outdoors	indoors
	1 2 3 4 5	
5. Which do you prefer most, working with people or with objects (including machines)?	people	objects
	1 2 3 4 5	
6. How important is making a great deal of money to you?	very important	not important
	1 2 3 4 5	
7. Do you like lots of variation in your daily activities, or do you prefer things to remain stable from day to day?	like change	prefer stability
	1 2 3 4 5	
8. Do you prefer being your own boss or working under a leader?	being my own boss	working under a leader
	1 2 3 4 5	

Exercises Assessing Your Interests and Skills

A. Answer the questions shown in the Interest Inventory on page 379. Write a short paragraph that summarizes what you find out about yourself.

B. To further determine your specific areas of interest, answer the following questions.

1. Of the courses that you have taken in school, which have you enjoyed most? Why?
2. Of the courses that you have taken in school, which have you enjoyed least? Why?
3. What extracurricular activities have you participated in? Which of these activities did you enjoy most and why?
4. What other public or group activities have you participated in outside of school?
5. Choose three of the following areas of employment or study and rank them, with 1 being the first choice.

Agribusiness (Farming)
Business and Office
Communications and Media
Construction
Engineering
Environment
Fine Arts and Humanities
Health and Medicine
Home Economics
Hospitality and Recreation
Manufacturing
Marketing and Distribution
Personal Services
Public Services
Scientific Research
Transportation

Obtaining More Information

Once you have conducted an interest inventory and assessed your skills, the next step is to find information on careers or schools that match your interests and skills. The following are excellent sources of such information:

1. **College catalogs or bulletins** provide in-depth information on specific fields of study.
2. **Employers or schools** may be contacted to answer specific questions about careers or fields of study.

3. ***The Federal Occupational Handbook*** contains information on thousands of jobs, including discussions of working conditions and training and skills required. It is available in most counseling offices and libraries.
4. **Your counselor** at school is another excellent source. He or she can provide you with reference materials as well as additional information about employment trends in various fields. If you have trouble identifying a particular field that interests you, you may want to take a vocational test. Such tests can provide valuable insights. Your guidance counselor can also help you determine the amount of education you will need to reach your career goals.
5. **Libraries** contain many important sources of information on careers and schools. These include reference works, college catalogs, books on specific careers or schools, and materials in verticle files. If you have specific career or school-related questions that you cannot answer by reference to materials known to you, discuss your questions with a reference librarian.

Exercises Obtaining Additional Information

A. Choose one of the occupational areas listed in Exercise B on page 380. Using one or more of the sources listed on page 380 and above, find two job classifications within this field that may be of interest to you (example: Health and Medicine: 1. Nuclear Medicine Technology, 2. Respiratory Therapy). Research each of these fields and list the following information:

1. The amount of education or training required
2. Locales of this education
3. Average annual salary
4. Skills required
5. Working conditions or environment

B. Based upon your interest inventory and your skills assessment, determine which of the jobs that you identified in Exercise A is most appropriate for you. Explain the reasons for your choice in a well-developed paragraph.

Part 3 Résumés and Interviews

Whatever your plans after high school, there is a good chance that you will have to present yourself to others through résumés and interviews. Both are methods commonly used by colleges and employers to screen applicants.

Organizing a Résumé

A résumé is a list of your experiences, education, skills, and references. Its purpose is to make a good impression on an employer or admissions officer. To make a good impression, your résumé must contain certain essential information presented in an accepted form. It must also follow all rules of good writing, including punctuation, spelling, and grammar.

All résumés should contain the following information:

1. Personal data. Include your name, address, and telephone number, with area code.

2. Objective. State your purpose, such as obtaining employment or gaining admission to college. If you are applying for a particular job, your objective should be very specific. If you are seeking any of a number of jobs in a particular area of employment, your objective may be more broad.

SPECIFIC OBJECTIVE: Position as delivery person for Medical Supplies Department of Bethany Hospital.

GENERAL OBJECTIVE: Employment that provides opportunities for learning and advancement in the field of hotel/restaurant management.

3. Experience. List all paid employment that you have had in the past or that you now hold. You may also wish to include significant volunteer work. Begin with your most recent job, and work backwards. For each job, list the following information, in the following order:

Period employed
Name and address of employer
Position held
Duties performed

If you do not have any work experience, skip this section and expand the section on skills described below.

4. Skills. This section is optional, but should be included if you have little or no job experience. In this section, list your special talents and abilities under categories, as follows:

LEADERSHIP:	Treasurer of speech team; manager of track team; organizer of student council's canned food drive for needy families.
MACHINES OPERATED:	Computer terminal; posting machine; most other office machines (type: 50 w.p.m.).
MATHEMATICS:	Scored at 90th percentile on mathematics sections of the S.A.T.; have familiarity with basic algebra, geometry, trigonometry, and business math.

5. Education. List all schools you have attended, dates of attendance, and any special courses of study. Include all honors and awards and any vocational or specialized training that you have received. If your grade point average or class standing is exceptional, include this information. List your most recent school first and work backward.

6. Personal Qualifications and Skills. In this section, list any additional items that might interest the employer. Such items might include: curricular or extracurricular activities such as debate, football, or student government, health, hobbies or special interests, community or group activities, machines that you can operate, languages that you speak, other special skills, professional memberships.

7. References. List the names, job titles, and addresses of three people who will give you good references. One may be a previous employer, one a former teacher or school administrator, and one a family friend. Make sure that these people have given you permission to use their name.

Writing Your Résumé

To create your own résumé, begin by listing all of the information that you need for each of the sections of the résumé. Then, following one of the two models provided on pages 385 and 386, write several drafts of your résumé. Keep the following guidelines in mind:

1. Do not use complete sentences or begin statements with personal pronouns referring to yourself:

   WRONG: I can speak and write the French language fluently.

   RIGHT: Fluent in written and spoken French.

2. Do not make any reference to your sex, weight, height, age, race, or religion.
3. Do not state salary or wage expectations.
4. Use language that reflects positive attitudes. This includes using action words that describe specific skills or duties that you have performed.

   WRONG: Auto Mechanics: I've always been kind of interested in working on cars.

   RIGHT: Auto Mechanics: Performed most major and minor auto repairs; operated modern auto diagnostic machines; won *Certificate for Excellence in Automotive Service and Repair* given by Harold R. Willis Vocational/Technical High School.

5. If you are writing a résumé to be included among college admissions materials, emphasize your skills, academic performance, and curricular or extracurricular activities. Your objective should state when you hope to enter school and at what level. You may also include the specific program that you wish to pursue.

   OBJECTIVE: Admission to undergraduate studies, Fall term, 1986.

The following pages show two different styles of résumés.

JOSEPH A. KEENE

185 Amarillo Ave.
Waco, Texas 76701 Telephone: (817) 555-2947

OBJECTIVE

Position as Manager Trainee, Lazy J Steak House

SKILLS

Communications: Sports reporter for the Waco H.S. newspaper; won Voice of Democracy speech contest.

Leadership and Management: Organized successful fund drive for Waco H.S. football team; served two terms on student council; planned and led several Eagle Scout Explorer Troop hiking expeditions.

Business: Courses in accounting, office procedures, and business math at Waco H.S.; one term as treasurer of the student council, Waco H.S.

EXPERIENCE

Part-time cafeteria work, Waco H.S., September, 1984-May, 1985. Responsibilities included cleaning tables, stacking dishes, and janitorial tasks.

EDUCATION

Waco H.S., Waco, Texas, August, 1982-present

Course of Study: Business
Activities: Football team, Student Council, Newspaper and Yearbook
Class Rank: Top ten percent

REFERENCES

Mr. Barry Wheaton,
Director of Food Services
Waco High School
Waco, Texas 76701

Mr. Francis Zimmerman,
Football Coach
Waco High School
Waco, Texas 76701

RÉSUMÉ

MARIA R. GARCIA	256 N. Burnham Place Springfield, Massachusetts 01123 Telephone: (317) 555-3031
OBJECTIVE	Position in retail sales that will utilize my previous experience.
EXPERIENCE	
Sept. 1983 to May 1984	Sales Specialist, J.C. Penney Company, South Hamilton, Mass. Duties included arranging displays; checking inventory; stocking shelves; and selling electronic appliances. Averaged $2,500 in monthly sales. Studied home computer literature and thereafter sold 26 home computers.
May 1983 to Aug. 1983	Part-time Stock Clerk, Smith's Music Store, Pittsfield, Mass. Duties included arranging displays and stocking shelves. Reorganized sheet music shelves which increased sales dramatically.
EDUCATION	Salem High School, Salem, Massachusetts. Graduated with honors. Took courses in business, accounting, and office procedures.
PERSONAL	Excellent health Member of Junior Achievement Worked one summer as hospital volunteer Interests include diving and reading.
REFERENCES	Mr. Max Horton, Assistant Manager, J.C. Penney Company, 820 Waltham Drive South Hamilton, Mass. 01982 Dr. Ruth Leahy, Principal Salem High School Salem, Massachusetts 01970 Mr. John Kane, Business Teacher, Salem High School Salem, Massachusetts 01970

The first résumé was written by a teen-ager with little actual work experience. Therefore, it contains an extensive section on skills that highlights this person's abilities and potential. The second was written by a teen-ager who has had significant work experiences, so it employs a different format. You may decide for yourself which format best presents your own background.

When preparing the final copy of your résumé, use 8½" × 11" white paper. Type your résumé or have it typed. This creates a more professional appearance. Proofread the typed copy carefully for neatness, consistency in format, and correct capitalization, punctuation, and spelling. Finally, try to limit your résumé to one typed page. In no case should the resume be more than two pages in length.

Exercise Writing a Résumé

Choose one of the following objectives or one of your own and write a résumé. Use one of the forms shown on pages 385-386.

1. Part-time employment in a local retail store
2. Full-time summer employment at a camp or resort
3. Admission to a vocational or trade school
4. Admission to a college

Interviewing

Another method of presenting yourself to colleges and employers is the interview. These guidelines will help you to create a positive impression.

1. **Control your nervousness.** If you have made it as far as the interview stage, this means that your letter and résumé have already made a good impression. During the interview, answer questions honestly and confidently, focusing on your strongest skills and most valuable experiences.
2. **Present a good appearance.** The way you dress can be a very important factor in any interview. Present a good impression through your general good grooming and neatness. Wear clothes that are appropriate to the situation.

3. **Arrive promptly for your interview.** Appear at the place of the interview on time or a few minutes early. This demonstrates something about your reliability and shows courtesy toward the interviewer.
4. **Be courteous.** Greet the interviewer with a friendly introduction and a handshake. This is enough to get the interview off to a good start. When the interview is over, thank the interviewer for his or her time.
5. **Use proper communications skills.** Throughout the interview, listen closely to the questions and comments made by the interviewer. Maintain good eye contact, sit up straight, and avoid nervous hand gestures. Always take a few moments to think before speaking. Then make sure that you speak clearly and use correct grammar. Answer questions thoroughly but concisely. Avoid being too soft-spoken or too boisterous.
6. **Follow up the interview with a call or letter.** This will indicate to the interviewer that you are both polite and interested. If you write a thank-you letter, follow the guidelines for letter writing given in Part 1 of this chapter.

Finally, be prepared to answer questions such as those shown below. Remember to speak positively about both yourself and any former employers.

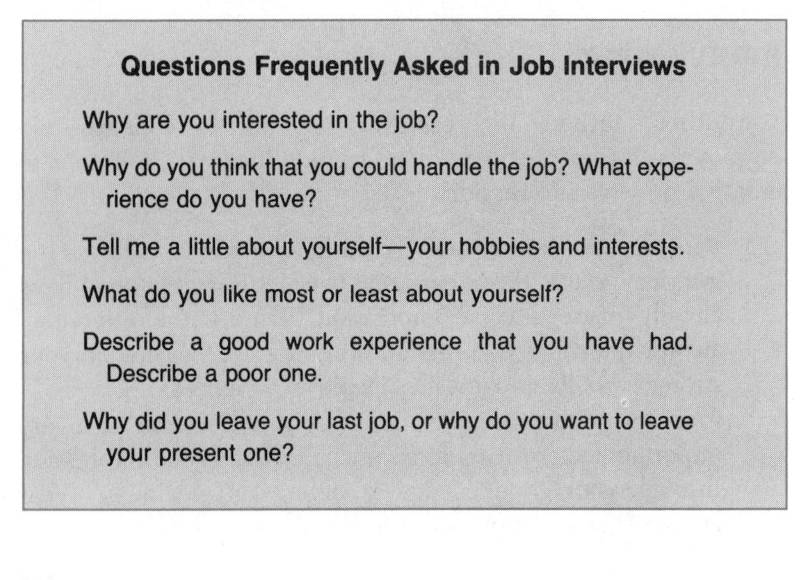

Questions Frequently Asked in Job Interviews

Why are you interested in the job?

Why do you think that you could handle the job? What experience do you have?

Tell me a little about yourself—your hobbies and interests.

What do you like most or least about yourself?

Describe a good work experience that you have had. Describe a poor one.

Why did you leave your last job, or why do you want to leave your present one?

Questions Frequently Asked in College Admissions Interviews

In what subjects did you receive your best grades?

In what subjects did you receive your worst grades?

What subjects do you like best? Why?

What subjects do you like least? Why?

What extracurricular activities have you participated in?

What is your class rank?

What are your hobbies and interests?

How do you spend your free time?

What books have you read recently besides those required for your classes? Tell me about them.

Why do you want to attend this particular college?

What courses do you wish to take in college?

What field of study do you wish to pursue?

What are your future goals?

Exercises Interviewing

A. Look at the list of questions on page 388. Choose a job that you might be interested in, and pretend that you are going to an interview for this job. Write out your answers to each of the questions on the list.

B. Look at the list of questions above. Pretend that you are going for a college interview. Write out your answer to each of the questions on the list.

C. Obtain a college catalog from your school or public library. Study the contents, and make a list of questions that you might ask an admissions officer.

Part 4 Applying to Colleges and Other Schools

Many careers require education after high school. If you wish to pursue such a career, the first step is to gain admission to a school or college that offers the necessary training.

Evaluating Your College Potential

If you are interested in attending college, you should first determine whether this is a realistic decision for you to make. Consider such factors as your grades in high school, your scores on entrance examinations (see Chapter 16), and the possibility of getting good recommendations from your teachers. Discuss these matters with a parent or guardian and with a high school counselor. If college does not seem a realistic immediate alternative, but you still wish to go to college, consider taking additional course work at a local community college or trade school. Then apply to the college of your choice after you have proved your ability to succeed academically.

Choosing a College

Once you decide that college is the best choice for you, you must then decide what college you wish to attend. There are nearly 3,000 two- and four-year colleges in this country. To narrow your choices, consider such factors as the academic reputation of the school, the programs offered, costs, location, size, facilities, and environment.

In making comparisons between colleges, two publications are extremely useful. They are *The College Handbook* and *Barron's Guide to Colleges*. They will help you answer the questions on the above chart and will provide you with the addresses of college admissions offices. Any further information that you need can be obtained by contacting or visiting the colleges of your choice.

Applying to Schools

After you have chosen the colleges to which you wish to apply, write to the admissions offices to obtain catalogs and application forms. (See the sample letter and application on pages 392 and 393.) State in your letters when you plan to attend. If you need financial aid or plan to live in student housing, request information about these subjects.

Information in Catalogs. The college catalogs that you receive in answer to your request will contain the following information:

1. Deadline dates for applications concerning admissions and financial aid.
2. Information on tuition, fees, and types of financial aid.
3. Explanations of entrance requirements.
4. Descriptions of programs and courses of instruction.
5. Descriptions of the facilities of the college.
6. Information concerning the faculty and staff.

Admission Requirements. Read the college catalog carefully to determine what requirements you must meet for admission. Colleges may require any or all of the following:

1. A completed application form. (See Part 5 for information on filling out forms and applications.)
2. Transcripts of courses and grades from your high school.
3. A report of your scores on the S.A.T., A.C.T., or other college entrance examinations. (See Chapter 16, Parts 2 and 3, for information on college entrance examinations.)
4. An application fee.
5. An essay written to demonstrate your writing abilities.
6. Letters of recommendation from your teachers.
7. An interview.
8. A résumé. (See Part 4 of this chapter.)

Note that your completed application and other materials requested by the college should be accompanied by a formal letter of application. (See the sample letter on page 377.) It is important that you begin the application process early so that you meet deadlines for submitting necessary information.

881 South Broadway
Boston, Massachusetts 12571
January 15, 1985

Director of Admissions
Admissions Office
Georgia State University
University Plaza
Atlanta, Georgia 30303

Dear Sirs:

I am a junior at Roosevelt High School, interested in attending a university that offers accelerated programs in Chemistry. Please send me the following information:

1. A catalog detailing the programs that you offer in chemistry.
2. Information on admissions and financial aid.

I would appreciate receiving this information as soon as possible, as I plan to visit universities with promising chemistry programs before making any formal applications.

Yours truly,

Anne Hancock

Anne Hancock

Undergraduate Application For Admission

University of Utah — **Salt Lake City, Utah 84112**

Date ______________________

Personal Data

1. Social Security No. ______________________

2. Legal name ☐ Mr. ☐ Miss ☐ Mrs. ______________________
Last Name — First — Middle
Names different from above, such as maiden name, that appear on your academic records. ______________________

3. Applying for 19 ___ yr. (Check one) Beginning: Summer Quarter ☐ Autumn Quarter ☐ Winter Quarter ☐ Spring Quarter ☐

4. Check appropriate status: ☐ Freshman ☐ Undergraduate transfer.

5. Birth date: ______________ 6. Birthplace (City and State): ______________

7. Home address:
____
Number and Street — City — State — Zip — Telephone (In case of emergency)

8. If you live in Utah, how long have you continually resided in this state? ______________

9. Please check all boxes that apply: ☐ Male ☐ Married ☐ Veteran ☐ Immigrant
☐ Female ☐ Unmarried ☐ U.S. Citizen ☐ Student Visa (A special application is required)

10. Applicant's parents: (List names even if deceased)

Father's Name	Mother's Name
Number and Street Address	Number and Street Address
City — State — Zip	City — State — Zip
Number of years resident of state above: ________	Number of years resident of state above: ________
Occupation ________	Occupation ________

11. Has either parent ever attended the University of Utah? ☐ Yes ☐ No

12. If both parents are deceased, who is guardian or nearest relative?
____
Name — Number and Street Address — City — State — Zip

13. Is above person your legal guardian? ☐ Yes ☐ No Applicant's relationship to above: ______________

Education

14. Have you ever attended the University of Utah? ☐ Yes ☐ No. If yes, when? Quarter ______ Year ______ as (Check one) Day ☐ Evening ☐ Special Student ☐

15. List in chronological order the last high school and all colleges you have attended, regardless of length of attendance and even if no work was completed:

Name of Institution	Location	Date Entered Mo.	Date Entered Yr.	Date Left or Will Leave Mo.	Date Left or Will Leave Yr.	Degree Earned or Expected	Yr. Degree Earned or Expected

Major Field of Study

16. Please select a major of interest to you by checking one of the areas listed below. This is for the purpose of assigning you a faculty advisor only. After you arrive at the University, you may change your major at any time. If you have not chosen a major or have no preference, then check the last item on the list: "No Preference."

__ Accounting (Pre)
__ Anthropology
__ Architecture (Pre)
__ Art (Pre)
__ Biology
__ Business (Pre)
__ Chemical Engineering
__ Chemistry
__ Child Development and Family Relations
__ Civil Engineering
__ Clothing and Textiles
__ Computer Science
__ Economics (Pre)
__ Education, Elementary certification (Pre)
__ Education, Secondary certification (Pre)
__ Electrical Engineering
__ Engineering
__ English
__ Finance (Pre)
__ French
__ Geology
__ Geography
__ German
__ Greek
__ Health Sciences
__ History
__ Home Economics
__ Industrial Engineering
__ Journalism and Mass Communications
__ Latin
__ Management (Pre)
__ Marketing (Pre)
__ Mathematics
__ Mechanical Engineering
__ Medical Technology (Pre)
__ Metallurgical Engineering
__ Meteorology
__ Mining Engineering
__ Music
__ Nursing (Pre)
__ Nutrition Science
__ Pharmacy
__ Philosophy
__ Physical Education
__ Physical Therapy (Pre)
__ Physics
__ Political Science
__ Pre-Dentistry
__ Pre-Law
__ Pre-Medicine
__ Psychology
__ Russian
__ Sociology
__ Spanish
__ Special Education (Pre)
__ Speech Communication
__ Theatre
__ No Preference

17. If you have any physical impairment or handicap, please check here and list nature of handicap. ☐ ______________
You will be sent information concerning available resources and services.

Signature

18. Additional comments which you consider pertinent to your application to the University of Utah: ______________

19. All the answers I have given in this application are complete and accurate to the best of my knowledge. If admitted, I agree to observe the rules and regulations of the University of Utah and to pay all fees and charges assessed thereunder.

____
Signature of Applicant

Freshman Applicant: Please give this application for admission, the application for financial aids (if desired) and the $15 application fee to your high school office.

Exercises Applying to Colleges and Other Schools

A. Write a letter requesting a college catalog. Use the address from a college catalog in the library or obtain one for the college of your choice. Make sure that your letter follows proper business letter form.

B. Using a college catalog from your library, answer the following questions concerning that school.

1. What is the amount charged per credit hour for tuition?
2. Does the college offer courses in Marine Science?
3. Are applicants to the college required to take the S.A.T.?
4. How many books are in the main library of the college?
5. Does the college enroll more than six thousand students?

Part 5 Using Skills To Find a Job

One of the decisions you make about your future may concern finding a job. You may want to work to earn money for college, to gain practical experience in a specific area, to help with expenses at home, or as an alternative to college.

Before you look for a job, determine what sort of job is best suited to your needs and availability. While you are in school, a full-time job will doubtless be out of the question.* Even a part-time job may require more time that you can devote to it. Therefore, the first step in any job planning that you do must be to consider your school, family, and social obligations to make certain that you have sufficient time. Do this by making up a schedule of your weekly activities and commitments. The next step is to assess your skills and interests to determine the type of work that you would most like to perform. (See Part 2 for information on assessing your interests and skills.)

*Federal and state laws protect teens from overwork and dangerous working conditions. Under Federal law, if you are fourteen or fifteen years old, you may work only up to three hours on a school day and up to eighteen hours per week. (Hours are extended during the summer.) State laws vary and supersede Federal laws. Check with your guidance counselor about your state's child labor laws.

Surveying the Job Market

Once you are certain that you have enough time for a job and have some idea of the areas and types of employment that are best suited to you, the next step is to survey the job market. There are many ways in which to find out about job opportunities and openings.

First, check employment ads in local newspapers. These are usually listed alphabetically by the type of job (Accountant . . . Welder). Most ads identify the job type and provide a telephone number or an address that you can use to contact the employer. These ads also commonly contain information on the qualifications and skills required of applicants.

Also check with guidance counselors, friends, and relatives. These people may know of specific job openings or be able to suggest avenues to explore.

Finally contact possible employers personally to see if jobs are available. When contacting a possible employer, make sure that you specify the type of job that you are looking for and the hours that you can work.

Contacting Employers

Your first contact with an employer may be to determine whether a job opening exists, or it may come after you have already learned this information. In either case, there are a few guidelines that you should follow.

Contacting Employers by Phone. If you contact the employer by phone, give your name and explain the type of job you are looking for. If you do not know of a specific opening, ask the employer if any openings exist. State the hours you are available. Speak briefly, clearly, and politely, giving particular attention to proper listening skills. During the call, write down any important information that you learn such as the employer's address or the date and time of an interview. Do not ask salary questions over the telephone unless the subject is raised by the employer. Save these for the interview.

Contacting Employers by Letter. If you apply for a long-term job or a position in a large company, you may wish to handle the application process more formally. Instead of calling the employer, write a letter of application such as the ones you learned about in Part 1. Along with your letter, you may wish to include a résumé.

Your letter of application should use the following four-part format:

1. **Purpose.** The first few lines of your letter should directly state the purpose—that you are applying for a specific position. Refer to an ad or person that told you about the job.

2. **Qualifications and References.** This is the most important section of your letter. State your age or grade in school and the date on which you will be available to work. Identify your experience and any skills that relate to the job you are seeking. List achievements that portray you as an effective worker. (This section may be shorter and more general if you are enclosing a résumé.)

   If you have any particular reason for looking for a job with a certain employer, include that in your letter. A veterinarian, for example, might be more interested in hiring you if he or she knows you plan to study in that field yourself. Remember that there are likely to be several applicants for any one job. You must find in yourself the extra asset that will make you appear more valuable to a potential employer.

   Finally, include references. Make sure that you have gotten permission from these people first. List their names, positions, addresses, and telephone numbers. Teachers and former employers are good references.

3. **Request for Application and/or Interview.** Ask for an application and an interview. Tell the employer exactly when and where you can be contacted by phone and include your phone number.

4. **Thank You.** Always thank a prospective employer for the time he or she spent actually reading your letter.

Following is a sample letter of application:

605 West Main Street
Springfield, Massachusetts 21670
January 21, 1985

Mr. Frank Jones, Manager
Great Outdoors Amusement Parks, Inc.
100 Cascade Way
Salem, Arkansas 54132

Dear Mr. Jones:

According to a recent article in Business Outlook, Great Outdoors expects record crowds this summer. If so, then perhaps you will need additional staff members experienced in providing the customer with prompt and courteous service.

You may note from the enclosed résumé that I have spent the past two summers, serving customers for Short Takes, a fast food restaurant here in Springfield. The experience has helped me learn how to provide people with fast, efficient service.

In addition to my work, I am a member of the basketball team at Springfield High School. Despite these activities, I have achieved a 3.4 grade average.

I will be available the first week in June when school recesses for the summer. I could work until the end of August.

Since the summer is only months away, I would appreciate an interview at your earliest possible convenience.

Respectfully yours,

Mary Johnson

Mary Johnson

Completing Job Applications and Other Forms

If you are asked to complete a job application, be sure to read through all directions carefully before making any marks on the form. Procedures as simple as filling in your name may vary from form to form. Also, notice any special requirements given, such as "Print" or "Please type." Finally, proofread the application once you have completed it. A neat, accurate job application will tell your prospective employer a great deal about your work habits and your ability to follow directions. Therefore, be very careful when filling out applications to ensure that you make a good impression.

If you have not sent a job application to the employer before going to your initial interview, make sure that you take the information to complete such an application to the interview with you. Most application forms require the following information:

Content of Job Application Forms

Personal Data	Name, address, phone, date of birth, social security number
Schools Attended	Names, cities and states, dates of attendance, subjects studied, activities
Employment History	Names, places, supervisors, dates, job titles, duties, reasons for leaving previous jobs, previous wages or salaries
Skills and Achievements	Job-related skills, honors or awards, volunteer positions (Examples: *type 60 wpm, speak Spanish fluently, biology lab assistant)*
References	Names, titles, addresses, relationship to you, telephone numbers

In addition to the job application form, there are several other work-related forms that you may have to complete after accepting a position. The forms listed on the following page are among the most common:

Social Security Applications. Before you can begin working, you must apply for a social security card by filling out a social security application form. These forms are available from your local office of the Department of Labor.

Work Permits. Most states require that teen-agers obtain work permits and present these to their employers before actually beginning to work. To obtain an application for a work permit, see your prospective employer or your guidance counselor. To apply for the permit, you will need a birth certificate and, in some states, a physician's statement of health.

W-2 Forms. These are used for tax purposes. Obtain one of these from your employer after accepting a position.

Health Permits. For certain jobs, especially jobs in food service, you must have a permit certifying your state of health. If your employer does not have the appropriate application form, he or she will be able to tell you where to obtain one.

When completing any application or form, there are a few basic guidelines that you should follow:

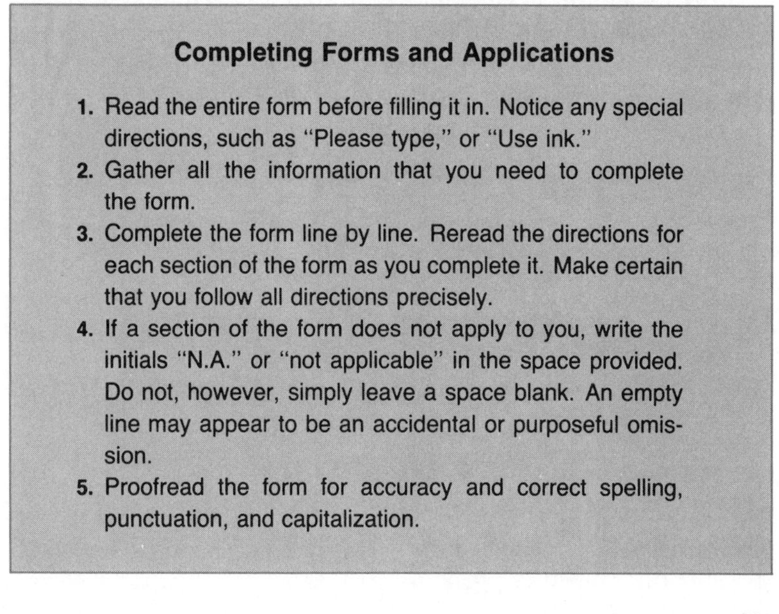

Completing Forms and Applications

1. Read the entire form before filling it in. Notice any special directions, such as "Please type," or "Use ink."
2. Gather all the information that you need to complete the form.
3. Complete the form line by line. Reread the directions for each section of the form as you complete it. Make certain that you follow all directions precisely.
4. If a section of the form does not apply to you, write the initials "N.A." or "not applicable" in the space provided. Do not, however, simply leave a space blank. An empty line may appear to be an accidental or purposeful omission.
5. Proofread the form for accuracy and correct spelling, punctuation, and capitalization.

Exercises Finding a Job

A. Read each of the following employment ads and determine your suitability for the position. Then, for each ad, write a short paragraph explaining why you would or would not apply. In your paragraphs, describe your experience, skills, interests, availability, and personal qualities.

Gas Station Attendant

Part-time, weekends only. Some auto care exp. preferred.

Cashier

Evenings, Bolton's Department Store, Women's Wear. Good math abilities and positive personality a must.

Usher

Perm. part-time. Sonov Cinema. Duties include ticket sales, candy counter, janitorial.

B. Write a letter to an employer in your area requesting consideration for a part-time job. Be sure to mention the type of job you are seeking, the hours that you can work, information about your skills, and a request for an interview.

SUMMARY AND APPLICATIONS

1. Learning to write effective business letters can help you to obtain information, settle claims, order merchandise, apply to schools, and gain employment.
2. All business letters contain the following parts: inside address, heading, date, salutation, body, closing, and signature. Letters may be in block or modified block form.
3. Before choosing a career or field of study, carefully assess your interests and skills.
4. A good résumé presents your experiences, education, skills, and references in a way that makes a positive impression.
5. Before applying to colleges and other schools, consider such factors as academic reputation, programs offered, costs, location, size, and facilities. Obtain catalogs and application forms. Follow admission requirements precisely.
6. To find a job, contact prospective employers by phone or by letter to set up interviews. Prepare résumés and complete applications as needed.

Applications in Other Subject Areas

Fine Arts / Humanities. There are many jobs in the areas of fine arts and the humanities, but these are generally less well-known than jobs in business or the professions. Choose two of the following areas and do some research, using the resources described in this chapter. For each area, list three possible jobs and explain in a brief paragraph what further schooling or training is needed.

Dance	Theater
Painting/Drawing	Film
Music	Sculpture/Ceramics

All Subjects. Choose some broad area of high school study that is of interest to you. Using a college catalog as a reference, list four possible areas of specialization or career training under the general area of study that you have chosen.

Chapter 18

Public Speaking and Group Discussion

As a high school student, you are often called upon to speak in public. You present oral reports and demonstrations. You participate in discussions with classmates and with fellow club or team members. You may even be involved in theater, student government, or some other activity that requires speaking before groups of students, parents, or teachers.

Learning how to speak effectively in such situations is excellent preparation for the public speaking and discussion that will be required of you in later life. The skills that you learn in this chapter will help you to present ideas with confidence and poise. They will also help you to ensure that the groups in which you participate function efficiently to achieve their goals.

Part 1 Public Speaking

Even people whose jobs or situations do not require public speaking on a regular basis occasionally find that they must deliver a speech. The speech may be a simple introduction, announcement, or demonstration; or it may be a fully-developed formal presentation. In either case, speaking before people can be disconcerting or even frightening unless you are properly prepared. Fortunately, learning a few simple guidelines will help you to make a success of any speech that you deliver.

Preparing a Speech

The steps required to prepare a speech are similar to the steps in the process of writing. (See Chapter 7.)

Choose and narrow your topic. Pick a subject that you know well so that you can keep the attention of your audience by providing fresh, specific details. After choosing a general topic, narrow it to fit the allotted time and to suit your audience.

Define your purpose. Your purpose will determine the type of speech that you will deliver. The following chart describes the three major types of speeches and their purposes.

Types of Speeches

Type	Purpose	Examples
Expository	To inform or explain.	The duties of student council members. How to save money by performing simple auto repairs.
Persuasive	To move an audience to take some action or to adopt a point of view.	Why high schools should offer courses in computer science. Reasons for learning a foreign language.
Entertainment	To amuse or entertain an audience.	The superstitions of soccer players. How not to run for political office.

Of course, any particular speech may combine elements of each of the preceding types. A persuasive speech, for example, might contain a humorous introduction and a great deal of background explanation or information. However, any speech should have one major purpose that determines most of its content and organization.

Identify your audience. When narrowing your topic, bear in mind what your audience already knows about it. Your final speech should not explain the obvious; however, it must include any essential information with which your audience is unfamiliar. Make certain, also, that the complexity of your ideas, vocabulary, and sentence structure is suited to the general age and sophistication of the audience.

Develop a statement of your main idea. This statement, usually a single sentence, will determine what information you will gather. When you are writing your speech, include this statement near the end of your introduction.

Gather information related to your main idea. Information may be gathered from personal experience, from other people, or from reference works. (See Chapter 7, page 111 and Chapter 8, pages 132–136, for more details on gathering information for use in compositions and speeches.)

Organize your information. Disregard any information not directly related to your main idea. Organize the remaining information as you would for any composition. (See Chapter 7, pages 112–114.)

Write the speech. Your speech should include an introduction, a body, and a conclusion. You may choose to write out the speech completely, as you would a composition. Some speakers, however, are comfortable simply recording the main points in outline form on note cards.

The **introduction** serves two purposes: It should gain the attention of your audience and state the main idea of your speech. The chart on the next page gives some common methods of introducing a speech.

Types of Introductions

1. **A story or anecdote.** An incident from personal experience can help the audience to identify with the speaker.
2. **A question.** Asking the audience for a show of hands in answer to a question breaks the ice and makes your listeners feel that they are participating.
3. **A startling fact or statistic.** A startling statement jars your listeners, focusing their attention on the unexpected news.
4. **A promise.** Promising to give your listeners some useful information appeals to their needs or interests and gets their attention.
5. **An exhibit.** Holding up something for people to look at is one of the easiest ways of focusing attention.

The **body** of your speech should develop your main idea by providing supporting facts, details, or examples. If you are speaking to inform, the body will answer the questions *Who? What? When? Where?* and *How?* If you are speaking to persuade, the body will give facts that support your opinions and suggestions for implementing any actions that you want your audience to take. If you are entertaining, the body will contain experiences and anecdotes that will amuse your audience.

The **conclusion** of an informative or persuasive speech should summarize the major points made in the body of the speech and restate the thesis or main idea. Concluding statements are especially important in persuasive speeches because they make a final appeal to the audience for support and possible action. The conclusion of an entertainment speech should be a high point of amusement rather than a summary.

Once you have finished writing the rough draft of your speech, revise the speech as follows:

1. Check to see that all of your ideas have been thoroughly developed and well supported.
2. Use the revision techniques described in Chapters 3, 4, and 6 to correct sentence structure, clarity, or variety.

3. Check your paragraphs for unity and coherence. (See Chapter 8, pages 144–149.)
4. Refer to the chart on evaluating speeches on page 408. Make sure that your speech meets these requirements.

Write your final draft and proofread it for errors.

The following chart summarizes the steps required to prepare a speech:

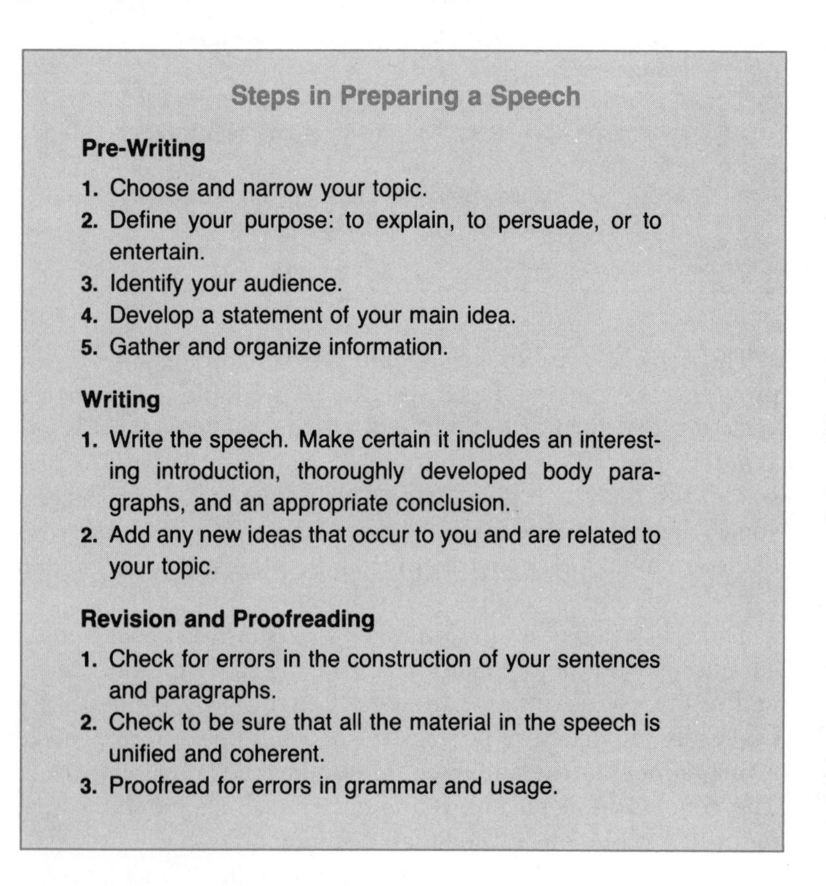

Steps in Preparing a Speech

Pre-Writing

1. Choose and narrow your topic.
2. Define your purpose: to explain, to persuade, or to entertain.
3. Identify your audience.
4. Develop a statement of your main idea.
5. Gather and organize information.

Writing

1. Write the speech. Make certain it includes an interesting introduction, thoroughly developed body paragraphs, and an appropriate conclusion.
2. Add any new ideas that occur to you and are related to your topic.

Revision and Proofreading

1. Check for errors in the construction of your sentences and paragraphs.
2. Check to be sure that all the material in the speech is unified and coherent.
3. Proofread for errors in grammar and usage.

Practicing Your Speech

Practice your speech aloud many times. If possible, use a tape recorder to check your delivery. Pay particular attention to pace, pitch, pausing for emphasis, variation in volume and intensity, and appropriateness of tone or emotional color. Maintain proper posture and use facial expressions and gestures that reflect the content of the speech. Check these nonverbal elements of your speech by practicing before a mirror. Finally, invite your friends or family members to listen to your delivery and to make suggestions for improvement.

Delivering Your Speech

Fear is probably the biggest obstacle you will need to overcome before you deliver your speech. Even professional speakers never completely lose their stage fright. In fact, a certain amount of stage fright is useful. It prepares your body to meet an unusual situation with clearer thinking and more energy. Remember, preparation and practice are the keys to overcoming fright and developing confidence.

When you are delivering your speech, act confident even if you do not feel confident. Talk naturally to your audience. Do not read or recite the entire speech, but refer to notes or an outline as necessary. Throughout the speech, maintain proper eye contact by looking directly at your audience or slightly above the heads of audience members. Be enthusiastic about your subject; speak clearly and distinctly; do not rush your delivery; vary your pace, volume, pitch, and tone; and use proper facial expressions and gestures.

Listening to and Evaluating Speeches

Whenever you are listening to a speech, make the speaker feel at ease by giving him or her your complete attention. Maintain eye contact with the speaker, and keep a positive expression on your face. Do not make unnecessary noise or movements. These are distracting and rude.

If you are asked to evaluate a speech given by another person, be positive in your approach. Discuss the speech and its delivery, not the speaker. Make your comments as specific as possible, using the following guidelines for proper speaking:

Guidelines for Evaluating Speeches

CONTENT:

Introduction

_____ arouses interest

_____ is brief and to the point

_____ is appropriate to the topic

Body

_____ supports thesis or main idea

_____ contains no irrelevant material

_____ main ideas are clear

_____ main ideas are well developed

Conclusion

_____ is brief

_____ provides a summary of major points or draws attention back to thesis

PRESENTATION:

Non-verbal

_____ speaker has good posture

_____ speaker is relaxed and confident

_____ speaker has good eye contact

_____ gestures and facial expressions are natural and appropriate

Verbal

_____ speaker is not too quiet or too loud

_____ speaker's articulation is clear

_____ speaker's pace is not too slow or rapid

_____ speaker's pitch is not too high or low

_____ speaker varies volume, pace, pitch

_____ speaker uses pauses effectively

Exercises **Public Speaking**

A. Choose one of the following general subject areas or a general subject of your own. Then, narrow this subject to produce a topic that is appropriate for a three-minute speech.

School	United States Presidents
Politics	Television
Sports	Cars
Current Events	Fashion
Hobbies	Fads
Movies	Art
Famous Entertainers	Music

B. Choose one of the following topics and write a statement of a main idea for a three-minute persuasive speech.

Year-round school
Job vs. college
The legal voting age
The draft
The legal driving age

C. Imagine that you are writing a humorous speech on "The Least Important Events in History." Write an amusing story or anecdote that could be used as an appropriate introduction to this speech.

D. Choose a topic having to do with entertainment: soap operas, videos, sidewalk theatre, or whatever interests you. Write a thesis statement for a three-minute expository speech on your topic. Then write two possible introductions for this speech. Choose from the following types of introductions: questions, startling facts or statistics, promises, exhibits.

E. Choose a topic of your own and develop a three-minute speech for presentation to your class. Follow the steps given in the chart on page 406.

Part 2 Discussion

The saying "Two heads are better than one" is a cliché, but, like many clichés, it contains an element of truth. By combining ideas, a group of people can often accomplish purposes that are beyond the abilities of an individual working alone. For this reason, most groups, including students in classes and members of teams or clubs, hold discussions regularly.

The Purposes of Discussion

Discussions are most effective when they serve a purpose that is clearly identified from the outset. Groups may hold discussions for any of the following reasons.

1. To explore ideas
2. To exchange information
3. To resolve mutual problems
4. To plan a course of action

In order to accomplish their purpose, the people who participate in a discussion must understand the roles that they are expected to play, how to prepare for the discussion, and how to carry out their roles in a spirit of cooperation.

The Organization of a Discussion Group

When a group meets for discussion, it is a good idea to choose a **chairperson** to lead the discussion and to maintain order. A group may also choose to elect a **secretary** to take notes on what is said. Other group members then act as **participants,** discussing the topic under the guidance of the chairperson.

The Stages of a Discussion

Discussions usually begin with a statement of the subject and purpose of the discussion. This statement is usually made by the chairperson.

Once the entire group understands the goal that the group is attempting to accomplish, the next step is to define any key terms that will be used in the discussion. This will help group members to avoid needless arguments and misunderstandings. At this point, group members may also wish to narrow the discussion topic to avoid irrelevance or vagueness.

In the next step, the group discusses and analyzes the discussion topic in detail. What happens during this step varies according to the nature of the topic and the purpose of the group.

Finally, as the discussion draws to a close, one group member, usually the chairperson or the secretary, summarizes the major points made during the discussion, describes any agreement that the group has reached, and explains any course of action that the group has agreed upon.

Preparing for a Discussion

You cannot give what you don't have. Before you can contribute to a pooling of ideas, you must have ideas. You must take time to prepare yourself mentally. This can be done by asking yourself the following questions.

1. What is the question or topic to be discussed?
2. What facts are already known about the question?
3. What unknown facts need to be explored or researched?
4. What other issues or factors are relevant to the question or topic?
5. What is the goal of the discussion?
6. What are my ideas and opinions about the topic?

Leading a Discussion

If you are asked to serve as the chairperson of a discussion group, there are several duties that you will need to carry out. The following guidelines will help you to fulfill your responsibilities as a group chairperson.

The Responsibilities of a Chairperson

1. Prepare for the discussion.
2. Introduce the topic and state the goal of the discussion.
3. Allow time for the introduction, the discussion, and a short summary of the conclusions reached.
4. Maintain order in the discussion group.
   a. Allow only one person to speak at a time.
   b. Insist that members of the group ask to be recognized and remain respectful toward one another.
5. Encourage everyone to contribute to the discussion.
6. Ask stimulating questions to keep the group interested in the topic. Encourage creative and critical thinking. Remember that your role is to guide participants toward conclusions, not to impose conclusions of your own on the group.
7. Keep the discussion on track by guiding the group toward a generally-accepted conclusion, or consensus. Do not allow the discussion to wander into unimportant or irrelevant matters.
8. Take notes and be prepared to summarize the key points at the end of the discussion.

Participating in a Discussion

You already know that it is your duty to prepare mentally for a group discussion. Once the discussion begins, you as a group member should follow these guidelines.

The Responsibility of a Participant

1. Speak only when the leader recognizes you.
2. Voice your ideas. You are there because your opinion is as important as that of anyone else.
3. Support your statements with concrete evidence.
4. Speak correctly and distinctly.
5. Listen carefully and politely to others. Take notes on what

is said by other group members, and refer to these when you speak.

6. Be courteous and tactful, especially when voicing disagreement.
7. Try to understand the viewpoints of other group members. Ask questions for clarification.

Exercises Group Discussion

A. Assume that you are part of a group discussing the idea of increasing the amount of driver's training needed to qualify for a license. Identify each statement below as a strong or weak contribution to a discussion and give your reasons.

1. Everybody knows that teenage drivers are reckless.
2. Patti, we haven't heard from you yet. I know you recently got your license. What can you tell us from your experience?
3. I disagree, Jack. You're just saying that because your parents won't let you get a license.
4. In summary, I would say that we are all agreed that more hours on the road should be required of all new drivers.
5. According to Sheriff Brandon, 60% of last year's accidents here in town involved drivers under the age of 23.
6. I really haven't thought much about the topic, so I don't think I should say much at this time.
7. Driver's training is important, but what about the safety of large cars versus small cars?

B. Assume that you are going to participate in a discussion of the following topic.

> Should parents allow young children to view prime time television programs?

Determine what key terms in the preceding question need to be defined at the beginning of any discussion on the question. Write five questions that you might ask to prepare yourself for this discussion. List three other ways you might prepare. If your teacher directs you to do so, join a group and discuss this question.

Part 3 Parliamentary Procedure

To ensure that meetings are conducted in an orderly fashion, many groups follow a set of rules for discussion that are known collectively as **parliamentary procedure.** These are the rules followed by most legislative bodies and formal organizations.

Conducting Meetings

In most formal groups, a certain number of members must be present to begin a meeting. This number is called a **quorum,** and may range from 20% to one more than half of the total membership of the group. A quorum guarantees that any action taken at a meeting represents the will of the majority. Once it is determined that a quorum is present, the president or chairperson announces, "This meeting will come to order."

The president or chairperson then conducts the meeting according to an established order, or **agenda.** The president or chairperson usually proceeds in the following order to conduct the meeting:

The Order of Business

1. Call the meeting to order.
2. Hear and approve the minutes of the previous meeting. The minutes are a summary of previous business.
3. Hear reports of officers and standing committees. These are permanent committees within the group or organization.
4. Hear reports of special committees. These are temporary committees set up to serve a particular purpose.
5. Clear up any unfinished business from the previous meeting.
6. Ask for new business.
7. Adjourn the meeting.

Motions

To propose an action during a meeting, a group member must use the parliamentary procedure known as the **motion.** At least two members must be in favor of a motion before the group can consider it. The first member makes the motion in an affirmative manner; that is, the member suggests that the club do something positive. An example of such a motion would be as follows:

"I move that our club participate in the marathon."

A second member immediately supports or seconds the motion:

"I second the motion."

To conduct yourself properly at a meeting, learn the following procedure for making a motion.

How To Make a Motion

1. The member stands and addresses the person in charge by the appropriate title, such as "Madame Chairwoman" or "Mr. President."
2. The member waits to be recognized by the presiding officer, who will either nod or say his or her name.
3. The member states the motion in brief, clear language.
4. Another member immediately seconds the motion without waiting to be recognized.
5. The presiding officer says, "It has been moved and seconded that . . . " and then restates the motion.
6. The presiding officer conducts a discussion of the motion. Discussion proceeds as it does in any formal discussion. A participant asks to be recognized by the chair and speaks only when given permission.
7. The presiding officer puts the motion to a vote.
8. The presiding officer announces the result of the vote by saying "The *Aye's* have it. The motion is carried." or "The *No's* have it. The motion is defeated."

Amending a Motion

Motions can be changed in the same way sentences can be revised. When someone makes a motion, other group members may see ways to improve the motion to make it more acceptable to all. The process of changing or rewording a motion is called **amending a motion.**

The following are standard ways of amending a motion:

1. Amending by striking out words
2. Amending by inserting words
3. Amending by substituting words

Suppose that at a meeting you introduce the following motion: "I move that our team purchase three new soccer balls." The motion is then seconded and opened for discussion. After some discussion, another member may choose to amend the motion by stating, "I move to strike out 'three' and insert 'five.' " This amendment must then be seconded and discussed. After discussion, the group must vote "yes" or "no" on the amendment before it can vote on the original motion. Amendments are a means of wording motions to express the wishes of the majority. Therefore, every amendment has to be voted on and settled before the final vote on the motion is taken.

Other Types of Motions

Each motion must be dealt with before the club can take up any new business. One way to deal with a motion is to amend it and then vote on it. Sometimes, however, members are not ready to vote on a motion. They may need more time to think, or they may wish to wait until more members are present. In such cases, a member can make a special motion:

1. "I move that this question be referred to a committee."

   If this motion passes, the president appoints a special committee to study the motion and report on it at a future meeting.

2. "I move that we table the motion."

   This is a motion to put aside or postpone a final vote on the motion until a later date.

On the other hand, sometimes a member may feel that discussion on the motion has gone on long enough. In this case, the member may say, "I move the previous question." This is a motion to end debate and proceed to a vote.

If a member feels that the discussion is becoming unproductive or that only a limited amount of discussion is necessary, he or she may introduce the following type of motion: "I move that debate on this matter be limited to fifteen minutes."

These motions are all ways of dealing with specific proposals or motions that have been put before the group. Motions themselves may not always be entirely new ideas. Sometimes the following motions may be used to clear up old business.

1. A motion to take up a matter previously tabled
2. A motion to reconsider an action already decided upon
3. A motion to strike out a motion previously passed

There are also two special motions that can be used to make sure that business is being conducted properly.

If you feel that a mistake has been made in parliamentary procedure, you may say "Point of order" and ask that the mistake be righted. The presiding officer will rule on the matter, and business will continue. Or, if you do not understand something that has occurred, say "Point of information," and ask the presiding officer for the information that you need. Neither of these two motions requires a second. They also do not need to be debated or put to a vote. They are simply useful tools for making sure that a meeting proceeds in an orderly fashion.

Analyzing Parliamentary Procedure

The following is a portion of a student council meeting conducted according to parliamentary procedure. Read it and be prepared to answer the questions that follow.

PRESIDENT: Our last item of unfinished business is the motion before the floor to send Rita Hernandez as the school's representative to the state Student Council Convention. At the last meeting you voted to delay action on the motion until today so that I could determine if Rita is available and willing to represent our school. Is there any further discussion on the motion?

(No one rises to discuss the motion further.)

PRESIDENT: It has been moved and seconded that the Student Council send Rita Hernandez as the school's representative to the State Student Council Convention to be held June 24 to June 27. All those in favor of the motion say "Aye."

MEMBERS: (Those in favor of the motion say, "Aye.")

PRESIDENT: Those opposed, say "No." (No one responds.) The *Aye*'s have it. The motion is carried. Congratulations, Rita. We are proud to send you as our representative. That concludes our old business. Is there any new business?

WANDA: Mr. President.

PRESIDENT: Wanda.

WANDA: It has been brought to my attention that since our school is so new, we do not yet have a motto. I think the Student Council should take some action to establish a school motto. I would like to hear some more ideas on the subject.

BILL: Mr. President.

PRESIDENT: Bill.

BILL: Several of us feel that all the Seniors should be able to take part in the selection of a motto. We think some sort of contest sponsored by the Student Council might be a good idea. Therefore, I move that the Student Council sponsor a contest open to all seniors to choose a school motto.

HOWARD: I second the motion.

PRESIDENT: It has been moved and seconded that the Student Council sponsor a contest open to all seniors to choose a school motto. Further discussion is now in order.

ANITA: I support the idea of a contest.

PRESIDENT: Anita, do you wish to be recognized?

ANITA: Oh, yes, Mr. President.

PRESIDENT: Anita.

ANITA: I support the idea. However, I think the contest should be open to all students. This will generate more school spirit.

RORY: Mr. President.

PRESIDENT: Rory.

RORY: I agree with Anita. Therefore, I move to amend the motion by striking out "seniors" and inserting "students."

TOBY: I second the motion.

PRESIDENT: (The president repeats the motion to amend and calls for further discussion. There is none. The amendment is put to a vote.) It has been moved and seconded that "seniors" be stricken out and "students" be inserted. Those in favor say "Aye." (Students respond.) Those opposed, "No." (Only two respond.) The *Aye*'s have it. The motion is so amended. Discussion on the amended motion is now in order.

RACHEL: (After she is recognized.) It seems to me that we have been too hasty. We are near the time agreed on for adjournment, and many details need to be worked out. For instance, who will judge the contest and how long should the contest run? Therefore, I move that the motion be referred to a committee appointed by the chair, with instructions to report their recommendations at the next meeting.

LINDA: I second the motion. (The President repeats the motion and calls for discussion. There is no further discussion. A vote is taken, and the motion is referred to a committee.)

PRESIDENT: The *Aye*'s have it. The motion is referred to a committee. I now appoint Rachel, Bill, Wanda, and Anita to constitute a committee to study the motion to sponsor a contest, open to all students, to choose a school motto. The committee will report on their recommendations at the meeting to be held two weeks from today. Is there any further new business? (No response.) Now, as you know, the Entertainment Committee has scheduled a special program for this time. Since there is no further business, the meeting stands adjourned.

Exercise Following Parliamentary Procedure

Answer these questions about the preceding sample meeting.

1. Write a brief explanation of each of the following parliamentary procedures. Then tell which ones were used in the preceding discussion. Point out specific examples.

following an agenda
establishing a quorum
amending a motion
demanding a point of order
calling for the question
tabling a motion
discussing a motion
referring to a committee
adjourning a meeting

2. What items on the agenda might have preceded the part of the meeting shown on the previous pages?

3. In the preceding discussion, one student committed a violation of proper parliamentary procedure. What was it?

SUMMARY AND APPLICATIONS

1. Learning how to prepare and deliver speeches and how to conduct yourself in discussions will help you to present ideas with confidence and poise.
2. Speeches should be prepared in accordance with the steps of the process of writing.
3. When delivering or evaluating a speech, keep in mind eye contact, posture, facial expressions, gestures, volume, articulation, pace, pitch, pausing, variation, and emotion.
4. In a discussion, both the chairperson and the participants should attempt to fulfill the duties outlined in this chapter.
5. Formal meetings follow the rules of parliamentary procedure to ensure that business is conducted in an orderly fashion.
6. Learning the order of business and the various kinds of motions will help you to participate effectively.

Applications in Other Subject Areas

Social Studies / Sociology / Mass Media. The ability to listen critically to the speeches of others is important. It means concentrating on the actual content of the message. Watch and listen to speakers in any of the situations listed below. Ask yourself how much the speaker's appearance, expressions, voice, and gestures are affecting you. Then analyze the content of the speech. Finally, write a few paragraphs that rate the content of the speech, as well as how its impact was affected by the speaker's delivery.

a town meeting
a pep assembly
a TV editorial
a campaign rally
(school, local, or national)
a televised speech

Math / Science / Humanities. Imagine that your class is the school board. Organize a group discussion on the question "Should our high school place greater emphasis on courses in math and science or on courses in the humanities?" Research the topic and conduct your discussion according to parliamentary procedure.

Handbook

A detailed Table of Contents of the Handbook appears in the front of this book.

How To Use the Handbook

This Handbook is your reference book. In it the concepts of grammar, usage, and mechanics are organized so that you can study them efficiently and refer to them quickly.

To use the Handbook well, you should first leaf through it to become familiar with its organization and contents. Note especially the following:

Organization of the Handbook

Grammar Sections 1–4 define and explain the elements of English grammar. Refer to these pages when you have questions about grammar in your speaking or writing.

Usage Sections 5–9 are a guide to English usage. When you are puzzled about which form of a word to use in your writing, turn to the appropriate part of these Sections.

Forms and constructions marked STANDARD are accepted as standard usage—the kind of usage that is appropriate at all times and in all places. Forms and constructions marked NONSTANDARD are not.

Mechanics Sections 10–16 give rules for capitalization, punctuation, spelling, and the formation of plurals. Use these Sections when proofreading or when you have questions about mechanics.

Good Form Sections 17 and 18 present the accepted forms for manuscripts and outlines.

The Handbook includes exercises that test your understanding of the concepts explained. These exercises are the first step in putting what you learn here to practical use. The next step is to apply the concepts in your own writing and speaking.

1.0 The Classification of Words

The words in our language can be organized into categories that can be studied separately and then used together in predictable patterns. English grammar groups words into eight major groups, which are called **parts of speech.** The eight parts of speech are given below.

nouns	adjectives	conjunctions
pronouns	adverbs	interjections
verbs	prepositions	

In addition to these eight categories, there are three kinds of words that can be used as various parts of speech. They are formed from verbs, and are therefore called **verbals.** The verbals are the *infinitive*, the *participle*, and the *gerund*.

This Section of the Handbook will explain these classifications and show you how they function in our language. As you study the parts of speech, you will gain a better understanding of how we link words together to communicate.

1.1 The Noun

We identify people, places, things, and ideas by using certain words as labels.

A noun is the name of a person, place, thing, or idea.

Often, nouns name things that we can perceive through our senses, such as sights, sounds, odors, tastes, and textures. Nouns can also name things that are abstract and not observable through the five senses. Such abstract nouns include thoughts, hopes, beliefs, memories, and so on.

PERSONS	PLACES	THINGS	IDEAS
Chris Evert Lloyd	Borneo	gift	honesty
uncle	arena	telephone	grace
author	island	sneaker	anxiety

A **common noun** is the name of a whole group of persons, places, things, or ideas. It is a name that is common to the whole group: *camera, glass, soldier, theater, theory.*

A **proper noun** is the name of an individual person, place, thing, or idea.

A proper noun always begins with a capital letter.

COMMON NOUNS	PROPER NOUNS
comedian	Eddie Murphy
car	Plymouth
country	England
holiday	Memorial Day

As the above list shows, a noun may consist of more than one word. Each word in a proper noun is capitalized.

Any word that can be immediately preceded by *the* is a common noun: *the* bridge, *the* forest, *the* language. Many proper nouns, but not all of them, can also be preceded by *the: the* Pacific Ocean, *the* Astrodome, but not *the* Abraham Lincoln or *the* France.

Exercise A: Find all the nouns in the following sentences. Label each one as a proper noun or a common noun.

1. The herd of cattle was overtaken by a blizzard.
2. During World War II many soldiers were in Europe.
3. Not all tribes were nomadic, as the Blackfeet were.
4. A group was formed to change the name of America to Columbia in honor of Christopher Columbus.
5. Neither the President nor his aides had a comment.
6. Six clowns and a huge dog climbed out of the little car.
7. Mastery of a foreign language can lead to exciting careers, such as a translator at the United Nations.
8. Every planet, including Earth, revolves around the sun.
9. Our swimmers won every meet except for the finals.
10. The Ford Foundation gave a grant to medical researchers in several parts of the world.

Exercise B: Writing Rewrite the following passage, filling in the spaces with appropriate nouns. Use at least five proper nouns.

On ______ we had a holiday from school, so ______ and I decided to take a long bicycle trip to ______. Before we started, we went to ______ to buy some energy snacks for the road. ______, the owner, told us that if we rode along ______ we would be able to see the new ______ that had been built there. We started out from ______ and followed the suggested route. Although we did not stop for sightseeing, we rode past ______, ______, and ______. Exhausted but satisfied, we returned around 9:00 that ______.

1.2 The Pronoun

Our speaking and writing would sound awkward if we had to repeat the full name of every person, place, or thing each time we wished to mention it.

Janice trained *Janice's* dog well.

To prevent this repetition, we sometimes use other words in place of names. These words are **pronouns.** They may be used in a sentence in any way that a noun is used.

A pronoun is a word used in place of a noun.

The noun for which the pronoun stands and to which it refers is its **antecedent.**

Tom had forgotten *his* books. (*Tom* is the antecedent of *his.*)

The *passengers* were reading *their* papers. (*passengers* is the antecedent of *their*.)

Ms. Brown is the *teacher* to *whom* Bob spoke. (*teacher* is the antecedent of *whom*.)

Sometimes the antecedent of a pronoun appears in a preceding sentence.

Maria lost her *keys*. *She* could not find *them* anywhere. (*Maria* is the antecedent of *she; keys* is the antecedent of *them*.)

There are six kinds of pronouns:

personal pronouns
compound personal pronouns
indefinite pronouns
demonstrative pronouns
interrogative pronouns
relative pronouns

Personal Pronouns

When a pronoun is used in place of a person's name, it is called a **personal pronoun.** Personal pronouns may also refer to things.

Did Kate say *she* plays the oboe?
I threw out the album because *it* was warped.

Personal pronouns may be categorized in several ways.

Person. If a pronoun refers to the person speaking, it is a **first-person** pronoun. If a pronoun refers to a person being spoken to, it is a **second-person** pronoun. A pronoun that refers to a person or thing spoken about is a **third-person** pronoun.

First Person (the person speaking) I, me, my, mine we, us, our, ours
Second Person (the person spoken to) you, your, yours
Third Person (the person or thing spoken about) he, him, his, she, her, hers, it, its they, them, their, theirs

Number. Pronouns that refer to *one* person, place, thing, or idea are **singular.** Pronouns that refer to *more than one* person, place, thing, or idea are **plural.**

SINGULAR: Randolph washed the car, and *I* waxed *it*.
PLURAL: Randolph washed the cars, and *we* waxed *them*.

Gender. Pronouns that refer to males are in the **masculine gender.** Pronouns that refer to females are in the **feminine gender.** Pronouns that refer to things are in the **neuter gender.**

MASCULINE: *He* was the tallest boy in *his* class.
FEMININE: *She* was the tallest girl in *her* class.
NEUTER: *It* was the tallest tree in the forest.

The neuter pronoun *it* is used to refer to things. The feminine pronouns are sometimes used to refer to countries, ships, and airplanes. Animals may be referred to by the neuter pronoun, *it* or *its*, or by the masculine or feminine pronouns if the gender of the animal is known.

Case. Personal pronouns change their form for different uses in sentences. This change of form is called **case.** There are three cases: *nominative, possessive,* and *objective*.

NOMINATIVE: *They* praised the surgeon.
POSSESSIVE: The surgeon was grateful for *their* praise.
OBJECTIVE: The surgeon praised *them*.

The table below shows the person and number of all three cases of personal pronouns.

Personal Pronouns

SINGULAR			
	NOMINATIVE	POSSESSIVE	OBJECTIVE
FIRST PERSON:	I	my, mine	me
SECOND PERSON:	you	your, yours,	you
THIRD PERSON:	he, she, it	his, her, hers, its	him, her, it

PLURAL			
	NOMINATIVE	POSSESSIVE	OBJECTIVE
FIRST PERSON:	we	our, ours	us
SECOND PERSON:	you	your, yours	you
THIRD PERSON:	they	their, theirs	them

Possessive Pronouns. Special forms of personal pronouns are used to show ownership or belonging. These pronouns are called **possessive pronouns.**

You are wearing *my* jacket. (ownership)
She enjoyed being with *her* cousins. (belonging)

Some personal pronouns have two possessive forms. One form is used in place of a noun: *mine, yours, hers, his, ours, theirs*. The other is used as a modifier before nouns: *my, your, her, his, our, their*.

Molly saved that piece of cake and ate *mine*. (used in place of a noun)
That was *my* piece of cake that Molly ate. (modifies *piece*)
The victory was *ours*. (used in place of a noun)
Our victory was sweet. (modifies *victory*)

Exercise: Find the personal pronouns in the following sentences. Find the antecedent of each pronoun, if there is one.

1. The mayor told the reporters that they could come into her office.
2. Isaac, your sister wants you to pick up her assignments.
3. Julie and Tony wrote the song. They work well together.
4. The male seahorse carries its young in a pouch.
5. Brooke Shields, a movie star since childhood, began her college career at Princeton.
6. The *Columbia* kept on its original course in spite of atmospheric changes.
7. Some frogs live in the desert. They are only active for a few days each year.
8. The work was all Elaine's, but the idea was mine.
9. Sarah keeps pigeons on the roof, but she does not bring them into the house.
10. Twenty artists displayed their work at the fair. They sold most of what they brought.

Compound Personal Pronouns

A **compound personal pronoun** is formed by adding *-self* or *-selves* to certain personal pronouns, as follows:

FIRST PERSON: myself, ourselves
SECOND PERSON: yourself, yourselves
THIRD PERSON: himself, herself, itself, oneself, themselves

These are the only acceptable compound personal pronouns. Forms such as *hisself* or *theirselves* are nonstandard.

Compound personal pronouns are used *intensively* for emphasis or *reflexively* to refer to a preceding noun or pronoun.

The admiral *himself* gave the order. (intensive)

Sue cut *herself* on the broken glass. (reflexive)

A compound personal pronoun must have an antecedent.

INCORRECT: The plan was approved by the board and myself.
CORRECT: The plan was approved by the board and me.
CORRECT: I myself approved the plan.

Exercise: Supply an acceptable compound personal pronoun in each of these sentences. Write its antecedent.

1. I ______ will give the signal.
2. Jim, you should give ______ more time to write.
3. They braced ______ for the next announcement.
4. We have only ______ to blame.
5. Bill hurt ______ by diving into shallow water.
6. The deed ______ was praiseworthy.
7. I ______ decided on the lighting of the stage.
8. Maynard Ferguson ______ accompanied the singer.
9. Carolyn found ______ in a dangerous situation.
10. Girls, you can be proud of ______ for winning the game.

Indefinite Pronouns

A pronoun that does not refer to a specific person or thing is an **indefinite pronoun.** Usually an indefinite pronoun has no antecedent, but sometimes it may refer to a preceding noun or pronoun.

The *players* were tired. *Some* were stretched out on the ground. (The antecedent of the indefinite pronoun *Some* is *players*.)

Furthermore, an indefinite pronoun itself may be the antecedent of a personal pronoun.

Everyone brought *his* own towel. (The antecedent of *his* is the indefinite pronoun *Everyone*.)

There are two main groups of indefinite pronouns.

SINGULAR INDEFINITE PRONOUNS

another	anything	either	everything	no one
anybody	one	everyone	neither	someone
anyone	each	everybody	nobody	somebody

PLURAL INDEFINITE PRONOUNS

both	many	few	several

The pronouns *all, some, any, most,* and *none* may be singular or plural, depending upon their meaning in the sentence.

All the snow *has* melted. (singular)
All the shovels *have* been sold. (plural)

Some of the money *is* being used for a party. (singular)
Some of us *are* invited to his home. (plural)

None of my homework *was* finished. (singular)
None of the problems *were* easy. (plural)

Demonstrative Pronouns

The pronouns *this, that, these,* and *those* are used to point out which thing or things are being referred to. Since they point to, or demonstrate, what is meant, they are called **demonstrative pronouns.** They always refer to a definite person or thing in the sentence or in another sentence.

This is the *book* my uncle wrote. (*This* refers to *book*.)

On the shore we saw five *boxes*. *These* contained our provisions. (*These* refers to *boxes*.)

Note: The demonstrative pronouns *this, that, these,* and *those* may also be used as adjectives to modify a noun: *this* bus, *those* squirrels.

Interrogative Pronouns

Pronouns that are used to ask questions, such as *who, whose, whom, which,* and *what,* are called **interrogative pronouns.**

Who saw the fire?
To *whom* did you wish to speak?
The pen isn't mine. *Whose* is it?
What is your answer?
Which do you prefer?

Relative Pronouns

The pronouns *who, whose, whom, which,* and *that* can be used to combine ideas, as in this example:

Schliemann was the archaeologist *who* discovered Troy.

Because such pronouns *relate* one idea to another, they are called **relative pronouns.** (See Section 3.6 for more information on the use of relative pronouns.)

Exercise A: Write each pronoun in the following sentences. Then tell whether it is indefinite, demonstrative, or interrogative.

1. Those are the apples Dustin picked.
2. Everyone came in costume to the party.
3. Who knows how to compute batting averages?
4. Have all of the ballots been counted?
5. This is Rita's cousin.
6. What is Arnold's phone number?
7. Which is the club in charge of the canned food drive?
8. That is a good topographical map of the moon.
9. Neither of the letters made sense.
10. Both of the twins are excellent skaters.

Exercise B: Follow the directions for Exercise A.

1. Someone must have left the door unlocked.
2. The sales clerk said those are excellent jogging shoes.
3. That is the road to the fairgrounds.
4. The hikers were hungry, for many had not eaten breakfast.
5. Some of the visitors were from Japan.
6. Who saw the last game of the World Series?
7. This is a very difficult dance step to master.
8. If those are not brushes, the paint won't go on easily.
9. None of the players was hurt.
10. Lee hid all of Donna's birthday gifts.

1.3 The Verb

Every sentence must contain a word that tells what is happening. This word is the **verb**.

A verb is a word that expresses an action, condition, or state of being.

Most verbs change their form (their sound or spelling) to show past time and present time. They are the only words to do so. This fact can help you decide which word is a verb.

Jerry *sings* ballads and show tunes. (present)
Jerry *sang* ballads and show tunes. (past)

The arrival of more troops *alters* the situation. (present)
The arrival of more troops *altered* the situation. (past)

Most verbs also change their form to show the difference between singular and plural in the third person.

Dave *plays* ping-pong competitively. (third person singular)
The other boys *play* for enjoyment. (third person plural)

Verbs can be divided into two main categories: **action verbs** and **linking verbs.**

Action Verbs

Action verbs tell what the subject is doing. The action may be visible, or it may be a mental action, which is not visible.

Helen *hit* the ball. (visible)
Estelle *thought* about her mistake. (not visible)

Linking Verbs

Some verbs do not express action. Instead they link the subject of a sentence to a noun, a pronoun, or an adjective. Hence they are called **linking verbs.**

Vicky *is* vice-president. (*is* links the subject *Vicky* to the noun *vice-president.*)

The most common linking verb is *be* and its forms. Other linking verbs have to do with the senses or express the condition or placement of the subject.

Linking Verbs

Forms of *To Be*	Sensory Verbs
She *was* inquisitive.	That tune *sounds* familiar.
I *am* a coin collector.	The milk *tasted* sour.
The pianos *were* Steinways.	Ian *appeared* healthy.
You *are* superstitious.	The air *felt* humid.
George *is* a dancer.	Charlie Brown *looked* sad.
Others: *be, been, being*	That pizza *smells* delicious.

Verbs of Condition or Placement	
The crowd *became* restless.	The driver *stayed* alert.
The wind *remained* steady.	The fruit *grew* round and orange.
The dancers *seem* prepared.	

Some verbs can be both a linking verb and an action verb.

Cary *grew* silent. (linking)
We *grew* eggplants and zucchini last summer. (action)

The child *felt* ill. (linking)
Jim *felt* his bruised arm tenderly. (action)

Main Verbs and Auxiliaries

Many verbs consist of more than one word. They consist of a **main verb** and one or more **auxiliaries,** or helping verbs. Together, a main verb and its auxiliaries are called a **verb phrase.** The last word in the phrase is the main verb.

Three verbs can be either main verbs or auxiliaries.

DO	HAVE	BE		
do	has	is	was	be
does	have	am	were	been
did	had	are		being

AS MAIN VERB	AS AUXILIARY
This will *do* the job.	I *do* like carrot cake.
You *have* the key.	We *have* seen the exhibit.
The doors *were* shut.	The girls *were* laughing.

The most frequently used auxiliaries are the forms of *be* and *have*. Here are other common auxiliaries:

must	may	shall	could	would
might	can	will	should	

AUXILIARY	MAIN VERB	VERB PHRASE
was	planning	was planning
had	said	had said
does	enjoy	does enjoy
could be	gone	could be gone
should have	been	should have been
was being	performed	was being performed

Often parts of a verb are separated by a modifier or modifiers that are not part of the verb.

We *had* just *arrived*. The rain *had* not quite *stopped*.

Exercise A: Write the verb in each of these sentences. Include all the words that make up the verb phrase. Do not include words that separate an auxiliary from a main verb.

1. Sally is busily building a weather station.
2. When are you leaving for Toronto?
3. She and I have always been adventurers.
4. Jerry will have reached Dallas by now.
5. The captain is being transferred next month.
6. The seeds of the plants were widely scattered.
7. Do you and your neighbors get together very often?
8. The helicopter had apparently run into a power line.
9. The gymnasts were all practicing for the meet.
10. Dr. Seeley, the chief surgeon, will operate.
11. The extent of his injuries has not yet been determined.
12. The stowaway was questioned by the ship's officers.
13. How will the new law affect you personally?
14. For the best results, you should preheat the oven.
15. Paula may not have gotten the part, after all.

Exercise B: Write each verb. Tell whether it is an action verb or a linking verb.

1. We all sat lazily around the campfire.
2. Carol forgot her dental appointment.
3. The astronomer saw the comet in the southwestern sky.
4. The king seemed depressed that afternoon.
5. Harry looked suspiciously at the falafel.
6. Cautiously, he tasted it.
7. Surprisingly, it tasted delicious.
8. Three exotic masks hung on the wall.
9. The weathered old fisherman wore a yellow slicker.
10. Your piano sounds flat to me.

11. The foreign diplomat appeared annoyed.
12. Sam felt in his backpack for his Swiss Army Knife.
13. We all became ill from the fumes.
14. The candidate for Congress sounded sincere.
15. A glowing red sun hovered above the horizon.

Exercise C: Writing Write two sentences for each verb. In one, use the verb as an action verb. In the second, use the verb as a linking verb. You may add auxiliaries if you wish.

1. smell	3. grew	5. looked	7. taste
2. felt	4. sound	6. remain	8. appear

Transitive and Intransitive Verbs

Action verbs may be transitive or intransitive. A **transitive verb** carries over the action from the subject to the object of the verb. This object is the word that comes after the verb and tells *who* or *what* receives the action. (See Section 2.8.) An **intransitive verb** expresses an action that is complete in itself; it does not carry action over to an object.

TRANSITIVE	INTRANSITIVE
Mom *painted* the ceiling first.	The movie *ended*.
Someone *rang* the bell.	The workers *left*.
Mary *enjoyed* the game.	The concert *began* early.

Note: Some of the intransitive verbs are followed by adverbs or other modifiers that tell *where, when, why, how,* or *to what extent*. Be careful not to mistake these modifiers for objects.

Many verbs may be transitive in one sentence and intransitive in another.

INTRANSITIVE	TRANSITIVE
Everyone *sang*.	Everyone *sang* the old songs.
Did you *call?*	*Did* you *call* the doctor?
I *could* not *see*.	I *could* not *see* the signal.

Exercise A: Find the verb. Tell whether it is transitive or intransitive. If it is transitive, write down the object of the verb.

1. Ancient Romans wore togas.
2. Legal cases jam the courts.
3. The thief posed as a safety inspector.
4. Phil Esposito slapped the puck into the net.
5. The eruption of Mt. Vesuvius buried three towns.
6. The troops crouched in the trenches.
7. Karen works for a detective agency.
8. Lea trained hard for the Olympics.
9. My cousin Aretha enlisted in the army.
10. Glaciers formed much of our country's terrain.
11. With two seconds on the clock, the Celtics scored a basket.
12. Alex waited by the stadium entrance.
13. Brian accepted Elyse's suggestion.
14. One commuter took the wrong bus.
15. Carolers sang "Jingle Bells" in the village square.

Exercise B: Writing Tell whether the verb in each of the following sentences is transitive or intransitive. Then write new sentences, using the transitive verbs as intransitive verbs and the intransitive verbs as transitive verbs.

1. Will you call after the rehearsal?
2. The manager of the store accidentally tripped the burglar alarm.
3. Every one of the children recited nervously.
4. Gerald de Nerval walked his pet lobster on a ribbon.
5. The UFO's moved through the night sky silently.
6. We will have to stand the speakers on top of each other.
7. The back door opens onto a redwood deck.
8. The rugged sailors fished for salmon in the icy waters of the North Sea.
9. The elves hammered through the night and into the morning.
10. Read one of the short stories in the anthology tonight.

1.4 The Adjective

Nouns and verbs alone cannot convey all of what we want to say and write. We also need **modifiers,** words that describe or limit the meanings of other words. One type of modifier is the **adjective.**

An adjective is a word that modifies a noun or pronoun.

Adjectives are used to tell *which one, what kind, how many,* or *how much* about nouns and pronouns.

WHICH ONE: this, that, these, those
WHAT KIND: healthy, pale, strong, lively
HOW MANY: some, all, few, four, twenty
HOW MUCH: little, much, plentiful

That new student has *three older* brothers.
Several professional athletes entered *this* marathon.
A *famous* lyricist wrote *those clever* parodies.

Notice that demonstrative pronouns can also be used as adjectives: *those* flowers, *that* wrench.

The Articles

The articles, *the, a,* and *an,* are considered adjectives because they modify the nouns they precede. The word *the* is called a **definite article** because it often points to a specific person, thing, or group.

The words *a* and *an* are called **indefinite articles.** Indefinite articles express the idea that a noun is not unique, but one of many.

The operation proceeded smoothly.
(*The* indicates a specific operation.)
The surgeon performed *an* operation of great delicacy. (*an* indicates that there are other operations of the same kind.)

Use *a* before words that begin with a consonant sound. Use *an* before words that begin with a vowel sound. Remember, it is the sound, not the spelling, that determines the correct choice.

a feather	*an* honorary degree
an ostrich	*a* university

Proper Adjectives

A **proper adjective** is formed from a proper noun. The proper adjective is always capitalized.

NOUN	ADJECTIVE	NOUN	ADJECTIVE
Switzerland	Swiss	Ireland	Irish
Greece	Greek	Talmud	Talmudic
Europe	European	Congress	Congressional

Predicate Adjectives

An adjective does not always precede the noun or pronoun it modifies. Frequently an adjective is separated from the noun or pronoun it modifies by a linking verb.

Phil seems *quiet*. We were *concerned*.

An adjective that follows a linking verb and modifies the subject is a predicate adjective.

Exercise A: Find each adjective and tell which word it modifies. Ignore the articles.

1. A loud noise woke me up.
2. An Indian family lives across the street.
3. Ron creates metal sculptures from empty cans.
4. The old chair was uncomfortable.
5. The new neighbors have a green tandem bicycle.

6. Simple, natural poetry has strong appeal.
7. Sandra seemed worried after the German test.
8. Many European immigrants adopted American customs.
9. In the dense forest was a small, sunny clearing.
10. Both back tires look low to me.

Exercise B: Follow the directions for Exercise A.

1. Hawaiian pineapples are an important export.
2. A minor mechanical defect caused the rocket to misfire.
3. In the aquarium swam a vicious piranha.
4. The hands on the old clock seemed immobile.
5. The tropical forests of Brazil are dense and humid.
6. I am aware that the risk is great.
7. The additional money will put us on a sound financial basis.
8. Few American students learn Oriental languages.
9. The impatient customer sounded angry.
10. Any movie by Steve Martin is clever and odd.

Exercise C: Writing Add adjectives to the following sentences to make them more vivid and precise. Some sentences may require proper adjectives.

1. The ______, ______ radiators spurted ______ steam all over the room.
2. A ______ evening includes ______ music and ______ food.
3. The lid of the coffin squeaked open as the ______ vampire stared at the ______, ______ moon.
4. The skiers looked forward to the ______ fireplace and a ______ meal after spending the day on the ______ slopes.
5. The ______ embassy was picketed by ______ demonstrators demanding ______ treatment.
6. The class enjoyed reading *Romeo and Juliet* and other ______ plays; however, the ______ language sometimes proved ______.

7. The players were ______ and ______ when they came off the field, but nothing could keep them from feeling ______.
8. A ______, ______ woman strode down the street brandishing a ______ umbrella.
9. Four ______ camels stared at the ______ visitors to the zoo.
10. The sounds of the farmhands returning from the ______ fields made a ______, ______ hum over the countryside.

1.5 The Adverb

The adverb is another type of modifier. It, too, can add color and interest to your writing.

An adverb modifies a verb, an adjective, or another adverb.

MODIFYING A VERB: Rick smiled *mysteriously*.

MODIFYING AN ADJECTIVE: It was a *most* disagreeable odor.

MODIFYING AN ADVERB: The music ended *rather* abruptly.

Adverbs tell *where, when, how,* or *to what extent:*

WHERE: A chill wind blew *outside*.
WHEN: The Prime Minister arrived *late*.
HOW: The chimps chattered *noisily*.
TO WHAT EXTENT: The dress was *completely* ruined.

Many adverbs are formed by adding *-ly* to an adjective: *cautious—cautiously, quick—quickly, soft—softly, wise—wisely.* However, not all modifiers ending in *-ly* are adverbs. The following, for example, are adjectives: *lively, homely, friendly, lovely, ugly, lonely.*

There are also many adverbs that do not end in *-ly*. The negatives *no, not,* and *never* are almost always adverbs. Many words that express time, such as *now, ever, almost,* and *soon* are always adverbs.

Some words may be either adjectives or adverbs.

ADJECTIVE	ADVERB
a *low* bridge	The plane flew *low.*
a *long* story	Don't stay *long.*

Directive Adverbs

Adverbs that tell *where* (place or direction) about the verb are called **directive adverbs.** They generally follow the verb.

The parakeet got *out.*
The prospector looked *up.*
A cheery fire glowed *inside.*
The cyclist had traveled *far.*

Many directive adverbs are combined with verbs to make idioms: *give out, give up, give in, give off.* An **idiom** is a group of words with a meaning different from the literal meanings of the individual words.

Position of Adverbs

A directive adverb normally follows the verb it modifies. An adverb modifying an adjective or another adverb usually comes immediately before the word it modifies. Other adverbs may be positioned in various parts of the sentence.

DIRECTIVE: Two of the posters fell *down.*

ADVERB MODIFYING MODIFIER: It was a *very* scary story.

OTHER ADVERBS: *Abruptly,* he slammed on the brakes.

He *abruptly* slammed on the brakes.

He slammed on the brakes *abruptly.*

Exercise A: Find each adverb in the following sentences. Tell which word or words it modifies.

1. Thomas Jefferson's influence extends far.
2. His unusually brilliant works were published recently in a small literary magazine.
3. The door will probably open if you press harder.
4. Emmy always arrives late.
5. Uncle Ed usually dresses rather carelessly.
6. The March Hare darted here and there.
7. Jon accepted the job quite eagerly.
8. Sue took out her frustrations on the lump of clay.
9. The fish doesn't smell very fresh today.
10. You should not have taken my remark so seriously.
11. In the morning I move more slowly.
12. Huffily, the actress stormed across the set and slammed her dressing room door.
13. Our team won because they fielded better.
14. Postal rates are probably going up again.
15. Here comes the mayor now.

Exercise B: Writing Rewrite each sentence, adding adverbs that answer the questions in parentheses.

1. Tina performed her routine ______. (how?)
2. Leave ______ if you expect to catch the bus. (when?)
3. Some rocks fell and ______ injured a worker. (to what extent?)
4. The town was ______ deserted. (to what extent?)
5. Will you ______ return to Squirrel Lake? (when?)
6. The shortstop fumbled the ball ______ because the sun was in his eyes. (how?)
7. The blizzard began ______. (when?)
8. The satellite's radio is ______ sending valuable information. (to what extent?)
9. The hot air balloon floated ______ above the trees and the crowds of people. (how?)
10. The cable car was ______ crowded. (to what extent?)

1.6 The Preposition

A sentence derives its meaning from the way the words within it relate to each other. One part of speech used to show a relationship between two or more words in a sentence is called the **preposition.**

There are seventeen one-syllable prepositions in English.* They are used to show the following relationships.

LOCATION: at, by, in, on, near
DIRECTION: to, from, down, off, through, out, past, up
ASSOCIATION: of, for, with, like

There are also some two-syllable prepositions.

about	along	below	during
above	among	beneath	except
across	around	beside	inside
after	before	between	outside
against	behind	beyond	over
			under

A number of prepositions have been formed by combining two one-syllable prepositions.

into	without	within
upon	onto	throughout

A **compound preposition** is formed by combining a modifier with a preposition or by grouping prepositions.

according to	in place of	on account of
prior to	out of	instead of
in regard to	owing to	because of
in front of	subsequent to	aside from
by means of	apart from	as to

*The word *but* may be used as a preposition with the meaning of *except*. The word *as* may be used as a preposition with the meaning "in the capacity of:" *As* president, you must set a good example.

Objects of Prepositions

A preposition never appears alone. It is always used with a word or group of words that is called its **object.** The preposition relates its object to some other word in the sentence. Together, the preposition, its object, and any modifiers of the object, form a **prepositional phrase.** Look at the phrases in the sentences below. The object of the preposition is shown in heavy type.

The firefighters dashed *into the* **store**.
The procession moved slowly *down the long* **aisle**.

The object of a preposition usually follows the preposition. An exception can occur in a sentence that contains an interrogative pronoun or a relative pronoun.

We do not know **whom** this ticket was left *for*.
Whom did you give it *to*?

The object of a preposition may be a single word or a group of words.

WORD: We went into the *cave*.
WORD: Before his *speech,* he consulted his notes.
WORD GROUP: After *reading the article,* I changed my mind.
WORD GROUP: Bob was ready for *whatever might happen*.

Exercise A: Find the prepositions. Tell the object of each one.

1. Have you seen the new lion cubs at the San Diego Zoo?
2. Carlos packed his gear into his backpack.
3. The escaping prisoner crouched among the mail sacks.
4. Add those egg shells to the compost pile.
5. Joggers shouldn't run on hard pavement.
6. Which county are the most covered bridges in?
7. For two years we have lived in New York.
8. Before leaving the house, please close the windows.
9. Which TV network is *Soundstage* on?
10. The daring performer dove off the cliff into the ocean.

Exercise B: Follow the directions for Exercise A.

1. The new school will stand on the site of the old one.
2. The captain of the ship held the boat against the wind.
3. No one was allowed beyond that point except the police.
4. Besides the trophy, Jack wants the thrill of victory.
5. Tanya placed the key beneath the mat outside the door.
6. The Raiders scored after the two-minute warning.
7. From whom did you get this strange bit of information?
8. Prior to the presentation of evidence, he had already passed judgment on the case.
9. He sold book covers to whoever wanted them.
10. During World War II, English children were removed from large cities.

1.7 The Conjunction

Another kind of word used to show relationships between words or groups of words in a sentence is the **conjunction.**

A conjunction is a word that connects words, phrases, or clauses.

There are three kinds of conjunctions: coordinating, correlative, and subordinating conjunctions.

Coordinating Conjunctions

Conjunctions that connect similar sentence parts are called **coordinating conjunctions.** The conjunctions *and, but, or,* and *yet* can all be used to join things of the same kind or order.

We are studying history *and* biology.
Dick worked rapidly *but* carefully.
Myra dove into the water *and* down to the bottom.
We can paint *or* stain the bookcases.
Close the door, *but* leave the window open.
The hammock was old *yet* serviceable.

For and *so* may also be used as coordinating conjunctions to connect groups of words that would otherwise stand alone as complete sentences.

> We went into the city, *for* our supplies were low.
> The land was dry, *so* Jerold planted a cactus garden.

The word *nor* is used as a coordinating conjunction only when it is preceded by another negative word.

> Two of the hikers have *no* blankets, *nor* do they have any warm clothing.
> The rooster was *not* in the coop, *nor* were any of the hens.

Correlative Conjunctions

Some conjunctions are used in pairs: *not only . . . but (also); either . . . or; neither . . . nor; both . . . and; whether . . . or*. These conjunctions are called **correlative conjunctions.**

> We must decide now *whether* to fight *or* to give way.
> *Both* the star *and* his understudy were ill.
> *Neither* time *nor* tide waits for any man.
> *Either* carpentry *or* electronics will be Mandy's choice.
> The test was *not only* difficult *but* unfair.

Conjunctive Adverbs

One group of adverbs can be used like conjunctions. They are called **conjunctive adverbs.** These adverbs join groups of words that could stand alone as sentences. A semicolon comes before a conjunctive adverb, and a comma follows it.

> I like to work with children; *furthermore,* I need the money.
> Marie injured her ankle; *consequently,* she had to miss the race.

The most common conjunctive adverbs are listed below.

accordingly	hence	nevertheless	therefore
consequently	however	otherwise	thus
furthermore	moreover	also	still

Note: There is a third type of conjunction: the **subordinating conjunction.** It is discussed in Section 3.5.

Exercise: Identify the conjunctions and conjunctive adverbs. Tell whether the conjunctions are coordinating or correlative.

1. Either you or I should go.
2. Doris limped slowly and painfully to the locker room.
3. Neither Jan nor Nancy could keep score.
4. The world leaders held a summit conference; however, little was accomplished.
5. For running you should not only wear proper shoes but also do adequate stretching exercises.
6. Both Mom and Uncle Ben attended the University of Hawaii.
7. Andrea thought Eric was going out of town; otherwise, she would have asked him to the dance.
8. Florence searched for her father's high school yearbook in the attic and in the garage.
9. Neither the children nor their parents enjoyed the play.
10. The class trip was postponed, for a snowstorm was predicted.
11. The strange man did not have any money, nor did he have a bus token.
12. The astronauts appeared alert and poised while they waited to enter the space shuttle.
13. Whether I shop early or wait until the last minute, I never seem to be prepared for the holidays.
14. The tour guide for our trip should speak either Italian or German.
15. There was nothing to do when the bus broke down, so we sang songs and played guessing games to pass the time.

1.8 The Interjection

An **interjection** does not have any specific relation to the other parts of a sentence. It is interjected, or "thrown into," the sentence. An interjection expresses strong feeling, so it is usually followed by an exclamation point.

An interjection is a word or word group used to express surprise or other emotion. It has no grammatical relation to other words in the sentence.

Oh!	Ah!	For heaven's sakes!	Hurrah!
Ouch!	Ha!	Congratulations!	Great!

1.9 Words Used as Different Parts of Speech

Some words are always the same part of speech. For example, *am* is always a verb, and *I* is always a personal pronoun. Most of the time, though, the part of speech of a word depends on how it is used in a sentence.

Arthur found a precious *stone*. (noun)
We built a *stone* fence. (adjective)
The angry mob *stoned* the embassy. (verb)
The sky was clear, *but* rain was predicted. (conjunction)
No one *but* Wilma has the right answer. (preposition)

To determine the part of speech of a word, you must consider how it is used in the sentence.

Verb or Noun?

Some words may be used as either verbs or nouns. To decide whether the word is being used as a noun or a verb, determine whether it names something (noun) or expresses an action or state of being (verb).

Would you like a *drink* of water? (noun)
I *drink* only skim milk. (verb)

Ron's *plants* were raised from seed. (noun)
Heidi *plants* her bulbs in late fall. (verb)

Noun or Adjective?

A word that names a person, place, thing, or idea is a noun. When the same word modifies another noun, it is an adjective.

Aluminum is now used in building. (noun)
An *aluminum* pan conducts heat rapidly. (adjective)

The holiday falls on *Sunday*. (noun)
Sunday games are well attended. (adjective)

Adjective or Pronoun?

The words *this*, *that*, *these*, and *those* may be used as demonstrative pronouns or as adjectives. If the word is used alone in place of a noun, it is a demonstrative pronoun. If it is used before another noun, it is an adjective.

This is my desk. (pronoun)
These are Jim's books. (pronoun)

That story is hard to believe. (adjective modifying *story*)
Those jeans are faded. (adjective modifying *jeans*)

Similarly, the words *what*, *which*, and *whose* may be used alone as pronouns or before nouns as adjectives.

What is your answer? (pronoun)
What town is this? (adjective modifying *town*)

Which is your choice? (pronoun)
Which coat is yours? (adjective modifying *coat*)

Whose is this? (pronoun)
Whose story do you believe? (adjective modifying *story*)

The words *your, my, our, his, her, their* are forms of the personal pronouns used to show possession. They always perform the job of adjectives. *Mine, yours, hers, ours,* and *theirs* are always pronouns. The word *his* may be used either way.

That dog of *hers* is a nuisance. (pronoun)
The yellow boat is *his*. (pronoun)
This is *his* paper. (adjective)

Adverb or Adjective?

Several words have the same form whether used as adjectives or adverbs. To tell the part of speech of such a word, determine what other word in the sentence it modifies. If the word modifies a noun or pronoun, it is an adjective. It will specify *what kind, which one, how many, how much*. If the word modifies any other kind of word, it is an adverb.

We played *hard*. (adverb telling *how* about *played*)
Dad brought some *hard* candy. (adjective telling *what kind* about *candy*)

Adverb or Preposition?

Some words may be used either as prepositions or as adverbs. To determine how such a word is being used, apply this simple test. A preposition is never used alone. It is always followed by a noun or a pronoun as part of a phrase. If the word is in a phrase, it is probably a preposition. If the word has no object, it is probably an adverb.

The council turned our request *down*.
(*down* is an adverb. It has no object.)
The basketball rolled *down* the stairs.
(*down* is a preposition. It has an object, *stairs*.)
Herb turned the lights *on*. (adverb)
The puzzle is *on* the table. (preposition)

Exercise A: Determine the part of speech of each italicized word in the sentences below.

1. The knight searched the forest *for* the dragon.
2. We looked in vain, *for* he had already gone.
3. The hero of the story has money, good health, intelligence—everything *but* character.
4. Many are called, *but* few are chosen.
5. We found the shovel again *after* the January thaw.
6. There was a frightened silence *after* the announcement had been made.
7. *These* are Douglas fir trees.
8. Where did you find *these* old magazines?
9. *Which* state has the highest budget for tourism?
10. *Which* is your favorite flavor of ice cream?
11. The men worked *hard* digging the *hard* soil.
12. My watch is *fast;* it always runs *fast*.
13. A ginger cat leaped *off* the roof.
14. Don't take *off* the bandage yet.
15. The dark, heavy drapes allowed no light *in*.

Exercise B: Writing Identify the part of speech of each italicized word. Then write a new sentence using the word as indicated in parentheses.

1. *What* time is it? (pronoun)
2. *Which* is the highest waterfall in South America? (adjective)
3. The three hour movie didn't seem *long*. (verb)
4. Steve is attending a *trade* school in Detroit. (verb)
5. We will never know the *whole* story. (noun)
6. The soccer *match* was tied. (verb)
7. My brother is planning a wedding in *June*. (adjective)
8. Gretchen taught us a German folk *dance*. (verb)
9. That *algebra* problem was hard to solve. (noun)
10. The mayor spoke about the *good* of the city. (adjective)
11. How can you put *up* with his constant whining? (preposition)

12. How can Jenny *work* at the restaurant with a broken ankle? (noun)
13. *For* three days, the crew wandered without food. (conjunction)
14. A *future* in computer programming sounds interesting to me. (adjective)
15. The patient finally felt *well* enough to go home. (adverb)

1.10 Verbals

There is a special class of words that are made from verbs but not used as verbs. They are called verbals. There are three kinds of verbals: **infinitives, participles,** and **gerunds.** Verbals are used as various parts of speech.

1.11 The Infinitive

An **infinitive** is a verb form that is usually preceded by the word *to*. When *to* is used before a verb, it is called the "sign of the infinitive." The infinitive occurs in the following forms:

ACTIVE PRESENT: to follow
ACTIVE PERFECT: to have followed
PASSIVE PRESENT: to be followed
PASSIVE PERFECT: to have been followed

The infinitive may be used as a noun. It may be the subject or object of a verb. It may be a predicate noun or an appositive.

To survive was now their only ambition. (subject of *was*)
Jan always wants *to win*. (object of *wants*)
Jack's chief ambition is *to fly*. (predicate noun)
His dream, *to win* the contest, was realized. (appositive)

The infinitive may also be used as a modifier. Used as an adjective, it may modify nouns and pronouns.

Ms. Anders is the person *to see*.

In this race, Rod is the one *to beat*.

As an adverb, the infinitive may modify adjectives, adverbs, or verbs.

The game was painful *to watch*. (modifies the adjective *painful*)

Sally arrived too late *to audition*. (modifies the adverb *late*)

We came *to hear* the music. (modifies the verb *came*)

See Sections 2.14 and 3.6 for additional details on the use of infinitives.

1.12 The Participle

The **participle** is a verbal that is used as an adjective. There are several forms of the participle.

PRESENT PARTICIPLE:	carrying
PAST PARTICIPLE:	carried
PERFECT PARTICIPLE:	having carried
PASSIVE PERFECT PARTICIPLE:	having been carried.

The present participle ends in *-ing*. The past participle usually ends in *-ed, -d, -en,* or *-t*.

The participle is always used as an adjective to modify a noun or a pronoun. In the examples below, the arrow indicates the word modified by the participle.

Stumbling, he just managed to save himself from falling off the dock.

Having been rejected, Terry walked aimlessly around town.

The girls, *smiling* suspiciously, walked out of the kitchen.

1.13 The Gerund

The **gerund** is a verbal noun that always ends in *-ing*. It is used in almost every way a noun can be used.

> *Swimming* is good exercise. (subject of verb)
> Maria does not enjoy *cooking*. (object of verb)
> After *eating*, relax for a while. (object of preposition)
> *Seeing* is *believing*. (subject and predicate noun)
> Kim's favorite sport, *skiing*, was expensive. (appositive)

1.14 Participle, Gerund, or Verb?

All present participles, all gerunds, and some verbs in verb phrases end in *-ing*. To distinguish among them, ask yourself the following questions:

1. Is the word used as an adjective? If so, it is a present participle.
2. Is the word used as a noun? If so, it is a gerund.
3. Is the word preceded by an auxiliary verb? If so, it is a verb in a verb phrase.

PRESENT PARTICIPLE: Satellites are sometimes reported as unidentified *flying* objects. (*flying* is an adjective modifying *objects*.)

GERUND: *Flying* was Daedalus's goal. (*Flying* is a noun, the subject of *was*.)

VERB: Charlie Brown has been *flying* his kite for many years. (*flying* is part of the verb phrase, *has been flying*.)

Exercise A: Find the verbals in the sentences below. Label them as infinitives, participles, or gerunds. There may be more than one verbal in a sentence.

1. A winding trail led down to the bottom of the mountain.
2. Hungry and frightened, the cub tried to find its mother.

3. Cooking is a chore to some people and a delight to others.
4. A dam was built to harness waterpower for the growing community.
5. Most cases of poisoning result from drugs or common household products.
6. In the hurdle event, Arthur is the one to beat.
7. The police force went on strike to secure better working conditions.
8. The newly married couple drove off in a car covered with paper flowers.
9. Andy's hobby, gardening, led him to a career in horticulture.
10. Over the summer holidays, Ken developed the habit of snacking.

Exercise B: Tell whether the italicized word or words in each sentence are verbs, present participles, or gerunds.

1. Before *painting*, be sure the wood on the boat is dry.
2. Some people enjoy *interviewing* for jobs.
3. The runners returned to the locker room, *sweating* and *panting*.
4. You have been *making* the same point for a half hour.
5. *Howling*, the bloodhounds greeted the rising of the full moon.
6. Maureen attributed her proficiency on the cello to *practicing*.
7. Are you *having* anything to eat before the performance?
8. Who is *going* with you to the orthodontist this afternoon?
9. *Skidding* and *sliding*, the bus made its way down the icy street.
10. *Sleeping* can be one of life's great pleasures.

Exercise C: Writing Write ten sentences. Each sentence must include at least one verbal. After each sentence, identify the verbal, tell what kind it is, and explain how it is used in the sentence.

REINFORCEMENT EXERCISES

The Classification of Words

A. Identify common and proper nouns. For each sentence below, write the nouns used in the sentence. Next to each noun, write *P* if it is a proper noun, and *C* if it is a common noun.

1. F. W. Ofeldt designed the first motorboat for a company in New York.
2. The car was stopped by the thick hedges.
3. Lauren and Terry volunteered to serve on the clean-up committee.
4. The first-place trophy was awarded to Paxton High School last Tuesday.
5. Uranium, used in nuclear reactors, is not a rare mineral.
6. Dorothea Lynde Dix was a pioneer in the movement for better treatment of the mentally ill.
7. Iodized salt provides the body with iodine.
8. The first American to orbit Earth was John Glenn.
9. Armadillos are nocturnal creatures.
10. Termites closely resemble ants but are actually related to cockroaches.

B. Recognize pronouns. Write each pronoun in the following sentences. Then tell whether it is a personal, a compound personal, an indefinite, a demonstrative, an interrogative, or a relative pronoun.

1. They navigated Burma's chief river, the Irrawaddy.
2. These are the chairs that need to be refinished.
3. Gregory asked if he could be excused.
4. "What can I do for you?" the security guard asked.
5. Aaron likes to type the final draft of his papers himself.
6. Anyone could see who was going to win the match.
7. That is the last game of the series.
8. Who among you has heard of the American railroad engineer Casey Jones?

9. Avicenna, who interpreted the works of Aristotle, was an Islamic philosopher.
10. Those are the heroic rescue workers mentioned by the President himself.

C. Identify different types of verbs. Write the complete verb in each sentence. Then tell whether each verb is an action or a linking verb. If it is an action verb, tell whether it is transitive or intransitive.

1. The fudge banana pie tasted terrible.
2. Ms. Manderly is moving the filing cabinet away from the window.
3. The judge at the county fair tasted preserves all afternoon.
4. Will you sing in the chorus this year?
5. The paramedic felt the leg for signs of a broken bone.
6. Amanda looked triumphant at the end of the race.
7. The young campers felt homesick only on the first night.
8. Our old dog was panting heavily in the oppressive heat.
9. I will be Frankenstein's monster for Halloween this year.
10. The band might have sounded better on disc than on tape.

D. Identify adjectives. For each sentence below, write the adjectives and tell which words they modify. Remember to look for predicate adjectives. Do not list articles.

1. To early Christians, the dragon was a symbol of sin, but to the Chinese, the magnificent, mythical monster was a symbol of kingship.
2. The Arctic explorers were tense after walking on the slippery glacier all day.
3. Traveling on transcontinental trains can be romantic, relaxing, and elegant.
4. Which of the seven flavors of ice cream tasted best to you?
5. The President requested that manufacturers of foreign cars impose a voluntary quota on exports to America.
6. Willem Bilderdijk is one of the great Dutch poets.

7. Todd felt sorry for the tiniest puppy in the huge litter.
8. Maya Plisetskaya is a ballerina who studied at the Bolshoi.
9. The armadillo is covered with hard, bony plates.
10. Anthrax, a fatal disease for cattle, is caused by a tiny microorganism in the blood.

E. Identify adverbs. In the sentences below, find the adverbs. Then tell what words they modify, and the part of speech of those words.

1. Deena said, "Go inside or you will catch a cold."
2. The lost campers vowed they would never again travel without a compass.
3. The flags hung limply on the hot, still afternoon.
4. It is not very often that we get such a famous visitor.
5. The flock of birds headed directly north as the season began to change.
6. Georgina looked hopefully at the awards that sparkled brightly on the judges' stand.
7. David approached the unusually friendly dog very cautiously.
8. The food quickly disappeared as the hikers filed into the lodge.
9. It soon became painfully obvious that the rain was not going to stop.
10. "What a strange plant!" said the biologist curiously.

F. Recognize prepositions. Each sentence below contains at least one prepositional phrase. Write out each prepositional phrase and underline the object.

1. One of Jean Dubuffet's paintings hangs in our museum.
2. A bird's nest is generally made of vegetation and dirt.
3. The giant panda was hiding between the two tall drums.
4. The pandas that live in the National Zoological Park in Washington, D.C., were presents from China.
5. Phillipe operated on the patient who had a torn cartilege.
6. The private detective glanced nervously at the three figures standing on the corner.

7. More than ten thousand window panes fell out of the John Hancock Tower in Boston.
8. Ruth stood alone among the silent, protecting pines.
9. The mail carrier arrived at an apartment building with a huge package.
10. I am going to the skating rink with Kerry.

G. Identify conjunctions. Identify the conjunctions and conjunctive adverbs in the following sentences. Label each conjunction as a coordinating or correlative conjunction.

1. Each Southern state decided whether to stay with the Union or to secede.
2. Both Alaska and Hawaii became part of the United States in 1959.
3. Sponges do not move; therefore, people once thought they were plants.
4. The diners could not decide between the excellent spaghetti and the delicious mostaccioli.
5. The children could sleep on the back porch or they could sleep in the tent.
6. The quarterback was small but powerfully built.
7. Carol had no money, but she did have confidence in her ability to earn some.
8. Insects are tiny animals; however, swarms of them can destroy whole sections of a country.
9. The author entitled her work *Buy This Book*, for she believed in a direct approach.
10. Neither the original manuscript nor the final revision was in readable form.

H. Use words as different parts of speech. Determine the part of speech of each italicized word. Then use each word in a new sentence as a different part of speech.

1. If you *play* the trumpet that *loud* you will wake up the whole neighborhood.
2. You can *judge* the speed skating, and I will judge the *floor* hockey.

3. A *cross* expression was on Jackie's face as her friends walked *up* to her.
4. The *cereal* box with the coupon we wanted was on the *top* shelf.
5. The Wilsons' four-year-old-son *skis* better than I do.
6. *Down* the mountainside clambered the *Swiss* mountaineers.
7. The surgeon arrived *late* for the *show* because her office called with an emergency.
8. *Six* are generally enough to make a pleasant *dinner* party.
9. Jeremy required *six* stitches when he tripped *over* the brick.
10. A *down* jacket and wool socks will help you keep out the *Arctic* chill.

I. Identify verbals. Find each verbal in the following sentences. Identify it as an infinitive, a participle, or a gerund.

1. Reacting angrily, the cook threw the skillet at the huge dog.
2. Rowing is a strenuous but health-building activity.
3. Knowing what poverty could mean, the lottery winner gave much of his wealth to the poor.
4. Julio enjoyed playing chess even more than he enjoyed winning.
5. The drama club is going to see a production of Miller's *Death of a Salesman*.
6. Watching golf on television is not one of my favorite Sunday activities.
7. Mission control was keeping a close eye on flying conditions.
8. Completing a job is often much harder than beginning it.
9. My brother-in-law is in training for the Boston marathon.
10. We did not bring our books with us, thinking we would only have to wait for a few minutes.

MIXED REVIEW

The Classification of Words

A. Identify each italicized word in these sentences as noun, verb, adjective, adverb, preposition, conjunction, interjection, participle, infinitive, or gerund.

1. *They attended* a concert at the Hollywood Bowl.
2. Tony made fudge *with* walnuts *and* marshmallows.
3. *Either* Della *or* Andrea could play the part *well*.
4. *Traveling* in the West, *Doug* visited a ghost town.
5. *After* the game *we* congratulated the team.
6. *Each season many* of the new TV shows are canceled.
7. *Who sponsors* the All-Star Game?
8. Deena *applied* glaze to her *pottery* mug.
9. Chris taught *herself* to play folk guitar *expertly*.
10. The *frightened* dog ran *too* fast *for* me to catch it.
11. *Wow!* I have never seen such *passing!*
12. *Since* June, we have *not* seen Derek.
13. Lucille has a watch *that* displays time, date, and temperature.
14. Some *young* people *serve* in the Senate *as* pages.
15. We go *to* the *community* center to see *silent* films.
16. *Encouraged* by her coach, Anne decided *to try* out for the Olympic team.
17. Van Gogh sold *only* one painting in *his* lifetime.
18. Helicopters are *sometimes* used for *aerial* photography.
19. *Dense,* gray smoke began *to creep* into our classroom.
20. The *government* accused spies of *stealing* national secrets.

B. For each sentence below, list the other word that is the same part of speech as the italicized word.

1. *Both* Cindy and Mindy were elected to the committee.
2. The *Irish* wolfhound was being walked by a dignified butler.
3. Marshall twisted in the air and landed *on* his feet.

4. The lyrebird *is* an Australian bird that runs on the ground.
5. Titanium is a *metal* that does not corrode easily.
6. Ask yourself whether *you* really want to do this.
7. Now is the time to proceed *cautiously.*
8. *Ouch!* Oh! I broke it!
9. *California* is sometimes referred to as the bear state.
10. Dinosaurs *became* extinct after mammals appeared on Earth.

C. Each of the words listed below can be used as more than one part of speech. Write two sentences for each of the words, using them as the parts of speech given in parentheses.

1.	fire	(verb, noun)
2.	these	(adjective, pronoun)
3.	staple	(adjective, verb)
4.	in	(adverb, preposition)
5.	park	(noun, verb)
6.	record	(noun, verb)
7.	truth	(noun, adjective)
8.	what	(adjective, pronoun)
9.	off	(adverb, preposition)
10.	baseball	(noun, adjective)

USING GRAMMAR IN WRITING

The Classification of Words

A. Adjectives and adverbs make your sentences vivid and precise. Write a paragraph in which you describe a common everyday occurrence, such as getting a glass of orange juice out of the refrigerator or raising a window shade in the morning, using adjectives and adverbs to make the scene as interesting as possible.

B. Sometimes when people write or speak, their pronoun references are ambiguous. In other words, the pronouns have two possible nouns that they might refer to. Read the paragraph below, then rewrite it, substituting nouns for any unclear pronoun references.

> Julia looked at her older sister. She thought she was a good photographer. No, she thought she was a *great* photographer. Why, then, didn't she have any confidence in herself? Why did she insist upon calling her photographs, "these silly things"? Margot wasn't that way about other things, only about her photography. Perhaps, thought Julia, it meant so much to her, more than anything else, and that was why she seemed to belittle it. Perhaps she was afraid of having it criticized, and so she criticized it herself, before anybody else could.

C. Make up a list of the ten things you would like to accomplish most in the next five years, using infinitives for the various items in the list. (For example, *to travel* extensively in Asia, *to graduate* from college, etc.) Then make a list of the ten things you enjoy doing most, using gerunds for the items on the list. Using these lists, write a few paragraphs that describe your ideal future.

CUMULATIVE REVIEW
The Parts of Speech

Recognizing the Parts of Speech and Verbals. Number your paper from 1 to 16. Decide whether each italicized word or phrase in the paragraph below is being used as a *Noun, Pronoun, Verb, Adverb, Adjective, Conjunction, Preposition, Gerund, Infinitive,* or *Participle*. Write your answer next to the corresponding number. Remember that the part of speech of a word often depends on how it is used in the sentence.

In 1644 the *French* [1] mathematician, scientist, *and* [2] philosopher Blaise Pascal constructed an *adding* [3] machine that he called the Pascaline. This machine contained six wheels, *along* [4] the edges of *which* [5] were written the numbers zero to nine. Above these *interlocking* [6] wheels were six tiny windows, each large enough *to show* [7] one digit. To add two or more numbers, one simply dialed digits on each wheel and read the sum that appeared in the windows. By *making* [8] an adjustment inside the machine, one could *also* [9] use the machine to subtract.

Pascal *had been inspired* [10] to invent the machine by watching his father, who was a tax collector, labor *late* [11] into the night, adding up his collections. Both Pascal and his father believed that *this* [12] new machine would make *calculating* [13] easier. They borrowed money *from* [14] friends and *associates* [15] and constructed as many machines as they could afford. *However,* [16] they lost their investment, because only a few of the machines were purchased.

2.0 The Parts of a Sentence

In Section 1, you learned about the types and functions of individual words. Words used in isolation, however, have little use in communication. Although the meaning of a single word message such as *Stop!* or *Warning* is easily understood by almost everyone, we usually depend on more elaborate combinations of words to convey meaning.

In order to be clear, these groups of words must be arranged in very specific orders, or patterns. You would not, for instance, say something like *Me that record hand*. You would know that the correct pattern is *Hand me that record*. You acquired knowledge of these patterns in early childhood as you listened to and mimicked the speech of others. However, you may never have given much conscious thought to exactly how these patterns work.

In Section 2, you will learn more about how groups of words are organized into sentences. This knowledge will help you to make your own use of language more effective.

2.1 The Sentence

Sentences are used to make statements and ask questions. To be a sentence, a group of words must express a complete thought, idea, or question. A preliminary definition of a sentence is given below:

A sentence is a group of words that expresses a complete thought.

INCOMPLETE: The boy with the compass (What about him?)
COMPLETE: The boy with the compass is our leader.

INCOMPLETE: Kay Jones, the manager of the bicycle factory (Did what?)
COMPLETE: Kay Jones, the manager of the bicycle factory, talked to our class.

INCOMPLETE: Coming up the path (Who did what?)
COMPLETE: Coming up the path, Jane saw a snake.

Exercise A: Which of these groups of words are sentences?

1. Down through the brush to the edge of the water
2. An enormous moose with a great spread of antlers and a shaggy winter coat
3. We were startled
4. Having nothing to protect myself with
5. I reached for the biggest stick in sight
6. Harry climbing a tree
7. Betty stood right in the middle of the portage and aimed her camera
8. The guide laughing
9. The moose a harmless animal
10. Actually, the moose usually avoids people
11. This one looked us over for a moment
12. Turned and crashed off through the brush
13. Once the guide by himself
14. There stood a huge black bear
15. The guide did not stop to exchange greetings

Exercise B: Writing Some of the following groups of words are not complete sentences. Identify these and make them into sentences. Write *Sentence* for the groups that are complete.

1. The change in seasons
2. Usually arriving twenty minutes after the bell
3. By practicing every chance he got
4. Over the icy river hovered a helicopter
5. Several new services provided by the telephone company
6. Boxes and crates piled up to the ceiling
7. A plant sale brought the student council the needed cash
8. Register your group over at the main desk
9. The town established a curfew
10. No amount of paint or wallpaper

2.2 Kinds of Sentences

One way to classify sentences is according to the purpose of the speaker or writer.* There are four principal purposes for sentences; therefore, there are four kinds of sentences.

1. The **declarative sentence** is used to make a statement. The statement may be one of fact, wish, intent, or feeling. It is followed by a period.

The moon is 238,000 miles from the Earth.
I would like to visit the Grand Canyon.

2. The **imperative sentence** is used to state a command, request, or direction. Although the subject of an imperative sentence is usually not expressed, it is always understood to be the pronoun *you*. An imperative sentence is usually followed by a period.

(You) Toss another log on the fire.
You go straight to the doctor.

(*For classification of sentences by form, see Section 3.)

3. The **interrogative sentence** is used to ask a question. It is always followed by a question mark.

Do you know all the lyrics?
You are a freshman in college?

4. An **exclamatory sentence** is used to express strong feeling. It is always followed by an exclamation point.

What a beautiful rainbow! Look at this mess!

Exercise A: What kind of sentence is each of the following?

1. What are you serving for dinner?
2. Ted and Paula are my closest friends.
3. How much did you pay for that jacket?
4. Have a good time on your canoe trip.
5. My sunburn really hurts!
6. Rhode Island is the smallest state in the country.
7. Please give me your address and phone number.
8. What a talented singer he is!
9. Wash the vegetables before you cook them.
10. Sally Ride first rode the space shuttle in 1983.

Exercise B: Writing Identify each sentence type shown below. Then rewrite each sentence to be the type indicated in parentheses. You may have to add or replace words.

1. Brazilians speak Portuguese. (interrogative)
2. That was a terrific movie. (exclamatory)
3. Our car has a five-speed floor shift. (interrogative)
4. Just set the cups on the sink. (interrogative)
5. Meet me at four o'clock sharp. (declarative)
6. Anyone who wants to buy tickets may do so on Thursday. (imperative)
7. The last one out should lock the door. (imperative)
8. Get your homework done before you go. (declarative)
9. Could you guard your opponent? (imperative)
10. Avoid that rotting bridge at all costs. (exclamatory)

2.3 Subject and Predicate

Every complete sentence is made up of two parts. (1) The **subject** is the person, thing, or idea about which something is said. (2) The **predicate** is the idea expressed about the subject.

Every sentence contains a subject and a predicate.

The subject of the sentence is the person, place, thing, or idea about which something is said.

The predicate tells something or asks something about the subject of the sentence.

The predicate of a sentence affirms, denies, declares, or asks something about the subject. Together, the subject and the predicate express a complete thought.

A sentence is a group of words expressing a complete thought by means of a subject and a predicate.

SUBJECT	PREDICATE
Ice	melts.
The ice on the pond	melts fast under the spring sun.

2.4 The Simple Predicate

No matter how many words there may be in a predicate,* the most important one is always a **verb.** The verb is the key word in the predicate, and in the entire sentence.

The simple predicate of the sentence is the verb.

The simple predicate, or verb, may consist of only one word. It may also be a phrase consisting of a main verb and its auxiliaries: *have gone, might have gone, is running, had been running*. The words making up the verb may be interrupted by a modifier. The modifier is not part of the verb.

*The **complete predicate** consists of the verb, its modifiers, and complements.

had not *been seen*	*had* just *come*
was never *completed*	*is* quickly *improving*

The verb may also be *compound,* which means "having more than one part of the same kind." The parts of a compound verb are joined by a conjunction (*and, or, neither-nor,* etc.).

We **arrived** late *and* **left** early.
The audience *neither* **laughed** *nor* **applauded.**

2.5 The Simple Subject

Every sentence has a **subject.** The complete subject is the word or words that the verb tells about. To find the subject, form a question by placing *who* or *what* before the verb.

Herb arrived early.		Dead limbs fell in the storm.	
VERB:	arrived	VERB:	fell
WHO ARRIVED?:	Herb	WHAT FELL?:	Dead limbs
SUBJECT:	Herb	SUBJECT:	Dead limbs

The **simple subject** is the key word or words of the complete subject. It is the sentence part that the verb refers to. The simple subject of the verb may be a single word or a group of words such as a phrase or a clause.

The *otters* slithered across the ice. (word as subject)
Having a goal is important. (phrase as subject)
What they wanted is not clear. (clause as subject)

Although an entire phrase may be the simple subject, a single word within a phrase can never be a subject.

One *of the paintings* was finished.
(Only one was finished. *One* is the subject. The word *paintings* lies within the prepositional phrase and is the object of the preposition *of*.)

Marion, *together with her cousins*, is at the flea market. (*Marion* is the subject of *is; cousins* is the object of the preposition *together with*.)

The subject of the verb may be compound. The parts of a compound subject are normally joined by a conjunction.

Books, papers, *and* **magazines** littered his desk.
Crates of eggs *and* **cartons** of butter spilled along the road.
Either a **dry cell** *or* a **magnet** will do.

Diagraming. The simple subject and verb of a sentence are diagramed as follows:

Dogs bark.

Dogs | **bark**

Single word modifiers are placed on slanted lines below the words they modify.

Your dogs bark loudly.

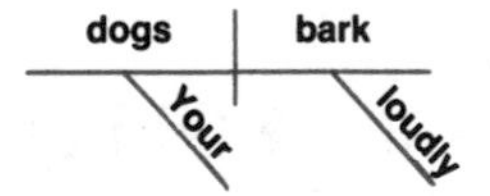

Exercise A: Find each verb and its simple subject. Some parts may be compound.

1. One of my sisters wears contact lenses.
2. The driver carefully avoided the potholes.
3. I had not seen my grandmother for nearly a year.
4. All of the spectators cheered and applauded.
5. Greg and Monroe are not playing this quarter.
6. My family, together with our dog, went on vacation.

7. Unusual camera angles and odd characters are the trademarks of Hitchcock's films.
8. The students and faculty were being entertained.
9. None of the students had ever seen the film before.
10. The cowhands roped the calves and branded them.

Exercise B: Follow the directions for Exercise A.

1. The baseball flew high into the air and crashed through a store window.
2. None of us saw or heard anything unusual.
3. People in the stands and players on the field stood in silence.
4. The serious tone of Corinne's remarks surprised everyone.
5. The people of this town will never forget your generosity.
6. Clothing, food, and money, together with offers of jobs, poured in on the homeless flood victims.
7. Streams and rivers became swollen and flooded the valley.
8. One member of the film crew flew to Denver and scouted out locations.
9. All but one of the workers stayed after five and helped us.
10. A fortune is not my idea of success.

2.6 Subjects in Unusual Positions

The most common sentence pattern in English places the subject before the verb. In certain situations, however, the usual subject-verb order is altered.

Questions. In most questions the subject appears between the words making up the verb phrase.

VERB	SUBJECT	VERB
Will	you	call?
Have	they	finished?
Is	Jess	going?
Could	he	have played?

The subject also falls between parts of the verb phrase in questions beginning with the interrogative words *where, when, why, how,* and *how much*.

> When *are* you *leaving?*
> How *could* he *forget* the tickets?

The interrogative pronouns *who* or *what* may function as the subject of the sentence. When this occurs, the subject will usually precede the verb in normal order.

> Who called? What happened?

Sentences Beginning with *There* and *Here*. Sometimes sentences begin with the word *There* or *Here* immediately followed by some form of *be: There is, There was, There will be, Here is, Here were,* and so on. In these sentences *Here* and *There* are introductory words used to get the sentence started. They are never the subject of the verb. In this kind of sentence, the subject follows the verb.

> Here is the answer to your question. (*answer* is the subject.)
> There were five parents present. (*parents* is the subject.)
> There will be a meeting tonight. (*meeting* is the subject.)

Note: Not all sentences beginning with *Here* and *There* follow the above pattern. In the following sentences, *Here* and *There* are adverbs modifying the verb: *There is the campsite. Here we can speak privately.*

Sentences in Inverted Order. Experienced writers and speakers often place the subject after the verb for emphasis or for variety of style.

> Out of the house poured heavy black *smoke*.
> Down the narrow passage crawled the *explorer*.
> Over the hills rolled the *fog*.

Finding the Subject of the Verb. To find the subject of the verb, find the verb first. Then form a question by placing *who* or *what* before the verb. If the sentence is not in normal order, this procedure will still work. However, restating the sentence may help to make the subject and verb more obvious.

INVERTED: From the crowd came a mighty roar.
NORMAL: A mighty roar came from the crowd.

Exercise A: Find each verb and its subject.

1. Where have the extra cartons been put?
2. Have we run out of chocolate milk again?
3. There are several boxes of paper clips in my desk drawer.
4. Out of the shadows comes a warning whisper.
5. Here in a desperate effort the workers piled sandbags.
6. Here stood the first capitol of the state.
7. After the brief shower, out came the children again.
8. Has anyone ever seen an electron?
9. From the bleachers snaked rolls of streamers.
10. Why are there no buses today?

Exercise B: Find the subject and verb of each sentence in the passage below. Notice how the variety adds interest to the story.

Tucked away in newspapers and magazines are amazing tales of human daring and determination. Some of these stories challenge the understanding of the reader.

In France, a mountain climber scales sheer cliffs with no equipment except his bare hands.
A runner from New Zealand jogs across Death Valley twice in twenty-five hours.
Alone in a sailboat, a blind sailor travels from San Francisco to Honolulu.

Why did these people attempt such dangerous feats? What were they trying to achieve? They may have been searching for fame. There may also have been a need for recognition involved. Perhaps, though, there simply runs through each of these people the spirit of the true adventurer.

Exercise C: Writing Using the passage in Exercise B as a model, write your own paragraph. Use as many different types of sentences as possible to add variety.

2.7 Complements

A sentence can express a complete thought with only a subject and a verb: *Mikhail dances*. More often, though, additional words must be used after the verb to complete the meaning. These words are called **complements.**

SUBJECT	VERB	COMPLEMENT
Leonard	held	the *trophy.*
Meredith	gave	*me* the *ticket.*
The grass	looked	*withered.*

There are three main kinds of complements: **direct objects, indirect objects,** and **predicate words.**

2.8 The Direct Object

An action verb may carry action from the subject to another word in the sentence. The verb connects these words to each other. The **direct object** is the word to which the action is carried from the subject.

The direct object is a word or group of words to which the verb carries the action from the subject.

The direct object may tell what receives the action of the verb, or what results from the action of the verb.

RECEIVER OF ACTION: Janet hit the *ball*. (hit what?)
RESULT OF ACTION: Janet scored a *run*. (scored what?)

RECEIVER OF ACTION: Ed painted the *canvas*. (painted what?)
RESULT OF ACTION: Ed completed a *portrait*. (completed what?)

The direct object may be a single word or a group of words such as a phrase or a clause.

Kari repaired the *motor*. (word)
We want *to encourage you*. (phrase)
John enjoyed *having you here*. (phrase)
I know *what you mean*. (clause)

The direct object may be compound.

The fire destroyed our *clothes* and *books*. (destroyed what?)
We planned *to swim* or *to play tennis*. (planned what?)

A **transitive verb** is an action verb that carries its action from the subject to an object. An **intransitive verb** is an action verb that is not followed by an object. A verb may be transitive in one sentence and intransitive in another.

The birds *were singing*. (intransitive)
The birds *were singing* a lively song. (transitive)

The spectators *cheered*. (intransitive)
The spectators *cheered* the pitcher. (transitive)

The action in action verbs is not always visible. However, the verb still carries the thought from the subject to the object, which makes the verb transitive.

Kato *has* a good idea. (has what?)
Lynn *knows* the answer. (knows what?)
You *will need* a coat. (will need what?)

Direct Object or Adverb? A direct object answers the question *what?* or *whom?* after an action verb. An adverb following an action verb tells *where, when, how,* or *to what extent* about the verb in the sentence.

The car struck a concrete *post*. (direct object telling *what* was struck)
The men in the search party turned *back*. (adverb telling *where* they turned)
The bus arrived *later*. (adverb telling *when* it arrived)

Diagraming. To diagram a sentence with a direct object, write the direct object on the horizontal line with the subject and verb. Separate the verb from the direct object with a vertical line that does not cross the main line.

Dogs distrust strangers.

Dogs	distrust	strangers

Exercise: Find the verb and its direct object.

1. Our dog chases cars and motorcycles.
2. The carpenter built a family room and deck on the back of the house.
3. The Hogans recently bought a snowmobile.
4. We rode our bikes along a beautiful nature trail.
5. The library does not have the record.
6. The boys' soccer team challenged the girls' team.
7. Who hid the chocolates under the stove?
8. The archaeologist found the bones of a mastodon in the tar pit.
9. Does Nathan have the skills he needs?
10. His long, rambling speech bored the class and the teacher.
11. Have you read "A & P" by John Updike?
12. Our physics class visited the space center at Houston.
13. Esther admits that she was rude.
14. Shana wrote this year's school play.
15. Thoreau built a small house by Walden Pond for $28.12.

2.9 The Indirect Object

If a sentence has a direct object, it may also have an **indirect object.** The indirect object complements the verb by telling *to* or *for whom,* or *to* or *for what* the action of the verb is performed.

The indirect object of the verb tells *to* or *for whom*, or *to* or *for what*, something is done.

We told the *police* our story. (to whom? *police*)
Mother wrote *Mary* an excuse. (for whom? *Mary*)
Dad wrote the *store* a letter of complaint. (to what? *the store*)

Like other parts of a sentence, an indirect object may be compound.

The conductor gave *Sarah* and *Bret* their cues.

The words *to* and *for* do not appear before indirect objects. When *to* or *for* precedes the noun, the noun is simply part of a prepositional phrase.

Don gave *Sue* the signal. (*Sue* is the indirect object.)
Don gave the signal to *Sue*. (*Sue* is the object of the preposition *to*.)
The office made *me* a reservation. (*me* is the indirect object.)
The office made a reservation for *me*. (*me* is the object of the preposition *for*.)

Diagraming. An indirect object is written on a horizontal line below the verb. The two lines are joined by a slanted line.

Heidi gave Billy her cold.

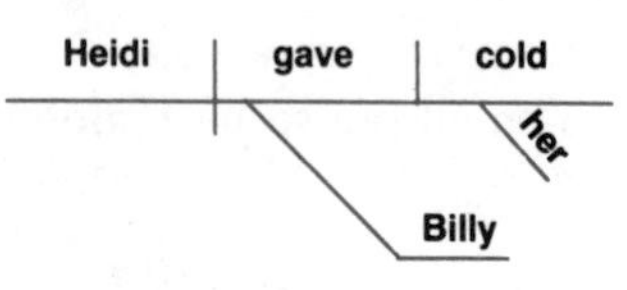

Exercise: Find the direct and indirect objects in each sentence.

1. Greg told an understanding friend his problems.
2. The owner of the wallet gave Joyce a generous reward.
3. The law allows a prisoner one phone call.

4. The coach paid Marty and his teammate a compliment.
5. Catlin shrugged and handed the sheriff the money.
6. Has anyone ever told you the story of Cook's heroic death?
7. The astronauts sent the space center transmissions concerning the meteor shower.
8. The doctor showed us his daughter's letters from Africa.
9. She made herself an absolutely amazing costume.
10. They sent us a trick hat and some disappearing coins.
11. Actually, the dog brings Dad his slippers every evening.
12. One company offered my aunt and uncle jobs in Brazil.
13. A reluctant usher at last found us two seats.
14. Most colleges now offer students scholarships and loans.
15. Governor Winthrop granted the colonists their request.

2.10 Predicate Words

A linking verb connects the subject of a sentence to a word in the predicate. This word is called the **predicate word.** A subject may be linked in this way to a **predicate noun,** a **predicate pronoun,** or a **predicate adjective.**

The next speaker will be Dr. Delaney. (predicate noun)

The writer was someone unknown. (predicate pronoun)

The driver seemed ill. (predicate adjective)

Because the predicate word refers back to the subject of the sentence it is sometimes called a **subject complement.**

Diagraming. To diagram a linking verb and a predicate word, write the predicate word on the main horizontal line. Separate it from the verb by a line that slants toward the subject.

Anne feels better.

Anne | feels \ better

Bob is chairperson.

Bob | is \ chairperson

Exercise A: Find the predicate words in the following sentences. Tell whether each is a predicate noun, a predicate pronoun, or a predicate adjective.

1. Barbara was editor of the yearbook.
2. The details of the accident sound frightening.
3. Charles seems very happy these days.
4. Ms. Hawkins is the adviser of our science club.
5. The responsibility will be mine.
6. Clark's argument sounded very unreasonable to the rest of the members.
7. The most surprised person in the crowd was Wallace.
8. The reports of the fight were unfair to our friends.
9. The security officer seemed uneasy about something.
10. The winner of the raffle could be you.

Exercise B: Make five columns. Head them *Subject, Verb, Direct Object, Indirect Object,* and *Predicate Word*. Place those parts of the following sentences in the proper columns. Not every sentence will contain all five parts.

1. The cough medicine tastes bitter.
2. Juan is the class treasurer this year.
3. The highway needs repairs after that harsh winter and rainy spring.
4. Jennifer brought the hamburgers and buns.
5. Cliff read us his book report.
6. Four of the crash survivors told the press their story.
7. Nobody will arrive for the meeting before nine o'clock.
8. Cups of coffee were served to everyone.
9. The noise of the airplane's motor nearly deafened me.
10. The doctor's advice sounded sensible.
11. The story of Betty's courage gave us a thrill.
12. All this time, Jerry has been looking very smug.
13. Ms. Lawrence handed the boys their papers.
14. Laura appeared nervous and uneasy upon mention of the missing boat.
15. The government paid Ms. Higson a liberal pension.

2.11 Compound Parts of Sentences

Any part of a sentence may be compound. That is, the sentence may include more than one part *of the same kind*. Look at the examples below. Notice that the compound parts are joined by commas and conjunctions.

COMPOUND SUBJECT: A *row* of trees and a *clump* of bushes blocked our view.

COMPOUND PREDICATE: The students *put down their books* and *picked up their rakes*.

COMPOUND VERB: The birds *sang* and *chattered*.

COMPOUND DIRECT OBJECT: We need *flour*, *sugar*, and *eggs*.

COMPOUND INDIRECT OBJECT: The coach gave *Rita* and *Nancy* some advice.

COMPOUND OBJECT OF PREPOSITION: Mrs. Cirillo left her fortune to the *museum* and the *hospital*.

COMPOUND PREDICATE WORD: The wind was *cold* and *fierce*.

Diagraming. Compound parts are diagramed as follows:

Ed and Judy *(compound subject)* stayed and worked *(compound verb)*.

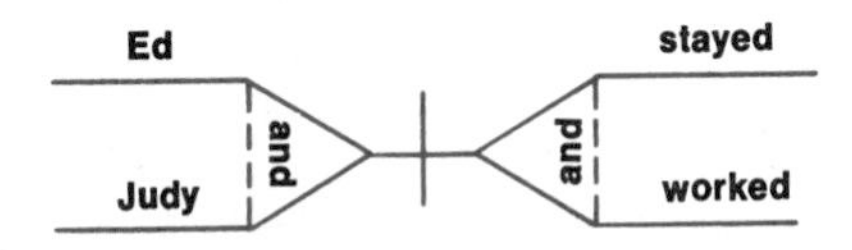

Ernie designed and built *(compound verb)* his new electric piano *(single complement shared by two verbs)*.

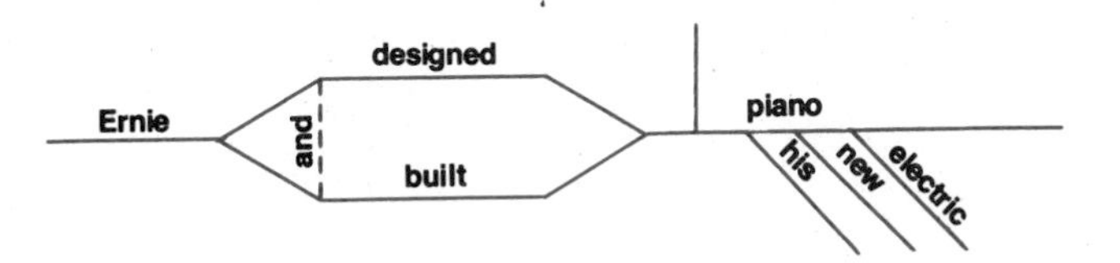

The coach gave Leo and John *(compound indirect object)* the plays and signals *(compound direct object)*.

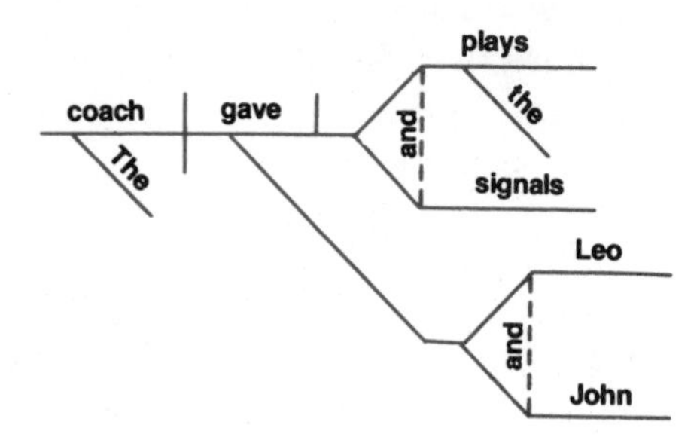

The lights from the streets and houses *(compound object of the preposition)* were dim and hazy *(compound predicate adjective)*.

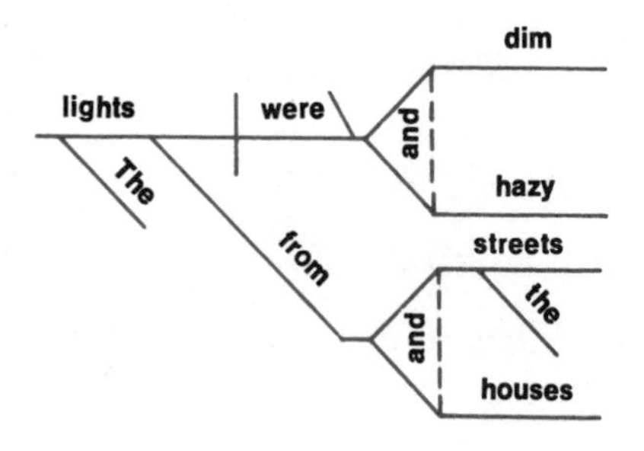

The students enjoyed the talk but disliked the film *(compound predicate)*.

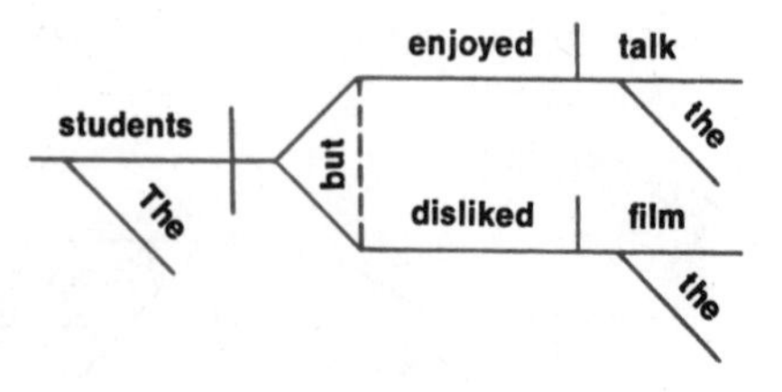

Exercise: Find the compound parts of the following sentences. Label them *Subject, Verb, Direct Object, Indirect Object,* or *Predicate Word*.

1. The audience seemed restless and altogether bored.
2. State police and truckdrivers brought the marooned motorists hot food and blankets.
3. The older man seemed uneasy and apprehensive.
4. Willard presented his résumé and recommendations.
5. Rex barks but never bites.
6. I gave Joy and her sister a Mexican belt and a pair of handmade earrings.
7. The hikers found Indian pipes and other wild plants.
8. A good athlete is responsible and dedicated.
9. Exploration of other planets seems possible and probable.
10. In the Far East great civilizations flourished and died thousands of years ago.
11. The arc lights over the stadium blinked and went out.
12. Astronauts need courage, patience, and stamina.
13. Barges and tugboats have multiplied recently on our inland rivers.
14. Over the radio Stella's voice sounded clear and full.
15. Valleys, ridges, and mountains are on the ocean floor.

2.12 The Phrase

You know that single words can function as different parts of speech. Groups of words can function this way, too.

A phrase is a group of words without a subject and a verb, used as one part of speech.

A phrase is used as one part of speech. A **verb phrase,** for example, is two or more words used as a verb: *could go, might have gone*. A **noun phrase** is two or more words used as a noun: *Lincoln Highway, Empire State Building*. Phrases may also be used as adjectives or adverbs.

2.13 The Prepositional Phrase

The prepositional phrase consists of the preposition and its object. It may also include modifiers of the object.

> *After that very long speech*, we grew restless.
> The dog crawled *under the low wooden fence*.

The object of a preposition is always a noun, a pronoun, or a group of words used as a noun.

> The ditch was full *of* water. (*water* is the object of *of*.)
> We looked everywhere *for* her. (*her* is the object of *for*.)
> *Before* leaving the ranch, we filled the radiator. (*leaving the ranch* is a group of words used as a noun. It is the object of *Before*.)
> Give the candy *to* whoever wants it. (*whoever wants it* is a group of words used as the object of *to*.)

A prepositional phrase acts as a modifier for some other word in the sentence. When a prepositional phrase modifies a noun or a pronoun, it is an **adjective phrase.** An adjective phrase is placed directly after the noun or pronoun it modifies.

> My coat is the one *with the red lining*. (*with the red lining* modifies the pronoun *one*.)

> The quarrel *between the two families* grew bitter. (*between the two families* modifies *quarrel*.)

Note: An adjective phrase can modify a subject, direct object, indirect object, or predicate word. Be careful not to confuse a noun or pronoun in an adjective phrase with the subject, object, or predicate word it modifies.

> Three *of the dishes* were broken. (*of the dishes* modifies the subject, *Three*.)

> She likes anything *with chocolate*. (*with chocolate* modifies the direct object, *anything*.)

When a prepositional phrase modifies a verb, an adjective, or an adverb, it is an **adverb phrase.** An adverb phrase tells *where, when, how,* or *to what extent* about the word it modifies.

The dog had been sleeping *on the bed*. (*on the bed* tells *where* about the verb *had been sleeping*.)

The guests arrived late *in the evening*. (*in the evening* tells *when* about the adverb *late*.)

Maya performed *with precision*. (*with precision* tells *how* about the verb *performed*.)

Tom was happy *beyond his wildest dreams*. (*beyond his wildest dreams* tells *to what extent* about *happy*.)

Sometimes two or more prepositional phrases follow each other. Either both phrases modify the same word, or one phrase may modify the object in the preceding phrase.

We arrived *at the camp* *in the morning*. (Both phrases modify *arrived; at the camp* tells *where* and *in the morning* tells *when* about the verb.)

We found the diary *in the middle* *of a box* *of rubbish*. (*in the middle* modifies the verb *found; of a box* modifies *middle; of rubbish* modifies *box*.)

Diagraming. In a diagram, a prepositional phrase and its modifiers are positioned below the word modified.

Jerry took a picture *of the fish*. (adjective phrase)

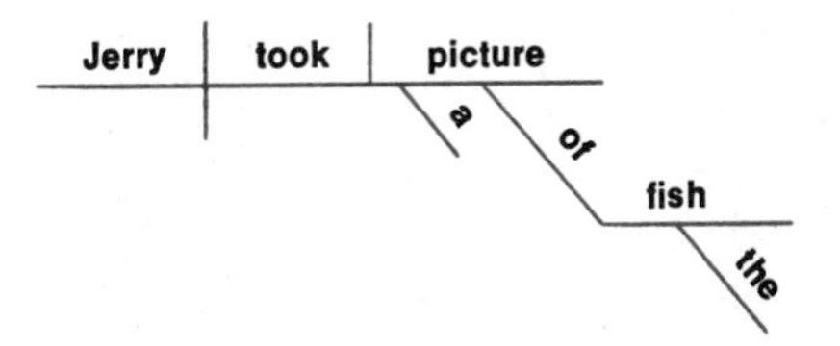

The cars arrived late *in the evening*. (adverb phrase)

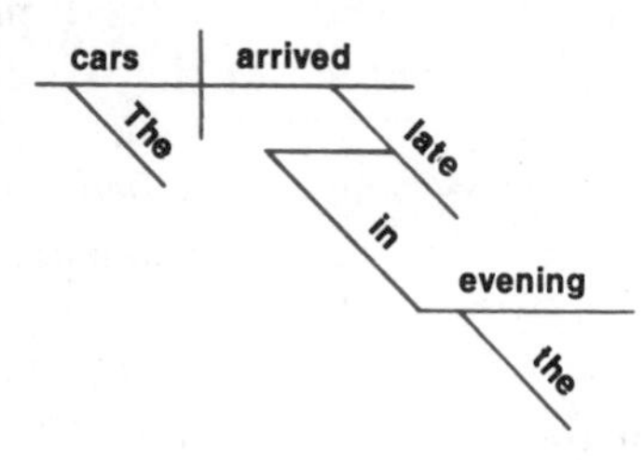

The kite was caught *in the tree*. (adverb phrase)

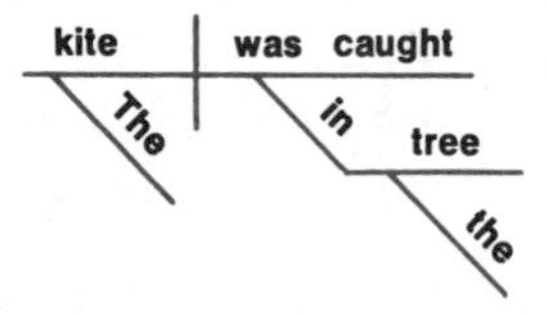

The stack *of books on the porch* got soaked. (adjective phrases)

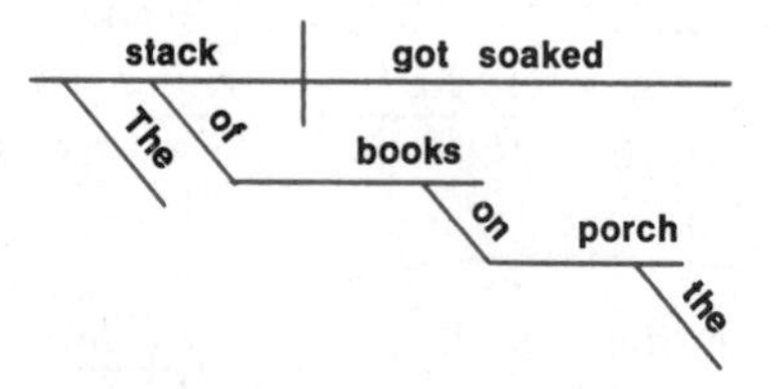

Exercise A: Write each prepositional phrase and the word it modifies. Then tell if the phrase is an adjective or adverb phrase.

1. The report gave us no idea of John's desperate plight.
2. The story of our adventure appeared on the front page.
3. The satellite can be seen early in the evening.
4. After this treatment, the water will be free of germs.
5. He earned money in the kitchen of the camp.
6. This stack of mail arrived in one day.
7. Several of the explorers were lost for hours in the cave.
8. A wave of resentment swept over the group.
9. This is a book of stories about Africa.
10. A flash of light appeared suddenly in the western sky.

Exercise B: Follow the directions for Exercise A.

1. Late at night, we heard someone at the door.
2. There was a plastic toy in every box of popcorn.
3. The officer motioned us forward with a wave of his hand.
4. The storm window fell to the ground and broke into a million splinters of glass.
5. From the outset, Nancy did the job with great energy.
6. In the afternoon, the President appeared on the street.
7. Janet was first off the starting block and won with ease.
8. The chorus will sing at County Center on Friday evening.
9. Paula brought several of the tables in her station wagon.
10. The hat was in the water at the bottom of the well.

Exercise C: Writing Rewrite the following sentences adding prepositional phrases that supply the information asked for.

1. The new school will stand on the site ______. (which?)
2. The captain of the trawler steered his boat ______. (where?)
3. Jack wants to win the race ______. (when?)
4. ______, English children were evacuated from London. (when?)
5. Tanya placed a key beneath the mat ______. (which one?)
6. We lit the fire ______. (how?)
7. No one was allowed ______. (where?)
8. The Raiders scored a touchdown ______. (when?)
9. The house ______ is going to be sold at auction. (which one?)
10. ______, he judged the case. (when?)

2.14 The Infinitive Phrase

You remember that an infinitive is a verbal that usually begins with *to: to work, to think, to be*. An infinitive can have both modifiers and complements. Together, an infinitive, its modifiers, and its complements make up an **infinitive phrase.**

We learned *to operate a power saw.*
I refuse *to believe in magic.*
The lights began *to flash rhythmically.*

When an infinitive is modified by an adverb or adverb phrase, these modifiers are also part of the infinitive phrase.

The driver had **to think** *quickly.*
The pirates began **to dig** *with all their might.*

Note: Most good writers do not place an adverb between *to* and the rest of the infinitive.

NONSTANDARD: He wants to quickly eliminate his debt.
STANDARD: He wants to eliminate his debt quickly.

Separating the two parts of the infinitive with an adverb is an error called a **split infinitive.**

When an infinitive is formed from a transitive verb, it may have both direct and indirect objects. These complements are part of the infinitive phrase.

George was unable **to control** *his laughter.*
It was Suzie's intention **to give** *Malcolm the keys.*

An infinitive formed from a linking verb, such as *to be* or *to seem,* may have a predicate word as a complement. This predicate word is part of the infinitive phrase.

Amy wants **to be** *captain.*
Alex had **to appear** *confident.*

Like other phrases, an infinitive phrase is used like a single part of speech. An infinitive phrase can act as a noun, an adjective, or an adverb. When an infinitive phrase is used as a noun, it can be a subject, an object, or a predicate noun.

SUBJECT: *To save lives* was the paramedic's goal.
DIRECT OBJECT: The instructor said *to stop at the light.*
PREDICATE WORD: Dana's dream was *to be a Nobel prize winner.*

An infinitive phrase can also be used as an adjective to modify a noun.

That is not the way *to settle your differences*.
(The infinitive phrase modifies the noun, *way*.)
Consuelo is the candidate *to beat*.
(The infinitive modifies the predicate noun, *candidate*.)

An infinitive phrase may be used as an adverb to modify a verb, an adjective, or an adverb.

Josie worked *to earn money for college*.
(The infinitive phrase modifies the verb *worked*.)
These berries are good *to eat*.
(The infinitive phrase modifies the adjective *good*.)
They came too late *to see the pre-game show*.)
(The infinitive phrase modifies the adverb *late*.)

Diagraming. The infinitive phrase is diagramed as follows:

We hope to buy a new car soon.

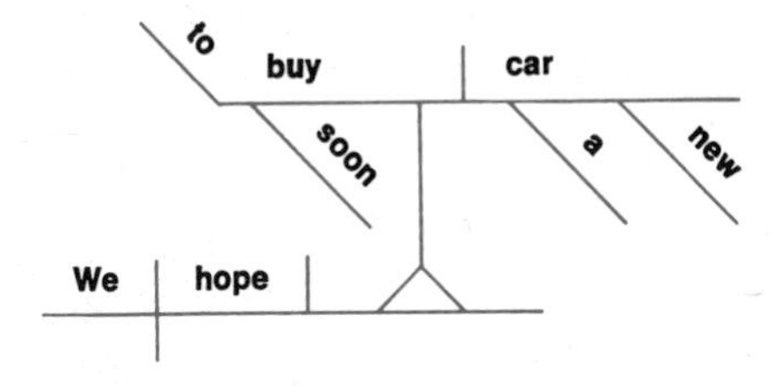

To find an empty box was not easy.

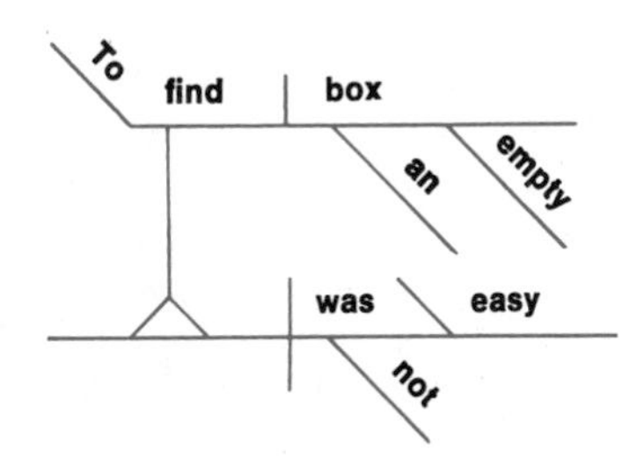

Exercise A: Find the infinitive phrases in the sentences below.

1. Would you like to keep score for us?
2. To climb the next cliff seemed impossible.
3. Roy's purpose was difficult to understand.
4. Our decision was to postpone the election.
5. The audience was asked to refrain from applause.
6. The school board plans to build two schools next year.
7. The ranger asked the inconsiderate picnickers to leave the park immediately.
8. To publish the controversial book now would be unwise.
9. Eric's plan is to enlist in the Navy right after high school.
10. Roy tried to speak softly.

Exercise B: Find the infinitive phrase in each sentence below. Label each as *Subject, Direct Object, Predicate Word,* or *Modifier*. If the phrase is a modifier, indicate what word it modifies.

1. It was impossible to complete the work on time.
2. Tomorrow's assignment is to read Act I of *Julius Caesar*.
3. The pilot decided to land in the open field.
4. Before the Wright brothers succeeded, many people had tried to invent a flying machine.
5. This is the right time of year to plant the bulbs.
6. You have come too early to see the changing of the guard.
7. To clean this fabric you must use dry cleaning fluid.
8. To climb Mt. Everest was the ultimate goal.
9. That suit is too good to wear in the rain.
10. The conductor told them to sing the chorus again.

Exercise C: Writing Find and correct the split infinitive in each sentence.

1. Cynthia tried to completely forget the incident.
2. The plan was designed to thoroughly mislead the police.
3. You should try to occasionally experiment with new foods.
4. I would like to eventually see the Pacific Ocean.
5. Try to quickly finish your work.

2.15 The Participial Phrase

A participle is a verbal that usually ends in *-ing*, *-ed*, *-d*, *-t*, or *-en*. It is used as an adjective: the *frightened* children, the *flying* geese, the *half-eaten* apple.

Like other verbals, a participle may have complements and modifiers. A participle together with its complements and modifiers make up a **participial phrase.**

When a participle is modified by an adverb, a phrase, or a clause, these modifiers are part of the participial phrase.

Arriving late, we sat at the rear.
(*late* is an adverb modifying the participle, *Arriving*.)

Practicing at odd hours, Herb soon learned the game.
(*at odd hours* is a phrase modifying the participle, *Practicing*.)

When a participle is completed by an object or predicate word, these complements are part of the participial phrase.

Covering our footprints, we walked through the sand.
(*footprints* is the direct object of the participle, *Covering*.)
Tossing Laurie the keys, Kelly walked angrily away.
(*Laurie* is the indirect object and *keys* is the direct object of the participle, *Tossing*.)
Mario walked to the stage, *looking happy*.
(*happy* is a predicate adjective, a complement for the participle, *looking*.)

Like individual participles, participial phrases can modify nouns, pronouns, and words being used as nouns.

Delayed by snow and fog, the plane started an hour late.
(The participial phrase modifies the noun, *plane*.)

Knowing what you need, you can shop more wisely.
(The participial phrase modifies the pronoun, *you*.)

Place a participle or participial phrase as close as possible to the word it modifies. If a participle or participial phrase is misplaced, it may appear to modify the wrong word. This type of error is called a **dangling participle.**

DANGLING PARTICIPLE: *Turning plump and red in late summer,* the gardener lovingly watched his prize-winning tomatoes.
(The misplaced phrase incorrectly modifies *gardener.*)

CORRECTLY PLACED PARTICIPLE: The gardener lovingly watched his prize-winning tomatoes *turning plump and red in late summer.*

Diagraming. The participle and the participial phrase are diagramed as follows:

Chuckling quietly, the stranger walked away.

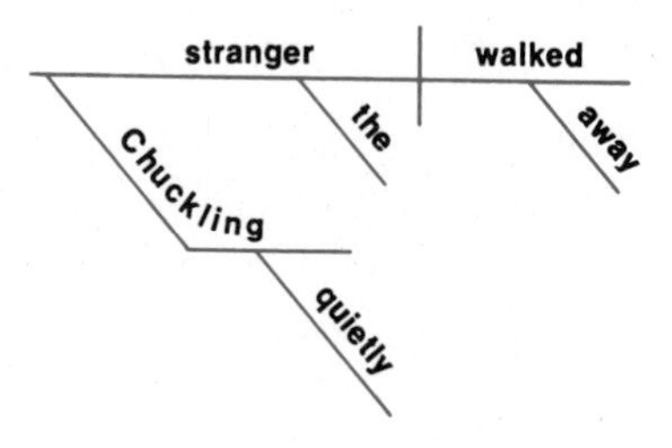

Closing the door softly, Don left the room.

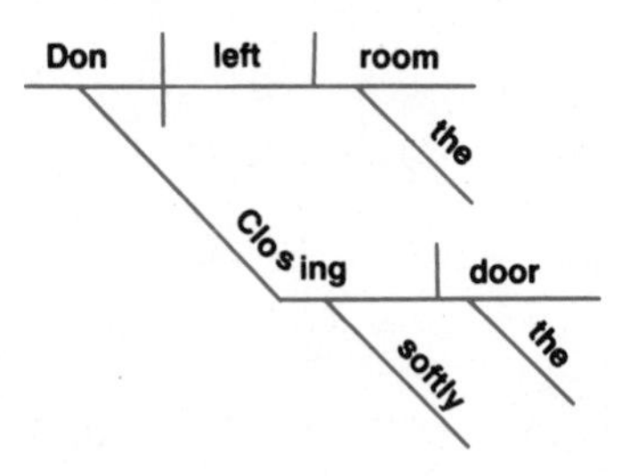

Exercise A: Find the participial phrase. Tell the word each phrase modifies. Remember that phrases may be made from past participles or present participles.

1. Having delivered the message, Hamilton retired to a nearby inn.
2. A package addressed to Ms. Barnes arrived this morning.
3. Discouraged by a lack of men and supplies, the rescue team turned back.
4. Tom drove for the goal line, carrying two tacklers with him.
5. Astonished by her answer, he tried to think of what to say next.
6. Having been notified of her election, Senator Hayes started for Washington.
7. Rose stepped onto the stage, carrying a clothes basket.
8. The prospectors, wearied by the long climb, lay down on the ledge.
9. Standing quietly, Mr. Peters waited for the crowd to calm down.
10. Two prisoners emerged, driven out by the tear gas.
11. We jumped up and down, trying to attract attention.
12. Mr. Hunter declined to run for office again, having twice been defeated.
13. The people working on the ledge are protected by safety belts.
14. The photograph, discolored with age, clearly showed Jean's features.
15. We have been waiting, hoping the storm will stop.

Exercise B: Writing Find the dangling participle in each sentence. Rewrite the sentence to correct the error.

1. The photographer took pictures of the herd of antelope circling in a helicopter.
2. Fastened to the bulletin board with a thumbtack, I saw your class picture.

3. Carefully arranged on a platter, the judges sampled the blueberry muffins.
4. Calder's mobiles were admired by the dealers, suspended on fine steel wires.
5. Whispering softly, the horses were soothed by their trainer.
6. The autumn leaves were admired by thousands of tourists turning from green to gold.
7. Bruised and covered with mud, Steven threw out the pumpkin.

2.16 The Gerund Phrase

A gerund is a verbal that is used as a noun. It always ends in *-ing*: *sleeping, believing, sewing*. Together, a gerund, its complements, and its modifiers make up a **gerund phrase.**

A gerund may be modified by single words or whole phrases. Because the gerund is a verb form, it may be modified by adverbs. Because it is used as a noun, it may be modified by adjectives.

Quick thinking is essential in tennis.
(*Quick* is an adjective modifying the gerund, *thinking*.)
Max enjoys *working quietly*.
(*quietly* is an adverb modifying the gerund, *working*.)
Writing under pressure causes mistakes.
(*under pressure* is a phrase modifying the gerund, *writing*.)
Giving Jerry the tickets created a mix-up.
(*Jerry* is the indirect object and *tickets* is the direct object of the gerund, *Giving*.)
Being class representative turned out to be hard work.
(*representative* is a predicate noun, a complement of the gerund, *Being*.)

Like the gerund alone, the gerund phrase is always used as a noun. It can be a subject, an object, or a predicate word.

SUBJECT: *Talking in the audience* is a discourtesy to the speaker.

DIRECT OBJECT: We enjoyed *watching the Sox win their division*.

PREDICATE WORD: Angela's hobby is *building plant stands*.

OBJECT OF THE PREPOSITION: By *acting quickly*, the canoers saved the paddles.

Diagraming. The gerund and the gerund phrase are diagramed as follows:

Swimming is good exercise.

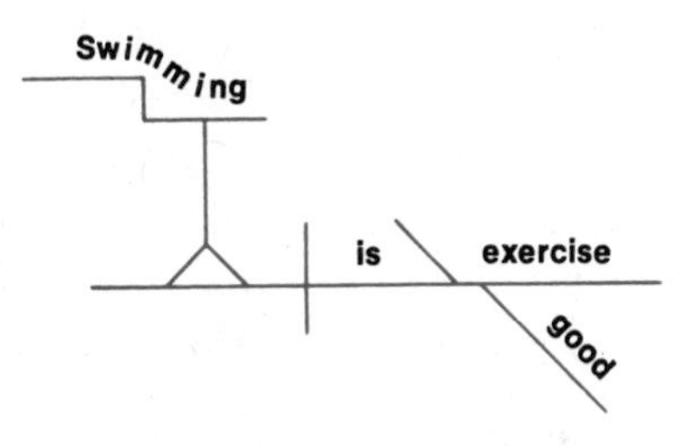

Quick thinking saved the day.

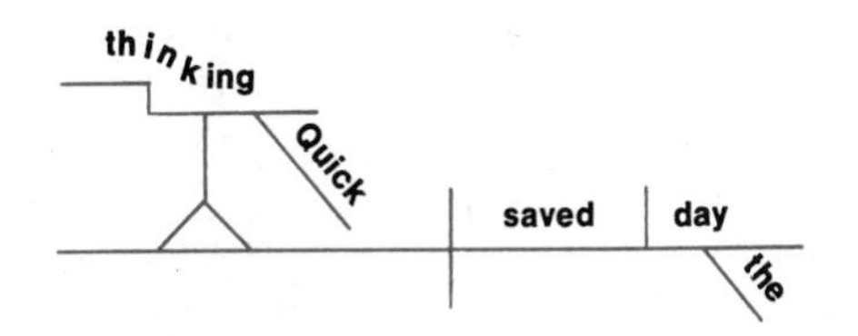

We enjoyed hearing the organ.

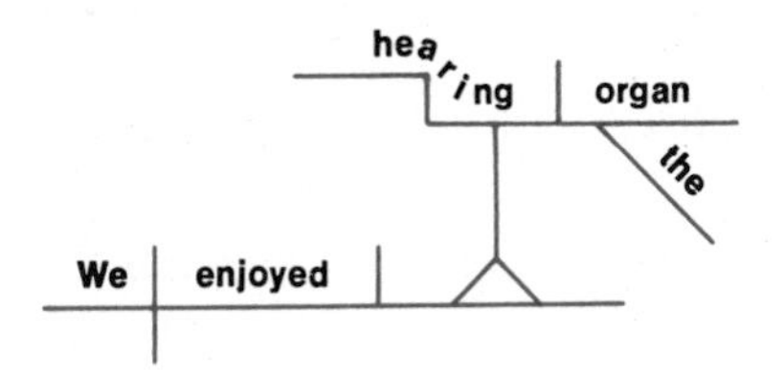

After rowing across the lake, we rested.

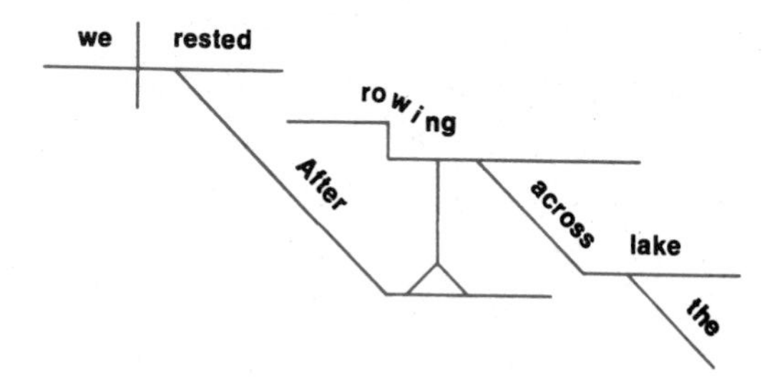

Exercise A: Find the gerund phrases in the following sentences.

1. Sawing the wood tired me out.
2. Please sign the guest book before leaving the lodge.
3. Playing a harpsichord is a rare skill.
4. Jane's mistake was reading the directions carelessly.
5. Upon arriving, Jack came immediately to my apartment.
6. Read the fine print before signing the contract.
7. Complaining about the weather does no good.
8. Have you tried heating the milk first?
9. Hearing you talk reminds me of Uncle Art.
10. All of us enjoyed reading your editorial.

Exercise B: Find each gerund phrase in the following sentences. Tell whether it is being used as a subject, direct object, object of the preposition, or predicate word.

1. Brushing your teeth will help prevent decay.
2. After learning of Wendell's record, the college granted him a scholarship.
3. Spending more than you earn is a short road to trouble.
4. Some people do not enjoy listening to classical music.
5. Mr. Wright got a ticket for parking too close to the corner.
6. Driving a hansom cab through Central Park was the elderly man's greatest pleasure.
7. For finishing last, Scott was awarded a consolation prize.
8. One approach is asking for an interview directly.

9. By researching various kinds of insulation, Joanie was able to save her family $150 in heating bills.
10. The assignment included looking up fifty words.

Exercise C: Find the verbal phrases in the following sentences. Label them *infinitive, participial,* or *gerund.*

1. Thinking fast, he smothered the flames with his jacket.
2. By analyzing the pollen spores in ancient fabrics, specialists can determine the material's place of origin.
3. Surrounded by sea and mountains, Portugal is about the size of Indiana.
4. Hoping we wouldn't be late, we rushed through dinner.
5. It is hard to imagine a more difficult assignment.
6. Running daily helps to build up your calves.
7. We wanted to see the aurora borealis.
8. Being a perfectionist can be hard on your nerves.
9. The function of an enzyme is to speed up chemical processes.
10. Lafayette left in the spring, hoping to return soon.

2.17 The Appositive Phrase

An **appositive** is a noun or pronoun placed immediately after another word in a sentence to identify it or provide more information about it. An appositive is usually set off by commas.

The poet, *Gwendolyn Brooks,* explained how she writes.
Dr. Roscoe, *the mayor,* spoke first.

An **appositive phrase** consists of the appositive and its modifiers, which themselves may be phrases or clauses.

The chairperson presented the trophy, *a tall silver cup with handles.*) (The italicized words are the appositive phrase, identifying *trophy*. The adjectives *tall* and *silver* modify the appositive *cup*, as does the adjective phrase *with handles.*)

Ms. Kramer's car, *a newly painted old Buick*, was stolen. (The appositive phrase identifies *car*. The adjective *old* and the participial phrase *newly painted* modify the appositive *Buick*.)

Note: The compound personal pronoun used intensively is not regarded as an appositive. It is used for emphasis and does not explain or identify the word to which it refers:

Diagraming. The appositive is diagramed as follows:

Dr. Thomas, my new teacher, studied in Germany.

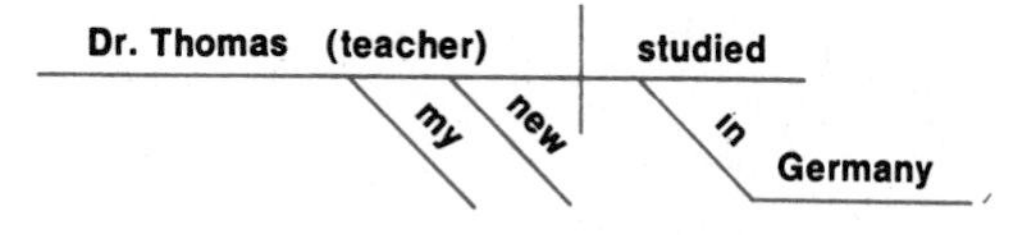

2.18 A Review of Diagraming

English sentences convey meaning because the words and word groups within them are arranged in specific patterns. A diagram helps show how words are grouped and how the groups are related to each other. A review of diagraming follows.

The simple sentence is composed of subject-verb-complement. These words are placed on the base line of the diagram. The indirect object is placed below the verb.

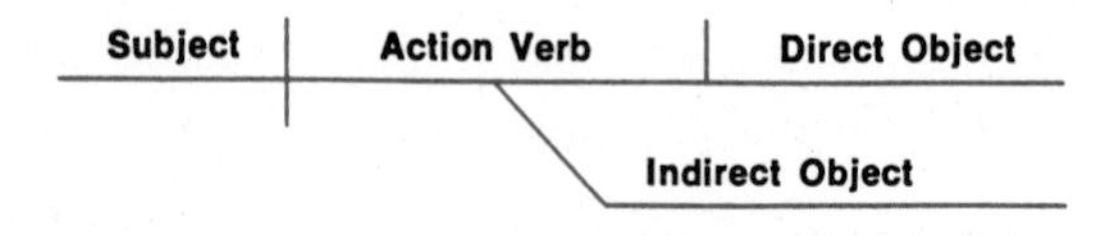

The introductory word *There* or *Here* is placed above the base line. Note the slant line after the linking verb.

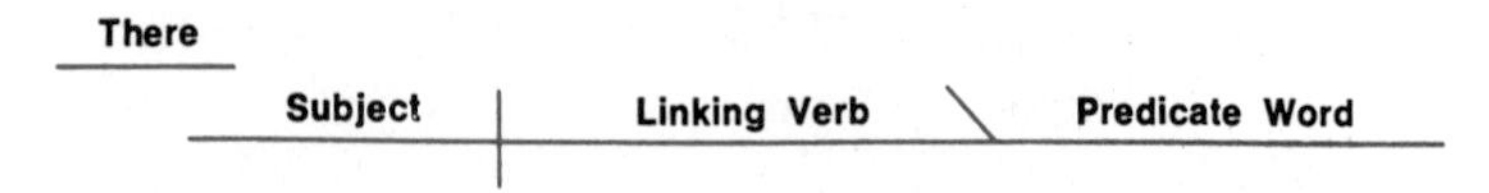

The subject of an imperative sentence, *you* (understood), is placed in parentheses.

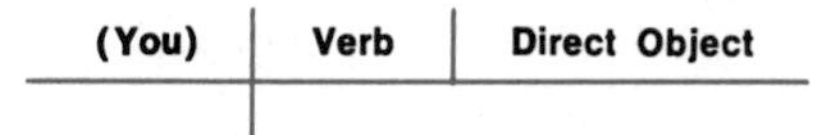

A single-word modifier is placed on a slant line below the word it modifies. An adverb modifying an adjective or adverb is placed as shown below.

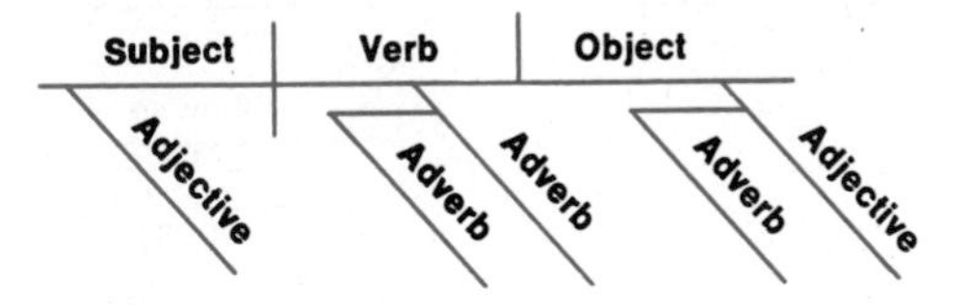

The prepositional phrase is attached to the word it modifies.

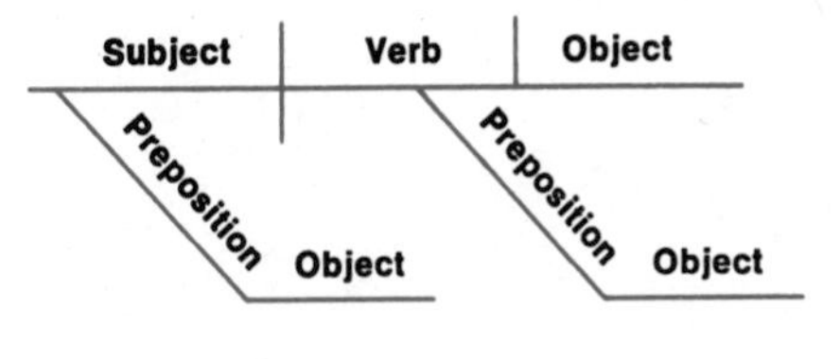

The participial phrase is shown as follows:

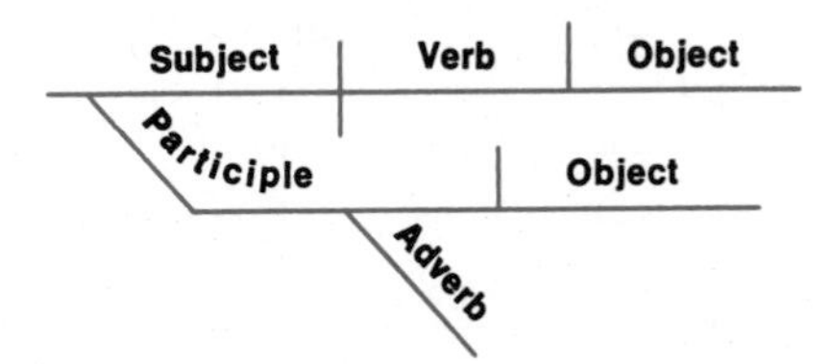

The infinitive phrase is shown in this way:

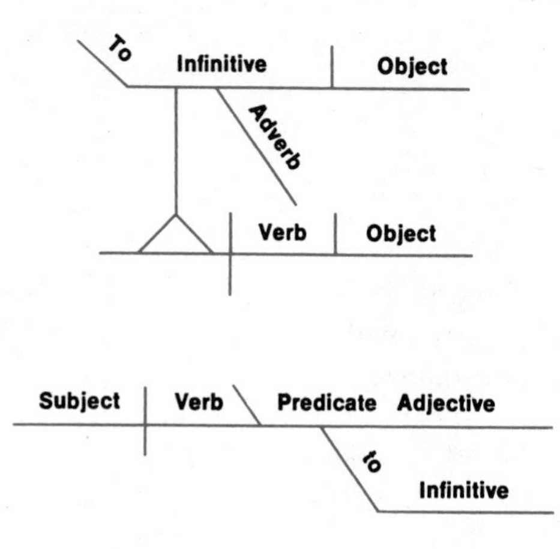

The gerund phrase is placed above the base line unless it is the object of a preposition.

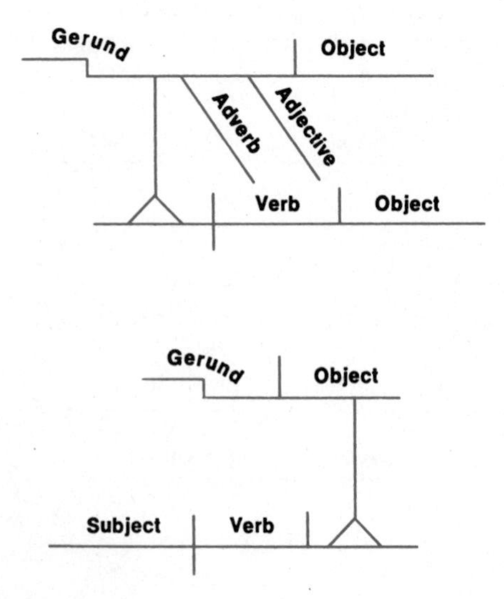

2.19 The Basic Sentence Patterns

As you have seen, sentences can be made up of many different types of word groups put together in endless combinations. Yet within the infinite number of English sentences that can be constructed, certain patterns recur. In fact, the word order of most English sentences can be classified as one of seven **basic sentence patterns.** Knowledge of these patterns will give you a clearer understanding of how our language works.

Pattern One

N	V	(ADVERB OR PREPOSITIONAL PHRASE)
A hurricane	struck.	
The plane	has departed.	
She	skis	beautifully.
Theatergoers	waited	in the lobby.
Len and he	are driving	through the mountains.

In their simplest form, Pattern One sentences consist of a noun *(N)* followed by a verb *(V)*. Frequently, the pattern is completed by an adverb or a prepositional phrase. Verbs in Pattern One sentences are *intransitive verbs*.

Note: In many of these patterns, you will find pronouns, gerunds, and infinitives in columns labeled *N*. Keep in mind that these words may be used as nouns.

Pattern Two

N	V	N
Carlos	plays	the trumpet.
We	were expecting	some praise.
Everyone	applauded	the mayor.
The Bears	scored	a touchdown.
Losing	reveals	character.

The verbs in Pattern Two sentences are *transitive verbs*. The noun following the verb in this pattern is a *direct object*. The transitive verb carries the action in the sentence over from the subject to the object.

Most of the thousands of transitive verbs in English occur only in Pattern Two sentences. However, some transitive verbs occur in sentences that have two nouns following the verb. Such sentences are shown in Pattern Three and in Pattern Seven.

Pattern Three

N	V	N	N
The coach	gave	Nina	a stopwatch.
Cheryl	has told	us	her plans.
He	showed	Maria	the letter.
The airline	will send	Leslie	her luggage.

In Pattern Three sentences, the first noun following the verb is the *indirect object;* the second noun is the *direct object*. The two nouns refer to different people or things. Remember this when you examine the Pattern Seven sentences.

Pattern Four

N	LV	N
The leader	has become	a tyrant.
Ms. Abrams	remained	our counselor.
That	is	a spaniel.
Seeing	is	believing.

Be, become, and *remain* are the verbs most often used in Pattern Four sentences. They are *linking verbs (LV)*. The noun following the linking verb in a Pattern Four sentence is a *predicate noun*. The predicate noun and the subject are connected by the linking verb, and refer to the *same* person or thing.

Pattern Two, which has a similar form *(N-V-N)*, uses transitive verbs and the two nouns refer to *different* people or things.

In the sentences below, notice how the noun relationship changes when a linking verb becomes a transitive verb:

Kathleen was the co-captain. (N-LV-N)
Kathleen nudged the co-captain. (N-V-N)

My sister has become an actress. (N-LV-N)
My sister has interviewed an actress. (N-V-N)

Pattern Five

N	LV	ADJ
Her laugh	is	contagious.
Shotputters	must be	strong.
She	became	sleepy.
To finish	appeared	hopeless.

Verbs in Pattern Five sentences are also linking verbs. The most common ones in this pattern are *be, seem,* and *become*.

The adjective *(Adj.)* following the verb in this pattern is a *predicate adjective*. This word further describes the noun and is connected to it by the linking verb.

Pattern Six

N	LV	ADV
The doctor	is	away.
Pranksters	have been	here.
They	are	around the corner.
Tryouts	will be	tomorrow.

The verb in a Pattern Six sentence is always some form of the linking verb *be*, such as *am, is, are, were, be, being,* or *been*.

The adverb *(Adv.)* or adverbial phrase that follows the linking verb refers to time or place. Adverbs such as *loudly, carefully, wildly,* never occur in this pattern (See Pattern One).

Pattern Seven

N	V	N	N
Practice	made	Jamie	a winner.
I	consider	you	my friend.
The President	declared	Hartford	a disaster area.
The archbishop	crowned	Elizabeth	queen.
Some people	consider	snakes	good pets.

Both Pattern Three and Pattern Seven sentences have the same order: noun-verb-noun-noun. The difference is that the two nouns following the verb in Pattern Three sentences refer to different people or things. The first noun following the verb in Pattern Three is called the *indirect object;* the second noun is the *direct object*. The nouns following the verb in Pattern Seven sentences, however, refer to the same person or thing. The first noun following the verb in Pattern Seven is the direct object, while the second noun is an *object complement*.

With some of the verbs that occur in Pattern Seven, an adjective can replace the second noun.

Training will make our dog a champion.
Training will make our dog manageable.

English sentences are seldom as simple as the basic sentences listed above. In order to convey meaning adequately, we usually need to expand the basic patterns by adding modifiers and more complicated constructions. No matter how complicated or how long a sentence becomes, however, it will always have one of the basic patterns as a foundation.

Exercise A: Identify the sentence pattern in each sentence.

1. That movie is a thriller.
2. This hayride has been enjoyable.
3. Rod lit the birthday candles.
4. The strangers were on horseback.
5. Our strategy worked.

6. Josh passed Sue a note.
7. The cast took another bow.
8. Trisha named Andrea her successor.
9. Blair will be the committee chairperson.
10. Revolutionaries plotted against the government.

Exercise B: Write two different sentences that follow each of the sentence patterns listed below.

1. Noun Verb
2. Noun Verb Noun
3. Noun Verb Noun Noun
4. Noun Linking Verb Noun
5. Noun Linking Verb Adjective

Exercise C: Writing You are given a sentence that follows one sentence pattern. Identify this pattern. Then, rewrite the sentence so that it follows the sentence pattern in parentheses.

1. Joyce gave a generous reward. (N-V-N-N)
2. The investigator felt baffled. (N-V-N)
3. My neighbor is very talented. (N-LV-N)
4. The pilot flew through the narrow passage. (N-V-N)
5. The team was in a huddle. (N-LV-ADJ)
6. Beth has been a trendsetter. (N-V)
7. Sean may become a famous magician. (N-V-N)
8. We handed the usher our tickets. (N-V-N)
9. This volcano is Mount St. Helens. (N-LV-ADJ)
10. The jury found Clemons innocent. (N-V-N)

REINFORCEMENT EXERCISES

The Parts of a Sentence

A. Write complete sentences. If any of the groups of words below are sentences, write *S*. If they are not sentences, make them into sentences by adding appropriate words.

1. The Spanish explorer, Francisco Vasquez de Coronado
2. Using satellite pictures to find likely sites of oil deposits
3. One of the main industries of the Inner Hebrides, islands of northwest Scotland, is tourism
4. The city's baseball team, which hadn't won a pennant in twenty years
5. A small African antelope called the klipspringer
6. Thanks to inflation
7. A rusted exterior and a mud-soaked interior
8. The word *vinegar* means "sour wine"
9. Volunteered to work in the zoo rather than pay the fine
10. St. Johns is the capital of Newfoundland

B. Write different kinds of sentences. Tell whether each sentence is declarative, interrogative, exclamatory, or imperative. Then rewrite the sentence to be the type indicated in parentheses.

1. The sloth is a slow-moving animal that lives in trees. (interrogative)
2. Did you take the formula to Dr. Bracken? (imperative)
3. The first American black to receive a Nobel Peace Prize was Ralph Bunche. (interrogative)
4. This is a wonderful film. (exclamatory)
5. August was named for Augustus Caesar. (interrogative)
6. Do migrating birds breed in the country they inhabit in the summer? (declarative)
7. How different she looks! (interrogative)
8. Research the subject and write a report on it. (declarative)
9. Who can bring a slide projector? (imperative)
10. My sister has written a marvelous novel. (exclamatory)

C. Identify the verb and its simple subject. Find the verb and its simple subject in each of the following sentences. The verb or the subject may be compound.

1. The wave climbed and then crashed down on the buoy.
2. The largest tribe of Indians in the United States is the Navajo tribe.
3. Garfield and Heathcliffe are popular comic strip cats.
4. Inspectors had recently examined the mine.
5. The dancers dipped and swayed like the shadows of bending trees.
6. Gilbert and Sullivan joined their talents in 1875.
7. Henry VIII and Katharine of Aragon were the parents of Mary Tudor.
8. The original seven United States astronauts were carefully selected for their experience and for their ability to withstand stressful situations.
9. Brett and Karen called their sister's fiddle music "noise pollution."
10. David Garrick acted in Shakespearean plays and wrote some plays of his own.

D. Find subjects and verbs in unusual positions. For each sentence below, find the verb and its simple subject.

1. Next to the patio entrance grew a wahoo, better known as a burning bush.
2. Beneath the beach chairs and across the towels scurried the crab.
3. There will be no break until the sandbags are in place.
4. Did the steward drop the tray on Dr. Fumo's lap?
5. There were three topics left to choose from.
6. Within the old oaken chest lay mineral-encrusted treasures.
7. Nearly three hundred years ago, Jean Francois Arouet adopted the pen name of Voltaire.
8. Should we order one large pizza or two small ones?
9. Here are the thief's footprints.
10. Is the city making plans for a new airport?

E. Identify objects and predicate words. Find direct objects, indirect objects, and predicate words in the following sentences.

1. The sky looked ominous to the wary crew.
2. The usher handed us programs.
3. Mary McLeod Bethune founded the National Council of Negro Women.
4. The ranger showed the hikers various methods of survival.
5. The basenji is a dog native to Africa.
6. He grows African violets for profit and relaxation.
7. Sheila bought Michael a ticket to the World Series.
8. The credit for the award is hers.
9. Sing a song of the open road.
10. I have to give the old car a paint job.

F. Find compound parts. Find the compound sentence parts in the following sentences. Label them *Subject*, *Verb*, *Direct Object*, *Indirect Object*, or *Predicate Word*.

1. Lava can be either thick or fluid.
2. Bowling and polo are both thousands of years old.
3. The keeper flung the seals and walruses some raw fish.
4. We visited Oahu, Kauai, and Maui.
5. Belva Ann Lockwood argued and lobbied for the right of women to practice before the U.S. Supreme Court.
6. My grandfather once made my sister and me a treehouse.
7. He used maps and diagrams to highlight his talk.
8. Joseph Merlin and James Plimpton contributed to the development of the roller skate.
9. Dizzy Dean pitched and joked his way into baseball lore.
10. Link was a top athlete and a class officer.

G. Use prepositional phrases. To each sentence add the type of prepositional phrase indicated. Circle the word each phrase modifies and underline any additional prepositional phrases.

1. The crow cawed harshly and landed. (adverb)
2. A sigh of relief came from the crowd. (adjective)

3. We picnicked near the beach. (adverb)
4. Leah and Carl sat down and discussed their argument. (adverb)
5. The building was constructed with substandard materials. (adjective)
6. The triptych, an ancient writing tablet, was found by one of the assistants. (adverb)
7. The Earth is traveling at a speed of 67,000 miles an hour. (adverb)
8. Scientists recorded the size of the crater after the eruption. (adjective)
9. The number of different home computers available is increasing daily. (adverb)
10. For two decades, radio astronomers have attempted to locate intelligent life in outer space. (adjective)

H. Identify verbal phrases. Find the infinitive, participial, and gerund phrases in the following sentences. Label each phrase. Some sentences may contain more than one type of phrase.

1. Hoping for an unusual setting, the producer wanted to use Stonehenge as a film location.
2. The South American oilbird feeds itself by searching for fruit at night.
3. Tracing crazy patterns on the water, the motorboat appeared out of control.
4. Frustrated by the long lines, the customer tried to show her irritation by complaining to the manager.
5. Inventing crossword puzzles is more difficult than it appears.
6. The Chinese were the first to use more than one name.
7. Who first attempted to build a canal connecting the Atlantic and Pacific Oceans?
8. Mohammed vowed to visit Mecca before the year was over.
9. Texas helped create Big Bend National Park by giving seven hundred thousand acres to the government.
10. The farmer found a badger digging a tunnel.

I. Use appositive phrases. Rewrite the sentences below, changing the second sentence of each pair into an appositive phrase.

1. Wilt Chamberlin coaches women athletes. Wilt Chamberlin was the NBA scoring leader for seven consecutive years.
2. Kent opened the present. The present was a gift certificate for $25 to his favorite store.
3. The will was read by the attorney. The attorney was a family friend.
4. Mrs. S.M. Child is probably not related to Julia Child. Mrs. S.M. Child wrote a 19th century cookbook.
5. One batman is allowed to every company of a British regiment on foreign service. A batman is a person in charge of cooking utensils.
6. The first general congress of the colonies was held at Albany. Albany is now the state capital of New York.
7. They made sandwiches for dinner. The sandwiches were concoctions of peanut butter, ham, and mustard.
8. Carl Sagan founded the Planetary Society. The society is an organization of space advocates.
9. Rona reads everything that Robert Ludlum writes. Ludlum is a popular author of spy novels.
10. The platypus has a bill like a duck and hatches its young from eggs. The platypus is an unusual kind of mammal.

J. Understand sentence patterns. Identify the pattern in each sentence below. Then write a new sentence in that pattern.

1. The clown's tattered umbrella quickly fell apart.
2. The rain fell softly onto the dusty ground.
3. Marcie loaned her brother ten dollars for the repair.
4. The controversial play was a huge success.
5. Sap from the maple trees is collected in the spring.
6. The blueberry milkshake tasted delicious.
7. The Australian boat won the competition.
8. Mitch decorated the apartment with vivid orange and blue.
9. The conductor gave us each a transfer.
10. The radio emits powerful signals.

MIXED REVIEW

The Parts of a Sentence

A. Make six columns. Head them *Subject, Verb, Direct Object, Indirect Object, Predicate Word,* and *Prepositional Phrase*. Place the parts of the following sentences in the proper columns.

1. Selina gave me two books about ceramics.
2. William Boyd was Hopalong Cassidy in early Westerns.
3. After the meal, Sheila felt refreshed and renewed.
4. The director offered Juan a part in a movie.
5. Has Anne Murray released a new album recently?
6. The debaters seemed confident about their performance.
7. The pilot had flown helicopters and planes in the Air Force.
8. Lee and Colleen took the driver's test during vacation.
9. Fitness has become a fad in recent years.
10. Secret Service agents closely guard the President.
11. This stable offers lessons and trail rides.
12. The shuttle coasted down the runway.
13. Ricardo and his sister visited relatives in San Juan.
14. The horses pranced and whinnied in their stalls.
15. Bonita turned and walked away.
16. Each day Ruth practices the trumpet and the drums.
17. Judith loaned Jeff and Kristin her notes.
18. Lauren showed us the best campsites in the park.
19. The cook heaped pepperoni and sausage onto the pizza.
20. Marietta is secretary and treasurer of the Latin club.

B. Identify the verbal phrases and the appositive phrases in the following sentences. Tell whether each verbal phrase functions as a subject, object, or modifier.

1. We decided to call Felicia in Israel on her birthday.
2. James A. Garfield, the twentieth President of the United States, was assassinated in 1881.
3. To hike from Mexico to Canada is my grandfather's ambition.

4. We made an effort to see the star shower last July.
5. Biking over the Rocky Mountains requires ten or fifteen gears.
6. Pausing only to refuel, the cars raced around the track.
7. By planning each move in advance, my uncle always wins at chess.
8. Chinua Achebe, the most famous Nigerian novelist, wrote *Things Fall Apart* and *No Longer at Ease*.
9. Known for its iris gardens, Montclair attracts thousands of visitors to New Jersey in the spring.
10. Phillip was too tired to stay up for the New Year's celebration.

C. Identify the basic sentence pattern of each of the following sentences. Some sentence parts may be compound. Then write one additional sentence that follows the same pattern.

1. I want onions, tomatoes, and pickles on my hamburger.
2. Carlos plays and sings in a jazz band.
3. Clark Gable and Vivian Leigh starred in *Gone With the Wind*.
4. Two infamous pirates were Bluebeard and Captain Kidd.
5. Grandmother gave Beth and me tickets to *My Fair Lady*.
6. Holgrave handed Dr. Santos the scalpel and sponge.
7. Rhonda and David seemed extremely happy after the ceremony.
8. Portuguese is the official language of Mozambique.
9. The patient remained conscious throughout the operation.
10. Dr. Chambers gave the class a lecture on daily life in the Old West.

The Parts of a Sentence

A. Imagine that you are a radio announcer reporting a sports event at your school. Write a paragraph of such a sportscast using appositive, infinitive, participial, and gerund phrases to create a more vivid impression of the action. Remember to give the position of each player the first time you mention him or her. Also remember that this sort of account is usually characterized by comments on the coach's, teams', and players' backgrounds as well as by exciting descriptions of present action.

B. Many outdoor activities can be hazardous if proper safety precautions are not taken. Pretend that you were one of a pair of swimmers, canoers, hikers, or mountain climbers who failed to take the necessary precautions. Write a journal entry in which you record what happened to you. In your account, include dialogue and create a sense of urgency by using imperative, interrogative, and exclamatory sentences in addition to declarative ones.

C. Descriptive writing is used to set the mood for a story. This is why many mystery and horror stories contain a great deal of description. Write the first paragraph of such a story. In your paragraph, describe a place that is odd or curious. Use prepositional phrases to show the locations of objects in this place.

D. One way to increase the interest level of a piece of writing is to vary the way you begin your sentences as well as the types of sentences you use. Knowing this can aid you greatly when you revise your work. Write two or three paragraphs on the topic of your choice. Check to see how many different sentence patterns you have used and whether you have ever varied traditional subject-verb order. Then rewrite your paragraphs, varying your sentence beginnings and adding one or two new types of patterns.

3.0 Sentence and Clause

In Section 2 you learned that sentences can be classified according to the purpose of the speaker: *declarative, imperative, interrogative,* and *exclamatory*. Among other uses, this classification helps you to determine the final punctuation mark for the sentence.

Sentences can also be classified according to form. There are three basic sentence forms: the *simple sentence,* the *compound sentence,* and the *complex sentence*. There is also a fourth form, the *compound-complex sentence,* which is actually a combination of two of the other forms. Understanding these forms will help you to write varied and more interesting sentences.

3.1 The Simple Sentence

A simple sentence contains only one subject and predicate. Both the subject and the predicate may be compound.

The term *compound* means having two or more parts of the same kind.

COMPOUND SUBJECT: The *inventor* and the *manufacturer* of the device went to Washington. (The inventor went; the manufacturer went.)

COMPOUND PREDICATE: The device *turns on electrical appliances* and *switches them off again*. (The device turns on electrical appliances. The device switches them off again.)

COMPOUND SUBJECT AND COMPOUND PREDICATE: The *Student Council* and the *principal have read our petition* and *approved our plan*. (The Student Council and the principal have read; the Student Council and the principal have approved.)

All the preceding sentences are simple sentences with compound parts. One has a compound subject with one predicate. The next has one subject with a compound predicate. The last has a compound subject and a compound predicate. No matter how involved each of the sentences is, they are all simple because there is a single subject-verb connection.

The following sentence has two subjects and two predicates. It is not simple; there are two subject-verb connections.

S. V. S. V.
The *women worked;* the *men rested* in the shade.

This form, the compound sentence, is explained in detail later in this Section.

The Compound Predicate. The compound predicate is useful for combining two or more ideas into a single sentence. As a general rule, do not use a comma or semicolon to separate the parts of a compound predicate.

S. V. V.
Violent *winds felled* telephone poles and *uprooted* trees.

S. V. V.
Each of the boys *went* out and *bought* a white sweater.

The compound predicate consists of two or more verbs having the same subject.

Exercise A: Identify the compound subjects and compound predicates in the following sentences.

1. My hands, ears, and feet were frostbitten.
2. I either walk or take a bus home.
3. The orchestra and chorus rose from their seats and bowed to the audience.
4. The baby neither slept nor ate all day.
5. Arnette ran outside and jumped onto her bicycle.
6. Randy dried the dishes and put them away.
7. The youth group held a car wash and ran a bake sale to raise money for charity.
8. Bob and Linda scraped off the old finish and painted all day.
9. Cary designed and built that intricate model bridge in only two weeks.
10. José bought a box of candy but ate only the chocolates.

Exercise B: Writing Rewrite the following sentences, making all the predicates compound.

1. Tammy caught five large trout. Tammy cleaned five large trout.
2. Two of the players collided. They fell along the sidelines.
3. The instructor handed out the tests. She left the room.
4. Karen cleans stalls at the stable. Karen exercises horses at the stable.
5. Frances and Alan looked tired. They also looked uncomfortable.
6. The dictionary did not have word etymologies. It was also outdated.
7. Alan Alda wrote this episode. He directed this special.
8. The confident salesman leaned back in his chair. He put his feet up on the desk.
9. The club will earn the money by washing cars. The club might borrow the money instead.
10. The landlord and the tenants smelled smoke. They ran from the building.

3.2 The Compound Sentence

The compound sentence consists of two or more simple sentences put together.

There are two ways to join the parts of a compound sentence: (1) with a comma and a coordinating conjunction *(and, but, or, for, nor);* or (2) with a semicolon.

> The lights dimmed, *and* the play began.
> The invitation was attractive, *but* we could not accept it.
> You can drive slowly and survive, *or* you can drive fast and become a statistic.
> We knew the car well, *for* we had once owned it.
> We heard Ted Nugent's new album; it's his best yet.

The parts of a compound sentence may also be joined by a conjunctive adverb (*then, therefore, however, moreover, hence, consequently,* etc.) The conjunctive adverb is preceded by a semicolon and followed by a comma.

> We finally found the gate; *however,* it had been locked.
> Dad stained the cabinet; *then,* he coated it with shellac.
> We produced the show on a small budget; *hence,* the costumes and scenery were simple.
> The wood was water-soaked; *consequently,* it was useless for building.

Diagraming. The compound sentence is diagramed on two parallel base lines, as follows:

The car was nearly full, but we piled in.

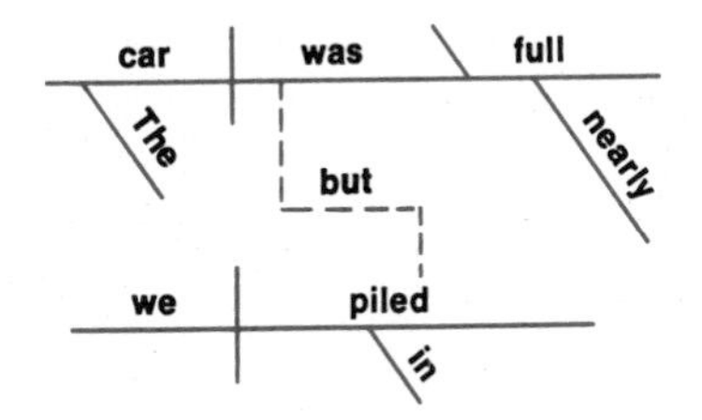

The campers sawed the logs; their counselor stacked up the pieces.

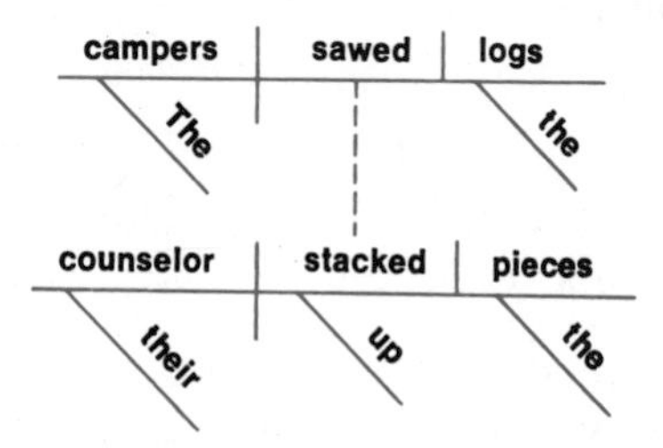

Compound Sentences and Compound Predicates. In the compound predicate every verb has the same subject. In the compound sentence, each verb has a different subject. This difference can be seen readily in the following diagrams.

SIMPLE SENTENCE WITH COMPOUND PREDICATE:

Alice restored several antiques and sold them.

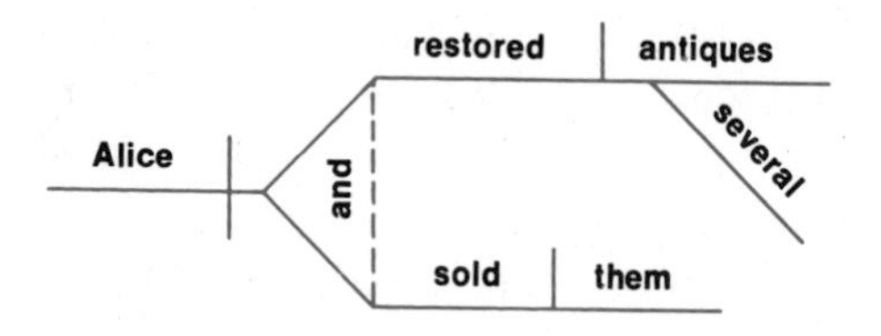

COMPOUND SENTENCE:

Alice restored several antiques, and her friends sold them.

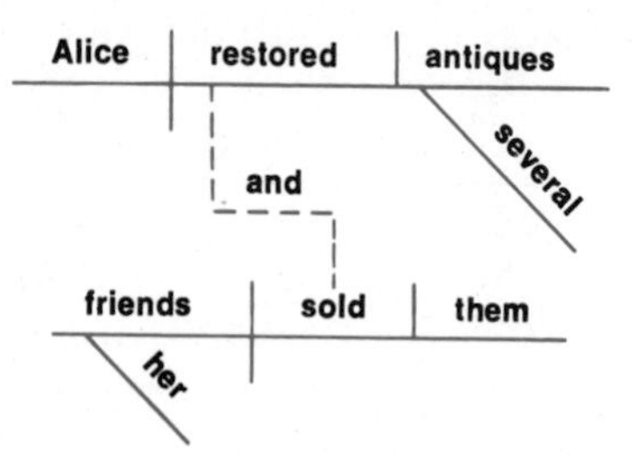

Exercise A: Decide which of the following sentences are compound and which are simple. In the simple sentences identify all compound predicates.

1. The fruit was delicious, and the flowers were beautiful.
2. Lightning does not strike the earth but rises from it.
3. Skiers ride the chairlift or take the towrope.
4. You can sell tickets, or you can be the head usher.
5. Ray went on a strict diet, but he lost only a few pounds.
6. Mr. MacDonald neither plays the bagpipes nor dances the Highland fling.
7. A huge meteor struck Siberia in 1906 and plunged far down into the earth's crust.
8. Reggie Jackson strutted to the plate and hit a home run.
9. I enjoy summer, for I can relax and go to the beach.
10. We think of air as weightless, but actually we carry a thousand pounds of it on our shoulders.

Exercise B: Writing All the following are compound sentences. Rewrite them as simple sentences. Use compound subjects or compound predicates.

EXAMPLE: The radiator whistled out steam; it seemed like it was about to explode.
The radiator whistled out steam and seemed like it was about to explode.

1. We caught a train at noon, and we arrived two hours late.
2. The desert looks barren; however, it can be productive.
3. Leslie took a supersonic plane from London; he arrived in New York before his time of departure.
4. Mango is now grown in the United States; papaya is now grown in the United States.
5. From the earth the sky looks blue; from space it is black.
6. I worried about failing the exam, but I passed easily.
7. The factory reduced machinery noise by 15 percent; it cut the errors of machine operators in half.

8. The art classes went to the Grant Wood exhibit at the museum, and the English classes also went to the Grant Wood exhibit at the museum.
9. Trevor and I finished our game of Frisbee, and we went for a swim.
10. Max went to the movies with some friends; Fran went with them.

3.3 The Clause

In order to understand complex or compound-complex sentences, you must be familiar with one of their basic elements. This element is the **clause.**

A clause is a group of words containing a verb and its subject.

A simple sentence has a subject and a verb. Therefore, it can be said to consist of one **clause.** Each part of a compound sentence also has its own verb and subject. A compound sentence, therefore, contains two clauses. Each clause in a compound sentence can be written separately as a simple sentence.

A clause that can stand by itself as a sentence is a main clause.

Our definition of a compound sentence can now be refined. A compound sentence consists of two or more main clauses. Not all clauses can stand by themselves, however. A **subordinate clause** contains a subject and a verb but does not express a complete thought and cannot stand alone.

A clause that cannot stand by itself as a sentence is a subordinate clause.

Often a subordinate clause is introduced by a subordinating conjunction such as *after* or *until*. (See Section 3.5.)

After he (S.) had gone (V.) . . . (What happened?)

Until you (S.) finish (V.) your work . . . (What?)

A relative pronoun can be the subject of a subordinate clause.

> Salk is the scientist *who discovered an immunization against polio*. (*who* is the subject of the clause.)
> Is this the magazine *that reviews foreign films*? (*that* is the subject of the clause.)

Phrase or Clause? A clause has a subject and a verb. A phrase does not.

> We saw Jack *coming down the road*. (phrase)
>
> s. v.
> We saw Jack *as he was coming down the road*. (clause)
>
> The carton *of crayons* broke open. (phrase)
>
> s. v.
> The carton *that held the crayons* broke open. (clause)

Exercise A: Are the italicized words in each sentence a phrase or a clause?

1. *Since Ken began babysitting*, he has learned a great deal.
2. The children ran into the playground, *laughing loudly*.
3. Not until morning did we learn *what was in the sack*.
4. We did not know *who was coming to pick us up*.
5. Suddenly, we saw an ancient car *coming up the road*.
6. The person *to whom you spoke* is the show's director.
7. I prefer flying *to going by boat*.
8. We fled the hall *with the warning still in our minds*.
9. *With this information*, you can proceed safely.
10. The captain heard the distress call *as the ship approached*.

Exercise B: Label each clause in the sentences below, *Main Clause* or *Subordinate Clause*.

1. The electrician broke his leg when his ladder slipped.
2. Candice is going to Florida, but her sister must stay home.
3. After she saw the sky show, Jamie wanted to be a pilot.

4. Neither the teachers nor the students heard the bell.
5. Because the piano was out of tune, the choir had to sing *a capella*.
6. Mary collects paperweights; Kara collects glass and ceramic monkeys.
7. Marnie paid for her car what her grandfather once paid for his house.
8. These papers must be sorted, stapled, and filed before we can leave.
9. Until you are confident behind the wheel, you should take an experienced driver with you.
10. The cheerleaders tried to keep the crowd hopeful, but even they were discouraged.

3.4 The Adjective Clause

An adjective clause, like a single word adjective or an adjective phrase, modifies a noun or pronoun.

An adjective clause is a subordinate clause used to modify a noun or pronoun.

Most adjective clauses begin with an **introductory word.** Examples are given in the sentences below. As you will see in the third and fifth sentences, however, sometimes an adjective clause may appear without an introductory word.

This is the park *where I once played*. (*where* is an introductory word.)

This is the season *when tornados occur*. (*when* is an introductory word.)

There is the car *I want*. (no introductory word)

There is the car *that I want*. (*that* is an introductory word.)

The book *you asked for* is on reserve. (no introductory word)

The book *that you asked for* is on reserve. (*that* is an introductory word.)

In the first two sentences above, the introductory words modify the verbs in the adjective clause: *where* modifies *played*, and *when* modifies *occur*. The clause as a whole is used to modify a specific noun. For these two sentences, the nouns are *park* and *season*.

Relative Pronouns. *Who, whose, whom, which,* and *that* sometimes introduce adjective clauses. When they do, they are called **relative pronouns.**

Relative pronouns refer to a word in the main clause and also are used in place of that word. The word in the main clause is both the antecedent of the pronoun and the word modified by the adjective clause. An adjective clause introduced by a relative pronoun is sometimes called a relative clause.

Naomi is the girl *who used to deliver our papers*.
(*girl* is the antecedent of *who* and is modified by the adjective clause.)
Here comes the man *whose seat you took*.
(*man* is the antecedent of *whose* and is modified by the adjective clause.)
The lake, *which lies at our doorstep,* is filled with fish.
(*lake* is the antecedent of *which* and is modified by the adjective clause.)

The relative pronoun functions in two ways in the sentence. It introduces the clause, and it is also used as a sentence part within the clause.

Esther is the girl *whom you met at my house*.
(*whom* is the direct object of *met* within the clause.)
The cause *for which I appeal* is just.
(*which* is the object of the preposition *for*.)
My father is a man *who likes hard work*.
(*who* is the subject of *likes*.)

Use of the relative pronouns *who* and *whom* is sometimes confusing. When the relative pronoun is the subject or predicate word in the clause, use *who*. When it is a direct object, indirect object, or object of a preposition, use *whom*. Notice that the case of the relative pronoun is *not* necessarily the same as that of its antecedent.

> It is *she whom* we wish to elect. (*whom* is in the objective case because it is the direct object of the verb *elect*. It does not agree in case with its antecedent, *she*.)

The pronouns *which* and *that* also require special attention. Use *that* to introduce adjective clauses that are essential to the meaning of the sentence. Use *which* to introduce nonessential clauses.

> There is the painting that he loves so much. (*that he loves so much* is essential to the sentence.)
> The painting, which he loves so much, is not for sale. (Here, the clause is not essential to the sentence.)

Diagraming. The adjective clause is joined to the word it modifies in the main clause. A dotted line leads from this word to the introductory word. Note that the relative pronoun is placed to show its use in the clause.

The purse that you found belongs to Ms. Weber.

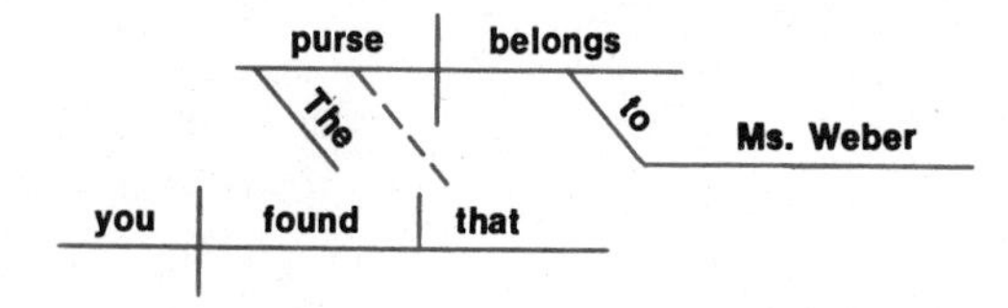

This is the place where the accident occurred.

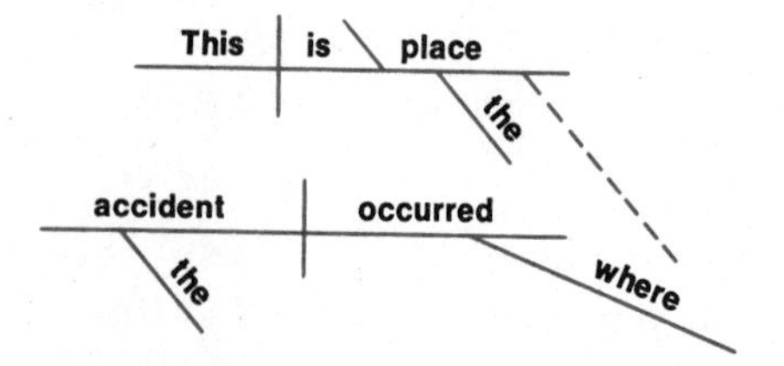

Exercise A: Find each adjective clause in the following sentences and the word each clause modifies.

1. The record that you requested will be played soon.
2. The line of cars, which stretched for miles, crept slowly toward the exit ramp.
3. March is the month when cold winds blow.
4. Anna is a girl whose personality is warm and outgoing.
5. Is this the corner where we turn left?
6. There's the spot where the dog buries his bones.
7. Is this the book you were reading?
8. Jim Bridger is the scout who discovered South Pass.
9. The goal for which we are striving is a clean environment.
10. Everyone who intends to work in science must study mathematics.

Exercise B: Writing To each sentence below, add an adjective clause containing the material in parentheses. Be sure to use the correct form of any relative pronoun.

1. We enjoyed the letters ______. (You wrote them from Japan.)
2. Dr. Wilson is a woman ______. (Everyone admires her.)
3. The boys camped on a high point ______. (They could see across the lake from there.)
4. The officers found the place ______. (The money had been hidden there.)
5. This is the building ______. (It must be torn down.)
6. You put too much sugar in those cookies ______. (You baked them.)
7. Dillon is the young actor ______ in that movie. (The director selected him to play the lead.)
8. One trap held a lobster ______. (The lobster weighed eight pounds.)
9. Do you have the tools ______ for changing tires? (The tools are the ones you need.)
10. Irwin finally got the book. (He had been wanting it.)

3.5 The Adverb Clause

The adverb clause, like the single-word adverb and the adverb phrase, modifies verbs, adjectives, and adverbs.

An adverb clause is a subordinate clause used to modify a verb, an adjective, or an adverb.

Adverb clauses tell *where, when, why, how, to what extent,* and *how much* about the words they modify.

ADVERB CLAUSES MODIFYING VERBS

We **found** the boat *where we had left it.* (tells *where*)
When the sirens sound, everyone **leaves.** (tells *when*)
We **left** early *because we were tired.* (tells *why*)
Bob **acted** *as if he meant business.* (tells *how*)

ADVERB CLAUSES MODIFYING ADJECTIVES

Bob is as **tall** *as his father is.* (tells *to what extent*)

Our school is **bigger** *than it used to be.* (tells *how much*)

ADVERB CLAUSES MODIFYING AN ADVERB

We played **harder** *than our opponents.* (tells *how much*)

Subordinating Conjunctions. Adverb clauses are introduced by **subordinating conjunctions.** These words introduce the clause and relate it to the word it modifies. The relations they express are *time, place, cause, result, exception, condition, alternative, comparison,* and *purpose.*

The most common subordinating conjunctions are these:

after	because	so that	whatever
although	before	than	when
as	if	though	whenever
as if	in order that	till	where
as long as	provided	unless	wherever
as though	since	until	while

When a subordinating conjunction is placed before a clause, the clause can no longer stand alone.

> The World Series is over. *(complete)*
> *When* the World Series is over . . . *(incomplete)*
> *Until* the World Series is over . . . *(incomplete)*

A subordinating conjunction may tie either of the two main clauses to the other. The writer decides which clause to subordinate depending on the meaning he or she wishes to express.

> *Although* Bob worked hard, he stayed on the second team.
> *Although* Bob stayed on the second team, he worked hard.
>
> *Because* everyone seemed satisfied, the plans were not changed.
>
> Everyone seemed satisfied *because* the plans were not changed.

Subordinating conjunctions enable you to show many different relationships between ideas. By using these conjunctions carefully you will be able to express your ideas clearly.

TIME:	as, after, before, since, until, when, whenever, while
CAUSE OR REASON:	because, since
COMPARISON:	as, as much as, than
CONDITION:	if, although, though, unless, provided (that)
PURPOSE:	so that, in order that

The following sentences illustrate how the relationship between ideas changes when the subordinating conjunction changes.

> *After* the doctor arrived, I felt better.
> *Because* the doctor arrived, I felt better.
> *Until* the doctor arrived, I felt better.

Some clauses omit words when there is no possibility that the reader or listener will be confused. These clauses are called **elliptical clauses.** *Ellipsis* simply means "omission of a word."

While we were driving, we were comfortably cool.
While driving, we were comfortably cool.
When he is playing the trumpet, he closes his eyes.
When playing the trumpet, he closes his eyes.

Diagraming. The adverb clause is diagramed on a separate line:

When the boat arrived, we jumped aboard.

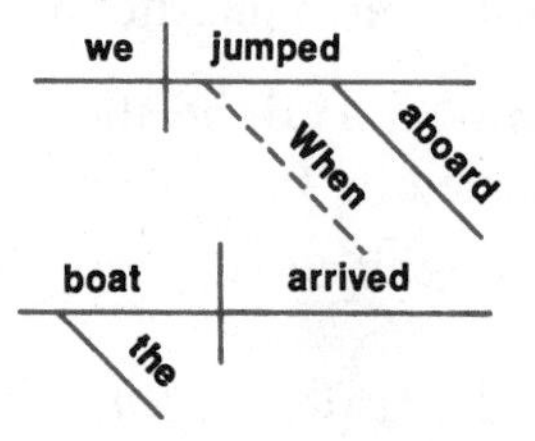

Exercise A: Find each adverb clause and the word or words it modifies.

1. When a high wind rises, the bay is not safe for sailing.
2. No one is as talented an actress as Rosa is.
3. When the Wilsons arrive in Arizona, they will rent a car.
4. The sale will continue until all the baked goods are gone.
5. Barry went for a walk since he had time to spare.
6. You will only receive letters if you write some.
7. The woodwinds played more sweetly than the strings did.
8. No one entered the house while we were here.
9. The concert was just ending as Margie drove up.
10. Aaron hurt his ankle when he was running for the bus.

Exercise B: Writing Add adverb clauses containing the information in parentheses to each of the sentences below.

1. We will begin the meal. (*Time:* Everyone is seated.)
2. Alison uses acrylic paints. (*Cause:* They dry quickly.)
3. You can take tennis lessons. (*Condition:* You have your own racquet.)
4. We will take the bus. (*Exception:* We go to Santa Maria.)

5. Charlie can whistle loudly. (*Comparison:* Paul can whistle loudly, too.)
6. Jocelyn worked hard on Friday. (*Purpose:* She wanted to go swimming on Saturday.)
7. You should breathe deeply and evenly. (*Time:* You jog.)
8. Phil read the instructions. (*Purpose:* He could operate the machine properly.)
9. This plant will flourish. (*Place:* There must be shade.)
10. My bike was stolen. (*Time:* I was shopping.)

3.6 The Noun Clause

A noun clause is a subordinate clause used as a noun.

A noun clause may be used in any way that a noun is used. It may be used as a subject, a direct object, an indirect object, a predicate noun, an object of a preposition, or an appositive.

Who you are is important. (subject)
The old man knew *where the fish were*. (direct object)
The policeman will give *whoever caused the accident* a ticket. (indirect object)
The mystery to me is *how this machine works*. (predicate noun)
There is no excuse for *what John did*. (object of preposition)
The fact *that I am his son* made no difference. (appositive)

Introductory Words. Noun clauses may be introduced by some of the same words that introduce adverb clauses: *when, where*. When they are part of a noun clause, these words are not subordinating conjunctions. They are **introductory words** used as adverbs within the noun clause.

Noun clauses may also be introduced by the same words used to introduce relative clauses: *who, whose, whom, which, that, when, where*. When they are part of a noun clause, these words are not relative pronouns. They serve as subjects or objects within the noun clause.

We looked **where** *the guide pointed*. (adverb clause modifying *looked*)

Denise knows **where** *your car is*. (noun clause as object of *knows*)

Are you the one **who** *painted this picture?* (relative clause modifying *one*)

Who *wrote this* is a mystery. (noun clause as subject of *is*)

Sometimes a noun clause may be written without an introductory word. A direct quotation, for example, is a noun clause that does not have an introductory word. Every direct quotation preceded by words such as *he said, I replied, Tony asked,* is a noun clause with no introductory word. Indirect quotations are noun clauses that begin with an introductory word.

He said *that the coat fits*. (noun clause as object of *said*)
He said, "*The coat fits*." (noun clause as object of *said*)

Infinitive Clauses. When a noun clause is made from an infinitive and its subject, it is called an **infinitive clause.** An infinitive clause may also include modifiers and complements. When the subject of such a clause is a pronoun, use the *objective* case.

We felt safe with *her to follow*.

Since the subject of an infinitive clause sometimes follows the main verb and looks like an object, it is often mistaken for the object of the main verb. In the following example, the entire infinitive clause is the direct object of the verb.

The landlord thought *us to blame*.

Gerund Clause. A noun clause may also be made from a gerund and its subject. This type of clause may also include modifiers and complements. When the subject of a gerund is a pronoun, use the possessive case.

His leaving without his briefcase was cause for concern. (*His* is a pronoun, subject of the gerund *leaving*. Notice that it is in the *possessive* case.)

Diagraming. The noun clause is diagramed as shown below. Note that the use of the noun clause determines its position in the diagram.

We thought that he was satisfied.

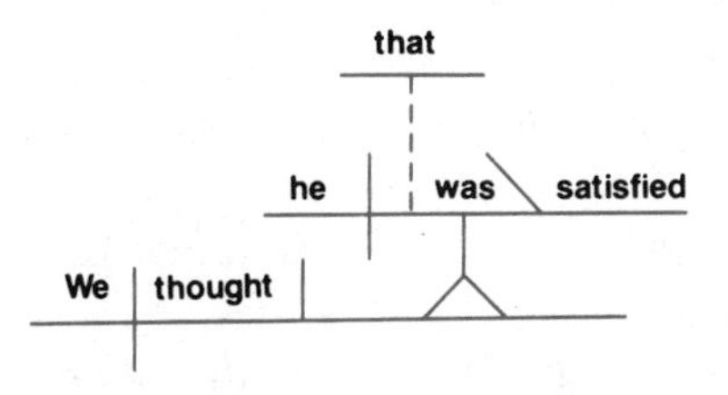

She saved a place for whoever was late.

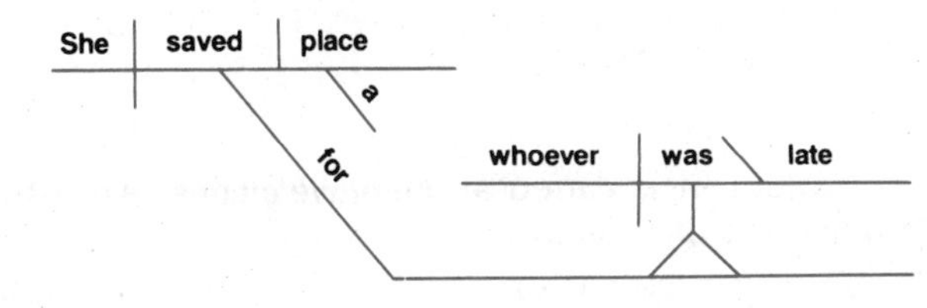

Exercise A: Identify each noun clause. Tell whether it is used as a subject, direct object, indirect object, object of a preposition, predicate word, or appositive.

1. No one knew where Jack had gone.
2. This key is not what I was looking for.
3. Mr. Callan said we would read two of Hemingway's novels.
4. What the doctor discovered has not been made known.
5. Do you remember who discovered oxygen?
6. The expedition was prepared for whatever might arise.
7. Mr. Sanders told whoever was listening the actual facts surrounding the disappearance.
8. The charge that we had ignored our orders was proved false.
9. We were amused by what Jenny had to say.
10. His standing in the rain resulted in a bad cold.

Exercise B: Writing Write a noun clause for each sentence below, using the information given in parentheses.

1. It resulted in some restrictions in the use of DDT. (*Subject:* Rachel Carson wrote about pesticides.)
2. The lifeguard could see something. (*Direct object:* The swimmers were tiring.)
3. The shipping agent can tell you that. (*Direct object:* The time the boat will arrive.)
4. The principal announced something. (*Direct object:* Friday will be a holiday.)
5. My only complaint is this. (*Predicate noun:* The food is inedible.)
6. The bloodhounds found this. (*Direct object:* The convict was hiding.)
7. It never occurred to him. (*Subject:* He could be wrong.)
8. Anyone can see this. (*Direct object:* Robert is a talented actor.)
9. The thought disturbed Jennie. (*Appositive:* Someone else might win the election.)
10. Donald disagreed with that. (*Object of the preposition:* Claire had suggested.)

Exercise C: Find the subordinate clause in each sentence. Identify it as an adjective clause, an adverb clause, or a noun clause.

1. The audience applauded when the play ended.
2. Sell those used books to whoever will buy them.
3. A gigantic chocolate sundae is what I would like.
4. As the horizon lightened, we could see the ducks rise from the marsh.
5. Is Ms. Rosin the math teacher whom you had last year?
6. The horse that I was riding would not obey me.
7. I'll expect you tomorrow unless you call me.
8. Mr. Duncan discovered that his house had been robbed.
9. Anne Sexton is one writer whose poems fascinate me.
10. Marlene's dream is that she will become a talk show host.
11. After many weeks had passed, we found our lost cat.

12. The knowledge that the project was almost finished gave us new energy.
13. As our lead narrowed, the coach warned us to stay alert.
14. I couldn't see who the stranger was.
15. "Garfield" is one newspaper comic strip that I read daily.

3.7 The Complex Sentence

You have learned about the different types of clauses that may occur in sentences. You are now ready to study the two remaining classifications of sentences.

The complex sentence consists of one main clause and one or more subordinate clauses.

In a complex sentence the subordinate clause is always used as a noun or a modifier. If it is used as a modifier, the subordinate clause modifies a word in the main clause.

You can stay *until the bell rings*. (Clause modifies *can stay*.)

If the rain continues, the game will be called. (Clause modifies *will be called*.)

This is the tool *that you need*. (Clause modifies *tool*.)

Here is the boy *whom you called*. (Clause modifies *boy*.)

In each example above, the main clause can stand as a sentence by itself: *You can stay, the game will be called, This is the tool, Here is the boy.*

The subordinate clauses cannot stand alone because their meaning is incomplete.

until the bell rings . . . (What then?)
If the rain continues . . . (What will happen?)
that you need . . . (What is needed?)
whom you called . . . (Who was called? What about him?)

Complex sentences containing noun clauses are somewhat different. The noun clause is used as a noun *within the main clause*. The noun clause, therefore, is part of the main clause.

What you need is sleep. (Noun clause is subject of *is*.)
We are worried about *what happened yesterday*. (Noun clause is object of preposition *about*.)
John said *that the door was locked*. (Noun clause is object of *said*.)

In some of these sentences neither the main clause nor the noun clause can stand by itself. Nevertheless, each of these sentences has a main clause and a subordinate clause, and each of them is a complex sentence.

Exercise A: Find each main clause and subordinate clause.

1. Here is a picture of the hotel that is to be built next year.
2. This is the town where my father was born.
3. *Star Wars* is the only movie that I've seen five times.
4. Karen does not know yet how many will attend.
5. May I borrow the book that you were talking about?
6. Yaws, which is a crippling disease, can be cured quickly with the right medicine.
7. It was now clear that the bus could not be repaired.
8. When the bell rings, the safety crews spring into action.
9. No one knows where the treasure was buried.
10. It was a science teacher who sponsored the project.

Exercise B: Indicate whether each sentence below is simple, compound, or complex.

1. Since rain is predicted, I'll wear my raincoat.
2. Into the bushes ran the frightened cat.
3. The van that carried our furniture got two flat tires.
4. The cast, together with the stage crew and orchestra, held a dress rehearsal.
5. Tracy completed the beginning photography course and signed up for the more advanced class.

6. Modern engineering achievements and scientific advancements are spectacular, but they depend upon pure research.
7. A recording studio uses a tape machine that has at least four tracks.
8. To our surprise there were four solutions to the puzzle.
9. Some scientists believe that to supply the food needs of the future we must learn to farm the seas.
10. What to do with chemical wastes is a major concern of environmentalists.
11. We were worried by the grinding noises coming from the engine of Bob's car.
12. There was no chance now of getting home before dark.
13. We could not move the sick man, nor could we leave him.
14. The traveler thanked his host, picked up his pack, and started climbing up the trail.
15. The movie was boring, but the popcorn was great.

3.8 The Compound-Complex Sentence

A compound-complex sentence consists of two or more main clauses and one or more subordinate clauses.

The compound-complex sentence has several identifiable characteristics. The main clauses are joined by a coordinating conjunction (preceded by a comma), a conjunctive adverb (preceded by a semicolon), or a semicolon alone. The subordinate clause modifies a word in one of the main clauses or acts as a noun within one of them.

MAIN CLAUSE	MAIN CLAUSE	SUBORDINATE CLAUSE
We came home,	and we saw	that the door was open.

MAIN CLAUSE	MAIN CLAUSE	SUBORDINATE CLAUSE
Try it;	however, don't blame me	if you fail.

MAIN CLAUSE	MAIN CLAUSE WITH NOUN CLAUSE AS OBJECT
Sue has a goal;	she hopes that she will be a lawyer.

Exercise: Find the two main clauses and the subordinate clause in each compound-complex sentence.

1. Don't ask me, for I was at home when the accident occurred.
2. I'm hungry, but I won't touch the cream pie that I baked for Dad's birthday.
3. Stan planned his trip carefully, but before he could even start, an emergency forced him to cancel it.
4. My car is very old; consequently, it needs parts that are hard to find.
5. Uncle George and I enjoy our conversations, so I was disappointed when he left early.
6. Melinda knew where the gift was hidden, but she kept silent.
7. Stand up and speak clearly if you know the answer.
8. Until her parents returned, the baby would not eat; nor would she play with her toys.
9. We painted the table, but it did not dry because the air was too damp.
10. Karen stood proudly on the stage, but when she opened her mouth to speak, she began to tremble.

3.9 The Sentence Redefined

Now we may present the complete definition of a sentence. First, it will be helpful to review the difference between a phrase and a clause and between a main clause and a subordinate clause.

A **phrase** is a group of words used together within a sentence as a single part of speech. A phrase may be used as a noun, a verb, an adjective, or an adverb. A phrase does *not* contain a subject and verb.

A **clause** is a group of words that contains a verb and its subject. It may be used within the sentence as a noun, an adjective, or an adverb.

PHRASE: Driving to the station . . .
PHRASE: Behind the tree . . .

s. v.
CLAUSE: While *we were driving* to the station . . .

s. v.
CLAUSE: When *he hid* behind the tree . . .

A main clause can stand by itself as a sentence. A subordinate clause cannot stand by itself.

MAIN CLAUSE MAIN CLAUSE
The sky was cloudy all day, but no rain fell.

The sky was cloudy all day. *(complete)*
No rain fell. *(complete)*

SUBORDINATE CLAUSE MAIN CLAUSE
Although the sky was cloudy all day, no rain fell.

Although the sky was cloudy all day . . . *(incomplete)*
No rain fell. *(complete)*

Phrases and clauses are sentence parts. Every sentence has at least one main clause. A sentence may also include any number of additional phrases or clauses. The complete definition of a sentence, then, has three parts.

A sentence is a group of words that

1. expresses a complete thought,
2. contains at least one main clause with a subject and verb, and
3. may contain phrases and subordinate clauses in addition to the main clause.

REINFORCEMENT EXERCISES

Sentence and Clause

A. Identify the subject and predicate in simple sentences. Copy the following sentences. Underline the subject once and the predicate twice. Some subjects and predicates are compound.

1. Barns, empty buildings, and hollow trees are homes for owls.
2. Millet can be planted in May and harvested in September.
3. A dictionary and a thesaurus are a writer's tools.
4. The carpeting and drapes were ruined by the flood.
5. Chef Luis roasted the chicken and grilled the fish.
6. Bob Fosse wrote the screenplay and directed the film.
7. Ethan and Ira Allen fought for American independence and argued for Vermont statehood.
8. Doug applied the veneer and swept up the sawdust.
9. Both the United States Air Force Academy and West Point accept women for training.
10. Will you and Rowena meet me at the football game?
11. Silk, rayon, and nylon can be used to make velvet.
12. The Phoenicians and Romans traded in Algiers.
13. Gilbert Tennat and Jonathon Edwards helped start the Great Awakening.
14. Randy read his notes, outlined some ideas, and wrote a rough draft of his composition.
15. Wales, Scotland, England, and Northern Ireland make up Great Britain.

B. Identify simple and compound sentences. Some of the sentences below are simple, and some are compound. Write *S* for the simple sentences and *C* for the compound sentences.

1. Julia Child hosts a TV program; she is a famous chef.
2. Harlech Castle and Conway Castle are in Wales.
3. Polypropylene and wool are both used for insulation.
4. Harvard and Yale compete in athletics and cooperate in academic research.

5. Andrew Carnegie built libraries throughout the United States; consequently, he is highly respected today.
6. Bears forage for berries and fish from mountain streams.
7. Kelly enjoyed cross-country skiing, but she disliked snowshoeing intensely.
8. Lonnie saw the accident and described it to the police.
9. The United States, Canada, and the Soviet Union rank as the largest producers of aluminum, but only the Soviet Union has large supplies of bauxite.
10. Felix Mendelssohn wrote an opera about the Lorelei myth, and Heinrich Heine wrote a poem about it.

C. Identify phrases and clauses. Tell whether the italicized group of words in each sentence is a phrase or clause.

1. *When Tom visited Australia,* he saw the Great Barrier Reef.
2. *Because of the heavy fog,* all airport traffic was suspended.
3. *Before the Pennsylvania Hospital was founded,* a hospital existed in New Amsterdam.
4. *After I heard the thunder,* I rolled up the car windows.
5. *At the sound of the bell,* two bears on unicycles pedaled into the center ring.
6. Stephen King, *who writes popular horror novels,* once acted in a movie based on one of his stories.
7. *Unless you have studied American history,* you may not have heard of the mound builders.
8. *Diving from an enormous height,* the eagle plucked its prey from the ground.
9. Read the directions *before you connect the printer.*
10. *The finest production at the theater festival this year* was the new drama by James Leonard.

D. Identify adjective clauses. Find the adjective clauses in the following sentences and tell what words they modify.

1. The electric piano that Hilda bought is portable.
2. *Star Trek,* which starred William Shatner, went off the air years ago.

3. Melanie, who wears contact lenses, asked for eye drops.
4. Here is the ward where premature babies are kept.
5. Tennessee Williams, whose plays often received bad reviews, is now considered a great American author.
6. According to *Consumer Reports*, this is the car that gets the best gas mileage.
7. Students of Africa should learn Swahili and Hausa, which are both spoken by over ten million people.
8. In *The Great Gatsby*, Fitzgerald tells of a time when Manhattan was an island wilderness.
9. A computer firm that declared bankruptcy was Osborne.
10. The Portuguese are the ones who invented the three-masted ship.

E. Identify adverb clauses. Find each adverb clause and tell which word or words it modifies.

1. Though few opportunities existed for women in her day, Jane Austen made a name for herself as a novelist.
2. Asthma victims suffer when there is pollution in the air.
3. The campaign manager is not as confident as the candidate is.
4. Security guards appeared on the runway immediately after the plane landed.
5. Jill studied veterinary science because she loves animals.
6. While you wait in line, I will look for a parking space.
7. He is more excited about seeing the Olympics than I am.
8. If the weather is nice on Saturday, we will ride our bikes to the forest preserve.
9. Many small colleges will close in the next few years unless they receive more private donations.
10. Ballet dancers must train harder than many athletes do.

F. Identify noun clauses. Find the noun clauses. Tell whether each is used as a subject, direct object, indirect object, object of a preposition, predicate word, or appositive.

1. The teacher asked Martin to read aloud.
2. Shelly liked my idea that we start our own newspaper.

3. Lane did not agree with what the coach had decided.
4. What had made the odd, clicking noise remained a mystery.
5. Mrs. McFarland frowned and asked where the pie had gone.
6. Steve and Greg shouted that they were safe.
7. We will give whoever wins the play-offs the trophy.
8. What Floyd asked was that we listen with open minds.
9. The book was about how Lincoln rose to the Presidency.
10. The newspaper article reported that the Japanese beetle was accidentally introduced into the United States.

G. Identify complex and compound-complex sentences. Tell whether each of the following sentences is complex or compound-complex.

1. Liquid air, which resembles water, freezes foods instantly, but it leaves them extremely brittle.
2. The letter *A*, which is the first letter in many alphabets, comes from the Egyptian hieroglyphic for "ox."
3. Jonathan is studying photography; however, his sister thinks that he should become a pharmacist.
4. After the floods receded, volunteer workers rebuilt the town, and the residents returned to their homes.
5. When football was first played, teams could have up to thirty players.
6. If the crowd is small, the actors may be discouraged; nevertheless, the show will go on.
7. Assam is a state in the Republic of India in which elephants, tigers, leopards, and bears are common.
8. The people who built the pyramids had primitive tools, yet they accomplished an incredible architectural feat.
9. Much of classical literature was destroyed when the Library of Alexander was burned.
10. Laura Ingalls Wilder, who wrote her first book at the age of 65, is famous for her children's stories.

MIXED REVIEW

Sentence and Clause

A. Indicate whether the words in italics are main clauses or subordinate clauses. Then tell whether each subordinate clause is an adjective, adverb, or noun clause.

1. Baked beans and brown bread are popular foods in New England, and *chili and flautas are popular foods in the Southwest.*
2. King Sunny Ade, *who is a Nigerian rock musician,* has helped popularize "JuJu" music.
3. Randy wondered *where he should look for information on colleges.*
4. *After the war was over,* Churchill wrote a book on painting.
5. Tiny crystals *that cover the surface of pearls* break light into little rainbows of color.
6. *When tomatoes were first introduced into Europe,* many people thought that they were poisonous.
7. Glaciers, like rivers, are constantly in motion, but their movement is so slow *that they appear stationary.*
8. *If Carla captures your bishop and your queen,* you will doubtless lose the game.
9. The fact *that one million seals may congregate in a rookery* indicates how social the animals are.
10. Megan named her dog "Byte" *because she is interested in computers,* not because the dog is dangerous.
11. Is that a lute, or *is it some other type of stringed instrument?*
12. The king *who united the West Africans and formed the Ashanti empire* was named Osei Tutu.
13. Cindi looked for her younger brother in the arcade; *however, he had already gotten a ride home.*
14. *Although he failed to reach the North Pole,* the Norwegian explorer Otto Sverdrup made valuable observations on his arctic journeys.

15. That unusual breed of dog has been around for nearly two thousand years, but *only recently has it been introduced into the United States*.

B. Identify each of the following sentences as simple, compound, or complex. In addition, find the subordinate clauses and tell whether they are adjective, adverb, or noun clauses.

1. Lemont works at the Humane Society in his free time.
2. Lisa wondered if the other students would agree to her proposal.
3. Sharks have two rows of teeth that grasp and slash.
4. Chip rebuilds and sells antique cars that he finds in junk yards.
5. Tarantulas are frightening, but they are actually fairly harmless.
6. Elliot prefers the radio stations that play soft rock.
7. Our school has varsity, junior varsity, and sophomore soccer teams.
8. When we visited the National Air and Space Museum, we saw the Spirit of St. Louis.
9. The type of cat that is most common in America is the tabby.
10. Consumer experts say that some advertising is deceptive.
11. If no good movies are playing, we can simply go to a restaurant and talk.
12. Janice did the research, and Marty wrote up the lab report.
13. Anne Frank kept a diary during her years in Amsterdam.
14. The waitress asked us what we wanted to eat.
15. Miguel and his sister bought some new records and cassettes.
16. Connors won the first set, but the match went to Borg.
17. Some fans found out where Michael Jackson was staying.
18. The Heimlich maneuver can save people who are choking.
19. The Bee Gees held a benefit concert and gave the proceeds to Reese Memorial Hospital.
20. Because fuel prices have risen, small cars have become quite popular.

USING GRAMMAR IN WRITING

Sentence and Clause

A. Imagine that you have achieved greatness in some highly publicized field such as acting or politics. The year is 2001, and you have been asked to write a brief autobiographical statement to be included in the *Dictionary of Prominent Americans*. Write such a statement about yourself. In this brief autobiography, use adjective, adverb, and noun clauses to describe yourself and your actions and to relate periods of your life to one another (Example: "After I graduated from high school . . .").

B. Imagine that you are a reporter for a newspaper in a small town in the Midwest. You get a call from a local farmer who tells you to drive to a nearby wheat field where you will get the story of your life. When you arrive, you find several townspeople and some military personnel standing around a gleaming metal box that towers thirty feet into the sky. The box contains no doors, and it seems simply to have appeared in the field overnight. Using this idea as a basis, write a short story describing how the box is opened, where it came from, and what it contains. Add variety to the story by using sentences of the following types: simple, compound, complex, and compound-complex.

C. Retell a familiar story for children, using only simple sentences. Then tell the story once again, this time using compound complex, and compound-complex sentences. Which story was easiest to write? Which story do you think is the most interesting? Which is more suitable for children? Why?

For an additional challenge use the plot line of the children's story but substitute settings and characters that would make the story interesting to someone of your own age. Use a variety of sentence types.

CUMULATIVE REVIEW
Usage (I)

Understanding How Words Are Used. Study each italicized word, phrase, or subordinate clause. Decide whether it is being used as a *Subject, Verb, Adjective, Adverb, Appositive, Predicate Word, Direct Object, Indirect Object*, or *Object of a Preposition*. Write each word and your answers next to the correct number.

1. Geoffrey loves *watching* the planets through his *telescope*.
2. *Which* is better adapted to desert life, the rattlesnake or the tarantula?
3. Look *carefully* before *entering the intersection*.
4. Paris *began* as a *fortified* island in the Seine river.
5. *Did* you *call* Marietta, or did you receive a *call* from her?
6. The *hard-working* beekeeper went *out* to the hives.
7. One water sport, *wind-surfing*, is a popular *form* of recreation along the coasts.
8. The *Renaissance* artist Raphael influenced painters for *centuries*.
9. Do you know *who invented the hot fudge sundae?*
10. Phrenology, *which is the study of the skull*, was a *kind* of pseudo-science *popular* in the nineteenth century.
11. Prizes went to *those* who held *specially marked* tickets.
12. Ice *floats* in water because water expands *as it freezes*.
13. Jim's hobby, *collecting movie memorabilia*, has led *him* to do extensive research.
14. *Playing baseball* is still *one* of our most popular activities.
15. The possibility of fortune and fame gives *acting* its *appeal*.
16. Janice hopes *to become an interpreter* for a foreign *firm*.
17. *Some* of the performers mixed with the crowd *waiting outside the stage entrance*.
18. The sparrows had fixed *themselves* a *nest* in the eaves.
19. Scientists *have been studying* alternatives to *fossil* fuels.
20. *Completing the restorations* should not be very *difficult*.

4.0 Complete Sentences

You know that a sentence must express a complete thought. Sometimes, however, we find ourselves communicating ideas in a few words or incomplete phrases. This is perfectly acceptable in conversation, where gestures and facial expressions can supplement our words. It becomes awkward in written work, however, for the reader has no way of finding out what the missing ideas or subtleties are.

To avoid this type of confusion, you must write sentences that communicate your ideas clearly. To do this, you must learn to avoid two types of sentence error: (1) the sentence fragment, and (2) the run-on sentence.

4.1 Fragments Resulting from Incomplete Thought

A **sentence fragment** is not a complete sentence. It is only a part, or fragment, of a sentence.

Behind the bookcase.
Confused by the noise.
Windblown and suntanned.

Fragments may occur when your thoughts are racing ahead of your hand. You might start to write a second idea before completing the first, or you might accidentally leave out an important part of the sentence.

Suppose you wanted to say something like this:

> Bob and Millie went to the carnival. After it had closed, they stopped for ice cream. They went home a short time later.

However, as your thoughts were moving on to the next idea, you actually wrote this:

> Bob and Millie went to the carnival. After they stopped for ice cream. They went home a short time later.

The second group of words is not a sentence. It causes confusion. The reader may think you meant to say, "Bob and Millie went to the carnival after they stopped for ice cream."

Exercise A: Writing Find the sentence fragments. Make each fragment a complete sentence by adding words or changing the punctuation.

1. Then we saw Boots. Running down the road as fast as he could go.
2. The plan to give everyone two choices in the election.
3. After we had climbed up a long succession of hills.
4. We had trouble from the outset. To begin with, something wrong with the motor.
5. Judge Marcia Turner, an old friend of Bob's mother.
6. The taxi turning around in the middle of the block.
7. No one saw us. Into the back of the auditorium, closing the door quietly.
8. There is a prize. The student entering the best experiment in the science fair.
9. The truck halfway up the mountain road.
10. When rain comes to the desert, a brightly-colored carpet of tiny flowers.

Exercise B: Writing Three of the following groups of words are sentences. The rest are fragments. Find the fragments and add words needed to make them sentences.

1. Floods were driving people from their homes.
2. The crops ruined by water and mud.
3. River mud through the doors and windows.
4. Cleaning up afterwards takes great courage.
5. The lifework and savings of many completely gone.
6. The Red Cross aid to many people.
7. Some buildings were washed away.
8. Few residents thinking of moving away.
9. A new start right along the river edge.
10. Flood control by replanting forests in the mountains.

4.2 Fragments Resulting from Incorrect Punctuation

A complete sentence begins with a capital letter and ends with a punctuation mark: *period, question mark,* or *exclamation point*. A complete thought must be included between the capital letter and the end mark.

Many sentence fragments result when the writer inserts an end mark before he or she has written a complete thought. This sentence error is called a **period fault.**

FRAGMENT: *At the start of the game.* It began to rain.
SENTENCE: At the start of the game, it began to rain.

FRAGMENT: The boys were very quiet. *While the picture was being shown.*
SENTENCE: The boys were very quiet while the picture was being shown.

FRAGMENT: *Although Kay could not swim.* She was not afraid of the water.
SENTENCE: Although Kay could not swim, she was not afraid of the water.

Exercise A: Writing Combine each idea in Column A with a fragment from Column B to make ten complete sentences.

	COLUMN A	COLUMN B
1.	We went camping over the weekend.	Simply to prove that they could do it.
2.	I would like you to meet Aunt Laura.	Who painted *Raft of the Medusa*.
3.	We tore down the goalposts.	To Dr. Feingold.
4.	Many reptiles make interesting pets.	Originally compounded of every known spice.
5.	The mountaineers climbed Pike's Peak.	Who is one of my favorite people.
6.	Marmalade is a sweet preserve.	In spite of the rain.
7.	Gericault was the nineteenth century painter.	After the final touchdown had been scored.
8.	Frangipani is a French perfume.	Especially chameleons.
9.	Mr. Roos said to return the permission slips.	Made from bitter oranges.
10.	Cable television is providing many job opportunities.	For students with a background in communications.

Exercise B: Writing Find the fragments. Correct them by changing the punctuation and capitalization.

1. After the dentist began drilling. I became more nervous.
2. The queen devised a clever plan. To fill her empty coffers.
3. Starting in the garage. Flames spread quickly through the house.
4. A crowd had gathered at the airport. Waiting for the President's plane.

5. Although she did not like handball. Faye played with us.
6. When we arrived at the picnic grounds. It was time to eat.
7. We finally found the scissors. In the refrigerator.
8. No one can help you. If you do not help yourself.
9. I like every kind of vegetable. Except turnips.
10. Jeff didn't appreciate good writing. Until he tried to write a story.

4.3 Phrases as Fragments

A sentence fragment may also occur when a writer mistakes a phrase for a sentence. A phrase is a group of words that does not contain a subject and a verb. Therefore, it cannot be a sentence.

A long prepositional phrase is sometimes written as a sentence fragment.

FRAGMENT: The students worked hard. *At the beginning of the school year*.

SENTENCE: The students worked hard at the beginning of the school year.

A verbal phrase may also be incorrectly used as a sentence. This occurs at times because a verbal looks and functions somewhat like a verb. However, a verbal is not a complete verb and cannot be used as the main verb of a sentence.

Gerunds and participles that end in *-ing* are most frequently confused with main verbs. The following rule can help you avoid writing sentence fragments.

No word ending in *-ing* can be a complete verb unless it is a one-syllable word like *sing, ring,* or *bring.*

FRAGMENT: Delaying the inning.

SENTENCE: The manager caused a disruption, delaying the inning.

FRAGMENT: Skiing on steep slopes.

SENTENCE: Lisa enjoys skiing on steep slopes.

If an *-ing* word is preceded by *is, are, was,* or some other form of *be,* the two words together are a verb.

PARTICIPLE	COMPLETE VERB
going	is going
seeing	was seeing
playing	had been playing
disturbing	were disturbing

A long infinitive phrase sometimes is incorrectly used as a sentence. It often has everything a sentence requires except a subject.

FRAGMENT: Chuck has a plan. To go down the back road at night.

SENTENCE: Chuck has a plan. His scheme is to go down the back road at night.

FRAGMENT: Cheryl was delighted. To have the unexpected opportunity to meet and talk with the prominent scientist.

SENTENCE: Cheryl was delighted to have the unexpected opportunity to meet and talk with the prominent scientist.

Another common sentence error occurs when a noun and an appositive are used together as a complete sentence. Although the combination may sound like a sentence, it is only a fragment because it lacks a verb.

FRAGMENT: Sue Mathews, *an outstanding sports writer*

SENTENCE: Sue Mathews is an outstanding sports writer.

SENTENCE: Sue Mathews, an outstanding sports writer, awarded the trophies.

FRAGMENT: The speech, *a tribute to the retiring president*

SENTENCE: The speech was a tribute to the retiring president.

SENTENCE: The speech, a tribute to the retiring president, was written by two staff members.

Exercise A: Writing Rewrite the following groups of words to make complete sentences. You may need to add words.

1. Lana, pretending she knew how to ski.
2. Steve Cauthen, a very young jockey.
3. Charlene received a letter. From a friend in Mexico.
4. You must be relieved. Finding your wallet.
5. The hikers needed to rest for an hour. To recover from the long climb.
6. A chance at the pennant becoming more and more real.
7. The President rushed back to the capital. Learning of the disaster through a radio announcement.
8. The Navy started at once. To search the area for the plane.
9. The farmer saying he had no use for tractors.
10. The speech, a summary of the nation's foreign policy regarding Latin America.

Exercise B: Follow the same directions as for Exercise A.

1. No one liked Lynn's suggestion. To raise money by having a sale.
2. The captives could see their only possible escape route. Over the wall and through the woods.
3. Watching the movie, a story of early days in Montana.
4. Joy figured out the trouble. Dust settling on the camera lens.
5. Mr. Cooley, encouraged by the excellent response of the class.
6. The families of the miners anxiously awaiting news at the mouth of the mine.
7. Each of the scouts had a special task. To find talented athletes.
8. The announcement, a warning to all who lived in the village.
9. Two strange ships, one a fishing trawler and the other a yacht.
10. Another satellite circling the moon and sending back messages.

4.4 Clauses as Fragments

Another type of fragment is caused by a subordinate clause used alone as a sentence. Placing a subordinating conjunction before a sentence changes it to a subordinate clause.

SENTENCE: We watched the players warm up.
SUBORDINATE CLAUSE: As we watched the players warm up . . .

If an end mark is placed before or after a subordinate clause that is not part of a complete sentence, a fragment results.

INCORRECT: When the game started. Jack forgot his fears.
CORRECT: When the game started, Jack forgot his fears.

INCORRECT: Helen took the test early. Because she was going on a trip.
CORRECT: Helen took the test early because she was going on a trip.

Exercise A: Rewrite the word groups below to eliminate the fragments.

1. We never could find out. Who donated the money.
2. When he reached his office. He heard the news.
3. The defeat was hard for Paul to accept. Since he had worked so hard for so long.
4. The victory of our team was thrilling. Although it had never been in doubt.
5. Dr. Bell decided to return to Hawaii. Where she had spent so many years.
6. Erin swam out to the boat. Which had obviously been abandoned.
7. No matter what the newspapers say. The story is false.
8. Visit us again. Whenever you can.
9. Do not remove the cap. Until you are ready to use the ink.
10. Do not disturb them. If the boys are still sleeping.

Exercise B: Copy the following paragraphs, changing the fragments to sentences by correcting the punctuation or by adding needed words. Some of the sentences are already correct.

> Jefferson mounted his horse and made his way. Through the snow and sleet to his beloved Monticello. Of all the houses yet built by man. None was ever so much a part of the owner. The structure bearing all over it the marks of his creative genius. The bricks that formed the walls. The nails that held down the floors. And much of the furniture were made on the plantation.
>
> On the top of the house was a weathervane. Which marked the direction of the wind. Over the main doorway hung a great clock. With one face for the porch and another for the hall. One of its weights turning over a metal plate to show the day of the week.
>
> In his library, the first collection of books in America. Here too were his swivel chair, another of his inventions, and tables with revolving tops. A few years later, reduced almost to poverty. Jefferson sold his collection of books. To pay off the debts that had accumulated while he was President.

4.5 Run-on Sentences

When two or more sentences are written as though they were one, they result in a **run-on sentence.** This error usually occurs when the writer fails to use a period or other end mark at the end of each sentence.

RUN-ON: The Drama Club had a bake sale it was a great success.

CORRECT: The Drama Club had a bake sale. It was a great success.

RUN-ON: The doctor cut off the bandage he then cleaned the wound.

CORRECT: The doctor cut off the bandage. He then cleaned the wound.

When two complete sentences are incorrectly joined by a comma, the sentence error is called a **comma fault.** This is the most common type of run-on sentence.

COMMA FAULT: Debby arrived late, her car had stalled.
CORRECT: Debby arrived late. Her car had stalled.

COMMA FAULT: Jack sang a solo at the concert, he has a tenor voice.
CORRECT: Jack sang a solo at the concert. He has a tenor voice.

COMMA FAULT: We were watching the first snowfall, it came early this year.
CORRECT: We were watching the first snowfall. It came early this year.

Notice the pattern in the preceding examples. Each pair of sentences is closely related, and the second sentence begins with a personal pronoun: *her, he, it*. Watch for this pattern in your writing to avoid the comma fault.

4.6 Avoiding the Run-on Sentence

If you want to combine short sentences into one longer sentence you may do so in one of three ways.

1. Sentences may be joined with a comma and a coordinating conjunction.

   RUN-ON: Fliss gave her opinion she regretted it immediately.
   CORRECT: Fliss gave her opinion, but she regretted it immediately.

2. Sentences may be joined with a semicolon.

   RUN-ON: Choose your program wisely it will set the course for your future.
   CORRECT: Choose your program wisely; it will set the course for your future.

3. Sentences may be joined with a semicolon and a conjunctive adverb.

RUN-ON: Rain fell all through the game, there were many fumbles.

CORRECT: Rain fell all through the game; consequently, there were many fumbles.

Exercise A: Writing Correct each of the following run-on sentences in one of these ways: (1) by using a period and a capital letter; (2) by using a semicolon; or (3) by using a comma and *and, but,* or *or*.

1. Heidi stayed at school to work on the paper then she walked home.
2. The paper appears every week, however, I read it only every two or three weeks.
3. Getting out the paper is hard work, it has to be done after school.
4. Ray is the editor, he is a senior.
5. It is a small paper, it has a big circulation.
6. It was dark and foggy we drove right past the house we were looking for.
7. Pat can't buy a car until next year, she doesn't have the money now.
8. Roberta enjoyed helping in the yard she was the only one who did.
9. Burt did not know the assignment, consequently he did not know what to study.
10. Dad found a pen in the desk, however it was not his.
11. Jean recognized the car, it was her cousin's.
12. Ernie did not know that he was to make a speech, nevertheless, he did very well.
13. Rain had been falling for several days, the roads were muddy.
14. Don started to erase the error then he tore up the paper and started over again.
15. No one was talking, we were all studying.

Exercise B: Writing The first part of a sentence is given on each line below. Add a second main clause, beginning it with the word in parentheses at the end of the line. If the word is a conjunctive adverb, place a semicolon before it and a comma after it. If the word is a personal pronoun, use a semicolon or use a comma with a coordinating conjunction.

1. First, I tried the dictionary (then)
2. The idea came from Dan Malone (he)
3. The average class size is already over thirty students (moreover)
4. The old station wagon has been used for seven years (it)
5. Kay had been training for the event for years (nonetheless)
6. The passengers got out of the bus to stretch their legs (they)
7. Some students fail to go to college because it costs too much (however)
8. Jim did not think that the interview was very important (consequently)
9. Arriving in the city, we went right to the convention center (then)
10. This is my room (it)
11. The temperature outside was well below zero (however)
12. Some of the workers have too many responsibilities (for example)
13. The test was hard (in fact)
14. This is my friend Betty (she)
15. I know this is my sweater (it)

REINFORCEMENT EXERCISES

Complete Sentences

A. Correct fragments resulting from incomplete thoughts. Rewrite the following fragments to make complete sentences.

1. To ease the pain of the wound
2. Jumping like a gazelle at the sound
3. Woods and streams and meadows full of flowers
4. Tons of molten lava, pouring from the volcano
5. Dancing his way to stardom
6. The lion, a symbol of courage
7. Finally returned the script to the director
8. After visiting Canada and Alaska
9. Jogging, swimming, weight lifting, and canoeing
10. Tiny rubber lizards that appeared enormous on TV

B. Correct fragments resulting from incorrect punctuation. Correct these by changing the punctuation and capitalization.

1. Alfred Lord Tennyson wrote many long poems. Including *Idylls of the King*.
2. One native South American predator is the ocelot. A medium-sized member of the cat family.
3. Mildew can attack plants, food, clothing, and books. Especially in damp climates.
4. Named after the Greek god Titan. The Titanic was a magnificent ship.
5. Tennis was exported from France to England. In the thirteenth century.
6. Natural rubber is fairly unimportant to modern manufacturing. Having been replaced, for most purposes, by synthetic products.
7. The garden was planted in red, yellow, and orange nasturtiums. Which are also known as Indian cress.
8. Navigators in the northern hemisphere rely on Polaris. A star in the constellation Ursa Minor.

9. Commemorating a Hebrew victory recorded in the Book of Esther. Purim is still celebrated by Jews today.
10. In *Our Town*, his famous play about small town life in turn-of-the-century America. Thorton Wilder uses a simple set consisting of a bare stage and a few chairs.

C. Correct fragments that are phrases. Correct the fragments below by connecting them to complete sentences.

On October 12, 1972. Naomi Thompson Clinton, of Columbia, South Carolina, saved the life of Harold Martin. A twenty-five-year-old truck driver. Martin's tractor-trailer collided with another truck. Carrying drums of gasoline. Several of these drums of gasoline rolled onto the road and caught fire. Martin was thrown out of his truck. Into the flames on the pavement. Ms. Clinton ran to him. Dragging him out of the burning area, smothering the flames on his clothes, and risking her own life in the process. Ms. Clinton was able to rescue the unfortunate truck driver. He survived. With minor injuries. As a result of her actions, Naomi Clinton received a medal. From the Carnegie Hero Fund Commission.

D. Correct fragments that are clauses. Rewrite the following word groups to create complete sentences.

1. The car never starts. When the outside temperature falls much below freezing.
2. Melissa was not satisfied with her accomplishments. Although she played second violin for the orchestra.
3. Give the messenger this check. If the package arrives.
4. Since great mineral wealth lies on the ocean floors. Techniques have been developed for underwater mining.
5. Spinoza was a philosopher. Who supported himself grinding lenses.
6. My parents took a trip to Seattle. Where they first met.
7. My phone privileges were suspended for a week. Because I tied up the line all evening.
8. Heidi could not decide what to be. Until Halloween night.

9. Until that dog learns to heel. I am not taking it for a walk.
10. My brother wishes he could change his birthday. Which falls on April Fool's day.

E. Correct run-on sentences. Correct the run-on sentences below.

1. Some animals hibernate in winter, this means that they enter a sleep-like state.
2. There are scores of Indian reservations in the United States they cover more than fifty million acres.
3. This is one of the smallest of the African antelopes, it is about the size of a jack rabbit.
4. Lou Gehrig was a famous New York Yankee he was nicknamed the "Iron Horse."
5. The crafted objects found by archaeologists are called artifacts the natural objects are called ecofacts.
6. Male parakeets have blue noses females have brown.
7. Elizabeth ruled England Philip ruled Spain.
8. It wasn't a new magazine I read it two months ago.
9. We were asked to write on Emily Dickinson but we could choose to write on Walt Whitman instead.
10. We thought it was a strange-looking rabbit then we learned that it was a chinchilla.
11. Maude Adams was a famous American stage actress, she first appeared on stage when she was nine months old.
12. The alligator turtle is large, nevertheless, it is as slow as its smaller relatives.
13. Mike wore his jogging suit it was navy with gray stripes.
14. Davy Crockett was born in 1786 he died in 1836.
15. Lusitania was an ancient Roman province it covered the area now known as Portugal.
16. Many people like spring I like autumn best.
17. One form of alabaster is hydrous calcium sulphate another is carbonate of lime.
18. The phalanger is an Australian animal these cat-like creatures live in trees.
19. My brother collects things his room looks like a museum.
20. P.J. worked after school Ann did, too.

MIXED REVIEW

Complete Sentences

A. Revise the following fragments and run-on sentences to make complete sentences.

1. Tracy got sunburned, she is beginning to blister.
2. Some people believe that attitudes affect health. That the mind can overcome disease.
3. A robbery had been reported, two police officers answered the call.
4. Ms. Agnelli directs the band, she also plans marching formations.
5. Hundreds of fans waited in line overnight. To get tickets to the Stray Cats concert.
6. Checking several sources before writing her article. The reporter made certain that her information was accurate.
7. Matt Dillon, already a well-known star.
8. Yvonne ordered Chinese food, she loves egg rolls.
9. What do you do in homeroom? Besides take attendance.
10. Some towns have curfews, ours doesn't.
11. Jon returned from the optometrist, he had gotten contact lenses.
12. Crepes must be cooked carefully, they burn easily.
13. The driving simulator, which tests reaction time and driving know-how.
14. Jenny was elected class president, Jordan became vice-president.
15. On weekends I watch hot air balloon races. In nearby Antioch.
16. The sales representative tried to sell us a microwave coffeepot. By emphasizing its safety features.
17. This doctor uses acupuncture, she claims the results are amazing.
18. Agatha Christie's mysteries are not always as complicated. As *Murder on the Orient Express*.

19. Psychological research has explored many areas. Including what makes people fall in love.
20. A guest speaker explained the juvenile justice system to our government class, she also discussed the rights of minors.

B. Identify the following as complete sentences, fragments, or run-ons. Rewrite any fragments and run-ons to make complete sentences.

1. A barrister, which is the English equivalent of a lawyer.
2. Marguerite Higgins was a war correspondent during World War II, she gained even greater fame covering the Korean War.
3. A colorless, flammable gas, ethylene is used in the plastics industry.
4. Geology, the study of rock formations.
5. The mongoose is known for its ability to kill rats and mice. And snakes.
6. Sandra was deeply moved by the book. Which was *The Grapes of Wrath*.
7. Assignments completed at school and assignments completed at home.
8. She kept a diary during her youth. Which was spent in Charleston, South Carolina.
9. One of the world's chief trade routes, the Mediterranean Sea is also visited by tourists.
10. The bird watchers studied the green, blue, and red bird, it was a motmot that had flown far from its Mexican home.
11. Hawthorne wrote *The House of the Seven Gables*. Also *The Scarlet Letter* and *The Blithedale Romance*.
12. Peat is like coal, both are made of once-living materials.
13. Known as the Desert Fox. Erwin Rommel was a German general of World War II.
14. The sun faded the furniture. Because George would not close the drapes.
15. The price of gasoline and the high interest rates.
16. My mother made a vow. To visit her birthplace in Naples.

17. Mr. Franey found his glasses. Resting on top of his head.
18. Millions of people enjoy the art of Norman Rockwell. A thoroughly American painter.
19. Which most people don't believe.
20. The most beautiful place I have ever seen.

C. Find and correct the sentence fragments and run-on sentences in the following paragraph. Look for incomplete ideas, phrases or clauses used alone, complete sentences separated by commas, and sentences that are not indicated by proper punctuation and capitalization.

Hezekiah Bradley Smith was one of the most colorful figures of a colorful time. He lived in post-Civil War America. A period known for Indian wars, riverboat gamblers, and the near impeachment of a President. An eccentric industrialist who began his career as a cabinetmaker. Smith started a furniture factory in a blacksmith's shack he made a fortune as a manufacturer of windowblinds, then he bought an entire town. Which he renamed Smithville next, he ran for Congress on the Democratic and Greenback ticket. During his campaign, in order to arouse curiosity and to attract votes. Smith rode through New Jersey in a grand procession. That included a bandwagon, numerous horses, and Smith's own carriage. Pulled by a harnessed moose. Smith won his first congressional race, however, he lost his second bid for public office. After which he returned to his business, the H. B. Smith Machine Company. Became the nation's foremost manufacturer of bicycles.

USING GRAMMAR IN WRITING

Complete Sentences

A. Advertisers often use sentence fragments to add "punch" to their advertising copy. Below is a newspaper ad written in this manner. Rewrite it, turning all fragments into complete sentences. Do not create any run-on sentences as you rewrite. Remember that imperative sentences may have *you* as an understood or implied subject.

> **SOUNDS!**
>
> **A complete sound system!** Includes receiver, turntable, cartridge, and speakers. *And* tape deck! Not one tape deck, but two! For recording from one tape to another. That enough? We think so. Drop by today. Special sale ends Sunday.

B. Dictionary definitions are often used in reports to define key terms. However, dictionaries usually define words in fragments in order to save space. Therefore, someone who uses a dictionary definition in a report must rewrite it to make it into a complete sentence. Look up any two nouns in a dictionary, and write out the definitions given for each. Then, rewrite each definition so that it is not a fragment.

C. Playwrights often have their characters speak in fragments and run-ons, especially in comic or highly emotional situations. Write a short scene from a play in which you have a quiet, introverted character who speaks in brief phrases or fragments and an excitable, extroverted character who runs his or her sentences together, creating run-ons. Then, rewrite the speeches, using only complete sentences. Which treatment is most effective? Why?

CUMULATIVE REVIEW
The Sentence (I)

Kinds of Sentences. The paragraphs below contain simple sentences, compound sentences, complex sentences, and compound-complex sentences. Number your paper from 1 to 10. Next to the number corresponding to each sentence, write either *S*, *CD*, *CX*, or *CD-CX* to identify the type of sentence it is. Also write *INT* next to the number of the interrogative sentence, and *E* next to the number of the exclamatory sentence.

(1) College and professional athletes are learning some moves these days that were unknown to the brawny players of previous seasons. (2) If you attend a training session of the Philadelphia 76ers, for example, you will see more than just jump shots and free throws. (3) John Kilbourne, who is the 76ers' conditioning and flexibility coach, has introduced dance classes as part of the team's regular training, and the program has had remarkable success. (4) In the first year of these classes, the 76ers had their lowest injury record in five years, and the team emerged, at the end of the season, as world champions!

(5) What brought about these dramatic results? (6) Kilbourne explains that dance helps develop balance, rhythm, coordination, flexibility, strength, and endurance. (7) It also helps people to relax and, at least in the case of the 76ers, the unusual exercise builds motivation. (8) As Philadelphia superstar Moses Malone puts it, "When you weigh 255 pounds, anything that helps you move better is important." (9) The Philadelphia management concurs. (10) Other teams may not follow the 76ers' lead for a few years, but sports people in the know will tell you that tap and ballet are here to stay.

CUMULATIVE REVIEW
The Sentence (II)

Correcting Fragments and Run-ons. On your own paper, rewrite the following passage. Correct all sentence fragments and run-on sentences. You may have to change or add a few words.

In 210 B.C., the first emperor of China, Ch'in Shih Huang Ti, was buried under a huge mound of earth called Mount Li. An ancient tomb left undisturbed for over two thousand years. In 1974, farmers digging a well about a mile from this mound made an extraordinary discovery. A life-size warrior made of clay. Since then, excavations have unearthed many more of these warriors, along with life-size horses and chariots of clay, archaeologists believe that they will eventually uncover six thousand figures. A guardian army that was meant to watch over the dead emperor throughout eternity.

Ch'in began construction of his tomb when he first became emperor at age thirteen, seven hundred thousand people worked for thirty-six years on the project. A historian who wrote about 100 B.C. described how these laborers filled the underground tomb with models of palaces, miniature rivers, and oceans. And how they set up crossbows that would kill anyone who tried to enter the tomb.

Excavations of royal tombs from the earlier Shang Dynasty have unearthed the skeletons of real warriors, women, servants, and horses. Who were buried live with kings and high officials. By burying clay warriors to keep him company in the kingdom of the dead. Emperor Ch'in was probably reviving their ancient tradition. This may explain why each of the statues found in Ch'in's tomb has an individual face, each statue was a substitute for an actual living soldier.

5.0 Verb Usage

Verbs may cause more problems in speech and writing than any other part of speech. This is because most verbs have several forms, each of which is used for specific purposes. In order to use verbs correctly, you must be familiar with these forms and the different situations in which they are used.

Most of the several thousand English verbs cause no problems in usage. These are **regular verbs** that follow a specific pattern of change. There are about sixty verbs, however, that change form in irregular ways. These **irregular verbs** will be the focus of most of this Section.

5.1 The Principal Parts of Verbs

All forms of a verb are made from the three **principal parts.** These parts are called the **present infinitive** (or **present**), the **past,** and the **past participle.**

The past and past participle forms of a **regular verb** are formed by adding *-ed* or *-d* to the present infinitive.

PRESENT	PAST	PAST PARTICIPLE
walk	walk*ed*	walk*ed*
look	look*ed*	look*ed*
excuse	excus*ed*	excus*ed*

An **irregular verb** does not follow this pattern to form its past and past participle. Instead, it may follow any of roughly five other patterns.

PRESENT	PAST	PAST PARTICIPLE
hit	hit	hit
bring	brought	brought
choose	chose	chosen
ring	rang	rung
see	saw	seen

The **present participle** of both regular and irregular verbs is formed by adding *-ing* to the present form. The present participle is sometimes considered a fourth principal part.

PRESENT	PRESENT PARTICIPLE
cry	cry*ing*
think	think*ing*
chew	chew*ing*
ask	ask*ing*
tell	tell*ing*

5.2 Irregular Verbs

Because the principal parts of irregular verbs are formed in a variety of ways, it is sometimes difficult to decide on the right form. The rule given below is helpful in making this decision.

The past tense form is used alone. The past participle form is used with forms of *be* or *have*.

Joyce *rang* the front door bell. (past)
Joyce *had rung* the front door bell. (past participle with form of have)

In order to make the right choice of verb form, therefore, you need only become familiar with the past and past participle forms of the most frequently used irregular verbs.

There are five groups of irregular verbs. They are classified by the ways in which they form their principal parts.

Group 1. The easiest of the irregular verbs are those that have the same forms in all principal parts.

PRESENT	PAST	PAST PARTICIPLE
burst	burst	(have) burst
cost	cost	(have) cost
hit	hit	(have) hit
hurt	hurt	(have) hurt
put	put	(have) put
set	set	(have) set
shut	shut	(have) shut

Group 2. A second group is composed of verbs that have the same form for the past and the past participle.

PRESENT	PAST	PAST PARTICIPLE
bring	brought	(have) brought
catch	caught	(have) caught
dive	dived *or* dove*	(have) dived
fight	fought	(have) fought
flee	fled	(have) fled
fling	flung	(have) flung
get	got	(have) got *or* gotten
lead	led	(have) led
lend	lent	(have) lent

PRESENT	PAST	PAST PARTICIPLE
lose	lost	(have) lost
say	said	(have) said
shine	shone	(have) shone
sit	sat	(have) sat
sting	stung	(have) stung
swing	swung	(have) swung

*Where two forms are given, both are standard usage, but the first is more common.

Exercise A: Choose the standard form from those given.

1. The little girl was crying because she (lost, losed) her key.
2. The children all screamed when the balloon (bursted, burst).
3. Several good points were (brought, brung) out in Janet's talk.
4. Dainis Kula (flinged, flang, flung) the javelin over three hundred feet in the 1980 Olympics.
5. The great liner slowly (swang, swung) out into the channel.
6. The street light (shined, shone) into my eyes all night long.
7. Randi thought she had (caught, catched) her cold while skating.
8. The general (led, leaded) his army through the narrow pass.
9. The ointment (stinged, stang, stung) the wound.
10. The state library has (lent, lended) us the books we need.

Exercise B: In the sentences below, the present form of the verb is given in parentheses. Substitute either the past or the past participle.

1. We had (sit) in the bleachers for three hours waiting for the rain to stop.
2. We had plenty of food but no one had (bring) a can opener.
3. By nightfall, everyone had (flee) the flooded town.
4. The guide (lead) us deeper into the cave.
5. Harriet (lend) me her warm coat.
6. I wish I knew how many pens I have (lose) this year.
7. All day long the sun (shine) hot and bright.
8. A man on deck (fling) a rope to the little craft bobbing in the waves below.
9. Suddenly, a dazzling light (shine) in our eyes.
10. After sunbathing on the deck, Ramon (dive) into the cold, refreshing water.

Group 3. Another group of irregular verbs adds ***-n*** or ***-en*** to the past form to make the past participle.

PRESENT	PAST	PAST PARTICIPLE
bear	bore	(have) borne*
beat	beat	(have) beaten
bite	bit	(have) bitten
break	broke	(have) broken
choose	chose	(have) chosen
freeze	froze	(have) frozen
speak	spoke	(have) spoken
steal	stole	(have) stolen
swear	swore	(have) sworn
tear	tore	(have) torn
wear	wore	(have) worn

Exercise A: Choose the standard form from those given.

1. The company (bore, beared) the expense of Gwen's trip.
2. We have already (beaten, beat) the best teams in the league.
3. The drill had (bit, bitten) deep into the rock.
4. As a result of the accident, two windows (broke, broken) in the laboratory.
5. Two students were (chose, chosen) to write the bulletin.
6. The meat had (frozen, froze) solid in the locker.
7. Has anyone (spoke, spoken) to the class adviser about your plans?
8. Joan's purse was (stole, stolen) on the train.
9. Grant had (swore, sworn) never to go back to Millville.
10. Gary (tore, teared) the final draft of his composition as he removed it from the notebook.
11. When the rain started, I was sorry I had (worn, wore) my new shirt to the game.
12. The coach had (borne, bore) an extra burden all year long.
13. The beach (beared, bore) evidence of a great storm at sea.

*Note that *borne* retains the final *e*.

14. My friends were badly (beaten, beat) in the second round of the tournament.
15. Our mail carrier was (bitten, bit) by a stray dog this morning.
16. The high jump record was (broke, broken) again last winter.
17. Mary, you couldn't have (chose, chosen) a more difficult topic.
18. The pond (froze, frozen) early in November.
19. The wind had (tore, torn) the election posters down.
20. The band hasn't (worn, wore) its new uniforms yet.

Exercise B: The present form of the verb is given. Substitute past or past participle, whichever the sentence requires.

1. By that time, we had (wear) out our welcome.
2. Helen had never (speak) before about losing the election.
3. During the night, the boys (steal) quietly out of camp.
4. The jury was immediately (swear) in.
5. The vegetables are (freeze) soon after they are picked.
6. Terri (choose) A *Separate Peace* for her report.
7. The radio reports that the dam has (break).
8. Sue (bite) into some stale candy.
9. Ms. Williams has never (break) her promise to us.
10. In the first inning, Rob had (beat) out a bunt.
11. The plane (bear) an unusually heavy load of gasoline.
12. Ricardo (tear) the wrapping paper off the package.
13. The coffee pot handle has been (break) for three months.
14. The witness (swear) she had been nowhere near the fire.
15. By morning, the windows were (freeze) shut.
16. Mr. Jennings reported that someone had (steal) his lawnmower.
17. A huge gash had been (tear) in the ship's bow.
18. The enemy attack was easily (beat) off.
19. The first night, we were (bite) by mosquitoes the size of crows.
20. Has anyone (speak) to you about paying your class dues?

Group 4. Seven verbs in English change an ***i*** in the present form to an ***a*** in the past and to a ***u*** in the past participle. Study these seven verbs as a group. They are the only verbs that follow this pattern.

PRESENT	PAST	PAST PARTICIPLE
begin	began	(have) begun
drink	drank	(have) drunk
ring	rang	(have) rung
sing	sang	(have) sung
sink	sank *or* sunk	(have) sunk
spring	sprang *or* sprung	(have) sprung
swim	swam	(have) swum

Exercise A: Choose the standard form from the two given.

1. The guests had (drank, drunk) a whole case of ginger ale.
2. All over the nation, bells were (rung, rang) in celebration.
3. The choir (sung, sang) very well this morning.
4. A Spanish galleon loaded with treasure had once (sunk, sank) off this shore.
5. The diver had (sprung, sprang) high above the pool.
6. The excavation for the new hotel was (began, begun) last month.
7. Tom (drank, drunk) the cocoa while it was too hot.
8. Has anyone (rang, rung) for the elevator yet?
9. Ellen felt that she could have (swam, swum) for hours.
10. The girls knew that they ought to have (sang, sung) better.

Exercise B: The present form is given in parentheses. Substitute the past or past participle, whichever the sentence requires.

1. Suddenly, everyone (begin) to laugh.
2. Have you (drink) this new kind of cola?
3. Has anyone (ring) the Liberty Bell in the last hundred years?
4. The boys' chorus (sing) an old hunting song.
5. We arrived in the morning and (swim) all afternoon.

6. The trap was (spring) on Friday night.
7. Ruth had (swim) out to the raft.
8. At last the replies (begin) to come in.
9. Dick (drink) the lemonade in one gulp and dashed off.
10. The church bells were (ring) for half an hour to announce the armistice.
11. Angela had never (swim) the backstroke in a race before.
12. A deep crater was (sink) into the side of the mountain by the meteorite.
13. Something had (spring) out of the bushes.
14. Fred had (sing) so much that he was hoarse.
15. In the fall, business had (begin) to get better.

Group 5. Another group of irregular verbs forms the past participle from the present form rather than from the past form.

PRESENT	PAST	PAST PARTICIPLE
blow	blew	(have) blown
come	came	(have) come
do	did	(have) done
draw	drew	(have) drawn
drive	drove	(have) driven
eat	ate	(have) eaten
fall	fell	(have) fallen
give	gave	(have) given
go	went	(have) gone
grow	grew	(have) grown
know	knew	(have) known
ride	rode	(have) ridden
rise	rose	(have) risen
run	ran	(have) run
see	saw	(have) seen
shake	shook	(have) shaken
slay	slew	(have) slain
take	took	(have) taken
throw	threw	(have) thrown
write	wrote	(have) written

Exercise A: Choose the standard form from those given.

1. The wind (blew, blowed) the roof off the house.
2. The flood waters (came, come) right up to our front door.
3. No one could have (did, done) more to help us.
4. The sheriff (drawed, drew) his gun faster than anyone else.
5. Alice and Bob had (drove, driven) all night to get home.
6. Hank finally admitted that he had (ate, eaten) too much.
7. Several of the decorations had (fell, fallen) down.
8. The Burton family (give, gave) the church a new bell.
9. By the time we arrived, everyone else had (went, gone).
10. These flowers were (growed, grew, grown) from seed.
11. Someone must have (knew, known) we were coming.
12. Andy had never (rid, rode, ridden) on a camel before.
13. The pumps (run, ran) all night to keep the ship afloat.
14. Tony was badly (shook, shaken) by his failure to win.
15. The entire garrison was (slew, slayed, slain) by the enemy.
16. The doctor's bag had been (took, taken) by mistake.
17. The catcher (throwed, threw) the ball into center field.
18. *The Heart Is a Lonely Hunter* was (wrote, written) by Carson McCullers.
19. A secret message had been (wrote, written) on the back of the stamp.
20. The children had (throwed, threw, thrown) papers all over.

Exercise B: The present form is given in parentheses. Substitute the past or past participle, whichever the sentence requires.

1. The hurricane had (blow) the roofs off houses.
2. Nobody knows why Jenkins (come) to our town.
3. The professor had (do) everything she could for us.
4. The trucks were (draw) up in a neat row.
5. Ms. Case (drive) the school bus last year.
6. Have you ever (eat) pineapple ripened in the field?
7. The price of chocolate bars has (rise) again.
8. Dr. Gray (give) the school a collection of books.
9. Everything has (go) wrong today.

10. The huge tree had (grow) right around the rock.
11. The students all (know) what was coming next.
12. The plane (ride) the jet stream across the Atlantic.
13. Bob (run) all the way home to tell us the good news.
14. The storm had (shake) much of the fruit off the trees.
15. Two of the guards were (slay) during the night.

5.3 The Progressive and Emphatic Forms of Verbs

The Progressive Forms

The **progressive forms** of verbs show ongoing action. To make the progressive form, add a form of the verb *be* to the present participle.

We *are staying.*
He *is working.*
The boys *were laughing.*
No one *will be leaving.*
Jayne *has been studying.*
The band *had been practicing.*
We *must be leaving.*
They *might have been waiting.*

The Emphatic Forms

Special emphasis can be given to a statement by using *do, does,* or *did* with the present form of the verb. These are examples of **emphatic forms.**

I *did hear* you talking.
We *do appreciate* your help.
Jean *does look* angry.

PRESENT: I *like* your cooking.
PRESENT EMPHATIC: I *do like* your cooking.

PAST: I *thought* about your offer.
PAST EMPHATIC: I *did think* about your offer.

Exercise A: Find each verb. Decide whether it is in the progressive or emphatic form.

1. Where are you going for spring vacation?
2. Rhonda is having second thoughts about going to gymnastics camp.
3. I do think about you often.
4. The porpoise was bouncing the ball out in the ocean.
5. Allan has been studying Hebrew for ten years.
6. We did try to find the owner before bringing the dog to the animal shelter.
7. The suspect had been loitering around the bank.
8. You did finally remember your lines.
9. Alicia will be dancing in Sunday's recital.
10. Were Jake and Dan laughing about their argument?

Exercise B: Writing Rewrite each sentence, changing the italicized verb to the form indicated in parentheses.

1. Although his works may not live as literature, Erle Stanley Gardner *wrote* as many as 10,000 words per day. (emphatic)
2. The tour guide *told* the travelers about the ancient city of Jericho. (progressive)
3. According to one theory the universe *expands* constantly. (progressive)
4. I *think* that Americans should travel in America as well as abroad. (emphatic)
5. According to anthropologists' estimates, the age of humankind *gets* older all the time. (progressive)
6. Marcus *said* he would play in the concert. (emphatic)
7. A special group *investigates* unsolved crimes with the help of psychics. (progressive)
8. Victor Hugo *wrote* his first novel in 1823. (emphatic)
9. The dodobird actually *existed* at one time on the island of Mauritius. (emphatic)
10. Scientists *will find* even more uses for the laser in the future. (progressive)

5.4 Verb Tense

The word **tense** means "time." Most verbs change their forms to tell present, past, and future time. There are three simple tenses (present, past, and future) and three perfect tenses (present perfect, past perfect, and future perfect) for each verb.

1. Present tense. The present tense is formed from the present or simple form of the verb.

The present forms of verbs usually tell of a condition that exists at the present moment.

The packages *are* in the garage. (right now)
The milk *smells* sour. (at this moment)

The simple or present forms of verbs, however, are not usually used to tell of actions that are going on at the moment. We do not say, "I read." We are more likely to use the **progressive form** "I am reading," or the **emphatic form** "I do read." An exception is in the description of ongoing sports events:

Jackson *fumbles* the ball and Central *recovers*.

The present forms of verbs are also used to tell of repeated or regular and habitual action.

We *go* to the lake every summer.
Dale *sings* in the choir on Wednesday evenings.
The store *closes* at seven o'clock.

The present forms of verbs are also used to tell of something that is generally true or true at all times.

All living things *need* oxygen.
The Greeks did not know that the earth *circles* the sun.

The **historical present tense** tells of some action or condition in the past as though it were occurring in the present.

The doctor *picks* up the key and *opens* the safe while Sherlock Holmes *watches* intently.

2. Past tense. Past time is usually told by the past tense, which is the second principal part of the verb: *We talked, they ran, nobody stirred.* Continuing past action is shown by the **past progressive:** We *were having* a good time.

3. Future tense. Future time is shown by using *shall* or *will* with the present form of the verb: *We shall go, you will hear.*

Future time may be shown by the present tense together with an adverb or phrase that tells time. Future time may also be shown by the use of a form of *be* with *going to*.

> We *see* the science films *tomorrow.* (*tomorrow* is an adverb telling time.)
> We *have* the wind with us *from now on.* (*from now on* is an adverb phrase telling time.)
> I *am going to* leave for New Orleans in December.

4. Present perfect tense. The present perfect tense is formed by using *has* or *have* with the past participle (third principal part) of the verb. This tense is used to refer to some indefinite time in the past.

> We *have heard* this story many times.
> Alice *has* already *seen* the picture.

The present perfect is also used to show action that began in the past and continues into the present.

> We *have lived* here for six years. (We still live here.)
> We *have been walking* all day. (present perfect progressive)

5. Past perfect tense. The past perfect tense is formed by using *had* with the past participle (third principal part) of the verb. The past perfect tense tells of an action completed in the past before some other action.

EARLIER	LATER
We *had finished* the job	before Dad *came* home.
Ellen *had been* happy	until that letter *arrived.*
We *had been waiting* an hour	before the doctor *came.*

6. Future perfect tense. The future perfect tense is formed by using *will have* or *shall have* with the past participle of the verb (third principal part). This tense is used to tell of one action completed in the future *before* some other action in the future.

Before autumn *is* over, we *will have raked* thousands of leaves.
Before the doors *close,* the exhibit *will have had* three hundred visitors.
By the time the sun *sets,* we *will have driven* three hundred miles.

Note: In the examples above, the verb in the present tense indicates far future action. The second verb, in future perfect tense, indicates future action that will occur *before* the action of the first verb.

A conjugation is a list of the forms of a verb. Verbs are usually conjugated in the order given here.

Conjugation of *Walk*

Principal Parts:
walk, walked, walked

Present Participle:
walking

Present Infinitive:
to walk

Perfect Infinitive:
to have walked

Present Tense

FIRST PERSON:	I walk	we walk
SECOND PERSON:	you walk	you walk
THIRD PERSON:	he, she, it walks	they walk

Present Progressive: I am walking, you are walking, etc.
Present Emphatic: I do walk, you do walk, he does walk, etc.

Past Tense

FIRST PERSON:	I walked	we walked
SECOND PERSON:	you walked	you walked
THIRD PERSON:	he, she, it walked	they walked

Past Progressive: I was walking, you were walking, etc.
Past Emphatic: I did walk, you did walk, etc.

Future Tense

FIRST PERSON:	I shall (will) walk	we shall (will) walk
SECOND PERSON:	you will walk	you will walk
THIRD PERSON:	he, she, it will walk	they will walk

Future Progressive: I shall be walking, you will be walking, etc.

Present Perfect Tense

FIRST PERSON:	I have walked	we have walked
SECOND PERSON:	you have walked	you have walked
THIRD PERSON:	he, she, it has walked	they have walked

Present Perfect Progressive: I have been walking, you have been walking, he has been walking, etc.

Past Perfect Tense

FIRST PERSON:	I had walked	we had walked
SECOND PERSON:	you had walked	you had walked
THIRD PERSON:	he, she, it had walked	they had walked

Past Perfect Progressive: I had been walking, you had been walking, he had been walking, etc.

Future Perfect Tense

FIRST PERSON:	I shall have walked	we shall have walked
SECOND PERSON:	you will have walked	you will have walked
THIRD PERSON:	he, she, it will have walked	they will have walked

Future Perfect Progressive: I shall have been walking, etc.

Exercise A: Find each verb and tell its tense.

1. Frankly, I doubt Joe's story.
2. Jess tore his jeans on the wire fence.
3. Mickey Rooney has had a lifelong career.
4. There in the nest were two young robins.
5. I have never tasted mango ice cream before.
6. They will probably deny the whole story.
7. The acrobat swung herself deftly over the bar.
8. Will you have eaten by that time?
9. Heather's first bicycle is still in the garage.
10. The trainer said that I had torn a ligament.

Exercise B: Writing Identify the tense of each verb. Then rewrite each sentence with at least one verb in the tense given.

1. The phone rang after I dozed off. (past perfect)
2. Tomorrow is my parents' anniversary. (future perfect)
3. Rafael was hired because of his Spanish. (past perfect)
4. The storekeeper was surprised as young Abe Lincoln walked in the door. (historical present)
5. Niagara Falls receded a quarter of a mile. (present perfect)
6. General Bradley will send reinforcements. (past)
7. I went to the coast of Maine every summer. (present)
8. Women have taken an important role in many areas. (future)
9. Food will be scarce because people will hoard it. (present)
10. *Drama* has come from a Greek word meaning *to do*. (past)

5.5 Voice and Mood

You have seen that verbs can be used in a variety of tenses to establish a time frame for the sentence. Verbs can also be used in the progressive form and the emphatic form to help convey the writer's exact meaning. In addition to these frequently used verb forms, there are other, more subtle forms that verbs can take to achieve special purposes.

The Active and the Passive Voice

When the subject *performs* the action expressed in the verb, the verb is in the **active voice.** When the subject *receives* the action of the verb, the verb is in the **passive voice.** The passive voice is formed by using some form of *be* with the past participle of the verb.

ACTIVE: Don *swept* the *floor* clean.
PASSIVE: The floor *was swept* clean.

ACTIVE: Someone *calls* the plays.
PASSIVE: The plays *are being called*.

The object in the active form becomes the subject in the passive form. A transitive verb can be put into the passive voice because it has an object.

An intransitive verb cannot be in the passive voice because it has no object. There is no word to become the subject.

The chairperson *introduced* the speakers. (active)
The speakers *were introduced* by the chairperson. (passive)

The president *promoted* Karen. (active)
Karen *was promoted* by the president. (passive)

The active voice is often livelier and more forceful than the passive voice. It also makes clear who is responsible for the action in the sentence.

PASSIVE: The window was broken. (Who did it?)
ACTIVE: Edith broke the window. (The *doer* is clear.)

Most writers prefer to use the livelier active voice whenever possible. Writers also avoid mixing the passive and active voices in the same sentence or passage.

Exercise A: Find each verb. Tell whether it is active or passive.

1. The town was heavily bombarded by the enemy.
2. At dawn the enemy attacked the town.
3. You will certainly be invited to the party.
4. Ted has already been driven home.
5. This lesson will not be forgotten.
6. The injured man was carefully laid on a stretcher.
7. America's relations with Taiwan have changed.
8. His actions were carefully observed by the FBI.
9. Candace is still writing thank-you notes.
10. The leader of the union will probably seek a compromise.

Exercise B: Writing Change the active verbs to passive. Change the passive verbs to active. You may have to add words.

1. The *Daily News* bought the pictures.
2. The team was given a pep talk by the coach.
3. Talks were delivered by representatives of India, West Germany, and Australia.
4. Patrice had been appointed chairperson by the president of the student council.
5. The wind blew the homecoming decorations all over the field.
6. The announcement was made by the principal that United Nations Week would be observed by the school.
7. A very old man rang the church bells every Christmas.
8. Our soccer team beat last year's champions with a last-second goal.
9. Police released a description of the suspect.
10. The loud thunder awakened me from a deep sleep.

Mood

The mood of a verb is used to show the writer's attitude about the reality of what is being stated. The **indicative mood,** which we use most of the time, indicates that we are talking or writing about a fact. That is, we are speaking of something that has happened in the past, is happening now, or definitely will happen in the future.

The dog *ran* across the street.
The light show at the planetarium *is* spectacular.
Will you *try* out for the basketball team this year?

The **imperative mood** is used to express a command, a directive, or a request. The imperative mood has only one tense—the present. It has only one person—the second.

Keep your hands off the door. *Help* me.
Take the first turn to the left. *Move* quickly.

The **subjunctive mood** is used to express a wish, a command, or a condition that is doubtful or contrary to fact. The forms of the subjunctive mood are like those of the indicative mood except in the third person singular of the present tense where the *s* ending is omitted.

INDICATIVE: He *takes* every precaution.
SUBJUNCTIVE: We insist that he *take* every precaution.

The subjunctive form of the verb *be* is a special case. With this verb, the form in the present tense for all persons and numbers is *be*.

Bob moved that the meeting *be* adjourned.
If this *be* a dream, don't wake me.

The past subjunctive form of the verb *to be* is *were*.

I wish I *were* going to the party.
If Jean *were* playing, we would have a better chance.
I wish Michael *were* the president.

The primary uses of the subjunctive are given below.

1. *Were* and *be* are often used instead of other forms of *to be:*
   a. To express wishes

      I wish I *were* a dancer.

   b. To express conditions that are doubtful or contrary to fact after *if, as though,* and *although*

      If I *were* John, I would get out of town fast.

2. *Were, be,* and the third person subjunctive forms of other verbs are often used:
   a. To express commands or requests after *that*

      The general commanded that each soldier *receive* an extra day's rations.
      She requests that Mary *do* the dishes.

   b. In certain isolated, ancient phrases:

      Come the harvest . . .
      Be that as it *may* . . .
      Do what you *will* . . .
      Heaven *prevent* . . .

Exercise: Tell whether each italicized verb is in the indicative, subjunctive, or imperative mood.

1. *Get* out of the car fast.
2. Elaine *has been* my best friend for three years.
3. The chilled hikers *warmed* their hands near the fire.
4. It is necessary that Ralph *take* this medicine twice a day.
5. Please *leave* your papers on the desk.
6. The time this project takes will prove well spent, *be* it two months or two years.
7. Mars is the planet that *is* physically most like Earth.
8. If I *were* you, I would get that overdue book back to the library.

9. I *wrapped* the present in old comic strips.
10. *Remove* your boots before you come into the house.
11. *Peel* the potatoes and cut them into cubes.
12. Alan always talks as if he *were* the smartest person in the entire world.
13. We *go* to my grandparents' house every Thanksgiving.
14. My parents insist that I *be* home by 10 o'clock on school nights.
15. Juan, *locate* the equator on the globe.

5.6 Commonly Confused Verbs

There are three pairs of verbs that are often confused. Not only do they look alike, but their meanings are similar. To use these verbs correctly, it is important to know the correct meaning and principal parts of each verb.

***Lie* and *lay*.** The verb *lay* means "to put or place something." The verb *lie* has many meanings, all of them having in common the idea of "being in a horizontal position, or to remain, or to be situated."*

Lie is always an intransitive verb. It never has an object. *Lay* is a transitive verb. It almost always has an object. The principal parts of these verbs are as follows:

PRESENT	PAST	PAST PARTICIPLE
lay	laid	(have) laid
lie	lay	(have) lain

Lay the diagrams on the table.
I *laid* the plans there for Ms. Weber to see.
Jean *had laid* the gloves on the heater.

If you're feeling ill, *lie* down on the couch.
The cat *lay* in a sunny area.
Greg *should have lain* down sooner.

*There is a homonym meaning "to tell an untruth." The principal parts of this verb are *lie, lied, lied*.

***Sit* and *set*.** The verb *sit* usually means "to rest with the legs bent and the back upright," but there are many other related meanings. The verb *set* means "to put or place something."

Sit is an intransitive verb; it never has an object. *Set* is a transitive verb; it almost always has an object. The principal parts of the verbs are as follows:

PRESENT	PAST	PAST PARTICIPLE
sit	sat	(have) set
set	set	(have) set

Don't *sit* on that antique chair.
Harriet *set* the crate on the floor.

***Rise* and *raise*.** The verb *rise* means "to go to a higher position." The verb *raise* means "to lift to a higher position."

Rise is intransitive; it never has an object. *Raise* is transitive; it always has an object. Things *rise* by themselves; they are *raised* by something else. The principal parts of these verbs are as follows:

PRESENT	PAST	PAST PARTICIPLE
rise	rose	(have) risen
raise	raised	(have) raised

The magician made his assistant *rise* into the air.
She *rose* as if weightless.
After she *had risen* several feet, he brought her down.

It is not difficult to *raise* plants.
I *raised* my flowers from seed.
Have you *raised* any?

Note: The rules of usage for the English language are full of exceptions. Here are some exceptions to the rules concerning the confusing verb pairs:

Then hens are *laying* well. (intransitive)
The sun *sets*. (intransitive)
The mixture will *set* in an hour. (intransitive)

Exercise A: Choose the standard form from those given.

1. Our books (lay, laid) where we had left them.
2. Tim had (lain, laid) down for a nap.
3. No one ever (lay, laid) eyes on him again.
4. You may (lie, lay) your coats on the bed.
5. Last week we (lay, laid) the cornerstone for the school.
6. The animals were (lying, laying) comfortably in the shade.
7. Betsy told the dog to (lie, lay) down.
8. This factory has (lain, laid) idle for six months.
9. Carl and his father were (lying, laying) a new floor.
10. The wagon wheel had (lain, laid) beside the trail for years.
11. Your book was (lying, laying) in the middle of the hall.
12. The blame for the confusion has been (lain, laid) on Andy.
13. When we returned the following year, the tools were still (lying, laying) under the bushes.
14. Why don't you (lie, lay) down for a few minutes?
15. The ambush party (lay, lied) noiselessly among the rocks.
16. The plans had been (lain, laid) carefully.
17. Judy (lain, laid) her books on the counter.
18. Phil's coat was (lying, laying) on the floor.
19. Helen (lay, laid) the letters beside her purse.
20. The keys were (lying, laying) on the kitchen table.

Exercise B: Choose the standard form from those given.

1. Please (sit, set) the table for dinner.
2. May I (sit, set) down next to you?
3. Now that spring is here, the sun will (sit, set) later.
4. While (sitting, setting) in the armchair, Henry fell asleep.
5. Karen (sat, set) her suitcases on the conveyor belt.
6. Please (sit, set) aside a half hour to discuss your art project.
7. (Sit, Set) still so the dentist can examine you.
8. Mr. Randolph (sits, sets) on the New York stock exchange.
9. Yvonne has (sat, set) the gift on Ms. Cougut's desk.
10. Eight plants (sit, set) on the window sills in the kitchen.
11. Let's (sit, set) up the booths before we go home.

12. Before Jackson (sat, set) down, he poured the orange juice.
13. Fred and Claire have (set, setted) the date for their wedding.
14. We (sat, set) the huge package down carefully.
15. My friends (sat, set) in the front row of the bleachers.
16. (Sitting, Setting) in the car for so long made me sleepy.
17. The campers (sat, set) a pot of water on the fire.
18. Parents are invited to (sit, set) in on any of our classes.
19. The counselor helps the seniors (sit, set) their career goals.
20. When Tina returned, six people were (sitting, setting) in her Volkswagen.

Exercise C: Choose the standard form from those given.

1. The outlying provinces had (risen, raised) in revolt.
2. Immediately, the merchants (rose, raised) their prices.
3. A storm of protest (rose, raised) against the new taxes.
4. Sally had (risen, raised) the window noisily.
5. Suddenly, balloons were (rising, raising) all around us.
6. In the spring, the river (rose, raised) above its banks.
7. The curtain was (rising, raising) as we got to our seats.
8. For many years, fine crops have been (risen, raised) here.
9. The spectators (rose, raised) when the judge entered.
10. Costs of production have continued to (rise, raise).
11. We had not intended to (rise, raise) such a commotion.
12. The sun is (rising, raising) earlier each day now.
13. Beth was hesitant to (rise, raise) her voice.
14. A strange odor seemed to (rise, raise) from the old trunk.
15. From the audience there (rose, raised) a mighty cheer.
16. A thin column of smoke was (rising, raising) in the hills.
17. Every morning when the sun came up, the campers (rose, raised) the flag.
18. Uncle Harry has (risen, raised) by six o'clock every morning for over forty years.
19. Mr. DiAngelo (rises, raises) prize-winning marigolds.
20. To signal the musicians, the conductor (rose, raised) her arms.

REINFORCEMENT EXERCISES

Verb Usage

A. Use past and past participle forms correctly. In the following sentences, the present form of the verb is given in parentheses. Substitute either the past or the past participle, as necessary.

1. Our little boat had (spring) a leak in the middle of Glenmere Lake.
2. The crime novelist, H. R. F. Keating, (sit) at his desk for the photograph.
3. For hundreds of years, Scots and Saxons (slay) one another on the battlefield.
4. Have you (break) your New Year's resolution yet?
5. You should have (put) the cat out before bedtime.
6. Harold Baines (dive) for the line drive.
7. The damp sheet had (freeze) solid as it hung on the line.
8. During the Middle Ages, small kingdoms (spring) up all over Europe.
9. Suzanne should not have (drink) so much lemonade.
10. The young jockey had (ride) only in European races.
11. The children were fascinated by the stingray they (see).
12. The custodian had (set) the temperature control too high.
13. Chuck knew he had (lose) the race when another runner breezed by him.
14. Mike McKool (speak) in the Texas State Senate for over forty-two hours in 1972.
15. Janet (tear) up her first poem and started over.
16. Alex has not (choose) his courses for next year yet.
17. Is it true that Sherlock Holmes once solved a case by noticing how far the parsley had (sink) into the butter?
18. Pioneers (drive) horses and oxen across the plains and mountains.
19. The editor could not believe that his prize-winning reporter had (write) such a poorly-researched piece.
20. Aviva had scarcely (begin) to wax her car when it began to rain.

B. Use the progressive and emphatic forms of verbs. Rewrite each sentence, changing the italicized verb to the form indicated in parentheses.

1. Although Uncle Ted is now in good health, he *suffered* a heart attack. (emphatic)
2. The lawyer argued that the Bill of Rights *guaranteed* such a freedom. (emphatic)
3. Watch the high jumper: he *does* the Fosbury Flop. (progressive)
4. The man in the green-tinted glasses *reads* science fiction. (progressive)
5. The biography of Georgia O'Keeffe *included* several photographs, didn't it? (emphatic)
6. As part of her costume, the actress *wore* an Egyptian snake bracelet. (progressive)
7. The jeweler *ground* the diamond chips into a fine powder. (progressive)
8. Our host *said* there are ghosts in this house, didn't he? (emphatic)
9. The Prime Minister announced that Canada *has* an abundance of wheat. (emphatic)
10. Ursula le Guin *speaks* about the idea of the fourth dimension. (progressive)

C. Identify verb tenses. Find each verb and tell its tense.

1. Several porpoises were dancing in the bay.
2. One of the bookcases is leaning perilously.
3. Tracy will have completed his part in the exchange program by July.
4. Shortly before his death, President Grant had been working on his memoirs.
5. By June, the track team will have run hundreds of miles.
6. Clouds of dust rose from the gravel road.
7. Unlike blackberries, dewberries trail along the ground.
8. The group has finished its album ahead of schedule.
9. The Senior Choir will be performing in the shopping center.
10. Our cat had raided the kitchen cabinets.

D. Use active verbs. Rewrite each sentence in the active voice.

1. Those wonderful ice sculptures were created by the art students for the school's Winter Festival.
2. Copper was first used about ten thousand years ago.
3. *Charlie and the Chocolate Factory* was published by Alfred A. Knopf.
4. Achilles' heel was pierced by an arrow.
5. Those valleys were carved out by a glacier.
6. The storm center was drawn in the wrong place on the map by the new weatherperson.
7. Candlefish were dried and burned by West Coast Indians to produce light.
8. Montreal is identified by almanacs as the world's second largest French-speaking city.
9. *Ballad of a Sad Cafe* was written by Carson McCullers.
10. Periodically, the animals in the park are tested for rabies by officials from the Department of Natural Resources.

E. Use commonly confused verbs correctly. Choose the correct verb form from those given in parentheses.

1. By the time the guests arrive, you should be (sitting, setting) the bowls of snacks out.
2. A new floor has been (lain, laid) in the gymnasium.
3. Through the spyglass, the captain saw that the pirates were (raising, rising) the skull and crossbones.
4. Mr. Wicklow (sit, set) out his petunias too early.
5. The organizers of the race (rose, raised) the entrance fee.
6. The baby (set, sat) in the highchair to eat its meal.
7. Every night the Egyptian pharoah would (lie, lay) down to sleep on a bed of gold.
8. There was a small indentation on the pillow where the cat had (lain, laid) in the sunlight.
9. Chief Joseph instructed his followers to (lay, lie) down their weapons.
10. Even before she awoke, she sensed that the wind had (risen, raised).

MIXED REVIEW

Verb Usage

A. In the sentences below, the present form of the verb is given in parentheses. Substitute the past or the past participle to fit the meaning of the sentence.

1. The king and queen could have (bear) anything but the knight's treachery.
2. The horseshoe twirled around the post and (sink) into the clay.
3. Rina (speak) about the need to volunteer some time to community groups.
4. Because we live in Minnesota, we have (see) more lakes than our cousins who live in Arizona.
5. The tense patient accidentally (bite) the dentist.
6. The insurance company replaced the car because it would have (cost) more to repair than to replace.
7. As part of his daily duties, the cleric (ring) the church bells.
8. Steve had (write) his report, but Richard had not even started his research.
9. Raoul (catch) the ball and tagged the runner as he slid toward second base.
10. The restless parrot had (tear) up all the newspapers.

B. Choose the standard form from those in parentheses.

1. Dad says the doctor's bill (hurt, hurted) more than the broken arm.
2. A hose in the car's engine (burst, bursted).
3. The helicopter (rose, raised) from the clearing and hung suspended in the air above the trees.
4. The ground will be (froze, frozen) until springtime.
5. The mechanic (rose, raised) the car on a hydraulic lift.
6. Only a team with a superior defense could have (beat, beaten) us.

7. Someone has (broke, broken) the computer's access code.
8. Have you ever (drank, drunk) well water?
9. The curator carefully (sat, set) the fragile statue on its pedestal.
10. Yolanda (sat, set) in the career center, reading pamphlets.
11. Camilla had never (rode, ridden) the waves on a surfboard.
12. Few students (knowed, knew) of the secret entrance.
13. A bottle of sulfuric acid had (fell, fallen) in the lab.
14. Gus (lay, laid) money on the counter.
15. Regina (lay, laid) on the wooden raft in the pond.
16. Working is more profitable than (lying, laying) around all summer.
17. Two cameras had (began, begun) shooting the scene.
18. Ian and Sylvia were two Canadian performers who (sang, sung) songs of life in the North Country.
19. Survivors (fleed, fled) the site of the earthquake.
20. Katy (flinged, flung) her jacket into her locker.

C. Some of the following sentences contain errors in verb usage. Rewrite these sentences, correcting any errors. If a sentence does not contain any errors, write *Correct*.

1. Susan asked the movers to set the piano in the den.
2. The hills raised before the weary travelers like mountains.
3. Felicia was gave a farewell party by her friends.
4. Mark had swum in high school, in college, and in international competition.
5. Tourists flung coins into the fountain for good luck.
6. The stage crew lay the huge amplifier on its side.
7. One of the keepers noticed that a lock on the lion's cage had been broke.
8. The Congresswoman wondered whether she should have ran for the Presidency.
9. The first snowfall of winter lay upon the tiny New England town.
10. The playwright and the two stars have knowed one another for years.

USING GRAMMAR IN WRITING

Verb Usage

A. One way to make writing more interesting and lively is to avoid overuse of common verbs. For example, any of the following verbs could be used in place of the verb *to say: declare, state, aver, affirm, allege, insist, recite, quote, babble, utter, whisper, pronounce, cry, exclaim, shout, chatter,* or *gossip*. Make a similar list of more precise synonyms for the verb *to walk*. Then write a brief essay on the subject of the body language of walking. In your essay, use verbs to describe different kinds of walking, and explain what personality traits are revealed by the way in which a person walks.

B. Assume that you have been asked by your principal to speak to a group of incoming freshmen about extracurricular activities. Briefly describe the activities and past accomplishments of several clubs and teams at your school. Then, explain what students will gain from membership in these organizations. Use the past, present, and future tense of verbs.

C. The impact of a piece of writing often depends on the writer's use of verbs. Precise, vivid words used in the active voice make a better impression than general verbs used passively.

To improve your skill in using verbs, imagine a very dull scene such as a person watching television or eating dinner, or a group of people riding an elevator or escalator. Using strong verbs, make the scene as fascinating as possible. You may want to use exciting modifers as well. You may find that the result of this exercise is a humorous piece, or one that sets a mood of tension or fear. You may even intentionally try to achieve such an effect.

CUMULATIVE REVIEW
The Sentence (III)

Writing Good Sentences. Rewrite each sentence on your own paper. Follow the directions given in parentheses.

1. We would like two hamburgers with onions, and my other friend would like a salad. (Change to a simple sentence with a compound direct object.)
2. The slow movement of the concerto was played much too quickly by the harpsichordist. (Change the passive verb to an active verb.)
3. Ms. Martin called to ask whether you have returned the books. (Add a clause beginning with *that*.)
4. My favorite video was being shown on two different television stations at the same time. (Add an appositive phrase.)
5. Martin sang along with the chorus. (Add a subordinate clause beginning with *while*.)
6. The dinosaurs disappeared suddenly sixty-five million years ago. An asteroid struck the earth and caused massive extinction of plant life. (Change to one complex sentence.)
7. The district attorney granted immunity from prosecution to the defendant. (Change this NVN sentence to one with a NVNN pattern.)
8. The old lion stretched out under a juniper tree. (Add a participal phrase.)
9. Lucille raised enough money to purchase a painting. (Add a prepositional phrase.)
10. The new highway was supposed to be finished this year. It probably will not be finished. The state has used all the money in its highway renovation fund. (Change to one compound-complex sentence by using the coordinating conjunction *but* and the subordinating conjunction *because*.)

6.0 Agreement of Subject and Verb

If the subject of a sentence is singular, the verb must also be singular. If the subject is plural, the verb must be plural. In grammar, this correspondence of parts is called *agreement*.

When people speak, they sometimes fail to make the subject and verb agree *(he don't, we was, you was)*. Agreement errors are easier to avoid in writing. They can be found and corrected during revision.

6.1 Subject-Verb Agreement in Number

There are two numbers in grammar: **singular** and **plural.** A word is singular in number if it refers to one person or thing. A word is plural if it refers to more than one person or thing.

Regular verbs and most irregular verbs change form to show singular or plural only in the third person, present tense. For these verbs, the third person singular present form ends in *s*.

I, you, we, they — walk

he, she, it — walks

A singular verb is used with a singular subject.

A plural verb is used with a plural subject.

The subject determines whether the verb is singular or plural. The verb does not agree with any other part of the sentence.

The lock (singular) *opens* easily.
The locks (plural) *open* easily.

The program (singular) *is* lively.
The programs (plural) *are* lively.

The verb *be* presents a special problem in agreement. It changes form in the third person to show singular and plural in the past as well as the present. This verb also changes form in the first person, present and past, to show singular or plural.

Present Tense		Past Tense	
SINGULAR	PLURAL	SINGULAR	PLURAL
I *am*	we *are*	I *was*	we *were*
you *are*	you *are*	you *were*	you *were*
he, she, it *is*	they *are*	he, she, it *was*	they *were*

Common errors with *be* are *you was, we was, they was*.

6.2 Words Between Subject and Verb

A verb agrees only with its subject. Sometimes a word or several words may separate the subject and the verb. These words have no effect upon the agreement of the subject and verb.

The *truck*, loaded with boxes of apples, *is* in the ditch.
(*truck* is the subject.)
One of the pictures *shows* our camp.
(*One* is the subject.)
The old *maps* of the country *show* the coastlines accurately.
(*maps* is the subject.)

The words *with, together with, along with, as well as* are prepositions. The objects of these prepositions have no effect upon the number of the verb.

> The *doctor*, together with the nurses, *was working* feverishly.
> (*doctor* is the subject.)
>
> Your *voice,* as well as your clothes, *gives* a pleasing impression.
> (*voice* is the subject.)
>
> The *President,* along with his cabinet, *makes* the final decision.
> (*President* is the subject.)

Exercise: Choose the standard form of the verb.

1. If you (was, were) at the meeting, why didn't you speak up?
2. We know that one of the men in the mine (was, were) injured.
3. (Has, Have) the package of tools been found?
4. Mr. Murphy, as well as the other members of the club, (regrets, regret) your leaving.
5. The state income tax, in addition to real estate taxes, (helps, help) pay for the cost of schools.
6. The leaders of this community-improvement project (needs, need) your assistance.
7. The cost of many of these proposals (is, are) too great.
8. The decision of the manager, backed by the directors, (stands, stand).
9. The streets in this old American community (was, were) very narrow.
10. Do you know whether the sale of tickets (has, have) started?
11. We could hardly believe that the speakers at the forum (was, were) in earnest.
12. The assistants at this shop (is, are) all skilled in electronics.

13. The director, together with the actors, (is, are) taking a break.
14. Memories of the Old West (is, are) likely to be exaggerated.
15. A float with streaming banners (was, were) parked on the lawn.
16. The lake, as well as the streams, (is, are) polluted.
17. One counselor, with her campers, (was, were) fishing.
18. A collage made out of fabrics (is, are) my art project.
19. The students, along with the faculty, (has, have) made the school carnival a huge success.
20. The members of the board (was, were) hostile to the idea.

6.3 Indefinite Pronouns

There are both singular and plural indefinite pronouns. Some are always singular, and some are always plural. Others may be singular or plural depending on their use in a sentence.

SINGULAR

anybody	each	everyone	anyone
anything	either	everybody	someone
everything	neither	no one	somebody
another	one	nobody	

PLURAL

several few both many

Each of the books *has* pages missing.
Neither of the coaches *wants* to complain.
Everybody in the stands *was* excited.

Several in this deck *are* bent.
Few in our class *have* failed.
Both doors at the front *were* open.

SINGULAR OR PLURAL

some most all none any

Some, most, all, none, and *any* are singular when they refer to a quantity. They are plural when they refer to a number of individual items.

Some of the film *was* destroyed. (quantity)
Some of the tickets *were* returned. (number)

Most of the show *is* hilarious. (quantity)
Most of the players *are* excellent. (number)

All the pie *was* eaten. (quantity)
All the pictures *were* lost. (number)

Exercise: Choose the standard form of the verb.

1. Neither of the books (interests, interest) me.
2. Most of the people (has, have) returned to their seats.
3. Not one of the scientists (knows, know) the answer.
4. Either of those coats (looks, look) good on you.
5. Not one of my friends (has, have) called me.
6. Few in our little town (has, have) been out of the state.
7. Both cars (is, are) low on gas.
8. (Has, Have) either of the boats been found?
9. It was clear that one of the planes (was, were) in trouble.
10. Several students in this class (has, have) made that mistake.
11. Everyone in the old wooden stands (was, were) in peril.
12. One of the passengers (has, have) picked up my bag.
13. Everyone in the villages (was, were) decorating the streets.
14. Neither of these mountains (is, are) as high as Mt. McKinley.
15. One of the visitors (has, have) lost a camera.
16. We believe that some of these fish (is, are) poisonous.
17. Everybody on these islands (is, are) friendly.
18. You will find that few of the courses (is, are) very difficult.
19. (Is, Are) either of these bikes yours?
20. Each of the rooms (is, are) overcrowded.

6.4 Compound Subjects

Compound subjects joined by *and* are plural.*

Good lighting and thoughtful composition *make* pictures interesting.

Singular words joined by *or, nor, either-or, neither-nor* to form a compound subject are singular.

Neither your manner nor your argument *is* convincing.
Either Carl or Jess *has* your jacket.
Dad or Mother *drives* us to school every day.

When a singular word and a plural word are joined by *or* or *nor* to form a compound subject, the verb agrees with the subject that is nearer to it.

Neither the firefighters nor their chief *knows* how the fire started.
The first paragraph or the last two paragraphs *are* unnecessary.

Exercise: Writing Rewrite these sentences, correcting the errors in subject-verb agreement. Two of the sentences are correct.

1. Neither the chairs nor the desk have been delivered.
2. The sidewalks and the street is covered with ice.
3. Neither the papers nor the radio has told the true story.
4. Either a squirrel or a cat have driven off the birds.
5. The stores and the school cooperates on part-time work.
6. A salad or a hot dish are served every noon.
7. Neither the union nor the manager have compromised.
8. The winner and the runner-up receives prizes.
9. The members of the jury and the judge seems bored.
10. Two bills and an advertisement is all we got in the mail.
11. A glass of milk and toast is not an adequate breakfast.

*If the words making up the compound subject are habitually used together to refer to a single thing, the subject may be used with a singular verb: *bread and butter, macaroni and cheese,* etc.

12. Have either Ms. Hahn or her secretary come in yet?
13. Neither the clerks nor the manager know the price.
14. Bob or Helen go to the mainland once a week.
15. Neither fish nor oysters agree with me.

6.5 Subject Following Verb

Sometimes the subject of the sentence comes after the verb. When this occurs, the speaker or writer must think ahead to determine whether the verb should be singular or plural.

The verb often precedes the subject in sentences beginning with *There* and *Here* and in questions beginning with *Who, Why, Where, What, How.*

NONSTANDARD: Here'*s* the skates for Dick.
STANDARD: Here *are* the skates for Dick.

NONSTANDARD: There'*s* two reasons why the project failed.
STANDARD: There *are* two reasons why the project failed.

NONSTANDARD: Who'*s* the three people in the office?
STANDARD: Who *are* the three people in the office?

NONSTANDARD: What'*s* the orders for today?
STANDARD: What *are* the orders for today?

NONSTANDARD: Onto the field *comes* the team and the band.
STANDARD: Onto the field *come* the team and the band.

6.6 Predicate Words

A linking verb agrees with its subject. The predicate word has no effect on the number of the verb.

NONSTANDARD: Dwindling resources *is* one problem.
STANDARD: Dwindling resources *are* one problem.

NONSTANDARD: One problem *are* dwindling resources.
STANDARD: One problem *is* dwindling resources.

6.7 *Don't* and *Doesn't*

Forms of the verb *do* often cause problems in agreement. The word *does* and the contraction *doesn't* are used with singular nouns and with the pronouns *he, she,* and *it*. The word *do* and the contraction *don't* are used with plural nouns and with the pronouns *I, we, you,* and *they.*

DOES, DOESN'T	DO, DON'T
the cat does	the cats do
he doesn't	we don't
she doesn't	you don't
it doesn't	they don't

Exercise: Choose the standard form from the two given.

1. (Doesn't, Don't) the owner of these lots live around here?
2. (Here's, Here are) the answer to your question.
3. (What's, What are) the best colors for this room?
4. (Where's, Where are) the directions for the projector?
5. We knew there (was, were) a good reason for the delay.
6. Judy's contribution (was, were) both time and money.
7. Mr. Ross, of all people, (doesn't, don't) approve of the plan.
8. Down the stretch (comes, come) the three runners.
9. Fertilizers and lime (is, are) the garden's greatest need.
10. The paint on the bricks (doesn't, don't) come off easily.
11. Out of these experiments (comes, come) new knowledge.
12. (Who's, Who are) the people in your car?
13. (Here's, Here are) the books you ordered.
14. Beneath these buildings (runs, run) an underground stream.
15. The photographs in the yearbook (is, are) her work.
16. My biggest problem (is, are) my experiments.
17. The picture of the girls (doesn't, don't) resemble them.
18. His main worry (is, are) defects in the camera.
19. (What's, What are) the plans for the picnic?
20. Over near the fence (stands, stand) a famous monument.

6.8 Collective Nouns

A collective noun names a group of people or things: *committee, club, team, herd, crowd.*

A singular verb is used with a collective noun when the group acts together as a single unit. A plural verb is used with a collective noun when members of the group act separately, as individuals.

The jury *is* ready with its verdict. (united action)
The jury *were* arguing noisily. (separate actions)

The crew *works* well together. (united action)
The crew *were* reading in their bunks. (separate actions)

If a collective noun is used with a singular verb, it must also have singular pronouns refer back to it. If a collective noun is used with a plural verb, it must also have plural pronouns refer back to it.

NONSTANDARD: The group *has* (singular) changed *their* (plural) decision.
STANDARD: The group *has* changed *its* decision.

6.9 Nouns Plural in Form

Not all nouns that end in *s* are plural. Some nouns have the plural form, but they stand for only one thing: *news, mumps, measles.* These nouns are used with a singular verb.

Mumps *becomes* more painful as you get older.
The news *is* not good.

Words ending in *-ics* like *economics, athletics, civics,* and *politics* may be either singular or plural. They are singular when they are used to refer to a school subject, a science, or a general practice. When preceded by *the, his, some, all,* and singular modifiers, the nouns are usually plural. Note the examples on the following page.

Politics *is* everyone's business. (singular)
His politics *are* known to everyone. (plural)

Ethics *is* a study of right and wrong. (singular)
The man's ethics *were* questionable. (plural)

6.10 Titles and Groups of Words

A singular verb is used with titles of books, plays, stories, poems, TV shows, films, musical compositions, and other works of art. A singular verb is also used for the names of countries. These words, even though they may be plural in form, refer to a single thing.

A Tale of Two Cities was written by Charles Dickens.
Fireflies is not the kind of music I like.
The United States *has* bases all around the world.
The United Nations *meets* in New York.

Any group of words referring to a single thing or thought is used with a singular verb.

What we need *is* dollars.
"To be or not to be" *is* a line from *Hamlet*.

6.11 Words of Amount and Time

A singular verb is usually used with words or phrases that express periods of time, fractions, weights, measurements, and amounts of money.

Three hours *is* too much time to spend on this lesson.
Three-fourths of the job *is* completed.
Five dollars *seems* too much to charge.
Forty pounds *is* too heavy to carry.

A prepositional phrase may separate the subject and the verb. The verb must still agree with the subject. If the subject is considered a single thing, the verb must be singular. If the subject refers to several things individually, the verb is plural.

> Sixty pounds of potatoes *was* what we ordered.
> Sixty of the passengers *were* saved.

Exercise: Choose the standard form from the two forms given.

1. The crowd in their usual fashion (was, were) having a noisy party.
2. Taking their time, the crew (was, were) repairing the damage.
3. Politics in a business office (is, are) dangerous.
4. My brother's politics (seems, seem) to change every four years.
5. Dietetics (offers, offer) several interesting career choices.
6. The West Indies now (has, have) a new government.
7. The herd (come, comes) every day to drink at its regular time.
8. Two pounds of shrimp (is, are) enough for us.
9. The team (was, were) excited about their new uniforms.
10. Two-thirds of the earth's surface (is, are) under water.
11. Two-thirds of the cars inspected (has, have) some safety defect.
12. Ron believes that athletics (is, are) overemphasized in college.
13. Deprived of its leader, the gang (was, were) slowly falling apart.
14. Physics (causes, cause) me more trouble than any other class.
15. *The Three Musketeers* (tells, tell) the story of four men, not three.
16. Twelve of the band members (was, were) late for rehearsal.
17. Numismatics (is, are) the study of coins and medals.
18. Two thousand cans of food (was, were) collected.
19. Five days (is, are) too long to wait for a reply.
20. The United States still (has, have) some island territories.

6.12 Relative Pronouns

A relative pronoun may be singular or plural depending on its antecedent. If the antecedent is plural, the relative pronoun is plural. If the antecedent is singular, the relative pronoun is singular.

A relative pronoun agrees with its antecedent in number.

When a relative pronoun is used as subject of the verb in the relative clause, the number of the verb depends upon the number of the pronoun's antecedent.

These are the *designers* (plural) who (plural) *are planning* our new house.

Janet is the *girl* (singular) who (singular) *plays* the drums in the school orchestra.

Phil is one of those *boys* who *are* always happy. (*boys* are always happy.)

Liz is the only *one* of the girls who *has* a scholarship. (Only *one* has a scholarship.)

Notice that in the last two examples, there are two words which seem like they might be the antecedent for the relative pronoun. Examine such sentences carefully to determine the true antecedent. Usually the meaning of the sentence shows which of the two actually *is* the correct antecedent.

Exercise A: Choose the standard form from the two given.

1. Carlotta is the only one of the aides who (works, work) closely with the Governor.
2. This is one of those stories that (seems, seem) to have no ending.
3. Shelly is the one person in our lab group who (likes, like) chemistry.

4. This is the only one of the papers that (is, are) worth keeping.
5. Aren't you one of the brothers who (owns, own) the farm?
6. This is the longest of the tests that (is, are) to be given.
7. You are not the only one of the students who (has, have) been worrying.
8. Here are two new metals of the kind that (resists, resist) great heat.
9. Joe is one of the students who (has, have) been to Washington.
10. There are three good points in the paper that (has, have) just been read.

Exercise B: Follow the directions for Exercise A.

1. I am the only one of the cast members who (doesn't, don't) have the flu.
2. Algebra is one of the subjects that (is, are) difficult for me.
3. Jim is one of those moviegoers who (talks, talk) all the time.
4. One of the children who (is, are) playing in the yard is my sister.
5. Weeds are the plants that (grows, grow) fastest in our garden.
6. It is Meg who (is, are) most qualified to be scorekeeper.
7. Isn't Mrs. Cohen one of the parents who (works, work) in the library?
8. This ballad is the only one of the songs that (is, are) hard to sing.
9. Everyone who (lives, live) in Newfoundland has seen the northern lights.
10. Two-thirds of the trucks that (has, have) been loaded are filled with coal.

REINFORCEMENT EXERCISES

Agreement of Subject and Verb

A. Choose the correct verb. Identify the subject in each of the following sentences. Then choose the standard form of the verb.

1. Tracy Nelson, one of the best blues singers, (record, records) in Studio C.
2. Seven choreographers (has, have) been fired by the movie director.
3. The chefs, along with the restaurant owner, (eat, eats) only after the last customer has been served.
4. The first of the tanks (contain, contains) a sand shark.
5. Your attitudes, as well as your tone, (is, are) insulting.
6. The boll weevils on the cotton (was, were) a cause for concern among local growers.
7. The leaves of this plant (react, reacts) to loud sounds.
8. The three women, each a professor at a major university, (was, were) honored by the Academy.
9. The horse pulling the cart (stop, stops) at every red light.
10. We (sponsor, sponsors) a child in South America by paying for her education.

B. Choose verbs that agree with indefinite pronouns. Identify the subject in each of the following sentences. Then choose the correct form of the verb.

1. No one really (believes, believe) in goblins, elves, and trolls anymore.
2. Many (hope, hopes) that they will live to see world peace.
3. Both of them (is, are) planning to work for a year before going to college.
4. All the papers (was, were) scattered on the floor.
5. Either of the twins (is, are) responsible enough for the job.
6. Each of the science fair projects (was, were) judged individually.

7. Most of the marathon contestants (collapse, collapses) before the event is over.
8. Everyone in the stands (shout, shouts) whenever a touchdown is made.
9. Few of the voters (wish, wishes) to stay home.
10. Several of the swimmers (compete, competes) at the state level.

C. Choose verbs that agree with compound subjects. Find the errors in subject-verb agreement in the following sentences. Rewrite any sentences containing errors. If a sentence does not contain any errors, write *Correct*.

1. Neither the Articles of Confederation nor the Constitution were accepted readily.
2. Ethnic studies and women's studies is offered at many colleges.
3. Are Fran or Eloise planning to help paint the mural?
4. Greenhouses and plastic caps extend a plant's growing season.
5. Neither the calculator nor computers helps in this situation.
6. Both oysters and shrimp is high in cholesterol.
7. My mother and Mr. Johnson is running for P.T.A. president.
8. Neither pretzels nor chocolate appeals to me right now.
9. Both the harp and the French horn is difficult to master.
10. Murals and frescoes require detailed planning in advance.

D. Choose verbs that agree with their subjects. Choose the correct form from among those given in parentheses.

1. His most valuable collection (is, are) his ancient pieces of armor.
2. There (is, are) many job opportunities for students in the summer.
3. From the jungle (comes, come) the cries of the night-stalking animals.
4. How (do, does) amphibians breathe when the lake is frozen?

5. There (was, were) the missing cats, hiding under my brother's bed.
6. The Rifkins (doesn't, don't) leave town over the holidays.
7. Around the bases (run, runs) Ron Kittle, waving to the grandstand.
8. That pumpkin (doesn't, don't) look ripe to me.
9. There (is, are) crumbled cookies and a crushed sandwich at the bottom of my knapsack.
10. (Who is, Who are) the stars who have agreed to appear at the benefit?
11. Which (is, are) the softest of the cotton flannels?
12. Here (comes, come) the cheerleaders from Central High.
13. Checkers and chess (is, are) Mr. Holton's favorite games.
14. Down the rocky cliffs (cascades, cascade) the water from the Alder River.
15. A beekeeper (don't, doesn't) worry about an occasional sting.

E. Make subjects and verbs agree. The subjects of some of the following sentences are collective nouns. Identify the subject of each sentence. Then choose the proper verb form.

1. The council (was, were) divided on the issue.
2. The Union of Soviet Socialist Republics (is, are) the largest nation on earth.
3. The volleyball team (was, were) submitting their ideas for new on-court strategies.
4. When you are waiting for important news, even thirty minutes (seem, seems) like a long time.
5. Nine-tenths (do, does) not make a whole of anything.
6. Teresa thought that economics (was, were) a required course.
7. Some people said that Abraham Lincoln's politics (was, were) difficult to comprehend.
8. The Florida Keys (extend, extends) far into the ocean.
9. *Leaves of Grass* (is, are) a collection containing all the poems by Walt Whitman that he wanted to preserve.
10. The companies (belongs, belong) to the American Retailers Association.

F. Use correct verbs after relative pronouns. Find the antecedent of each relative pronoun. Then choose the verb that agrees with this antecedent.

1. Sharon Grambo is one of the dancers who (teach, teaches) at the Munsler Academy of Dance.
2. This is one of those books that (leave, leaves) you breathless until the last page.
3. Mary Travers is one folk singer of the 1960's who still (records, record) today.
4. Here are two pieces of evidence that (contradict, contradicts) your assumption.
5. The red-brick apartment house is the only one of the buildings that (remain, remains) standing today.
6. Doug Henning and David Copperfield are magicians who (has, have) enormous followings.
7. These are the types of deer that (roams, roam) in herds.
8. The sausage-and-mushroom spaghetti sauce is the one that (get, gets) my vote.
9. Matthew is one of those students who (excel, excels) in everything.
10. This is the only one of the coupons that (expire, expires) today.

MIXED REVIEW

Agreement of Subject and Verb

A. Choose the standard form of the verb from the two forms given in parentheses.

1. Tony's photo of folk dancers (captures, capture) their motion.
2. This class, as well as the advanced class, (uses, use) the kiln.
3. (Does, Do) the signatures on this document look authentic or forged?
4. Everyone in the stands (is, are) throwing confetti.
5. Neither of these combinations (opens, open) my locker.
6. Either the orchestra or the dancers (is, are) off by one beat.
7. One of the biggest pearl fisheries (is, are) in Baja, California.
8. There (is, are) many job openings for nurses.
9. The editorial, together with the news reports, (was, were) persuasive.
10. Either the reed or the quill (was, were) the earliest pen.
11. Neither the President nor his advisers (expects, expect) his foreign policy to satisfy everyone.
12. Here (is, are) the fossilized footprints of a dinosaur.
13. (Doesn't, Don't) he belong to a fan club?
14. The committee (has, have) announced its decision for the prom.
15. Obstetrics (is, are) the field of medicine that my sister is studying.
16. *The Washington Post* is one of the newspapers that (is, are) known for investigative reporting.
17. Fifty feet (is, are) the width of the playing field.
18. Two boxes of silver (was, were) found in the wreckage.
19. *The Adventures of Augie March* (was, were) written by Saul Bellow.
20. You are the only tenor who (is, are) singing a solo.

B. Correct any errors in subject-verb agreement in the following sentences. If the sentence is correct, write *Correct*.

1. Six apples has fallen on Newman's head.
2. The hoof marks on the old corral post was an indication of the fierce struggle.
3. The car with the two flat tires appears to be abandoned.
4. Many was the times I regretted not being able to sing.
5. Wings is giving a benefit concert at the stadium on Wednesday.
6. Experts on cold weather stress that mittens is warmer than gloves.
7. One of the clerks told me that more of the sweaters is expected soon.
8. Is football or rugby played in Australia?
9. Neither Nina nor Julie plans a career in acting.
10. Trimming and pruning helps keep a plant healthy.
11. What's the reasons that Chandra gave for not trying out for the team?
12. If Michael Jackson and Paul McCartney makes another record together, I want a copy of it.
13. The fencing team practices in the local Y.M.C.A.
14. A hundred pounds of clay last the potter a month.
15. Don't the color of the car's interior appeal to you?
16. Mathematics are a subject with a fascinating history.
17. One of the finest players in the history of baseball were Jackie Robinson.
18. This is one of those legends that grow with time.
19. The poet said that stone walls and iron bars does not a prison make.
20. The United States are one of the world's greatest powers.

Agreement of Subject and Verb

A. Make a list of your three favorite musical groups. Then list your favorite songs by each of these groups. Write a short composition describing your own tastes in music and using these groups and songs as examples. Be sure to make the verb of each sentence agree with its subject.

B. Choose five television commercials and analyze the contents of each. What elements are common to all of them? What elements are found in some of them, but not all? Write a composition comparing and contrasting the contents and techniques of commercials. In your composition, use indefinite pronouns, (some, everyone, none, all, most, each, every, many, several) and relative pronouns (who, which, that) whenever possible. Make sure that your subjects and verbs agree.

C. You have been invited to a screening of a new movie, *Journey into Confusion*. The producers of the movie are eager to get your reactions so that they can make final changes in the movie before releasing it nationwide. They have therefore passed out a list of the following phrases to each of the viewers in order to elicit comments. Write a brief review of the movie for these producers. Assume that the movie was either the best or the worst piece of cinema you have ever seen in your life.

This movie is . . .
Both the lead and the supporting characters . . .
The only one of the actors . . .
Neither the producers nor the director . . .
The scenery, as well as the special effects, . . .
Several of the costumes . . .
Most of the dialogue . . .
The best of the scenes . . .
Each one of my friends . . .

7.0 Pronoun Usage

In grammar, the term *inflection* has a special meaning. It means "a change in form to show how a word is used in a sentence." Prepositions, conjunctions, and interjections do not change form. All other parts of speech do. Usually, the change in form is just a change in spelling:

NOUN:	boy	— boy's	— boys	— boys'
VERB:	walk	— walks	— walked	— walking
ADJECTIVE:	big	— bigger	— biggest	
ADVERB:	hard	— harder	— hardest	

Sometimes, however, the change involves the use of a completely new word:

VERB:	go	— went	— gone
ADJECTIVE:	bad	— worse	— worst
PRONOUN:	I	— me	— mine

Pronouns change their form, or **case,** in both ways. The **case** of a pronoun indicates how it is used in a particular sentence. There are three cases of pronouns: **nominative, possessive,** and **objective.** The three cases for the personal pronouns and *who* are shown on the following page:

NOMINATIVE	POSSESSIVE	OBJECTIVE
I	my, mine	me
we	our, ours	us
you	your, yours	you
he	his	him
she	her, hers	her
it	its	it
they	their, theirs	them
who	whose	whom
whoever	whosever	whomever

Indefinite pronouns change form only when they are used as modifiers. Then, they are in the possessive case.

NOMINATIVE	POSSESSIVE	OBJECTIVE
everyone	everyone's	everyone
nobody	nobody's	nobody
anyone	anyone's	anyone

The pronouns *this, that, these, those, which,* and *what* do not change their forms to indicate case.

7.1 The Pronoun as Subject of a Verb

The nominative form of the pronoun is used as subject of a verb.

When there is only one subject in a sentence, there is no problem in choosing the correct pronoun form. The problem arises when the subject is compound. The compound subject may be made up of pronouns or of both nouns and pronouns.

To decide which pronoun form to use in a compound subject, *try each part of the subject by itself with the verb.*

John and (I, me) rode in the team bus.
(John rode; I rode, *not* me rode.)
The Clarks and (they, them) are neighbors.
(The Clarks are; they are, *not* them are.)
Nathan and (she, her) worked at the library.
(Nathan worked; she worked, *not* her worked.)

The plural forms *we* and *they* sound awkward in many compounds. They can be avoided by recasting the sentence.

AWKWARD: The boys and we are ready.
BETTER: We and the boys are ready.

AWKWARD: We and they planned to meet later.
BETTER: We planned to meet them later.

7.2 The Predicate Pronoun

A **predicate pronoun** is a pronoun linked to the subject by the linking verb *be*.

The nominative pronoun form is used as a predicate pronoun.*

The rule applies to all verb phrases built around forms of *be: could have been, can be, should be,* etc.

It *was* **I** whom they wanted.
Could it *have been* **he** who called?
It *must have been* **they** that we heard.

If the nominative case sounds awkward, try to rephrase the sentence.

AWKWARD: The chairpersons are she and Tom.
BETTER: Tom and she are the chairpersons.

AWKWARD: It was we who ordered the food.
BETTER: We are the people who ordered the food.

7.3 The Pronoun as Object of a Verb

The objective pronoun form is used as direct or indirect object.

Choosing the correct pronoun form for an object is a problem only when the object is compound. A compound object may be made up of pronouns or of both nouns and pronouns.

*Standard usage permits the exception in both speech and writing of *It is me*.

To decide which pronoun form to use in a compound object, *try each part of the object by itself with the verb.*

The coach gave Stuart and (I, me) little hope.
(gave Stuart; gave me, *not* gave I)
The invitation included Jane and (he, him).
(included Jane; included him, *not* included he)
Mr. Alden asked both (they, them) and (we, us) for help.
(asked them, *not* asked they; asked us, *not* asked we)
Will you tell (she, her) and (I, me) what's wrong?
(tell her, *not* tell she; tell me, *not* tell I)

Exercise A: Choose the standard form from those given.

1. Anita and (I, me) will make all arrangements.
2. Ted invited her and (I, me) to the party.
3. The guests of honor were Maria and (I, me).
4. How many goals did (he, him) and Chuck make?
5. Tell Betty and (she, her) the whole story.
6. She and (I, me) volunteered to help the Red Cross.
7. (They, Them) and the Reimers went to Aspen.
8. Dad gave Chuck and (I, me) a ride to town.
9. Was it (he, him) who called the fire department or was it (them, they)?
10. He and (she, her) were on the bus.
11. (She, Her) and her mother have flown to Detroit.
12. Will you lend Cathy and (I, me) your records?
13. Our boss gave Greg and (I, me) a raise.
14. The girls and (we, us) are putting on a skit.
15. I have a suspicion that it was (she, her).

Exercise B: Choose the standard form from those given.

1. The accident taught (he, him) and (I, me) a lesson.
2. It could have been (she, her), but I doubt it.
3. It was (he, him) who notified the police.
4. The usher gave (he, him) and (I, me) a program and showed (we, us) to our seats.

5. The Carlsons and (I, me) are going to the first game of the World Series.
6. Have you been avoiding Jack and (I, me)?
7. That must be (he, him) at the door.
8. Why don't you give (they, them) and (we, us) some help with this computer program?
9. Was it Charlotte and (she, her) who wrote that script?
10. Have you and (she, her) had an argument?
11. The song sent Lilla and (we, us) into fits of laughter.
12. The waiter asked (he, him) and (I, me) what we would have.
13. If I were (she, her), I'd accept the invitation.
14. Is it (she, her) whom you are dating?
15. Melissa showed Ben and (I, me) the correct way to vault.

7.4 The Pronoun as Object of a Preposition

The objective pronoun form is used as object of a preposition.

Deciding which pronoun form to use as object of a preposition is a problem only when the object is compound. The compound object may contain pronouns, or both nouns and pronouns. To decide which pronoun to use in the compound object, *try each part of the object by itself with the preposition*.

Ms. Broch has a special job for you and (I, me).
(for you; for me, *not* for I)
We heard good things about (they, them) and Martin.
(about them, *not* about they)
The judge awarded the ribbons to Ellen and (we, us).
(to Ellen; to us, *not* to we)

The preposition *between* often causes errors in pronoun usage. To avoid these errors, only use objective pronoun forms after *between*.

between you and her, *not* between you and she
between her and me, *not* between she and I

7.5 The Pronoun Used with a Noun

In a construction such as *we girls* or *us boys,* the use of the noun determines the case form of the pronoun.

We boys will prepare the food.
(*boys* is the subject of *will prepare;* the nominative pronoun is therefore required.)
The agency offered us girls a job.
(*girls* is the indirect object of *offered;* the objective pronoun is therefore required.)

To decide which pronoun form to use in a construction such as *we boys* or *us girls*, try the pronoun by itself with the verb or preposition.

This year the choice is easy for (we, us) voters.
(for us, *not* for we)
The driver asked (we, us) passengers to help him.
(asked us, *not* asked we)
(We, Us) honor students can apply now for scholarships.
(We can apply, *not* Us can apply.)

Exercise A: Choose the standard form from those given.

1. In the Fourth of July procession Corky walked behind him and (me, I).
2. I live just a block away from Bess and (she, her).
3. The manager was fair to Bob and (I, me) when we asked about part-time jobs.
4. The shadow of the big oak fell across Ann and (I, me) as we sunbathed.
5. Between you and (me, I), this is the worst play I have ever seen.
6. The decision is strictly up to the officer and (he, him) and his parents.
7. (We, Us) writers often keep a journal of ideas for future writing projects.
8. The petition should be signed by (us, we) students.

9. I sat between Alec and (he, him) at my sister's high school commencement.
10. The package is for (she, her) and (me, I).
11. Did you hear the wonderful news about (he, him) and his brother Andy?
12. The secret must be kept between (us, we) two.
13. The sandwiches are to be distributed among (us, we) campers.
14. The free movie tickets were won by Sally, Betsy, and (them, they).
15. (We, Us) two are the only tuba players in the school marching band.

Exercise B: Choose the standard form from those given.

1. I haven't heard a word from either Judy or (she, her) since they left on vacation.
2. The proceeds were shared between the school and (us, we) club members.
3. Everyone did well on the test except (we, us) two.
4. I'll tell Harry, Charlene, and (him, he) that the performance is sold out.
5. The letters are for you, Paula, and (me, I).
6. Give Frank and (I, me) another chance.
7. The job of decorating the gym for the dance was given to Joe and (I, me).
8. He rode his bike right between Clara and (me, I).
9. You will have to choose between (her, she) and (I, me).
10. The school board appealed to (we, us) juniors and seniors to set an example.
11. The solo parts were given to (she, her) and Jules.
12. The prize money was divided evenly between Nelson and (he, him).
13. A congratulatory telegram was sent to (we, us) players.
14. The decision of the judges was hard on (us, we) two.
15. Marnie and (I, me) will meet the exchange students at the airport on Saturday.

7.6 *Who* and *Whom* in Questions

Pronouns used to ask questions are **interrogative pronouns.** Within the sentence, the pronoun may be the subject, object, predicate word, or object of a preposition. To use the pronouns *who* and *whom* correctly, you must understand how they are used in the sentence.

Who is the nominative form. It is used as the subject of the verb or as a predicate pronoun.

> Who gave you this information? (*Who* is the subject.)
> Your aunt is *who*? (*Who* is the predicate pronoun.)

Whom is the objective form. It is used as the object of the verb or the object of a preposition.

> Whom do you want? (*Whom* is the object of *do want*.)
> *To whom were these packages sent?* (*whom* is the object of the preposition *To*.)

Exercise: Choose the standard form from those given.

1. (Who, Whom) can spell *embarrass?*
2. (Who, Whom) did the referee penalize?
3. (Who, Whom) revived 3-D movies?
4. (Who, Whom) do you think we just saw?
5. (Who, Whom) received a telegram?
6. (Who, Whom) are you thinking about?
7. For (who, whom) will you vote?
8. (Who, Whom) is that odd individual?
9. (Who, Whom) can that be in that werewolf costume?
10. (Who, Whom) wrote this paper?
11. (Who, Whom) was the award given to?
12. (Who, Whom) was that biography about?
13. The winning song was performed by (who, whom)?
14. (Who, Whom) invented peanut butter?
15. (Who, Whom) did the nominating committee select to be chairperson?

7.7 *Who, Whom,* and *Whose* in Clauses

The pronouns *who, whom,* and *whose* may be used as relative pronouns to introduce adjective clauses or as introductory words in noun clauses. These pronouns also perform jobs within the clauses they introduce.

The use of the pronoun within the clause determines whether the nominative, objective, or possessive form is used.

Natalia Makarova is a ballet dancer *who left Russia*. (The nominative form *who* is the subject within this adjective clause.)

Everyone wondered *who the masked person was*. (This noun clause is the direct object of the verb *wondered*. Within this noun clause, the nominative form *who* is the predicate pronoun.)

The woman *whom the king married* was an American. (The objective form *whom* is the direct object of the verb *married* within this adjective clause.)

The primary determines *whom the party will endorse*. (This noun clause is the direct object of the verb *determines*. Within this clause, *whom* is the direct object of the verb *will endorse*.)

The man *whose car was dented* called the police. (*whose* is a possessive pronoun within this adjective clause.)

Whoever and *whomever* follow the same rules as *who* and *whom* when used as introductory words.

Whoever plays honestly wins my respect. (Within this noun clause, the nominative form *whoever* is the subject.)

Give the tickets to *whoever wants them*. (This noun clause is the object of the preposition *to*. (Within the clause, *whoever* is the subject of the verb *wants*.)

It is important to cooperate with *whomever you elect*. (The noun clause is the object of the preposition *with*. Within the noun clause, *whomever* is the direct object of the verb *elect*.)

Exercise: Choose the standard form from those given.

1. The architect (who, whom) designed this building is I. M. Pei.
2. These are the cousins (who, whom) I had never met before.
3. Brecht is the playwright (who, whom) wrote *Mother Courage*.
4. I pity (whoever, whomever) Chris Hanburg tackles.
5. The writer (who, whom) uses words precisely has impact.
6. You may invite (whoever, whomever) you like.
7. Does anyone know (who, whom) Jane Addams was?
8. (Whoever, Whomever) is named editor of the school paper should have good writing skills.
9. Our dog will gallop over (whoever, whomever) is in his path to get to his dinner.
10. The pseudonym assured that no one would know (who, whom) the author was.
11. A public defender represents (whoever, whomever) is charged with a crime.
12. The man (whose, whom) dog we found tried to give us a reward.
13. The entire team cheered the player (who, whom) scored the winning touchdown.
14. Annie Sullivan is the teacher about (who, whom) *The Miracle Worker* was written.
15. Scholarships are awarded to (whoever, whomever) needs them most.

7.8 Pronouns in Comparisons

A comparison is sometimes made by using a clause that begins with *than* or *as*.

Jean is better at math *than* Bob *is*.
We have as much time *as anyone else has*.
Jeff admires you more *than he admires me*.

The final clause in the comparison may be left incomplete.

Alyson uses the computer more than Greg (does).
You have a better chance than he (has).
Doug has as much experience as anyone else.

To decide which pronoun form to use in an incomplete comparison, complete the comparison.

Phil got more help than (I, me).
(Phil got more help than *I got*.)
The editor gave Pam a longer assignment than (I, me). (The editor gave Pam a longer assignment than *she gave me*.)

7.9 Pronouns with Infinitives

The objective form of the pronoun is used as the subject, object, or predicate pronoun of an infinitive.

The director asked *him to work* more quietly.
(*him* is subject of *to work*.)
They took *her to be me*.
(*her* is the subject of *to be*, and *me* is the predicate pronoun following *to be*.)
The whole town turned out *to hear him*.
(*him* is the object of *to hear*.)
We didn't expect the instructor *to be her*.
(*her* is the predicate pronoun following *to be*.)

7.10 Pronouns with Participles and Gerunds

Both gerunds and present participles are formed from verbs and end in *-ing*. If an *-ing* verbal is used as a noun, it is a gerund. If it is used as a modifier, it is a participle.

A participle may be used with a pronoun in either the nominative or the objective form.

The officers saw *him creeping* through the cornfield. (*creeping* is a participle modifying *him*.)

Thinking fast, *she* came up with the answer. (*Thinking* is a participle modifying *she*.)

A gerund must be used with a pronoun in the possessive form.

They disliked *his watching* so much television. (*watching* is the gerund object of *disliked; his* is the subject of *watching*.)

Their voting made a difference in the outcome of the election. (*voting* is the gerund subject of *made; Their* is the subject of *voting*.)

Sometimes you must examine the meaning of a sentence carefully in order to determine which pronoun form to use.

Their singing left much to be desired. (*singing* is a gerund, the subject of the verb *left*.)

We heard *them singing* at their work. (*singing* is a participle modifying *them*.)

7.11 The Pronoun as an Appositive

The form of a pronoun used as an appositive is determined by the use of the noun with which it is in apposition.

The co-captains, *Louise* and *I*, called the team together. (*Louise* and *I* are in apposition to *co-captains*, which is the subject of *called*. Therefore, the nominative form of the pronoun is required.)

For our friends, *Jo* and *her*, the parting was sad. (*Jo* and *her* are in apposition to *friends*, which is the object of the preposition *for*. Therefore, the objective form of the pronoun is required.)

We gave the winners, *Ross* and *him,* a warm welcome.
(*Ross* and *him* are in apposition to *winners,* which is the indirect object of *gave*. Therefore, the objective form of the pronoun is required.)

To determine which form of the pronoun to use in apposition, try the appositive by itself with the verb or preposition.

The losers, Phil and (her, she), were good sports.
(Phil and she were, *not* Phil and her were.)
The tickets are from two of your admirers, Stan and (I, me).
(The tickets are from me, *not* from I.)

7.12 Compound Personal Pronouns

Compound personal pronouns are used only when their antecedents appear in the same sentence.

STANDARD: My canary likes to preen itself.
STANDARD: We reserved the seats for ourselves.

NONSTANDARD: The same rule applies to yourself.
STANDARD: The same rule applies to you.

NONSTANDARD: Pat and myself will be in charge.
STANDARD: Pat and I will be in charge.

Exercise: Choose the standard form from those in parentheses.

1. Cheri would rather take Leonard than (he, him) to the prom.
2. The leaders, Bonnie and (I, myself, me), will have the greatest responsibility.
3. The Australians played better tennis than (we, us).
4. My companion was younger than (I, me, myself).
5. The award was presented by two juniors, Larry and (he, him).
6. My parents were excited about (me, my) making the team.
7. They disapproved of (his, him) climbing the mountain.

8. No one saw (my, me) eating that second sundae.
9. No one can make the decision but (you, yourself).
10. His parents objected to (his, him) reading at the table.
11. Jim is unhappy about (you, your) moving to Ohio.
12. Nobody in the audience laughed except (us, ourselves).
13. Will you go swimming with Janice, Joyce, and (me, myself)?
14. Grace has a better chance than (him, he).
15. Sonia and (I, myself) will make the arrangements.
16. John urged him as strongly as (I, myself).
17. The people who called were the well-known pranksters, Nick and (she, her).
18. Nancy invited my sister and (I, me, myself) to her wedding.
19. The judges were impressed by (him, his) fancy skating.
20. Tell one of us, either (he, him) or (I, me), what happened.

7.13 Pronouns and Antecedents

A pronoun must agree with its antecedent in number, gender, and person.

Agreement in Number. If the antecedent of a pronoun is singular, a singular pronoun is required. If the antecedent is plural, a plural pronoun is required.

Indefinite pronouns that are singular in meaning must be paired with singular pronouns. The following indefinite pronouns are always singular.

another	either	nobody
anyone	everybody	no one
anything	everyone	one
each	everything	somebody
	neither	someone

Each of the racers has *his* car ready.
Everyone has a right to *his* or *her* own opinion.
One of the lifeguards dived from *her* chair.

The indefinite pronouns *all, some, any, most,* and *none* may be referred to by a singular or plural pronoun, depending on the meaning intended.

Some of the maple syrup *has* lost *its* flavor.

Some of the students *have* seen *their* pictures.

All the equipment *was* in *its* proper place.

All the backfield *were* playing *their* best game.

For more information on agreement with indefinite pronouns see Sections 1.2 and 6.3.

Collective nouns may be referred to by either a singular or plural pronoun, depending on the meaning intended.

The football team *has its* new plays.
The football team *have* been awarded *their* letters.

Note: In all of the foregoing examples, the collective nouns and indefinite pronouns are used as subjects. The number of the verb and the number of the pronoun referring to the subject must be the same.

NONSTANDARD: Some of the band *are* wearing *its* new gold and blue uniforms.
STANDARD: Some of the band *are* wearing *their* new gold and blue uniforms.

NONSTANDARD: None of the door-to-door salesmen *was* doing *their* best.
STANDARD: None of the door-to-door salesmen *were* doing *their* best.
STANDARD: None of the door-to-door salesmen *was* doing *his* best.

Two or more singular antecedents joined by *or* or *nor* are referred to by a singular pronoun.

Either Jack or Hal will bring *his* record player.
Neither the president nor the treasurer was in *her* office.

Agreement in Gender. A pronoun must be the same gender as the word to which it refers. *He, his,* and *him* are masculine pronouns. *She, her,* and *hers* are feminine pronouns. *It* and *its* are neuter pronouns.

The otter was floating on *its* back. (neuter)
The doctor dropped *her* bag. (feminine)
The waiter was taking *his* time. (masculine)

When a singular pronoun refers to both masculine and feminine antecedents, there are two acceptable pronoun uses. Historically, the masculine *his* was used. It still is considered standard usage. Today some people use the phrase *his or her* to avoid what they consider to be sexist language.

STANDARD: Every student will want *his* picture in the school yearbook.

STANDARD: Every student will want *his or her* picture in the school yearbook.

Agreement in Person. A personal pronoun must be in the same person as its antecedent. The words *one, everyone,* and *everybody* are in the third person. They are referred to by *he, his, him, she, her, hers*.

NONSTANDARD: *Everyone* should report to *your* cabin soon.
STANDARD: *Everyone* should report to *his or her* cabin soon.

NONSTANDARD: *I* find that night-driving is extremely hard on *your* eyes.
STANDARD: *I* find that night-driving is extremely hard on *my* eyes.

Exercise: Writing Correct the errors in agreement in these sentences. Make sure that both verb and pronoun are correct.

1. Most of the rides lost its thrill after the first time.
2. Everyone has a right to their own opinion.
3. Each of the winning essays had their good points.

4. Either Jim or Guy will lend us their history notes.
5. Will each student please turn in their schedule tomorrow?
6. The cast took its places on stage.
7. One should always write ahead for your hotel reservations.
8. Each of us need to start thinking about their career now.
9. Neither Brad nor Hugh answer their telephones.
10. If one tries hard enough, you can usually finish the reports in an hour.
11. Everyone applying for the scholarship must bring their birth certificate.
12. I avoid watermelon because it upsets your stomach.
13. No one who makes your own ice cream will be satisfied with commercial brands.
14. Can Jessica or Lori bring their tape-recorder to school?
15. Everybody in the office has made their vacation plans.

7.14 Indefinite Reference

To avoid any confusion for the reader, every personal pronoun should refer clearly to a definite antecedent.

INDEFINITE: The color is attractive, but *they* didn't do a good job on the ceiling.
BETTER: The color is attractive, but the painters didn't do a good job on the ceiling.

INDEFINITE: *It* says in the book that outer space is not empty.
BETTER: The book says that outer space is not empty.

INDEFINITE: Mark wants to be a pilot because he thinks *it* is exciting.
BETTER: Mark wants to be a pilot because he thinks flying a plane is exciting.

INDEFINITE: You should apply now if *they* will let you.
BETTER: You should apply now if the college will let you.

Avoid using the pronoun *you* when it does not refer to the person spoken to.

INDEFINITE: In those days, *you* were thrown into jail if *you* could not pay *your bills*.
BETTER: In those days, debtors were thrown into jail if they could not pay their bills.

INDEFINITE: In a jet plane *you* have fewer dials to watch.
BETTER: In a jet plane there are fewer dials to watch.

Exercise A: Writing Revise the sentences below to remove all indefinite reference of pronouns.

1. In a dictatorship, you are not allowed to criticize the government.
2. In a business office, they don't let you come to work late every day.
3. The roof is leaking; it is ruining the plaster and causing the paint to peel.
4. In the introduction, it says that this is a true story.
5. When the symphony concert begins, they close the doors and refuse to seat latecomers until intermission.
6. On Easter Island, when people died, they buried them in a cave.
7. We worked very hard on the plans for our science exhibit, but it doesn't show.
8. We signaled the bus driver frantically, but it kept right on going.
9. Jane played some tennis and won it easily.
10. In this hospital, they give you very good food.

Exercise B: Writing Follow the directions for Exercise A.

1. During these cold months, you get a lot of stalled cars on the highways.
2. On the first page, it tells what topics are covered in the book.
3. Since Mike gets good grades, they let him take extra courses.
4. They say that the younger generation has too much freedom and too little responsibility.

5. I would like to become a veterinarian since it helps animals.
6. It says in the directions that you should write the correct answers on the blank lines.
7. The pie was warm, but they served the rest of the dinner cold.
8. A hundred years ago, you often didn't go to school past the fifth grade because you had to go to work.
9. Ingrid used several tools to pry the board loose, but it just didn't work.
10. Do you think they ever dreamed that the Constitution would remain the fundamental body of law for two centuries?

7.15 Ambiguous Reference

The word *ambiguous* means "having two or more possible meanings." The reference of a pronoun is ambiguous if the reader cannot tell which word the pronoun is referring to. This situation arises whenever a noun or pronoun falls between the pronoun and its true antecedent.

AMBIGUOUS: Take the screens off the second story windows and paint *them*.

BETTER: Paint the screens after you take them off the second story windows.

AMBIGUOUS: The police chased the bandits until *their* car broke down.

BETTER: The police chased the bandits until the police car broke down.

AMBIGUOUS: Before we could move the sled down the road, *it* had to be repaired.

BETTER: We had to repair the sled before moving it down the road.

AMBIGUOUS: Sue told Ellen that *she* had failed the test.

BETTER: Sue had failed the test, she told Ellen.

Exercise A: Writing Revise the sentences below to remove all ambiguous pronoun references.

1. Marion interrupted Sarah to say that her mother had come.
2. Marcy's picture was in yesterday's paper, but I can't find it.
3. Bill moved the car out of the garage and cleaned it.
4. We took the books out of the cartons and stacked them in the garage.
5. When Sarah hung the picture on the wall, it looked better.
6. Fred told George that he was next on the program.
7. Francesca asked her mother whether she was invited.
8. Frank tried a new battery in the flashlight, but it didn't work.
9. When I tried to glue the handle onto the cup, it broke.
10. When the reporter interviewed the warden, he was not very friendly.

Exercise B: Writing Follow the directions for Exercise A.

1. Ms. Pappas has seen productions at each of the city's playhouses and has liked every one of them.
2. Larry played soccer with his younger brother until he got tired.
3. When the surgeon came into Kathy's room, she looked worried.
4. Andy told Pedro that he got an "A" on the biology test.
5. Will you and Dan please help me get the sail off the boat so I can repair it?
6. Mary took the laces out of her gym shoes and bleached them.
7. Lisa and Sandy went for a ride on her bike.
8. Dad told Phil that the last piece of pie was his.
9. Mr. and Mrs. Davis have six children, but they are very easygoing.
10. When the puppy tripped over the broom, I picked it up.

7.16 Vague Reference

The words *this*, *which*, *that*, and *it* are sometimes used to refer to a preceding idea or chain of ideas. The reader may be confused if the reference is vague.

VAGUE: Bruce had had a tiring day, and hadn't eaten breakfast. *This* made him irritable.

BETTER: Bruce was irritable because he had had a tiring day and hadn't eaten breakfast.

VAGUE: There is no place in our town for young people to meet on weekends, *which* is the reason they drive to other towns for entertainment.

BETTER: The young people in our town drive to other towns for entertainment because there is no place for them to meet here on weekends.

VAGUE: The boys had never been in trouble before. *That* made the judge more lenient.

BETTER: When the judge learned that the boys had never been in trouble before, he was more lenient.

Exercise A: Writing Revise the sentences below to remove all vague references of pronouns.

1. Many of us were late for practice, which upset the director.
2. Many areas have an inadequate water supply and this is why the conversion of sea water is important.
3. The wind had blown the snow into huge drifts; it delayed the progress of the rescuers to the marooned town.
4. Mary's English paper had taken all her time, and this made her uneasy about the French test.
5. The freshman class had a paper drive two months ago, which is the reason we can't have one now.
6. The mayor promised to fund a recreational center. It sounded good to us.
7. Don bought a 1973 car, which was a mistake.
8. Ellen spoke very well, and everyone liked it.

9. Scientists have discovered layers of atmosphere with heavy radiation, and this may delay manned space flight.
10. Jerry let the cut bleed, which was the right thing to do.

Exercise B: Writing Follow the directions for Exercise A.

1. The weather was bad. That is why we took so long.
2. The judges were impressed by Paul's exhibit but gave the award to another project. This frustrated him.
3. Our swimmers never give up. It makes me proud.
4. The zoo is quite crowded today, which isn't unusual.
5. The debating club won many trophies last year; this makes it a popular organization.
6. Charles isn't able to pay his rent and car loan on time. This makes him very nervous.
7. Each year, some 45 billion gallons of untreated water are discharged into rivers and lakes, which is shocking.
8. The fix-it shop does excellent repairs and guarantees the work. That alone is worth the money.
9. A person needs protection for any accident occurring while at work. This is one benefit of an insurance plan.
10. When a subject is interesting, it is easy to study, but it is difficult when the subject is dull.

Exercise C: Writing Revise the sentences below to remove vague, indefinite, or ambiguous reference of pronouns.

1. Henry's closet is quite small, which is why his clothes are always scattered around his room.
2. We tried to pack the book in this box, but it was too big.
3. At the university, they expect you to take care of yourself.
4. We started painting early, and by noon it was dry.
5. Felicia drove all night, and this exhausted her.
6. Don't pour the soup into the dish if it is cold.
7. When you work in a bank, they give you a lot of holidays.
8. When the woman spoke to the waitress, she smiled.
9. If you don't practice now, you must do it in the morning.
10. In our family you can't be late for meals.

REINFORCEMENT EXERCISES

Pronoun Usage

A. Use pronoun forms correctly. Choose the correct pronoun form from those given in parentheses.

1. Was it Robin Williams and (he, him) who played in the film, *The Survivors?*
2. The rope held (he, him) and (I, me) without snapping.
3. (She, Her) and the mechanic agreed that the alternator needed to be replaced.
4. Weston and (I, me) worked on the camouflage for the tent.
5. The best runners on the team are (he, him) and (I, me).
6. (They, Them) and the other volunteers repaved all the driveways in that complex.
7. Sandra first heard (they, them) on "Soul Train."
8. The salamander avoided (he, him) and (I, me).
9. Stuart and (I, me) are doing a science project on plastics.
10. It was (she, her) who taught classical guitar.

B. Use pronouns correctly. Choose the correct pronoun from those given in parentheses.

1. Phil was told to report to the supervisor and (I, me).
2. Karl dedicated his poem to Mrs. Baxter and (he, him).
3. Just between you and (me, I), I think the latest fashions look bizarre.
4. Nearly everyone arrived at the show before (we, us).
5. My uncle wrote a short story about my friend and (I, me).
6. It was to (us, we) voters that the pamphlet was addressed.
7. When you are in Canada, send a card to Jo and (me, I).
8. Mrs. Grisby does not want to interfere in the debate between you and (he, him).
9. Dr. Bowen gave (we, us) mountain climbers instructions in emergency first aid.
10. I will be thinking of you and (her, she) up here in the cold when I am lying on the beach in Florida.

C. Use *who* and *whom* correctly. Choose the correct pronoun from those given in parentheses.

1. (Who, Whom) has read the book about black holes, white holes, and quasars?
2. The author of *The Sun Also Rises* is (who, whom)?
3. To (who, whom) is that mysterious letter addressed?
4. (Who, Whom) knows what causes cakes to rise?
5. By (who, whom) is the photograph being taken?
6. Is Dali the painter (who, whom) you have chosen for your slide presentation?
7. With (who, whom) are you going to the game?
8. (Who, Whom) did the choreographer choose to dance the lead?
9. (Who, Whom) cut this pineapple into such jagged sections?
10. To (who, whom) did you wish to speak?

D. Use *who* and *whom* in clauses. Choose the correct pronoun from those given in parentheses.

1. The agent made contact with (whoever, whomever) drove the surveillance van.
2. Olof Ohman was a farmer (who, whom) found a stone with Scandinavian lettering in Minnesota, in 1898.
3. Scientists (who, whom) study the weather are called meteorologists.
4. Simón Bolívar is one South American hero (who, whom) is known worldwide.
5. The athletes (who, whom) I admire most are skiers.
6. The audience at the awards ceremony had already guessed (who, whom) the winner was.
7. Give the message to (whoever, whomever) answers.
8. The manager asked (who, whom) wanted responsibility for the new pet department.
9. She is the artist (who, whom) weaves wall hangings out of cashmere wool.
10. The author (who, whom) wrote *The Source* and *The Covenant* is James Michener.

E. Use pronouns correctly. Some of the following sentences contain errors in the use of pronouns. If a sentence is correct as it stands, write *Correct* on your paper. If a sentence is incorrect, change the pronoun as necessary.

1. Hernando threw the shot put further than I.
2. The two newscasters, Jane Pauley and him, commented on the pre-convention festivities.
3. It was her and I that were finally chosen.
4. When it comes to computers, no one is as fanatic as him.
5. Both the coach and the team manager were surprised at him finishing the lap in less than forty seconds.
6. To all the climbers, both the professionals and us amateurs, Blackfoot Glacier presented quite a challenge.
7. Several mazes were built for the psychology class by Coretta and myself.
8. The president of the company worried about their carrying the explosives.
9. All the botany students but yourself are going to tour the nursery.
10. Ms. Quinn, the correspondent from *Newsweek*, told the Chinese ambassador that she wanted to believe him.

F. Use pronouns that agree with antecedents. Find the antecedent of the italicized pronoun in each of the following sentences. If the pronoun agrees with its antecedent, write *Correct* on your paper. If the pronoun does not agree with its antecedent, change the pronoun as necessary.

1. Each of the candidates delivered *their* speeches to extremely small audiences.
2. None of the ambassadors was revealing *their* plan.
3. Some of the flock of geese had lost *their* way.
4. One should know good speaking skills to improve *your* ability to do well in interviews.
5. Neither the rabbit nor the fox had lost *their* winter coat.
6. After a brief adjournment, the council returned to *its* seats.

7. The whale escaped *its* pursuers by diving below the ice and surfacing on the other side.
8. The ballerina was laughing over *her* mistake.
9. Every loser should save *their* ticket stub for the second raffle.
10. One should make sure that the horse is calm before *you* attempt to bridle it.

G. Correct indefinite or ambiguous pronoun reference. Rewrite the following sentences to remove all indefinite or ambiguous pronoun reference.

1. Mason Profitt was a popular rock band, but they don't say what became of it.
2. Separate the buffalo from the zebras and feed them.
3. We heard that Dr. Thompson's manuscript was lost in the mail and were really sorry about it.
4. Because the oven temperature was too high for the bread, it burned.
5. We tried to understand the legal language on the contract, but it was too difficult.
6. The jazz exercises are fun, but they didn't tell me how difficult they would be.
7. She removed the passport from her desk and placed it in her briefcase.
8. The prom committee might hire Junction instead of the Halftones which will make some people happy because they are not as popular.
9. The task of the survey team was to trace the path of the Mississippi into the Gulf of Mexico and to make a map of it.
10. It says that the mayor is going to sponsor a film festival.

MIXED REVIEW

Pronoun Usage

A. Choose the standard form from those given in parentheses.

1. (Who, Whom) does your terrier like best, the veterinarian, or the mail carrier?
2. The nominating committee made (its, their) recommendations after they had reviewed the grades and experience of the candidates.
3. Rice was a steady diet for Mona and (me, myself) while we lived in Samoa.
4. We could not imagine (them, their) moving into the country.
5. The leading scorers on the basketball team are (he, him) and (I, me).
6. Neither Alexis nor (she, her) will leave until the decorations are all hung.
7. These two scientists—Dr. Madden and (she, her)—visited the Amazon jungle to study anacondas and other large snakes.
8. One of the ski instructors left (their, his) equipment in the lodge.
9. Carla taught Max and (I, me, myself) how to ring the bells of the carillon.
10. In the summer a house-sitting service is run by George and (we, us).
11. Anyone (who, whom) has never walked on snowshoes before is likely to develop sore shins.
12. (They, Them) and I work at the Candlelight Dinner Theatre as ushers.
13. (We, Us) Earthlings may not be the only life forms in the universe.
14. Juan won even more prizes at the carnival than (me, I).
15. After the bell rang, the only people left in the hall were Ms. Valenti and (I, me).
16. To (who, whom) was that special delivery package addressed?

17. There is no doubt that this submarine sandwich was ordered by (you, yourself).
18. Leave your car with (whoever, whomever) is working as parking attendant.
19. Do you know (who, whom) will ride on the junior float this year?
20. As Robert Frost neared seventy, many people expected the Nobel Committee to offer (he, him) the prize in literature.

B. Some of the following sentences contain errors in pronoun usage. Rewrite these sentences, eliminating the errors. If there are no errors in a particular sentence, write *Correct*.

1. Wendy, Josh, and me tried out the new toboggan.
2. Neither Sal nor Chuck will bring their guitar.
3. Two famous French singers are Jacques Brel and she.
4. Ms. Blair showed Cindy and I her antique doll collection.
5. The team bus transports them and the cheerleaders.
6. The lead role in *The Rainmaker* is played by she.
7. It didn't sound like her on the phone.
8. Unfortunately, us two could not jump the battery.
9. The band reworked its formation after they realized it was too confusing.
10. Whom do you think will be competing in the finals?
11. We knew that him cooking the dinner was a treat.
12. At the public library, there is a special lounge for us students.
13. Johnny Carson introduced his guests, John Travolta and she.
14. Two of the linemen, Bailey and myself, were offside.
15. The students in charge of the floats are Joyce, Ann, and me.
16. Everyone took their own luggage onto the train.
17. All the gymnasts admire their coach.
18. Each of the lifeguards will get his or her assignment.
19. On weekends, everybody should forget your worries.
20. Julio volunteers at the hospital because it is rewarding.

Pronoun Usage

The following poem is from Edgar Lee Master's *Spoon River Anthology*. The character speaking in the poem is Albert Schirding. Several of the transitional pronouns have been removed and replaced by the words or phrases to which they refer. Rewrite the poem, replacing the italicized words and phrases with pronouns. When you change a noun to a pronoun, you may also have to alter the corresponding verb.

Jonas Keene thought *Jonas Keene's* lot a hard *lot*
Because *Jonas Keene's* children were all failures.
But Albert Schirding knows of a fate more trying than
having children who are all failures:
The fate is to be a failure while your children are
successes.
For Albert Schirding raised a brood of eagles:
The eagles flew away at last, leaving *Albert Schirding*
A crow on the abandoned bough.
Then, with the ambition to prefix Honorable to *Albert*
Schirding's name,
And thus to win *Albert Schirding's* children's admiration,
Albert Schirding ran for county superintendent of schools,
Spending *Albert Schirding's* accumulations to win—and
lost.
That fall *Albert Schirding's* daughter received first prize in
Paris
For *the daughter's* picture, entitled, "The Old Mill"—
(*The picture* was of the water mill before Henry Wilkin put
in steam.)
The feeling that *Albert Schirding* was not worthy of *Albert*
Schirding's daughter finished *Albert Schirding*.

8.0 Adjective and Adverb Usage

Adjectives and adverbs are used as modifiers. Some adjectives look like adverbs, and some adverbs look like adjectives. To avoid confusing these parts of speech, learn the characteristics of each that are presented in this Section.

8.1 Distinguishing Between Adjectives and Adverbs

Usually an adverb is formed by adding an *-ly* ending to an adjective.

ADJECTIVE	ADVERB
swift	swiftly
careless	carelessly
omnivorous	omnivorously

A few adverbs, however, have the same form as the corresponding adjective.

ADJECTIVE	ADVERB
a *fast* sprinter	runs *fast*
a *high* branch	reaches *high*
a *hard* decision	thought *hard*

Most adjectives and adverbs that are spelled alike have only one syllable. Adjectives with two or more syllables usually add an *-ly* ending to form an adverb.

Philadelphia has many buildings of *historical* interest.
This is an *historically* accurate reproduction.

Some adverbs have two forms. One has an *-ly* ending. The other does not. Each is considered correct in certain contexts.

drive *slow*	eat *slowly*
sing *loud*	chewing *loudly*
dive *deep*	sleep *deeply*

The first adverb in each of these pairs can also be used as an adjective: a *slow* leak, a *loud* voice, a *deep* pool. These modifiers may be distinguished by the way they are used in a sentence.

8.2 Using Adjectives and Adverbs Correctly

To decide whether to use an adjective or an adverb, identify which word you want to modify. Adjectives modify nouns and pronouns. An adjective can also be used as a predicate word. Adverbs modify verbs, adjectives, and other adverbs.

A *gelatinous* creature stepped out of the space craft. (The adjective *gelatinous* modifies the noun *creature*.)

The creature looked *transparent*. (The predicate adjective *transparent* is linked to *creature* by the verb *was*.)

The creature crawled *slowly* across the lawn. (The adverb *slowly* modifies the verb *crawled*.)

It was a *highly* intelligent being. (The adverb *highly* modifies the adjective *intelligent*.)

To determine whether a modifier is an adjective or an adverb, determine the part of speech of the word that it modifies.

8.3 The Placement of Adverbs

A modifier that is placed directly before an action verb, an adjective, or another adverb is always an adverb.

Pigs *often* roll in the mud. (modifies the verb *roll*)
Sometimes they get *quite* dirty. (modifies the adjective *dirty*)
A pig *very* definitely requires constant care. (modifies the adverb *definitely*)

When an adverb comes after the word it modifies, it is sometimes tempting to use an adjective instead.

NONSTANDARD: Sheri sings beautiful.
STANDARD: Sheri sings beautifully.

A word that comes after an action verb and that modifies the verb is an adverb.

8.4 Adjectives with Linking Verbs

A linking verb is usually followed by an adjective rather than an adverb. The adjective is linked to the subject which it modifies. The choice of adjective after the verb *be* does not cause any confusion. However, most of the other linking verbs may also be used as action verbs.

look	appear	smell	stay	grow	seem
sound	feel	taste	remain	become	act

Use an adjective to modify the subject after a linking verb. Use an adverb to modify the verb after an action verb.

The owner of the car *appeared suddenly*.
(*appeared* is an action verb modified by an adverb.)

The officer *appeared angry*. (*appeared* is a linking verb followed by a predicate adjective.)

Betty *looked quickly* at her ticket.
(*looked* is an action verb modified by an adverb.)

Gary *looked happy.*
(*looked* is a linking verb followed by a predicate adjective.)

To determine whether a verb is used as a linking verb or an action verb, substitute a form of *be* for the verb. If the sentence still makes sense, the verb is a linking verb.

The speaker *seemed* (uneasy, uneasily).
(*The speaker was uneasily* does not make sense. *The speaker was uneasy* makes sense; *seemed* is a linking verb here.)

The speaker *looked* (uneasy, uneasily) at the clock.
(*was* will not make sense with either modifier; *looked* is an action verb here.)

Exercise A: Choose the standard form from those given in parentheses.

1. You can (easy, easily) finish the job in an hour.
2. The sky remained (clear, clearly) all day long.
3. The mechanics stayed (steady, steadily) on the job until it was finished.
4. The rancher seemed (uneasy, uneasily) about the rapidly approaching storm.
5. Mary felt (happy, happily) about her report card.
6. Darla (quick, quickly) picked up her camera and ran to the open door.
7. Phil thought he would (certain, certainly) fail the test because he did not study.
8. You can run a small car more (economical, economically) than a large one.
9. The poem sounds (strange, strangely) in French.
10. Vanessa's knee was hurt (bad, badly) in the first half of the basketball game.

Exercise B: Decide whether the italicized modifier is standard or nonstandard. If it is nonstandard, substitute the standard form.

1. With algebra I can solve this problem *easy*.
2. Darnell sounded *angrily* over the telephone.
3. Football is played *differently* in Canada.
4. The repair job was not done *careful*, and the lawn mower broke down again.
5. Marta gazed *unhappily* at her ruined photographs.
6. The left shoe now seemed to fit *perfect*.
7. Our dog smells each new arrival *suspiciously*.
8. The boys had lost their way *completely*.
9. Ms. Brown thinks that Jane acted *disrespectful* to her when they were boarding the plane.
10. Allen and Brad gave their report *perfect*.

8.5 *This—These; That—Those*

This and *that* modify singular words. *These* and *those* modify plural words. The words *kind, sort,* and *type* require a singular modifier.

NONSTANDARD: *These* kind are my favorites.
STANDARD: *This* kind is my favorite.

NONSTANDARD: *These* sort of shoes hurt my feet.
STANDARD: *This* sort of shoe hurts my feet.

8.6 *Them—Those*

Those may be either a pronoun or an adjective. *Them* is always a pronoun and never an adjective.

NONSTANDARD: Where did you put *them* tools?
STANDARD: Where did you put *those* tools?
STANDARD: Where did you put *them*?
STANDARD: *Those* are my tools.

8.7 *Bad—Badly*

In standard usage, *bad* is always used after linking verbs. Use *badly* to modify action verbs, adjectives, and adverbs.

He felt *bad*. (*not* he felt badly)
The yard looked *bad*.

It was a *badly* executed design.
The avalanche damaged the car *badly*.

8.8 *Good—Well*

Good is an adjective. It modifies nouns and pronouns. Do not use *good* to modify verbs, adjectives, or adverbs.

Well is an adjective and an adverb. As an adjective *well* means "in good health." As an adverb *well* means "properly or expertly performed."

It took a long time for Cindy to feel *well*.
Our dog guards the house *well*.

8.9 *Fewer—Less*

Fewer is used to describe things that can be counted. *Less* refers to quantity or degree.

Jack has *fewer* colds than he used to have.
There is *less* snow today than yesterday.
This lamp gives *less* light than the other one.

Exercise: Tell if the italicized words are standard or nonstandard usage. Substitute a standard form for each nonstandard one.

1. Supposedly there are *less* problems with this new film.
2. Glen likes *those* cookies; he can never get enough of *them*.
3. He certainly had enough of *these* cookies yesterday.

4. The report of Ruth's illness sounds *badly* to me.
5. Stir the mixture *good* before adding the milk.
6. Harriet feels *badly* about losing her jade earring.
7. Ted had *fewer* first-place votes than George.
8. You will have *less* interruptions if you work in the library.
9. I have never seen *these* kind of fish before.
10. Have you sold *them* tires yet?
11. I don't think Julie is well; she looks *badly* to me.
12. You can see just as *good* from the balcony.
13. Those plums are not as sweet as *these* kind.
14. We have seen *less* tourists here this year.
15. My grandfather doesn't hear so *good* any more.

8.10 Comparative and Superlative

Adjectives and adverbs describe words and tell what their qualities are. These qualities may be compared by using the **comparative** or the **superlative** form. The comparative is used to compare two things. The superlative is used to express the highest degree of a quality when three or more are compared.

COMPARATIVE ADJECTIVE: Your brownies are *chewier* than the commercial kind.
SUPERLATIVE ADJECTIVE: The sun is the *brightest* star in the sky.
COMPARATIVE ADVERB: Jill runs *faster* than Elaine.
SUPERLATIVE ADVERB: Of all the planes, Milo's can fly *lowest*.

Adjectives in Comparisons

The **comparative** form of adjectives is made in two ways.

1. Most adjectives of one syllable and a few adjectives with two, add *-er* to form the comparative.

hard—harder wise—wiser
mighty—mightier happy—happier

2. Most adjectives with two syllables and all adjectives with more than two syllables use *more* and *less* to form the comparative.

hopeful—more hopeful	ridiculous—more ridiculous
cautious—less cautious	crowded—less crowded

Like the comparative, the **superlative** is formed in two different ways. Adjectives that form the comparative with *-er* form the superlative with *-est*. Adjectives that form the comparative by adding the words *more* and *less*, form the superlative with *most* and *least*.

ADJECTIVE	COMPARATIVE	SUPERLATIVE
great	greater	greatest
clear	clearer	clearest
warm	warmer	warmest
funny	funnier	funniest
wrinkled	more wrinkled	most wrinkled
miserable	less miserable	least miserable
abstract	more abstract	most abstract
colorful	less colorful	least colorful

Irregular Comparison Using Adjectives

The comparative and superlative forms of some frequently-used adjectives are irregular. They are made by changing the words themselves.

ADJECTIVE	COMPARATIVE	SUPERLATIVE
good	better	best
well	better	best
bad	worse	worst
ill	worse	worst
little	less *or* lesser	least
much	more	most
many	more	most
far	farther *or* further	farthest *or* furthest

Adverbs in Comparisons

Like adjectives, adverbs have comparative and superlative forms. The comparative form is made in two ways.

1. Most adverbs of one syllable form the comparative by adding *-er*.

   The team worked *harder* today than yesterday.
   Missy practiced her dance routine *longer* than Juliana.

2. Most adverbs ending in *-ly* form the comparative with *more* and *less*.

   Jenny proofreads *more carefully* than Josh.
   The second window opened *less easily*.

The superlative form of the adverb is formed with *-est* or the words *most* and *least*. Adverbs that form the comparative with *-er* form the superlative with *-est*. Those that use *more* and *less* for the comparative use *most* and *least* for the superlative.

ADVERB	COMPARATIVE	SUPERLATIVE
fast	faster	fastest
early	earlier	earliest
closely	more closely	most closely
accurately	less accurately	least accurately

Irregular Comparison Using Adverbs

A few adverbs have irregular comparative and superlative forms.

ADVERB	COMPARATIVE	SUPERLATIVE
well	better	best
much	more	most
little	less	least
late	later	latest, last
far	farther, further	farthest, furthest

Exercise A: Find each adjective. Tell whether it is in comparative form or superlative form.

1. It was the worst play I had ever seen.
2. Houston is larger than Dallas.
3. He was the most mischievous person I knew.
4. Who is older, Peg or Bill?
5. We chose the longest and most scenic route.
6. Can't you find a more recent encyclopedia?
7. The Cullinan diamond is the largest ever discovered.
8. Ellis is undoubtedly the best dancer in the class.
9. The quarterback is often the smallest and lightest person on the team.
10. There are more sailboats in the harbor today.

Exercise B: Find each adverb. Tell whether it is in the comparative or the superlative form.

1. My digital watch keeps time more precisely than the grandfather clock in the hall.
2. She can play tennis more easily with her left hand.
3. Try to type less quickly and more accurately in the future.
4. Which of our batters can hit the ball farthest?
5. The ancient Egyptians made cloth more skillfully than twentieth century machines.
6. Which of the skaters executed the turn most gracefully?
7. Princess Di dresses more fashionably than other members of the royal household.
8. The stars appear to shine more brightly in the country.
9. Why do crickets chirp loudest when you are trying to get to sleep?
10. You accompany the singer better on the accordian than on the piano.

Exercise C: Writing Write ten pairs of sentences. Ten should show adjectives used in the comparative and superlative forms. Ten should show adverbs used in the comparative and superlative forms.

8.11 The Double Comparison

To make the comparative form of an adjective or adverb, add *-er* or use the word *more* or *less*. It is nonstandard to use both.

To make the superlative form of an adjective or adverb, add *-est* or use the word *most* or *least*. It is nonstandard to use both.

NONSTANDARD: My dress is more prettier than yours.
STANDARD: My dress is prettier than yours.

NONSTANDARD: Nathaniel is the least likeliest candidate I have ever seen.
STANDARD: Nathaniel is the least likely candidate I have ever seen.

NONSTANDARD: Those boys play more rougher than anyone else in school.
STANDARD: Those boys play rougher than anyone else in school.

NONSTANDARD: The spectators watched less closer as the day wore on.
STANDARD: The spectators watched less closely as the day wore on.

8.12 Illogical Comparisons

The word *other*, or the word *else*, is required in comparisons of an individual member with the rest of the group.

ILLOGICAL: Our team has scored more points than any team in the league. (Our team is also in the league.)
CLEAR: Our team has scored more points than any *other* team in the league.

ILLOGICAL: Helen is as talented as anyone in her class.
CLEAR: Helen is as talented as anyone *else* in her class.

The words *than* or *as* are required after the first modifier in a compound comparison.

ILLOGICAL: Natalie is as tall if not taller than Joy.

CLEAR BUT AWKWARD: Natalie is as tall as, if not taller than, Joy.

BETTER: Natalie is as tall as Joy, if not taller.

ILLOGICAL: Paul had as much reason to be optimistic if not more than I did.

CLEAR: Paul had as much reason to be optimistic as I did, if not more.

ILLOGICAL: Your chances of getting into a good college are as good if not better than Bert's.

CLEAR: Your chances of getting into a good college are as good as Bert's, if not better.

Both parts of a comparison must be stated completely if there is any chance of its being misunderstood.

CONFUSING: I trust her more than Lisa.

CLEAR: I trust her more than Lisa does.

CLEAR: I trust her more than I trust Lisa.

CONFUSING: Ohio State beat Purdue worse than Indiana.

CLEAR: Ohio State beat Purdue worse than Indiana did.

CLEAR: Ohio State beat Purdue worse than it defeated Indiana.

ILLOGICAL: The income of a doctor is greater than a nurse.

CLEAR: The income of a doctor is greater than that of a nurse.

BETTER: A doctor has a greater income than a nurse has.

Exercise A: Writing Revise these sentences to make the comparisons clear.

1. We will sing this part a little more softer.
2. Is the career of an engineer more exciting than a lawyer?
3. We have read more of Willa Cather's stories than Eudora Welty.

4. This traveling bag is much more lighter than mine.
5. This year our classes are as large or larger than they were last year.
6. My sister has more sweaters than anyone I know.
7. Chicago's O'Hare Airport is busier than any airport in the country.
8. We have as much homework if not more than college students.
9. Alana worked as long at the radio station as the photo lab.
10. Life in a city is more exciting than the country.

Exercise B: Writing Follow the directions for Exercise A.

1. We waited for Lynn longer than Betty.
2. Your chances of winning the diving competition are as good as Julie.
3. German is as hard if not harder than French.
4. More people in the world eat rice than any food.
5. Please be a little more quieter.
6. The ranchers disliked the settlers more than the Indians.
7. Bill is faster than any person in his class.
8. We see Tom more often than his family.
9. *A Tale of Two Cities* is as good or better than *Oliver Twist*.
10. We could have come more sooner if Janet had been well.

8.13 The Double Negative

The double negative is an error that occurs when a second negative word is added to a construction that is already negative. This error occurs most often when the adverb *not* is contracted to *n't*.

NONSTANDARD: I *don't know nothing* about the accident.
STANDARD: I *don't know anything* about the accident.

NONSTANDARD: We *don't* have *no* papers.
STANDARD: We *don't* have *any* papers.

Hardly, barely, or *scarcely,* used with a negative word, is nonstandard.

NONSTANDARD: There *wasn't hardly* anyone in the pool.
STANDARD: There *was hardly* anyone in the pool.

NONSTANDARD: I could*n't barely* hear the orchestra.
STANDARD: I could *barely* hear the orchestra.

Exercise: These sentences cover all the problems of adjective and adverb usage in this Section. Choose the standard form from within the parentheses.

1. Gina (had, hadn't) hardly any money left.
2. You can (easy, easily) push the car down the hill.
3. The boys in the class were not acting (helpful, helpfully).
4. Look (careful, carefully) before you back up.
5. There (were, weren't) scarcely any trees left on the farm.
6. If you look (alert, alertly), you will make a good impression.
7. The car was damaged (bad, badly) in the crash.
8. Wipe your shoes (good, well) before you come in.
9. You can't get (them, those, that) kind (no, any) more.
10. We (had, hadn't) barely enough gas to get home.
11. The auditorium (was, wasn't) hardly half filled.
12. The milk tastes (bad, badly) to me today.
13. We grew (uneasy, uneasily) when Henry failed to come back.
14. Beth didn't do very (good, well) on the last test.
15. We prefer (them, this, these) sort of movie to westerns.
16. Mark is making (less, fewer) typing errors than before.
17. Of the two cities, New York is the (cleaner, cleanest).
18. The rest of the class were sitting (quiet, quietly).
19. We had never seen a (more lovelier, lovelier) day.
20. There are (less, fewer) stairs to climb in our new house.

REINFORCEMENT EXERCISES

Adjective and Adverb Usage

A. Use adjectives and adverbs correctly. Rewrite the following sentences, correcting errors in the use of modifiers. If a sentence contains no errors, write *Correct*.

1. The weather forecaster said that one should drive slow on entrance ramps and bridges.
2. We were surprised that the soup tasted sweetly.
3. From the bandstand across the river, we could hear the lovely sound of a concertina.
4. You can see the cilia on the paramecium move if you look close enough.
5. The passengers looked calmly in spite of the turbulence.
6. Herman's friends took the news very hard.
7. Huck was terrible curious to explore the abandoned boat.
8. The detectives looked careful around the scene for clues.
9. Ms. Santos appeared flushed, but she didn't have a fever.
10. Colleen did wonderful on her exam in French class.

B. Use troublesome modifiers correctly. Rewrite the following sentences correcting errors in the use of modifiers. If a sentence contains no errors, write *Correct*.

1. You shouldn't believe *those* kind of fables.
2. You'll soon feel *good* again if you get some rest.
3. I play backgammon *badly,* but I excel at Chinese checkers.
4. *This* kind of vacation is more tiring than it is relaxing.
5. *These* sort of jazz band can be heard in New Orleans.
6. *Less* people attended the hockey game than attended the basketball game.
7. *Them* silverfish are insects that feed on starch and paper.
8. The discussion was going good until you made that insensitive remark.
9. The dog looked *badly* after its encounter with a badger.
10. The local college has one of *them* new scoreboards.

C. Correct improper comparisons. Revise the following sentences, correcting all errors in comparison.

1. The large, gray female was the smarter of the three mongrel puppies.
2. Court jesters were more wittier than today's clowns.
3. To me, the metamorphosis of a butterfly is more interesting than a frog.
4. In the playoffs between the Orioles and the White Sox, the Orioles had the best team.
5. The film we just saw was much better than any movie that's been out this year.
6. I trust Claxton more than Randolf.
7. Sandy knows the game *Dungeons and Dragons* better than Mark.
8. Italy is more fascinating than any country.
9. Vicki is as pleasant as if not more pleasant than Terry.
10. The local residents valued the trees more than the contractors who wanted to build on the site.

D. Correct double negatives. Rewrite the following sentences, correcting the double negatives.

1. Lleweleyn had never pitched no horseshoe game before.
2. During the 1930's, there wasn't nobody who didn't listen to the radio.
3. Leslie hadn't never heard of the singer Al Jarreau.
4. Unlike baking powder, baking soda doesn't contain no starch.
5. Sidney felt as if she hadn't barely closed her eyes before the alarm rang.
6. The desert air didn't hardly contain no water vapor.
7. Winnie didn't scarcely appreciate being pushed into the muddy river.
8. Nobody on the speeding train couldn't stop it.
9. Please don't put out no more of those kiwi fruits.
10. Wouldn't none of the new basketball jerseys fit you?

MIXED REVIEW

Adjective and Adverb Usage

A. Choose the standard form from those given in parentheses.

1. The technicians (could, couldn't) barely track the satellite.
2. Martin did (fewer, less) pushups than Kiyoshi.
3. The carolers made a (joyful, joyfully) sound.
4. Andrés Segovia is more famous than (any, any other) classical guitarist.
5. Fred's grandfather spoke Yiddish (better, more better) than he spoke Hebrew.
6. The roasted roots and bulbs tasted (delicious, deliciously) to the lost hikers.
7. The decorator of the restaurant chose the furnishings (well, good).
8. There weren't (any, no) metal tools during the Stone Age.
9. The collector displayed his baseball card collection (proud, proudly).
10. The king cobra is one of the (longer, longest) and (more, most) deadly of all snakes.
11. Can you solve (them, these) puzzles before the hour is up?
12. Americans eat beef (more often, most often) than they eat pork.
13. Chandra hadn't (ever, never) visited Chicago before.
14. The biologist pointed (quick, quickly) to the frog's intestine.
15. I've never noticed (them, those) old totem poles before.
16. The soil of that overworked section of ground seems very (poor, poorly).
17. Of all the Presidents, Herbert Hoover is perhaps the (more misunderstood, most misunderstood).
18. Olivia (had, hadn't) barely recovered from the strenuous swim meet when she entered the bicycle race.
19. The effects of such a long period of malnutrition sound (serious, seriously).
20. Juan read the poetry selection quite (beautiful, beautifully).

B. Some of the following sentences contain errors in the use of modifiers. Identify these sentences and rewrite them. If a sentence is already correct, write *Correct*.

1. The lawyer argued forceful for her client's freedom.
2. Emily seemed happily when she heard the results of the examination.
3. Does the electric engine appear efficient?
4. That school offers less vocational courses than our school.
5. The handwriting analyst looked closely at certain letters.
6. This kinds of rock groups fade in popularity.
7. Who borrowed them musical scores?
8. Marcia felt bad about losing her friend's scarf.
9. The goalie has the harder job of all the players.
10. The relay team swam good in yesterday's meet.
11. If they aren't ripe, apples taste badly.
12. Linda won't eat no desserts that contain a lot of sugar.
13. We could pitch a tent or sleep in the open air, but a tent would be warmer.
14. When the band performed bad, the audience was disappointed.
15. Dehydrated food is the most easiest kind for campers to fix.
16. America hasn't barely begun to use metrics.
17. "60 Minutes" may be more informative than any TV show.
18. Next year's team will have less seniors on it.
19. We could hardly hold back our laughter.
20. Sandra had a better sense of direction than anyone in the wilderness course.

USING GRAMMAR IN WRITING

Adjective and Adverb Usage

A. Choose one of your favorite popular songs and design your own video to accompany it. Make two columns on a piece of paper and label them *Audio Track* and *Visual Track*. Write the lyrics of the song in the *Audio Track* column. Then, next to each verse of the song, describe a visual scene that complements the verse. Use adjectives and adverbs throughout to make your descriptions vivid and precise.

EXAMPLE:

Audio Track	Visual Track
Who are you? Who's behind the mask? What must I do, What things should I ask?	close shot of a mask with one half wildly elaborate, and the other half starkly simple

B. Stilts, which today are used mainly by circus performers, may have originated in the Landes region of France, where they were used by shepherds to cross very soft, wet ground. Imagine that you are such a shepherd several hundred years ago, and that, after a hard day's work, you are going to participate in a stilt race. Write a description of this race. Use both adjectives and adverbs to describe your own attempts and those of your friends. Try to include some modifiers in both comparative and superlative forms.

C. Choose two similar films, television shows, or books and write a review comparing them to one another and to other books or shows of their kind. Use comparative and superlative modifiers in your review.

9.0 The Right Word

If you wish to communicate effectively, an important concept to understand is the distinction between **standard usage** and **nonstandard usage.** Standard usages are words and phrases that are acceptable at all times and in all places. Nonstandard usages are words and phrases that are not acceptable everywhere.

Nonstandard usages may be perfectly acceptable in casual conversation. In other situations, however, they may brand the user as careless or untrained in the English language. Consequently, skillful use of English requires a thorough familiarity with standard usage. (If you would like more information on the levels of standard and nonstandard usage, consult Chapter 3 in this book.)

The word lists that follow provide a guide to some commonly confused and misused words and expressions. Refer to these lists when you have questions about standard usage. If your question is not covered on one of these lists, consult a good dictionary.

9.1 Words Commonly Confused

accept, except To *accept* is "to agree to something or to receive something willingly." To *except* is "to exclude or omit." As a preposition, *except* means "but" or "excluding."

I hope you will *accept* my apologies.
Students with low grades are *excepted* from the team.
Everybody *except* Scrooge loves holidays. (preposition)

adapt, adopt To keep the meanings of these words straight, look at the second syllables. *Adapt* means "to make *apt* or suitable; to adjust." *Adopt*, on the other hand, means "to *opt* or choose as one's own; to accept."

The dressmaker *adapted* the pattern to fit.
After the accident, Cary *adopted* a new outlook.

advise, advice *Advise* is a verb; *advice* is a noun. You *advise* someone. What you give that person is *advice*.

affect, effect *Affect* is a verb meaning either "to influence" or "to pretend." *Effect* as a verb means "to accomplish or to produce as a result." As a noun, *effect* means "result."

The drought *affected* this season's harvest of melons.
The child *affected* her great-aunt's manners.

We hope *to effect* a permanent change in pay scales.
What *effect* can one vote have? (noun)

agree to, with, on You agree *to* something such as a plan of action. You agree *with* someone else, or something such as spinach does not agree *with* you. You agree with others *on* a course of action.

allusion, illusion An *allusion* is a reference to something. An *illusion* is a false idea or faulty interpretation of the facts.

The book makes vague *allusions* to the Kennedy family.
My dog has an *illusion* that he is a person.

already, all ready *Already* is an adverb meaning "even now" or "previously." *All ready* is an adjective phrase meaning "completely prepared."

It is *already* midnight.
Are you *all ready* for school to start?

altogether, all together *Altogether* means "entirely" or "on the whole." *All together* means that all parts of a group are considered together.

Her visit was *altogether* unexpected. (entirely)
The cast rehearsed *all together* the night before the play.

among, between *Between* expresses the joining or separation of two people or things. *Among* refers to a group of three or more.

NONSTANDARD: We had a lively discussion *between* the four of us.
STANDARD: We had a lively discussion *among* the four of us.
STANDARD: There are no secrets *between* him and me.

amount, number *Amount* is used to indicate a total sum of things. It is usually used to refer to items that cannot be counted. *Number* is used to refer to items that can be counted.

The dairy processes a large *amount* of cheese.
The farmer harvested a large *number* of pumpkins.

angry at, with You are angry *with* a person and angry *at* a thing.

bad, badly See Section 8.7.

being This completely acceptable present participle is often misused in the awkward phrases *being as* and *being that*. Instead of these phrases, use *since* or *because*.

NONSTANDARD: *Being that* I am the leader, I'll decide.
STANDARD: *Since* I am the leader, I'll decide.

beside, besides *Beside* means "at the side of." *Besides* means "in addition to."

My best friend stood *beside* me at tryouts.
Besides skill, the judges also looked for enthusiasm.

between *Between* is not followed by a singular noun.

NONSTANDARD: *Between each house* was a row of bushes.
STANDARD: *Between* the houses was a row of bushes.

borrow, lend *Borrow* and *lend* are verbs. You *borrow from* someone. You *lend to* someone.

NONSTANDARD: Did I *borrow* you my bike?
STANDARD: Did I *lend* you my bike?
STANDARD: Did you *borrow* my bike?

bring, take *Bring* means motion toward someone or some place; *take* means motion away from someone or some place.

May I *bring* my friend home? (toward here)
I will *take* the dog to the veterinarian. (away from here)
November *brings* chilly weather. (toward us)

can, may *Can* means "able or having the power to do something." *May* is used to ask or to grant permission. It also expresses the probability of something happening.

Terri *can* paddle a canoe. (ability)
May we watch television? (permission)
The train *may* arrive late. (probability)

Could is the past tense of *can; might* is the past of *may.*

continual, continuous *Continual* means "occurring repeatedly or at intervals over a long period." *Continuous* means "extending without interruption in space or time."

The faulty alarm system was *continually* causing problems.
The din from the construction was *continuous* through the afternoon.

differ from, with One thing or person differs *from* another in characteristics. You differ *with* someone when you disagree with him or her.

different from, different than In most situations *different from* is better usage than *different than*. However, there are some situations in which *than* must be used to avoid awkward expression.

> Your translation of Molière's plays is *different from* mine.
> My elementary school looks *different than* it did when I was six years old.

disinterested, uninterested *Disinterested* means "neutral; unbiased by personal advantage." *Uninterested* means simply "having no interest."

> NONSTANDARD: A good judge is fair and *uninterested*.
> STANDARD: A good judge is fair and *disinterested*.

Exercise A: Writing Rewrite these sentences to make them follow standard usage. Some words are already used correctly.

1. Can we please bring some candy on the bus?
2. Good advise usually affects a person's decision.
3. A large amount of students chatted between themselves.
4. Being that I am on a diet, I eat no food accept carrot sticks between each meal.
5. Only altogether uninterested people should be chosen for juries.
6. The chefs agreed with how to adapt the recipe for large groups of people.
7. The trick-or-treaters felt badly when they could not find a bell to ring besides the door.
8. Coaches get angry at teams that do not work together.
9. Opticians differ with ophthalmologists in the number of years they train.
10. If I work continually on this project, it will be finished in a few hours.

Exercise B: Follow the directions for Exercise A.

1. Can I take back the pen that I borrowed you?
2. By the time Jessie got home, it was all ready ten o'clock.
3. You can learn to except a certain amount of compliments.
4. He differs from me on a lot of issues beside energy.
5. Between each serve, I listened to the tennis pro's advise.
6. Many athletes are uninterested in tournaments between all the conference schools.
7. Carrie will bring her sister anywhere accept here.
8. The delegates finally agreed with the adapted proposals.
9. The diesel engine is all together different from the fuel-pump engine.
10. Some dieters are under the allusion that weight-reducing aids will have an instant effect.

eager, anxious These words are not synonyms. *Anxious* indicates "experiencing uneasiness caused by anticipated anger or misfortune." *Eager* means "longing or enthusiastic."

NONSTANDARD: The class seemed *anxious* to begin.
STANDARD: The student was *anxious* about the test.
STANDARD: However, she was *eager* to finish.

emigrate, immigrate To *emigrate* is to leave one's homeland. To *immigrate* is to enter a country in order to settle there.

fewer, less See Section 8.9.

formally, formerly *Formally* means "in a formal manner." *Formerly* means "previously."

The candidate *formally* accepted the nomination.
Jan *formerly* worked as a dogsitter.

further, farther; furthest, farthest *Farther* is used for comparisons of distance and *further* for any other comparisons.

My house is *farther* from school than yours. (distance)
Further research is necessary. (extent)

good, well See Section 8.8.

hanged, hung Criminals are *hanged*. Things are *hung* on walls, hooks, or elsewhere.

The swindler was *hanged* at sunset.
The butcher *hung* the hams from hooks.

imply, infer A speaker or writer suggests or *implies* something. The reader, listener, or observer comes to a conclusion or *infers* something on the basis of what is heard.

The editor *implied* that teenagers are lazy.
I *infer* that you disapprove.

in, into *In* means "inside something." *Into* tells of motion from the outside to the inside of something.

NONSTANDARD: Toni dashed *in* the classroom fifteen minutes late.
STANDARD: Toni dashed *into* the classroom fifteen minutes late.

NONSTANDARD: I dropped my homework *in* a puddle.
STANDARD: I dropped my homework *into* a puddle.

is where, is when The use of *where* or *when* in a definition is nonstandard unless the definition refers to a time or place.

NONSTANDARD: A slalom is *where* you ski over a zigzag, downhill course.
STANDARD: A slalom *is* a ski race over a zigzag, downhill course.
STANDARD: A zigzag, downhill course is *where* a slalom race is held.

it's, its *It's* is a contraction for *it is*. *Its* is a possessive pronoun meaning "belonging to it."

kind, sort, type See Section 8.5.

lay, lie See Section 5.6.

learn, teach To *learn* means "to gain knowledge or instruction." To *teach* is "to provide knowledge" or "to instruct."

After the counselors *learn* the song, they will *teach* it to the campers.

leave, let *Leave* means "to go away from." *Let* means "permit." The principal parts of these verbs are *leave, left, left,* and *let, let, let*.

NONSTANDARD: Please *leave* Carla finish her dinner.
STANDARD: Please *let* Carla finish her dinner.
STANDARD: A witness should not *leave* the scene of a crime.

like, as, as if The use of *like* as a conjunction is not fully established in writing. It is better to use *like* as a preposition.

NOT ACCEPTED: I feel *like* you do about vegetarian food.
BETTER: I feel *as* you do about vegetarian food.

NOT ACCEPTED: Cal acted *like* he didn't expect a gift.
BETTER: Cal acted *as if* he didn't expect a gift.
STANDARD: *Like* any cat, Garfield wants prompt service.

most, almost *Almost* is an adverb meaning "nearly." *Most* is an adjective meaning "the greater part."

NONSTANDARD: *Most* everywhere you go, people are talking about computers.
STANDARD: *Almost* everywhere you go, people are talking about computers.

of, have When *could have, might have, must have,* and similar phrases are spoken, they usually come out as contractions: *could've, might've, must've,* and so on. Because the contracted form *'ve* sounds like *of*, some people mistakenly write *could of, might of, must of*.

NONSTANDARD: You *must of* touched poison ivy.
STANDARD: You *must have* touched poison ivy.

only The placement of this word can change and sometimes confuse the meaning of a sentence. For clarity, it should be positioned before the word(s) it qualifies. Notice the difference in meaning:

Ten people are invited *only* to the ceremony.
Only ten people are invited to the ceremony.

percent, percentage *Percent* is correctly used only when preceded by a number. When there is no preceding number, *percentage* is correct.

About *50 percent* of the students attended the play.
Only a small *percentage* of the cast members had performed before.

raise, rise See Section 5.6.

real, really In precise usage *real* is an adjective, and *really* is an adverb.

NOT ACCEPTED: A laser beam is *real* powerful.
BETTER: A laser beam is *really* powerful.

their, they're, there *Their* is a possessive pronoun meaning "belonging to them." *They're* is a contraction for "they are." *There*, like *here*, refers to a place.

to, too *To* is a preposition used to introduce prepositional phrases: *to the beach, to me*. *To* is also the sign of the infinitive: *to* be. *Too* is an adverb meaning "overly" or "also."

unique *Unique* means "one of a kind." Therefore, it is illogical to qualify the word, as in "somewhat unique." A few other absolute words that do not take comparatives or superlatives are *equal, fatal, final, absolute*.

NONSTANDARD: This necklace is *rather unique*.
STANDARD: This necklace is *unique*.

NONSTANDARD: The wound was *completely fatal*.
STANDARD: The wound was *fatal*.

way, ways *Ways* is misused when it refers to distance.

NONSTANDARD: Our hotel is a long *ways* from the beach.
STANDARD: Our hotel is a long *way* from the beach.
STANDARD: There are as many *ways* to make chicken soup as there are cooks.

your, you're *Your* is a possessive pronoun meaning "belonging to you." *You're* is a contraction meaning "you are."

Exercise A: Writing Rewrite these sentences to make them follow standard usage. Some words are already used correctly.

1. Randi hopped into the pond like a frog would.
2. I wish we had been formerly introduced.
3. Most joggers wear this kind of a shoe.
4. The country's emigration laws limit the number of people who can settle their.
5. Criminals are seldom hung nowadays.
6. I imply from your comments that you would of preferred a different kind of class.
7. I hope they will leave us go a little way further down the expressway.
8. Quadrophonic sound is when a receiver has four speakers.
9. A certain percent of people have rather unique names.
10. Only humans are the animals who can reason.

Exercise B: Writing Follow the directions for Exercise A.

1. At the beginning of summer we lowered the boat in the water.
2. The museum hanged the expressionist paintings in a rather unique way.
3. We decided to be real lazy and just lay around all day.
4. I am real anxious to see my favorite uncle, who was formally a firefighter.
5. Did the principal infer that she would leave us put up all these posters?
6. Fifty-one percentage is needed only to pass the bill.

7. We must of walked a real long ways.
8. A knockout is where a boxer is knocked down and can't get up off the mat within ten seconds.
9. I should of explored the topic farther as my teacher and my dad advised.
10. Will Joel's parents leave him go on the trip or will he have to stay home with his sister?

9.2 Words Commonly Misused

a lot This pair of words is misused *a lot*. Some people combine the two words to make one. The misspelling *alot* is nonstandard. Also, the phrase is overused. Substitute other expressions like "a great deal" for variety.

all of The *of* is unnecessary except before pronouns.

NONSTANDARD: Childers sent *all of* the invitations.
STANDARD: Childers sent *all* the invitations
STANDARD: Childers sent *all of* them.

all right This pair of words is sometimes misspelled as one. *Alright* is nonstandard.

anywhere, nowhere, somewhere, anyway *Anywheres, nowheres, somewheres,* and *anyways* are nonstandard.

had of, off of The *of* is unnecessary and nonstandard.

NONSTANDARD: If Paul *had of* come, we would have won the game.
STANDARD: If Paul *had* come, we would have won the game.

NONSTANDARD: The plate rolled *off of* the table.
STANDARD: The plate rolled *off* the table.

kind of a, sort of a The *a* is unnecessary and nonstandard.

NONSTANDARD: What *kind of a* party do you want?
STANDARD: What *kind of* party do you want?

majority This word can be used only with items that can be counted. It is nonstandard if used in speaking of time or distance.

NONSTANDARD: The *majority* of the book was in English.
STANDARD: *Most* of the book was in English.

seldom ever The *ever* is unnecessary and nonstandard. Use *seldom, very seldom,* or *hardly ever* instead.

Exercise: Writing Rewrite the following sentences, correcting any errors in usage.

1. This is the kind of a day that always makes me feel alright.
2. The crying child had fallen off of her bicycle.
3. Edith's parents seldom ever scold their children.
4. The majority of the time should of been spent making paper flowers.
5. It's alright to cry when you are depressed.
6. The person who had been tapping at the window was nowheres in sight.
7. All of the dishes needed to be washed.
8. If you think about all of the hours you put in sleeping, you will realize that it is alot.
9. Somewheres in all this mess I left my keys.
10. Alot of people would love to train for the Olympics.

REINFORCEMENT EXERCISES

The Right Word

A. Use commonly confused words correctly. Some of the following sentences contain errors in word choice. Rewrite these sentences, correcting any errors. If a sentence contains no errors, write *Correct*.

1. Do vaporizers differ with humidifiers in any way?
2. Train rides do not agree with me; they give me severe motion sickness.
3. Nikki adviced me to take photographs of both natural and artificial surfaces.
4. In the Polynesian game *ula maika*, players try to knock over an amount of pins with balls of stone.
5. The landslide was altogether too close for comfort.
6. As bees, termites live in large colonies organized along caste lines.
7. Rex did not want to borrow me his trivia book before the contest.
8. By the time the zoologists reached the eagle's nest, the eggs had all ready hatched.
9. Marnie likes every kind of vegetable accept artichokes.
10. Can I write a report on the supposedly haunted houses of England?
11. The rodeo rider must of broken his ribs half a dozen times.
12. Many sports commentators were formally professional football players.
13. Most all stomach ulcers are treated with alkaline drugs and a controlled diet.
14. The book inferred that the government did not deal fairly with the Native American tribes.
15. This information is only to be discussed between us three.
16. Great white sharks do not travel the oceans in schools like anchovies do.
17. During earlier times, criminals were hung for minor offenses.

18. A bear can rake berries from a bush by using it's claws.
19. Gray hair is usually due too a loss of melanin, a pigment that produces hair color.
20. The drama teacher promised to leave me design the backdrop for *Oklahoma*.

B. Use commonly misused words correctly. Rewrite the following sentences, correcting any errors in usage.

1. What kind of a bridge are we supposed to design?
2. Kim knows alot about Korean history and culture.
3. I seldom ever attend soccer games, though I was given a season ticket.
4. The majority of the novel was told in flashback.
5. Cindy said that she didn't want to camp out anyways.
6. What sort of a film is Alfred Hitchcock's *Rear Window*?
7. Somewheres in all of this mess is my notebook.
8. My mother said it is alright for you to spend the weekend at our house.
9. The plate glass fell off of the truck and broke in the busy intersection.
10. All of the birds that nested in our yard have flown south.
11. Misha asked Harold what kind of a job he wanted.
12. Clancey would be happy to take a vacation anywheres where it is warm.
13. If I'd of known that you like fudge, I would have saved you some.
14. It cost alot of money to grade and pave the streets.
15. The trainer felt the player's forearm to determine whether it was alright.

MIXED REVIEW

The Right Word

A. Rewrite these sentences to make them follow standard usage.

1. Trees effect the temperature of nearby houses, making them warmer in winter and colder in summer.
2. The naturalist explained that moas were different than dodos, though both were extinct birds of New Zealand.
3. Everyone remembered his or her lines accept the fellow with the walk-on part.
4. The pitcher and the catcher could not agree on a uniform system of hand signals.
5. Would American history be different if Coronado had of discovered the "city of gold"?
6. Julie wants to study law like her father did.
7. On the basis of what Morris said about his eating habits, the doctor inferred that the rash might be an allergic reaction to strawberries.
8. At the banquet, the President formerly announced his intention to run for office a second time.
9. Their are alot less people in the arcades these days.
10. Seldom ever has a book such as *The Right Stuff* been made into a movie.
11. The Eskimos have adopted to the icy cold climate of the Arctic.
12. Did Luzinski's home run go further than Kittel's?
13. Harris painted pictures on slate and hanged them on the prison walls.
14. In Seattle it rains the majority of the time.
15. I should of known that Admiral Chester Nimitz served in World War II.
16. The three shot putters decided between themselves who would represent the school.
17. The librarian wouldn't leave me check out more books until I paid the fine.
18. Did you ask Emily and Hector if their going to the prom?

B. Some of the following sentences contain errors in word usage. Rewrite these sentences correcting the errors. If a sentence contains no errors, write *Correct*.

1. Our team was anxious to accept the championship trophy.
2. Beside the shirt, I will borrow you a tie to go with it.
3. During the half time show, the coach acted like he was worried, to.
4. Can we please see that extremely unique saddle?
5. The majority of the playing field is muddy.
6. The mother cats had already trained their kittens.
7. Our trail guide let us ride beside the stream.
8. The cross-country course only ends a short ways from here.
9. The mechanics adopted the engine and put it in the Chevy.
10. A polemic is a type of speech in which one person differs from another.
11. Our drama coach was formally a professional actress.
12. Melissa lost her keys somewheres in the vast depths of her purse.
13. If the show had of started on time, we would of missed part of the first act.
14. The interior decorator hung the sketches altogether on one wall.
15. Keep this wallet, and put you're money in one of it's compartments.
16. We divided the huge amount of tickets among all of the clubs in the school.
17. A large amount of patients feel alright after tonsillectomies.
18. My brother seldom ever agrees to me, but he rarely gets to angry at me either.
19. The advice of experts is that smoking has a bad effect on the lungs.
20. Since Jon yawned and snoozed, his friends implied that he was not interested in science fiction films.

USING GRAMMAR IN WRITING

The Right Word

A. The nonstandard words and phrases covered in this Section are common in casual conversation, but they should be avoided in most formal situations. Often, they mark the user as careless or untrained in the English language, and can create a poor impression of that person.

Write out an imaginary interview between an employer and two candidates for a position as a guide at a local zoo. First write out the questions that the interviewer might ask. Then write the responses of the two candidates. Let one candidate answer using standard English, and let the other use some of the nonstandard construction you have just studied. You may want to perform this interview for your class along with two other students to emphasize the difference the proper use of language can make.

B. The term *dialect* refers to the variations in vocabulary, pronunciation, and grammatical constructions that occur in different sections of the country. (See Chapter 2 at the front of this text.) Sometimes dialect includes a number of nonstandard words and phrases. Everyone, however, speaks some sort of dialect. This results in a rich and colorful language.

Go to the library and find a collection of American folklore. Look for a story that has been recorded in the original dialect. First look for nonstandard language. Then rewrite the story using only standard English. Read both versions carefully. What are the positive aspects of each one? What are the negative aspects?

C. A person's speech can tell as much about him or her as clothes, habits, and gestures. For this reason, writers often develop a character's personality through the use of dialogue.

Write a short scene for a play or story that involves two people. Make the personalities of these characters as different as possible, but only by giving each of them a distinct way of speaking. Allow only one of your characters to use nonstandard language.

CUMULATIVE REVIEW
Usage (II)

Using the Correct Form of Words. Write the correct word from those given in parentheses.

1. (Fewer, Less) than ten people were in the lobby.
2. The mission (brung, brought) back valuable information.
3. The pipes in our kitchen (burst, busted) overnight.
4. The President did not agree (to, with, on) the bill, and he was very angry (at, with) those who had supported it.
5. A large (amount, number) of coats (lay, laid) on the bed.
6. I objected to (him, his) saying that I worked less.
7. He had (swang, swung) the bat before the pitch was even (threw, thrown).
8. What the team needs most (is, are) better pitchers.
9. Helen felt (uncomfortable, uncomfortably) in her boots.
10. (Who, Whom) did that message concern?

Finding Errors in Usage. Identify the errors of agreement or form in the following sentences, and rewrite each incorrect sentence. Write *C* if a sentence is already correct.

1. Neither of the other astronauts were qualified to do that kind of experiment.
2. Whom was it that said she could run faster than me?
3. Politics don't usually interest me, but this campaign has been lively.
4. An hour was all the time he had to lay out the materials.
5. The reporter hadn't barely finished her article when new information came over the wire.
6. Bob did not feel good when he walked in the hospital.
7. The politician left the audience imply from his statements that the other candidate was a kind of thief.
8. It is all right with me if Linda or Silvia is included.
9. The majority of the trip was all together delightful, but hardly nobody beside me drove the car.
10. The boss appreciated her working late on Saturdays.

10.0 Capitalization

10.1 Proper Nouns and Adjectives

A **common noun** is not capitalized. It is a name that is held in common by an entire group of persons, places, or things. A **proper noun** is capitalized. It names an individual person, place, or thing. Adjectives formed from proper nouns are called **proper adjectives.** They are also capitalized.

COMMON NOUN	PROPER NOUN	PROPER ADJECTIVE
country	Russia	Russian
state	Texas	Texan
book	Bible	Biblical
poet	Chaucer	Chaucerian

If a proper noun or adjective occurs with a prefix, capitalize only the parts that are capitalized when used alone. Prefixes, such as *pro-*, *un-*, and *anti-*, are not capitalized.

pro-Irish   un-American   pre-Revolutionary

There are many kinds of proper nouns. The rules given in this Section will help you decide whether or not to capitalize a word when you are writing.

10.2 Geographical Names

In a geographical name, capitalize the first letter of each word except articles and prepositions.

The article *the* is not part of a geographical name and is not capitalized.

CONTINENTS:	Africa, Europe, North America
BODIES OF WATER:	the Gulf of Mexico, the Bay of Fundy, the Flint River, the Baltic Sea, the Strait of Magellan, the Rio Grande, Lake Baikal
LAND FORMS:	the Sahara Desert, the Himalayas, Sea Island, Mount Everest, the Black Hills
POLITICAL UNITS:	the People's Republic of China, the Province of Ontario, Kankakee County, Newcastle Township, Salt Lake City
PUBLIC AREAS:	Yosemite National Park, Mammoth Cave, the Grand Canyon, Fort Laramie, Trafalgar Square
ROADS AND HIGHWAYS:	Los Angeles Freeway, Fifth Avenue, U.S. Highway 1, Green Street, London Road, Route 12, Ohio Turnpike

10.3 Common Nouns in Names

A common noun that is part of a name is capitalized. A common noun used to define or refer to a proper noun is not capitalized.

PART OF THE NAME	REFERENCE OR DEFINITION
New York State	the state of Arizona*
Carson City	the city of Boulder
Gettysburg Battlefield	the battlefield at Gettysburg
the Sinai Desert	the desert in the Sinai

*In official documents, words like *city, state,* and *county* are capitalized when they are part of the name of a political unit: *the County of York, the State of Ohio.*

10.4 Words Modified by Proper Adjectives

The word modified by a proper adjective is not capitalized unless adjective and noun together are a geographical name.

GEOGRAPHICAL NAME	MODIFIED NOUN
the Pacific Ocean	the Pacific coastline
the Hawaiian Islands	Hawaiian customs
the Roman Empire	Roman numerals

10.5 First Words

Capitalize the first word of a sentence, a direct quotation, and a line of poetry.

Her love of singing is evident.

"My agent told me," he said, "that you wanted to see me."

The other day I chanced to meet
An angry man upon the street—
A man of wrath, a man of war,
A man who truculently bore
Over his shoulder, like a lance,
A banner labeled "Tolerance."
—from "The Angry Man" PHYLLIS McGINLEY

10.6 *A.D., B.C., I, O*

Capitalize the abbreviations *A.D.* and *B.C.*, the pronoun *I*, and the interjection *O*.

The abbreviations B.C. and A.D. are used with the number of a year: 43 B.C., A.D. 900.

The interjection *O* occurs in poetry, in the Bible, or in prayers or petitions: *O Lord, O King*. It is not the same as the explosive interjection *oh* which is capitalized only at the beginning of a sentence.

Exercise: Copy the following sentences; supply necessary capitals.

1. how many American ex-presidents are living today?
2. the hudson river is an arm of the atlantic ocean.
3. there are still many nations that are neither pro-russian nor pro-american.
4. more than seven thousand islands make up the republic of the philippines.
5. the atlas mountains extend 1,500 miles along the edge of the african continent.
6. cleopatra died in 30 b.c., ending the dynasty of the ptolemies.
7. i would like to travel back to a.d. 1066.
8. the joshua tree monument is located in southern california.
9. there are more than seventy colleges in the state of ohio.
10. the number of english-speaking people is growing in the far east.
11. the roman alphabet has replaced arabic script in turkish schools.
12. there is a swiss national anthem, but there is no swiss language.
13. the french language is spoken in the province of quebec.
14. patrick henry said, "give me liberty or give me death."
15. the mississippi river flows into the gulf of mexico.

10.7 Directions and Sections

Capitalize names of sections of the country but not of directions of the compass.

The South is now heavily industrialized.
The West was a place of adventure during the 1800's.
To the north lies Kalamazoo.
Some people head south during the winter.
Los Angeles is east of Reno, Nevada.
You will find mountains to the west of here.
Many people are resettling in the Southwest.

Capitalize proper adjectives derived from names of sections of the country. Do not capitalize adjectives made from words telling direction.

a southernly wind	an Eastern city
a westbound train	a Midwestern college

Exercise: Copy the following sentences, supplying the necessary capitals. Some sentences are already correct.

1. Every year the west gets thousands of new residents.
2. We are traveling north to spend the summer.
3. The north wind usually brings cold weather.
4. A mass of hot, moist air is moving eastward.
5. The eastbound train heads north at this junction.
6. The people of the east will be warmed by winds moving north.
7. A southern factory moved its entire plant to the midwest.
8. The northeast will benefit greatly from the new seaway.
9. We are driving east, but we will go by the southern route.
10. The southern papers are carrying stories about the northwest.
11. My cousin says I speak with a midwestern twang.
12. A woman from the south has been named president of a midwestern college.
13. The western mountains are more spectacular than those in the east.
14. You can get southern fried chicken two blocks north of here.
15. Many people from the midwest go south for the winter.

10.8 Languages, Races, Nationalities, and Religions

Capitalize the names of languages, races, nationalities, and religions and the adjectives formed from them.

Russian ballet	Islam	Mormon
a French tutor	Indian	Welsh
Japanese customs	Methodist	Austrian

Do not capitalize the names of school subjects unless they are specific course names. Languages, however, are always capitalized.

geometry	Geometry II
social studies	Western Civilization
speech	Communications II
Latin	Latin I

10.9 Organizations and Institutions

Capitalize important words in the names of organizations, buildings, firms, schools, churches, and other institutions. Do not capitalize *and* or prepositions. Capitalize an article (*a, an,* or *the*) only if it appears as the first word in a name.

the New York Philharmonic
University of Pennsylvania
Lutheran General Hospital
Book-of-the-Month Club
Standard Gas, Incorporated
Library of Congress
Chicago and Northwestern Railroad

Note: In brand names, capitalize only proper nouns and adjectives: *Kellogg's cereals, Kellogg's Rice Krispies; Ford station wagon, Ford Tempo.*

Exercise: Copy the following sentences, supplying necessary capital letters.

1. The boston pops will present a benefit concert at radio city music hall.
2. The detroit public library has an exhibit of dutch paintings.
3. For the puerto rican schools, american texts are printed in spanish.
4. My sister, a math instructor, teaches geometry II at montclair high school.

5. The tahitian people may have a peruvian ancestry.
6. The language of the egyptian people is arabic.
7. The university of minnesota has several german professors on its staff.
8. The united states oil company is offering two scholarships this year.
9. My uncle has just bought a volvo station wagon.
10. There is a sale of florida grapefruit and hawaiian pineapple at best's market.
11. The smithsonian institution has a display of indian pottery.
12. The chicago public library has a fine collection of books on early american history.
13. The ticket agent said that american airlines flies into several european countries.
14. The university of southern california offers courses in japanese.
15. The budapest string quartet gave a concert at the library of congress.

10.10 Titles of Persons

Capitalize words that show rank, office, or profession, when they are used with a person's name.

Chief Michaels	Senator Edwards	Professor Kingsfield
Colonel Flagg	Bishop Jackson	Judge Wright
Doctor Parelli	Mayor Byrne	Captain Smith

The titles of high officials are capitalized even when they are used without the official's name.

the President of the United States	the Governor
the Secretary of State	the Pope
the Prime Minister	the Bishop

The prefix *ex-* and the suffix *-elect* are not capitalized when attached to titles: *ex-President Nixon*, the *Senator-elect*.

10.11 Family Relationships

Capitalize the name of a family relationship when it is used with a person's name.

Aunt Mitzi   Uncle Stan   Grandma Moses   Cousin Norm

In addition, when words like *mother, father, dad,* and *mom* are substituted for a particular person's name, capitalize them. Do not capitalize them if they do not refer to a particular person or if they are modified by a possessive pronoun, as in *your mother*.

Bob asked Dad for his advice.
Does Todd have an older brother?
I saw your father at the airport.

10.12 Titles of Books and Works of Art

Capitalize the first word and every important word in the titles of books, stories, plays, articles, poems, motion pictures, works of art, and musical compositions.

The only words considered not important are conjunctions, articles (*a, an,* and *the*), and prepositions containing fewer than five letters. But even these words are capitalized when used as the first word in a title.

The Old Man and the Sea   "The Lottery"
The Crucible   "The Unknown Citizen"
Whistler's Mother   "Stairway to Heaven"
Time After Time   "The Road Not Taken"

Exercise: Copy each word that requires a capital.

1. Did you know that aunt mary lives near judge white?
2. pearl s. buck won the pulitzer prize for *the good earth*.
3. I met general miller, who is senator-elect.

4. There is to be a meeting of the british prime minister and our secretary of state.
5. My mother will drive us out to see uncle bob.
6. It was announced today that governor rhodes and his aide will fly to washington.
7. The paper reports that judge roberts is to be president of the new college.
8. For his birthday, we gave uncle dennis a copy of *mastering the art of french cooking* by julia child.
9. My parents cried when the orchestra began playing "pomp and circumstance."
10. Supposedly president lincoln wrote the gettysburg address on the back of an envelope.
11. I'm going to read "the charge of the light brigade" for my class presentation.
12. We left aunt sarah and father looking at rembrandt's *portrait of a young man*.
13. Do you know the story of chief joseph?
14. The lieutenant will speak to captain foster about your cousin's furlough.
15. Because dr. carey was away, we got another doctor to look in on uncle walt.

10.13 The Deity

Capitalize all words referring to the Deity, the Holy Family, and religious scriptures.

God	the Virgin Mary	the Bible	the Torah
Jehovah	the Holy Ghost	the Almighty	the Koran
Allah	the Gospel	Krishna	the Talmud

Capitalize personal pronouns but not relative pronouns that refer to the Deity.

May the Lord let His countenance shine upon you.
Praise God from whom all blessings flow.

10.14 Days, Months, Holidays

Capitalize the names of days of the week, of months, and of holidays. Do not capitalize the names of the seasons.

Wednesday	New Year's Eve	summer
June	Presidents' Day	winter

10.15 Historical Names

Capitalize names of historical events, documents, and periods.

the Bill of Rights	the Neo-Classic Period
the Hundred Years' War	the Great Depression

Exercise: Copy the words that require capitals.

1. There are many books about the westward movement.
2. How many men signed both the declaration of independence and the constitution?
3. The battle of leyte gulf occurred during world war II.
4. Schools will not be closed on election day.
5. Thanksgiving day comes on a thursday in november.
6. The pentateuch is the first five books of the old testament.
7. When did the industrial revolution begin?
8. The era of good feeling began after the war of 1812.
9. The first stone age produced advances in tool-making.
10. The seeds of world war II were planted in the treaty of versailles.
11. In sunday school, the teacher read the part of the bible where god gives moses the ten commandments.
12. It seems un-american not to have a parade with a marching band on the fourth of july.
13. I read the upanishads, a group of sacred vedic texts.
14. My report is on robert e. lee, a civil war general.
15. Michelangelo painted during the italian renaissance.

REINFORCEMENT EXERCISES

Capitalization

A. Use correct capitalization. Capitalize the following phrases.

1. a spanish sombrero
2. pro-american forces
3. new dehli, in india
4. the arctic ocean
5. contemporary french sculpture
6. the birth of st. francis in a.d. 1182
7. the jean lafitte national park in new orleans, louisiana
8. lake tanganyika, between the countries of tanzania and zaire
9. a volkswagon rabbit with a diesel engine
10. the san francisco skyline

B. Use correct capitalization. Correctly capitalize the following phrases. Then use each phrase in a sentence.

1. the koran, the sacred book of moslems
2. *the awakening*, a novel by the american author, kate chopin
3. the aztecs, an ancient mexican civilization
4. german potato salad
5. new year's day, on january 1
6. the latest catalog from montgomery ward
7. the white house, in washington, d.c.
8. oxford university
9. relations between the east and the west
10. aunt frieda's tour of the southern states

C. Use proper capitalization. Rewrite the following sentences, supplying necessary capitals.

1. margaret thatcher, the prime minister of britain, visited the queen at windsor castle.
2. in the past fifteen years, uncle philip has owned a chevrolet, a ford, a datsun, and a chrysler.
3. this section of vancouver is the second largest chinese community in north america.

4. this spring the court theatre, which is affiliated with the university of chicago, will present a production of henrik ibsen's *the wild duck*.
5. abraham, a central figure in christianity, islam, and judaism, appears in the old testament, the torah, and the koran.
6. aliage is a perfume manufactured by estée lauder.
7. serbo-croation is an eastern european language that has two different alphabets.
8. clovis became king of the franks in a.d. 481.
9. doctor richards, of the smithsonian institution, cataloged the museum's pre-stone age artifacts.
10. a saudi oil tanker exploded as it passed through the strait of hormuz.

D. Use proper capitalization. Follow the directions for C.

1. thousands of people of irish descent paraded up fifth avenue.
2. a great many american books have been translated into the japanese language.
3. at the head of the great lakes lies the city of duluth.
4. the students went to stratford, connecticut, to see a shakespearean play.
5. the misty vicksburg battlefield was filled with silent echoes.
6. the school's most popular course is introduction to psychology.
7. the state university of new york is made up of many different colleges scattered across the state.
8. you can buy crest toothpaste on sale at sun drugs.
9. my western civilization II teacher studied history at indiana university.
10. the english firm is called connery and son, limited.

MIXED REVIEW

Capitalization

A. Write the words requiring capital letters.

1. alexander the great lived from 356–323 b.c.
2. she had tickets for mom, dad, and me to attend the kansas state vs. loyola game at the rosemont horizon.
3. short yiddish skits such as *the orphans* and *the last hour of life* were shown at the pavilion theatre.
4. a u-haul truck was stranded in the north-bound lane of the bluegrass parkway.
5. shintoism and buddhism are common japanese religions.
6. aramaic is a language that dates back to pre-biblical times.
7. the states of oregon, washington, and california make up the area known as the pacific northwest.
8. the space shuttle *columbia* made several flights, all beginning at kennedy space center.
9. the ob and lena rivers, in the eastern part of the soviet union, both flow northward.
10. runnymede is the meadow where king john was forced to sign the magna charta.
11. the people of elizabethan england were fond of travel books such as those about richard hakluyt's voyages.
12. was *the golden hind* sir francis drake's ship?
13. the ex-senator became president-elect in november.
14. the new york yankees once dominated the world series.
15. my favorite math course was plane geometry I, but i also did well in algebra II.
16. i camped in big bend national park on the rio grande.
17. the book *women's running* was written by dr. joan ullyot.
18. the xerox corporation does not want people to say "xeroxing" when they really mean "photocopying."
19. the national press photographers association and the university of missouri school of journalism put out a book on photojournalism.
20. the hawaiian god lono often took the form of a shark.

B. Follow the directions for Exercise A.

1. luis made german chocolate cake with pure dutch chocolate.
2. the odesta community pool closes on labor day.
3. our school offers courses in french, spanish, and german.
4. on monday, senator white was a guest speaker in our history class.
5. the longest cave system is at mammoth cave national park in kentucky.
6. the vice-president was vacationing in the adirondack mountains when president mckinley was shot.
7. for christmas, grandma gave me the book is there life after high school?
8. in 1886, dr. john s. pemberton, of atlanta, georgia, invented coca-cola.
9. there are several arabic manuscripts at the library of congress.
10. private colleges like yale, stanford, and vanderbilt set high standards for admission.
11. even though the star trek series was taken off the air, mr. spock and captain kirk still have millions of fans.
12. the story "spring victory" tells of a terrible winter in the kentucky hills.
13. the stratford company in ontario stages shakespearean plays.
14. the first woman in space was a soviet, jr. lt. valentina v. tereshkova.
15. i know your mother and father think *gandhi* has been the best film of the '80's.
16. a fortune was found in a spanish galleon off the coast of the dominican republic.
17. the warren commission reported on the assassination of president john f. kennedy.
18. meryl told the press, "the wilmington river is being polluted by malinot industries."
19. the egyptian pyramids were begun in about 3000 b.c.
20. old buildings in cities of the northeast are being renovated.

USING MECHANICS IN WRITING

Capitalization

A. People tend to associate with others who share their interests. Test this idea by answering the following questions and then asking the same questions of two of your friends.

1. What forms of entertainment do you most enjoy?
2. Name a book that really interested you. What was the subject of the book?
3. Name a television show or movie that you really enjoy. What kind of show or movie is this? Is it a comedy, a drama, or a variety show?
4. Do you read magazines or newspapers on a regular basis? If so, what magazines or newspapers?
5. What are your favorite subjects in school? What were your favorite particular classes?
6. Name two famous people whom you admire.
7. If you had your choice of any job with any company in the world, what job and what company would you choose?
8. What foreign country would you most like to visit, and what would you like to see while you are there?

Once you have gathered this information, write a composition describing the similarities and differences that you have noticed in your interests and those of your friends. In what ways are you alike? In what ways are you different? In your composition, be sure to follow the rules for capitalization.

B. Choose any famous person whom you admire. Do some research on that person, and write a short biography that includes all significant personal information and accomplishments. You may wish to write about an entertainer, a sports figure, or a political figure. Be as thorough as possible.

11.0 End Marks and Commas

11.1 Periods at the Close of Sentences

Place a period at the close of every declarative sentence and of most imperative sentences.

A period may also be used to set off a group of words that is not a complete sentence.

Stay away from that cage.
Oh, no. We were not near the fire.

11.2 Periods in Abbreviations

Place a period after every part of an abbreviation.

T. S. Eliot	Thomas Stearns Eliot
A.D.	Anno Domini
U. S. A.	United States of America
Washington, D. C.	Washington, District of Columbia

Since the 1930's it has become the custom not to use periods in abbreviations of certain government agencies and international organizations.

ICC	Interstate Commerce Commission
HUD	Department of Housing and Urban Development
UN	United Nations
USAF	United States Air Force

11.3 Exclamation Points

Place an exclamation point after an exclamatory sentence and after an exclamation set off from a sentence.

Hey! You can't leave now.
Go, team!
Follow that car!
How wonderful!
Penzell for President!
Ow! That hurt!

11.4 Question Marks

Place a question mark after an interrogative sentence or after a question that is not a complete sentence.

The word order in questions is not always inverted. Sometimes the word order of a declarative sentence is used as a question. In speech, the speaker raises his voice at the end of the sentence to show that it is a question. In writing, the question mark performs the same function.

Has the period ended?
Do you call these ordinary times?
The time? It is now ten o'clock.
The period has ended?
These are ordinary times?
It's ten o'clock?

Exercise A: Copy these sentences, using end marks and punctuation as required for sentences and abbreviations. Use question marks only for sentences in normal interrogative form.

1. Where are you going for your vacation
2. Dr A C Bryant will leave from the UN at 11:30 A M and arrive here at 1:30 P M
3. The U S Post Office at Third Ave and Fourth St is to be torn down
4. Watch out for that truck
5. Mr J Kellogg was elected president of the Midwest Regis Oil Co, Inc

6. Was Caesar assassinated in 44 B C
7. If Jack attends, will he be alone
8. The pastor is Rev John Marshal, D D
9. C J Carson, Jr spoke on "The U S A in A D 2000"
10. What a time we had

Exercise B: Follow the same directions as for Exercise A.

1. I asked the police officer to direct me to B Altman and Co
2. Do you really think we can get to the campground at Winamac, Ind by 9 P M
3. Dr and Mrs Abdul Mahmud have moved to Washington, DC, to work at the Islamic Center
4. Wow That's a tiger act even PT Barnum would envy
5. HUD helped relocate the displaced family to 4130 N Archer Rd, Apt 2E
6. Ms Ruth Jensen, RN, works for the FDA
7. Ouch That ointment stings
8. Let's ask Rep Bunin to speak at the PTA meeting next Sept
9. Jackie can't remember where she parked the car
10. Will you please return these books to the library before they close for the holiday

Uses of the Comma

11.5 Introductory Words

Introductory words such as *yes, no, well, why,* and *oh* are followed by a comma.

Oh, I meant to tell you about the car.
Well, you must have known Pat was arriving today.
Why, you can't see anything from here.

Certain adverbs that begin sentences are set off by commas. Examples are *besides, however, anyhow,* and *nonetheless*.

11.6 Introductory Phrases and Clauses

A participial phrase at the beginning of a sentence is followed by a comma.

An adverbial clause at the beginning of a sentence is followed by a comma.

A succession of prepositional phrases at the beginning of a sentence is set off by a comma.

A single prepositional phrase at the beginning of a sentence may be set off by a comma if it is followed by a natural pause when read.

Following the crowd, we came to a huge tent. (participial phrase)
When the first guests began to arrive, we were still making sandwiches. (adverbial clause)
In the lane at the end of the field, the band was forming. (succession of prepositional phrases)
Before the game, the marching band put on a show. (optional comma after single introductory prepositional phrase)

11.7 Transposed Words and Phrases

Words and phrases moved to the beginning of a sentence from their normal position are set off by a comma.

We were naturally afraid. (normal order)
Naturally, we were afraid. (transposed order)

There was obviously just one thing to do. (normal order)
Obviously, there was just one thing to do. (transposed order)

Bill was determined from the outset to win the scholarship. (normal order)
From the outset, Bill was determined to win the scholarship. (transposed order)

Take this road to get to the station. (normal order)
To get to the station, take this road. (transposed order)

Exercise A: Copy the following sentences, inserting commas where necessary. Two of the sentences are correct.

1. Clearly we had arrived too late.
2. From the start of the contest our swimming team was at a disadvantage.
3. Why everyone knows that you can't square a circle.
4. Arriving on time is difficult for Kevin.
5. To open the parachute pull this cord.
6. Coming from Eduardo the complaint was a surprise.
7. Although I had read the book before I enjoyed reading it a second time.
8. Hopefully Ann picked up the telephone.
9. Yes there is an easier solution to the problem.
10. To swim in competitive meets requires constant training.

Exercise B: Copy the following sentences, inserting commas where necessary. Two of the sentences are correct.

1. Following the path we plunged deeper into the woods.
2. Staying in good condition is essential.
3. As he picked up the paper Harry saw the key.
4. While looking through my desk I found my great-grandmother's letters.
5. No one at the lodge had told us about the fire.
6. Well I'm sorry that I didn't get all the shopping done.
7. Presently there is no crossing guard on that corner.
8. To stop severe bleeding pack the wound with a clean towel.
9. When the weather is cold I take the bus.
10. Because I fell asleep I missed the end of the movie.

11.8 Appositives

An appositive is set off from the rest of the sentence by commas.

The speaker, *a rocket expert,* talked about space flights.
Our science teacher, *Ms. Farrell,* will not be back next year.

11.9 Words of Direct Address

Words of direct address are set off by commas.

Sally, will you please see me after class?
You know, *my friends,* that taxes are necessary.
Will you see if the door is closed, *Janet?*

11.10 Parenthetical Expressions

A word or phrase used to explain or qualify a statement is called a **parenthetical expression.** The same word or phrase may also be used as a basic part of a sentence. Commas are used to set off these words or phrases only when they are parenthetical; that is, only when they can be left out of the sentence without affecting the meaning.

I think every person should receive a free education.
Schuyler Colfax was, *I think,* Vice President under Grant. (parenthetical)
Of course Brad was right.
It was Sue, *of course,* who found us. (parenthetical)

Parenthetical expressions are set off by commas.

Here are some expressions often used parenthetically:

of course	I believe (hope, think)	on the other hand
in fact	I suppose	as a matter of fact
indeed	for example	

Conjunctive adverbs (see Section 1.7) used parenthetically within the sentence are set off by commas. Conjunctive adverbs include *therefore, moreover, nevertheless, however, consequently,* and so on.

The class, *therefore,* had been fully warned.
The school, *moreover,* is locked up on weekends.
Diane said, *however,* that she would do the job.

Words like *however, therefore,* and *consequently* are occasionally used to modify a word in the sentence. As modifiers they are an essential part of the meaning of a sentence. Since they are essential, they are not set off by commas.

Nadia waited for an hour, but no one came. She was therefore justified in leaving for home.
We were consequently mystified by your letter.
Jack could not get up the hill however hard he tried.

11.11 Dates, Addresses, Geographical Names

In dates and addresses of more than one part, set off every part after the first from the rest of the sentence.

Mr. Lovell has a cabin near Boulder. (one part)
Near Boulder, Colorado, he built a summer cabin. (two parts, the second set off by commas)
Our vacation begins on June 15. (one part)
The Louisiana Territory was purchased on April 30, 1803. (two parts with a comma after the first)
The store relocated to 8204 Sherman Avenue, Birch Harbor, Maine 04613, for the owner's convenience. (three parts, the second and third set off by commas)

Note: The day of the month and the month are one item. The name of the street and the house number are one item. The name of the state and the ZIP code are one item.

November 17   39 Forest Street   New Jersey 07042

Exercise: Copy these sentences, inserting necessary commas.

1. Melanie quoted her authority one of the inventors.
2. The third act a ventriloquist was the audience's favorite.
3. You see Francis there is no way of avoiding responsibility.
4. The house was in fact perfect for them.

5. Henry's reputation to be sure has exceeded his performance.
6. The 1912 Stutz for example is a classic car.
7. Eve found the statement a quotation from Emerson.
8. We had finished the job as a matter of fact before you called to inquire about it.
9. The story was nonetheless hard to believe.
10. The main factory is located at Dayton Ohio.
11. From San Diego California we flew to Tucson Arizona.
12. Please mail the package to me at 14 East Seventeenth Street New York N.Y. 10003.
13. The stock market crashed on Thursday October 24 1929.
14. In January 1914 the first assembly line was organized in an American automobile plant.
15. Orville Wright made his first successful flight on December 17 1903 at Kitty Hawk North Carolina.
16. After all students the success of this program depends upon you.
17. Their house you know is for sale.
18. My father was born on April 7 1943 in Seattle.
19. We shall wait therefore until the new models come out.
20. My friends the answer to this problem as you can readily see is not a simple one.

11.12 Nonrestrictive Modifiers

A **restrictive clause** points out the person or thing it modifies. Without the restrictive clause, the meaning of the sentence is confused or incomplete.

The book *that I want* is by Cornelia Otis Skinner. (The clause tells *which* book.)

We want to hire a man *who can cook*. (The clause tells an essential characteristic of the man wanted.)

The person *who enjoys reading* is never lonely. (Without the clause, the sentence has no specific meaning.)

Restrictive clauses are not set off from the rest of the sentence by commas.

A **nonrestrictive clause** presents added information. It is not needed to keep the meaning of a sentence intact. A nonrestrictive clause may be dropped without changing the meaning of a sentence.

Linemen, *who are just as important to football success as the backs*, seldom get any of the glory.
These shoes, *which are certainly better looking*, cost more than I can pay.

Nonrestrictive clauses are set off by commas from the rest of the sentence.

Use the word *that* to introduce restrictive clauses and the word *which* to introduce nonrestrictive clauses.

The farm *that* we passed a mile back sells apples and pumpkins.
The farm, *which* has a beautiful yellow barn, sells apples and pumpkins.

Participial phrases that identify or point out the thing or person they modify are restrictive.

The woman *standing on the chair* is the director. (Without the phrase, the sentence loses its specific meaning.)
The paper *attached to the handle* gives the directions for using the sharpener. (The phrase identifies the paper.)

Nonrestrictive participial phrases merely add meaning. They are not essential and can be dropped without making the meaning of the sentence incomplete.

Climbing fast, we arrived at the top out of breath.
Sue Reynolds, *carrying the flag*, advanced to the stage.

Nonrestrictive participial phrases are set off from the rest of the sentence by commas. Restrictive phrases are not set off by commas.

Exercise: Number your paper from 1–20. Decide whether the adjective clause or the participial phrase is restrictive or nonrestrictive. After each number write *restrictive* or *nonrestrictive*. Copy and insert commas in the sentences in which commas are needed.

1. The committee appointed by the President has finished its report.
2. The typing manual dog-eared from long use was open on the desk.
3. This is the book that I've been telling you about.
4. Dr. Powers who lives next door is a famous surgeon.
5. The winner of the olympic medal overwhelmed by applause could scarcely speak.
6. The boat now coming into view belongs to a large oil company.
7. We were skeptical of the story that the salesperson told.
8. Melanie returned to the library only the books that she had read.
9. The first bus which was crowded with passengers rushed right past us.
10. This report which is very persuasive must be read with great care.
11. Here are the contracts that you must sign.
12. Hoping to hear from the employer Rick stayed at home all day.
13. So this is the typewriter that you ordered.
14. The last song which I had never heard before was enchanting.
15. Tina paid for these concert tickets which she couldn't use.
16. The merchants alarmed by rising costs decided to reduce expenses.
17. The kit that you asked for has finally arrived.
18. We left the path which had become impassable and struggled through the brush.
19. The price named by Mr. Andrews is not acceptable.
20. Dana Jones is the person who owns the TV repair shop.

11.13 Compound Sentences

Place a comma before the conjunction that joins two main clauses in a compound sentence.

We must win this game, *or* we will be out of the running.
I tried to do the third problem, *but* I couldn't remember how to do square roots.
The elevator has stopped running, *and* everyone is going to be late to work.
Jeff could not repair his car, *nor* could he find a mechanic who could.

When the main clauses are quite short, the comma may be omitted.

John arrived early but Paul was late.
The train arrived and we got on.

11.14 Series

A **series** is a group of three or more items of the same kind.

SERIES OF NOUNS: *Dogs*, *children*, and *clowns* were suddenly mixed in a tangled mass.
SERIES OF VERBS: The old car *coughed*, *lurched* forward, then *shuddered* to a stop.
SERIES OF ADJECTIVES: The food was *greasy*, *tasteless*, and *insufficient* for our hunger.
SERIES OF PHRASES: We searched *under the rug*, *behind the pictures*, and *in the desk drawers*.

Commas are used to separate the parts of a series.

Do not place a comma after the last item in a series. The use of a comma before the conjunction joining the last two items in a series is optional. However, to avoid confusion, it is preferable to use a comma before a conjunction.

Do not use a comma if all parts of the series are joined by *and, or,* or *nor*.

We swam and ate and slept for five days.
Milk or water or even ink would have tasted good to us.

11.15 Coordinate Adjectives

Commas are placed between coordinate adjectives that modify the same noun.

The hot, humid day drew to a close.
The blinding, blistering, interminable heat bore down on us.

If you are not certain whether adjectives are coordinate, try placing an *and* between them. If it sounds natural, they are coordinate, and a comma is needed.

PROBLEM: The loud irritating noise persisted.
NATURAL: The loud *and* irritating noise persisted.
SOLUTION: The loud, irritating noise persisted all day.

PROBLEM: It was a light, warm pleasant room.
NATURAL: It was a light, warm, *and* pleasant room.
SOLUTION: It was a light, warm, pleasant room.

PROBLEM: Turn left at the big red barn.
NOT NATURAL: Turn left at the big *and* red barn.
SOLUTION: Turn left at the big red barn.

In general, it is safe to omit the comma before numbers and adjectives of size, shape, and age.

the little old man   a huge round dome

Exercise: Copy these sentences, placing commas where they are needed. Some of the sentences are correct.

1. Dan has his work permit and he is looking for a job.
2. The fine big bonfire soon restored the spirits of the weary travelers.

3. The customers arrived poured over the counters and demanded immediate service.
4. Janet had gone to bed early but she was too excited to sleep well.
5. You can pay for the tires now or you can send us a check or money order later.
6. The two overstuffed sofas had been moved out of the living room.
7. The happy tired victorious crew staggered over the rocks and fell on the sand.
8. Detectives looked in the attic in the basement and in every closet.
9. The grossbeaks are attracted by the little red berries on those bushes.
10. Harry's rude thoughtless reply to our question bothered us all day.
11. The repairs have been completed but the store cannot deliver the chairs until tomorrow because no one will be home to accept them today.
12. Desks chairs and files had been pushed carelessly against the walls.
13. The parade travels up Fifth Avenue through the park and down Park Avenue.
14. Heat electricity and light are all forms of energy.
15. We knew Kay was at the concert but we could not find her.
16. The local newspaper puts editorials on the front page news items in its editorials and errors of fact everywhere.
17. The yellowed surface of the beautiful old oil painting was covered with tiny cracks.
18. The travelers lingered in the cool refreshing shade of the oak tree.
19. The three young athletes have given the team new spirit and dedication.
20. We knew the boys knew their abilities and knew their families.

11.16 Clarity

Use a comma to separate words or phrases that might be mistakenly joined in reading.

In certain situations, words or phrases in a sentence may be mistakenly read together. The first situation occurs when the conjunctions *but* and *for* are mistaken for prepositions.

CONFUSING: Mom came back for the key was missing.
CLEAR: Mom came back, for the key was missing.

CONFUSING: All the boys slept quietly but one talked in his sleep.
CLEAR: All the boys slept quietly, but one talked in his sleep.

A second source of confusion is a noun following a verbal phrase.

CONFUSING: Before painting Emily sanded the surface.
CLEAR: Before painting, Emily sanded the surface.

CONFUSING: To float a swimmer must arch his back.
CLEAR: To float, a swimmer must arch his back.

A third source of confusion is the word that may be adverb, preposition, or conjunction at the beginning of the sentence.

CONFUSING: Above the stars shone brightly.
CLEAR: Above, the stars shone brightly.

CONFUSING: Inside the house was neat and clean.
CLEAR: Inside, the house was neat and clean.

11.17 Words Omitted

Use a comma when words are omitted from parallel word groups.

Lana brought a stereo; Clint, a pile of records.
In *As You Like It* Orlando is a hero; Touchstone, a clown.
The sun was hot, and the water, cold.

Exercise A: Copy these sentences, placing commas where necessary to avoid confusion.

1. We turned back for the wind was rising.
2. None of the group was happy about the decision but Meryl was completely crushed.
3. Beyond the hills were bare of trees.
4. The victor left in triumph and his opponent in anger.
5. Outside the gates had been closed and barred.
6. Below the bricklayers were working quietly.
7. Mark went to the university to study and Bert to have a good time.
8. All the men were pleased but Harry was simply delighted.
9. Kris opened the door for the doctor was coming.
10. To eat the old men used chopsticks.
11. Above the monkeys chattered noisily in the trees.
12. For the costume party I can be Tarzan; you Jane.
13. Kendra must have been late for the program had already begun.
14. Within the family was fast asleep.
15. To burn fire needs oxygen.

Exercise B: Writing Write five sentences that require commas for clarity and five sentences that need commas for sense when words are omitted. You may want to refer back to the example sentences for 11.16 and 11.17 in this Section. Make sure your sentences are punctuated correctly.

REINFORCEMENT EXERCISES

End Marks and Commas

A. Use end marks correctly. Punctuate the following sentences as necessary.

1. Hey This man is ill Is there a doctor or a nurse in the auditorium
2. The USA and the USSR are both members of the UN Security Council
3. Rep Byron Dorgan, of N Dakota, introduced an amendment to the tax bill
4. Ms Marshall received her MA from Stanford and her Ph D from UCLA
5. Dr Perez told the desk clerk to give him a wake-up call at 6:30 AM
6. One of the most interesting questions raised by the pyramids is how the Egyptians managed to build them without pulleys
7. The coast guard patrol boat received an SOS signal from a plane that was having engine trouble
8. Hit the ground That sounds like the roar of a tornado
9. Can you believe it I just won a quarter of a million dollars
10. Will the Rev William LeFevre perform the marriage ceremony

B. Use commas after introductory words and phrases. Insert commas where needed in the following sentences.

1. No Francis Bacon did not write any of the plays attributed to Shakespeare.
2. After the invention of the electric light life styles in America changed dramatically.
3. Naturally we were anxious to learn how to use the new home computer system.
4. When Bryant wrote his most famous poem he was only nineteen years old.

5. The dinosaurs were reptiles; however some of them may have been warm-blooded.
6. Working around the clock the department store employees were able to complete their year-end inventory in only three days.
7. In the loam beneath the fallen trees the bears found grubs and worms.
8. When taking a test be certain to read and understand the directions before beginning.
9. Why did you know that beetles were the most common creature on earth!
10. After skiing all day without wearing a sunscreen Colleen suffered from severe sunburn.

C. Use commas correctly. Insert commas where necessary in the following sentences.

1. Squids as a matter of fact have ten arms.
2. Sigmund Freud the father of psychoanalysis was interested in the effects of early childhood experiences on later behavior.
3. Indiana by the way produces more pumpkins than any other state in the country.
4. George Steinbrenner owner of the Yankee Trader Restaurant also owns the New York Yankees.
5. Sarah please stop at Ticketron on your way home from dancing class.
6. The banjo I believe was originated in the southern United States.
7. Werner Heisenberg the German physicist proved that it is impossible to make observations that are absolutely accurate.
8. Walt Whitman and Herman Melville were both born on May 31 1819.
9. Oahu, Kauai, Hawaii, and Maui the four major Hawaiian islands depend on tourism for the largest part of their income.
10. The offices of the magazine entitled *The Movies* are located at 310 Madison Avenue New York New York.

D. Use commas to set off nonrestrictive modifiers. Identify the italicized phrases and clauses in the following sentences as *restrictive* or *nonrestrictive*. Then, rewrite the sentences, inserting commas where necessary. Remember that commas are *not* used to set off restrictive modifiers.

1. The march *that Navajos call the "Long Walk"* was ordered by U.S. Army troops in 1864.
2. Emily Dickinson *whose poetry is now included in most anthologies of American verse* was largely unknown during her lifetime.
3. The person *who takes the first step* is as much a pioneer as the person who completes the journey.
4. *Hoping for a sale* the clerk willingly demonstrated the new computerized chess board.
5. Tides *which are caused by the moon* occur on opposite sides of the earth at the same time.
6. Kahlil Gibran *who was born in Lebanon* became famous for his books of inspiration and wisdom.
7. A plane *carrying food and medical supplies* arrived just in the nick of time.
8. No one really knows *who invented the game of baseball.*
9. The present *that intrigues me most* is the one in the tiny box.
10. *Using its wings for support* the lyrebird leaped away from the huge cat.

E. Use commas correctly. Insert commas in the following sentences as necessary. One sentence is already correct.

1. Mary Decker ran the three thousand meters and Marianne Dickerson ran the marathon.
2. Students wrote the play designed the set and played all the parts.
3. I usually read books but lately I've been reading newspapers.
4. A basketball player must have power strength and skill.
5. The bright yellow tent looked even brighter against the freshly-fallen snow.

6. The green mold-covered object was an old tennis ball.
7. "Either dinosaurs became extinct or they became invisible," jested the professor.
8. The skier swayed regained his balance jumped sped down the hill and slalomed.
9. Hector did not have any money nor had he remembered to bring a bus token.
10. Astronomical observatories were built by the ancient Celts Mayans and Koreans.
11. Mary Alice and Megan were the first three across the finish line.
12. The long hot summer did not end until October.
13. On our way to Texas we drove on Routes 55 30 and 45.
14. *HOMES* is an acronym for the Great Lakes: Huron Ontario Michigan Erie and Superior.
15. Recognizing shapes sizes and figures are skills a child must have in order to learn to read.

F. Use commas for clarity. Punctuate the following sentences as necessary.

1. Above the Austrian competitor was preparing to dive.
2. Before jumping Kerry checked her parachute once again.
3. Michele baked the bread; Norton the pies; and Vicki the cakes.
4. I thought I had delivered all the pizzas but one had fallen behind the seat.
5. Porter liked rock; Yvonne baroque music.
6. Serving Cathy outscored her opponent two-to-one.
7. Brenda dropped the apple for a worm was in it.
8. To play draw the bow across the strings.
9. While shampooing Max was singing at the top of his lungs.
10. After breaking the tip of the bat flew into the stands.

MIXED REVIEW

End Marks and Commas

A. Copy these sentences, inserting the necessary punctuation.

1. No send the gift to Mrs. V C Marshall's downtown office not to her home
2. When you witnessed the accident were you wearing your contact lenses
3. Wallace you know is a Scottish name
4. Clothing made of polypropelene a synthetic fiber keeps moisture away from the body
5. Incredibly the crystal goblet bounced but did not break
6. At last I thought you'd never get here
7. When it is 6 P M in Sudbury Ontario is it 4 P M in Calgary Alberta
8. All the paintings were good but one was outstanding
9. Carla wore a leotard leg warmers socks and tennis shoes
10. Corn beans and squash were often planted together by the Indians of the East Coast
11. The catalog from the Metropolitan Museum of Art in New York City New York arrived before the holidays
12. I'm not sure he understands what a Roman numeral is for he was unable to write one
13. Rudyard Kipling the author of *Jungle Book* and other stories about India also wrote *Captains Courageous* a book about whaling
14. Didn't you know Kevin that the square root of zero is zero
15. Yes the secretary bird an African species is a skillful snake-killer
16. The I R S seldom if ever audits young tax payers
17. Without asking the guest answered the telephone
18. The large circular red spot on Jupiter may be a storm
19. In the summer we enjoy going to the beach; in the winter to the mountains
20. The television special which concerned illiteracy in the U S was repeated the next week

B. Copy these sentences, inserting the necessary periods, commas, question marks, and exclamation points.

1. Yes A C Nielsen Company a national survey organization rates television programs
2. Stories songs and riddles are all part of folklore
3. Could you tell me sir which tape deck has the fullest strongest sound
4. The Ecology Club will meet I believe at 3:30 P M on Tuesday March 6
5. When the subway train lurched forward Bradley dropped his packages
6. The industrial arts classes constructed a house at 222 Thorny Circle Northbrook Illinois
7. Beginning next semester we will study public speaking
8. Hinsdale's swim team having won another championship was greeted with a parade
9. Amy answered the want ad for the job she had was uninteresting
10. We savored our pizza which was loaded with sausage onions and cheese
11. Ice formed on the tracks and the train could not move
12. Fortunately Mr Ogden and the service station owner were able to start our car
13. On May 28 1934 the first surviving quintuplets were born
14. Did Cal take the course in sheet metals; Sara the one in masonry
15. Flashy fast-stepping bands played at the Superdome in New Orleans Louisiana
16. To win Marni must exercise diet and get enough sleep
17. Mr I M Villainous plotting revenge decided to foreclose the mortgage
18. Naturally all activities scheduled for Saturday June 6 have been cancelled
19. Run Terry It's after you
20. Does the FDA a consumer protection agency test dyes flavorings and preservatives

USING MECHANICS IN WRITING

End Marks and Commas

A. In emergency situations, people are naturally inclined to panic. However, this natural reaction is often inappropriate because most emergencies raise questions that must be thought about carefully and rationally. Write a short skit that would demonstrate this lesson to young children. Create two characters and place them in an emergency situation. Use exclamation marks and question marks to indicate the state of panic that the emergency causes in one of your characters. Use periods to indicate that your other character is dealing with the situation in a reasoned, logical manner.

B. Imagine that you have been given the opportunity to travel backward or forward in time. What period would you choose? Whom (or what!) would you like to meet? Write a composition describing your ideal "vacation in time." In your composition, list the people that you would like to meet, using a series of names separated by commas, and explain why you would like to meet them. Also, discuss the things you would like to see or do. If any of these people, places, or activities would be unfamiliar to your reader, explain them, using parenthetical expressions, appositives, and restrictive or nonrestrictive modifers. Make sure that you punctuate the various elements of your composition correctly.

C. Imagine that you are writing a guide to your community for people from another area. Your purpose is to explain to these people what they can look forward to when they come to visit. Remember that your audience probably will not be familiar with any of your local landmarks. Therefore, you will have to use appositives and restrictive or nonrestrictive phrases and clauses to explain what these places are. In your composition, follow the punctuation rules given in this Section. If you wish, this guide may be humorous.

12.0 The Semicolon, the Colon, the Dash, and Parentheses

12.1 Semicolons Between Main Clauses

A semicolon is placed between the main clauses of a compound sentence when they are not joined by a conjunction.

Clauses may be joined together into a compound sentence if they are closely related in thought. The relationship is expressed more clearly than if the clauses were written as separate sentences.

Sometimes the best way to join main clauses is to use a semicolon instead of a conjunction. This is especially true when *and* or *but* adds little meaning to the joined clauses.

> Our opponents were alert, *but* we were not.
>
> Our opponents were alert; we were not.
>
> Allen always volunteers to help at the Special Olympics, *for* he finds the experience very satisfying.
>
> Allen always volunteers to help at the Special Olympics; he finds the experience very satisfying.

12.2 Semicolons and Conjunctive Adverbs

A semicolon is used between main clauses joined by conjunctive adverbs or by phrases like *for example, in fact, for instance.*

The test was long and difficult; *however,* everyone in the class managed to finish it on time.
The cosmopolitan high school has many advantages; *for example,* it brings together students of many different interests.

Note that the conjunctive adverb or phrase is followed by a comma in the examples above.

12.3 Semicolons Between Word Groups Containing Commas

If a sentence contains too many commas, the reader may become confused. If commas precede the conjunction between main clauses, another comma at this point would lose its value as a guide to the reader. Use a semicolon instead.

A semicolon is used between main clauses joined by a conjunction if the clause before the conjunction contains commas.

Rob won't try Mexican, Greek, or Chinese food; nor will he taste anything that looks at all unusual.
We had canned soup, canned beans, and canned milk; but no one had a can opener.

A semicolon is used between a series of phrases if they contain commas.

The auctions will be held on Monday, September 10; Tuesday, September 11; and Friday, September 14.
Leo painted a picture of Maria, his mother; Christopher, his nephew; and Julio, his cousin.
The prize winners came from Waukegan, Illinois; from Denton, Texas; and from Hillside, New York.

Exercise: Indicate where a semicolon should replace a comma in the following sentences. Two sentences are correct.

1. Gordon's jokes are getting out of hand, for example, today he put hot sauce in the catsup dispenser.
2. The secretary opened the door, she asked us to wait.
3. First, the footlights wouldn't work, then the curtain got stuck halfway open.
4. Abigail's grades have improved, in fact, she has the second highest average in the class.
5. The fire alarms sounded, and we lost half of our audience.
6. Jack applied at Northwestern, Stanford, and Duke, he was finally accepted at all three.
7. The senior class has $1,200 in its treasury, the junior class, $800, and the sophomore class, only $500.
8. We were still one hundred miles from home, but we decided not to stop for dinner.
9. I had lost my raincoat, Mary, her umbrella, and Andy, a set of keys.
10. Vi Collins, a local humorist, served as toastmaster, and Ed Bryan, the Amherst coach, made the main speech.
11. The winter weather was severe, as a result, the roads were badly damaged.
12. Ben has another car, he bought it for almost nothing.
13. The rain began coming down harder, nevertheless, the umpires refused to halt the game.
14. In the first half we were badly outclassed, then, in the second half, the tide turned.
15. The editor came from Burma, the printer, from India, and the authors, from Thailand.

12.4 Colons To Introduce Lists

The colon is used to call attention to the items that follow it. The list that follows the colon is usually an explanation or the equivalent of what was stated before the colon.

A colon is used to introduce a list of items.

When a list is preceded by *the following* or *as follows,* a colon is generally used. A colon is not used before a series of modifiers or complements immediately following the verb.

His grades are as follows: English, A; history, B; science, D; and math, C. (list)
The new traffic control system will be introduced in the following cities: Buffalo, St. Louis, and Duluth. (list)
The virus is found in wastes, in milk, and in water. (series of modifiers)
Her virtues are patience, wisdom, and understanding of human motives. (series of complements)

A colon should never follow a sentence fragment.

INCORRECT: Remember to bring: paint, brushes, drop cloths, and turpentine.
CORRECT: Remember to bring the following items: paint, brushes, drop cloths, and turpentine.

12.5 Colons with Formal Quotations

A colon is used to introduce a formal quotation or statement.

Theodore Roosevelt based many of his actions on his pet proverb: "Speak softly and carry a big stick."

12.6 Colons Before Explanatory Statements

A colon is used between two sentences when the second explains the first. The second sentence begins with a capital letter.

We soon learned the answer: Someone had sawed halfway through the supporting plank.
We now knew what to expect from the new manager: She was going to be a strict disciplinarian.

12.7 Other Uses of the Colon

A colon is used (1) after the formal salutation of a letter, (2) between the hour and minute figures of clock time, (3) in Biblical references, (4) between the title and subtitle of a book, (5) between numbers referring to volume and pages of books and magazines.

Dear Dr. Fry:	*The Wide World: A Geography*
6:15 A.M.	Volume II: pages 65–72
Genesis 2:4–7	

12.8 The Dash To Show Break in Thought

A dash is used to show an abrupt break in thought.

In dialogue, the break in thought is often caused by uncertainty or hesitancy as in the first example below.

"Mitosis is—well, it's a change—I mean it's when a cell breaks up or something."

We went down to the—oh, I wasn't supposed to mention that.

We would like—but what do our likes have to do with the situation?

12.9 The Dash with Interrupters

A dash is used to set off a long explanatory statement that interrupts the thought.

There was a feeling of excitement—a feeling that now something explosive might occur—among the courtroom spectators.

This honored guest—a man who had once slept on park benches—arose to address the distinguished group of scholars.

12.10 The Dash Before a Summary

The dash is used after a series to indicate a summarizing statement.

Writs of assistance, the quartering of soldiers in private homes, the insolent searches by royal officers—all these irritations the people of Boston had suffered with growing unease.

Bottles, rags, old tin cans, discarded clothing and papers—these were his stock in trade.

Exercise: Find the sentences that are incorrectly punctuated. Copy them, inserting semicolons, colons, and dashes.

1. Will the following students please report to the office Scott Brooks, Arlene Slavin, and Beth Miller.
2. Katherine's favorite sports are hockey, swimming, badminton, and tennis.
3. Harry began his paper with a quotation from Emerson "A foolish consistency is the hobgoblin of little minds."
4. The title is *Prestidigitation The How-to of Magic Tricks*.
5. The story you are looking for is in *The American Heritage*, Volume IV pages 9–34.
6. We found the road easily, it was well marked.
7. The girls at least some of them felt that no one should hold two important offices.
8. Dr. Jones got up to speak, however, there was little response from the audience.
9. Old tintypes, crumpled letters, and flowers pressed between pages of a book these were some of the treasures we found in our grandparents' attic.
10. You will need the following a work permit, a statement from your parents, and a letter of recommendation.
11. My main job preferences are forestry, farm engineering, and heavy construction.
12. Ann closed with these words "We have a long way to go. Yet, if we work together, we can succeed."

13. I never agreed with oh, I guess I did.
14. Bob recognized the car at once, it was the car his sister had sold to Harry Borden.
15. The conference dates are as follows September 9–12, December 20–22, and March 8–11.

12.11 Parentheses To Enclose Supplementary or Explanatory Words

Commas, dashes, and parentheses all set off supplementary or explanatory material. To determine which marks to use, consider how close in thought the explanatory words are to the main sentence. Commas set off material that is close to the main thought of the sentence. Dashes set off material that is more loosely related, and parentheses set off material that is so distantly connected that it actually could be written as a separate sentence.

There are few occasions in high school writing when parentheses are needed. The safest course for the student is to use commas, or even dashes, to set off parenthetical matter. If the material is so distantly related as to require parentheses, the passage might better be rewritten as a separate sentence.

COMMAS ADEQUATE: The antique car, *which was stored in a warehouse,* was driven in the parade.

DASHES REQUIRED: The vegetables were sautéed—that is, they were lightly fried in butter.

PARENTHESES APPROPRIATE: "By and large, physicists have done their best work before they are thirty (mathematicians even earlier, biologists perhaps a little later)."

—J. BRONOWSKI, *The Ascent of Man*

PARENTHESES AVOIDED: By and large, physicists have done their best work before they are thirty. Mathematicians peak even earlier; biologists, perhaps a little later.

12.12 Punctuation Within Parentheses

Commas, semicolons, and periods are placed outside the closing parenthesis. The question mark and exclamation point are placed inside if the parenthetical material is itself a question or exclamation; otherwise, outside.

Let the mixture simmer over a slow fire (do not boil).
Jack plays two instruments; Jean, three (if you include the guitar); Grace plays four.
We did not stop (who would have?) to see what had happened.
Everyone thought Gustave was joking (as if he ever joked!) when he called out from his truck as it passed us.

12.13 Brackets

Brackets are used to enclose corrections or material inserted by a writer who is quoting someone else's material.

"The 18th Amendment, ratified in 1918 [1919] formally brought Prohibition to the country." (correction)
The critic stated in his column: "I have always found her [Lina Wertmuller] to be a fascinating director." (explanatory word inserted by the writer)

12.14 Ellipses

Indicate the omission of unused parts of a quotation by ellipses: three dots (. . .) to indicate an omission within a sentence and four dots (. . . .) to indicate an omission at the end of a sentence.

In short, . . . to maintain one's self on this earth is not a hardship but a pastime, if we will live simply and wisely. . . .
—HENRY DAVID THOREAU

REINFORCEMENT EXERCISES

The Semicolon, the Colon, the Dash, and Parentheses

A. Use semicolons correctly. The following sentences contain errors in punctuation. Delete commas and add semicolons as necessary.

1. Grandmother loved the hanging Spanish moss, I did not.
2. Pete visited Nashville, Tennessee, Bowling Green, Kentucky, Springfield, Missouri, and East St. Louis, Illinois.
3. The season featured many fine artists, however, I bought tickets only for the Boston Pops and Lionel Ritchie.
4. Soapstone is a soft rock of mineral talc, it is also called steatite.
5. The ancient Egyptians and Greeks used vinegar as a food, a food preservative, a medicine, and a cleaner, and it is still used these ways today.
6. Titanium was discovered by William Gregor of England, but it was named by Martin Klaproth of Germany.
7. William Faulkner was her favorite novelist, Emily Dickinson, her favorite poet, and Bruce Springsteen, her favorite musician.
8. Gretta had fair skin as a result, she did not tan easily.
9. Jordan has memorized all the Presidents' middle names, for example, he says that Harding's middle name was Gamaliel and Hayes's middle name was Birchard.
10. The wind chill factor can make the air feel much colder than it actually is, in fact, sometimes a temperature of zero degrees can feel like fifty-four degrees below zero.
11. The ancient birthstone for May was the agate, today, it is the emerald.
12. Florida is called the Sunshine State, California, the Golden State, and Louisiana, the Pelican State.
13. The turkey buzzard looks something like a turkey, it actually is a member of the vulture family.

14. The movie had wonderful acting, a superb score, and beautiful sets unfortunately, the poor direction all but destroyed it.
15. Lamprey eels are common in the Atlantic coast of Europe they may also be found in the Mediterranean.

B. Use colons and dashes. The following sentences contain errors in punctuation. Correct these errors by adding colons and dashes as necessary.

1. Among the famous works describing utopias are the following *Erewhon*, *Looking Backward*, and *A Modern Utopia*.
2. We can choose topics for our term papers from among the following effects of the Civil War on industrialization, carpet baggers in the post-Civil War South, and the plight of the former slaves.
3. Well, of *course* I mean 12 30 P.M. 12 30 A.M. is in the middle of the night!
4. Turn right at the Watch out!
5. Burning bush, wahoo, and arrow wood these are three names given to the same plant.
6. The story line is interesting oh, have you read it already?
7. Cal said he was from "ruburbia" the land beyond the suburbs.
8. The pamphlet provided the following statistic "In the last 10 years, more than 250,000 people have been killed in alcohol-related crashes."
9. The book was entitled *Space The Last Frontier*.
10. Only then did I understand the confusing images represented a dream.

MIXED REVIEW

The Semicolon, the Colon, the Dash, and Parentheses

A. Rewrite the following sentences, inserting necessary semicolons, colons, and dashes.

1. All the parts of the dog's fur the back, the belly, and even the tip of the tail were covered with mud.
2. Hoyt checked an atlas, Ilene, an almanac.
3. The novel ended with these words "From the depths there rose a long-drawn rumbling roar. The outlet to Deception Pass closed forever."
4. Africa is a continent of contrasts, for example, the Sahara is nothing like the Congo.
5. The following rodeo riders set records Larry Mahan, Jim Shoulders, and Tom Ferguson.
6. Strangely enough, Mrs. Eisler had lived in London, England, London, Canada, and London, Kentucky.
7. The page contained ads for carrying cases, straps, lenses, and film, but it did not contain an ad for cameras.
8. The judge pronounced the sentence not guilty.
9. Dee Brown wrote *Bury My Heart at Wounded Knee An Indian History of the American West*.
10. Old bills, receipts, checks, they all fell out of the desk.
11. Nearsightedness is the condition of having difficulty seeing things that are far away farsightedness is the opposite condition.
12. The resort offered many winter sports bobsledding, cross-country skiing, snow-shoeing, and ice skating.
13. The rucksack was skillfully packed, as a result, it contained all that I needed.
14. Sandro Munari won the Targa Florio, Bobby Unser, the Indy, and Helmut Marko, the Le Mans.
15. Hand me the paint before too late!
16. *Hill, Dumont, Maki, Jurek,* and *Zola* all these last names mean "hill" in different languages.

17. The winner I think I have a chance is going to receive a $10,000 scholarship.
18. Bruce was fascinated by the history of firefighting he wanted, in fact, to be a firefighter.
19. Tunya made the announcement The Bayanihan Philippine Dance Company would perform.
20. Lucia I knew it wasn't the doctor's first name.

B. Rewrite the following sentences, inserting the necessary semicolons, colons, and dashes. Delete commas as necessary.

1. Down jackets are very warm, they are good for outdoor sports in cold weather.
2. Trains, buses, planes they were all shut down by the week-long blizzard.
3. An aerial stunt pilot is performing a oh, he did a double back loop!
4. Olga skied in a down-hill race yesterday, she placed third.
5. At 6 30 we watched the news, at 7 30 we switched to our favorite comedy show.
6. Turn right I mean left at the next corner.
7. The commentator closed with these words "The world hunger problem will not go away. Can we ignore it any longer?"
8. The store held a sale, in fact, prices were cut in half.
9. The article appears in *World History An Introduction* Volume 2 pages 64–67.
10. Mark used the proper tools, read all the directions, and worked slowly, but the bicycle he put together fell apart in one week.
11. For lunch, Kimberly had yogurt, Lisa, a sandwich, and Rob, a salad.
12. The movie was produced on a low budget, nevertheless, it is one of the year's best releases.
13. The lineup was as follows Ken, center, Bo and Les, forwards, and Ted and Gino, guards.
14. Karen knew why Lee was late his car was undependable.
15. I was not worried I knew better that anything would go wrong.

USING MECHANICS IN WRITING

The Semicolon, the Colon, the Dash, and Parentheses

A. Think of an object that has many parts—an object with which you are quite familiar. It might be a computer, the engine of a car, a leaf, a baseball field, or anything else. Write a description of the object. Do not use exact or technical terms except in parentheses (and be certain to use as many exact or technical terms as you can). For example, in describing a baseball field, you might write: "Several feet behind the crouching catcher is a tall screen made of heavy wire (the backstop). Its purpose is to protect the spectators sitting in the area." Write a description of the object that is detailed enough so that a person who is completely unfamiliar with the object can visualize its parts and correctly identify them.

B. Imagine a humorous character whose speech pattern is such that he or she is constantly interrupting himself or herself with side thoughts, commentary, irrelevancies, and omitted details. Write a paragraph in which this character is trying to give a friend a simple message but cannot get to the point because of all the self-interruptions. Use parentheses, dashes, and ellipses to indicate the turns and lapses in your character's speech.

C. Study a copy of a will or another such legal document. Notice how many colons, semicolons, dashes, and parentheses such documents contain. Then imagine that you are very old and very wealthy. Write your own will, using as many colons, semicolons, dashes, and parentheses as possible.

13.0 The Apostrophe

An **apostrophe** used with a noun shows possession or ownership: *Ms. Carr's station wagon, Tom's bat, the dentist's chair*. It may also show membership, a source or origin, an identifying characteristic, or location.

MEMBERSHIP:	Brett's fraternity, mother's team
SOURCE OR ORIGIN:	Mexico's art, Ed's idea
IDENTIFYING CHARACTERISTIC:	Jack's laugh, peacock's plumage
LOCATION:	New York's Bowery, Gary's factories

To avoid leaving out essential apostrophes, learn the rules in this Section and proofread your writing carefully.

13.1 The Possessive of Singular Nouns

The possessive form of a singular noun is usually made by adding an apostrophe and s ('s) to the noun.

Charles + 's = Charles's	teacher + 's = teacher's
family + 's = family's	dog + 's = dog's

Note: A few proper nouns ending in *s* may take the apostrophe only: *Jesus', Moses'*. In general, however, the correct way to make a singular noun possessive is to add an apostrophe and *s*.

13.2 The Possessive of Plural Nouns

If a plural noun does not end in *s*, add both apostrophe and *s* (*'s*) to form the possessive.

men + 's = men's oxen + 's = oxen's
alumni + 's = alumni's children + 's = children's

If a plural noun ends in *s*, add only the apostrophe to form the possessive.

senators + ' = senators' Joneses + ' = Joneses'
guitarists + ' = guitarists' bears + ' = bears'

Exercise: Write *Correct* for each sentence in which the possessive form is correct. If the form is incorrect, write it correctly.

1. The salespersons experiences with the new product are interesting.
2. This season, men's fashions are more casual.
3. James's report was hard to understand.
4. The defense attorneys' statement seemed to surprise her client.
5. We were looking for the Coleman's car.
6. The mayor met with the transport worker's committee.
7. The state's attorney rose to address the jury.
8. We could barely hear the speaker's voices.
9. The senator's spouses were entertained at the White House.
10. The parents were invited to the teachers meeting.
11. The reporter's newspapers expect them to hunt out the truth.
12. The childrens' doctor is an old friend of ours.
13. We listened in awe to the womans' bitter attack.
14. An actors' employment is not continuous.
15. All fifty states were represented at the Governor's Conference.
16. The firefighters' voices receded as they entered the building.

17. The boy's uniforms have not been ordered.
18. The student's diplomas will be mailed to them in two weeks.
19. Chris's shoes hurt his feet.
20. The childrens names were sewn on their coats and inside each mitten.

13.3 The Possessive of Compound Nouns

A **compound noun** is one word that has been made by joining two or more words together. Some compound words have hyphens between the parts.

Only the last part of a hyphenated noun shows possession.

mother-in-law + 's = mother-in-law's
editor-in-chief + 's = editor-in-chief's
attorney-general + 's = attorney-general's

Nouns such as *the Queen of England, the President of the United States, the Secretary of State* form the possessive by adding an apostrophe and *s* to the last word only: *the Secretary of State's name*. However, this awkward construction can be avoided by using an *of* phrase.

the itinerary of the Queen of England
the children of the President of the United States
the name of the Secretary of State

13.4 Joint Ownership

When the names of two or more persons are used to show joint ownership, only the name of the last person mentioned is given the possessive form. Add an apostrophe or an apostrophe and *s* in accord with the spelling of that name.

Mom and Dad's idea
Nicole and Barry's project

The rule applies also to firm names and to names of organizations.

McGinnis and Company's guarantee
Procter and Gamble's products
the Department of Urban Renewal's report
Hainert, Hanson, and Wright's new location

13.5 Separate Ownership or Possession

If the names of two or more persons are used to show separate ownership, each name is given the possessive form.

Capra's and Ford's movies   Parker's and Stein's satires

This construction may become awkward. It can be avoided by using an *of* phrase.

the movies of Capra and Ford
the satires of Parker and Stein

13.6 The Possessive of Indefinite Pronouns

Use an apostrophe and s to form the possessive of indefinite pronouns.

someone + 's = someone's   nobody + 's = nobody's
another + 's = another's   anyone + 's = anyone's

The apostrophe and *s* are added to the last word in forms like *everyone else, nobody else, no one else:*

nobody else's   everyone else's

The apostrophe is not used to form the possessive of personal pronouns. (See Section 1.2.)

NONSTANDARD: their's, your's, her's, our's, it's
STANDARD: theirs, yours, hers, ours, its

13.7 Expressions of Time and Amount

When used as adjectives, words expressing time and amount are given the possessive form.

a day's wages	three days' wages
an hour's time	two hours' time
a dollar's worth	five dollars' worth

Exercise: Copy the italicized words, changing them to show ownership or possession correctly.

1. Jerry will be staying at his *sister-in-law* house.
2. *Betty* and *Velma* papers were corrected first.
3. The drop in business is *nobody* fault.
4. We bought ten *dollars* worth of crepe paper for decoration.
5. Have you seen *Altman and Henry* new store?
6. The accident cost me three *weeks* pay.
7. *Jack and Jill* story is a very sad one.
8. We looked into *Marsh and Company* offer.
9. The *commander-in-chief* flag was flying.
10. An *hour* delay now may cost a *week* time next January.
11. Both *Jackson* and *Balfour* stores will be open tonight.
12. The *editor-in-chief* job is to determine editorial policies.
13. I had left the restaurant with *someone else* hat.
14. The *Smiths* and *Browns* houses were open for inspection.
15. We couldn't find the *Attorney-General* name.

13.8 Apostrophes To Show Omissions

An apostrophe is used to show omission of letters or figures.

the gold rush of '49	1849
o'clock	of the clock
doesn't	does not
I'd	I would

13.9 Plurals of Letters, Words, Numbers, and Signs

An apostrophe is used to show the plurals of letters, words, numbers, and signs used as words.

Are there two *c*'s or two *s*'s in *occasion?*
There are too many *but*'s in this agreement.
It is easy to confuse *7*'s and *1*'s.
I accidentally used <'s instead of >'s.

Note: Letters, numbers, signs, and words used as words are italicized in print. They may be underlined or placed in quotation marks in manuscript or typescript. (See Section 14.7 for additional information on the uses of italics and underlining.)

Exercise A: Copy the following sentences, inserting an apostrophe (and *s*) where needed. This exercise reviews all the uses of apostrophes.

1. Do you capitalize the *ands* in a title?
2. Doesnt Jeffs phone number have two 6s in it?
3. There wasnt much unemployment during the 20s.
4. The players dont hear the spectators cheers.
5. Its too early to tell whether Mueller and Sons petition will be granted.
6. The bus wont leave until seven oclock.
7. Bobs and Jacks desks were piled high with gifts.
8. This mornings paper has one of Charles stories in it.
9. My grandparents home is in Wisconsin.
10. We cant tell whos winning.
11. Dartmouth used to be a mens college, didnt it?
12. The waitress smile was reassuring.
13. The states capitol is being rebuilt.
14. The witnesses stories were not even similar.
15. Ten years work was destroyed in five minutes time.
16. The womens coats had been delivered to the mens department.

17. Spielbergs and Coppolas movies are usually popular.
18. If you dont put up a warning sign, someones likely to get hurt.
19. Ross letter was the first to arrive.
20. My brother-in-laws voice could be heard plainly.

Exercise B: Write the possessive singular and the possessive plural of each of the following words:

1. child
2. heiress
3. deer
4. salesperson
5. minute
6. baby
7. hostess
8. horse
9. county
10. class
11. trolley
12. hour
13. country
14. bus
15. box

Exercise C: The following sentences contain errors in the use of apostrophes. Copy the sentences, correcting all errors.

1. Its a long way to the Wassmans' cottage.
2. Al has started to work at Laidlaw's and Brown's store.
3. The factory has been using one of Gerald's and Company pumps.
4. Frieda's and Donna's exhibit won first prize.
5. Robert Frost and Marianne Moore's poetry readings are available on records.
6. This years' profits are higher than last years.
7. The neighbors dont' know when Jess's trunk arrived.
8. Jefferson's and Madison's partnership was known to everyone.
9. We saw your cat at Bob Jone's garage.
10. Someones' car had run over the children's toys.
11. The foreman's voice rang out above the worker's voices.
12. Won't you be staying at your brother's-in-law house?
13. Bess' sister works at B. Little's and Company store.
14. We went to Brentano's Book Store after we had gone to Chris' house.
15. Lewis's and Clark's expedition gave the nation a better understanding of it's western territory.

REINFORCEMENT EXERCISES

The Apostrophe

A. Use the possessive form of nouns. Some of the following sentences contain errors in the use of apostrophes. If a sentence contains an error, rewrite the word correctly. If a sentence does not contain an error, write *Correct*.

1. The locomotives single whistle blast frightened the campers.
2. The *Stockholm*'s prow crushed the *Andrea Dorias* starboard side.
3. The trainers greatest pleasure was to help each other learn more about the behavior of dolphins.
4. Louisianas' counties are called parishes.
5. Diana Ross is one of my favorite performers, but this album is not Rosses best work.
6. When you were young, did you read Kipling's *Just So Stories?*
7. Why do womens' shirts and mens' shirts button on opposite sides?
8. Virginia Woolf's last novel was *Mrs. Dalloway.*
9. One of Ghanas main exports is cacao beans.
10. The childrens room will be designed with safety and convenience in mind.

B. Use apostrophes to show ownership. Rewrite the sentences below using the correct possessive form.

1. My sisters father-in-laws birthday is on the same day as hers.
2. Carlotta found somebodys wallet on the bus and turned it over to the police.
3. "That mistake will cost me a years pay," groaned Ms. Exeter.
4. The reporter brought his column to the editor-in-chiefs attention.

5. The historical tour included visits to Washington and Jefferson's homes.
6. Fitzgeralds stories about the Roaring Twenties capture the decades particular flavor.
7. If we don't feed them in separate rooms, our dog will eat it's lunch and the cats, too.
8. My grandmother always warns me against using someone elses comb.
9. Lewis's and Clarks book told the story of their famous expedition.
10. This paper with the "A" on it must be your's.

C. Use apostrophes for omissions and plurals. Rewrite the following sentences, correcting any errors. If a sentence contains no errors, write *Correct*.

1. In older romantic novels, the characters used words such as *mustnt* for *must not* and *shant* for *shall not*.
2. Dont you think its too late for apologies?
3. The book was entitled *The Crash of* 29.
4. Every typesetter knows what *picas* and *points* are.
5. Milt loved to repeat the old cliché, "I would if I could, but I cant, so I wont."
6. I cant remember how many *l*s there are in Llewellyn's name.
7. *I* and *II* are Roman, not Arabic, numerals.
8. The binary number had fifteen *0*s and three *1*s in it.
9. The baby's sweatshirt read "Class of 05."
10. The teacher circled all the *thing*s in my composition.

MIXED REVIEW

The Apostrophe

A. Rewrite the following sentences, correcting all errors in the use of the apostrophe. If a sentence has no error, write *Correct*.

1. My poems theme is that perhaps the world is nothing more than a dream.
2. The Senator-elects resignation was entirely unexpected.
3. Isnt it awful that some people call that plant a mother-in-laws tongue?
4. Finn's and O'Reillys Hardware Store sold nothing but bolts, nuts, and nails.
5. The Secretary of State's face looked grim.
6. The contributors' names appeared on the inside cover of the program.
7. Is your speech full of *you knows*?
8. Many businesses have phone numbers that end in two or three *0*s.
9. Theyre going to study fossil remains in Africas interior.
10. Faulkners and Hemingways styles are quite different from one another.
11. Chris' signature appeared on the note but he denied any knowledge of it.
12. My humorous essay was entitled, "How I Survived the Summer of 85."
13. Gordon Lightfoot gave a concert for the workers in Albertas oil fields.
14. Im reading a book on the movie stars of the 30s.
15. Terry and Kim's solar battery won first prize in the science fair.
16. The ranger asked if the campfire was our's.
17. The flag was lowered and sixty second's silence was observed.
18. The banners slogans all called for peace.
19. We applauded Marcus' touchdown.
20. With a splint and tape, I repaired the rabbits foot.

B. Rewrite the following sentences, correcting all errors in the use of the apostrophe.

1. Dun's and Bradstreet's report may affect the value of that stock.
2. Milwaukee and Chicago's zoos are very large.
3. I bought the Moody Blue's new album.
4. Coretta wore Bess' costume to my sister-in-laws Halloween party.
5. Someone's books are on Ms. Thomsons desk.
6. Most of the guest's costumes were very elaborate.
7. How many *no*s have we counted on these ballots?
8. Last years swimming coach wont be returning.
9. No ones excuse was as original as Henrys'.
10. Didnt you see that mans tattoos?
11. I like these three radio station's music.
12. Wanda has *x*s and *o*s written all over her letter.
13. Many peoples' cars are faster than her's.
14. The babie's crying disturbed the neighbors.
15. The mens' dispute was over a golf score.
16. We ate six dollars worth of pistachio nuts.
17. Dale likes Oak Lakes' beach because of it's white sand.
18. The outcome depended on one representative's-at-large vote.
19. Don't string your sentences together with *and*s.
20. Lavinia and Aaron's families live in adjoining townhouses.

The Apostrophe

A. Do some research on a specific area of interest in which different types of special equipment, terms, and symbols are used. Here are some subjects that might be narrowed for this purpose:

weather forecasting
theater
broadcasting
medicine
special effects
journalism
archaeology
professional sports
movie-making
computers

Write a short, informal talk that provides an overview of the subject that you have chosen. In this overview, explain the subject, the duties of the different people involved, and the types of equipment and terms used by these people. Try to use possessive nouns and pronouns, as well as the plural forms of some of the special terms. Since the talk will be informal, you may also use contractions.

B. Write an essay in which you express your personal opinion about something you think should *not* happen in the next few years. Write your paper using contractions such as *shouldn't, can't,* and *won't*. Then, rewrite the paper, eliminating all the contractions. Observe how this change affects the tone of your essay.

C. Write a review of an imaginary variety show in which everything goes wrong. Include the following acts in your review, and use the possessive forms of their names:

Gregory and His Dancing Bears
Tina and Chris (magicians who work as a team)
Markowitz and Company (a group of comedic actors)

14.0 Quotations

14.1 Direct and Indirect Quotations

Quotation marks are used to enclose a direct quotation.

In a direct quotation, words are written exactly as the speaker said them.

> The witness answered, "I have known her for three years."
> "The defendant," he said, "has been guilty of negligence."

Quotation marks are not used with an indirect quotation.

An indirect quotation reports the meaning expressed by the speaker but does not give the exact words.

> INDIRECT: The hostess announced that the musicians would be an hour late.
> DIRECT: "The musicians will be an hour late," the hostess announced.

14.2 Punctuation of Direct Quotations

1. In dialogue, the first word of a quotation is capitalized.

Kim said, "To ski or not to ski—that is the question."

When a writer uses only a portion of material taken from another source, the first word is not capitalized.

Let us, too, act "with justice for all" in our own times.

2. The speaker's words are set off from the rest of the sentence.

Note the placement of commas in these examples:

The officer said, "No one is to leave this room."
"No one is to leave this room," said the officer.

3. When the end of the quotation is also the end of the sentence, the period falls inside the quotation marks.

Henry said, "You can have dinner at my house."

4. If the quoted words are a question or an exclamation, the question mark or the exclamation point falls inside the quotation marks. In this situation no comma is needed.

"Have we missed the train?" Joan asked.
"The story is utterly false!" Harry shouted.

5. If the entire sentence is a question or an exclamation, the punctuation falls outside the quotation marks.

Did the witness say, "I was not present"?
The imposter even said, "You are welcome in my house"!

6. The colon and the semicolon at the close of a quotation fall outside the quotation marks.

These were the items listed as "indispensable": laboratory tables, Bunsen burners, metal trays, and storage cabinets.
Read Hemingway's "A Clean, Well-Lighted Place"; then compare it with *The Old Man and the Sea*.

7. **Both parts of a divided quotation are enclosed in quotation marks. The first word of the second part is not capitalized unless it begins a new sentence.**

   "I believe we can now hope," the doctor said, "for a complete recovery."
   "We cannot give up hope," the doctor said. "The human body has many hidden resources."

8. **In dialogue, a new paragraph and a new set of quotation marks show a change in speaker.**

   "Scientific research today is well organized," the speaker said. "Scientists work in teams, each investigating one aspect of a problem."

   Wayne asked politely, "Isn't it true that many inventions and discoveries are just a matter of luck?"

   "Yes, indeed," answered the speaker with a laugh. "We call it *serendipity*. You need a little luck in science as well as in other fields."

14.3 Quotations Within Quotations

Single quotation marks are used to enclose a quotation within a quotation.

Mary reported, "Phil had trouble saying, 'There is where their wares are sold.' "
"I thought he was saying, 'Stand aside and let the passengers off,' " Luisa replied.

14.4 Long Quotations

A quotation may be several paragraphs in length. A speech or an address is a long quotation.

In long quotations, begin each paragraph with quotation marks. Place quotation marks at the end of the last paragraph only.

Exercise A: Copy the following sentences, adding the necessary punctuation marks and capital letters.

1. Judy asked has everyone been warned about the new speed limit on the highway
2. This fire was no accident the chief quickly retorted it was a set fire
3. I do not know Jean admitted whether the attic door was closed or not
4. Did the speaker say you are all invited
5. Did you hear Leo say we don't need your help Paul asked
6. Watch that left linebacker Burt shouted
7. We will never really know Ruby said how much Ms. Barber has done for us
8. Ms. Rice asked how many of you know which play the line To be or not to be comes from
9. The officer asked whether we had seen any strangers in the neighborhood
10. I heard him shout the money has been stolen Karen insisted
11. Are you for us or against us Bob demanded
12. Did you hear someone whisper Go away
13. Has everyone boarded the bus asked Marion
14. I never knew before said Colin how good water can taste
15. Do you really know asked Helen who won first prize in photography?

Exercise B: The following passage is adapted from O. Henry's short story "The Third Ingredient." In it, a young woman named Hetty confronts a young man whom she had invited to dinner upon assuming he had nothing to his name except an onion. Rewrite the passage, adding correct punctuation and paragraphing correctly.

> Don't lie to me Hetty said, calmly. What were you going to do with that onion? The young man suppressed a cough and faced her resolutely. I was going to eat it said he with emphatic slowness just as I told you before. And you have

nothing else to eat at home? Not a thing. What kind of work do you do? I am not working at anything just now. Then why said Hetty, with her voice set on its sharpest edge do you lean out of windows and give orders to chauffeurs in green automobiles in the street below? The young man flushed, and his dull eyes began to sparkle. Because, madam said he, in accelerando tones I pay the chauffeur's wages and I own the automobile—and also this onion—this onion, madam. He flourished the onion within an inch of Hetty's nose. Then why do you eat onions she said, with biting contempt and nothing else? I never said I did retorted the young man, heatedly. I said I had nothing else to eat where I live. I am not a delicatessen storekeeper. Then why pursued Hetty, inflexibly were you going to eat a raw onion? My mother said the young man always made me eat one for a cold.

Exercise C: Writing Write a dialogue between two people during which each speaker quotes another person. Use single quotation marks, quotation marks, and new paragraphs to indicate a change of speaker.

14.5 Setting Off Titles

In print, italics are used to indicate titles of books, magazines, newspapers, movies, long pamphlets, or bulletins. In your own writing, underline titles to indicate italics.

To indicate a television show or part of a book, magazine, or newspaper use quotation marks.

Use quotation marks to enclose the titles of chapters and other parts of books and to enclose the titles of stories, poems, essays, articles, and short musical compositions.

In *Coping with the Mass Media* I liked "A Nation of Videots."

I read an article called "Here Come the Robots" in *Time* magazine.

14.6 Words Used in Special Ways

Words used in special ways or special senses are enclosed in quotation marks.

Quotation marks may be used by a writer to show that he or she is using a word as someone else has used it. Using quotation marks indicates that the writer does not accept this use of the word.

Slang words and phrases are also enclosed in quotation marks to indicate that the writer does not accept them as standard usage.

> Among these "juvenile delinquents" are many class officers and natural leaders of the student body.
> Are these what you call "simple directions"?
> They were locked up overnight in the local "slammer"; they were released in the morning.

Note: When a comma or period immediately follows the quoted word, it is placed *inside* the quotation marks. A semicolon or colon is placed *outside* the quotation marks, as in the example above. If the quoted word appears at the end of a question or exclamation, the question or exclamation point is placed *outside* the quotation marks. See the second example.

14.7 Words Used as Words

A word referred to as a word is italicized in print. In writing, the word is underlined.

> I dislike the word *impossible*. (If this sentence were handwritten, *impossible* would be underlined.)

When a word and its definition appear in the same sentence, the word is italicized, and the definition is placed in quotation marks.

> The word *perspicuity* means "clearness of expression."

Exercise: Copy the following sentences. Insert quotation marks where necessary. Indicate italics by underlining.

1. The quiz, as she called it, turned out to be a full-scale test.
2. The book by former astronaut Michael Collins is called Fire on the Moon.
3. I have just read Eudora Welty's short story A Visit of Charity.
4. The word critical may also mean dangerous.
5. Dana's book Two Years Before the Mast influenced the lives of many sailors.
6. What does the writer mean by the phrase natural causes?
7. You can find A Way You'll Never Be in Hemingway's Winner Take Nothing.
8. We must stop calling these countries underdeveloped nations.
9. The word serendipity means an aptitude for making fortunate discoveries by chance.
10. The editorial in today's Boston Globe is titled The unCouncil.
11. The first piece I learned to play on the piano was Twinkle, Twinkle, Little Star.
12. Idioms are phrases such as let the cat out of the bag that can't be taken literally.
13. In Edna St. Vincent Millay's Poems Selected for Young People, my favorite is The Philosopher.
14. The note was signed A friend.
15. One new song simply repeats the word love over and over.

REINFORCEMENT EXERCISES

Quotations

A. Punctuate direct and indirect quotations. Rewrite the following sentences, inserting proper punctuation and necessary capital letters. If a sentence is correct as it is, write *Correct*.

1. Jessica said that she took part in a one-day ascent of Mt. Washington.
2. Let me explain the features and benefits of this stereo said the salesperson.
3. The director explained when Juliet says wherefore art thou Romeo she is *not* asking where he is.
4. Do you think Ken asked that we will finish our work in time to catch a movie?
5. Matthew said that I could improve my French by listening to one of the radio stations that broadcasts out of Quebec.
6. My grandfather was born in Brooklyn said Cynthia in 1920.
7. The director announced that we would reshoot this scene fifty times, if necessary.
8. Will everyone fit at one table? asked Celeste.
9. Wow Ken shouted did you see that catch?
10. Was it Roosevelt who said walk softly and carry a big stick?

B. Use quotation marks and underlining. Rewrite the following sentences, correcting any errors in punctuation and capitalization.

1. Erika asked what does the phrase third world nations mean?
2. I believe, said the instructor, that the quotation less is more comes from a poem by Robert Browning.
3. It took us three days to figure out the so-called easy directions that came with the kit.

4. Did Langston Hughes write the poem Dream Deferred asked Julius.
5. The song called Gus: the Theatre Cat is taken from T. S. Eliot's collection of childrens' poems, Old Possum's Book of Practical Cats.
6. Heraclitus the book stated is known for his proverb Nothing endures but changes.
7. Country music fans are particularly fond of Tom T. Hall, whom they have nicknamed The Storyteller.
8. The word mah-jongg comes from the Chinese word ma-ch'iao and means house sparrow.
9. Stravinsky's most famous work is a ballet entitled Le Sacre du Printemps, or The Rite of Spring.
10. Some people use the word theater, some use cinema, and some use movie house.

MIXED REVIEW

Quotations

A. Copy the following sentences, inserting the necessary quotation marks, capitals, and punctuation. Indicate italics by underlining.

1. The secret of my craft said the magician lies in misdirecting the audience.
2. Carly whispered did he ask Who will confess to the crime?
3. Hooray shouted the first runner to reach the finish line.
4. To comedians, the phrase to mug means to make exaggerated facial expressions.
5. The painting Starry Night by Van Gogh inspired a song of the same name.
6. The songwriter received very little money for his work, but he did achieve a certain succes d'estime.
7. I think, Philip said, that it was Margo Jones who wrote Everything in life is theatre.
8. Did Lara actually ask Who goes there
9. In Spain the term Moors was used to designate Muslims.
10. Shirley Jackson wrote short stories, such as The Lottery, as well as novels such as The Haunting of Hill House.
11. In Italy, foreign tourists are called gli stranieri, which means the strangers.
12. Yes, the movie critic for the Daily News did write the only good thing about this movie was the fact that it ended Lance said.
13. What do you mean by whatchamacallit, asked Mr. Burgess patiently.
14. Holy cow the sports announcer screamed the ball is out of the park.
15. Why don't you buy a used car asked Simon instead of spending all of your savings on a new one?
16. Tomorrow's assignment is to read Flannery O'Connor's short story, Everything That Rises Must Converge, announced Ms. Olsen.

17. What was the origin of the word hippie?
18. Many of Jules Verne's books, such as Twenty Thousand Leagues Under the Sea, predicted the future with startling accuracy.
19. My great uncle said that he wanted to live to see the next century.
20. Sheila asked what did the Elizabethans mean by the phrase a fond fellow?

B. Copy the following sentences, inserting necessary punctuation and capital letters. Indicate italics by underlining.

1. Who are your favorite athletes Rick asked.
2. Would you rather go now JoAnn asked or after dinner?
3. Look out below the fire marshal shouted.
4. The human body our biology teacher said is a machine.
5. Why did MacLeish entitle his poem Eleven?
6. The comedian said his remarks were off the cuff.
7. Katherine Mansfield wrote the story called The Garden Party Jennifer said.
8. Jan asked did the referee say Strike three?
9. Lisa writes a column, Sports Scene, in the newspaper.
10. Stay happy my doctor said laughter is the best medicine.
11. Can you believe said Ron she asked who did the dishes.
12. Aunt Betty felt under the weather, so she stayed in bed.
13. One of my brother's friends still uses the word groovy.
14. The motto of the Times is all the news that's fit to print.
15. Two Gwendolyn Brooks poems Bradley likes are The Bean Eaters and We Real Cool.
16. Shakespeare wrote The course of true love never did run smooth.
17. Bob asked did the role of Fanny Brice in Funny Girl make Barbra Streisand famous?
18. Have you ever watched Dr. Who on public television asked the science fiction fanatic in our class.
19. The little favor my mom asked me to do turned out to be a three hour shoveling job.
20. Lewis Carroll coined the words chortle and jabberwocky.

USING MECHANICS IN WRITING

Quotations

A. Imagine that you are a music critic for a magazine devoted to popular music. Choose a type of popular music that you enjoy (rock, new wave, blues, country, folk, or gospel), and write an essay on common themes in this music. Mention specific songs and albums. Also use quotations from song lyrics to support the points that you make in your essay.

B. The following is a passage from a book on the legends of King Arthur. Rewrite this passage, inserting quotation marks and other punctuation as necessary. Indicate a change of speaker by beginning a new paragraph.

EXCALIBUR

As Arthur rode with Merlin, he sighed. How can I do battle for my kingdom when I have no sword? Be of good cheer Merlin answered for nearby is a sword that shall be yours. So saying, Merlin led the King down a path deep into the woods until they came upon a shining blue lake. In the middle of the lake, Arthur saw an arm clothed in white, mysterious and wonderful. High above the blue water, the raised arm held a sword encased in a rich scabbard embellished all in gold. Behold said Merlin there is the sword I spoke of. As Arthur still stared at the wondrous sight, a damsel rose up out of the water and walked toward them on the rippling waves. What damsel is that? Arthur asked. The Lady of the Lake Merlin answered. She lives beneath the water in a palace of rock. When the Lady of the Lake came close, Arthur spoke. What sword he asked is it that yonder hand holds above the water? I would have it for my own. The sword Excalibur is mine the lady replied in a voice that was deep and yet soft, like water falling over stones on a winter's morning. Yet now you shall have the sword.

CUMULATIVE REVIEW

Capitalization and Punctuation

Using Capitalization and Punctuation Correctly. Copy the paragraphs, correcting errors in capitalization and punctuation.

One of the oddest, figures in history was king ludwig II of bavaria Known to subsequent ages as "mad king ludwig this mysterious monarch was born in munich on august 15 1845 and ruled bavaria until he was deposed in 1886. . .

When he was a child the future king lived with his parents members of the royal wittelsbach family in a restored castle in the bavarian Alps. Showing the influence of these surroundings young ludwig became obsessed with stories of the mysterious romantic heroes of the german middle ages In 1864 ludwig's father died and Ludwig became king inheriting the resources to indulge his passion for the Days of Old.

One of ludwig's first acts as King was to befriend richard wagner the debt-ridden composer of romantic operas shared Ludwig's love of medieval germanic folklore and legends. ludwig paid wagner's debts gave him an annual income and even tried to have an opera house built solely to première wagner's masterpiece opera the ring of the nibelung. ludwig then turned to what was to be his major preoccupation in life building castles.

In 1869 ludwig built the fairy-tale castle of neuschwanstein at the foot of mount tegelberg. Over the next few years the king spent all that he had plus an additional 21 million Marks which he borrowed from the Bavarian treasury to build two more amazing castles linderhof a castle in the french style decorated throughout with 24-carat gold and herrenchiemsee a castle modeled on the french palace of versailles.

Ludwig also had plans for other castles, the bavarian government had grown tired of ludwig's wastefulness and removed him from power. The obsession of Bavaria's strange king had come to an end.

15.0 Spelling

Almost everyone has at least some trouble with spelling. For some people, the problem may involve only a few difficult or "tricky" words; for others, spelling may be difficult with even short, relatively simple words.

If you have trouble with spelling, you may be consoled by the fact that other students for generations back have also had trouble, and many have learned to improve. There is no simple way to teach you to spell. If you are concerned about the problem, however, here are several helpful suggestions.

1. Proofread your writing. Many errors in spelling are caused by carelessness or haste. Even the best speller may sometimes write "your" for "you're" or "its" for "it's." Leave yourself time to check your writing carefully before turning it in.

2. Learn to look at the letters and patterns in a word. We learn to read by recognizing whole words or parts of words. However, when we write, we must pay attention to each letter. It is also helpful to break up a difficult word into its parts and memorize the spelling of each part. Finally, look for familiar patterns, such as double letters and *-ies* endings.

3. Keep a list of your spelling errors. You spell most words correctly. If you concentrate on the few words you misspell—the ones you keep on your personal list—you may show quick improvement.

4. Practice on your own spelling problems. One recommended procedure is to use a pack of flash cards. Print your problem words on cards in large letters. Take a card from the pack. Look at every letter and let the order of the letters sink into your mind. Pronounce each part of the word separately. Turn the card over. Write the word on a piece of paper. Turn the card over again and compare what you have written with the correct spelling of the word.

5. Memorize and apply the few rules of spelling given below. Be sure you understand the rules, or your memory work will be wasted. Practice using these rules so that their use becomes automatic and you can write *recommend, weird, disappoint,* and so on, quickly.

Exercise: Divide these words into syllables. Do not be concerned as to whether they conform to the dictionary division. Just make sure that every word part has a vowel sound. Once you have divided the words, look at each part separately to fix the spelling in your memory.

1. abbreviate
2. accommodate
3. athletics
4. boundaries
5. candidate
6. competitive
7. desperate
8. disappear
9. extraordinary
10. immediately
11. incredible
12. laboratory
13. library
14. mischievous
15. necessary
16. probably
17. quantity
18. sophomore
19. occasional
20. preparation

15.1 The Final Silent e

When a suffix beginning with a vowel is added to a word ending in a silent e, the e is usually dropped.

approve + al = approval
write + er = writer
move + ing = moving
creative + ive = creative
desire + able = desirable
pore + ous = porous
structure + al = structural
statue + ary = statuary

When the final silent *e* is preceded by *c* or *g*, the *e* is usually retained before a suffix beginning with *a* or *o*.

outrage + ous = outrageous
manage + able = manageable
change + able = changeable
notice + able = noticeable

When a suffix beginning with a consonant is added to a word ending in a silent *e*, the *e* is usually retained.

base + ment = basement
blame + less = blameless
care + ful = careful
lone + ly = lonely

The following words are exceptions: *truly, argument, judgment, wholly, awful.*

15.2 Words Ending in *y*

When a suffix is added to a word ending in *y* preceded by a consonant, the *y* is usually changed to *i*.

There are two exceptions: (1) When *-ing* is added, the *y* does not change. (2) Some one-syllable words do not change the *y*: *dryness, shyness.*

funny + er = funnier
party + es = parties
carry + ed = carried
luxury + ous = luxurious
fuzzy + ness = fuzziness
carry + ing = carrying

When a suffix is added to a word ending in *y* preceded by a vowel, the *y* usually does not change.

enjoy + ing = enjoying
delay + ed = delayed

EXCEPTIONS: day + ly = daily, gay + ly = gaily

Exercise A: Rewrite the sentences below filling in the blanks with a *single* word that has the meaning given in parentheses.

1. The ideal age for ______ varies from one culture to another. (getting married)
2. Dr. Grue will not tolerate ______ of thinking in your writing. (condition of haze)

3. My great-grandfather had his ______ birthday this month. (he was ninety)
4. The ballet dancer jumped ______ over the hurdles. (with ease)
5. That was the most ______ picnic we ever went to. (we could enjoy it)
6. The workers were having a heated ______ when the representative from ______ arrived to negotiate the dispute. (they were arguing) (the ones who manage)
7. The ______ doll on the shelf has always been my favorite. (most homely)
8. The road was ______; so the ______ had to go slowly and carefully on the hill. (covered with ice) (a vehicle that carries things)
9. John tripped ______ over his laces as he entered the ______ class. (in a clumsy manner) (teaching how to dance)
10. A ______ sound preceded the spacecraft's ______. (characterized by mystery) (it disappeared)

Exercise B: Add the suffixes as shown and write the new word.

1. lazy + ly
2. delay + ing
3. handy + ly
4. crazy + ness
5. appraise + al
6. shame + ful
7. busy + ness
8. continue + ance
9. breezy + ly
10. locate + ion
11. create + ion
12. carry + er
13. bully + ing
14. educate + or
15. bury + al
16. notice + able
17. carry + age
18. peruse + al
19. amuse + ment
20. fuzzy + er
21. thirty + eth
22. true + ly
23. shy + ness
24. whole + some
25. play + ing
26. pare + ing
27. hairy + est
28. baste + ing
29. history + an
30. victory + ous

15.3 The Suffixes *-ness* and *-ly*

When the suffix *-ly* is added to a word ending in *l*, both *l*'s are retained. When *-ness* is added to a word ending in *n*, both *n*'s are retained.

occasional + ly = occasionally
natural + ly = naturally
stubborn + ness = stubbornness
mean + ness = meanness

15.4 The Addition of Prefixes

When a prefix is added to a word, the spelling of the word remains the same.

dis + satisfied = dissatisfied
il + legible = illegible
im + movable = immovable
mis + use = misuse
re + commend = recommend
mis + spell = misspell
trans + plant = transplant
co + author = coauthor

15.5 Words with the "Seed" Sound

Only one English word ends in *sede: supersede.*
Three words end in *ceed: exceed, proceed, succeed.*
All other words ending in the sound of *seed* are spelled *cede: secede, accede, recede, concede, precede.*

Exercise A: Find the spelling errors in these sentences. Spell the words correctly.

1. Usualy the uneveness of the pages makes a bad impression.
2. The snow actualy dissappeared while we were talking about it.
3. The thiness of the paper is realy an advantage.
4. The lawyer certainly wouldn't reccommend anything ilegal.
5. Mispelling can gradualy be overcome.

6. It will be unecessary to tranship the freight hereafter.
7. Eventualy, the man's meaness faded away.
8. The two samples of handwriting were quite disimilar.
9. The signature was virtualy ilegible.
10. The plainess of the food made Jack disatisfied.
11. Nothing succedes like success.
12. The flood waters are receeding.
13. The iregularity of the trail exceded our expectations.
14. Alex proceded to show us how unatural our fears were.
15. Naturaly, we are willing to concede that the door was locked.

Exercise B: Add the suffixes and prefixes as indicated.

1. un + needed
2. ir + relevant
3. dis + appoint
4. mis + state
5. re + examine
6. dis + similar
7. casual + ly
8. clean + ness
9. dis + solve
10. im + measurable
11. dis + agree
12. heavy + ly
13. dis + appear
14. visual + ly
15. ir + radiate

15.6 Words with *ie* and *ei*

When the sound is long e (ē), the word is spelled *ie* except after c.

I BEFORE E

thief	grief	niece
chief	achieve	relieve
yield	brief	piece

EXCEPT AFTER C

ceiling	receive	deceit
conceive	perceive	receipt

Exceptions: *either, neither, financier, weird, species, seize, leisure*. You can remember these words by using a *mnemonic device* (memory aid) such as the following sentence: *Neither financier seized either weird species of leisure.*

Exercise A: Correct the spelling errors in these sentences.

1. My neice is coming for a brief visit.
2. I believe that this moth you found in the feild is a new speceis.
3. The warrior would not yeild his shield.
4. We were releived to see that the cieling was undamaged.
5. The chief of police gave us a receipt for the fine.
6. It was a very wierd piece of business.
7. We couldn't tell whether deciet or conceit caused the trouble.
8. The firefighter siezed the trapped boy's hand.
9. The chief dancer weilded a heavy bronze sword.
10. The prisoner concieved a weird plan of escape.

Exercise B: Copy the words listed below, filling the blank spaces with *ie* or *ei*.

1. dec__t
2. bel__f
3. rel__ved
4. perc__ve
5. ch__f
6. p__r
7. th__f
8. w__ld
9. shr__k
10. w__rd
11. p__rce
12. retr__ve
13. spec__s
14. s__ze
15. y__ld

15.7 Doubling the Final Consonant

Words of one syllable, ending in one consonant preceded by one vowel, double the final consonant before adding a suffix beginning with a vowel.

1. The words below are the kind to which the rule applies.

plan   sit   shun   red

These words double the final consonant if the suffix begins with a vowel.

plan + ing = planning   shun + ed = shunned
sit + er = sitter   red + est = reddest

2. The rule does not apply to the following one-syllable words because *two* vowels precede the final consonant.

clear speak coat shoot

With these words, the final consonant is *not* doubled before the suffix is added.

clear + est = clearest coat + ed = coated
speak + er = speaker shoot + ing = shooting

3. The final consonant is doubled in words of *more* than one syllable when these conditions are met:

When they end in one consonant preceded by one vowel.
When they are accented on the last syllable.

oc•cur′ com•pel′ sub•mit′ pa•trol′

The same syllable is accented in the new word formed by adding the suffix:

oc•cur′ + ence = oc•cur′rence
com•pel′ + ing = com•pel′ling
sub•mit′ + ed = sub•mit′ted
pa•trol′ + er = pa•trol′ler

If the newly formed word is accented on a different syllable, the final consonant is not doubled.

con•fer′ + ence = con′fer•ence
de•fer′ + ence = def′er•ence

Exercise A: Copy these words, indicating with an accent mark (′) where each word is accented.

1. differ
2. refer
3. concur
4. omit
5. excel
6. limit
7. allot
8. control
9. travel
10. remit
11. panic
12. propel
13. defer
14. impel
15. begin
16. patrol
17. abet
18. admit

Exercise B: Add the ending indicated, and write the new word.

1. travel + ing
2. patrol + ing
3. thin + er
4. big + est
5. brag + art
6. feel + ing
7. stop + er
8. admit + ance
9. refer + al
10. begin + er
11. got + en
12. weak + en
13. propel + er
14. distil + er
15. allot + ed
16. refer + ence
17. forget + ing
18. defer + ing
19. repeat + ed
20. dispel + ed
21. hot + er
22. set + ing
23. murmur + ing
24. expel + ed
25. wit + y
26. fur + ier
27. shop + er
28. upset + ing
29. benefit + ed
30. control + er

15.8 Words Often Confused

capital is the city or town that is the seat of government in a country, state, or region. It also means "most important."
capitol is a building in which the state legislature meets.
the Capitol is the building in Washington, D.C., in which the United States Congress meets.

des'ert refers to a wilderness or a dry, sandy region with sparse, scrubby vegetation.
de•sert' means "to abandon."
dessert (note the change in spelling) is a sweet such as cake or pie served at the end of a meal.

hear means "to listen to, or take notice of."
here means "in this place."

its is a word that indicates ownership.
it's is a contraction for *it is* or *it has*.

loose means "free or not fastened."
lose means "to mislay or suffer the loss of something."

principal describes something of chief or central importance. It also refers to the head of an elementary or high school.
principle is a basic truth, standard, or rule of behavior.

stationary means "fixed or unmoving."
stationery refers to paper and envelopes used for writing letters or other correspondence.

their means "belonging to them."
there means "in that place."
they're is a contraction for *they are*.

to means "toward," or "in the direction of."
too means "also" or "very."
two is the number 2.

weather refers to atmospheric conditions such as temperature or cloudiness.
whether helps express choice or alternative.

who's is a contraction for *who is* or *who has*.
whose is the possessive form of *who*.

your is the possessive form of *you*.
you're is a contraction for *you are*.

Exercise A: Choose the right word from those given.

1. The (capital, capitol) dome has just been painted.
2. The voters of Alaska chose a new (capital, capitol) city.
3. What are you having for (desert, dessert)?
4. Don't (desert, dessert) me now!
5. He was driving (to, too) fast for conditions.
6. (To, Too, Two) people were sitting in the park.
7. I didn't (hear, here) the alarm clock.
8. (Its, It's) too late to get to the bank.
9. Our village buys (its, it's) water from the next town.
10. Don't (loose, lose) the receipt for your sweater.
11. My bicycle seat keeps coming (loose, lose).
12. The (principal, principle) of Logan High is Ms. Cross.
13. Jessica taught me the (principals, principles) of chess.
14. I wish I had some personal (stationary, stationery).
15. The dancers practiced (their, there) routines.

16. (There, They're) aren't any orange sodas left.
17. I can't decide (weather, whether) or not to go.
18. (Who's, Whose) five-dollar bill is this?
19. You can pick up (your, you're) coat on Saturday.
20. I'm glad (your, you're) bringing the radio.

Exercise B: Follow the directions for Exercise A.

1. The weather service predicts hot weather for another day because of a (stationary, stationery) front.
2. Sacramento is the (capital, capitol, Capitol) of California.
3. In spring, the (desert, dessert) comes alive with flowers.
4. Please put the papers (hear, here) on my desk.
5. After lunch, we went (to, too, two) the beach.
6. (Whose, Who's) in charge of designing our float this year?
7. Poor health was the (principal, principle) reason why Ms. Koval quit her job.
8. On our class trip to Washington, D.C., we had our picture taken on the (capital, capitol, Capitol) steps.
9. Ask the boys why (their, there, they're) taking so long to get to class.
10. The first word in a sentence begins with a (capital, capitol) letter.
11. The Constitution contains the (principals, principles) by which our country is to be governed.
12. Did you (hear, here) Journey in concert?
13. After dinner, Teresa ordered cannoli and spumoni, (to, too, two).
14. (Who's, Whose) portrait is hanging in the main hallway?
15. Have you chosen the topic for (your, you're) speech?
16. If you move the desk (their, there, they're), it will block the doorway.
17. One chimpanzee stuck out (its, it's) tongue at us.
18. Paulo worried that he would (loose, lose) his wallet.
19. The (weather, whether) in Arizona is warm and dry.
20. A (stationary, stationery) oil well has been constructed just off the coast.

A List of Commonly Misspelled Words

abbreviate	ab-bre-vi-ate	balance	bal-ance
absence	ab-sence	bargain	bar-gain
accidentally	ac-ci-den-tal-ly	becoming	be-com-ing
accommodate	ac-com-mo-date	beginning	be-gin-ning
accompanying	ac-com-pa-ny-ing	believe	be-lieve
achievement	a-chieve-ment	benefited	ben-e-fit-ed
acknowledge	ac-know-ledge	bicycle	bi-cy-cle
acquaintance	ac-quaint-ance	biscuit	bis-cuit
across	a-cross	bookkeeper	book-keep-er
address	ad-dress	bulletin	bul-le-tin
all right	all right	bureau	bu-reau
altogether	al-to-geth-er	business	busi-ness
always	al-ways	cafeteria	caf-e-te-ri-a
amateur	am-a-teur	calendar	cal-en-dar
analyze	an-a-lyze	campaign	cam-paign
annihilate	an-ni-hi-late	candidate	can-di-date
anonymous	a-non-y-mous	cellophane	cel-lo-phane
answer	an-swer	cemetery	cem-e-ter-y
apologize	a-pol-o-gize	certain	cer-tain
appearance	ap-pear-ance	changeable	change-a-ble
appreciate	ap-pre-ci-ate	characteristic	char-ac-ter-is-tic
appropriate	ap-pro-pri-ate	colonel	colo-nel
arctic	arc-tic	colossal	co-los-sal
argument	ar-gu-ment	column	col-umn
arising	a-ris-ing	commission	com-mis-sion
arrangement	ar-range-ment	committed	com-mit-ted
ascend	as-cend	committee	com-mit-tee
assassinate	as-sas-si-nate	comparative	com-par-a-tive
associate	as-so-ci-ate	compel	com-pel
attendance	at-tend-ance	competitive	com-pet-i-tive
audience	au-di-ence	complexion	com-plex-ion
auxiliary	aux-il-ia-ry	compulsory	com-pul-so-ry
awkward	awk-ward	conscience	con-science
bachelor	bach-e-lor	conscientious	con-sci-en-tious

conscious	con-scious	eminent	em-i-nent
consensus	con-sen-sus	emphasize	em-pha-size
contemptible	con-tempt-i-ble	enthusiastic	en-thu-si-as-tic
convenience	con-ven-ience	environment	en-vi-ron-ment
corps	corps	equipped	e-quipped
correspondence	cor-re-spond-ence	especially	es-pe-cial-ly
courageous	cou-ra-geous	etiquette	et-i-quette
courteous	cour-te-ous	exaggerate	ex-ag-ger-ate
criticism	crit-i-cism	excellent	ex-cel-lent
criticize	crit-i-cize	exceptional	ex-cep-tion-al
curiosity	cu-ri-os-i-ty	exhaust	ex-haust
cylinder	cyl-in-der	exhilarate	ex-hil-a-rate
dealt	dealt	existence	ex-ist-ence
decision	de-ci-sion	expense	ex-pense
definitely	def-i-nite-ly	experience	ex-pe-ri-ence
dependent	de-pend-ent	familiar	fa-mil-iar
descent	de-scent	fascinating	fas-ci-nat-ing
description	de-scrip-tion	fatigue	fa-tigue
desirable	de-sir-a-ble	February	Feb-ru-ar-y
despair	de-spair	feminine	fem-i-nine
desperate	des-per-ate	financial	fi-nan-cial
dictionary	dic-tion-ar-y	foreign	for-eign
different	dif-fer-ent	forfeit	for-feit
dining	din-ing	fourth	fourth
diphtheria	diph-the-ri-a	fragile	frag-ile
disagree	dis-a-gree	generally	gen-er-al-ly
disappear	dis-ap-pear	genius	gen-ius
disappoint	dis-ap-point	government	gov-ern-ment
discipline	dis-ci-pline	grammar	gram-mar
dissatisfied	dis-sat-is-fied	guarantee	guar-an-tee
economical	e-co-nom-i-cal	guard	guard
efficient	ef-fi-cient	gymnasium	gym-na-si-um
eighth	eighth	handkerchief	hand-ker-chief
eligible	el-i-gi-ble	height	height
eliminate	e-lim-i-nate	hindrance	hin-drance
embarrass	em-bar-rass	horizon	ho-ri-zon

humorous hu-mor-ous
imaginary im-ag-i-nar-y
immediately im-me-di-ate-ly
incidentally in-ci-den-tal-ly
inconvenience in-con-ven-ience
incredible in-cred-i-ble
indefinitely in-def-i-nite-ly
indispensable in-dis-pen-sa-ble
inevitable in-ev-i-ta-ble
infinite in-fi-nite
influence in-flu-ence
inoculation in-oc-u-la-tion
intelligence in-tel-li-gence
interesting in-ter-est-ing
irrelevant ir-rel-e-vant
irresistible ir-re-sist-i-ble
knowledge knowl-edge
laboratory lab-o-ra-to-ry
legitimate le-git-i-mate
leisure lei-sure
lieutenant lieu-ten-ant
lightning light-ning
literacy lit-er-a-cy
literature lit-er-a-ture
loneliness lone-li-ness
luxurious lux-u-ri-ous
maintenance main-te-nance
maneuver ma-neu-ver
marriage mar-riage
mathematics math-e-mat-ics
matinee mat-i-nee
medicine med-i-cine
medieval me-di-e-val
microphone mi-cro-phone
miniature min-i-a-ture
minimum min-i-mum
mischievous mis-chie-vous
missile mis-sile
misspell mis-spell
mortgage mort-gage
municipal mu-nic-i-pal
necessary nec-es-sar-y
nickel nick-el
ninety nine-ty
noticeable no-tice-a-ble
nuclear nu-cle-ar
nuisance nui-sance
obstacle ob-sta-cle
occasionally oc-ca-sion-al-ly
occur oc-cur
occurence oc-cur-rence
opinion o-pin-ion
opportunity op-por-tu-ni-ty
optimistic op-ti-mis-tic
original o-rig-i-nal
outrageous out-ra-geous
pamphlet pam-phlet
parallel par-al-lel
parliament par-lia-ment
particularly par-tic-u-lar-ly
pastime pas-time
permanent per-ma-nent
permissible per-mis-si-ble
perseverance per-se-ver-ance
perspiration per-spi-ra-tion
persuade per-suade
picnicking pic-nick-ing
pleasant pleas-ant
pneumonia pneu-mo-ni-a
politics pol-i-tics
possess pos-sess
possibility pos-si-bil-i-ty

practice	prac-tice
preference	pref-er-ence
prejudice	prej-u-dice
preparation	prep-a-ra-tion
privilege	priv-i-lege
probably	prob-a-bly
professor	pro-fes-sor
pronunciation	pro-nun-ci-a-tion
propeller	pro-pel-ler
prophecy	proph-e-cy
psychology	psy-chol-o-gy
pursue	pur-sue
quantity	quan-ti-ty
questionnaire	ques-tion-naire
realize	re-al-ize
recognize	rec-og-nize
recommend	rec-om-mend
reference	ref-er-ence
referred	re-ferred
rehearse	re-hearse
reign	reign
repetition	rep-e-ti-tion
representative	rep-re-sent-a-tive
restaurant	res-tau-rant
rhythm	rhythm
ridiculous	ri-dic-u-lous
sandwich	sand-wich
schedule	sched-ule
scissors	scis-sors
secretary	sec-re-tar-y
separate	sep-a-rate
sergeant	ser-geant
similar	sim-i-lar
sincerely	sin-cere-ly
sophomore	soph-o-more
souvenir	sou-ve-nir
specifically	spe-cif-i-cal-ly
specimen	spec-i-men
strategy	strat-e-gy
strictly	strict-ly
subtle	sub-tle
success	suc-cess
sufficient	suf-fi-cient
surprise	sur-prise
syllable	syl-la-ble
sympathy	sym-pa-thy
symptom	symp-tom
tariff	tar-iff
temperament	tem-per-a-ment
temperature	tem-per-a-ture
thorough	thor-ough
throughout	through-out
together	to-geth-er
tomorrow	to-mor-row
traffic	traf-fic
tragedy	trag-e-dy
transferred	trans-ferred
truly	tru-ly
Tuesday	Tues-day
tyranny	tyr-an-ny
twelfth	twelfth
unanimous	u-nan-i-mous
undoubtedly	un-doubt-ed-ly
unnecessary	un-nec-es-sar-y
vacuum	vac-u-um
vengeance	venge-ance
vicinity	vi-cin-i-ty
village	vil-lage
villain	vil-lain
weird	weird
wholly	whol-ly
writing	writ-ing

REINFORCEMENT EXERCISES

Spelling

A. Add suffixes to words ending in silent *e* or *y*. Combine the following base words and suffixes, being careful to spell the resulting words correctly.

1. ferry + ed
2. definite + ly
3. like + able
4. play + ing
5. wary + ly
6. care + ful
7. manage + able
8. exercise + ing
9. lonely + ness
10. happy + er
11. argue + ment
12. delete + ion
13. service + able
14. line + ing
15. suave + ly
16. bury + ed
17. deploy + ed
18. merry + ly
19. lease + ing
20. skate + ing

B. Identify misspelled words. Find the misspelled words in the following list and spell them correctly. Some words are correct.

1. preceed
2. forlorness
3. partialy
4. prosede
5. unnaware
6. ilogical
7. truly
8. missadventure
9. disstasteful
10. supersede
11. acceed
12. leanness
13. hatefuly
14. conceed
15. waness
16. airyly
17. receede
18. excede

C. Spell words containing *ei* or *ie*. Rewrite the following sentences, correcting any errors in spelling. If a sentence is correct as it is, write *Correct*.

1. It is my beleif that the reign of the chief will be breif.
2. Do not yield; the relief troups have taken the field.
3. The financeir enjoyed his liesure.
4. Niether informer recieved a reward.
5. Cara perceived that a piece of the pie had been eaten.

6. A clown with the wierd green beard was performing on the peir.
7. The police seized the theif and retrieved the contents of the breifcase.
8. The carpenter asked for a receipt for the work that she did on our ceiling.
9. The priest read a brief peice from his journal.
10. This species communicates in shrill shreiks.

D. Add suffixes. Combine the following base words and suffixes, being careful to spell the resulting words correctly.

1. waltz + ing
2. delay + ed
3. war + ing
4. travel + ing
5. vary + ance
6. ally + ed
7. trim + er
8. shatter + ed
9. dig + er
10. yard + age
11. frill + ed
12. pop + ing
13. chop + ing
14. transmit + ed
15. bore + ed
16. excel + ed
17. shave + ing
18. fold + er

E. Use confusing words correctly. Choose the right word from those given in parentheses.

1. Jerome did his aerobic exercises on a (stationery, stationary) bicycle.
2. Do not ask (whose, who's) responsibility it is—do the job yourself.
3. The tarpaulin blew away because (its, it's) ropes were (loose, lose).
4. Our (principal, principle) was a very ethical person.
5. The Gobi is a (desert, dessert) in Asia, I believe.
6. Has the mayor decided (whether, weather) she will seek reelection?
7. The zookeeper led the animals into the exhibition area (too by too, two by two).
8. Does the (capitol, capital) of Iowa have a dome of gold?
9. (There, Their) was the chocolate (desert, dessert), beckoning to me.
10. (Your, You're) going (to, too) enjoy visiting the Wisconsin Dells.

MIXED REVIEW

Spelling

A. Combine the following words and word parts.

1. ethical + ly
2. defer + ence
3. geography + cal + ly
4. un + advise + able
5. engage + ing
6. worry + ed
7. custom + ary + ly
8. deploy + ed
9. barren + ness
10. haze + y
11. mis + apply + ed
12. handy + er
13. re + arrange + able
14. separate + ion
15. sing + ing
16. dis + continue + ed
17. faithful + ly
18. mat + ed
19. il + legal + ity
20. transmit + ed

B. Find the misspelled words in the following sentences and spell them correctly.

1. Joan carefuly moved the floral arrangment.
2. My brother and I generaly dissagree about food.
3. Are you disatisfied with the guideance services?
4. A wierd light appearred in the stary sky.
5. Makeing mischeif is one of there specialtys.
6. Whose read "An Occurence at Owl Creek Bridge"?
7. Ramon's name was accidentaly omited from the list.
8. Planes were circleing the airfeild, waiting to land.
9. Marcia submited the poster to the dean for approveal.
10. Emily prefered to go shoping at varyous flea markets.
11. Paul immediatly grabed the runaway dog.
12. The principle made a breif speech about studying.
13. The diners ate a strangly tart desert.
14. Justine reccomended a more managable horse.
15. The coach beleives our gym is well equiped.
16. "Research preceeds writeing," the librarian noted.
17. Which states formaly seceeded from the Union?
18. That is niether ilegal nor immproper.

USING MECHANICS IN WRITING

Spelling

A. Both scientists and architects have been developing "artificial environments"—small areas where weather, plant and animal life, and all other environmental features are chosen and controlled by people. Write a description of your idea of a perfect environment. You may also want to tell how some of the systems within it work. Your composition may be serious or humorous. Use at least fifteen words from the List of Commonly Misspelled Words in your composition. Make sure that you spell these words correctly.

B. Make up a simple but enjoyable game that you could teach to others. A word or number game is one possibility. Write out the rules of your game so carefully and completely that others can play the game after reading these rules. In your instructions, use as many words containing the "seed" sound as you can.

C. Imagine that you receive a sporting goods catalog in the mail. As you browse through it, you notice the following descriptions, each of which contains several spelling errors. Practice your proofreading skills by finding the errors in these product descriptions. Then rewrite each description, correcting the errors.

DUMBELL SET: Only twelve dollars. Perfect for dayly muscle-developping exercises. Wieght per dumbell: exactly six pounds.

SLANT BOARD: A realy terrific buy at $28.95 dollars. Usful for performing bent-legged sittups.

COTTON SWEATTSUIT: For liesure time or any time, an enticing bargain at $17.50. Made of pree shrunk cotton. Unnlike suits made of synthetic fibers, this cotton suit absorbs perspireation, helping to keep you dryer when you are exerciseing heavyly.

16.0 The Plurals of Nouns

16.1 Regular Formation of Plurals

The plural of most nouns is formed by adding *-s*.

herd + s = herds	truck + s = trucks
theater + s = theaters	counter + s = counters

16.2 Plurals Formed with -es

The plural of nouns ending in *s, sh, ch, x,* and *z* is formed with *-es*.

dress + es = dresses	birch + es = birches
bush + es = bushes	tax + es = taxes

16.3 Plurals of Nouns Ending in *y*

When a noun ends in *y* preceded by a consonant, the plural is formed by changing the *y* to *i* and adding *-es*.

candy	candi + es = candies
salary	salari + es = salaries
jury	juri + es = juries
party	parti + es = parties

When a noun ends in *y* preceded by a vowel, the plural is formed by adding *-s*.

driveway + s = driveways
convoy + s = convoys
alley + s = alleys
weekday + s = weekdays
monkey + s = monkeys
cowboy + s = cowboys

16.4 Plurals of Nouns Ending in *o*

The plural of a noun ending in *o*, preceded by a vowel, is formed by adding *-s*.

trio + s = trios
rodeo + s = rodeos
folio + s = folios
radio + s = radios
patio + s = patios
studio + s = studios

The plural of most nouns ending in *o*, preceded by a consonant, is formed by adding *-s*, but for some nouns of their class the plural is formed by adding *-es*.

piano + s = pianos
solo + s = solos
auto + s = autos
soprano + s = sopranos
tomato + es = tomatoes
potato + es = potatoes
echo + es = echoes
hero + es = heroes

Some nouns ending in *o* with a preceding consonant may form the plural with either *-s* or *-es*: *grotto, mango, mosquito*. When you are in doubt about how to form the plural of a word ending in *o*, consult the dictionary. The plural form will follow the singular form.

16.5 Plurals of Nouns Ending in *f*, *ff*, or *fe*

The plural of most nouns ending in *f* or *ff* is formed regularly by adding *-s*.

cliff + s = cliffs
reef + s = reefs
puff + s = puffs
gulf + s = gulfs
tariff + s = tariffs
sheriff + s = sheriffs

The plural of some nouns ending in *f* or *fe* is formed by changing the *f* or *fe* to *ve* and adding -s.

leaf—leaves	knife—knives	life—lives
wife—wives	loaf—loaves	elf—elves
wolf—wolves	sheaf—sheaves	thief—thieves
half—halves	wharf—wharves	shelf—shelves

Pronouncing the plural form of these common words, can help you to spell them correctly. When you are in doubt, refer to a dictionary. If the plural form of a word is irregular, the plural will be given after the singular.

16.6 Nouns with Irregular Plurals

The plural of some nouns is formed by a change of spelling.

crisis—crises	medium—media
alumnus—alumni	mouse—mice
woman—women	ox—oxen
child—children	basis—bases
datum—data	phenomenon—phenomena
index—indices *or* indexes	hypothesis—hypotheses

The plural and singular forms are the same for a few nouns.

sheep	deer	Chinese
trout	corps	Portuguese
species	cattle	Swiss

16.7 The Plurals of Names

The plural of a name is formed by adding *-s* or *-es*.

Lina Porter—the Porters	Jim Fox—the Foxes
Abe Stein—the Steins	Lorraine Hopkins—the Hopkinses

16.8 The Plurals of Compound Nouns

When a compound noun is written without a hyphen, the plural is formed at the end of the word.

handful + s = handfuls tablespoonful + s = tablespoonfuls
leftover + s = leftovers placemat + s = placemats

When a compound noun is made up of a noun plus a modifier, the plural is made from the noun.

fathers-in-law (The phrase *in-law* is a modifier.)
courts-martial (The word *martial* is a modifier.)
attorneys-general (*general* modifies *attorneys*.)
hangers-on (*on* modifies *hangers*.)
bills of sale (The phrase *of sale* modifies *bills*.)

Exercise A: Form the plural of each of the following words.

1. birthday
2. piano
3. grass
4. hero
5. lash
6. studio
7. branch
8. dormitory
9. worry
10. teaspoonful
11. valley
12. country
13. photo
14. chief
15. knife
16. belief
17. thief
18. basis
19. phenomenon
20. hypothesis
21. handful
22. mother-in-law
23. smash-up
24. commander-in-chief
25. chief of police
26. justice of the peace
27. bill of lading
28. sergeant-at-arms
29. register of deeds
30. Circuit Court judge

Exercise B: Find and correct the errors in plural form.

1. UFO's often turn out to be easily explained natural phenomenons.
2. A researcher may try several hypothesis to solve a problem.
3. The commander-in-chiefs met to plan their strategy.
4. Allen took four teaspoonsful of the medicine.
5. How many loafs of bread did the thieves steal?

6. All the trucks and autoes were loaded with tomatoes.
7. Two of the altoes sang solos.
8. The heros visited several movie studios in Hollywood.
9. How many Secretary of States can you name?
10. The football coachs at our big university are well paid.
11. You will find none of the beautys of rural life in your citys.
12. Both of our sister-in-laws have pianos.
13. There were deep gullys along the highways.
14. You must leave your photoes at all the agencys.
15. We have tried at least fifty varietys of potatos on our farm.
16. What are the basis of these charges against George?
17. How many cupsful of flour do you need?
18. There is an annual meeting of the state attorney-generals.
19. In India the cattles are sacred and wander around the streets.
20. Are those flowers lily-of-the-valleys?
21. Of course, heroes in storys are required to do more than lift pianos and stop speeding trains.
22. The majoritys in the last election were small.
23. The Jones were selling tomatoes, and the Chiss's were selling loafs of bread.
24. I like the fall when the leafs start to change color.
25. The thiefs had broken into two motion picture studios.

REINFORCEMENT EXERCISES

The Plurals of Nouns

A. Form the plurals of nouns. Complete each of the following sentences with the proper plural form of the noun given in parentheses.

1. Our library has six sets of ______, but some are very old. (encyclopedia)
2. My mother and father love to listen to Viennese ______. (waltz)
3. There were fifty ______ in the firm, half of them women. (attorney)
4. The ______ in England were destroyed in the 1530's, during the reign of Henry VIII. (monastery)
5. The park department cut the low ______ off the trees to help them grow. (branch)
6. The baby ______ were the biggest attraction in the children's zoo. (monkey)
7. The costume designer sewed ______ on the pair of old jeans to be worn by the scarecrow. (patch)
8. The salesperson explained the use of various ______ for preserving antique wood furniture. (wax)
9. Ms. Greeves explained my ______ as nurse's aide in great detail. (duty)
10. Rapunzel watched her long ______ tumble down the length of the tower. (tress)

B. Form the plurals of nouns. Complete each of the following sentences with the proper plural form of the noun given in parentheses.

1. The prosperous-looking farm had two ______. (silo)
2. The ______ led a life of toil. (serf)
3. Malaria is spread by ______, isn't it? (mosquito)
4. By the end of the year, the lost-and-found had collected seven unclaimed ______. (scarf)

5. The cowboys competed in ______ all over the Southwest. (rodeo)
6. My uncle can tell a story about every one of the ______ in his collection. (banjo)
7. Several local ______ got together to catch the stagecoach robbers. (sheriff)
8. The butcher cut the roast in two ______. (half)
9. Jed and Nick were practicing a piece for two ______. (piano)
10. Lewis Thomas wrote a popular book of scientific essays called *The* ______ *of a Cell*. (Life)

C. Correct improper plurals. Rewrite the following sentences, correcting all errors in the formation of plurals.

1. Three Debbie's enrolled in the calculus course.
2. Four of the five senator-elects held press conferences.
3. The Lapps actually use reindeers to pull sleighs.
4. My brother-in-laws were out on the golf course when the rain began.
5. The muffins were flat because I only put two teaspoonsful of baking powder in the batter.
6. There has to be a logical explanation for the strange phenomenons that occur in this house.
7. Dan and Sandra Loren have a doormat that reads *The Loren's*.
8. Several specieses of butterflies were discovered by Professor Hindemuth.
9. All of the mediumes gave extensive coverage to the Presidential campaign.
10. How many Secretary of Defenses have served in the United States government since the Truman administration?

MIXED REVIEW

The Plurals of Nouns

A. Form the plural of each of the following words. You may need to check a dictionary for the correct spelling.

1. jack-of-all-trades
2. flash
3. datum
4. radio
5. sheep
6. wreath
7. poppy
8. bias
9. city
10. hoof
11. dragonfly
12. runner-up
13. handful
14. piccolo
15. calf
16. wife
17. lineman
18. Harris

B. Complete the following sentences with the proper plural forms of the words given in parentheses.

1. The anthropology students studied the ______ of the ancient Aztecs. (belief)
2. The area was hit by two ______ in one season. (tornado)
3. All the ______ were working, yet the lines kept getting longer. (cashier)
4. Four wild ______ came trotting down the road. (donkey)
5. Several ______ were sung by Luciano Pavarotti. (solo)
6. The ______ were grazing inside the preserve. (moose)
7. On our way home, we visited the ______. (Jones)
8. Marge baked a batch of ______ all for herself. (brownie)
9. The cosmetic cream promised to erase ______ from around the eyes. (crow's-foot)
10. The shield was decorated with ______. (half-moon)
11. The high winds knocked down several ______ in our neighborhood. (chimney)
12. The engineer discovered that the air ______ were blocked by cartons. (intake)
13. The managers drew up their initial ______. (lineup)
14. The angels in the high school production of *Everyman* were given gold ______ and gauze wings to wear. (halo)
15. Do ______ really bake cookies in hollow trees? (elf)

USING MECHANICS IN WRITING

The Plurals of Nouns

A. Write a humorous poem using the plurals of the following words. You may use the words in any order you wish. You might want to check the meanings of the words to make certain your poem makes sense.

buffalo, hero, cargo, echo, rodeo, dynamo, banjo, solo

B. Imagine that you are an explorer in the Himalayan mountains. You have come across an isolated village where an unknown language is spoken. In this language all objects and living things are named with singular nouns that end in *s, sh, ch, x,* or *z*. Compose a journal entry that you will send back to the museum for which you are working. Describe the people and life of the village, using words from the village language in their plural forms.

C. Your insurance company insists that you submit an inventory of your belongings before they will issue a homeowner's policy. Make a list of the contents of your room and attach an approximate value to each category. You do not have to itemize each category; simply give a number and what kind of thing it is (for example, 2 boxes of pencils—$2.50). Use plurals properly throughout.

CUMULATIVE REVIEW
Spelling and Plurals of Nouns

Proofreading for Spelling Errors. Write the misspelled words from each sentence correctly.

1. All the boys carryed portable radioes.
2. Wolfs and gooses cannot live peacefully together.
3. I am truely sorry that you and I had that arguement.
4. The reviewer refered to Miriam's performance as "createively concieved and brilliantly executted."
5. The experiment did not sucede because niether of the scientists recorded the measurements properly.
6. You will need two cupsful of that solution to reproduce the phenomenons we observed.
7. Whenever there are crisises, Luis always remains calm.
8. Both of my sister-in-laws jog or swim dayly.
9. All of the Jones'es are likable people.
10. Finaly, practical watch's have returned to jeweller's shelfs.

Using the Correct Word. Write the correct word from the two given in parentheses.

1. The (principals, principles) of both schools agreed to (accept, except) the state's recommendations.
2. (Whose, Who's) chemistry notes did you (lose, loose)?
3. Albany, the (capital, capitol) of my state, is (further, farther) from my home than is the city of New York.
4. The stricter requirements (adapted, adopted) by my school have (already, all ready) (affected, effected) students.
5. (Your, You're) arm will soon regain (its, it's) strength.
6. (There, Their, They're) are several excellent books about meteorology, the science of (weather, whether).
7. The pink dress is (all together, altogether) unsuitable.
8. The researchers reported that (their, they're, there) close to finding a solution.
9. Everyone (accept, except) Cynthia wore jeans on the hike.
10. By the time Carlotta was ready for (desert, dessert), Martin had eaten (alot, a lot) of the pie.

17.0 Good Manuscript Form

Just as a good personal appearance makes a favorable impression on those you meet, so a neat, legible paper impresses your readers. Good manuscript form assures a receptive audience for what you have to say. Many high schools and colleges have regular forms that students are expected to follow. Others require manuscripts to follow the form described below.

17.1 Legible Writing

A well-typed paper is generally easier to read than one written by hand. However, few high schools require students to type their papers. When a paper is written by hand, it should be written in pen with dark blue or black ink. Individual letters should be formed carefully: *a*'s and *o*'s should be distinctly different; *u*'s and *i*'s should also be distinct; *i*'s must be dotted and *t*'s crossed.

17.2 Margins and Spacing

The margin at the top, the bottom, and the right side of each page should be one inch. Make the left margin slightly wider. The left margin should be perfectly straight; and the right margin, as even as possible. Avoid using an excess of hyphens to show breaks in words. Try not to have more than two successive lines end with a hyphen.

Double space all typed copy, and indent five spaces for each new paragraph. Put one space between words and two spaces after the end punctuation of a sentence. If material must be deleted, cover it with *x*'s, capital *M*'s, or correction fluid.

17.3 Proper Labeling

The proper heading of a paper will vary from class to class and from school to school. However, somewhere on the paper you must write your name, the course number, and the date. Usually these three lines of information are placed in the upper right-hand corner of the first page.

Each page after the first page should be numbered. Numbers are usually placed in the upper right-hand corner. Your name may be placed below the page number to guard against losing the page.

17.4 Placement of the Title

Put the title of your paper on the first page only. It should be centered two lines below the last line of your heading. Then skip two lines before you begin your first paragraph.

Capitalize the first word and all important words in the title. (See Section 10.12). Do not capitalize every letter but only the initial letters. The title should not be underlined or placed in quotation marks unless it is a quotation from some other source.

If a paper is longer than three or four pages, your teacher may ask you to supply a title page. This is a separate page containing the heading in the upper right-hand corner and the title centered on the page.

17.5 Preparation of Final Copy

The first draft of a paper is never written exactly as the writer would like it to be. A first draft should be read carefully, revised, and corrected. Then a final copy must be made. It, too, must be read carefully.

If there are errors on the final copy, they must be corrected neatly. If a word has been omitted, it should be written neatly above the line where it should appear, and its position indicated by a caret (‸). Other errors can be corrected by neatly drawing a line through a word and writing the correction above it. If a page contains more than two or three corrections, it should be recopied.

See Chapter 7, "The Process of Writing," for more information on revision and proofreading.

17.6 Numbers in Writing

Numbers that can be expressed in fewer than four words are usually spelled out; longer numbers are written in figures.

There were *twenty-four hundred* coins in the lot.
The estate amounted to *one million* dollars.
We had *twenty-two* dollars among us.
The check was written for $3,475.

A number beginning a sentence is spelled out.

Thirteen students answered the advertisement.
Twenty-five persons were injured.
Fifty percent of the merchandise was damaged.

17.7 Figures in Writing

Figures are used for dates, street and room numbers, telephone numbers, page numbers, temperatures, decimals, and percentages.

The date of the trial was June 6, 1871.
The address is 2214 East Superior Street, Room 306.
The telephone number is 647-1048.
The assignment began on page 243.
The patient's temperature was 102.4 degrees.
Pieces of mail must be at least .007 inch thick.
We had 60 percent of the students on our side.

Note: Commas are used to separate the figures in sums of money or expressions of large quantities. They are not used in dates, serial numbers, page numbers, addresses, or telephone numbers.

CORRECT: Our class had saved $1,276.50 for the trip.
CORRECT: The population of Alabama is 3,900,000.

INCORRECT: The first satellite went into orbit in 1,957.
CORRECT: The first satellite went into orbit in 1957.

Exercise: Copy these sentences, correcting any errors in the writing of numbers and figures. Some sentences are correct.

1. There are four hundred fifty students in our class.
2. 13 of the books on the list are now out of print.
3. The temperature was thirty-one and eight-tenths degrees.
4. The price asked for the house is $75500.
5. Did you say three percent or five percent?
6. Helen lives at 1,770 East End Avenue.
7. The engine number is MH 1,674,570.
8. The first prize is $1,000.
9. Dad's room number is three hundred twenty.
10. Over two thousand five hundred twenty copies were sold.
11. He was born in nineteen hundred six.
12. Beth's telephone number is 476-2,120.

13. The office is located at sixty-one Madison Avenue.
14. More than two hundred samples were taken in the test.
15. There were 300 telephone calls on the first day.

17.8 Abbreviations in Writing

Abbreviations may be used for most titles before and after proper names, names of government agencies, and in dates.

BEFORE PROPER NAMES:	Dr., Mr., Mrs., Ms., Messrs., Rev., Hon., Gov., Capt.
AFTER PROPER NAMES:	Jr., Sr., D.D.S., Ph.D.
GOVERNMENT AGENCIES:	TVA, FCC, AEC
DATES AND TIME:	A.D., B.C., A.M., P.M.

Do not use periods after abbreviations of government agencies.

Abbreviate titles only when they are used as part of a name. Do not write *The sec'y. of the board is a dr.* The titles *Honorable* and *Reverend* are not abbreviated when preceded by *the: the Honorable Harold Powell*. They appear with the person's full name, not just the last name. Do not use abbreviations for the President and Vice-President of the United States.

In ordinary writing, abbreviations are not acceptable for names of countries and states, months and days of the week, nor for words that are part of addresses or firm names.

UNACCEPTABLE:	My uncle lives in N.D.
BETTER:	My uncle lives in North Dakota.
UNACCEPTABLE:	It was good to be back in the U.S.
BETTER:	It was good to be back in the United States.
UNACCEPTABLE:	Ellen got a job with the Elgin Mfg. Co.
BETTER:	Ellen got a job with the Elgin Manufacturing Company.
UNACCEPTABLE:	I went to my first class on Mon., Sept. 28.
BETTER:	I went to my first class on Monday, September 28.

In ordinary writing, abbreviations are not acceptable for the following: names of school courses, *page, chapter, Christmas,* and words standing for measurements such as *bu., in., hr., min., sec.*

17.9 The Hyphen

A hyphen is used at the end of a line to divide a word between syllables.

> Some states require that students pass "mini-
> mum competency examinations" before they gradu-
> ate from high school.

Note: At least two letters of the hyphenated word should appear on each line.

Many compound words require hyphens. A good dictionary will indicate correct hyphenation.

hand-me-down	editor-in-chief	runner-up
mother-in-law	five-year-old	stand-in
double-decker	jack-in-the-box	helter-skelter

Words used together as an adjective before a noun are usually connected with a hyphen.

strong-willed person	life-size portrait
five-minute meeting	play-by-play account
multiple-choice test	deep-set eyes
stand-up comic	open-minded attitude

However, such words used after the noun are often not hyphenated.

STANDARD: A *well-dressed* model floated down the runway.
STANDARD: The model on the runway was *well dressed*.

Compound numbers between twenty-one and ninety-nine are hyphenated, as are fractions, like *three-fourths* and *three thirty-seconds*.

Sometimes a word needs a hyphen when a prefix or suffix is

added. The prefixes *all-*, *self-*, *co-*, and *ex-*, for example, often use hyphens. The practices are not consistent; for instance, *all-powerful* is hyphenated and *allover* is not. Check a dictionary when you are not sure whether or not a hyphen is used. Hyphens are certain to be used, though, when a prefix or suffix is added to a proper noun.

co-captain	pre-Civil War	President-elect
self-reliance	non-European	ex-mayor
mid-Atlantic	pro-Arab	all-star

Exercise: Correct the errors in abbreviation and hyphenation in the following sentences.

1. The Hon. W. C. Wyatt was born in Mass. fifty years ago.
2. Harry is going to work for U.S. Ink Corp. next Dec.
3. Four fifths of the Central H.S. graduating class is going on to college.
4. Dr. Buck and Chas. Giones were both born in Seattle, Wash.
5. You have an appointment scheduled with Wm. Jones next Mon. at 3 P.M.
6. On Tues. demonstrators staged a sit in on a ten acre battlefield.
7. The chem. assignment is to read Chap. 10.
8. My brother will be home for Xmas, and he will attend our holiday concert on Dec. 27.
9. Who is the treas. of the Phillips Mfg. Co.?
10. We are going to stop at Dallas, Tex. and Santa Fe, N. Mex. on our way to Cal.
11. Sophie is working at the First Nat'l Bank.
12. It is more than a thousand miles from Kan. City to L.A., but we made the trip in four hrs.
13. N.Y.'s long range plan is to build low income housing in mid Manhattan.
14. We elected my brother in law treas. of the co. last week.
15. Eliz. Wallace, my sister in law, cross examined the witness with double edged questions.

17.10 Italics for Titles

The word *italics* is a printer's term. It refers to a kind of type. When a writer wants to indicate that a word is in italics, he or she underlines it in the manuscript.

Titles of books, plays, movies, newspapers, magazines, works of art, and long musical compositions are printed in italics. The names of ships, trains, and airplanes are also printed in italics.

MANUSCRIPT FORM: We bought a recording of Mozart's Requiem.

PRINTED FORM: We bought a recording of Mozart's *Requiem*.

MANUSCRIPT FORM: West Side Story is actually a modern reworking of Shakespeare's Romeo and Juliet.

PRINTED FORM: *West Side Story* is actually a modern reworking of Shakespeare's *Romeo and Juliet*.

MANUSCRIPT FORM: The old London Times had a picture of the Titanic.

PRINTED FORM: The old *London Times* had a picture of the *Titanic*.

17.11 Italics for Foreign Words and Phrases

Many words in the English language have been borrowed from other languages. When the words are so widely used that they are considered part of the language, they are printed in regular type.

My grandmother always makes succotash as part of Thanksgiving dinner.
Police finally trapped the runaway prisoner in a narrow cul-de-sac.
The subway walls were covered with graffiti.

Foreign words and phrases that have not become naturalized in English are printed in italics and underlined in manuscript: *tout de suite, shalom*.

Check a dictionary when you are not sure whether or not a word should be underlined.

17.12 Italics for Words, Letters, or Figures

Italics are used for words, letters, or figures referred to as such.

Words, letters, or figures referred to as such are printed in italics. In manuscript or typescript, they are underlined as shown in the following examples.

PRINTED FORM: The word *err* is frequently mispronounced.
MANUSCRIPT FORM: The word err is frequently mispronounced.
PRINTED FORM: Some words change the final *y* to *i* when forming the plural.
MANUSCRIPT FORM: Some words change the final y to i when forming the plural.

17.13 Italics for Emphasis

Italics (underlining) are used to give special emphasis to words or phrases.

Use italics sparingly in your writing. Italic type is not as easy to read as regular (roman) type. Rely on a clear, direct style to give emphasis to important words.

Use italics (underlining) for emphasis only when it is necessary to make the meaning clear.

I know you *hear* me, but are you *listening*?
The P.T.A. is protesting *violence* on television, not *violins*, Ms. Latella.

17.14 Correction Symbols and Revision

Teachers generally make their comments in the margins of papers. Marginal notes on themes or reports indicate errors or awkward passages that require rewriting. Correcting the errors will help you prevent repeating them in future writing. Rephrasing awkward sentences will help you construct direct, meaningful sentences.

The following is a list of correction symbols used by professional copyreaders. Your teacher may use this system or another to indicate weaknesses in your writing. When a writer receives a manuscript bearing these marks, he or she must correct the errors and rewrite the paper.

ab *Abbreviation*. Either the abbreviation is not appropriate, or it is wrong. Consult a dictionary.

agr *Agreement*. You have made an error in agreement of subject and verb, or of pronoun and antecedent. See Sections 6 and 7 in your Handbook.

awk *Awkward*. The sentence is clumsy. Rewrite it.

cap *Capital letters*. You have omitted necessary capitals. Consult Section 10 in your Handbook.

cf *Comma fault*. You have joined two sentences together with a comma. Change the punctuation.

dang *Dangling construction*. You have written a verbal phrase in such a way that it does not tie up to another word in the sentence. Rewrite it.

frag *Sentence fragment*. You have placed a period after a group of words that is not a sentence. Join the fragment to an existing sentence or add words to complete the thought.

ital *Italics*. You have omitted italics that are needed.

k *Awkward*. See *awk* above.

lc *Lower case*. You have mistakenly used a capital letter where a small letter is required.

ms *Manuscript form*. You have not followed the proper manuscript form. See Section 17 in your Handbook.

no ¶ *No paragraph*. You have started a new paragraph too soon. Join these sentences to the preceding paragraph.

¶ *Paragraph*. Begin a new paragraph at this point.

nc *Not clear*. Your meaning is not clear. Rewrite the passage to say what you mean.

om *Omission*. You have left out words that are needed for clarity or smoothness of style.

p *Punctuation*. You have made an error in punctuation. See Sections 11–14 in your Handbook.

par *Parallelism*. You have committed an error in parallel structure. Consult Chapter 4.

ref *Reference*. There is an error or a weakness in the reference of pronoun to antecedent. See Section 7 in your Handbook.

rep *Repetition*. You have repeated a word too often, or you have repeated something you wrote in preceding sentences.

ro *Run-on sentence*. You have written two or more sentences as one. Change the punctuation.

shift *Shift*. You have shifted point of view or tense needlessly.

sp *Spelling*. You have misspelled a word. Consult a dictionary.

t *Tense*. You have used the wrong tense form. See Section 5 in your Handbook.

tr *Transpose*. You have misplaced a modifier; see Chapter 4. Your meaning would be clearer if a sentence or passage were placed at another point.

wd *Wrong word*. You have confused homonyms, or you have used a word that does not fit the meaning. See Section 9, or consult a dictionary.

REINFORCEMENT EXERCISES

Good Manuscript Form

A. Understand proper manuscript form. The following statements refer to good manuscript form. Tell whether these statements are true or false.

1. The title should appear, centered, on every page of the manuscript.
2. Number each page, beginning with page one.
3. Titles should be in upper and lower case letters; they should not be underlined.
4. The best way to delete material from a manuscript is by crossing it out completely with a wide-tipped black marker.
5. Both right and left margins must be even.
6. If a page has fewer than ten corrections, it is acceptable.
7. Insert words in a typed manuscript by using a caret and writing the words above the line in which they should appear.
8. Put your name, the name or number of the course, and the date in the upper right-hand corner of every page.
9. Do all handwritten papers in ink or in pencil.
10. Leave a one inch margin at the bottom and/or left side of the paper.

B. Write numbers and figures correctly. Rewrite the following sentences, correcting any errors in the writing of numbers or figures.

1. We will need at least 45 people to help at the polls on election day.
2. The temperature is supposed to climb to ninety-eight degrees this afternoon.
3. 3,000 people were killed by the *tsunami* that came after the earthquake.
4. The delivery company said that the package was delivered to 3,280 Hillcrest Lane.

5. Pages seven and eight were missing from my textbook.
6. Over 13,000 people showed up to run in the marathon.
7. The voter turnout in our district was over eighty percent.
8. The Declaration of Independence was adopted by the Continental Congress on July Fourth 1,776.
9. Yes, there were 138 students in my graduating class.
10. 73 people showed up to audition for just 5 parts.

C. Use abbreviations correctly. Rewrite the following sentences, correcting any errors in abbreviation. If a sentence is correct, write *Correct*.

1. Jack was elected sec'y., and Barbara was elected v.p.
2. "A fire alarm was coming from Jackson H.S.," the fire chief testified.
3. John photographed the hot air balloons in Albuquerque, N.M.
4. Casey was born on Sat., Oct. 22, 1973.
5. St. Paul is the capital of Minn.
6. I addressed the letter to Carl Kaplan, Phd.
7. We will be leaving on our fishing trip at 4:30 AM.
8. The year 42 BC is given for Tiberius Caesar's birth.
9. Our class has to read from p. 35 to p. 85 in one night.
10. The Hon. Beth Rubenstein presided over the court.

D. Use hyphens correctly. Rewrite the following sentences, correcting any errors in the use of the hyphen. If a sentence is correct, write *Correct*. You may have to use a dictionary to determine whether or not a word is hyphenated.

1. Hettie told the squad leader that she would need more than her say so to violate the rule.
2. At age thirty five, Mr. Fairfax had fought in two wars.
3. The ten minute conference turned into an all day session.
4. Al was surprised that his take home pay was so much less than he had expected.
5. It is important to do adequate warm ups before running or jogging for any length of time.
6. Our teachers are usually well dressed.

7. We veered quickly to the left to avoid a head on collision with a raccoon.
8. The Solidarity union members sometimes listen to pro American radio broadcasts.
9. Phil's speech was full of heavy handed sarcasm.
10. The philanthropist set up a not for profit corporation.

E. Understand the use of italics. Rewrite the following sentences, underlining words that would appear in italics if the sentence were printed.

1. Old English poems like Beowulf were originally recited de memoire by a bard.
2. How many s's are there in unnecessary?
3. Have you read Hemingway's The Sun Also Rises?
4. The play's director wanted a wide door, not a white one.
5. An experimental production of A Comedy of Errors was playing at the Goodman Theater.
6. Do psychologists still think that a new born child is a tabula rasa, or blank slate?
7. What is the origin of the £ symbol?
8. The Mona Lisa is protected by a bullet-proof covering.
9. Professor Baskin bought an electric gelati machine after visiting Italy.
10. Avoid using too many really's and very's in your formal writing.
11. I said bring dessert or a main dish, not both.
12. Tschaikowsky thought that the Nutcracker Suite was one of his poorest compositions.
13. Mrs. Klein said her son-in-law was a real mensch, but I personally don't think that he is very sensible.
14. Janice has six 7's in her phone number.
15. Are you on the phone with Bret again?

MIXED REVIEW

Good Manuscript Form

A. Rewrite the following sentences, correcting any errors in manuscript form.

1. The falling book, a copy of The American Heritage Dictionary, missed my head but fell on my foot.
2. What does the expression savoir-faire mean?
3. The stuntman enjoyed getting into death defying situations.
4. The cartoonist was required to finish the illustration no later than noon on Thurs., Jan. 6, 1,985.
5. Since I was very weak in physics, I was surprised to get seventy-two percent of the answers correct.
6. Smaller players quaked at his Goliath like size.
7. 10,000 scofflaws showed up to pay their traffic tickets the day before the new law went into effect.
8. Do you think there are too many articles on hunting in Sports Illustrated?
9. The clerk said that Time delayed its issue in order to include a cover story on the crisis.
10. When I dialed 7380091 the phone made a terrible click ing noise.
11. Of course I realize that four sixteenths equals one fourth.
12. The round trip airfare to Australia cost more than $1000 per person.
13. She was inaugurated pres. on Mar. 4 of last year.
14. We did not need a passport to cross the Can. border.
15. Many television shows are aimed at twelve year old audiences.
16. Lawrence Olivier has played in everything from Shakespeare's Henry V to the movie Marathon Man.
17. Are people considered senior citizens at 65?
18. Harry was thrilled to see his name appear in the by line.
19. 7,000 people showed up for the demonstration.
20. This morning Sally ran one mi. and swam for 30 min.

B. Rewrite the following sentences, correcting the errors in the writing of figures, and in the use of abbreviations, hyphens, and italics. Indicate italics by underlining.

1. Children watch an average of over 20000 commercials per yr.
2. Chuck will become a full fledged dr. on Mar. 25.
3. The passenger ship France is 1035 ft. long.
4. Procter and Gamble Co. is the largest advertiser in the U.S.
5. Lord of the Flies is similar to another novel, High Wind in Jamaica.
6. Fla. and Ha. depend on income from tourism.
7. Room Ten is the rehearsal room.
8. Much loved Charlie Brown is over 30 yrs. old.
9. 80 percent of Brown's pitches are sliders.
10. On Apr. 12, 1981, the space shuttle Columbia took its first flight.
11. The 2 leaders held a tête-à-tête in the Pres.'s office.
12. The long awaited yearbooks will arrive on Wed., Aug. 9.
13. The public library at 1,432 S. Oak St. is showing silent films.
14. In Sept., Mr. Lloyd will open his 25 acre apple orchard to the public.
15. From Jan. twelve to Feb. 15 the museum will have a doll-house exhibit.
16. How many k's are there in bookkeeping?
17. Your assignment is pp. 23–47 in the bio. book.
18. "What does the word gratuity mean?" Lois asked.
19. The Northern Theater Co. is presenting 4 plays by O'Neill.
20. Tennis magazine explained 15 ways to improve your game.

USING MECHANICS IN WRITING

Good Manuscript Form

A. Imagine that you have invented and/or produced a product that you want to sell. Consider its features and benefits (what it offers, and how it benefits the buyer). Estimate its manufacturing cost, how much you will sell it for to the dealer, and its sale price (how much the dealer will sell it for to the customer). Then plan a production and marketing schedule that describes how, when, and where you will make and sell your product. Write a report describing the product and these various considerations. Observe proper manuscript form throughout.

B. Create a small, fictional town. Make a list of some of the more prominent citizens, local landmarks, important historical events, and industries associated with your creation. Decide on its population and the kind of climate its citizens enjoy. You might even make up the title of a town song. For an interesting twist, you might want to create a town that only a lover of horror stories would enjoy. You might even want to choose a town in another time period or on another planet. Once you have your town firmly pictured in your mind, assume that you are its public relations agent. Write up a colorful brochure that tells an interested reader all about the town and why it would be a good place to visit. Make sure that you use proper manuscript form as you mention numbers, dates, and titles.

18.0 Outlining

The outline is useful for taking notes and for planning a composition. It can help a note-taker record information logically and concisely. It can help a writer organize ideas. An outline can also be used to put the ideas of a speech or talk in skeleton form for easy reference during presentation.

18.1 Outlines in Note Taking

In many situations, outlined notes are helpful. You may be doing background reading to gather information for a report or paper or studying for an important test. You may be listening to a lecture or a speech. In any case, outlining the information will help you to remember it, to see the author's or speaker's reasoning, and to summarize the material. You will find that you can learn more from your reading or listening if you make an outline.

For outlined notes, the goal is to pick out important ideas and their relation to each other. Before you begin to read an article or other written selection, look it over quickly. Note headings and titles. Such scanning can give you an idea of the organization of the piece. In a speech or lecture, listen for changes in topic and for explanations of main topics.

To write the outline, recognize and write down the main points as main headings. Use the examples or details that develop these main points as subheadings. Summarize the purpose of the talk or written piece at the top of the outline.

18.2 Outlines for Organizing Compositions

Before you can make an outline for a composition, report, or speech, you must gather information related to the topic of your paper. All the information you include must directly develop a single controlling point. Once you have gathered enough relevant information, the outline can help you plan the order in which you will develop your central argument.

First, think about the main idea of your paper and the ideas you will use to support it. Determine which ideas are most important. These will be the main headings of the outline. Then group the remaining ideas under the main headings. These will be the subheadings and their supporting details.

You will find that some ideas are most logically organized in time sequence, some in ascending order of importance, and some in order of complexity or familiarity. The correct order is the one that is clearest to the reader or listener.

The finished outline will give you a pattern to follow to keep your paper organized and focused. See Chapters 7, 8, and 10 at the front of this book for more information on organizing ideas during the writing process.

18.3 Kinds of Outlines

There are two basic kinds of outlines: (1) **topic outlines** and (2) **sentence outlines.**

A topic outline is useful for taking notes and for quick and informal organization of ideas. This kind of outline uses words or short phrases instead of complete sentences. An example of a topic outline is shown on the following page.

The Development of Rocketry

Statement of Purpose: to explain the major developments in rocketry through the beginning of the space age.

I. The early history of rocketry
   A. Invention by Chinese in thirteenth century
      1. Use of rockets in festivals and celebrations
      2. Use of rockets in warfare
   B. Development of early military rockets
      1. Congreve's explosives-carrying rocket
      2. Hale's finned rocket and the Mexican/American War

II. The development of modern rocketry
   A. Tsiolkovsky's theory of rocket power
   B. Goddard's invention of the liquid-fueled rocket
   C. Von Braun's invention of the V-2 guided missile

III. The coming of the space age
   A. High altitude rockets
   B. Rocket-powered planes
   C. Sputnik and Explorer I

As you can see, much of the information for this composition is in the mind of the person who made the outline. The outline itself merely provides a guide to the organization of ideas.

Sentence outlines are appropriate for use with complex material. They are also useful for notes that will be used long after the material is read or heard. In this case, you cannot rely as much on memory and must take notes in sentences that express complete thoughts. You might also use a sentence outline when someone else is going to read or use the outline.

An example of a sentence outline begins on the next page.

Beyond the Five Senses

Statement of Purpose: to show that animal sensory systems surpass the so-called five senses of human beings.

I. Humans are believed to have five senses.
   A. Aristotle first categorized the senses.
   B. Modern physics and physiology have reclassified the senses.

II. Photoreceptors are those sense organs that react to light.
   A. The human eye is a photoreceptor.
   B. Animals such as hawks have greater visual ability than humans.
   C. Other kinds of animal photoreception are also superior to that of humans.
      1. Insects have specialized eyes.
      2. Nocturnal animals can see in the dark.

III. Chemoreceptors are sense organs that react to chemicals.
   A. Both taste and smell in humans use chemoreception.
   B. Fish sense the chemical environment with their whole bodies.
   C. Some animals make distinctions that humans cannot. (example: deer can taste the difference between potassium chloride and sodium chloride.)

IV. Mechanoreceptors are sense organs that react to touch.
   A. Both touch and hearing in humans use mechanoreception.
   B. Hairs and antennae amplify touch sensations in animals.
   C. Sonar and echo-reception are animal specializations.

V. Thermoreceptors are sense organs that react to heat.
   A. Heat sensitivity in humans is generally not recognized as one of the senses.
   B. Snakes have highly developed thermoreceptors.
   C. Mosquitoes hunt by sensing infra-red radiations.

VI. Some animals respond to stimuli to which human beings are completely insensitive.
   A. Rats may have an X-ray receptor.
   B. Snails respond to the magnetic forces of the earth.

18.4 Outline Form

In general, the same procedure is used to write both topic outlines and sentence outlines.

1. Write the title above the outline.

2. Put the purpose statement a few spaces below your title.

3. Use standard outline form. The following is a sample arrangement of numerals and letters in outline form.

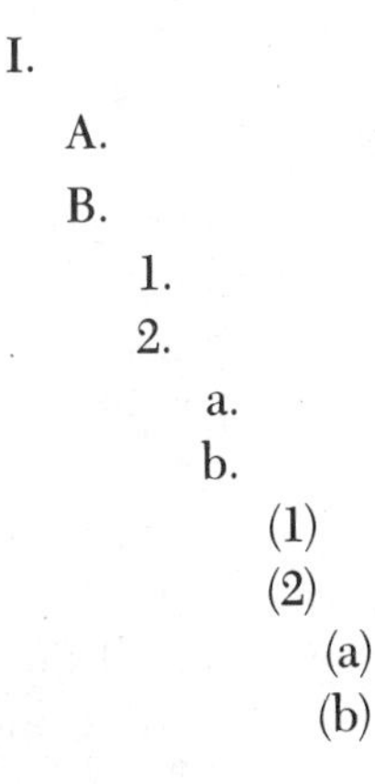

4. Number your main headings with Roman numerals. Use capital letters for headings under each main heading. Divide your subtopics in descending order of importance: first Arabic numerals, then small letters, then Arabic numerals in parentheses, then small letters in parentheses.

5. Indent subheadings placing the letters or numerals directly below the first letter of the first word in your preceding heading or subheading.

6. Do not use the words Introduction, Body, and Conclusion in your outline. These are merely organizational terms used to plan a composition.

7. Use only one idea for each heading or subheading.

8. Do not use a single subheading. Use either two or more, or none at all. A heading cannot be divided into fewer than two parts.

9. Begin the first word of each heading and subheading with a capital letter. In a sentence outline, make sure that all headings and subheadings are complete sentences, ending with a period. Do not use periods after headings or subheadings in a topic outline.

10. In topic outlines, make all main headings parallel in form. Make each group of subheadings parallel in form. For example, if the first main heading is a noun, all the other main headings must be nouns. If the first heading under the main heading is a prepositional phrase, the remainder of that group of headings must also be prepositional phrases.

Exercise A: The list on the following page contains all the ideas needed for a complete topic outline: a title, a group of main headings, and several groups of subheadings. Arrange all the ideas in outline form, using all the items given and numbering and lettering them properly as main headings and subheadings. Place the title at the top of the outline.

Sustains life
In art
Effect of the sun on the earth
Creates energy
Mass
In music
Future study of the sun
Movement
Mythology of the sun
The history of the sun
Size
In worship
Facts about the sun
Heat
In literature
Brightness
Affects on weather
Man and the sun

Exercise B: Revise the following topic outline to conform with the guidelines given in part 18.4 of this Section.

Sir Isaac Newton

I. Introduction: Modern scientists agree that Isaac Newton was one of the great figures in the history of science.

II. The Early Life of Newton.
  1. Born in 1642 at Woolsthorpe, Lincolnshire
  2. He was considered a poor student as a child
  3. Tinkered with gadgets as a boy
  4. Newton's student life
    a. Attended Trinity College, Cambridge

III. The discoveries of Newton
  1. Constructed a Reflecting Telescope
  2. Invented Integral and Differential Calculus
  3. Stated the laws of gravitation
    a. Also stated the laws of motion.
  4. President of the Royal Society (1703-1727)

IV. His professional life.
  a. Professor of mathematics at Cambridge
  b. Member of Parliament
  c. Associate member of the French Academy
  d. He explained the laws governing light and color.

V. Conclusion

REINFORCEMENT EXERCISES

Outlining

A. Understand proper outline form. Complete the following statements about proper outline form. If necessary, refer back to parts 18.3 and 18.4 of this Section.

1. There are two types of outline, the sentence outline, and the ______.
2. Roman numerals are used in outlines before ______.
3. Capital letters are used in outlines before ______.
4. In a topic outline, items under a single heading or of the same rank should be in ______ form.
5. A statement of the ______ should immediately follow the title.
6. The first letter of the first word of each outline entry should be ______.
7. End punctuation is not used in ______ outlines.
8. If an outline entry is broken into subheadings, there must be at least ______ subheadings.
9. The letter or numeral at the beginning of each outline entry should be placed ______.
10. Every outline should develop a single ______.

B. Use correct outline form. The outline that begins on this page contains several errors in form. Rewrite the outline correcting all mistakes.

Magic and Magicians

Statement of Purpose: To describe the art of magic as practiced by professional magicians.

1. The History of Magic

A. Magic and superstition in ancient times (Egypt, Greece, Rome, India)

B. Magic and theater in modern times.

II. Famous performers of magic
- –harry blackstone
- –harry houdini
- –albert goshman
- –paul rosini
- –david copperfield
- –doug henning

III. The techniques of magicians.
- a. Types of magic tricks
  1. sleight of hand.
  2. close-up magic.
  3. illusions.
  4. escapes.
  5. mentalist magic

MIXED REVIEW

Outlining

Read the following rough notes for a short report on the boomerang. First group similar ideas together. Devise possible headings for each group. Put the groups into the order in which you would present them. Finally, write up the ideas as a formal topic outline. Be sure to use the correct form. Remember, however, that there is no single correct way to present ideas. You may even want to combine or delete some of the ideas presented here.

curved, flat implement
sometimes used as a weapon
often used for sport
usually curved, each wing flat on bottom and curved on the top, one edge thicker than the other
made of wood or plastic
weight—1-80 ounces
length—1 to 6½ feet
width—½ to 5 inches
flight of boomerang depends on shape, size, wind, throw
returning boomerangs can fly 150 feet before returning
non-returning boomerangs can fly 300 feet
shape of boomerang (see above) causes lower air pressure above each wing—helps keep it airborne
two kinds of boomerangs—*returning* and *non-returning*
returning boomerang best known—when it is thrown, it spins forward, rises, and curves back to thrower
returning boomerang difficult to aim, used primarily for sport and in competition
non-returning boomerang used mainly for hunting and fighting—also used to light fires, cut, scrape, and as toys
non-returning boomerang hits target with great force
boomerangs may have been developed by prehistoric people
found in many parts of the world
generally associated with the Aborigines of Australia

USING MECHANICS IN WRITING

Outlining

A. Look at the outline you wrote in the Mixed Review for this Section. Using the outline, write a short report on boomerangs. Refer to Chapter 7, "The Process of Writing," at the front of this book for help with writing and revising your rough draft.

B. Write an outline for a paper explaining the various courses of study offered to students of your grade level at your high school. Classify the programs by the most general headings first. Such headings might include *Language Arts*, *College Preparatory*, or *Vocational Training*. Then break each heading down into component parts. Finally, list individual courses. When the outline is complete, write an essay for a student handbook, following the organization developed in the outline.

C. Look at the table of contents for the owner's manual of a car, stereo, television set, or household appliance. Notice that these contents pages very much resemble an outline. There are general headings, such as *Description*, *Operation*, *Special Features*, and *Repairs*, and then more specific subheads that break down each major head into more detail.

Select a possession of yours and imagine that you have just sold it. You have promised the buyer that you will provide a short owner's manual that explains how the item works. Begin by making an outline of the points you will cover. Be sure to organize these items in an order that the buyer will find most useful. Finally work from your outline to write your manual.

Sources of Quoted Materials

Educational Testing Service: For SAT questions selected from *Taking the SAT,* College Examination Board, 1983; reprinted by permission of Educational Testing Service, the copyright owner of the sample questions. Permission to reprint the SAT material does not constitute review or endorsement by Educational Testing Service or the College Board of this publication. William Morrow & Company, Inc.: For "Icebergs on the Move," from *Icebergs and Their Voyages* by Gwen Schultz; copyright © 1975 by Gwen Schultz, adapted by permission of William Morrow & Company. The University of Michigan Press: For a map from *A Word Geography of the Eastern United States;* copyright 1949. The authors and editors have made every effort to trace the ownership of all copyrighted selections found in this book and to make full acknowledgment for their use.

Cover

Homage to the Square: Sound. Josef Albers. Courtesy of The Josef F. Albers Foundation, Inc. Whereabouts of the painting unknown.

Editorial Credits

Editor-in-Chief: Joseph F. Littell
Editorial Director, English Programs: Joy Littell
Administrative Editor: Kathleen Laya
Managing Editor: Geraldine Macsai

Director of Secondary English: Bonnie Dobkin
Assistant Editor: Robert D. Shepherd

Associate Designer: Mary E. MacDonald
Handwritten Art: Amy Palmer
Cover Design: Joy Littell, Debbie Costello
Production Assistant: Julie Schumacher

Index